African Roots/American Cultures

African Roots/American Cultures

Africa in the Creation of the Americas

Edited by Sheila S. Walker

ROWMAN & LITTLEFIELD PUBLISHERS, INC.
Lanham • Boulder • New York • Oxford

ROWMAN & LITTLEFIELD PUBLISHERS, INC.

Published in the United States of America
by Rowman & Littlefield Publishers, Inc.
4501 Forbes Blvd, Suite 200, Lanham, Maryland 20706
http://www.rowmanlittlefield.com

12 Hid's Copse Road, Cumnor Hill, Oxford OX2 9JJ, England

British Library Cataloguing-in-Publication Information Available

Library of Congress Cataloging-in-Publication Data

African roots/American cultures : Africa in the creation of the Americas / edited by
Sheila S. Walker.
    p. cm.
  Includes bibliographical references and index.
  ISBN 978-0-7425-0165-2
    1. America—Civilization—African influences—Congresses. 2. African
diaspora—Congresses. 3. Africans—America—History—Congresses. 4. African
Americans—History—Congresses. I. Walker, Sheila S.

E20 .A4 2001
970—dc21

                                                                    00-068400

Printed in the United States of America

♾TM The paper used in this publication meets the minimum requirements of American
National Standard for Information Sciences—Permanence of Paper
for Printed Library Materials, ANSI/NISO Z39.48-1992.

To my parents
James O. Walker
and
Susan Walker Snell
For Everything

Africa is like Osiris. It has been torn apart and scattered over the earth. It is our responsibility to put it back together.

—Joseph Ki-Zerbo, historian, Burkina Faso

Contents

Figures

Acknowledgments

There are always more people to be thanked than is possible in the kind of undertaking that this book represents. I will try to do justice to the short list, in full acknowledgment that I cannot possibly express my gratitude to the long list that goes back several decades and spans several continents and quite a few islands.

This book is based on an international conference on the African Diaspora and the Modern World that I organized as director of the Center for African and African American Studies at the University of Texas at Austin in February 1996. Without anthropologist Dr. Deborah Mack, who collaborated on the millions of things involved in making such an event happen, the conference could not have taken place, and thus the book would not have been possible.

The conference was made possible by the support of UNESCO, the United Nations Educational, Scientific, and Cultural Organization. I am extremely grateful to special advisors to the director general, Ehsan Naraghi, who helped conceive the idea and bring it to fruition, and Ambassador Yaw Bamful Turkson, who represented the director general at the event, and to Mr. Sergei Lazarov, director of the Unit for Tolerance. And thanks are due to now former Director General Federico Mayor. I was also honored by the presence of history buff U.S. Congressman Donald Payne of New Jersey, then chair of the Congressional Black Caucus.

At the University of Texas the conference benefited from the encouragement and support of then dean of the College of Liberal Arts and now executive vice president and provost, Dr. Sheldon Ekland-Olson, as well as that of the Office of the President and the Institute of Latin American Studies.

I would also like to express my sincere gratitude to the many University of Texas colleagues who participated in the event in various ways, to Kelly Porterfield, who was the center's computer publications specialist, to the students in the African Diaspora Graduate Program in Anthropology, who were involved in the conference in myriad ways, as well as to the plethora of sometimes surprise volunteers, a few of whom showed up miraculously in our moments of greatest need.

For mentoring and other support beginning in graduate school I am grateful to historian of religions Dr. Charles H. Long. For the book, my deepest gratitude goes to Dr. Yvonne Daniel, my sister anthropologist who gave me the key feedback that allowed me to finish it. Without the amazing assistance of the center's computer publications specialist, Jennifer B. Jones, who helped with the zillions of revisions, did more research than either of us could ever have anticipated, and performed related tasks too numerous to imagine, the book would never have come to exist. I am thankful for translation and editorial assistance to Dr. Lisa Sánchez González. Thanks are also due to my teaching assistant, BC Harrison, for critical feedback and help when I needed it. And a deep thanks to Betty Nunley, senior administrative associate of the center, who made everything work.

I also extend my gratitude to all of those people in Africa and the African Diaspora who welcomed me, shared their cultures with me, and helped me understand them—and through them, us.

Sheila S. Walker
Professor, Department of Anthropology
Annabel Irion Worsham Centennial Professor
College of Liberal Arts
The University of Texas at Austin

*

Translator's Notes

Lisa Sánchez González

Translating the work of African Diasporan activists and researchers into English is an urgent project, one that creates specific challenges for North American scholars. This urgency is prompted by a number of social emergencies in the Americas. The so-called neoliberal economic project in Latin America and the Caribbean has further polarized wealth in national contexts in which communities of color—largely descendants of indigenous and African peoples—have always been shoved into the margins of nationalist imaginaries and socioeconomic power in the "modern" world, and who, consequently, are now experiencing U.S.-sponsored neoliberal "reforms" as a rising cost of living that is both emotionally and financially dire: even less food on tables that had little food to begin with, fewer and more exploitative and ephemeral jobs, young families torn asunder by the need to emigrate for employment, environmental poisoning in low-income communities and sacred ancestral lands, lack of access to education and to the most basic medical care, and high rates of infant and child mortality due to hunger, paramilitary violence, and curable or preventable diseases. Tragically, under these new policies and the regimes of power they advance, the most severely impacted constituencies are usually children.

People and researchers of color and conscience in the United States should therefore be concerned with how U.S. imperialism, aggravated or complemented by governmental and corporate corruption, racism, and sexism within specific Latin American nations, is impacting the daily lives of peoples across the Americas. The translated works of those who are entrenched in grassroots mobilizations by and for low-income communities of color offer English-language readers particularly relevant information and particularly keen analyses. Hence, part of the politics of this kind of translation is calling attention to how these chapters are once-removed not only from their original languages, but also from original contexts that are entangled, always on unequal footing, with our own in the United States.

Of course, this is not to characterize the contemporary scene in the Americas as apocalyptic, or to render the various African Diasporan communities represented in these chapters as a homogenous and irremediably victimized mass. One of the most important underlying themes of the South American chapters included in this volume concerns the legacies of survival and achievement in communities of color across the Americas, legacies that these communities are reclaiming and recycling to produce new knowledge, new strategies, and new tactics for solving or mitigating the problems and crises they face. This new knowledge includes a recuperation of African Diasporan history from archival sources and oral traditions, which has motivated these scholar–activists to create dynamic new conceptualizations of national history, culture, and cultural resistance. The new (or perhaps more accurately, "new-old") strategies emerging in Afro-Argentinean, Afro-Uruguayan, Afro-Venezuelan, Afro-Bolivian, and Afro-Paraguayan advocacy work call for cultural and political collaboration that transcends national boundaries and borders while attending to local community efforts in quite specific national and/or regional contexts. The tactical flexibility of this new African Diasporan political project is remarkable; it attests to a grassroots logic that shuttles between responding to the most immediate and localized human rights struggles and collectivizing the broadest constituency possible under an insurgent group identity and a progressive program for action.

Translating this work is also urgent because of the anglophone prejudice in contemporary African Diasporan research. Unfortunately, many people of color in the United States who are interested in a global African Diasporan vision are not fluent in the languages of their cousins in places like Haiti, Brazil, Puerto Rico, Nicaragua, and the Yucatán. Even worse, sometimes learning "standard" Spanish, French, or Portuguese in a North American classroom may not equip students to communicate effectively in their cousins' creolized ways of speaking. Too often U.S. researchers in Black history and cultural studies are uncomfortable dealing with non-anglophone traditions.

Added to these difficulties is the fact that, generally speaking, Latin American studies is still a rather young discipline firmly tied to government sponsorship; one that still prioritizes research that promotes state, military, or corporate interests or, in the arts, research that is often oriented to a kind of colorful coffee table book exposition of primitively styled folklore that is drained of all but the last drop of political relevance. And, truth be told, Latin American studies is not always welcoming to critical race studies, *especially* in the hands of politicized researchers of color. In critical response to these concerns, these chapters offer the monolingual English-speaking audience a unique opportunity to listen to these communities speaking to them (as closely as possible) on their own terms. Therefore, I hope that providing these translations to a broad English-language readership may help to foster a dialogue, or at least a first encounter, between constituencies that might not otherwise have the opportunity to meet, to speak, to listen, and to discuss common ground.

The languages with which I worked also posed some inherent challenges. Translating Spanish-language texts into English is never, even under the best of circumstances, an easy task. In a way, it is like re-creating a ceramic vase in wood, making a stool out of a rocking chair, or trying to trace the design of a Berber tile with a straightedge ruler. Spanish is a language that cools down and heats up depending on its environment; that flows in long, varied, but deliberate rhythms; that winds itself up, down, and around the subject in complicated patterns. English privileges a more predictable surface, linear tracks to the subject at hand, and the staccato of short, self-contained clauses firmly locked in concise syncopation with grammatically stiff sentences. My partial solution for bridging these fundamental differences was to invent and incorporate metaphor in places where I thought the Spanish was waxing eloquent but where there was no precise equivalent to express this elegance in English.

Added to the mere burden of this basic linguistic challenge were two other negotiations. First, translating the work of scholars (activists, organizers, autodidacts) who do not necessarily write in an academic style or format that is familiar to a North American audience. And second, balancing a respect for the intricacies of the Spanish-language essay tradition with my own sensibilities as an academic writer in the English language. My compromise for meeting both these challenges was to make the chapters somewhat structurally familiar while staying as true as possible to the unique stylization of the original. Nevertheless, I feel I must own up to the fact of my translatitious tendencies and English-language biases in these translations.

Where and if my efforts to capture the authors' stylistic tendencies with metaphoric and other devices are effective, complete credit should go to the original for inspiration; and wherever the prose becomes wooden and flat, it reflects my failure to strike the appropriate communicative balance between two languages and the expressive worlds they represent. I must also acknowledge the careful and consistent work of the editor, Dr. Sheila Walker, whose polyglot fluency across not only linguistic but also class and disciplinary lines never ceases to amaze me. Her work in editing the ultimate drafts of these translations provided a kind of final gloss that made these chapters more readable and the ideas I translated flow more fluidly one to the next.

As the adage goes, necessity is indeed the mother of invention, and translating this South American public intellectual work became a political necessity for me; one that, at many junctures, required careful but creative reinventions. After attending the conference "The African Diaspora and the Modern World," where the chapters included here were first presented, I was honored to be asked to reinvent these ideas in an artful way; to pay what tribute I could to the spirit of urgency I felt in the room during the presentations, especially those in Spanish and Portuguese; and to honor in turn the voices I heard there speaking to realities that I, as a politicized U.S. public university educator and as a "First World" woman of color, could not ignore nor dismiss as insignificant.

Moreover, I appreciate and admire the South American public intellectuals—both men and women—who shared their experiences and knowledge at the conference that gave birth to this book, most of whom are autodidactic scholars with scant resources for their research. I learned so much at this conference, and I was humbled by the Latin American participants' generosity of spirit as well as their efforts and successes as scholars under such relatively difficult circumstances compared with my own. Guided by their invitation to a genuine dialogue about *América* as a plurality of voices, of experiences, of political trajectories, as well as by their provocative new readings of the common ground all African descendants share, translating for this volume was a labor of love: labor, because it was a demanding and difficult task; of love, because sustaining me through all my negotiations with these chapters was a commitment to a vision of unity and mutual respect I heard calling to me in the originals.

¡Siempre p'alante!

Orthographic and Terminological Notes

Because the African Diaspora in the Americas speaks Portuguese, English, Spanish, French, Dutch, and various creole languages, and because some words also have spellings that reflect their African origins, many words have no single standard spelling. Spellings in this volume reflect the geography of the phenomena in question. Hence, the word *Orisha,* for example, referring to the spiritual beings of the Yoruba people from Nigeria and Benin in West Africa, many of whom were brought to the Americas during the transatlantic slave trade, is spelled *Orisa* (with the "s" having a "sh" sound) in Nigeria, *Orixa* or *Orisha* in Brazilian Portuguese (with the "x" having a "sh" sound), *Orisha* in English, and *Oricha* in Cuban Spanish. Some words are spelled according to European language as well as phonetic spellings, such as *callaloo/kalalu.* And some words of African origin, such as *candombe,* referring to the secular music/dance phenomenon of Uruguay and Argentina, have undergone linguistic modifications in the Americas, as evidenced in the Brazilian religious phenomenon *candomblé,* which comes from the same Bantu root.

And some terminology, a prime example being Kongo or Congo, reflects the complexity of historical and geocultural realities. The Bakongo, or Kongo ("ba," which is often omitted, being, in the Bantu language family, the pluralizing prefix for humans), people of the Kongo kingdom were divided by Portuguese, Belgian, and French colonialists into what are the three current nations of Angola, the Democratic Republic of the Congo (Congo-Kinshasa), and the Republic of the Congo (Congo-Brazzaville). The term Kongo-Angola or Angola-Kongo refers generally to the historical Kongo kingdom and its central African Bantu-speaking neighbors. In the Americas, the term Congo is used in various ways in different places—to refer to descendants of Central African people, as well as to designate peppers and peas.

Introduction

Are You Hip to the Jive? (Re)Writing/Righting the Pan-American Discourse

Sheila S. Walker

AFRICAN CONTRIBUTIONS TO THE AMERICAS—
AND TO THE STORY OF THE AMERICAS

The millions of Africans who survived the Middle Passage to the Americas during the transatlantic slave trade have not been acknowledged for the essential roles they played in the creation of the Atlantic and modern worlds. The extent of the contributions of these Africans and their African Diasporan descendants to the construction and definition of the Americas and of global civilization is only beginning to be taken seriously and to be seriously researched. The fact that everyone has been misinformed about them makes it easy to believe that these contributions were insignificant.

This volume is the result of an international conference on the African Diaspora and the Modern World that I organized in February 1996 as director of the Center for African and African American Studies at the University of Texas at Austin. Cosponsored by UNESCO (United Nations Educational, Scientific, and Cultural Organization), the conference was the principal event held in the United States under the aegis of the United Nations International Year for Tolerance.

The contributors to the volume are urhobophone/anglophone and yorubophone/francophone Africans, and African Americans and Euro-Americans—"American" used in the inclusive continental and insular Pan-American sense—from North and South America and the Caribbean. Lusophone, anglophone, and hispanophone, they represent the major languages of the Americas. The contributors are historians, including economic and culinary; linguists; creative writers and literary scholars; social, cultural, and physical anthropologists; journalists; filmmakers; music and dance scholars who are also musicians, composers, choreographers, singers, and dancers; and political and cultural activists. Many fit into several categories. The volume reflects both scholarly outsider and engaged insider points of view, and in the case of

1

African and African Diasporan scholars, both simultaneously. While also including the extremely valuable contributions of other scholars, this volume privileges the perspectives of Africans and African Diasporans in telling the stories of their own communities.

The contributors are committed to (re)writing and righting the story of the African presence in the Americas and to discovering and revealing old and new truths with which to replace old and new omissions, misrepresentations, and myths. A major intention is to help correct the partial, hence inaccurate, version that has been told of the story of the Americas; partial because the contributions of the Americas' now second-largest population have been consistently and systematically minimized, distorted, or ignored.

Until the early nineteenth century, hence for more than three hundred of the five-hundred-year modern history of the Americas, Africans and their descendants were the Americas' largest population. Therefore, the demographic foundation of the Americas was African, not European. According to historian Philip Curtin, in his seminal *The African Slave Trade: A Census*, "For the Americas, both North and South, Africans who came by way of the slave trade were the most numerous Old World immigrants until the late eighteenth century. And it is equally clear that more Africans than Europeans arrived in the Americas between, say, 1492 and 1770."[1]

And according to the introduction to the CD-ROM database *The Trans-Atlantic Slave Trade*, "As Europeans colonized the Americas, a steady stream of European peoples migrated to the Americas between 1492 and the early nineteenth century. But what is often overlooked is that before 1820, perhaps three times as many enslaved Africans crossed the Atlantic as Europeans. This was the largest transoceanic migration of a people until that day, and it provided the Americas with a crucial labor force for their own economic development."[2]

That some American nations officially encouraged European migration in the nineteenth century specifically to "whiten" their populations, which helps explain the precipitous decline in the proportion of African descendants that Romero Rodríguez and Lucía Molina and Mario López describe in this volume for Argentina, demonstrates this fundamental demographic fact. Curtin makes the point that "historians have too often regarded the Afro-American community created by the trade as an alien body on the periphery of national life."[3] Yet the fact that the Americas were demographically more African American than Euro-American during the first three centuries, when the foundations of the new societies were being laid, logically affirms that the African human and cultural presence had to be an important ingredient in their creation.

It is important to emphasize that these Africans who came to the Americas constituted not merely a "labor force," which in the context of slavery in the Americas connotes physical, not intellectual, labor. The transatlantic slave trade also involved the very deliberate selection of Africans on the basis of their specific knowledge and skills that were needed for the development of the Americas. Therefore, this largest human migration also constituted the world's first *massive brain drain and transfer of technology* from Africa to the Americas, which established the basis for contemporary power relations in the Atlantic world.

It is, thus, impossible to understand the past and present of the Americas without understanding the African presence in the Americas. Much of African American, and all-

American, history and behavior is explicable only in light of its African antecedents. Africa remains present in the nature of economic systems, in struggles for and concepts of freedom and justice, in technology and material culture, in the arts and the art of celebration, in popular culture, in spirituality and religion, in everyday language and gastronomy.

By offering new data, interpretations, and theories, this volume explicitly challenges the conceptualization of the Americas as a European construct and construction. Historian Howard Dodson, chief of the Schomburg Center for Research in Black Culture of the New York Public Library, the major library and archive of the Black experience in the world, argues in chapter 5 that it was the transatlantic slave trade that shaped the modern world by fostering the development of the levels of communication, trade, cultural exchange, and economic and political interdependence among the nations of Europe, Africa, and the Americas that characterize the modern era.

If African participation in the creation of the Americas has been ignored, Africans have been given even less credit for their roles in the development of modern Europe. Curtin says that "The traditional national histories of European states . . . tend to view the slave trade as something peripheral to their own social and political development."[4] Yet Europeans, Dodson asserts, reorganized their political, economic, social, and cultural institutions to carry out the vast trade in human lives that was the most important international commercial activity of the era. This commercial activity became a basis for European wealth, power, and imperialist expansion.

A major consequence of the slave trade, Dodson reminds us, was the peopling of the Americas with Africans, who formed much of the human foundation on which the Americas were built, and whose presence and activities were of key importance during the formative period of the new nations. In the necessary process of re-creating themselves in their new milieu, these Diasporan Africans invented and participated in the inventing of new cultural forms such as languages, religions, foods, aesthetic expressions, and political and social organizations.

Economic historian Joseph Inikori states in chapter 6, in agreement with Dodson and using quantitative data to support his contentions, that for the three and a half centuries between 1500 and 1850, it was the labor of African peoples enslaved in the Americas that was at the center of the economic development of the Atlantic world. During this period, large-scale commodity production in the Americas transformed the Atlantic Ocean into the busiest trading mart in the world, with trade among European countries depending heavily on American products. It was the forced migration of Africans to the Americas through the slave trade, and the forced labor of their descendants in the Americas through the plantation system, that made this large-scale production possible and profitable. Inikori contends that "According to recent estimates, 75 percent of the American products traded during the period were produced by Africans and their descendants in the Americas."

Why, one might wonder, should such critical information about the creation of the Americas and the Atlantic world come as such a surprise? In discussing this seminal role of Africans and their descendants in the development of the economies of the Atlantic world, Inikori notes that a fundamental problem in scientific discussions concerning the economics of the Atlantic slave trade and African slavery in the Americas has been conceptual. Using appropriate theories in order to pose the right questions, identify relevant evidence to seek, and interpret facts correctly is, he says, the real basis of empirical research. This seemingly obvious observation leads him to conclude that the African presence in the economic history of the Atlantic world has been invisibilized by theories and perspectives that have focused attention on other issues. Discussions of the origins of the modern economies of the Atlantic world have simply neglected to mention that it was Africans and their descendants who paid with their lives the high price of this development by providing the involuntary and unremunerated labor, both skilled and unskilled, that made it possible.

The literature on the economics of the Atlantic slave trade and African slavery in the Americas, Inikori contends, involves many obsolete or inappropriate theories that have discounted the role of the slave trade and slavery as key factors in explaining the comparative economic development of the continents of the Atlantic basin. Thus, the essential role of the twelve to fifteen million Africans and their descendants whose labor was the economic basis for the development of the Atlantic world has been erased by theoretical approaches that have "disappeared" them by focusing elsewhere.

In contrast to such empirical realities, a recent *Worth* magazine article titled "How America Got Rich" cites as the causes of the wealth of the United States a geographic advantage, being isolated by oceans from potential attackers; raw materials for trade and commerce and rich cropland; an *unfortunately* annihilated indigenous population, allowing a depopulated territory to develop without effective opposition; and a Western Christian culture fostering a sense of progress.[5] Curiously missing from this idyllic account, in the kind of mass-market publication that forges public opinion and what passes for knowledge, is any mention, however slight or indirect, of the enslaved labor force that was the basis of the creation of this immense wealth.

The contributors to this volume challenge inaccurate perspectives based on inadequate, limited, and unimaginative searches for information and interpretations that sometimes result from a failure to understand, or reluctance to give credence to, possible sources of unexpected knowledge. This includes genuinely acknowledging the authority of the oral tradition of community "keepers of culture," whose presence and knowledge anthropologist and museum professional Diana Baird N'Diaye (chapter 13) had to overcome considerable resistance to include in a Smithsonian Institution project. It also involves understanding what constitutes essential knowledge and where to find it, such as the knowledge anthropologist Yvonne Daniel (chapter 23) found "embodied" in African Diasporan sacred dance.

The contributors also challenge disobliging points of view and theories that deliberately or casually disempower African Diasporan subjects. Distinguished professor of history Joseph Harris, the dean of African Diasporan studies who organized the first international conference in the United States on the African Diaspora at Howard University in 1979, characterizes the African Diaspora as a worldwide phenomenon.[6] Since ancient times, Harris notes (chapter 4), Africans have traveled outside the continent in a variety of roles, often as free people, and have settled in and made important contributions to societies of Europe and Asia as well as the Americas. Offering evidence of the continuity of the consciousness of and identity with Africa by members of these global Diasporan communities, he maintains that Africa has remained present in their religion, music, dance, language, and oral traditions.

Harris attributes the pervasive ignorance of the global nature of the African presence to stereotypes of Africans as inferior, without a meaningful history, and uncivilized and so incapable of having contributed to world civilization. Functioning as unquestioned premises promoting the maintenance of theories that discount the possibility that Africans have been major actors in the creation of the Atlantic world, these myths persist in spite of all evidence to the contrary. Such myths account for the scholarly tendency, which Dodson and Inikori cite, to simply ignore the central role of enslaved Africans in the development of the Atlantic world.

Information provided here comes from new sources, some of whose existence is not only not commonly known, but that is even sometimes specifically denied. Afro-Uruguayan Tomás Olivera Chirimini (chapter 15), who, based on his archival and oral historical research produces Afro-Uruguayan performances for national and international audiences, read in a U.S. encyclopedia that there was no population of African origin in Uruguay. It felt odd, he said, to learn from such an authoritative source that neither he nor the community of which he was a part existed. And a list of populations of African origin in the Americas appropriately titled "Are We or Aren't We?" explicitly characterized as "zero"[7] the Afro-Argentinean population of whose current activities Afro-Argentinean Lucía Molina (chapter 21) and Afro-Uruguayan Romero Rodríguez (chapter 20) write.

Inspired by Olivera Chirimini's experience, I was curious to see what a current U.S. encyclopedia might say about the four African Diasporan populations of the Southern Cone of South America that are the subjects of the chapters by Olivera Chirimini, Molina, and Rodríguez. The *Encyclopaedia Britannica Online* says of Argentina: "Population estimates of the colonial period suggest that by 1810 Argentina had more than 400,000 people. . . . Ten percent were black and mulatto, either slaves or descendants of slaves who had been smuggled into the country through Buenos Aires. . . . It was the great wave of European immigration after the mid-1890s that molded the present-day ethnic and racial character of Argentina. The Indians and mestizos were pushed aside or absorbed, and the blacks and mulattos disappeared."[8]

The *Encyclopaedia* says of Bolivia: "The population of Bolivia consists of three groups—the Indians, the mestizos (of mixed Indian and Spanish descent), and the descendants of the Spaniards."[9] Of Paraguay it says: "The vast majority of the inhabitants are native Paraguayans, who are almost all mestizo (a mixture of Spanish and Indian)."[10] And of Uruguay: "The Uruguayans of today are predominantly of European origin, mostly descendants of 19th- and 20th-century immigrants. . . . Of the small number of Blacks in the country, most came southward from Brazil."[11] The contributors offer correctives to *Britannica's* (mis)representation of the realities of the African Diasporan populations of all four countries.

A good place to seek new ideas, data, and theories is outside the traditional academic discourses that have created and perpetuated the old ones that were based on the limited human composition, hence the limited worldview and concerns, of the scholarly establishment. Cultural leaders from African Diasporan communities, who have not been included in academic discourses about themselves, enrich the discourse here by telling their own stories based on their own experiences, perspectives, and interests. These are people about and for whom others have assumed the privilege of speaking—others who presume to represent them in their absence while neglecting to facilitate their presence. I met them during the research travels I undertook in my quest to understand the African Diaspora. Lucía Molina from Argentina, Gilberto Leal from Brazil, Romero Rodríguez from Uruguay, and Jesús García from Venezuela are all internationally recognized leaders who are actively engaged in the struggle to discover and use accurate knowledge about their histories in the interest of improving the lives of their communities in the present.

As thoughtful participants and respected leaders in, researchers about, and promoters of the continuing development of their own cultures, they may be reasonably considered to be authorities on them. Like many of the scholars, they are involved in recovering and documenting their communities' neglected stories as a corrective to misrepresentative official histories and exclusionary national identities. Where necessary, they are also challenging disempowering scholarly (mis)representations. Gilberto Leal (chapter 18), for example, contrasts the well-documented history of persistent Afro-Brazilian resistance to bondage with still-influential scholarly representations of Brazilian slavery as a benign institution with an accommodated enslaved population.

In using new perspectives, data, theories, and sources of knowledge, as well as new interpretations of old sources of knowledge, the contributors are challenging and changing the stories of the Americas, making them more accurate by including both peoples and points of view that have been systematically excluded. Scholars and nonscholars alike bring interests and perspectives to bear that were not only not formed in traditional academia, but that are, on the contrary, often based on their efforts to rediscover and reclaim a historical role and cultural heritage that the academic establishment has been complicit in trivializing, misdefining, and invisibilizing.

The fact that most of the scholars are members of African and African Diasporan societies allows them to view these societies from the point of view of participants whose native knowledge is further informed, and critically enriched, by the acquired perspective of a scholarly discipline, and often by comparative experience and research in several African and African Diasporan societies. They are, thus, researchers with privileged insights because of their dualistic gaze as insider–outsiders, whom Yvonne Daniel (chapter 23) would characterize as "observing participants."[12]

They also evidence what African American anthropologist St. Clair Drake termed a "vindicationist perspective," which has historically characterized much of African American intellectual life. According to Drake, "What came to be called 'vindicating the Negro' emerged to counteract White Racism. It involved correcting stereotypes, setting the record straight, and substituting a more accurate picture of reality."[13] The interest of the African and African Diasporan scholars represented here in accurately telling the stories of their own communities is necessarily different from that of scholars motivated by intellectual curiosity and a desire to develop or test theories, even when fueled by a commitment to honesty and justice. Their intention is to lend their voices to the telling of a truer, more inclusive story of the Americas, from which the integral and essential roles played by their ancestors and contemporaries is no longer omitted.

These insider scholars have a special perspective on and interest in what is defined as significant based on the logic of their own lives and the lives of their communities, as well as on their disciplinary training. Reflecting this common concern, Brenda Dixon Gottschild (chapter 3) says, "what is spoken or silenced depends on who is speaking, who is doing the documenting, from whose perspective, by whose criteria, and what is being recorded."

AFROGENIC INTERPRETATIONS OF AFRICAN DIASPORAN REALITIES

"Are you hip to the jive?" was a question I often heard my father, James Walker, and his friends ask when I was growing up in New Jersey. They were questioning whether or not you really understood what was really happening, as distinguished from what you only thought you understood about what might only appear to be happening—from the simplest to the most profound meanings of that understanding. To be hip to the jive and to hip others to the jive are the major tasks of the contributors to this volume.

In chapter 1, about discovering Africa in New Jersey, I note that in my efforts to understand behaviors for which my community lacked explanations satisfying to me, terminology was a key to an alternative way of authoritative knowing and interpreting. Explanations for valid behavior in the United States have been and continue to be Eurocentric. Behavior not fitting a Eurocentric model has tended to be interpreted, more or less subtly, as somehow pathological, rather than as logical and legitimate products of radically different histories and experiences.

In his foreword to *By the Work of Their Hands* by John Michael Vlach, historian Lawrence Levine cites some key scholarly texts that have specifically denied that U.S. African Americans have a distinctive cultural heritage. Levine says that scholarship, rather than understanding African Americans as "complex amalgams of African and European cultures," has characterized us as the result of "imperfect acculturation to Euro-American cultures." This respected scholarly tradition has, he says, "depicted African-Americans as the one group that had lost its entire indigenous culture . . . among all of the peoples that constituted the United States."[14]

Levine notes that Gunnar Myrdal states in *An American Dilemma* that "American Negro culture is not something independent of general American culture. It is a distorted development, or a pathological condition, of the general American culture." Levine also cites Nathan Glazer and Daniel Patrick Moynihan who, in their influential *Beyond the Melting Pot*, claim that "The Negro is only an American and nothing else. He has no culture and values to value and protect."[15]

Such perspectives remain alive and well, overtly or covertly, in spite of substantial empirical evidence to the contrary. These kinds of Eurocentric pathology interpretations of African American behavior, however, made no sense *to* me or to other reflective members of my community with whom I discussed them in my efforts to understand our culture. And they certainly made no sense *of* the culturally normal and normative behaviors that surrounded and intrigued me.

The problem was not that community members did not have interpretations. The problem was rather that I did not know how to interpret the revealing interpretations that were articulated in familiar everyday language of which I did not fully understand the implications. I was *not* hip to the jive. Only as a result of comparative experiences in Africa and the African Diaspora, which offered me a broader worldview and more complex interpretative schema, was I able to begin to discover terminological clues hinting at interpretations and at unexpected African origins and meanings for familiar African American behaviors. I found these linguistic hints in the ways in which people talked of the spirit by which they were filled and moved in religious celebrations; in the terms by which they referred to people and characterized behaviors and attitudes; in the names by which they called people; and in the words with which they designated their secular and sacred, regular and ritual cuisines.

I also discovered that the best way to understand this African Diasporan reality was literally on its own terms. And I learned that some of these terms remain African. The obvious idea of seeking to understand a culture in and on its own terms should not appear either surprising or revolutionary, until one seeks instances in which African Diasporan culture has been analyzed in and on African Diasporan terms. A recent book that stands out for doing so concerning African American women is anthropologist Leith Mullings's aptly titled *On Our Own Terms*.[16]

Terms about which I had been curious as I was growing up proved to be seminal in helping me understand African Diasporan behaviors. I had understood the meanings of the words but had had no idea of where they came from in the human geographical sense, or where they "were coming from" in the conceptual sense. The explanation was not in the Eurocentric system where I had been taught that I should seek and find explanations for all American behavior. It was rather in an alternative system that was not supposed to exist. But it does. I characterize this system as "Afrogenic."

Afrogenic simply means growing out of the histories, ways of being and knowing, and interpretations and interpretive styles of African and African Diasporan peoples. It refers to these communities' experiences, priorities, and styles, and their articulations of them while acknowledging that most human behavior is not intellectually articulated by the actors who perform it and that plural interpretations of similar behaviors are obviously possible.

Afrogenic also refers to the interpretations and interpretive methods of African and African Diasporan scholars as a result of our roles as community members whose academic positionality is necessarily mediated by this belonging. The perspectives and methodologies of these scholars manifest a creative tension resulting from our being products of the epistemologies and hermeneutics—the ways of authoritative knowing and interpreting—of our own communities, and of having also mediated through these primary sources other, sometimes competing or incompatible, epistemologies and hermeneutics encountered in the academy. Reciprocally, Eurogenic relates to experiences and interpretations of people of European and European Diasporan origins.

It is entirely possible, to say nothing of intellectually honest, for people who are not of African descent to manifest an Afrogenic perspective, as contributors to this volume clearly demonstrate. They can do so, and do so here, by acknowledging African and African Diasporan agency, by assuming the "blackness" as well as the "whiteness" of the

Pan-American experience, by challenging Eurocentric (mis)interpretations of Afrogenic behaviors, and by being committed to telling an inclusive and accurate story of the Americas. Although adding an Afrogenic approach does not, of course, exhaust the perspectives that must be considered in order to tell the full story of the Americas, since multiple indigenous American points of view can obviously not be conscientiously excluded, inclusion of the now second Pan-American population represents progress.

An Afrogenic perspective necessarily recognizes the special importance of terminologies associated with, and generated by, the experiences of African and African Diasporan communities. These are our privileged expressions and interpretations of our lives and of our ways of experiencing and seeing them, and of pointing out what is important in them. African Diasporan societies have consciously articulated and unconsciously acted out distinctive epistemologies and hermeneutics, which it behooves scholars to discover and use as points of departure and as road maps for descriptive and analytical efforts. Eliciting and providing such insider interpretations of reality, Afrogenic principles and priorities around which African Diasporan communities organize our social institutions and cultural production are part of the task undertaken by contributors to this volume.

Exemplifying such an Afrogenic perspective, linguist Olabiyi Yai (chapter 14), in discussing the need for a "terminological, epistemological, and hermeneutical overhauling" of approaches to understanding the African Diaspora, argues that it is "scientifically unsound to uncritically 'inherit' and endorse the conceptual tools forged by one's oppressors' organic intellectuals to discourse on oneself and one's realities." He urges as an antidote the use of African and African Diasporan creole terms "as media of scientific discourse."

One way to do so is to seek out and seek to understand the meanings and implications of African and African Diasporan terms that are in common usage, as Yai does with the African Diasporan concept of *nation*. Gilberto Leal (chapter 18) and Jesús García (chapter 17) use African terms to characterize African and African Diasporan resistance to enslavement in Brazil and Venezuela. Leal uses Yoruba terms, Yoruba culture being one of the African cultures best represented in contemporary Brazil, to characterize active and passive resistance to slavery. And García conceptualizes an Afro-Venezuelan "culture of resistance" in Kikongo terms that he learned while seeking unacknowledged origins and roots of Venezuelan life in the Republic of the Congo, culture of Central African Bantu-speaking origin being the dominant African influence in Venezuela.

The complex of terms that García uses expresses a worldview based on premises similar to those that Bantu speakers might have brought with them to the Americas, premises which, even if not consciously articulated in exactly the same way, could have served as the basis for their understanding of, survival in, and resistance to the oppressive situation in which they found themselves. Africans arriving in the Americas necessarily used African terms to designate their resistance to the system of enslavement, terms designating concepts that their descendants would have perpetuated in their continuing resistance to slavery and oppression. Some contemporary African Diasporan leaders are using such terms to conceptualize resistant behavior affirming African Diasporan agency in the past and present.

García's discussion of this Bantu linguistic complex that provides the philosophical basis of an Afro-Venezuelan culture of resistance is akin to the U.S. African American survival linguistic complex expressed in an African language that I discovered in New Jersey. I found the original meanings of the words in Africa but could not have found the linguistic complex there because it was developed in conditions of enslavement in the Americas. It is noteworthy that a term from this slavery era complex was revived during the 1960s Black consciousness movement, a recent high point of African American resistance, self-redefinition, and affirmation that radically modified U.S. society.

U.S. African Americans have used "hip" and "jive," words from Wolof, the principal language of Senegal, to make significant epistemological and hermeneutical statements about ways of knowing, understanding, and interpreting life. "Jive," from *jef*, which Senegalese Wolof speakers translate into French, their official national language, as *pas sérieux* (not serious), proves most useful for the extremely serious intellectual overhaul that Yai proposes. The issue is to discourse critically on our own experiences and realities both *in* and *on* our own terms. Doing so offers an Afrogenic corrective to the inherent contradiction of discussing ourselves in and on the Eurogenic terms of those who have appropriated for themselves the right to define us without our consent, for their interests not ours, and often in such a way that we are either insulted or are unable to recognize ourselves.

Along this line, the dearth of "slaves," as opposed to "enslaved Africans" or "enslaved people," in a volume on the African Diaspora is perhaps worthy of comment. This terminological preference corresponds to Mullings's observation concerning the discussion of slavery on terms other than our own. She notes that she and other African American students "squirmed with discomfort and embarrassment" when slavery was presented in U.S. history lessons, "knowing something was wrong, but bereft of the knowledge that could empower us." As presented, "the slaves were clearly pitiful things without history, volition, or agency." Only later did she become conscious that, "describing (them) as 'enslaved' (by someone) rather than 'slaves' (an inherent state of being) shifts the burden of culpability and transgression."[17]

The terminological choice expressed here refuses to collaborate in the reification of a condition that has been given the connotation, with scholarly collusion, of representing the entire existence of enslaved African and African Diasporan human beings. Although that may have been the intention of their enslavers, it was clearly not a result to which enslaved people acquiesced. This linguistic overhaul also conveys an assertion of a sense of the volition and agency of people who, albeit living in lifetime bondage, were actively engaged in re-creating their identities and in creating new dynamic cultures that have helped to define both the Americas and contemporary global society.

Concerning this issue of accurate representation and self-recognition, I had not expected to find that a dictionary would constitute a problem, nor had I anticipated bringing one into my chapter on discovering Africa in New Jersey. I had seen dictionaries as "objective" sources of word meanings and had not expected to find myself in an adversarial intellectual relationship with one that I was shocked to find so culturally insulting. I had, admittedly naïvely, never considered the extent to which the ways in which the people who construct dictionaries and determine the authoritative meanings of words, the building blocks of societal communication and interpretation, logically reflect prevalent biases as well as more general cultural currents.

"Hip" means to have one's eyes wide open, to be keenly aware, as well as to make others aware. "Jive," as Afrogenically used by U.S. African Americans, relates to the art of dissimulation. The dictionary, which probably does a fine job for Eurogenic words, defines dissimulation as "to hide under a false appearance,"[18] derived from "simulate," meaning "to give or assume the appearance or effect of, often with the intent to deceive."[19] It defines jive as a "special jargon or difficult slang" and as "glib, deceptive, or foolish talk,"[20] as if these three terms were comparable.

The idea of a special jargon is probably more accurate than intended when one considers U.S. African American English as a linguistic system originating in a situation of enslavement, and involving deliberate dissimulation and subterfuge as a fundamental and essential survival strategy. The definition of jive as glib and foolish talk, although accurate on a superficial level, represents a trivializing perception of a term involving much greater interpretative profundity, and reflects an external perception that fails to account for the considered intentionality, and the sense of deliberate agency, of consciously deceptive, jive-talking African and African Diasporan actors and actresses. The definition also indicates that the jive worked if it was understood so superficially.

Africans enslaved in the Americas found themselves in a situation in which they could not possibly tell the truth to their European and Euro-American enslavers who did not even acknowledge them as human beings. According to the introduction to *The Trans-Atlantic Slave Trade,* "for those Europeans who thought about the issue, the shipping of enslaved Africans across the Atlantic was morally indistinguishable from shipping textiles, wheat, or even sugar."[21]

These Africans would hardly reveal their truths to those who bought and transported them "tightly packed" or "loosely packed"[22] based on calculations of what percentage of African lives the enslavers could lose and still make a profit, in the holds of ships they specifically conceived and constructed to transport human beings as if they were inanimate merchandise referred to in French, for example, as *bois d'ébène* (ebony wood); who literally *worked them to death* in order to enrich themselves, as demonstrated by the skeletal remains that Michael Blakey (chapter 12) discusses from New York's African Burial Ground; and whose concept of truth, whatever it may have been, was obviously the antithesis of that of the people they sought, unsuccessfully, to dehumanize.

A telling example of ways in which European enslavers thought of African human beings in nonhuman, commoditized terms is found in the concept of a *pieza de India(s)* (a "piece of the Indies"), the "Indies" Columbus was seeking referring to the Americas he "discovered." Often shortened to pieza, the term, according to historian Leslie Rout, referred to "the theoretical mean used to define the ideal slave; an African male between the ages of eighteen and thirty, with no physical defects, and at least five feet tall."[23]

According to Philip Curtin:

Most *asiento*[24] contracts gave the quantities to be delivered in *piezas de India,* not individual slaves. A pieza de India was a potential measure of labor, not of individuals. For a slave to qualify as a pieza, he had to be a young adult male meeting certain specifications as to size, physical condition, and health. The very young, the old, and females were defined for commercial purposes as fractional parts of a pieza de India. This measure was convenient for Spanish imperial economic planning, where the need was a given amount of labor power, not a given number of individuals. For the historian, however, it means that the number of individuals delivered will always be greater than the number of piezas recorded. Market conditions in Africa made it impossible to buy only prime slaves and leave all the rest, but the extent of the difference varied greatly with time and place. The asiento of the Portuguese Cacheu Company in 1693, for example, provided for an annual delivery in Spanish America of 4,000 slaves, so distributed in sex, age, and condition as to make up 2,500 piezas de India.[25]

The concept of Africans and African Diasporans as fractional was not limited to Spanish America. The U.S. Constitution, in fact, designated enslaved African Americans as three-fifths of a person for purposes of federal apportionment of taxation and congressional representation:

> Representative and direct Taxes shall be apportioned among the several States which may be included within this Union, according to their respective Numbers, which shall be determined by adding to the whole Number of free Persons, including those bound to Service for a Term of Years, and excluding Indians not taxed, three fifths of all other Persons.[26]

Whereas Euro-Americans endeavored to define the total reality of the Africans they purchased to do with as they pleased, enslaved Africans and their descendants, who considered themselves full, not partial, human beings, insisted upon defining themselves by and for themselves *in* their own terms, some of which still maintain explanatory power. That enslaved Africans also succeeded in defining themselves *on* their own terms, in spite of all the powerful, colonial and national government-enforced efforts to make it impossible for them to do so, is evident in their creation of the many original cultures and cultural forms of the African Diaspora, as well as in their important recognized and unrecognized contributions to the cultures of all of the Americas and to global society.

To survive and even create in unimaginably adverse circumstances, Africans and their descendants had no choice but to practice artful dissimulation, subtle subterfuge, and serious jive in their interactions with whites whose interests were, by definition, antithetical to those of the people they considered their chattel, whom they included not on human census rolls but rather on property inventories along with their tables and chairs, with their cows and pigs. How else might a thinking person account for the "happy smiling darky" Euro-American stereotype for the human beings they kept imprisoned in generations of lifetimes of perpetual bondage?

An African American saying states that "I've got one mind for my master, and one mind for myself." I've got a jive version of what I think/believe/know for the person who tries to control me, and I keep my real truth for myself and my people. What was perceived as glib and foolish talk by those who were intended to be deceived often protected the profound truths of those who were consciously, carefully, and selectively deceiving.

The concept of jive as deception and dissimulation must, however, be applied in both directions. The first concerns the ways in which African Americans jived their white enslavers in order to resist their efforts at total control and joked among themselves about doing so. The other is the way in which white enslavers invented and presented jive versions, deceptive misrepresentative versions, of African, African Diasporan, and consequently Pan-American history to the world, and pretended that it was the truth, perhaps joking among themselves about "getting over" on their victims—both materially and intellectually. The dissimulative way in which the story of the Americas has been told, such that it denies, minimizes, and distorts African and African Diasporan roles in it, has been successfully jive in that it has deceived everyone, even convincing of its validity many of the very people whose experiences it has misrepresented.

Thus, a major task of African and African Diasporan scholars, and of all scholars committed to telling an accurate and honest story about the African Diaspora, therefore to telling an accurate and honest story about the Americas, is to become hip to the jive, to see and see through the jive, the dissimulation, the hiding of the presence of Africa in all of the Americas under false appearances with the obvious intention of deceiving. Having become hip to the jive ourselves, knowing what is really happening as opposed to what we have been told is happening, knowing that the version of "the truth" told by those who have assumed the authority to tell it is not true, our next task is to hip others to the falsely authoritative jive and to tell a more honest, because more inclusive, version of the truth.

"ORIGIN UNKNOWN": INVISIBILIZING AFRICANITY VERSUS "MADE IN AFRICA" OR *SI NO ES DEL CONGO, ES DE CARABALÍ*

I found Africa not only where I was not taught to expect to find it, but even where I was specifically taught not to expect it to be—in New Jersey. My later experiences in Africa and in the African Diaspora beyond New Jersey enabled me to begin to recognize signs and expressions—to understand what I had been seeing, hearing, saying, even tasting—and to perceive clues leading to explanations, interpretations, and various levels of meaning.

U.S. African American and other scholars and cultural leaders have been arguing throughout the twentieth century, and increasingly since the Black consciousness/Black nationalist/Pan-Africanist period of the 1960s, that the culture of U.S. African Americans, like that of other African descendants in the Americas, continues to reflect its African heritage. Although this fact should seem obvious, the firm belief of most people in the United States, including many African Americans, is that there is no such continuing African presence. Or if it exists, it exists mainly in music and dance and maybe the least mainstream versions of religion. Therefore, it can be found only in areas of expressive culture that are not part of what are considered the serious bases of society, such as political systems, economics, and technology, as my professors insistently, but unsuccessfully, tried to teach me during my graduate study in anthropology.

Even in areas of the Americas in which the African presence is unmistakable and acknowledged, such as Brazil, this presence tends to be folklorized rather than defined as an essential part of the foundation of the nation. This presumed absence of African culture worthy of serious respect has deprived U.S. and other African Diasporans of an accurate sense of meaningful origins to make profound sense of significant behaviors. It has deprived all Americans of a way to account for Pan-American Afrogenic behaviors of whose origins almost everyone is unaware, or maybe uninterested in recognizing or unwilling to acknowledge. It has also permitted the history and present of the Americas to be told in a partial, hence fictional, rather than complete, hence accurate, manner. The result is that what should be the commonly told story of all of us in the Americas is only the partially told story of some of us.

This declared or presumed absence allows the origins of words of probable African provenience, for example, words of useful interpretive value for understanding African Diasporan culture on its own terms, to be characterized as "unknown," rather than as "made in Africa," as I discovered in looking up "hip" and "jive" in a dictionary that boldly claims to be "The Voice of Authority." Looking words up in the dictionary, rather than being the banal act I had anticipated, proved to be an unanticipatedly Eurocentric experience, as I recount in chapter 1. The one word of the Wolof linguistic complex I identified for which an origin, a Eurogenic origin, was provided, misrepresented both the source of the word and the experiences of the African American speakers who most publicly used it.

This terminological example is symbolic of larger issues of interpretation in significant areas of the African Diaspora in which Africa is not, in what would appear to be a logical contradiction, assumed as the source of African Diasporan behaviors. Yet Eurogenic interpretations of such behaviors necessarily misinterpret them. A major result, as exemplified in the dictionary example, is the misattribution of African and African Diasporan contributions to the Americas, as John Vlach (chapter 10) discusses with respect to pottery in the United States. Such misattributions may qualify Afrogenic contributions as Eurogenic when the Eurogenic usages, as in the linguistic cases I cite, are either derivative from Afrogenic usages or are misrepresentations based on an apparent discounting of the possibility of an Afrogenic alternative.

Ironically, this failure to acknowledge African origins, in favor of seeking explanations for African Diasporan behaviors in Eurogenic premises and concepts, coincides with the perspective of those U.S. African Americans who have been successfully "miseducated," as African American historian Carter G. Woodson asserted in his 1933 book *The Miseducation of the Negro*,[27] to disavow their African origins and claim that they "ain't left nothin' in no Africa." It also coincides with the perspective of those hispanophone Americans who affirm their European ancestry and deny their African ancestry, but of whom others say, "*Si no es del Congo, es de Carabalí*" (If s/he's not from the Congo, s/he's from Calabar). Thus, "origin unknown" is preferable to "made in Africa" from the perspectives of antithetical groups of descendants of both enslavers and enslaved. There are, for balance, also people who claim African origins for African Diasporan behaviors but who, in the absence of adequate and adequately accessible research, are often unaware of the specific historical links.

The contributors to this volume encourage and demonstrate a perspective that involves looking at the Americas through a glass darkly, so to speak, as a corrective to the whitewash that has obscured the rich and complex multicolored mosaic that the societies of Pan-America really represent, whose origins are from the Congo and Calabar and elsewhere in Africa, as well as from various parts of Europe and the indigenous Americas. Brenda Dixon Gottschild (chapter 3) suggests that in order to understand what she terms the "Africanist" presence in the Americas, we should reverse positions and view American cultures as Africanist, looking at presumably Euro-American behaviors through an Afrogenic black light that highlights different forms, that shines light on things imperceptible in the usual Eurogenic white light—black light highlighting things invisibilized by white light, so offering different interpretive models.

In regard to looking at ourselves and our African Diasporan societies from an Afrogenic rather than Eurogenic perspective, Jesús García (chapter 17) says, similar to Olabiyi Yai (chapter 14), that we need to engage in a process of self-reconceptualization in order to free ourselves from the disorienting effects of Eurogenic concepts, norms, and terminologies. To think Afrogenically involves an active, deliberate, and vigilant process of mental decolonization. As a result of both Eurocentric formal education and the informal education of everyday life in the Americas, we have all been taught, as Shelley Fisher Fishkin says (chapter 2), to assume whiteness rather than blackness as the origin and explanation of American behaviors.

I began to discover this fact while seeking explanations of U.S. African American behaviors for which the whiteness hypothesis lacked explanatory value but for which an officially sanctioned alternative was lacking. I initially assumed, for example, that the name of an elderly African American woman I met was a modification of a European name, rather than considering the possibility that it might be an African name.

For those of us with extensive academic training, hence with years of being taught, tested on, and approved for our command of and ability to reproduce and retransmit Eurogenic concepts and arguments, this need for mental decolonization is especially essential. This Eurocentric learning was accomplished in academic environments characterized by an absence of a sanctioned Afrogenic intellectual balance with which to reconcile the difference between what we lived in our communities, so knew to be true, and what we were taught by others not from those communities and were expected to believe to be true, however unrepresentative of and irrelevant to our empirical reality. We were to believe what we were told, rather than what we saw with "our own lying eyes."

Exemplifying this situation, Mullings says of those of us who were working toward academic degrees during the transformative 1960s, as we also sought to decolonize our minds:

> It is perhaps difficult for many young students today to fully comprehend what it meant to have virtually no faculty of color, few courses that reflected our experiences, *and—almost always—highly distorted accounts of the lives of people of color.* . . . While seeking to transform the academy, we had to live within it; we rejected their models, but had to do so in their language. We knew that much of what passed as objective knowledge was at best inadequate and distorted and at worst racist, oppressive, and false. The student of color often labored to reformulate the paradigm without assistance from sympathetic faculty. In retrospect, this is not surprising when one considers that the critique entailed challenging not only the paradigms but also the institutions that supported them. (emphasis added)[28]

Those of us engaged in the multiethnic, international, multidisciplinary encounter that this volume represents are trying to provide balance to narrowly Eurocentric/Eurogenic perspectives on the Americas that by definition misrepresent us all.

My quest to understand the African basis of U.S. African American culture during my graduate studies was not only not encouraged, but was actively discouraged and even ridiculed by professors responsible for the evolution of my intellectual orientation. When I told my academic advisor how pleased I was to have come across Melville Herskovits's *The Myth of the Negro Past*,[29] which provided extensive African and African Diasporan data to support the idea that U.S. African Americans have an African heritage, he summarily dismissed such ideas as "rubbish." That is the kind of statement that sticks in your mind, especially coming from someone responsible for your academic success and hence your future career. Although the details vary, I know that my experience of the denial of the African presence in the Americas was not unique among African Diasporans in academia seeking to discover and defend an Afrogenic perspective on our own lives.

The empirical evidence that I encountered in the process of the mental decolonization that evolved during my wonderings and wanderings in Africa and the African Diaspora hipped me to the fact that Eurogenic explanations and theories emanating from the "(Euro)American way of life" could not possibly explain African Diasporan behaviors. Based on the assumptions of descendants of enslavers rather than descendants of the enslaved, such Eurogenic premises by definition obscure more plausible Afrogenic meanings, as my aforementioned dictionary experience demonstrated.

That my wonderings about U.S. African American behaviors and my discovering of answers in Africa and elsewhere in the African Diaspora led me to adopt an Afrogenic perspective on African Diasporan realities sounds simple and obvious. It is not so simple and obvious, however, in the context of the power relationships, intellectual and otherwise, on the basis of which the Americas were constructed and continue to function.

My wonderings led me to wander into what García (chapter 17) characterizes as "intellectual *palenques* and *quilombos*" (Spanish and Portuguese designations for autonomous communities created by Africans and African Diasporan "maroons" who liberated themselves from enslavement), which I understand as resistant spaces of Afrogenic thought, practice, and expression. These are spaces of intellectual marooning in which it is not only possible but even required to abandon Eurogenic models in the interest of mentally liberating Afrogenic reflection. This perspective allowed me to not only see the Africanity of much "blackness," but even to see the "blackness" of much presumed "whiteness." I learned empirically all over the Americas that "If it's not from the Congo, it's from Calabar," or elsewhere in Africa.

My analysis of the ordinary everydayness of the African presence in the lives of U.S. African Americans, and of all Americans, began with my quest to understand origins and meanings that would make sense of aspects of U.S. African American culture. Experiences elsewhere in the African Diaspora led me to understand that some of these meanings are most easily perceived through the mirror of cultural forms and styles from other societies whose Africanity remains more apparent and acknowledged, and that offer perspectives that allow the sometimes more subtle Africanity of the United States to appear in higher relief.

A growing understanding of the cultural continuum from Africa to the Americas led me to an understanding of commonalities, as well as the mosaic of uniquenesses, within the African Diaspora. This evolving comparative perspective also enabled me to use this discovered Africanity of the United States to identify Africanisms elsewhere in the Diaspora, including places in which they are even more present and simultaneously even less recognized. These Afrogenic cultural complexes often turned out to be defining elements of national cultures, hence constituents of the cultural repertoire of all Americans.

Whereas my quest was spurred by my interest in the origins of U.S. African American behaviors, Shelley Fisher Fishkin (chapter 2), literary scholar and professor of American studies and English, looks at U.S. Euro-American culture and contends that much of what has been assumed to be "white" is, in fact, not. She challenges the paradigm that has allowed the African presence to be neglected in telling the stories of who and what we all are in the United States. And she proposes a new understanding of "mainstream" U.S. culture that includes the African legacy and assumes that Euro-Americans have learned from African Americans as well as vice versa. Concerning those who continue to assert the whiteness of U.S. culture, she contends that "the white Anglo-Saxon Protestant civilization of the United States was itself shaped from the start by people and traditions who were not white, or Anglo-Saxon, or Protestant." The demographics of the origins of the Americas clearly reinforce Fisher Fishkin's argument and make the opposing one seem even more untenuous.

For Fisher Fishkin, the intellectual paradigm of the scholarly denial of the extent and diversity of African and African American roles in the creation of U.S. culture is based on the same racism that has denied African Americans full rights of citizenship in the nation and that has "allowed a patently false monocultural myth to mask and distort a multicultural reality." That the whiteness of U.S. culture continues to be simply and unquestionably assumed remains part of the enduring racist logic of the society, and hence the premise of both everyday behavior and intellectual production. Fisher Fishkin cites unexpected, even sacrosanct, areas of U.S. culture, including the classic works of literary icons, in which the African presence is clearly discernable from, of course, an Afrogenic perspective.

Her discussion of the African origins of elements of U.S. popular culture, well exemplified by cartoon character Bugs Bunny, points up several dynamics concerning the nonwhite origins of an all-American figure, origins that have broader applications and implications. Bugs Bunny, as it turns out, appears to be a mainstreamized version of the African American Br'er Rabbit. Part of the hare cycle common to the West African savanna and Sahelian areas, the stories, with the hare transformed into a rabbit, retained their educational and entertaining virtues in the African American oral tradition.[30] They were collected and put into the written tradition by white Americans who popularized them as mass culture. So the hip, jive-talking transgressive rabbit began his trajectory from black to white by coming to the Americas in the African oral tradition that was the basis of the African American oral tradition. When Br'er Rabbit was recast as Bugs Bunny and commercialized as an all-American icon, he quietly lost his "blackness" in the process, and his "whiteness" (okay, grayness) became assumed.

Like Fisher Fishkin, Brenda Dixon Gottschild (chapter 3), dance historian, critic, former professor of dance, and performer, also discusses the Africanity of another sacrosanct area of mainstream "high culture"—U.S. concert dance. Similar to Fisher Fishkin's contention concerning the African American presence in U.S. literary classics, Dixon Gottschild asserts that the "Africanist" presence is a defining ingredient of U.S. ballet and a characteristic that distinguishes it from its European origins and counterparts. Ironically, African Americans are still trying to become ordinary participants in concert dance troupes, as opposed to being mostly members of both well-respected and less known ethnic troupes. So their cultural presence has preceded their significant physical presence.

This seemingly contradictory situation of a defining Africanist cultural presence in the absence of a significant African American physical presence exemplifies well the "origin unknown" appropriation of Africanist culture without its Afrogenic identity, as with Bugs Bunny. But in this instance it occurs in a bastion of elite white culture, where it really is not supposed to be, as opposed to in popular culture where its presence, if recognized, comes as less of a shock. This precedence of the Afrogenic cultural presence over the Afrogenic physical presence contrasts with the situation in Argentina, for example, where the Afrogenic cultural presence remains, as Romero Rodríguez, Lucía Molina and Mario López, and I discuss, after the physical presence has almost been eliminated.

According to Dixon Gottschild, the Africanist aesthetic is readily apparent in U.S. culture to those who are aware that it exists, are interested in finding it, know how and where to look for it, and recognize it when they find it. The Africanist legacy is, she contends, an imperative, not a choice. It is rather a pervasive part of U.S. culture that all people in the nation embrace, even subliminally, whether or not they know or admit it. Most are unaware of this presence, and only a few are aware of its sources.

This pattern of forgetting, ignoring, denying, failing to see the Africanity of cultural elements that get appropriated as part of the national cultures of the Americas is a frequent theme in this volume. The Afrogenic nature of things gets "lost" as they become part of presumably white, Eurogenic, national cultures. Their African ancestry is not denied, because that would involve acknowledging the possibility of its original presence. It is rather forgotten, is quietly "disappeared," becomes "unknown," in an amnesia of former blackness, induced and enforced by authoritative voices of assumed whiteness.

It seems almost tautological to suggest, as Dixon Gottschild does, that looking from an Africanist perspective reveals the Africanist presence in American ballet. But given that this presence is assumed not to exist because of the "assumption of whiteness," the mere fact of presuming to look from an Afrogenic perspective is more revolutionary than it should logically be at this point in history, especially given the demographic construction of the Americas. The issue here, as echoed throughout this volume, is that those of us in the Americas who have not had the privilege of defining what constitutes knowledge are suggesting that we know something special and have something new to bring to this defining, especially when discussing our own communities' experiences. And what we have to reveal, as those who are hip to the jive have already perceived, is very often "hidden in plain view."[31]

A CENTENNIAL REVISITING OF THE DOUBLE CONSCIOUSNESS

[T]he Negro is sort of a seventh son, born with a veil, and gifted with second sight in this American world—a world which yields him no true self-consciousness, but only lets him see himself through the revelation of the other world. It is a peculiar sensation, this double-consciousness, this sense of always looking at one's self through the eyes of others, of measuring one's soul by the tape of a world that looks on in amused contempt and pity. One ever feels his two-ness—an American, a Negro; two souls, two thoughts, two unreconciled strivings; two warring ideals in one dark body, whose dogged strength alone keeps it from being torn asunder.[32]

In contrast with Du Bois's well-known tormented and disempowered concept of the "double consciousness" developed in the context of African American life at the beginning of the twentieth century, an informed and empowered sense of positive duality based on the "two-ness" of being both African American and American, each term used in both its individual national and its collective Pan-Diasporan sense, offers valuable constructs for understanding African Diasporan realities at the beginning of the twenty-first century.

The categories American and African American/African Diasporan are sometimes mutually exclusive and sometimes overlapping, sometimes antagonistic and sometimes complementary, but always a source of at least "two thoughts" of some kind of duality, or more likely multiplicity, of experience and/or perspective. This double or multiple consciousness, however, need no longer be a source of "unreconciled strivings." This splendid "gift" of "second sight" can, on the contrary, now function as a conscious source of both experiential and analytical riches—of simultaneously multiple, and necessarily critical, perspectives in response to the contradictions between one's own experiences and the "revelation[s] of the other world." And the idea of being "born with a veil," according to the U.S. African American epistemology with which I am most familiar, implies the ability to see beyond the ordinary realm that others see, even to perceive different dimensions of reality, hence a gift with empowering ramifications.

To function within one's own African Diasporan society, as well as in the larger (Pan)American society of which it is an integral and even foundational part, regularly performing both literal and metaphoric cultural code-switches, and to contemplate one's reality from both inside and outside, sometimes simultaneously, are, in fact, elements of a core definition of what it means to be part of the African Diaspora. The concept of "African American"—again with "American" used in the most inclusive Pan-American sense—facilitates a necessary definition of a double consciousness based on African origins and African American presents and presence.

This concept considers the pervasive African/African American presence in the fabric of Pan-America, while also respecting the rich variety of these historical and present presences. African Diasporan culture(s), both in the plural singulars of distinctive national cultures and in their common Pan-African substrata, constitute(s) a synergy of multiple African ethnic origins in dynamic interaction with the cultures of others encountered while African people were obligatorily reinventing themselves both individually and collectively as biologically and culturally new people in the new world they helped to create.

Even at the beginning of the twentieth century, having a double, or multiple, consciousness could prove to be an empowering experience, as the accomplishments of Arturo Alfonso Schomburg illustrate. Whereas some contributors to this volume are concerned with situating African Diasporan communities within, and acknowledging their contributions to, their larger national contexts, Lisa Sánchez González (chapter 7), literary critic, journalist, and professor of English, is concerned with situating a major African Diasporan intellectual in, and acknowledging his full contributions to, his plural sociocultural contexts. Arturo Alfonso Schomburg was the Afro-Puerto Rican bibliophile whose monumental efforts to document African Diasporan culture provided the foundation for the creation of the Schomburg Center for Research in Black Culture. Schomburg violated the "conspiracy of silence" that invizibilized the Africanity of important cultural figures in his quest to rediscover the erased history of people of African origin in the Americas and Europe. By bringing to light obscured information, popularizing it in his writings and public lectures, and making it available in the invaluable repository that his collection has become, Schomburg's activities serve as an excellent prototype for the work that many contemporary African Diasporan and other scholars are continuing.

Schomburg's inspiration to seek and gather materials on African and African Diasporan history and culture is overly familiar. A high school teacher's response to his query about the contributions of Africans and their descendants to the history of the Americas was that they had contributed nothing. Like others of us in the past and present who have been given such dismissive and negating responses in one way or another, Schomburg decided to prove the teacher wrong and to discover Africa's contributions to the Americas, as Molina and López, Rodríguez, and García say African Diasporan groups are currently doing in Argentina, Bolivia, Paraguay, Uruguay, and Venezuela. Sánchez González notes with no astonishment, as Fisher Fishkin, Dixon Gottschild, and I also found in seeking Afrogenic culture in the Americas several generations after Schomburg, that the more Schomburg looked for information on the contributions of Africans and their descendants to the Americas and Europe, the more he discovered.

In discussing Schomburg's accomplishments in the context of his identity as an Afro-Puerto Rican intellectual, Sánchez González critiques both Puerto Rican intellectual traditions that ignore Schomburg as Puerto Rican because of his blackness and U.S. African American and anglophone Caribbean intellectual traditions that fail to acknowledge the significance of his Puerto Rican origins. Both communities, based on dysfunctional intra-Diasporan blinders and limiting exclusivities of identification, thus invisibilize part of the multiply conscious transnational heritage that was the basis of Schomburg's broad interests, extensive accomplishments, and seminal contributions to the accurate telling of the story of the Americas and the Atlantic world.

Whereas Schomburg discussed the erasure of the blackness of important figures in Puerto Rican arts and letters, who were whitened in being included in the presumably "Euro"-Caribbean cultural tradition, Sánchez González interprets the fact of Schomburg's blackness as a tacit rationale for his not being centered in Puerto Rican intellectual traditions. The irony is that Schomburg promoted coalition-building across the lines of African Diasporan national identities and outlined the contours of the kind of

Pan-American African Diasporan consciousness that he himself exemplified, a consciousness that those who would narrow his identity have failed to understand. It is also a consciousness that has deep and firm empirical foundations in the commonalities of Pan-American African Diasporan culture, as demonstrated by the research and reflections of the contributors to this volume.

The Afrogenic double consciousness concept is especially relevant both epistemologically and hermeneutically to African Diasporan scholars who are researching our own and/or other African Diasporan communities. In our research personae we are both natives of sorts as well as scholars, scholar being a category that has until recently tended to signify the antithesis of native. We are both Diasporan insiders and academically disciplined outsiders, but outsiders much more familiar, in both the ordinary and the extended family meanings of the term, than the usual thoroughly outsider researchers have been. The insider/outsider conceptual and methodological approaches of African Diasporan scholars often involve applying the perspectives of academic disciplines to intuitions informed by the Afrogenic community knowledge, the native knowledge, of especially observant participants.

The idea of the double consciousness is also useful for highlighting the important issue of the significance of the African Diasporan native as scholar and scholar as native. Many of the contributors have begun their scholarly quests and developed their understandings based on their native knowledge and personal curiosities as members of the communities in question. To this experiential knowledge they have added academic training leading to dynamic and reciprocal interactions, rather than "warring ideals," between their roles as knowing natives and as inquiring intellectuals. Information, theories, and methods of knowing from each of these roles and positionalities challenges, nourishes, complements, and complicates the other. This was my experience in coming to an understanding of the Africanity of New Jersey.

Olly Wilson (chapter 8), musicologist, professor of music, and internationally known composer, says that his quest to discover the African conceptual basis of African American music was stimulated by what appeared to his ears to be obvious similarities between certain aspects of West African and U.S. African American musical genres. Thus it was as a participant in, as well as a scholarly researcher of, the musical culture of African America that he began to perceive these relationships. And it was as a dancer of African Diasporan sacred dances that Yvonne Daniel (chapter 23) learned the knowledge embodied in them, to which she applied her acquired anthropological perspectives to offer new insights and interpretations. Her intellectual authority for identifying and asserting the validity of an Afrogenic corporal epistemology is based on her "two thoughts," on her "second sight" in her dualistic positionality as both insider/dancer/participant and as observant scholar.

The concept of double consciousness, in addition to such methodological implications, is also key to looking at the African foundations of African Diasporan behaviors. Wilson says that there is a distinct set of musical qualities of African origin that is expressive of the collective cultural values of people of African descent in the Americas. The essence of this tradition is a common core of conceptual approaches to the process of music-making and to the ways in which music functions in society. The manifestations of this common core are infinite, with the particular forms reflecting the peculiarities of specific African Diasporan experiences. It is about a way of doing something, not simply something that is done, similar to Dixon Gottschild's characterization of the Africanist aesthetic as an attitude, a way of doing that permeates realms of behavior.

It was necessarily within the frameworks of meaning and belief that they brought with them that Africans in the Americas read their new environment. And it was through both the linguistic and the aesthetic languages they brought with them that they expressed these understandings. Thus, their music was formed by African cognitive assumptions and conceptual approaches to music-making—and to life in general—which were then shaped by their experiences in the Americas. It is precisely this duality, this double consciousness, Wilson says, that gives African Diasporan music its distinctive position as part of the broad fabric of shared American culture, with roots that remain fundamentally African.

In a similar vein, culinary historian and professor of English Jessica Harris (chapter 9) discusses African foods and cooking techniques that have remained not only in African Diasporan communities, but also in the national gastronomies of the Americas. Because enslaved Africans and African Americans were involved in the cultivation of food crops and were placed in charge of their enslavers' kitchens, their foods and foodways subtly defined the tastes of the Americas, usually without acknowledgment. Additionally, privations of the U.S. Civil War introduced formerly privileged white Southerners to foods previously relegated to African Americans. These foods, Harris contends, have come to characterize "Southern cuisine," with, again, their African origins forgotten.

Like Bugs Bunny, Southern food lost the Afrogenic identity of its creators and original consumers and was whitened for national consumption as a regional culinary tradition. I had noticed this phenomenon with gumbo, the "classic" version of which *Food & Wine*[33] magazine claimed was predicated on its Eurogenic roux base, rather than on the defining African okra that gave it its origin and name. It is ironic that the South, the historic bastion of the most severe racial segregation and oppression, remains the area in which white culture is the blackest, with foodways as intimate and essential, if unacknowledged, everyday Afrogenic reminders.

African Diasporan food traditions involve both dishes whose African origins are obvious, as its Bantu name proclaims for gumbo, and dishes that reflect African Diasporan gastronomic creations based on African culinary memories and the American realities of local crops and durable foods, such as salted and/or dried fish and meats, versions of which were also known in Africa, as well as the rejected innards and extremities of the animals eaten by privileged whites. Both traditions remain in African Diasporan and national gastronomies, sometimes even being touted as distinctive and defining features of the latter.

In discussing the African roots and American branches of U.S. African American material culture, John Vlach (chapter 10), anthropologist and professor of American civilization, describes how African Americans created objects based on African aesthetics, meanings, and purposes while using Euro-American techniques. Concerning the difference in importance that Euro-Americans and African Americans attribute to specific kinds of quilting patterns, for example, Vlach notes that although African Americans have been familiar with the geometric patterns preferred in Euro-American quilting, they have traditionally favored a strip style reminiscent of an aesthetic common to West African weaving. Thus, African Americans have applied African aesthetics to Euro-American production techniques to express Afrogenic meanings through Eurogenic media.

Wooden canes carved by African Americans often bore distinctive marks and adornments reflecting, Vlach says, African motifs symbolic of supernatural communication and human authority. So when an African American carved a snake or alligator on a walking stick, he may have intended and conveyed a different meaning than a similar animal carved by a white artisan. It is also quite possible, within the perspective of the Afrogenic double consciousness, that rather than these meanings being either/or, either of African or of Euro-American origin or inspiration, they were and are both/and for African Americans, who are part of both realities. Both Afrogenic and Eurogenic meanings are both real and significant, sometimes in different contexts, sometimes on different levels.

Vlach also notes that African American accomplishments in the area of material culture remain mostly unacknowledged and are often misattributed, hence are underresearched. This observation recalls my findings concerning the misattribution of African and African American culinary, and more especially linguistic, contributions to U.S. culture. In both cases, African and African Diasporan contributions have been denied or dismissed and Eurogenic sources substituted or prioritized, thus invisibilizing African and African Diasporan creations.

Were it not for the process of historical distortion, the fact that Africans brought knowledge and technical skills with them to the Americas would not come as such a surprise. South Carolina and Georgia Low Country planters, for example, specifically sought Africans from rice-growing regions of West Africa, who brought with them knowledge of the technology and tools of rice production and preparation. The failure to properly attribute African contributions to the material culture, hence to the knowledge-based technology of production in the Americas, although congruent with the myth cited by Joseph Harris that Africans had no knowledge or skills to bring with them, is logically, to say nothing of empirically, incongruent with the reality that Africans were brought to the Americas specifically to work. Hence they were selected for the specialized knowledge and skills that they had used to live in diverse environments in Africa, as well as for their ability to furnish manual labor.

But although they were brought to the Americas to work, Africans and their African Diasporan descendants did not just work. They also created new artistic forms in music and dance, from Argentina's tango to the jazz of the United States that is now acknowledged as the only indigenously American classical music. And in spite of doing grueling labor and being victims of tremendous and relentless efforts to kill their spirit, they succeeded in setting the standard for celebratory aesthetic jubilance for the Americas and increasingly for the world.

Cultural anthropologist John Stewart (chapter 11) describes the African Diaspora as the source of the globalization of a creolized African culture and aesthetic through the exporting of the exuberantly joyous Trinidadian carnival to North America, Europe, and beyond. As elsewhere in the Americas where carnival exists, Africans were initially prohibited from participating in Trinidad's elite white event. When allowed to participate, they took it over and Africanized it. The increasingly global carnival is a contemporary expression of the sharing with a receptive global society of an emphatically Afrogenic celebratory style.

Emerging out of Trinidad's multiethnic background, contributions from other ethnic sources were, Stewart says, grafted onto the African aesthetic and social sensibility evident in the music, dance, and overall style that remains at the core of Trinidad's carnival. This is similar to Wilson's assertion that there is an African aesthetic core onto which other musical influences have been grafted in the Americas. Stewart concurs with Wilson's view of African and African Diasporan music in noting that carnival plays roles that transcend mere entertainment, bringing together the secular and sacred in what he characterizes as "a great metaphysical force."

ACKNOWLEDGING OUR KNOWLEDGE(S) AND TELLING OUR STORIES—IN AND ON OUR OWN TERMS

> We wish to plead our case. Too long have others spoken for us. Too long has the publick been deceived by misrepresentations, in things which concern us dearly.

This statement is from the first page of the first issue of the first African American newspaper, from March 16, 1827. *Freedom's Journal* was founded by John B. Russwurm and Samuel E. Cornish in response to New York City newspapers' negative portrayals of, and overt attacks on, the free African American community. Some white editors, for example, used their publications to encourage the (re)enslavement of New York's free African American population.[34]

For Africans and African Diasporans to tell our own stories, to see ourselves through our own eyes, without others as either models or authorities for defining either reality or significance, offers a corrective to the problem Du Bois identified as our "looking at [our] self[selves] through the eyes of others," and our understanding ourselves through the prism of "the revelation of the other world" that "yields [us] no true self-consciousness," of, as Jesús García (chapter 17) says a century later, "seeing ourselves through borrowed eyes."

Actually, given the intellectual tradition of the Americas, this seeing might be better characterized as being through not so much "borrowed eyes" as through the "imposed eyes of others," since borrowing implies volition. Being hip to the jive involves having one's own eyes wide open to perceive the truth through the veil of others' mystifying and mythifying reality-negating revelations. In spite of the massive societal changes that have taken place since these words were written almost two centuries ago, contributors to this volume are still saying "We wish to plead our case. Too long have others spoken for us. Too long has the publick been deceived by misrepresentations, in things which concern us dearly."

We are also insisting upon seeing and portraying ourselves through the revelations of our own experiences and interpretations, as opposed to through the revelations of others based on their experiences and interpretations that are usually different from and sometimes antithetical to our own. And we are claiming the authority to be "voices of our own authority" speaking of and for the cultures that our communities have authored. On the basis of our dually or multiply conscious authority as both members of the communities and as scholars of these communities, we are challenging misrepresentations of them by both omission and commission.

The New York African Burial Ground Project, concerning such a significant issue as the rediscovered physical remains of African and African American ancestors, exemplifies many of the complex dynamics involved in our insistence upon telling our own stories, in this case via the stories of centuries-old Africans and African Diasporans who returned to tell theirs. Physical anthropologist Michael Blakey (chapter 12), director of the project, discusses the politics of omission and the distortions of history that were literally and metaphorically brought to light both by the discovery of New York City's colonial African cemetery and by the controversies generated by this discovery. These events, Blakey argues, exemplify the kinds of problems African Americans continue to face in the struggle for self-definition with, as Fisher Fishkin and others also contend, the major theoretical problem being the fundamental Euro-American racism that distorts perceptions of African Diasporan realities.

Members of the African American descendant community had to wage a battle to gain control of the Burial Ground and to place the scientific task of reconstructing our own ancestors' history in the hands of the leading African American research university. The locating of the project at Howard University in Washington, D.C., was made difficult by competing anthropologists at Lehman College of the City University of New York, who had taken initial possession of the African and African American ancestral remains and whose political allies mobilized in support of their attempts to obtain the lucrative research contract to study and interpret them. Blakey notes that taking control of telling our own stories is not just an intellectual issue. It is often also about the financial value of the business of controlling definitions of reality and determinations of what constitutes valid knowledge.

The struggle to empower scientists at Howard University rather than Lehman College to interpret African and African Diasporan skeletal remains offers a striking metaphor about the continuing economic value for whites of African and African Diasporan bodies, and about the continuing African American struggle to control our destiny on various levels, including this most intimate one of controlling our bodies. The 1990s efforts to liberate historic African and African American skeletal bodies from Euro-American control seem like a contemporary rerun of nineteenth-century efforts to liberate African and African Diasporan enslaved bodies from the lucrative bondage to whites that allowed for the building of the Americas and the Atlantic world.

Whites in the 1990s had no qualms about desecrating African American graves and had to be forced to stop by a coalition of African Americans from the community, the academy, and the city, state, and federal governments. White institutions and individuals sought to continue to violate African American bodies with impunity, further enriching themselves by using power politics to usurp the right to tell their version of the story of someone else's ancestors.

The issue here was not just about the right to define a people, but also about the economic benefits of doing so. Had Lehman College succeeded in maintaining control over the skeletal remains of the enslaved ancestors of the African American community, the previously obscured commodified relationships of slavery in colonial New York would have been recreated in contemporary New York. Slavery-style economic relationships would seem not to have changed significantly after two centuries of history and more than a century of emancipation. It is especially interesting to note that the graves of individuals whose lives were spent creating the economic basis for the development of the city are buried, in symbolic irony, under the southern Manhattan Wall Street area that is the financial center of New York City, the United States, the Americas, and the world.

The fact that politics and community activism were so important in a scientific project points up the fact that African Diasporans must fight in various ways for access to, and control of, both the data and the right to tell our own stories with it, especially when these stories contradict official versions. But if the stories told of African Americans' lives in and contributions to the construction of all of the Americas are not true, then the stories told about the history and present of all of the Americas are also not true.

An African sense of ancestral agency would recognize that Africans and African Americans who had not been able to tell their stories in the past had returned to tell them in the present. These ancestors would insist upon correcting the denigrating stories told about them by those who had enslaved them, benefited tremendously from their bondage, and then arrogantly denied the value of their work. They would have returned at this time to tell their stories through the contemporary voices of their descendants, who now have the scientific knowledge and institutions with the technical capacity to enable them to do so in a plethora of highly sophisticated ways.

A symbol found on one coffin was interpreted by the Howard University team as a *Sankofa* representing the Akan proverb *Se wo were fi na wo sankofa a yenkyi* (It is not a taboo to go back and retrieve if you forget).[35] The symbol refers to the wisdom of using an understanding of the past in planning and preparing for the future, of recognizing the value of and seeking to learn about and from those who are now ancestors as a basis for present and future life. The team that had initially taken possession of the skeletal remains had made the facile assumption that what appeared to them to be a geometricized heart shape represented the meanings associated with the Eurogenic heart-equals-love imagery most visibly evoked on bumper stickers, mugs, and T-shirts, and commercialized for Valentine's Day.

This probable misinterpretation resulting from the use of a Eurocentric cultural lens and this trivializing of a powerful African symbol highlight the obvious value of using an Afrogenic perspective in interpreting material remains and cultural expressions of African and African Diasporan people. Many of the people buried in the Burial Ground had been born in Africa. And given the African demographics of North America, some were very likely from the Akan-speaking area of present-day Ghana and Côte d'Ivoire from which the Sankofa symbol comes.

Archaeologist James Denbow suggests another, Central African, interpretation of the symbol. He says concerning early twentieth-century tombstones from the Atlantic coast of the Republic of the Congo that "Almost all of the tombstones have a heart as a central element." Noting that the shape represents a European stylistic convention introduced by missionaries who had converted Africans to Catholicism prior to the eighteenth century, he observes that "symbolic meanings associated with the heart" are "deeply embedded in Kongolese concepts of body and soul."[36] Denbow thus suggests that twentieth-century Kongo people have been utilizing a European symbol, modified and adapted to Kongo thoughts and needs, to make visual a concept profoundly rooted in their own culture. And he quotes a Kongo man as saying, "The heart rules the entire being. It is the center of all information and instruction. . . . The heart also stores up the memories of all past experience and gives man the power of action."[37]

There is a congruity between the West African Akan and Central African Kongo interpretations of the symbol. People from various areas of Africa met in the Americas and forged new identities based on commonalities they discovered. The idea that "the heart stores up memories of past experience and gives man the power of action" leads to using an understanding of the past as the basis for building the future. So, the heart-shaped symbol may have been intended to represent a Sankofa, or the similar meanings the Kongo associated with the heart, or/and something else that has not yet been suggested from elsewhere in Africa. Thus, one might reasonably presume that Africans would have used a familiar and meaningful African symbol, or that if they used a Eurogenic symbol, it would represent African meanings in as significant a context as a burial site for the transition of their loved ones to the status of revered ancestors. The Howard University researchers had a sense of both the Afrogenic and the Eurogenic interpretations of the symbol, as well as of their relative explanatory values.

In the context of the African Burial Ground, the Sankofa may be understood as referring symbolically to the fact that the literal and figurative coming to light of the historic ancestral remains offered the opportunity to learn from their scientific analysis something about how these Africans and African Americans had lived, and the roles they had played in the building of the City of New York. Their existence, their stories, and their contributions had been "forgotten," invisibilized, literally buried under the physical constructions, and the intellectual construction, of the modern city for which they helped create, and of which they continue to literally help constitute, the foundation.

The coming to light of this covered-up aspect of U.S. African American history, and of U.S. history, is symbolic of the larger issue of the both real and symbolic uncovering/discovering of the African Diasporan presence in the foundations of the societies of the Americas. What was figuratively uncovered with the literal uncovering of the ancestral skeletal remains was the metaphoric cover-up of the African/African Diasporan role in the creation of New York. If Africans and African Diasporans contributed little or nothing to the construction of New York City, the United States, the Americas, the Atlantic world, and global civilization, as has been systematically claimed and taught, the implication is that having contributed little, they/we are not entitled to much.

The retelling of the story of New York such that the presence and contributions of the individuals interred in the Burial Ground are included in the historical patrimony of the city should situate African Americans as rightful heirs to that legacy. If our ancestors did, however, participate in the building of the city, the nation, the Americas, the Atlantic world, and global civilization, then we their descendants should be entitled to benefit from the fruits of their labors.

The idea that Africans and African Diasporans may have contributed little or nothing is a logical and empirical contradiction in the context of enslavement. The implication is that the only human group whose presence and raison d'être in the Americas was predicated solely on their role as a labor force, as Curtin noted in describing piezas de India as units of labor rather than as individual human beings, did not do the work that they were often violently obliged to do in building the societies of Pan-America.

The process for African Diasporans of telling our own stories requires such a struggle because doing so involves changing the versions of the past and present of the Americas that others had an interest in fabricating and have an interest in maintaining. A story of newly American African efforts to speak for themselves in the context of contemporary museum representations exemplifies this point. Cultural anthropologist Diana Baird N'Diaye (chapter 13) discusses the politics of representation as manifest in the Smithsonian Institution's African Immigrant Folklife Study Project, which she founded and directs. The goals of the project were for researchers from Washington, DC, area African immigrant communities to study and share with the public ways in which their communities are preserving and transforming their lifestyles and creating new senses of community, culture, and identity in the United States. N'Diaye's experiences demonstrate the nature of the power relations involved in Africans' claiming the authority to represent and define themselves in the contemporary United States, and the right to determine what constitutes relevant and legitimate knowledge about their communities and who possesses it.

This new African presence in the United States represents a contemporary example of Joseph Harris's (chapter 4) description of the continuing global African Diaspora. Like people involved in the initial involuntary Diaspora to the Americas, members of this contemporary Diaspora are, albeit in much more volitional and favorable circumstances, also reinventing Afrogenic institutions and behaviors in a context that lacks many familiar things, makes many different demands, and offers many new resources and possibilities. This most recent African Diaspora further complicates the definition of African American and offers another take on the Du Boisian double consciousness by adding the actively transnational duality of those who are now both African and American.

Although the success of the project led her to downplay the obstacles, N'Diaye acknowledges that it was difficult to fund the project through the usual sources. The researchers, respected African-born culture bearers and scholars, brought to the project insider knowledge of the dominant discourses about their evolving identities and cultures, and knowledge of subtleties of practice and meaning unavailable to outsider scholars with which to determine which aspects of their communities to document and how to interpret them. In spite of academia's current claims of respect for the authority of "native voices," she notes, potential funders focused on the absence of the usual academically sanctioned "experts" and challenged the ability of African immigrant community members to research their own cultures seriously. Although some participants were credentialed scholars, the reviewers were unfamiliar with them so apparently did not consider their presence the kind of intellectual authority they were seeking.

Reciprocally, African immigrant community members complained about the ways in which Africa had been represented in Smithsonian exhibits, did not believe in the possibility of an authentic partnership, and were suspicious of the intentions of the institution. The project gained community trust through the production of programs and publications accurately reflecting African immigrant voices. Similar to the New York African Burial Ground Project, the African immigrant project was sustained largely because mainly African Americans in key positions insisted upon including the authoritative voices of the African community in telling their own stories.

The work of linguist Olabiyi Yai (chapter 14), ambassador to UNESCO from the Republic of Benin, on historic concepts of African *nations* in the Americas complements N'Diaye's contemporary analysis by shedding comparative light on common Afrogenic conceptual foundations in the creation of past and present Diasporan African communities and identities. Yai's analysis also highlights the special value of studies of the African Diaspora by scholars from African societies that have established a transatlantic presence in the Americas. His intimate native, and disciplined scholarly, knowledge of the African roots of African Diasporan practices gives him an especially valuable style of Afrogenic perspective in interpreting them. His form of double consciousness as related to the African Diaspora offers a privileged example of Dixon Gottschild's suggestion to reverse the perspective and look at the Americas through an Africanist light.

Yai's African(ist) perspective, an essential complement to African Diasporan perspectives, allows him to discover meanings and principles in the Diaspora of which members and scholars of these societies, lacking his broad experiential knowledge of the African roots of Diasporan phenomena, are unaware. Like the African immigrant researchers in Washington, he has an insider's "knowledge of subtleties of practice and meaning" not only "unavailable to outsider scholars," but sometimes also unknown to practitioners because of their historical distance from the origins of their practices.

Yai notes that some historians claim that it was enslavers who organized Africans into separate nations based on their ethnicities or regions of origin in a divide-and-rule strategy. This perspective assumes an absence of African agency in creating for themselves spaces of relative freedom. Allowed time for entertainment and Christian instruction in the context of the nation structures, Africans, Yai contends, reinvented Afrogenic institutions and practices cloaked in Eurogenic garb.

To maintain and (re)create as much culture as they did, Africans clearly had to use multiple techniques of camouflage and dissimulation. They had to be, and the results prove that they were, both hip and jive. This dissimulative resistance to imposed assimilationist efforts by appearing to conform on the level of visible behaviors, but with different intentions, meanings, and goals from those intended by their enslavers, is similar to Vlach's discussion of African foundations and meanings in African American material culture. All over the Americas Africans and their descendants who were hip to the jive cloaked African and African Diasporan meanings in Eurogenic garb, jiving those they intended to deceive into believing they had really acquiesced to their jive.

Depending on one's focus, one may highlight either the imposed Eurogenic meanings or the deep structural Afrogenic meanings of the same phenomena, such as with the interpretations of the nations. Given my discovery that Afrogenic meanings offer the only convincing explanations for African Diasporan behaviors in twentieth-century New Jersey almost two centuries after the end of the legal importation of Africans to the United States, I have to assume that in the eighteenth and nineteenth centuries, when Africans were arriving regularly from the continent and were continually infusing African Diasporan societies with new information and inspiration from old traditions, the meanings of African Diasporan behaviors were significantly more Afrogenic than Eurogenic.

The macrolevel of belonging to recreated African nations in the Americas based on notions of plural citizenships remembered from Africa that Yai discusses is similar to the multiple belonging of both Arturo Alfonso Schomburg and of the dynamically transnational new Diasporan Africans whom N'Diaye describes. In contrast, social anthropologist Patricia Guthrie (chapter 16) discusses a microsocietal level of (re)creating a sense of individual belonging that was designed to allow each person a place in the disrupted and reorganized situation of enslavement.

Enslaved Africans and African Americans were very often deprived of consanguine family ties and were obliged to develop new forms of social organization to recreate a sense of personhood and community. Guthrie describes a social institution developed during slavery by which everyone could be integrated into reinvented communities and given a role and sense of belonging. On St. Helena Island in the South Carolina Sea Islands, such an institution was "catching sense," the process by which children were provided with a human network and an eventual place in the adult social community. Similar to Yai's analysis of the concept of the nation in Africa and the African Diaspora, with the institution of catching sense what mattered was not simply a person's condition or place of birth, but rather values associated with and acquired in that place.

Musician, artist, and researcher Tomás Olivera Chirimini (chapter 15) is the cultural director of Montevideo's oldest Afro-Uruguayan organization, the Asociación Cultural y Social Uruguaya Negra (ACSUN), and the founder and artistic director of the Conjunto Bantú, a performance group that reenacts traditional Afro-Uruguayan pageantry. He analyses the evolution of the *candombe*, the core Afro-Uruguayan cultural complex that constitutes a major contribution to Uruguay's national identity. Candombe originally designated the music, dance, instrumentation, and locales of the eighteenth- and nineteenth-century social events of reconstituted African nations in Uruguay. In these nations, which Yai discusses in a Pan-American context, Africans of similar origins recreated a sense of identity and community based on old principles and new realities. Although ceasing to exist as such with the demise of the African-born population at the end of the nineteenth century, the African nations and the candombe have continued to reinvent themselves in new guises based on old foundations and new realities.

Candombe became a source of inspiration for artistic representation in painting, in popular and classical music and dance, and in the Uruguayan carnival. Candombe also became the foundation of contemporary Afro-Uruguayan self-expression and the key element of the national cultural identity by which Uruguayans celebrate their uniqueness. Thus, the presumably nonexistent Afro-Uruguayan population, which has always been hypervisible in cultural production, maintains obvious continuities of Afrogenic culture in a society that proclaims its European heritage while characterizing itself by its African heritage.

IN AND ON OUR OWN TERMS

The desire to and insistence upon telling our stories both in and on our own terms is part of a contemporary Pan-American African Diasporan dynamic. Where we look for information, which information is considered useful and valid, and who makes these determinations for what purposes are crucial issues. Also significant are the terms *on* which we understand and interpret the data, and the terms *in* which we tell the stories. Innovative sources of revisionist information can be found in old oral traditions, in new readings of old archives, in new understandings of old ways of structuring and characterizing experience, and in new definitions of kinds and sources of knowledge, some of which may be ancestral.

Jesús García (chapter 17), author, musician, filmmaker, and general coordinator of the Fundación AfroAmérica, is concerned with demystifying the absence of the African presence in the construction of the Venezuelan national identity. He is also concerned with the Eurocentric nature of the historical discourse taught in Venezuelan schools, which leads, among other negative results, to internalized negative self-perceptions among Afro-Venezuelans. Fortunately for García's worldview, the elders in his Afro-Venezuelan town told him a different story from that told in the schools, one featuring Afro-Venezuelans in tales, songs, and poetry. Everyday life provided him with an alternative vision and an antidote to the official version of Venezuelan history.

As in Venezuela, all over the Americas members of the African Diaspora, like all other Americans, have been systematically (mis)educated to see Africa as savage and ahistorical based on the kinds of myths evoked by Joseph Harris. These systematically inculcated (mis)perceptions have inclined African Diasporans not to want to identify with such a problematic past and to underestimate our ancestors' participation in the development of the Americas. This miseducation continues in both compulsory formal education and in the much more influential informal mass education with which we are bombarded by the media. I called the results of a study I did of films on Africa used in U.S. schools, "Tarzan in the Classroom: How 'Educational' Films Mythologize Africa and Miseducate Americans."[38]

García sought to resolve the contradiction between the national version of Venezuelan history and that of his elders by going to the same archival sources from which the official version came. There he found that the same national archives in which the exclusionary definers of the official history had found only part of the story also contained the data for telling the rest of the story. Historical documents corroborated his community's oral traditions about the Afro-Venezuelan presence and contradicted official stories that ignored or misrepresented this presence.

García's experience clearly demonstrates Inikori's and Dixon Gottschild's contention that the theory one seeks to prove and the worldview one seeks to support determine the data one chooses to look for, notice, declare significant, and use to prove one's points. He found an important African presence "hidden in plain view" in the same official sources used by those who told the story of Venezuela as if Africans had not been significant actors in the history of the nation.

On a visit to the African Burial Ground's Office of Public Education and Interpretation, I learned that public educator and researcher Marie-Alice Devieux had had a parallel experience at the New York Historical Society. When she told a white researcher there that she was seeking documentation of the enslaved African/African American presence in colonial New York, the man, who had been working for four months with documents from the period that interested her, assured her that there had been few Africans/African Americans in New York at the time and that most of them had been free. At the end of the day the man came to her with a pile of documents referring to the large enslaved African/African American presence in colonial New York. With "an incredulous look on his face," he told her that he had never "seen" that information before.[39]

In searching for evidence of the moral and political contributions of Afro-Venezuelans to the national concept of and struggle for independence, García found declarations of African and Afro-Venezuelan maroons who had been captured and tortured for seeking freedom from bondage. Such discoveries led him to critique theories positing that the freedom-seeking aspirations of Afro-Venezuelans were, rather than evidence of their own desire for freedom, in fact inspired by the French Revolution, a thesis upheld by presumably credible Venezuelan scholars. To the contrary, based on his archival research García contends that Afro-Venezuelan and other African Diasporan quests for freedom, as expressed, for example, in the creation of autonomous maroon communities, many of which predated the 1789 French Revolution, should be understood as models for American independence movements. Based on such Pan-American realities, he urges a study of comparative marooning and its impact on the construction of ideas of national independence in the Americas.

The Eurocentric idea that such movements were modeled on the French Revolution is part of the pervasive tendency of imposing inaccurate origins on African Diasporan phenomena, and in this case attributing the inspiration for Afrogenic freedom-seeking to a European phenomenon that had not yet occurred. García's exhortation is especially significant when related to the acknowledgment in the United States that the nineteenth- and twentieth-century African American abolitionist and civil rights struggles served as the impetus and models for other sectors of the population to seek their own greater freedom and increased rights.

White women's involvement in the nineteenth-century abolitionist movement preceded their seeking greater rights for themselves through the women's suffrage movement. And the mid-twentieth-century African American civil rights and Black liberation movements led to the women's liberation movement, to senior citizens' rights movements such as the Gray Panthers, whose name, albeit with much less militant implications, was copied from the Black Panthers, as well as to the assertions of the rights of other ethnic and self-identified groups. It should not be so difficult to imagine that the most unfree people in the Americas, on the basis of whose bondage the Americas were predicated, should be those people most inclined to fight for their freedom. Nor should it come as a surprise that their freedom struggles should serve as models for others, including those whose privilege was based on their subjugation.

Similarly, geologist Gilberto Leal (chapter 18), a founder of the Conselho Nacional de Entidades Negras (the National Council of Black Organizations) and coordinator of the Bahian politico-cultural organization Núcleo Cultural Níger-Okàn (Níger-Okàn Cultural Center), provides a retelling of Brazilian history that foregrounds Afro-Brazilian activism and resistance and challenges the still-alive scholarly and uncritical popular vision of Brazil as a "racial democracy." Those who are hip to the jive characterize this perspective as Brazil's "exquisite myth." Brazilian history was, Leal states, marked by frequent revolts against the violence of the slavocratic system, in flagrant contrast to the national myth of a benign system of slavery passively accepted by the enslaved. Official history has invisibilized this heroic aspect of Afro-Brazilian history by misrepresenting Afro-Brazilian resistance to oppression as banditry rather than as freedom-fighting.

Like García, Leal posits the freedom struggles of enslaved African Diasporans as models for national independence movements, and presents African and Afro-Brazilian active resistance to enslavement as the forerunner of and prototype for Brazil's quest for independence from Portuguese colonialism. He asserts that the seventeenth-century Quilombo of Palmares represented the first successful act of resistance against colonial control in Brazil, and that Zumbi, the last leader of Palmares, whose heroism Afro-Brazilians commemorate annually, should be considered a national hero of Brazil's independence.

Leal also illustrates Inikori's claims concerning the African role in the economic development of the Atlantic basin by discussing the omission in Brazil's official history of acknowledgment of the fundamental Afro-Brazilian role as the unremunerated labor force in the sugar, coffee, and mining industries that created the wealth of the nation. In line with Inikori's contention that the modern economies of the Atlantic world were based on enslaved African labor in the Americas, Leal asserts that the modern industrial nation of Brazil was built by Afro-Brazilians.

Brazilian historian João Reis (chapter 19) supports Leal's contentions concerning Afro-Brazilian resistance to enslavement by documenting the fact that uprisings of enslaved people and the creation of maroon communities were common all over the country throughout the history of Brazilian slavery. While acknowledging that inspirations for revolts came from various sources internal and external to Afro-Brazilian and Brazilian society, Reis alludes to links between and influences from intra-Diasporan contacts in noting that the effect of the 1804 Haitian revolution, known in Brazil as *haitianismo*, was a major inspiration for freedom-seeking Afro-Brazilians, and that the 1835 Revolt of the Malês in Bahia was a source of good news reported in the abolitionist newspaper *The Liberator*, in New York City.

The issue of resistance to enslavement among African Diasporans is obviously a very important issue because it is a key demonstration of agency and accomplishment. The acknowledgment of such agency creates an intellectual problem when the goal of a system is to disempower a people, enslavement representing the ultimate disempowerment. Demonstrations of agency and accomplishment have to be denied through dissimulatory intellectual tactics of nonacknowledgment, distortion of meaning, logic-defying interpretations, and misattribution.

Once the system of American slavery, predicated on the disempowerment of people of African descent, was in place, it became intellectually impossible to acknowledge something so contradictory as the premise that struggles for freedom among presumably powerless enslaved people could have inspired struggles for freedom from colonialism, in the form of national independence movements, among their enslavers. It is noteworthy that the acknowledgment of the African American freedom quest as a model for others in the United States is limited to other relatively disenfranchised groups, such as women and the elderly, and not extended to the national quest for independence that is part of the heroic formative story of the nation.

The Quilombo of Palmares is documented to have existed and to have resisted frequent attacks between 1605 and 1695. So the Palmares maroons were defending their autonomous community against colonial armies more than a century before both the French Revolution in 1789 and Brazil's independence from Portugal in 1822. The Haitian revolution that encouraged Afro-Brazilian freedom quests also preceded Brazil's independence and served as an important inspiration for Spanish-speaking American independence movements. Hence, Palmares' autonomy from Portuguese colonial rule predated all American independences. The historical data suggest that principles of freedom and independence so important to the American republics just may have been inspired by resistant quests for freedom on the parts of the very people whose lack of freedom the rulers and elites of these societies sought to perpetuate.

Romero Rodríguez (chapter 20), journalist, government advisor, and director general of Organizaciones Mundo Afro, a national federation of Afro-Uruguayan institutions, created the Red de Organizaciones Afro-Americanas (Network of Afro-American Organizations) to develop links and stimulate collaboration between Pan-American African Diasporan organizations. The network is an excellent example of the kind of transnational coalition-building with the goal of creating a Pan-American African Diasporan consciousness advocated by Arturo Alfonso Schomburg. Rodríguez illustrates ways in which African Diasporan populations of South America's Southern Cone are reclaiming their Afrogenic heritages to counteract the alienating effects of assimilationist cultural politics, and are affirming their distinctive identities and highlighting their significant roles in their national histories and cultures.

Afro-Bolivians are basing their newly rediscovered sense of identity around the Afrogenic musical and dance form *saya*, which had been disappearing as a result of their increasing assimilation into the larger society. And they are using that cultural rallying point as a basis for both the recovery of their oral history, often transmitted in saya lyrics, and for promoting community development. Afro-Paraguayans of Uruguayan origin continue to use the Afrogenic music and dance form *candombe*, discussed by Olivera Chirimini (chapter 15), in venerating their Afro-Catholic patron saint and use this symbol of their collective identity as a basis of the group solidarity manifest in their fight to secure community land rights.

Afro-Argentineans, who now exist in small and dispersed numbers, have also organized themselves to affirm their presence, identify and assert their contributions to Argentinean culture, and reclaim cultural spaces from which their ancestors were historically "disappeared." Unlike what is hidden in plain view, Afro-Argentineans vanished from public consciousness while remaining in full sight, albeit in diminished numbers. And Afro-Uruguayans, after suffering the physical destruction of their communities at the hands of a military government, are working not only on reclaiming their cultural heritage and asserting their significant role in the formation of Uruguay's national identity, but also on organizing and collaborating with other African Diasporan groups toward similar ends.

Although these groups have been integrally involved in the creation of their nations and have been important sources of economic development, military cannon fodder, and culture trivializingly characterized as "folklore," the significant change is that now, rather than downplaying their distinctiveness in seeking to assimilate, they are affirming and promoting their unique cultural forms and claiming their self-defined place within their national cultures. They are, thus, insisting upon being subjects of their own Afrogenic stories rather than objects of the Eurogenic (mis)representations of others. And they are asserting the right to (re)present themselves, for the benefit of their communities' interests, in and on their own terms.

In this vein, Lucía Molina and Mario López (chapter 21), founders of the Casa de la Cultura Indo-Afro-Americana in Santa Fe, Argentina, tell their version of the story of Argentina, providing an analysis of the systematic socioeconomic oppression and frequent military decimation, as well as of the intellectual gymnastics involved in "disappearing" the formerly numerous Afro-Argentinean population. The Afro-Argentinean presence became a source of cognitive dissonance in a society determined to define itself as European and to declare itself "white," in spite of a demographic and cultural history of a significant African presence that had to be very deliberately "forgotten." A recent *Washington Times* article says that "Argentines have a reputation today for a superiority complex sometimes tinged with a sense of satisfaction that their country is not home to a large nonwhite population, as is most of the rest of Latin America. . . . But the racial smugness is founded on a whitewashed history."[40]

Molina and López demonstrate that Africans and their descendants were present and playing active roles in important numbers during the formative period of the development of the Argentinean nation, and that they continue to exist dynamically and visibly while being declared officially absent. The authors also detail the intellectual context and content of this process of "disappearing," and its effects on both the Afro-Argentinean population that tried to "whiten" itself to conform to its supposed nonexistence, and on the larger population that continues to misrepresent itself to itself and to others by denying a significant aspect of its composition and evolution. Beyond the simple assumption of whiteness identified by Fisher Fishkin for the United States, and the absence of acknowledgment of the Afro-Venezuelan presence highlighted by García, Afro-Argentineans were, Molina and López argue, consciously and system(at)ically invisibilized while remaining visible, and were "disappeared" while continuing to appear by substituting desire for reality in a society for which the concept of "disappearing" people became a morbid cliché.

The insistence of these communities upon correcting the historical record to accurately reflect the presence in and contributions of their ancestors to the formation of the nation, and correcting the present record to accurately reflect their own continuing participation in nations that must be accurately defined as multiethnic, has pragmatic as well as intellectual goals related to issues of socioeconomic development. Documenting an historical presence can prove useful in questions of land tenure, a pressing issue in several African Diasporan communities. Insisting on being acknowledged as having a distinctive identity and on being counted as such in national censuses can provide a basis for making demands on public institutions and for obtaining support from national and international institutions for community development projects. And asserting the necessity of having their stories accurately told as an integral part of the official story of the nation through the educational process can help these communities internalize a sense of positive self-esteem and entitlement with which to fuel their struggles for equal rights and equitable participation in all areas of contemporary society.

Afro-Cuban filmmaker Gloria Rolando (chapter 22) highlights the importance of collecting and documenting, before it is too late, knowledge maintained in the oral traditions of African Diasporan communities. Afro-Cuban elders who drum, sing, and dance in the Yoruba and other African religious traditions recreated in Cuba are, she says, Caribbean *griots*, oral historians whom some would denigrate by characterizing them as performers of "folklore." Her exhortation to document and preserve their wisdom responds to the often-quoted statement by the distinguished Malian champion of the oral tradition, historian and diplomat Amadou Hampâté Bâ,[41] that "Each old person who dies in Africa is like a library that is burned."[42] This idea is also applicable to the African Diaspora in this still-pioneering era of data-gathering, as Rolando notes in saying that, like the Sankofa concept, "We have to return to the past to see what remains in the present."

Rolando also discusses her documentation of other African Diasporas subsequent to the transatlantic one, internal dispersions such as those in which Haitians, Jamaicans, and Barbadians arrived in eastern Cuba as a result of the sugarcane boom, in an economic migration that made more complex the ethnocultural composition of the island. She makes the point, similar to N'Diaye concerning the United States, that the African Diaspora continues within the Americas, creating further layering in a continuing dynamic of intradiasporan encounters and increasingly multiple consciousnesses.

And cultural anthropologist, dancer, and dance scholar and teacher Yvonne Daniel (chapter 23) ends the volume by going even further than those contributors who want the knowledge of African Diasporan culture-bearers to be included in the Pan-American discourse. Daniel argues for the recognition of a whole different way of knowing, an "embodied knowledge," a profoundly Afrogenic epistemological and hermeneutical system codified in the religious dances that celebrate the divine beings of African America. She characterizes the knowledge embodied in religious dance as another way, kind, and source of knowing the universe. This is a valid form of knowledge, she argues, echoing Wilson, Stewart, and Rolando, that needs to be recognized as such rather than devalued as mere entertainment.

Daniel, thus, takes the idea of the very necessary epistemological and hermeneutical overhaul proposed by Yai to a new level by asserting that it is not just the intellect, but rather the entire dancing body, that is the repository of Afrogenic knowledge. She argues for a new level of perceiving and understanding of something that is seen and discussed, but not on its own terms. It is not acknowledged for all that it signifies because of the application of inapplicable premises that obscure deep meanings in favor of trivializing interpretations.

From the perspective of Amadou Hampâté Bâ, the knowledge that Daniel says is embodied in dance may be considered libraries lost with the demise of each knowledgeable dancer. In this case, the library is the corpus of dancing bodies. Daniel, in fact, characterizes the dancers and singers whom Rolando thinks of as griots as African Diasporan archivists.

A dancer as well as an anthropologist and a member of an African Diasporan community that dances—all the roles one plays determining how one sees, moves in, and gathers data and theorizes about the world—Daniel challenges the limited kinds of knowledge and limited ways of accessing knowledge that have been considered reliable and important by scholars. Like Dixon Gottschild, she questions who can decide what is and is not valid knowledge and by which criteria. From multiply conscious perspectives, she questions the limited and limiting definitions and categorizations of the kinds of knowledge recognized by those who have claimed the power and authority to hegemonically define such issues. And she offers dance performance and its analysis as a privileged method—and a method clearly privileged by the African and African Diasporan cultures whose spiritual beings have selected dance as their preferred style of expression and communication—for really knowing these cultural systems.

In advocating dance as a methodology for knowing, Daniel asserts that without the deep knowledge that comes from participatory immersion, in combination with the study of institutions and social interactions, researchers cannot really understand African Diasporan ritual communities in which dance is such an essential form of expression. In essence, cultural blinders premised on the sensory limitations firmly encoded into academic styles of knowing inherently limit the ability to know by allowing only partial tools for making sense of holistic systems of human knowledge.

Africans and African Diasporans and our spiritual beings have defined music and dance as a profound style of expression of the divine essential to the functioning of the universe, representing the most fundamental principles of the cosmic system, and a privileged form of communication between humans and the divine. Yet this same behavior has been denigrated from a Eurogenic perspective, rather than respected as Afrogenic wisdom imparted by sages about the most important aspects of life. This situation exemplifies well the problem of failing to take seriously what a culture is conveying about itself, about its premises, its priorities, and its serious everyday concerns, in and on its own terms. Failing to acknowledge this reality, and imposing an exogenic perspective rather than accepting what the endogenic perspective is communicating, precludes understanding the culture in and on the terms by which it understands itself and presents itself to the world.

AFRICAN DIASPORAN PAN-AMERICAN PUZZLES

The contributions of Africans and their descendants to Pan-American life are so central and foundational that there is no way of discussing the Americas accurately and honestly without considering them. They were part of the agriculture that allowed the voluntary European and involuntary African immigrants to survive. They were part of the technology that allowed everyone to work and create. They were part of the economy that allowed the societies to develop and expand. They were part of the creation of the languages in which everyone learned to communicate. They were part of the definition of the nature of the spiritual, and of how to access and relate to it. They were part of the creation of all of the myriad cultural systems, forms, and styles in which all

African and European immigrant Americans organized themselves and expressed their identities.

Africans and their descendents waged the struggles necessary to free themselves from their enslavers and participated actively in the battles to free their enslavers from their European colonial rulers. Hence they were a formative part of the very definition of freedom and justice in the Americas. And although they were brought to the Americas only to work and worked *de sol a sol,* from "kin to cain't,"[43] they also taught the Americas how to celebrate life.

From the beginning of the European invasion and conquest of Native American territory, Europeans brought along Africans who, albeit involuntarily, participated integrally in the creation of the Americas with their dominant demographic presence and economic contributions, their specialized knowledge and skills, their enduring principles and attitudes, their influential tastes and preferences, and their profound understanding of life and insistence upon living it as joyously as possible. As foundational constituents of all of the societies of the Americas—although as unequal constituents who worked much more and benefited much less than Euro-Americans—they helped determine the basic forms these societies have taken and the ways in which they function today.

To understand the Americas it is, therefore, necessary to assume and acknowledge that these African contributions are part of their deep structure; and that as such they continue to express themselves in many ways seen and unseen, named and unnamed, somewhat known and mostly still to be known. This volume offers the beginning of an antidote to the inherently incomplete Eurocentric version of the Pan-American story.

The volume represents a fundamental challenge to the way in which the story of the Americas has been told, as if Africans and their descendants had not been the basis of the labor that made the development of both the Americas and Western Europe possible, and as if much of the cultural repertoire of everyone in the Americas were not of African/African Diasporan origin. The African and African Diasporan scholars and politico-cultural leaders and other conscientious scholars represented here offer new data about the African Diaspora from Buenos Aires to New York City, data from old sources such as new readings of historical documents, and data from unexpected sources such as the lives of long-deceased individuals. They also offer new perspectives on old sources of knowledge such as everyday language and the knowledge encoded in dance. And they uncover the Afrogenic nature of much culture unquestioningly assumed to be Eurogenic, such as U.S. canonical literature and elite concert dance. They, in essence, contradict and correct much of the prevailing story of the Americas.

This volume also represents the beginning of a comparative analysis of African Diasporan societies and phenomena from an Afrogenic perspective that focuses on African and African Diasporan agency, participation, and contributions. It represents a beginning of an attempt to respond to what might reasonably be considered the fundamental problem in the real understanding of the Americas. That problem, which is the result of an apparently deliberate distortion of the portrayal of historical reality in order to justify an unconscionable social system, is that of acknowledging the role of enslaved Africans and their descendants in the creation of the Americas.

Such an acknowledgment involves confronting the intellectual tradition/contradiction of justifying how good Christians could treat other humans in the inhuman ways that history makes obvious, while at the same time pretending to create democratic republics. A flagrant example of this fundamental contradiction was defining human beings not as people but as chattel like pigs and cows or as pieces of ebony, and claiming that they were uncivilized, while simultaneously "recruiting" these very same people specifically for their sophisticated technological knowledge in such fundamental survival areas as agriculture and mining, putting them in charge of growing and preparing food, and even entrusting them with the responsibility of taking care of the privileged children of their enslavers.

African American historian John Henrik Clarke said, "You cannot subjugate a man and recognize his humanity, his history and his personality."[44] Europeans and Euro-Americans subjugated Africans and their descendants and denied their/our humanity, history, and personality. Denial, however, does not make things go away, even if it may intellectually exclude or obscure problematic presences. Such denial rather obliges the deniers to lie, to dissimulate, about the presence of the subject of the denial in a variety of ways, such as "origin unknown," with or without Eurocentric misattribution. It requires imaginative styles of erasure and invisibilization such as *writing* African and African Diasporan subjects of denial out of selected parts of the story by simply *whiting* us out.

The dispersal of African people and culture throughout the Americas, the meetings of Africans with other peoples, and African adaptations of their original knowledge and behaviors to different natural and human environments, have created multiple refractions of Afrogenic culture. The purpose of this volume is also to look at this Pan-American Afrogenic culture holistically and comparatively, demonstrating African continuity and American creativity and highlighting commonalities and uniquenesses.

An important goal is to see ourselves, and to allow others to see us, through our own eyes, through the reflection of our own self-consciousness, rather than through either borrowed or imposed eyes. We endeavor to present ourselves in and on our own terms so as to allow ourselves and others to understand us from our multiple endogenic perspectives, rather than as filtered through the perspectives of inapplicable exogenic premises that distort our realities. Our Afrogenic perspectives offer both correctives and opportunities to become hip to jive scholarly and popular traditions that have propagated a story of the Pan-American African Diaspora that does not either conform to empirical reality or do justice to the much more complex story of the Americas.

As a result of my experiences and research, I have come to view the African Diaspora in the Americas as a vast, multidimensional puzzle in which some of the pieces were brought from Africa and have maintained recognizable identities, and other pieces were created in the Americas based on Afrogenic conceptual foundations. In this volume we see these two fundamental principles demonstrated in struggles for freedom and independence, in concepts of knowledge, in social organization and its philosophical bases, in technology and material culture, in gastronomy, in language, in music and dance, and in celebration.

My quest has been to seek out and identify these puzzle pieces, to figure out how they fit together, and to imagine how the resultant pictures might look. The chapters in this volume represent a step toward finding these pieces, figuring out the principles by which they are to be assembled, and assembling them to see some of the local, national, and international pictures that they compose. These principles of assembly are the common conceptual structures underlying variegated surface manifestations. There are obviously many more pieces to be sought and found, many more principles of assembly to be identified or figured out, and many more pictures to be seen.

To understand the African Diaspora it is necessary to seek, discover, recognize, identify, and properly interpret puzzle pieces that we have not known how to see, or have been told not to seek, so have not sought to find. We have not known how to see them because their presence has been obscured by authoritative assertions and unquestioned assumptions of their nonexistence. And even if these puzzle pieces have been perceived as in some way distinctive, meaningful interpretations have not been readily available in prevailing explanatory systems. Once these puzzle pieces are acknowledged to exist, seeing and distinguishing them and understanding their sometimes plural meanings and complex implications can be facilitated by the double/multiple consciousness of an Afrogenic perspective.

African Diasporan cultures and contributions to their national cultures have been misrepresented throughout the Americas in various ways. Afro-Uruguayans, who have been overrepresented in public culture since the eighteenth century and who have contributed to the national culture the ingredient by which Uruguay celebrates its uniqueness, have simply been claimed not to exist. The presence of as much Afrogenic culture as has been identified in everyday all-American life, in popular culture and even in "high" culture in the United States, a society in which African American culture, if it existed at all, was authoritatively defined as a pathological version of Euro-American culture, is bound to come as a surprise to practically everyone.

And there are still denials and distortions even in societies in which Afrogenic culture is commonly acknowledged as existing in religion, music, and dance, as in Brazil, Cuba, and Venezuela. Behaviors that might be respected as sources of important philosophical concepts are not usually acknowledged for their seriousness, and African Diasporan contributions to issues of national values and principles, and to heroic behaviors in defense of them as manifest, for example, in the quest for freedom, justice, and independence, have been misrepresented and misattributed.

It is not clear whether it is more deleterious to be told that you do not exist, as was the case for the Afro-Uruguayans, or not to have your existence doubted but rather to have it declared originless and pathological, as in the United States. Both this nonexistence and this pathology were claimed in contradictory situations in which the cultural creations of the communities that did not exist, or were pathological, were simultaneously appropriated by the same segments of the society that made these negative determinations.

Such inherent contradictions result from the fundamentally jive nature of the authoritative story told of the Americas. Complex intellectual gymnastics are required to make such an empirically problematic story seem coherent. Our goal in this volume is to help correct these misrepresentations and to help tell the story of the Americas honestly—by accurately including the excluded but historically, demographically, and culturally not only present but essential African-descended population.

The comparative study of African Diasporan societies and their roles in their nations, in addition to demonstrating similar patterns of misrepresentation, also highlights significant commonalities in both sociocultural forms and in the underlying principles that give them meaning. Looking at one African Diasporan society through the light of a principle understood from another, as some of the contributors do, and as others provide the theoretical and/or empirical bases for doing, is especially illuminating. That several contributors have independently made similar and complementary discoveries supports the point. García's conceptualization in African terms of an Afro-Venezuelan culture of resistance reinforced my understanding of the resistant survival linguistic complex expressed in African terms that I identified in New Jersey. And both analyses conform to Yai's exhortation to use African and African Diasporan terms as especially informed Afrogenic media for scientific discourse about these realities.

So researchers from Africa and North and South America have independently made complementary points about the African Diaspora based on Afrogenic, multiply conscious perspectives. We have looked at African Diasporan societies based on Afrogenic concepts elicited from or discernable in the cultures in question, which we have discussed using African and African Diasporan terms. We have drawn our understandings from viewing African Diasporan societies comparatively in the context of their conceptual continuity with their African roots, while also assuming African Diasporan agency and creativity. These findings suggest leads for seeking similarly resistant complexes of various kinds in other African Diasporan societies. Creole languages should, for example, be especially rich sources of such terminology and concepts given their origins and functions as literal and/or metaphoric maroon languages.

The Afrogenic double/multiple consciousness of most of the contributors allows us to perceive, through the realities of our own lives and those of our communities' behaviors, conceptual principles to which we can apply the results of our academic training in the dualistic methodology of an insider/outsider epistemological and hermeneutical approach. This Afrogenic approach has allowed for the identification of new sources of knowledge and ways of knowing, as well as new styles of expressing and methods of interpreting this knowledge. It has allowed Afrogenic rereadings of Eurogenic data and interpretations through Afrogenic eyes, in and on Afrogenic terms, to arrive at very different conclusions. This reversal of perspectives has made visible, noticeable, and significant what had been invisibilized, gone unnoticed, and been deemed insignificant.

Of course, this reversal of perspectives from Eurogenic to Afrogenic represents the normal perspective through which Africans and African Diasporans actually live and see the world; with the Eurogenic perspective as an imposed, or borrowed, perspective by which the lived Afrogenic reality has been externally interpreted and often misinterpreted. So our asserting of an Afrogenic perspective is simply saying that we are telling our own stories from our own points of view. But rather than simply assuming the logical legitimacy of an Afrogenic perspective on the part of people of African origin, centered in our own lived realities and predicated on our own sense of agency, in the intellectually Eurocentric context of the Americas, it is necessary to defend the validity of such an obvious point of view.

This "reversal" is an indispensable source of a corrective balance for understanding the Americas. It permits everyone who is interested to look at the Afro-Euro-Americas from the neglected perspective of their Afrogenic, not just their hyperbolized Eurogenic, reality. The fundamental issue is the inherent richness of having a double/multiple consciousness with which to make possible a complex, nuanced, and multidimensional understanding of the African Diaspora and of Pan-America.

The Americas have been (mis)(re)presented as a Eurogenic creation. From the information presented in this volume, it is clear that the Americas represent a much more complex puzzle than the one that has been presented as complete, in spite of its lacking so many crucial pieces. For these missing pieces, either blank "origin unknown" pieces or jive distorted pieces have been substituted. Only by adding the real Afrogenic pieces can the rich mosaic of the Americas be correctly portrayed.

In fact, the African Diaspora represents the intersection of at least three planes of multidimensional, intersecting, and interdependent puzzles. There is the transnational African puzzle of those cultures that have, over the past five centuries, managed to establish more or less evident overseas outposts in the Americas. This African substratum is now part of the foundational substance of the Americas, and appears in various forms in different places in myriad ways, many of which have yet to be decrypted. My experiences have led me into some small paths that hint at this larger vision. This is a surface that has hardly been scratched, of which there remain to be discovered both unplumbed depths and unsuspected manifestations.

Then there is the puzzle of the African Diaspora per se, of which some of the explanatory pieces for one society may be found in another, as I learned in trying to make intellectual sense of basic issues of language, naming, food, and the spirit, first in New Jersey, and then beyond. Only with a comparative vision was it possible to identify these pieces, discover their relevance, and assemble them to form a picture based on foundational principles, many of which still remain to be discerned.

And finally, an accurate Pan-American puzzle must be predicated on the intersection of these transatlantic African and African Diasporan puzzles with the Native American and European Diasporan puzzles of the Americas. We will now begin an Afrogenic Pan-American journey of puzzling discovery of the (un)familiar Africanity of everyday life in the Americas.

NOTES

1. Philip Curtin, *The African Slave Trade: A Census* (Madison: University of Wisconsin Press, 1969), 3.

2. David Eltis, David Richardson, Stephen D. Behrendt, and Herbert S. Klein, eds., *The Trans-Atlantic Slave Trade: A Database on CD-ROM* (Cambridge: Cambridge University Press, 2000), 3.

3. Curtin, *The African Slave Trade*, xv.

4. Curtin, *The African Slave Trade*, xv.

5. Walter Russell Mead, "How America Got Rich," *Worth* (Sept. 1999): 97–103, 149–150.

6. Colin Palmer, in "Defining and Studying the Modern African Diaspora," contextualizes the concept of African Diaspora most broadly by situating the modern (past five hundred years)

African Diaspora in the context of the original and earlier ones, beginning with the hominid Diaspora out of Africa to people the world 100,000 years ago; *Perspectives* [the American Historical Association Newsletter] 36, no. 6 (Sept. 1998): 1, 22–25.

7. Rodolfo Monge Oviedo, "Are We or Aren't We?" *Report on the Americas* 25, no. 4 (Feb. 1992): 19.

8. "Argentina: The People," *Encyclopaedia Britannica Online*, <www.search.eb.com/bol/topic?eu=117955&sctn=1> (accessed 28 Feb. 2000).

9. "Bolivia: The People," *Encyclopaedia Britannica Online*, <www.search.eb.com/bol/topic?eu=117955&sctn=1> (accessed 28 Feb. 2000).

10. "Paraguay: The People," *Encyclopaedia Britannica Online*, <www.search.eb.com/bol/topic?eu=119388&sctn=1> (accessed 28 Feb. 2000).

11. "Uruguay: The People," *Encyclopaedia Britannica Online*, <www.search.eb.com/bol/topic?eu=115670&sctn=1#32683> (accessed 28 Feb. 2000).

12. She discusses "observing participants" in *Rumba: Dance and Social Change in Contemporary Cuba* (Bloomington: University of Indiana Press, 1995), 21.

13. St. Clair Drake, *Black Folks Here and There: An Essay in History and Anthropology*, vol. 1, 4th ed. (Los Angeles: Center for Afro-American Studies, University of California, 1987), 32.

14. Lawrence Levine, "Foreword," in John Michael Vlach, *By the Work of their Hands: Studies in Afro-American Folklife* (Ann Arbor, Mich.: U.M.I. Research Press, 1991), ix–x.

15. Lawrence Levine, "Foreword," Gunnar Myrdal, *An American Dilemma* (New York: Harper, 1962), 928–29; Nathan Glazer and Daniel Patrick Moynihan, *Beyond the Melting Pot* (Cambridge: M.I.T. Press, 1963), 53.

16. Leith Mullings, *On Our Own Terms: Race, Class, and Gender in the Lives of African American Women* (New York: Routledge. 1997).

17. Mullings, *On Our Own Terms*, xii.

18. *Merriam Webster's Collegiate Dictionary*, 10th ed. (Springfield, Mass.: Merriam Webster, 1993), 336.

19. *Webster's Dictionary*, 1094.

20. *Webster's Dictionary*, 630.

21. Eltis et al., "Introduction," *Trans-Atlantic Slave Trade*, 3.

22. The relative merits of "tight" or "loose" packing of humans into the holds of ships was an important debate among enslavers—the concern being to ensure the greatest arrival rate in the Americas for the greatest number of Africans for the greatest profit of European and Euro-American enslavers.

23. Leslie B. Rout, *The African Experience in Spanish America: 1502 to the Present Day* (Cambridge: Cambridge University Press, 1976), xii.

24. An *asiento* was a license to trade in Africa, usually given by the Spanish Crown to foreign companies to supply enslaved Africans to Spanish colonies. Curtin, *The African Slave Trade*, 21.

25. Curtin, *The African Slave Trade*, 22, referencing Georges Scelle, *La Traite Négrière aux Indes de Castille*, vol. 2 (Paris: L. Larose and L. Tenin, 1906), 26–27.

26. *United States Constitution*, Article I, Section 2, Clause 3, 1787.

27. Carter G. Woodson, *The Miseducation of the Negro* (Washington, D.C.: Associated Publishers, 1933).

28. Mullings, *On Our Own Terms*, xiv–xv.

29. Melville Herskovits, *The Myth of the Negro Past* (Boston: Beacon Press, 1958 [1941]).

30. Some of the stories of Leuk, the trickster hare in the Wolof tradition of Senegal, were written as primary school teaching tools for francophone Africa in Léopold Sédar Senghor and Abdoulaye Sadji, *La belle histoire de Leuk-le-Lièvre* (Dakar: Nouvelles Editions Africaines, 1975).

31. Jacqueline L. Tobin and Raymond G. Dobard's *Hidden in Plain View: The Secret Story of Quilts and the Underground Railroad* (New York: Doubleday, 1999) is the provocative title of a recent study concerning ways in which U.S. African Americans used patchwork quilt patterns to map underground railroad routes of escape from slavery—"hiding" such prohibited information in plain view.

32. W. E. B. Du Bois, *The Souls of Black Folk* (New York: Vintage Books/Library of America, 1990 [1903]), 5.

33. "New Orleans Menu Glossary," *Food & Wine* (Oct. 1989): 122.

34. *Freedom's Journal* 1, no. 1 (16 Mar. 1827): 1.

35. Kwaku Ofori-Ansa, "The Meanings of Symbols in Adinkra Cloth," <www.users.erols.com/kemet/adinkra.htm> (accessed 10 Oct. 2000).

36. James Denbow, "Heart and Soul: Glimpses of Ideology in the Iconography of Tombstones from the Loango Coast," *Journal of American Folklore*, no. 445 (1999): 411.

37. Karl Laman, *The Kongo*, vol. 4 (Uppsala, Sweden: Almquist and Wiksells, 1968), 39, as cited in Denbow, "Heart and Soul," 412.

38. Sheila S. Walker with Jennifer Rasamimanana, "Tarzan in the Classroom: How 'Educational' Films Mythologize Africa and Miseducate Americans," *Journal of Negro Education* 62, no. 1 (Winter 1993): 3–23. A slightly different version appears in Janis Faye Hutchinson, ed., *Cultural Portrayals of African Americans: Creating an Ethnic/Racial Identity* (Westport, Conn.: Bergin and Garvey, 1997), 27–48.

39. Marie-Alice Devieux, personal communication, August 1999.

40. Jason Webb, "Modern Argentina Largely Ignores its Black Ancestry," *Washington Times* (28 Dec. 1999): 14A. ©Reuters News Agency. Reprinted with permission.

41. Amadou Hampâté Bâ and Jacques Daget, *L'empire peul du Macina* (Paris: Mouton, 1962); "Kaidara: récit initiatique peul," in *Classiques africaines,* ed. Amadou Hampâté Bâ and Lilyan Kestelroot (Paris: Julliard, 1969); *l'Etrange destin de Wangrin.* (Paris: UGE/Presse de la Cité, 1973); *Laaytere koodal (French and Fulah)—L'éclat de la grande étoile suivi du bain rituel: récits initiatiques peuls* (Paris: A. Colin, 1974).

42. Amadou Hampâté Bâ, "La parole africaine dans des instances internationales" speech at the UNESCO General Conference, Paris 1960, track five from the Radiodiffusion compact disc ARCL 31 *Les voix de l'écriture: Amadou Hampâté Bâ.* In arguing for the importance of recording Africa's oral traditions before it was too late, and requesting UNESCO assistance in doing so, Bâ's actual words were "Je considère la mort de chacun de ces traditionalistes comme l'incendie d'un fond culturel non-exploité" (I consider the death of each of these traditionalists to be like the burning of an unresearched cultural archive).

43. From sunup to sundown, so from when you kin (can) see the sun until when you cain't (can't).

44. John Henrik Clarke, as quoted in "The New Ring Shout," a mixed-media collaboration by sculptor Houston Conwill, architect Joseph DePace, and poet Estella Conwill Majozo, installed in the 290 Broadway Building adjacent to the African Burial Ground in New York City.

1

Everyday Africa in New Jersey: Wonderings and Wanderings in the African Diaspora

Sheila S. Walker

Say that on a typical Saturday morning your kids create a ruckus while watching Bugs Bunny on television. Later, your teenager and her hunky guy practice a hip rendition of a cool new dance. And that evening, after toting the young ones to the sitter, you and your spouse hang in a local jazz club to do your own thing.

You may not know it, but you just spent your day immersed in the fruits of a cultural importation from Africa.

That rascally rabbit sprang from an African heritage—along with jazz and many forms of dance. Some experts say the words "bug," "ruckus," "hunky," "guy," "cool," "tote," "jazz," and "do your own thing," are all Africanisms—American English words with roots in African culture.

These reflect only a few ways in which Africa has influenced Western society, language, and customs through what has come to be known as the "African Diaspora."[1]

I had my first intriguing experiences of Africa before I was five years old and before leaving New Jersey. Then it took me decades of wondering and wandering[2] in Africa and the African Diaspora in the Americas to figure out what I had seen, heard, said, and even eaten but had not really understood.

It was while attending a Candomblé ceremony in Salvador da Bahia, Brazil, that I found answers to questions remaining from a childhood experience in a Baptist church in Newark, New Jersey. On my first foray to grown-up church rather than Sunday school, I had been surprised to see well-dressed ladies with hats and purses "get happy," "shout," be "filled with the spirit," and generally behave in ways radically different from their everyday demeanor. The tautological answers to my questions—that they were moved by "the spirit," a spirit whose precise identity I could not ascertain—left me further perplexed.

It was while studying Wolof, the major language of Senegal, that I learned the origin of terms like *hip* (not the body part), *cat* (in its hip nonfeline sense), *dig* (not having to do with making holes in dirt), and *jive*, which had also intrigued me since my childhood in Kearny, New Jersey. When I was learning to read and write, these words, the first three of which I knew meant something else in addition to the standard English meanings, had seemed somehow different from other words, for reasons I didn't know. I also learned the source of that characteristically U.S. exclamation, *Wow!*[3]

It was while doing research for an article on African American naming behavior that I learned why the last name of a boy I knew in high school in East Orange, New Jersey, was Cuff, and of a man I later met skiing, Coffey.[4] It was while learning about places where Africans involuntarily boarded ships that transported them to the Americas during the transatlantic slave trade that I understood the meaning of Weda, the name of a girl from the same school. And it was in meeting an Afro-Colombian family named Mina and their friends Señor Biafara and Señora Lucumí de Carabalí on the Pacific coast of Colombia, after being assured that their culture included no vestiges of anything African, that I understood the immense value of having knowledge from one African Diasporan society to bring to the understanding of another one.

It was while living and traveling in West and Central Africa that I understood why okra and black-eyed peas are such fundamentals of U.S. African American soul food and of the diet of many more white Southerners than I could ever have suspected, as well as delicacies in Afro-Brazilian divine gastronomy.[5] And it was while eating *mondongo*, a cousin of U.S. *chitlins* and anglophone Caribbean *souse*, in Buenos Aires, and noting the contrast between it and Argentina's usual European fare that I understood that African culture persists in the Americas even where few people of visible African descent remain. Mondongo also exists elsewhere in the Americas, in areas with many people of African origin such as Venezuela and Panama, where I ate it with *ají congo* (hot pepper), and with few people of African origin, such as Mexico, where it is also known as *menudo*.

Discoveries begin with experiences whose meanings you don't understand, meanings that dawn subtly or suddenly. Discoveries may result from information shared by teachers whose identity as such may not be obvious and who may not even know that they are teachers. Nor may the learner—until understanding comes. These experiential understandings have led me to do research, and to intend to do more research, since these experiencings and discoverings are an ongoing process.

My decades of temporally and geographically dispersed, deliberate and nondeliberate wonderings and wanderings, seekings and discoverings, and realizations and revelations about the African Diaspora in the Americas have made me aware of a most fundamental fact. Contrary to everything I had been taught in both my socialization and in the information imparted to me throughout my extensive both ordinary and elite formal and informal education, my version of U.S. American culture—Northern, urban, middle-class, living in ethnically mixed neighborhoods, and always attending predominantly, even overwhelmingly, white schools—continues to reflect its African origins almost two hundred years after the official end of the importation of Africans to the United States during the transatlantic slave trade.

These discoveries also taught me that the African cultural presence in the Americas is not limited to people whose epidermal melanin reflects their recent African ancestry. Recent here means within the past five hundred years, as opposed to referring to all of the descendants of Lucy Afarensis, the 3.5-million-year-old African ancestress of all humans. This recent African presence is an integral part, to more or less a degree, of the culture of all members of all societies of the Americas, including the U.S. "mainstream" that some still claim to be its antithesis—relentlessly ignoring all empirical evidence to the contrary, even, or especially, in their own daily lives.

Scholars have recently begun to focus on the Africanity of the presumably non-African American mainstream culture of the United States. Examples include John Edward Philips's "The African Heritage of White America," William Pierson's *Black Legacy*, Shelley Fisher Fishkin's "Interrogating 'Whiteness,' Complicating 'Blackness'," and *Was Huck Black? Mark Twain and African-American Voices*, and Brenda Dixon Gottschild's *Digging the Africanist Presence in American Performance*.[6]

These dawning awarenesses prepared me to understand the cultural continuum from Africa to the Americas and the resultant commonalities between the societies of the African Diaspora. These revelations also demonstrated the necessity of having both African experience and knowledge, as well as a comparative perspective on the Americas, in order to understand the African Diaspora. Familiarity with unmistakably African forms in one society can cast light upon less obvious forms in others, including, and maybe even especially, those of which community members are unaware and which they may specifically deny.

I started to develop this familiarity first by living and traveling in much of Africa and then by doing field research on Afro-Brazilian religion in the state of Bahia and later in other parts of Brazil. I titled a popular article for *Essence* magazine, written after my first trip to Brazil, "Bahia: Africa in America," which also became the name of a documentary on Afro-Brazilian culture in which I participated.[7] I used what I learned in Brazil to better understand U.S. African American culture and used my resultant enhanced perspective, based on these two major points of reference, to look at other African Diasporan societies.

Experiences in West, Central, South, East, and North Africa, North, South, and Central America, and the Caribbean; in lusophone, anglophone, hispanophone, and francophone/creolophone countries; doing field work, consulting, and participating in professional conferences and various cultural activities furthered these comparative experiencings and understandings. I wrote the results of my research and experiences in both scholarly and popular forms, gave lectures often illustrated with my slides, and participated in nationally broadcast documentaries on aspects of the African Diaspora.

As a result of my field research in Brazil, "getting happy," "shouting," and being "filled with the spirit" in the New Jersey Baptist church began to make sense to me and to acquire intellectual significance. I began to view this behavior as an aspect, and for me a major symbol, of the cultural continuum from Africa to the Americas and the cultural commonalities in the African Diaspora. Viewing being "moved by the spirit" in a U.S. African American church through the mirror of "manifesting the Orishas," the Yoruba spiritual beings who survived the Middle Passage, in an Afro-Brazilian Candomblé ceremony highlighted for me the unmistakable behavioral and conceptual similarities between these Afro-North American and Afro-South American spiritual expressions. This kinship was apparent even though one behavior was "Christian" and the other was part of a spiritual system whose African identity remains obvious to all.

In both instances the relationship between the human and the divine is so intimate that the entering of spiritual beings into the bodies of worshipers, who literally *embody* the divine energies, is the essence of religious ceremonial. If the spirit does not "move" anyone, if worshipers do not dance the "holy dance," if the Orishas do not "manifest" their presence in the human community by dancing in the bodies of their entranced initiates the gestures symbolic of their roles in the cosmos and human life, no spiritual communion has taken place.[8]

Similar to people who "shout" the divine presence when they are "filled with the spirit" in the United States, in Brazil people in whose bodies the Orishas "incorporate" themselves also "shout" to announce this spiritual presence in the human community, in that each Orisha has a characteristic *grito*, a shout. The Orishas also dance in a counterclockwise *roda*, or ring/circle, reminiscent of the counterclockwise "ring shout" in which some U.S. African Americans used to and continue to "dance divinity," to borrow an expression from dance anthropologist Yvonne Daniel.[9]

Afro-Brazilians say, "I don't believe in a believer who doesn't move. And I don't believe in a god who doesn't dance." An Afro-Cuban woman, in comparing Catholicism with her worship of the Orishas, said, "We understand that their spiritual beings are content with just prayers. But ours like to dance." And in discussing the influence of African American religious culture on Euro-Americans in colonial Virginia, Mechal Sobel says that Euro-American spiritual beings also learned to like to dance, or be danced for, and that they learned from the people who knew best. She argues that aspects of the ecstatic behavior of Euro-American Christians were learned from African Americans.[10] Sobel also said that when she told scholars at Colonial Williamsburg and the College of William and Mary in Virginia that part of her research focused on the influence of African Americans on Euro-American culture, they told her she had misunderstood the situation. African Americans had, they corrected her, been influenced by, they had not influenced, Euro-Americans.[11] Apparently not convinced of such unidirectional cultural flow, she titled her book *The World They Made Together.*[12]

These incipient satisfactions of my wonderings, resulting from revelations during my wanderings (often substantiated by focused research), which helped resolve the mystery of the New Jersey church ladies, were the beginning of my discovery that elements of African sacred and/or secular culture exist in all of the Americas. This is true whether people of African origin are the overwhelming majority, as in most of the Caribbean; or an almost invisible minority, maybe even claimed not to exist at all, as in Argentina; or a more or less significant proportion in between, as in Brazil, Cuba, and the United States. Some of my experiential understandings have been buttressed by fieldwork and by reading the research of others where available. Other understandings, some more tentative and provisional than others, remain the speculative results of my experiences and research, in which the anthropologist has also sometimes been, simultaneously, her own "native informant."

Elements of African-derived culture in the Americas may take the form of religious institutions whose specific African roots are obvious, such as in the Orisha tradition in Brazil, Trinidad, and Cuba, of Yoruba origin from what are now Nigeria and Benin; and Vodun in Haiti, the Casa das Minas in Brazil, and Arará in Cuba, of predominantly Fon origin also from Benin. Or they may take the form of behavior whose African origins are unacknowledged, perhaps less apparent, and often explicitly disavowed, as in some U.S. African American Protestant churches.

Having learned the lesson that the ideal culture is Euro-American, with anything redolent of Africa being embarrassing at best, many U.S. African American spirit-moved Christians claim that they "ain't left nothin' in no Africa"—without being aware of just how much culture of African origin that insistent triple negation affirms by unsuccessful denial and protesting too much. Practicing anthropologist Loretta Johnson, in fact, contends that, "African Americans are never so African as when they go to church at eleven o'clock on Sunday morning."[13]

The African presence is an inextricable element of the fabric of the American nations and often a major definer of their popular cultures and collective identities. Hence, it is an integral part of the cultural repertoire of the populations of non-African as well as of African descent. This is especially true of the expressive culture by which individuals and societies enjoy themselves, declare their specificity, and celebrate their uniqueness— through their spirituality, language, cuisine, music, and dance.

In Argentina, for example, which had a very significant population of African descent until the mid-nineteenth century,[14] people go to nightspots called *milongas* to dance their national dance the *tango*, the name of which is probably from the Kikongo *tanga*, for a party, festival, or banquet.[15] They use the expression *"que quilombo,"*[16] "what a mess," and in cool weather eat spicy *mondongo*, all of Central African Bantu[17] origin. Mondongo is perhaps from *ndongo-ndongo*, a viscous soup, or from *Mundongo*, which can designate a person from the Ndongo kingdom or the food of the Ndongo people, many people from the Ndongo kingdom having been enslaved through the port of Luanda in Angola.[18]

In Montevideo, the presentation I saw of Uruguayan culture for foreign tourists in a chic nightclub had two parts: the tango performed by Euro-Uruguayans, and the *candombe* performed by Afro-Uruguayans. Both music–dance forms are of Central African origin. The tango developed from the candombe and was transformed by imported European styles.[19] When I asked a Euro-Uruguayan taxi driver in Newark, New Jersey, what the Uruguayan community in the area did to express its cultural identity, he said, "We get together and play candombe. That's our national music. I brought my drums with me from home."

The African Diasporan rhythms and dances that are major definers of the national expressive cultures of the Americas, and of how these countries present themselves to the world internally in presentations to tourists and externally in international performances, often have Central African Bantu or Bantu-derived or inspired names. The *marimba*, from the Kimbundu word for xylophone, is characteristic of Afro-Colombian and Afro-Ecuadorian music, among others, and is also the national instrument of Guatemala, which has only a small African-descended population. The marimba is also played nightly by Mexican mestizos to entertain diners at open-air restaurants in Veracruz's *zócalo* (the main public square). The Brazilian *samba*, the Cuban *rumba*, and the Puerto Rican *bomba* are all well-known popular dances of less well-known Central African origin.[20]

The African presence is also a part of the technological foundations of the Americas. For work in the mines of Minas Gerais in Brazil, Africans, referred to as "Minas," were preferred and were consequently most numerous. They were called Mina because they came from what the Portuguese called the Costa da Mina, the Coast of Mines or Mina Coast, the name "Gold Coast" in English being derived from these gold mines.[21] According to Charles Boxer in his study of colonial Brazil, the Minas "were believed to have almost magical powers of discovering gold." Less magically and more pragmatically, "some of the mining techniques used were apparently of West African origin, for the Portuguese evidently knew less about mining than did some of their slaves from the Western Sudan."[22]

The Gold Coast, now Ghana, is one of West Africa's major gold-producing regions. It was, in fact, gold that arrived in medieval and renaissance Europe via the trans-Saharan trade that attracted Europeans to that part of Africa.[23] One may reasonably assume that Europeans enslaved Africans with greater expertise in mining than they themselves had in order to acquire the benefits of the Africans' knowledge and skills. James Lockhart says, in fact, in his study of colonial Peru, that enslaved African and Afro-Peruvian artisans formed "the backbone of the skilled labor force working in the shops of Peruvian Spanish artisans. . . . A disproportionate number of Negro artisans were blacksmiths and swordsmiths, practitioners of these most basic trades of all, which made the whole Spanish conquest and occupation possible."[24]

Rice culture in the United States, which originally centered in the coastal Low Country of South Carolina and Georgia, was based on the knowledge and skills of people from Sierra Leone on West Africa's "Grain Coast" or "Rice Coast" who were involuntarily "recruited" because of their well-known expertise in rice production.[25] The "Carolina rice," or more honestly the "Sierra Leone rice," which so enriched nineteenth-century plantation owners that it was called "Carolina gold," was what W. E. B. Du Bois might have characterized as a "Gift of Black Folks,"[26] since the producers were not remunerated for their contributions to the nutrition, gastronomy, and wealth of their enslavers.

Peter Wood, in his study of African Americans in colonial South Carolina, says that "No development had greater impact upon the course of South Carolina history than the successful introduction of rice." Cultivated for export, it dominated South Carolina's economy for most of the eighteenth century. But, "rice was a crop about which Englishmen . . . knew nothing at all. . . . Even those Englishmen with farm experience were notably less familiar with the agricultural peculiarities of a southern Atlantic coastal climate than their Indian neighbors or their West African and Caribbean slaves."[27]

And according to Gwendolyn Midlo Hall about another area of the United States:

> The survival of French Louisiana was due not only to African labor but also to African technology. The introduction from Africa of rice seeds and of slaves who knew how to cultivate rice assured the only reliable food crop that could be grown in the swamplands in and around New Orleans. Converting swamps and coastal wetlands into rice paddies involved complex technology. *Oryza glaberrima*, a species of wet rice, was first domesticated along the middle Niger probably during the second millennium, B.C., independently of Asian rice.

There was a secondary region of domestication that intensified the productivity. It was located between the Sine-Salum and the Casamance River, which empties into the Atlantic between the Senegal and the Gambia rivers. By the sixteenth century, residents along the Gambia grew rice in the alluvial soil, using a system of dikes that harnessed the tides. This wet, or swamp, rice had a much higher yield than did dry rice. A large supply could be grown in a small area. The transformation of swamps into rice fields required a great deal of knowledge and skill as well as labor. . . . The captains of the first two ships that brought African slaves to Louisiana in 1719 were instructed to try to purchase three or four barrels of rice for seeding and several Blacks who knew how to cultivate rice, which they were to give to the directors of the company on their arrival in Louisiana. By 1720, rice was growing in great abundance all along the Mississippi River.[28]

Concerning the discrepancy between the image and the reality of the nature of the labor performed by enslaved Africans, Wood says that, "Scholars have traditionally implied that African laborers were generally 'unskilled' and that this characteristic was particularly appropriate to the tedious work of rice cultivation. It may well be that something closer to the reverse was true early in South Carolina's development." Noting that most of the work of all colonists, European as well as African, was tedious, he says, "but if highly specialized workers were not required, at the same time there was hardly a premium on being unskilled. It seems safe to venture that if Africans had not shown much competence in, or aptitude for, such basic frontier skills as managing boats, clearing land, herding cattle, working wood, and cultivating fields, their importation would not have continued to grow. . . . [W]ith respect to rice cultivation, particular knowledge, rather than the lack of it, was one factor which made Black labor attractive to the English colonists."[29]

Commenting on the reasons for such a discrepancy, Wood concludes that "it is only from the more closed society of later times, which placed a high premium on fostering ignorance and dependence within the servile labor force, that white Americans have derived the false notion that Black slaves were initially accepted, and even sought, as being totally 'unskilled.' The actual conditions of the colonial frontier meant that workers who were merely obedient and submissive would have been a useless luxury. The white slaveholders, whose descendants could impose a pattern of mannered outward docility on their Negroes, were themselves dependent upon a pioneer pattern of versatility and competence among their workers during these early years."[30]

Along the same lines, in *Rice and Slaves*, Daniel C. Littlefield, in his discussion of the selection of particular African ethnic groups for enslavement specifically because of their agricultural knowledge, notes that "blacks were active rather than passive (if often unwilling) participants in the founding of American civilization, that they were sometimes both physically and culturally better suited than their masters to the tasks of survival and construction in a new environment, and that Europeans were occasionally both perceptive and acquisitive of African capabilities."[31] Europeans and Euro-Americans learned not only the African technology of planting rice, but also the African taste for eating it. And Leland Ferguson, in discussing southern foodways, says that rice, an African crop that was a mainstay of early South Carolina's economy and diet, was "readily adopted by planter families."[32]

The transatlantic slave trade, the largest population relocation in the history of humankind, was thus not just an unskilled labor migration, as has been generally taught and believed.[33] The European and Euro-American commercialization and commodification of the lives of African human beings represented, more importantly, the world's first and most massive brain drain and transfer of technology—out of Africa and into the Americas. While devastating Africa, this forced transfer of not only working bodies, but also of especially selected brains, was the basis of the development, wealth, power, and hegemony of Western Europe and Euro-North America.

Elements of specific African cultures are present in the Americas as a result of the African and American geographies of European and Euro-American colonial and commercial exploitation of land and people. These dynamics determined which Africans were taken from where in Africa to where in the Americas, by which Europeans, during which periods, in which numbers, for which kinds of forced labor, in which kinds of natural and/or human-made environments—temperate or tropical plantations or farms, cattle-raising plains, mines, or urban areas.[34] Additionally, enslavers expressed preferences for Africans from specific areas and ethnic origins because of both their specialized knowledge and skills and their perceived demeanors.

According to Leslie Rout, "Dealers and slaveholders in each Spanish American region came to express a distinct preference for certain types of Blacks. In Peru, *congos* and *angolas* were considered jovial and docile, and for these reasons were highly valued. In Cuba and Colombia *lucumis* [Yoruba] were the choice since they were viewed as industrious workmen."[35] There was no consensus about these reputations. Concerning New Granada (Ecuador, Venezuela, Colombia, and Panama), where Africans constituted most of the mine workers in the seventeenth and eighteenth centuries, Robert West says, "Blacks from the Guinea coast were preferred by most miners, while those of the Congo and the Carabali Negroes were considered rebellious."[36]

My experiential discoveries in trying to satisfy my curiosities suggested that as the Yoruba and Fon cultures of Nigeria and Benin remain most obviously represented in the Americas in religious institutions, an area in which Akan[37] culture from Ghana and Côte d'Ivoire remains obvious is in names. Akan-speaking people name children according to their day of birth, and some of those day names have remained in the United States, Jamaica, Surinam, and elsewhere in the African Diaspora, as family rather than personal names. Cuff/Cuffee/Cuffy or Coffey/Coffee/Coffie from Kofi, the name for a boy born on Friday, is the origin of the surnames of my schoolmate, my skiing partner, and even some Euro-Americans. The use of day names as family names in conjunction with European first names now also exists in Africa as a result of the colonial influence.

Cuffee Slocum was the father of Captain Paul Cuffe (1759–1817), the affluent free African American shipbuilder who in 1815 transported thirty-eight free African Americans to Sierra Leone in the first successful Return to Africa movement. The names of the father and son show the transformation from the African to the American pattern. And musicologist Lorna McDaniel, in *The Big Drum Ritual of Carriacou*, about the African "nation dances" of the island, titles a chapter about a prominent Carriacouan family "Quashie Genealogy."[38] Kwasi, Quashie in the Americas, designates a boy born on Sunday.

In addition to the fact that there was a preponderance of Akan-speaking people in some areas of the Americas, the fact that there is a small number of day names, of which everyone has one, logically gave these names a mathematical survival advantage. Based on an analysis of newspapers and slave documents, Henning Cohen concluded that Cuffee and Cudjo for males, and Abba and Juba for females, were the most common Akan names in the colonial United States.[39] And Lorenzo Dow Turner, in discussing the perpetuation of African naming patterns among the Gullah people of South Carolina and Georgia, found that in the 1930s and early 1940s, Akan day names still existed, as did English translations of them that perpetuated the original African concept in a modified, less apparent, form.[40]

When I met elderly Miss Fiba in rural Georgia, I initially thought that her name was an African American modification of Phoebe. Then I learned that Efiba or Phibba/Fiba is an Akan name for a female born on Friday. The similarity with the European name might, I thought, have assisted the African name in persisting. Discussing ways in which enslaved Africans strove to retain names that reflected their identities, Peter Wood said, confirming my observation, that a common compromise was for Africans and their descendants to take English names similar in sound to African names. Thus, Phiba or Phibbi "was easily heard and perpetuated as Phoebe by whites."[41]

In the United States the name Cuffy became a generic term. H. L. Mencken suggested that from the eighteenth century until about 1880, "Cuffy" designated an African American.[42] Sterling Stuckey provides an example of that practice with a line, "Cuffee, with protruding lip" from the music of New York's annual Pinkster festival in which, from the mid-eighteenth to mid-nineteenth century, African Americans were the major participants.[43] And African American anthropologist and writer Zora Neale Hurston, in criticizing the ways in which some African Americans denigrated others they considered of lesser status, said that their attitude was, underscoring their derogatory use of the term, "If it was old cuffy, down with it!" and "old Cuffy just got to cut de fool, you know."[44]

The heroic leader of Accompong, one of Jamaica's extant maroon settlements, was Cudjo, meaning male born on Monday. In Paramaribo, Surinam, the Statue of the Unknown Maroon, which represents and honors the Africans who escaped from slavery and created the autonomous maroon societies that still exist in the interior of the country, is known as Kwaku, meaning male born on Wednesday. The fact that these real and symbolic maroon heroes had/have Akan names also alludes to the prominent involvement in revolts against enslavement of Akan people, known in the Americas as Coromantee or Kromanti, derived from the Dutch fort at Cormantine on the "Mina" coast of Ghana, an area from which many Africans were shipped to the Americas.[45]

The Mr. Coffey I met skiing had, I ascertained, an aunt named Essie Coffey, a totally Akan name, Esi or Essie designating a female born on Sunday. One of my worries since I began my interest in names has been that an African American with such a name might, in an uninformed moment of Afrocentric enthusiasm, decide to change what he or she perceives as a "slave name" to an "African" name of his or her choice or creation— without realizing that he or she already has an African name inherited from real African and African American ancestors.

The Akan name of a legendary trickster spider, Anansi or Kwaku Anansi, also remains well known in the Americas. The spider tales, which are widespread in the forest area of West Africa, are similar to those of the hare cycle from the savanna and the Sahel area of West Africa (Senegal, Mali, Guinea, Burkina Faso, Niger, etc.). With the hare transformed into a rabbit, these tales gave us Br'er Rabbit in the United States, except for Louisiana, where he's Compair Lapin; Compé Lapin in the francophone/creolophone Caribbean; and Tio Conejo in Colombia in South America.[46] In much of the anglophone Caribbean the Anansi tales are called "Nancy Stories" and the spider is B'Anansi (Brother Anansi). In the Bahamas the spider has become a trickster child called Boy Nasty.[47] On the predominantly Afro-Colombian Pacific coast of Colombia, Anancio in the town of Buenaventura or Anansé in the state of Chocó refers to a small house spider, presumably with "special powers."[48] Elsewhere in Colombia, Anansi has become a trickster man named Anancio, and in Grenada he can also be a man, because of his shapeshifter abilities.[49] And when the Gullah/Geechee people of Sapelo Island, Georgia, saw a spider catch a fly, they might say, "An' Nancy got um."[50]

One of the Uncle Remus tales from the southern United States is "Brother Rabbit Doesn't Go to See Aunt Nancy." According to storyteller Uncle Remus, every year the animals would pay a visit to Aunt Nancy, the daughter of "Mammy Whammy Big Money." Aunt Nancy ruled over all of the animals and would summon them with a gesture to her house, which looked like a fog. One year Br'er Rabbit decided not to pay the visit. Flying into a rage at this disobedience, Aunt Nancy said that she was going to find him and "shake hands with him." When the other animals asked her why she never shook hands with them, she stood up abruptly, not taking care to keep her cloak closed around her. The animals were shocked to see that Aunt Nancy had seven arms and was half woman and half spider. The house that looked like a fog was a web.[51]

So in the Americas, Anansi could designate a real spider, with or without "special powers," and was also transformed into a trickster boy and man, as well as a powerful, controlling half-spider woman. The hare from Africa's savanna and Sahel met the spider from Africa's forest in the southern United States, as Africans from those areas met each other in the Americas and, blending their cultural traditions, became a new people. One might speculate about the kinds of intra-African sociocultural dynamics and negotiations that the Uncle Remus story suggests were occurring in the Americas, in that the Akan Aunt Nancy had power over the animals, and the savanna/Sahelian trickster hare/rabbit was the only animal who dared to defy her. This element of the oral tradition hints at possible paths of fruitful research.

Weda, the name of my other high school classmate, Ouida(h) in its French spelling, was an important coastal town in what is now the (francophone) Republic of Benin, from which many African captives were shipped to the Americas. Weda/Ouida remains an African American female name, probably without the bearers' knowing its origin or significance. A friend of mine also had a school friend named Ouida. When asked about her name, Ouida said that she had inherited it from her mother, grandmother, and great-grandmother. But she had no idea why. It was, she said, "just a name."

A colleague recently told me that, "Ouida is a common Southern name," and said that he knew at least four Ouidas. "They're all white women," he added.[52] Several other white Southerners have since said the same thing. I have been unsuccessful in finding out the significance of their having such a name. African Americans might logically have the name for one of two reasons. Europeans and Euro-Americans frequently called Africans by the names of their places of embarkation in Africa. And Africans sometimes named their children for places of significance on the continent, although a point of involuntary embarkation on a slave ship would probably not be their choice unless they were from that place. Someone told me of a friend of hers named Onishus (I'm spelling this as I heard it, not knowing how he spelled it), which was a family name passed from father to son. My immediate reaction was "Onitsha," the site of a major predominantly Igbo population center and well-known market on the Niger River in eastern Nigeria. "Exactly," she said. The man's family had passed the name down for generations as a way of remembering where they came from in Africa.

But how would the name of an African port town become a common Southern white female name? It seems improbable that enslavers would have named their daughters for the African geography of their source of wealth through their commerce in human lives. One may speculate that an African American "mammy" might have called a white girl she took care of Ouida simply because to her it was a familiar name. I am not suggesting that she would have known its meaning and deliberately called a white girl by a name with such a connotation. It might have been considered pretty or maybe unusual in the white population and so become generalized. It seems improbable that Southern whites would have consciously chosen to adopt an African American name derived from an African toponym of enslavement.

I was pleased to be able to explain the African origins of their names to the people Elena Mina, Señor Biafara, and Señora Lucumí de Carabalí, whom I met in the town of Santander de Quilichao in the Valle del Cauca on the Pacific coast of Colombia. I told them that Africans in the Americas were often called by the names of their ethnic groups or larger regional groupings, or their points of departure from Africa. Hence, the people called Mina in the Americas probably left Africa from the Costa da Mina, often from the fort of Elmina in Ghana. That mina is also Spanish for "mine," in which many of the original "Minas" worked, probably helped the name to persist since it was familiar to hispanophone ears.

I told Señor Biafara that his name probably referred to an origin in the Bight of Biafra in what is now Nigeria, from which many Africans also came. And the name of Señora Lucumí de Carabalí, her maiden name being Lucumí and her married name Carabalí, alluded to both the Oyo subgroup of Yoruba people of Nigeria, who were referred to as Lucumí by some of their neighbors,[53] and the port of Calabar in the Bight of Biafra.

These Afro-Colombian family names also exist in various ways in other parts of the African Diaspora. In Cuba, one designation for the Yoruba religion is Lucumí, and one of the Afro-Brazilian religious institutions in São Luis, capital of the state of Maranhão, is the Casa das Minas. Carabalí turns up in a wonderful expression used in various parts of hispanophone America. When a presumably "white" person, who might not be so white according to more stringent U.S. criteria, discusses his or her European ancestors and denies any African ancestry, skeptical others might say, probably behind the person's back, *"Si no es del Congo, es de Carabalí"* (If s/he's not from the Congo, s/he's from

Calabar). The Afro-Colombians were pleased to learn something of their African heritage, about which they had had no information. And they were especially gratified to find out that their surnames represented something more than "just a name."

African languages have also persisted in various ways in the Americas. Yoruba, for example, is the liturgical language of Orisha worship in Brazil, Cuba, and Trinidad. And African linguistics are a foundation of the creole languages developed in the Americas by Africans and their descendants who were obliged to create new systems of communication. Among these African Diasporan languages, which reflect in their lexicons their sometimes plural colonial European language contexts, are Surinamese maroon languages such as Saramaka and Ndjuka, and Sranan, the national creole; Palenquero from the maroon community of Palenque de San Basilio in Colombia; the French Creoles of Haiti, Martinique, Guadeloupe, French Guiana, St. Lucia, Dominica, and Louisiana; Papiamento in the Netherlands Antilles; and the Caribbean and continental North, South, and Central American English Creoles. These English Creoles include the Gullah of the coastal Low Country and Sea Islands of South Carolina and Georgia, and its Black Seminole or Mascoga extensions in Texas, Oklahoma, and Nacimiento de los Negros in the state of Coahuila in northern Mexico. Ebonics, the U.S. African American vernacular that keeps infusing standard English with new terms and concepts, which has led to heated and emotional controversies for reasons that have everything to do with sociocultural attitudes and educational and economic realities and nothing to do with its validity as a linguistic system whose purpose, like that of all others, is human communication, is also a form of English Creole.

African languages also have a continued presence in the European colonial languages of the Americas. Books on the African linguistic presence in the Americas include, in addition to African American linguist Lorenzo Dow Turner's pioneering and seminal *Africanisms in the Gullah Dialect*, which initiated the discussion of the African roots of U.S. African American English: *Glosario de afronegrismos* about Cuba; *Quimba, Fa, Malambo, Ñeque: afronegrismos en el Perú; Aspectos del lenguaje afronegroide en Venezuela; África en Santo Domingo: su heréncia lingüística; Trinidad Yoruba; The Bantu-Speaking Heritage of the Southern United States; The African Heritage of American English; Africanisms in Afro-American Language Varieties; A influencia africana no português do Brasil; Dicionário banto do Brasil;* and *Glosario de afronegrismos uruguayos.*[54]

Afro-Peruvians characterize their gossip circuit as *"radio bemba." "Porque los negros son bembones,"* was the explanation I received in Lima, "because Black folks have big lips," referring to big mouths that talk a lot. *Bemba,* the *"-on"* being a Spanish augmentative, is a Bantu word for mouth, referring to the more ample dimensions of African, as compared to European, lips. This word is also found in the disobligingly named Puerto Rican song *"Negro Bembón,"* "Big-Lipped Black Man," which some claim is not meant offensively.

The beginning of my curiosity about these linguistic Africanisms came when my parents were teaching me to spell simple words like "cat." Knowing about the hairy quadruped, I wondered why my father and his friends used the same word to refer to other men. No one could explain the reason to me because no one in Kearny, New Jersey, spoke Wolof, the major language of Senegal. As I learned, and began to satisfy my curiosity, in an introductory language class decades later, a *kat* in Wolof is someone who does something, and *xipi* (the "x" representing a guttural sound like the Spanish "j") means to have one's eyes wide open, to be alert, to know what's happening—to be a *xipikat*, a hip cat.

Clarence Major, in his *Dictionary of Afro-American Slang*, an early compendium of African American terms, defines hip as, "sophisticated, independent, and wise; in fashion; alert and courageous," and claims "the reliability of [his] own ethnic experience. And the experience of others," as well as written sources, as the bases of his authority.[55] Hip is also a verb. To hip people to something is to make them aware of it. "Xippi!" meaning open your eyes, wake up, check out what's happening, is the title of a cassette by internationally known Senegalese singer Youssou N'Dour.[56]

A *jefbat*, giving us "jive cat," is a person who is *jef, pas sérieux*, not serious, as officially francophone Senegalese Wolof-speakers would say, and/or skilled in the art of dissimulation, which can be extremely serious. So, "Are you hip to the jive?" as my father and his friends would ask, questions whether or not you really know what's going on, if you can distinguish what is from what may only appear to be. Dig it? Do you understand?

"Dig it," which had also perplexed me since I didn't see the relationship between making a hole in the ground and understanding or appreciating something, also comes from Wolof. *Deggit*, meaning "we understand," from *degg*, "the truth," is the way a Wolof audience might respond to someone who says something powerful. This is akin to the African American "tell the truth" as an affirming and encouraging response in African-derived call and response style to a speaker, especially to a preacher in a church service, who says something powerful.[57]

Wolof also helped me with a 1960s term, all explanations of which had struck me as incorrect. In that era of the Black consciousness movement, many African Americans began to refer to whites as "honkies." One interpretation I heard of the word was that it referred to Hungarians. That made no sense, since most African Americans have no particular experience of or attitude toward Hungarians. Nor was it clear why a word designating Hungarians would be extended to all whites. Another explanation I found even less convincing was that the term referred to white males who drove into African American neighborhoods honking their horns to attract African American women for purposes of prostitution. Like Clarence Major, I used my "own ethnic experience" and the opinions of other members of the language community that used the term as the authority for my informed skepticism.

The most logical etymology I encountered was the Wolof *xonx nopp*, meaning red ears (xonx = red, nopp = ear), which designates a white person, like redneck. The Wolof term, in fact, suggests a possible inspiration for the word "redneck," which my dictionary defines as, "a white member of the Southern rural laboring class—sometimes used disparagingly."[58] Xonx nopp is a Wolof characterization of what happens to people of little melanin in bright sunlight. There is no doubt that more African Americans have met more white people whom they have characterized as rednecks than have met Hungarians.

In the racially polarized 1960s, African Americans and all Americans saw nightly on national television Southern whites brutalizing African American freedom-seekers by beating them with police clubs, attacking them with high-pressure water hoses, unleashing fierce dogs on them, bombing churches and killing little girls, and murdering civil rights leaders. It is thus easily conceivable that more African Americans would have thought of whites in general as rednecks, rather than, nonsensically, as Hungarians.

I have heard another African-derived word, *bukra* or *bakra* from *mbakara*, meaning white person in Ibo and Efik from southern Nigeria,[59] used by U.S. African Americans, initially by a man from Muskogee, Oklahoma, as well as by Ndjuka maroons in the interior of Surinam. Whereas in Jamaica bukra refers to a rich white person,[60] what I've heard in the United States is *po' bukra*.

I even met an affluent white South Carolinean who said that it wasn't until he went to college in the North in the 1950s that he realized that po' bukra, which he said was from Gullah and which he had thought was a single word, was not a generally known and accepted term for poor whites. That this term of obvious African origin remains in active use in the United States and elsewhere in the African Diaspora, even though it is not in my dictionary, supports the logic of the continued existence also of the Wolof term for whites, just as hip, jive, cat, and dig remained in African American linguistic environments before becoming generalized enough to a larger U.S. population to make their way into the dictionary.

Honky gained currency at a time when African Americans were redefining ourselves as Black/Afro-American/African American and also renaming whites with a word of unsuspected African origin. The fact that the word was similar to a term used by some other population to designate Hungarians allowed an explanation to be proposed for the African American usage that had absolutely nothing to do with the experience of the users, whereas a more plausible interpretation existed in another explanatory system.

Wolof is also the likely source of the expression "the fuzz," which also puzzled me, for the police, from *fas*, meaning horse. Fas perhaps initially referred to the mounted patrollers who guarded plantation areas to keep enslaved people from moving around freely beyond permitted limits and pursued those who fled from bondage. The horse was probably at least as fear-inspiring as the rider, perhaps even more so—as urban crowd-control mounted police, whom I first discovered as a child at parades in Newark, New Jersey, are aware. Being able to hip people in one's own language, warn them to watch out, if they could dig it, if they understood, to open their eyes wide and look out for the fuzz, patrollers, xonx nopp/honkies/red ears/rednecks on horseback, had obvious survival value. And the ubiquitous standard U.S. English exclamation "wow" means "yes" in Wolof.

These Wolof words that continue to exist in U.S. African American, and in some hip Euro-American English suggest not just random lexical items, but rather a linguistic complex focusing around issues of survival crucial for Africans and their descendants during the period of slavery when the words appeared in North America. The ability of enslaved people to communicate in a linguistic system unknown to their enslavers was an obviously useful survival tool. African Diasporan creoles have been characterized as "maroon languages," because they represent a style of resistant communication among the enslaved, in opposition to the presumably all-controlling system of slavery. Such systems of encoded communication represented one of many ways of creating spaces of relative freedom in a system designed to ensure the total control of the lives of enslaved individuals and communities.

Being hip, having one's eyes wide open, being alert to one's natural and human environment, knowing what was really going on, was clearly as important a survival skill as the ability to jive, to dissimulate, and also to see through the jive in interactions with those in control during both slavery and its continuing aftermath. Beginning with basic issues of physical survival, hip has come to be associated with matters of attitude, style, and fashion, crucial issues of a different order of knowing and being for those who have managed not only to survive, but even to thrive, in incipient twenty-first-century (African) America.

It occurred to me to check what a dictionary might have to say about my linguistic wonderings and revelations. I had at hand the 1994 tenth edition of the *Merriam-Webster's Collegiate Dictionary*,[61] which seemed particularly appropriate because it was described on the dust jacket as both "America's best-selling dictionary" and, even more importantly, as "The Voice of Authority." It is also the dictionary of choice on the University of Texas at Austin's homepage on the World Wide Web, with the same 1994 definitions of the words that I had sought.[62]

The introductory section promised to reveal "how words make it into the dictionary,"[63] and said that "an etymologist must know a good deal about the history of English."[64] I was pleased to read that within the "borrowings that have occurred within the Modern English period . . . we find such exotic language names as . . . Kimbundu (at banjo)."[65] I also found okra, which was said to be "of African origin; akin to Ibo *ókürù*."[66] And I found gumbo, "of Bantu origin; akin to Umbundu *ochinggombo*," and referring to both okra the vegetable and to "a soup thickened with okra pods or filé and containing meat or seafoods and usually vegetables."[67]

Interestingly, for the first entry for gumbo, the culinary reference being the second, the origin was said to be American French from *gombo*, "perhaps from Kongo *nkómbó*" meaning "runaway slave." This first meaning of gumbo was defined as designating the French Creole spoken "by blacks in southern Louisiana."[68] The suggestion was of a real or metaphorical association between the Creole language and those who escaped or sought to escape from slavery, hence a real or figurative maroon language. Some creoles in the Americas are still literally maroon languages, such as Ndjuka and Saramaka for the maroons of Surinam and Palenquero in the maroon community of Palenque de San Basilio in Colombia.

Some pregnant women in Africa eat okra to facilitate childbirth, the slippery consistency of the vegetable being associated with the idea of facilitating the easy slipping of the baby through the birth canal. Thus, the linguistic association between okra and seeking freedom from slavery may be that the "runaway slaves" were able to slip away from plantations, slip through guarded areas, and slip past patrollers, so were hard to hold on to like well-cooked okra.

I was encouraged to find that *hip* as an adjective meant "characterized by keen informed awareness of or involvement in the newest developments or styles," and as a verb, "to make aware; tell, inform."[69] Hip was said to be an alteration of hep, circuitously defined as hip. But, rather than the Wolof origin that I expected, given banjo, okra, and gumbo, I was disappointed to find hip/hep characterized as "origin unknown."[70]

I then looked up *jive*. The first definition given was "swing music or the dancing performed to it." That didn't sound right so I asked my father, as the authoritative source from whom I had first heard the word. My father and others of his generation agreed that it didn't sound right and said that it did not correspond to their usage. Jive referred to talking, not dancing, they said. Maybe that was how whites used the term, but not African Americans. So the dictionary's first definition was not the original meaning of the word as used by the African American speech community in which it originated.

The second definition was "(a): glib, deceptive, or foolish talk (b): the jargon of hipsters (c): a special jargon or difficult slang." As a transitive verb, jive was said to mean "to tease or cajole," and as an adjective, "phony." Jive, like hip/hep, was also characterized as "origin unknown."[71] Glib and foolish talk are rather trivializing definitions, as are tease and cajole. Whereas dictionaries are not about profundity of interpretation, one might reasonably expect them to be sources of definitions that facilitate rather than impede such interpretations. The terms phony, and more especially, deceptive, contribute to understanding the more profound implications of "jive" as referring to a concept of conscious, deliberate, strategic, and selective dissimulation, as does the idea of special jargon or difficult slang. That it is the jargon of the hip, the informed, makes perfect sense.

Fuzz was said to mean police, again with its origin unknown.[72] For "dig," the origin of which was Middle English, the first five definitions had to do with loosening with an implement or poking literally or figuratively. The sixth definition, totally unrelated to the others, which gave me hope of finding a different origin, was "(a): to pay attention to: notice . . . (b): understand, appreciate . . . (c): like, admire."[73] The seventh definition of "cat," the origin of which was also Middle English, and the first six meanings of which were about the quadrupeds, was "(a): a player or devotee of jazz (b): guy."[74] No different origin, however, was provided to account for the difference between these latter definitions of the two words and the Middle English ones to which they were clearly unrelated. "Honky," "a white person—usually used disparagingly,"[75] was said to "probably" be an alteration of Hunky, which was an alteration of Hungarian, referring to "a person of central or east European birth or descent—usually used disparagingly."[76] No origin, known or unknown, was mentioned for "wow."[77]

After saying, "In writing new etymologies this editor must, of course, be alive to the possible languages from which a new term may have been borrowed," the introduction to the dictionary said that "When all attempts to provide a satisfactory etymology have failed, the editor has recourse to the formula 'origin unknown.'" It continued that, "This formula seldom means that the editor is unaware of various speculations about the origin of the term but instead usually means that no single theory conceived by the etymologist or proposed by others is well enough backed by evidence to include in a serious work of reference, even when qualified by 'probably' or 'perhaps.'"[78]

Interestingly "Honky," referring to Hungarians, deserved a "probably," although the language community that used the word most recently and most publicly would disagree. In contrast, the origin of the other related words of common etymology, used primarily by the same African American language community, was said to be "unknown" without even a "perhaps." The important nuance may be that the words whose origins the dictionary does acknowledge as "akin to" African words, or "perhaps" of African origin, are not specifically associated with African Americans, so they could be seen as somehow coming into English directly from their "exotic" African linguistic origins. The Wolof-derived expressions, however, represent a linguistic complex derived from and mediated by the nonexotic U.S. African American population based on the experience of slavery.

"Americanisms That May Once Have Been Africanisms" is the title of a 1969 *Times of London* article[79] I came upon many years after its publication and subsequent to my introduction to Wolof and to the revelations offered me by conversations with Wolof speakers during frequent trips to Senegal. In the article, David Dalby posited Wolof as the origin of several words used in U.S. English. I was pleased to find that Dalby's position as a scholar of West African languages, in contrast with the best-selling Voice of Authority etymologist, supported my opinion as both a member of the language community that had contributed the words to a U.S. English mainstream enough for them to "make it into the dictionary," and as a scholar of Africa and the African Diaspora.

According to Dalby, "There has been much speculation about the origin of such well-known Americanisms as OK, guy, jive, hippy, cat (meaning 'person'), and dig (meaning 'to understand'). Fanciful explanations have been proposed, like the traditional derivation of OK from a misspelling of 'all correct' [the "fanciful" definition that my dictionary affirmed with absolute certainty, with neither a 'perhaps' nor a 'probably.'[80]] It would seem, however, that these and certain other Americanisms may originally have been Africanisms, taken to the New World by West African slaves."[81]

"OK," Dalby states, is from the Wolof *waw*, meaning yes, with the emphatic particle *kay*, giving *waw kay* the meaning "all right, certainly," which I heard often in Senegal. Dalby also suggests, supporting my growing loss of confidence in *Webster's* etymologist, that "the historical role of Black speech in the development of American English appears to have been underestimated. Just as Black Americans have often been unjustly regarded as passive agents in the course of American history, so they have been regarded as largely passive in the shaping of the American language." He goes on to say that:

> There has been contact between English and West African languages for more than 400 years, and it is a sad reflection of old attitudes toward Africans and Black Americans that the possible effects of this contact on the English language should have received so little attention. It should not be forgotten that Black Americans represented the largest non-British ethnic group in the North American colonies during the formative years of American English, and that the last African-speaking ex-slaves in the United States were still alive at the beginning of this century.[82]

Dalby cites as the source of this underestimation of the role of African languages in U.S. English the fact that "the traditional belief was that slaves lost all trace of their original African languages when they arrived in the new world, and that they were forced to imitate the language of their white captors as best they could." This belief, he states, was first challenged when Lorenzo Dow Turner drew attention in 1949 to the African survivals in the Gullah language of South Carolina and Georgia. Dalby notes that plantation owners tried to prevent Africans from speaking their languages in order to keep them from using them for secret communication, and that enslaved Africans "conceal[ed] African words, with their original African meanings, behind similar sounding words already existing in English: dig, cat, sock, bug, fuzz(y) and jam," in a process of "linguistic subterfuge."[83]

But *Webster's* etymologists, "knowing a good deal about the history of English," apparently did not consider the knowledge of a Reader in West African Languages at the School of Oriental and African Studies of the University of London, former chair of the Centre of African Studies, and esteemed enough by his academic colleagues to be director of the International African Institute for half a decade, to be "well enough backed by evidence to include in a serious work of reference, even when qualified by 'probably' or 'perhaps'." As a result, for this Wolof-based African American linguistic subterfuge survival complex, which suggests interesting interpretations of an important area of U.S. African American behavior, and which has left its linguistic imprint on mainstream society, "all attempts to provide a satisfactory etymology have failed." Yet respected Africanist historian Philip Curtin, in his classic work *The African Slave Trade*, cited Dalby as an especially thorough and careful linguist and in comparing two scholars' attempts to identify African word origins said, "Dalby's list will be the more accurate."[84]

I thought that the problem might be the dictionary etymologists' unfamiliarity with Dalby's research. When I noticed on the last page of the dictionary that I could write to the Language Research Service to ask about entries, I did so, asking why the Wolof origins of words like hip, jive, cat, dig, fuzz, and honky were not acknowledged. The patronizing response I received from an etymologist began by acknowledging Dalby's "genuine knowledge of African languages." The etymologist then went on, contradictorily, to question the validity of Dalby's linguistic observations and claims of a significant Wolof presence in the United States, which, apparently unaware of thirty-year-old scholarship, he characterized as a "hypothesis" that had "not been supported by subsequent research." The etymologist saw no reason to consider hip of African origin, allowed that dig might be, failed to mention jive, and saw no connection between horses and police. Hunky, he said, was "indubitably AAVE [African American Vernacular English]." Satisfied with the highly questionable Hungarian definition, he asks, "If there is a good explanation of this word without resorting to an exotic source, I see no necessity to bring in Wolof."[85]

"I do not," he goes on, "deny that there are Africanisms in AAVE, but do we really have to lift so many stones to find them?" As proof he offers the word "tote," "to carry by hand," to which he attributes a Bantu origin. "Is it plausible," he asks, "that this word should be so easy to find in documentation of early forms of AAVE [his example being the slave narratives] while many other Africanisms remained buried for so long, not to emerge until African Americans migrated north to large urban centers? I am afraid that I am not convinced."[86] It is telling that "tote," the only word the etymologist concedes as African in origin, is quintessentially associated with labor, hence almost inevitably associated with enslaved African Americans. The "implausible" Wolof words are, in contrast, associated with intellectual concepts, with a resistant, subversive form of cognition and communication that was deliberately not supposed to "emerge" to become known by whites.

Although the etymologist refers to Dalby's work, his asking why the Wolof words "remained buried so long" before "emerg[ing]" demonstrates his failure to understand the answer to his question that Dalby provides in the very article the etymologist cites:

> White ignorance of Black American language and linguistic culture has stemmed not only from traditional prejudice, but also from the fact that one of the main applications of Black

language has been to strengthen the in-group solidarity of Black Americans to the specific exclusions of whites, and to deceive, confuse, and conceal information from white people in general. Hence it is that an in-group Black expression will often be dropped from Black speech—or changed in meaning—as soon as it becomes widely known by non-Blacks . . . so that the first appearance in print of an originally Black expression may not necessarily mark the time of its birth, but in a very real sense the time of its "death," perhaps after a long life in unrecorded Black speech.[87]

The problems with the etymologist's response suggest that perhaps the underlying issue remains, as Dalby suggested decades ago, that African American versions of English are still not a "possible language" source in which to seek the origins of words. The definition of jive that my father failed to recognize is a good case in point. The fact that the first definition given by the dictionary for jive was a Euro-American usage, rather than the African American usage from which the former derived, suggests that for an African word used by African Americans to make it into the dictionary, it must have entered into the usage of whites, whose derivative definition then takes precedence over the original. I do not, unfortunately, suspect that *Webster's* is worse than other dictionaries along these lines, but as the best-selling Voice of Authority is merely representative of a more general Eurocentric worldview.

On the culinary side, okra and black-eyed peas, the vegetables themselves and some of their preparations, are mainstays of the African gastronomic presence in the Americas. I had never had okra at home in New Jersey because my father didn't like it for the standard reason, the notoriously slimy consistency it acquires when cooked beyond al dente—and it is always cooked beyond al dente in Africa and African America. We had it only once when I was an adolescent, mixed with greens, a common African American preparation. It wasn't slimy and was delicious.

I was, however, horrified at a later date to find a big bowl of very slimy stuff on the dining table of the family with which I was spending the summer on an exchange program in Cameroon in Central Africa when I was nineteen. "What's wrong with the consistency?" they wanted to know. "That's what makes the sauce stick so well to the *fufu*." Fufu is a cornmeal ball reminiscent of stiff grits that is a staple of the area of Cameroon where I was. Similar staples made with grains, tubers, or plantain are eaten under a variety of names in most of Africa. Not sticking to the fufu, I told my Cameroonian family, had not been a problem in New Jersey.

In any case, I had to eat the okra sauce or risk offending my wonderful Cameroonian host family. That I managed to begin to like it prepared me to enjoy okra sauce, stew, or soup from Senegal to Angola and in North, Central, and South America and the Caribbean. Once I traveled from Angola in Central Africa to Curaçao in the Netherlands Antilles. I dined on fungi and okra sauce before leaving Luanda and dined on fungi and okra sauce for dinner upon arriving in Willemstad forty-eight hours of ocean-crossing later. The slimy okra stuck deliciously to the cornmeal balls on both sides of the Atlantic.

Louisiana's "okra gumbo" is a redundant name reflecting the tasty synergy of the fortuitous meeting of West African Akan- and Ibo-speaking women and Central African Bantu-speaking women over a cook pot in the process of forging their new synergistic

African Diasporan identities. Okra, or okro in much of the anglophone Caribbean, comes from the Akan *nkruman* or *nkrumun*[88] and/or the Ibo *òkùrù*. And *ngombo* is the Bantu root for okra,[89] which gives *ochinggombo* in Umbundu; gombo in the French of Europe, francophone Africa, and the francophone/creolophone Caribbean; *quimbombó* in Cuba; and *quiabo* in Brazil.

The African redundancy of okra gumbo, emphasizing both the origin of the vegetable and its names, stands in contrast to the de-Africanized "okraless gumbo" that has become an acclaimed part of Louisiana's culinary repertoire. A "New Orleans Menu Glossary" in *Food & Wine* magazine stated that "Classically constructed gumbos contain shellfish, chicken, turkey, ham, duck or sausage, either alone or in almost endless combinations, cooked in a roux-based, assertively seasoned broth. The liquid can be thickened and flavored with filé or okra, but never both."[90]

While retaining the original African nomenclature, this "classic" gumbo, which might be more accurately characterized as faux gumbo, has lost its African foundation as its texturizer, thickener, and flavor, and a European foundation, the toasted flour roux contributed by Cajuns, occupies its place. The African base that was essential has become optional. Interestingly, my dictionary definition of gumbo contained only okra or filé, no roux. Some Cajuns, it seems, consciously avoid the use of okra in their gumbo, which might better be called "no-gumbo gumbo," because they associate okra with African Americans, many of whom now also use the roux base and consider okra optional.

Okra gumbo, in contrast to the nongumbo variations, is the northernmost version of *callaloo*, a dish widely enjoyed in the African Diaspora. *Kalulú is* a Kimbundu word from Angola designating a stew of okra, greens, palm oil, and dried and fresh fish, which is eaten with fungi. It was a typical food of the former Ndongo kingdom, from which many people were victims of the transatlantic slave trade.[91] Kalalú is also a common dish in São Tomé and Principe, where it is composed of greens and other vegetables, palm oil, smoke-dried fish, shrimp, and chicken.[92] *Kalalú* perhaps led, maybe in convergence with the Anglo-Saxon *colewort* (a nonhead-forming member of the cabbage family, such as kale),[93] à la Phibba/Fiba/Phoebe, to the name of the collard greens and kale that are nutritious African American soul food staples, now widely touted as cruciform anti-carcinogens and calcium-rich osteoporosis preventives.

Callaloo is found in various incarnations in most of the Caribbean, with people from each island being absolutely adamant about the special and distinctive qualities of their own version of the dish. It is a leafy green vegetable usually prepared like spicy spinach, maybe enhanced with salt fish or pigtails in Jamaica, as well as an iron-rich soup recommended for people suffering from anemia.[94] In the United States spinach leaves may be used. And in Martinique it is a rich greens and okra soup, maybe with a crab.

In Trinidad, according to my mother's friend Ivy,[95] it is a stew composed of callaloo bush (Trinidad's dasheen or cocoyam leaves being different from those, called baji in Trinidad, used in Jamaican callaloo) leaves and okro in equal proportion, such as "ten leaves and ten okros," with salt meat such as pigtails, shrimp, and coconut milk, and served over rice. Callaloo and crab is typically a Sunday dish that many consider the Trinidadian national dish.[96] It may be heated up with "congo pepper." I ate callaloo in three ways on the tiny island of Carriacou: as a small cup of soup as the first course in a fine restaurant, and as both a vegetable like greens and as the real local "callaloo soup," a stew with pigtails and provisions (tropical white sweet potatoes and yams, dasheen, etc.), in a guesthouse restaurant frequented by knowledgeable islanders.

In Haiti *calalou*, or in some parts of the island, *calalou gombo*, means okra, and *légumes calalou* is an okra stew prepared with beef or pork and including seafood in some areas, which is eaten with rice.[97] In Brazil *carurú*, an okra dish prepared with dried shrimp, onions, and palm oil, is the culinary basis of an Afro-Brazilian religious festivity that bears its name. When prepared for secular enjoyment, carurú may include coconut milk or ground raw peanuts or cashews.[98]

Webster's says that callaloo is "American Spanish," *calalú*, for "a soup or stew made of greens, onions, and crabmeat."[99] The dictionary fails to account for how the word got into American Spanish if it did not come from Iberian Spanish, although the dictionary had indicated that the linguistic definition of gumbo "perhaps" got into American French from [Ki]Kongo. Nor is calalú found more especially in hispanophone America than elsewhere, as the dictionary's proposed origin would lead one to expect. It is, in fact, equally present in the Portuguese-, English-, and French/Creole-speaking regions of the Americas, with no apparent diffusion from the Spanish-speaking areas. The common denominator of the distribution of callaloo is rather the Central African origins of the populations and the word, which might lead one to question again the limited sense of "possible language" origins considered by the Voice of Authority.

I ate black-eyed pea fritters called *acará* from Cameroon in Central Africa to Senegal at the ocean edge of West Africa. I also ate *acarajé* on the streets of Salvador da Bahia in Brazil, the *jé* being a Yoruba accretion meaning "to eat." In the Candomblé, acarajé is a favorite food of the Orishas Shangó and Oyá. Because of the Orishas's insistence on being not only "dancing divinities," as Yvonne Daniel says,[100] but also on being nourished by their favorite food offerings, culinary historian Jessica Harris characterizes them as "gourmet gods."[101] In addition to being offered as tasty sacrifices to Shangó and Oyá and being served as spiritually empowering communion food for people who attend ceremonies in their honor, in its secular incarnation acarajé is cooked and sold on the streets by Afro-Brazilian women who are initiates of the Orishas—in a soulful fast-food gastroapotheosis.

Before nourishing African spiritual beings and Afro-Brazilian and other human souls in Brazil, black-eyed peas nourished African bodies prior to their forced departure from the continent. Joseph N'Diaye, the original curator of the euphemistically named Slave House, a former holding pen for enslaved Africans now transformed into a museum on Gorée Island, Senegal, told visitors that *niébé*, black-eyed peas, were fed to African captives to help them survive the agonizing waiting period there and to fortify them for the torturous ocean voyage ahead.

It had not occurred to me until rather late in my discoveries of African Diasporan realities to wonder about the insistence of a great many U.S. African Americans, and quite a few Southern whites, upon consuming black-eyed peas on New Year's Eve, hence as ritual food. The black-eyed peas must be accompanied by greens—for money. Greens means collard, kale, mustard, or turnip greens or combinations thereof. Spinach, swiss chard, and the like do not fall within the category of the "mean greens" to which jazz trumpeter Eddie Harris was referring in his song of that name.[102]

New Year's Eve black-eyed peas and greens must be accompanied by hocks, "trotters," and/or (hog) "maws," which Brazilians characterize as the "non-noble" parts of the pig. These parts contrast not only positionally, but also philosophically, with the chops and loins and other more elevated, thus more noble, cuts on the top and outside of the animal to which African Americans refer when speaking of the good life as "living high on the hog." A friend's mother, in fact, serves a ham along with the essential black-eyed peas and rice and greens with ham hocks, demonstrating that she is both literally and symbolically living high on the hog.

I was, of course, fully aware that eating black-eyed peas for New Year's Eve, or maybe New Year's Day depending on the region, ensured luck for the new year, and I practiced the tradition assiduously. When asked to take a dish to a New Year's Eve party organized by some African friends, I automatically cooked black-eyed peas. In addition to being concerned with my own luck, I also felt responsible for theirs, in case they were unaware of how to ensure it. But during all of my wanderings and seekings of meanings, I never found an explanation, in spite of asking everyone whom I thought might know, for why black-eyed peas were indispensable to starting the new year right—beyond everyone's certainty that you had to eat them if you wanted to be lucky and prosperous.

This wondering was enhanced during one of my wanderings when I learned, by being at the right table at the right time, that in Martinique for Christmas, people eat what they call in Creole *pwa d'angole*, Angola peas, with non-noble pig parts, to ensure luck for the new year, *bien sùr*. Pwa d'angole are known in English as pigeon peas or *gongo/gunga/gungu* peas in Jamaica.[103] In Spanish they are *guandules* (Dominican Republic) or *gandules* (Puerto Rico), and *guandu* in Brazilian Portuguese[104] from *wandu*, a staple in Angola's historic Kongo kingdom.[105]

The holiday eating of pwa d'angole in Martinique suggested a phenomenon similar to the one with which I had grown up, with the name of the peas referring to the Central African point of African origin of some of the population. Mentally connecting the two sides of the Atlantic, it occurred to me that there just might be a symbolic relationship between the last supper black-eyed peas meal in Africa before leaving the continent through Gorée's (and other such places of horror) "door of no return," and the last supper of the old year–black-eyed peas meals in African America.

The black-eyed peas pretravel fattening regime was to help promote for the Africans who left Gorée the luck, rather than the fatal alternative, of surviving the Middle Passage across the Atlantic. If lucky enough to survive that challenging journey, they would have the opportunity to undertake another challenging journey through a life of perpetual bondage on the other side, ritually eating annual meals of black-eyed peas to try to ensure the luck of surviving each successive new year. It is probably no coincidence that an explanation for this more than physical survival food that had intrigued me also comes from the same Wolof speakers who provided the survival linguistic complex that had perplexed me.

The significance of the Wolof influence for African American, and even Euro-American culture is affirmed by Joseph Holloway:

Between 1670 and 1700, Africans were imported to South Carolina predominantly from "Guinea." The majority of these "Guinea" Africans were Wolofs and other Mandes, such as

Bambaras, Fulani, and Susus. The Wolofs, the most numerous of the African groups to arrive in the United States in the seventeenth century, were mostly house servants who had extensive and close contact with European-Americans. They were, perhaps, the first Africans whose cultural elements and language were assimilated by and retained within the developing culture of America. They also had greater opportunities for admixture and interaction with whites than other African groups in the years before 1700.[106]

And according to Gwendolyn Midlo Hall, two-thirds of the Africans taken to Louisiana during the French period were Senegambians, and Senegambia (Senegal and the Gambia) remained an important source of the slave trade for Louisiana throughout the eighteenth century. The related populations of the relatively homogenous culture area spoke closely related languages, Sereer, Pulaar, Wolof, and Malinke. Although few Wolofs were shipped from Senegambia during the 1720s, they were taken to Louisiana because important French colonists, including the director of the Company of the Indies in Louisiana that was responsible for enslaving Africans for the colony, expressed a preference for Wolofs, characterizing them as "good commanders of other *nègres*" who can be "easily encouraged to learn a trade." The director apparently "recommended that only Wolof slaves, male and female, young and old, be selected for any service in the home."[107]

Donna Marie Williams's *Black-Eyed Peas for the Soul* inevitably includes a story about black-eyed peas and luck. The author describes her father's efforts to teach her to prepare, and to properly appreciate, the larger implications of the nutritious legume that continues to nourish African American spirits and hearts as well as bodies:

"Black-eyed peas are a down-home food. When I was growing up in Jacksonville, Alabama, your great-grandma, my grandma, would cook 'em in molasses and serve it over rice. She'd cook 'em with ham, pig tails, bacon—whatever she'd have lying around, and she'd cook 'em in a pot as big as this kitchen on that tiny wood-burning stove. We'd be eating black-eyed peas for weeks. Every New Year's she'd cook a batch for good luck."

"Good luck?"

"Right, cook 'em on New Year's and you'll have good luck for the rest of the year," said Daddy.

"Sounds like some superstitious Negro nonsense to me," I said superciliously. But as soon as I said it, I regretted it. My father looked to heaven and shook his head sadly.

"You complain about your son not caring about our history—wonder where he got it from?" I deserved that.

"Daddy, I'm sorry. I didn't mean to crack, but you've got to admit—black-eyed peas, good luck, oh c'mon!"

. . . [H]e proceeded to tell me a story. It was a story about how my great-great-grandma had walked off the plantation with my great-grandma in hand and set up housekeeping in Jacksonville. Times were hard, but our family has the work ethic stitched into our genetic code. . . .

"There was never an easy time when I was growing up. We had to fight Jim Crow, the Ku Klux Klan, and other black folks. Sometimes, throwing kernels of corn on the ground with a prayer or fixing a big batch of black-eyed peas on New Year's Day was the only things that gave us hope for a better life. And somehow, some way, we'd manage to get over. That Negro nonsense, as you call it, gave us hope and a laugh when there wasn't nothing to laugh about."

I had been properly chastised. "I'm sorry," I said, my cheeks hot with shame.

"Don't put down something you don't know nothing about," he said.[108]

On the island of St. John in the U.S. Virgin Islands, the New Year's ritual food is callaloo, made with spinach, okra, fish, crab, and pigtails or other pork seasoning, served with fungi, and eaten, of course, to ensure luck for the new year.[109] And a U.S. colleague who grew up in the black-eyed peas tradition said that when she was living in California and learning to cook, her best friends were from Louisiana. For New Year's Eve they always ate a very rich real, not faux, okra gumbo, for which they might import special crabs from home. My friend, whose mother is the person who includes the ham in her ritual meal, now combines both the black-eyed peas and the gumbo traditions, ensuring herself multiple sources of luck from these plurally ancestral African foods.

Hence, there are significant ritual meals to begin the new year in much of African America that reflect their African origins in both nomenclature and ingredients. These meals are based on either black-eyed peas, or pwa d'angole, or on an okra dish called by the Bantu terms gumbo or callaloo. A principle even more fundamental than the specific foods eaten may have originally been the eating of food of African origin at the time of the year when enslaved people had the opportunity to express and enjoy themselves most freely and fully. They began the new year with a source of physical and spiritual nourishment that reminded them of both their African roots and their success in surviving yet another year against enormous odds.

It occurred to me that my interpretation might suggest that I think that most enslaved U.S. African Americans left Africa from Gorée Island, where black-eyed peas were meaningful, whereas the majority left from elsewhere. It might also suggest that I think that most Africans and African Americans ate black-eyed peas on New Year's Eve during slavery, whereas I do not think there was usually the possibility for that level of gastronomic volition on the part of the enslaved, or that there was that kind of gastronomic uniformity in any case. But then no one assumes that all of the European immigrants from whom the U.S. patriotic holiday Thanksgiving came ate the now de rigueur turkey with dressing at that first harvest meal that gave us the tradition.

When I asked people where the black-eyed peas custom came from, the usual response was on the order of the "I don't know. We've just always done it that way," with which anthropologists are familiar from asking people around the world why they do what they do. I had hoped that someone would give me an explanation based on either passed-down knowledge or historical research into the origins and evolution of this gastronomic tradition of eating black-eyed peas or an okra stew (or both in the case of my friend) to ensure luck for the new year, which I discovered to be so widespread in the African Diaspora.

The only person who had an explanation of why her family ate black-eyed peas for New Year's was a white woman from North Carolina. When I asked her why they ate them, she said, of course, "for luck." When I asked her if she had any idea of what was behind her family's eating them for luck, she said, "Our cook wouldn't come in our house if we didn't. She said it was bad luck to cross into the New Year without eating them. So she wouldn't cross the threshold into our house unless we had eaten them. You know, as I look back I realize that we ate black-eyed peas on New Years because our African American cook made us do it."[110]

In the absence of knowledge or research on the historical origins of the tradition, what is apparent is that the practice existed to enough of an extent, in the habits of enough of the population, or of a significant and influential enough segment of the population, to be perpetuated with enough of its importance intact, that people, African Americans and whites apparently influenced by African Americans, continue it today, in disparate areas of the Diaspora, even though they do not know the source of the meaning that continues to give it that importance. No one I have encountered, however, is interested in doing the kind of risky scientific testing of the theory that would involve forgoing the delicious ritual meal to see if the luck persists without it—although vegetarians do dare to leave out the non-noble pig parts.

According to a Senegalese friend, in addition to their nutritional value, black-eyed peas also serve a more than ordinary purpose in Senegal. Growing easily, even in drought conditions, and refertilizing the soil with their nitrogen, they symbolize abundance. People seeking improvement in their lives consult a *marabout,* a Muslim holy man, who usually tells them to offer charity to a beggar, sometimes in the form of cooked black-eyed peas. They are to give a food that portends abundance to someone in need, in a nourishing gesture both real and symbolic, in order to receive in exchange the desired abundance in their own lives. My friend said that an African American woman visiting her in Senegal had given black-eyed peas to a beggar on the advice of a marabout whom she had told of her desire to open a business. The business flourished.[111]

Black-eyed peas play a similar role as a medium of spiritual exchange in the Afro-Brazilian Candomblé. People prepare black-eyed peas as sacrifices to several of the Orishas in gratitude for their help and to request more blessings. People also symbolically eat black-eyed peas with the Orishas in communion feasts in order to absorb from the divine beings spiritual energy with which to enhance their lives.

These spiritual functions of the legume as a source of nutrition that goes way beyond the merely physical have satisfied my seemingly simple gastronomic inquiry with the kind of complex philosophical explanation that my attendance at the Afro-Brazilian Candomblé ceremony gave me for my curiosity about the Baptist church ladies in Newark. Again I had to wander widely in Africa and the African Diaspora to find explanations and interpretations to satisfy my wonderings about intriguing African American behaviors from back home in New Jersey.

The New Year's Eve black-eyed peas meal so essential to U.S. African Americans and some not-so-African Americans, when situated in the contexts of both the Senegalese and Afro-Brazilian meanings, takes on greater significance as a form of ritual expression of gratitude for the blessings of the previous year and of requesting further luck and abundance for the future. These elucidations of what seemed like a relatively simple culinary curiosity also further highlight the primary issue of the necessity of seeking deep explanations for African Diasporan behaviors in cultural continuities from Africa to the Americas and in commonalities among African Diasporan societies. This is especially true of behaviors for which satisfying explanations internal to the societies in question seem unavailable. Their profound meanings have obviously been forgotten, although the behaviors persist tenaciously because people understand that they are, for some reason, important.

That is the gist of the issue and the basis of my quest. The quest began with my questions about everyday behaviors that seemed somehow different, as if part of a different system, and for which no one could provide explanations that satisfied me. What I finally understood from the comparative perspective I acquired as a result of my wondering and wandering and deliberate research was that the norms I was assuming, on which African American life was presumably predicated, were the Euro-American norms that I had been taught to assume.

At the same time, I was participating in and observing behaviors that did not conform to those norms, norms that therefore lacked both explanatory ability and interpretative value. The issue, then, was to find sources of intellectually satisfying explanations in another conceptual system. The only logical source of explanation, certainly preferable to a dismissive "origin unknown," was the African heritage that continues to determine behavior in more or less obvious ways all over the African Diaspora.

The accepted truism, however, was, and for many people still is, that although elsewhere in the Americas behaviors reflecting specific African origins had been preserved, this did not happen in the United States because Africans from the same ethnic and language groups had been deliberately separated by their enslavers to both prevent conspiracies against the system of oppression and exploitation and to ensure the cultural destruction necessary to create a docile enslaved labor force. This explanation for the demise of African culture in general in the United States meant that there could not, of course, be evidence of specific ethnic identities, especially not in urban New Jersey.

Scholars such as Stanley Elkins, in his 1963 *Slavery: A Problem in American Institutional Life*,[112] contended that the enslavers' desires to transform Africans and their descendants into passive, malleable "Sambo" personalities had become the reality of the enslaved. To draw such a conclusion it was necessary to fail to notice, or to manage to ignore, evidence of the revolts and attempted revolts that clearly indicated the contrary, as had been documented twenty years earlier, for example, by Herbert Aptheker in his 1943 *American Negro Slave Revolts*.[113]

Although the Africanity of other multiethnic societies of the Americas, such as Brazil and Cuba, had been acknowledged decades earlier, that of U.S. African American society did not begin to be seriously considered by the scholarly establishment until the publication of anthropologist Melville Herskovits's groundbreaking and initially controversial 1941 book *The Myth of the Negro Past*.[114] The myth that Herskovits marshaled extensive cross-cultural fieldwork-based data from West Africa, South America, and the Caribbean to refute was that U.S. African Americans had maintained no culture of African origin because of the destructive effects of slavery.

The opposing position was most prominently defended by African American sociologist E. Franklin Frazier in his 1948 *The Negro Family in the United States* and later in his 1963 *The Negro Church in America*.[115] The two scholars engaged in the "Herskovits-Frazier debate" on the theme in a series of articles. This was an era in which African Americans were trying to assimilate into and gain full rights of citizenship in U.S. society. We wanted to emphasize our Americanity, not our Africanity, which would have been dysfunctional. Frazier's perspective, in contrast with Herskovits's, was clearly informed by the pragmatic situation and interests of the African American community, rather than by purely intellectual concerns.

A comment made at a conference on "The African Impact on the Material Culture of the Americas" expresses well the African American perspective that Frazier represented. "Before the dawn of the multicultural era, acknowledgement of the African— read savage—impact on African American culture was seen by some as another means of justifying second-class citizenship. If blacks were still retaining elements of their African heritage after more than three hundred years of exposure to 'civilization,' what hope was there that they might ever attain salvation. After all, integration was equated with assimilation."[116]

Since the beginning of the twentieth century African American scholars such as W. E. B. Du Bois, Zora Neale Hurston, Arturo Alfonso Schomburg, and Carter G. Woodson had been documenting the African origins of African American culture, the cultural continuity within the African Diaspora, and the roles of Africa and Africans in the Americas and globally in works including Du Bois' *The Souls of Black Folk: Essays and Sketches* (1903), *The Gift of Black Folks: Negroes in the Making of America* (1924), *Black Folk Then and Now: An Essay in the History and Sociology of the Negro Race* (1939), and *The World and Africa: An Inquiry Into the Part Which Africa Has Played in World History* (1946); Hurston's *Mules and Men: Negro Folktales and Voodoo Practices in the South* (1935), and *Tell My Horse* (1938); Schomburg's articles "The Economic Contribution by the Negro to America" (1916), and "The Negro Digs Up His Past" (1925); and Woodson's *The African Background Outlined* (1936), and *The Negro in Our History* (1947).[117] Their works were not, however, widely considered by the non-African American academic establishment.

The policy of separating captive Africans from the same areas did exist in both Africa and the Americas in some times and places so as to better control them through simple divide-and-rule tactics, as exemplified in the words of a British ship's captain in West Africa:

> As for the languages of the Gambia, they are so many and so different, that the Natives, on either Side the River, cannot understand each other; which, if rightly consider'd, is no small Happiness to the Europeans who go there to trade for slaves. . . . I have known some melancholy Instances of whole Ship Crews being surpriz'd, and cut off by them. But the safest Way is to trade with the different Nations on either Side the River, and having some of every Sort on board, there will be no more Likelihood of their succeeding in a Plot, than of finishing the Tower of Babel.[118]

For the Americas, Peter Wood says:

> In fact, most planters put great stock in the assertion that African language differences, occasionally reinforced by national antipathies, served to divide the slaves among themselves. . . . It was an article of faith among the English in late-seventeenth-century Barbados . . . that "the whites have no greater security than the diversity of the negroes' languages." Few masters acknowledged the fact that the accepted policy of mixing slaves from different backgrounds was itself an inducement to the evolution of a common pidgin.[119]

But issues of practicality and preference in the Americas also led to keeping Africans from the same groups together in the United States as elsewhere. My curiosities and discoveries began to reveal several specific African ethnic and regional cultural complexes in the United States, resulting from either fortuitous or purposeful concentrations of

Africans from the same groups, the latter based on sought-after skills selected or rebellious tendencies avoided. These discoveries led me to perceive similarities with, as opposed to differences between, the United States and other African Diasporan communities. I am convinced that my findings, inspired by initial childhood observations and curiosities, and substantiated by subsequent experiences and systematic research, represent merely the tip of the iceberg of what exists and becomes visible once one learns how to see.

Recent studies that support my observations by discussing specific African ethnic and regional identities maintained in the United States include Michael Mullin's 1992 *Africa in America*, Gwendolyn Midlo Hall's 1992 *Africans in Colonial Louisiana*, John Thornton's 1992 *Africa and Africans in the Making of the Atlantic World, 1400–1680*, and Michael A. Gomez's 1998 *Exchanging Our Country Marks*. Video documentaries that also do so include *Family Across the Sea* (1991) and *The Language You Cry In* (1999),[120] which portray the historical and cultural links between the Gullah and Geechee people of South Carolina and Georgia and the Mende people of Sierra Leone.

Most Africans were captured in groups as a result of systematic wars and raids, a cost-effective technique in a market based on an economy of scale. Also there were cultural and linguistic similarities between neighboring groups, and some people were multilingual due to proximity and mobility. The unquestioned assumption that Africans in the United States could not communicate with one another for purposes of cultural preservation has, however, influenced both data-seeking and theorizing concerning the African heritage of the United States.

This perspective has fostered a focus on the differences rather than the similarities between the Africanity of U.S. African American culture and that of the rest of the African Diaspora. Many differences might be more simply attributable to factors such as the relatively small numbers of Africans who arrived in the large territory of the United States, as compared to the relatively large numbers who arrived on small Caribbean islands, and the both relatively and absolutely large numbers who arrived in equally large Brazil. In addition, there was the relatively early end of the legal importation of Africans into the United States in 1808, as compared to generations later in Brazil in 1850.

This assumption of difference has successfully served the disempowering function of diluting the U.S. African American community's sense of its Africanity and of making its members think that they, in contrast with members of other Diasporan communities, cannot trace links to their African heritage. Many Afro-Brazilians, for example, trace cultural links with Yoruba people from Nigeria and Benin who arrived in northeastern Brazil in large numbers in the first half of the nineteenth century. These Yoruba were able to institutionalize their religion such that it remains an important and dynamic presence that helps define the national culture of Brazil.

U.S. African Americans are inclined to see ourselves as different from, rather than similar to, other Diasporan communities based on relative Africanity and to view African Diasporan populations as dispersed and oppressed national minorities, rather than as constituents of a diversely transnational Pan-African American community. The idea that any association with Africa was negative, so that being less African than other African Diasporans was positive, began to be countered by the 1960s Black consciousness/Black nationalist movement that promoted a Pan-Africanist worldview emphasizing continuities and commonalities.

Such a disavowing of African origins created the fundamental intellectual problem of depriving U.S. African Americans of sources of explanations and interpretations of behaviors, as well as precluding a Pan-American, rather than a limited national, perspective on African and African Diasporan contributions to the creation of the societies of the Americas. A focus on the African Diaspora and its links with its individual, plural, and synergized African heritages, and on the commonalities between African Diasporan communities, necessarily leads to more and better sources of relevant explanations and greater interpretive power.

Thus, in trying to understand everyday African American behaviors that I experienced in New Jersey in the areas of spirituality, language, naming practices, and ritual gastronomy, I learned that in order to understand them, I needed to know that as a result of area-specific factors, African cultural elements in the nations of the Americas are more or less obvious, more or less blended with one another as well as with non-African forms, and more or less pervasive in the larger society, or limited to the population defined as being of African descent. President Fidel Castro, for example, characterized Cuba as "an Afro-Latin society," acknowledging the African presence as an integral and inextricable component of the fabric of the national culture of all Cubans.

The United States, in contrast, is the only American nation that has simplistically divided its citizens into people of African origin and people of European origin, with any degree of African genetic heritage—the famous "one drop rule"—defining a person as African American. The associated assumption is that culture can also be color-coded. This binary construction mandates the fiction that African culture can only have remained in the population of obvious African origin and cannot be part of the "mainstream" that is, according to this peculiarly imperceptive and flagrantly counter-empirical worldview, a Euro-American preserve that has influenced, but has not been influenced by, African American culture.[121] The problem with this idea of cultural isolationism and mono-directionality of flow is that it is contradicted not only by the nature of culture, which so easily and ironically transgresses presumably impermeable social boundaries, but also by the facts. Witness white Southerners eating black-eyed peas for luck on New Year's and white Southern women blithely named Ouida.

Culture functions in a more dynamic, nonlinear manner than that posited by the binary theory and is certainly no respecter of epidermal melanin. Social definitions in the United States, coupled with enforced legal, and more casual post-legal, segregation, have created and reinforced a situation in which African culture remains mainly, but by no means exclusively, concentrated in the African American population.

The irony of the situation is that it is precisely this presumably peripheral, most African repository that continues to create dynamic new cultural forms that infiltrate the mainstream more and more obviously and aggressively, further muddying those already less than limpid waters. The commodification and commercialization of these cultural forms by the mainstream establishment only serves to further embed them therein and to further propagate them into U.S., Pan-American, and global culture.

NOTES

1. Juan R. Palomo, "Seeds of African Culture Sown in Life, Literature, Language," *Austin American-Statesman* (Feb. 18, 1996): 1A. This article was about the "African Diaspora and the Modern World" conference that I organized at the University of Texas at Austin, which provided the basis for this volume.

2. My idea of "wondering and wandering," came from Langston Hughes's book, *I Wonder as I Wander: An Autobiographical Journey* (New York: Rinehart, 1956), which inspired me when I was an adolescent who wondered, but had not yet gotten to wander.

3. In a required mid-1960s University of Chicago graduate linguistics class, my Euro-American professor, whose specialty was Nahuatl, the language of the Aztecs, authoritatively challenged my command of African American English in a paper I wrote. He insisted that "nitty-gritty," meaning "essence," should be correctly rendered as "gritty nitty"! This inspired me to do research on the African origins of African American English, an incipient area of linguistic research at that time. I wrote my first popular article on the topic for an African American publication that acknowledged my accurate command of the language: "Black English: Expression of the Afro-American Experience," *Black World* 20, no. 8 (June 1971): 4–16.

Recent works on the African origins of African Diasporan Englishes include Mervyn C. Alleyne's *Comparative Afro-American: An Historical Comparative Study of English-based Afro-American Dialects of the New World* (Ann Arbor, Mich.: Karoma Publishers, 1980) and *Theoretical Issues in Caribbean Linguistics* (Mona, Jamaica: Language Laboratory, University of the West Indies, 1982); and Salikoko Mufwene's *Africanisms in Afro-American Language Varieties* (Athens: University of Georgia Press, 1993) and *African American English: Structure, History and Use* (New York: Routledge, 1998).

4. The 1960s and 1970s Black consciousness/Black nationalist period, with its discarding of "slave names" and adopting of African and African-inspired names, led me to research the evolution of African American naming behavior. I wrote the results in both popular and scholarly versions: "What's in a Name?" *Ebony* 32, no. 8 (June 1977): 74–84, and "Noms et identité chez les noirs-américains/African American Names and Identity," *Ethiopiques: Revue socialiste de culture négro-africaine* (Dakar, Senegal), no. 8 (April 1979): 26–45. I received several responses to the *Ebony* article—from people such as a Mr. Cuffy and a Ms. Quashie, who were pleased to learn the African (Akan in both cases) origins of their names. I also heard from people who said that they had decided to change their names to something more meaningful based on the information I provided. To my knowledge the more scholarly version did not provoke the kind of nomenclatural modification that was an unanticipated, and gratifying, consequence of the popular version.

5. Questions about what people eat in Africa from people in the United States after my first stay in Cameroon in 1964, and my fieldwork in the Ivory Coast and travels around West, Central, and East Africa in 1971–72, inspired me to write another article for an African American publication on what, and especially how, Africans eat, and on the relationships between African and African American foods and foodways. The result was "How You Eat Is How You Be," *Essence* (September 1973): 62–63, 77. Subsequent publications by Jessica B. Harris on the foods of the African Diaspora and their continuities with, divergences from, and creative elaborations on their African gastronomic ancestors both make the point more extensively and offer recipes to make it less theoretically and more deliciously: *Hot Stuff: A Cookbook in Praise of the Piquant* (Flushing, N.Y.: Queens College/CUNY, 1987); *Iron Pots and Wooden Spoons: Africa's Gift to New World Cooking* (New York: Atheneum, 1989); *Sky Juice and Flying Fish: Traditional Caribbean Cooking* (New York: Simon and Schuster, 1991); *Tasting Brazil: Regional Recipes and Reminiscences* (New York: Maxwell Macmillan International, 1992); *The Welcome Table: African American Heritage*

Cooking (New York: Simon and Schuster, 1995); *A Kwanzaa Keepsake: Celebrating the Holiday with New Traditions and Feasts* (New York: Simon and Schuster, 1995), and *The Africa Cookbook: A Taste of the Continent* (New York: Simon and Schuster, 1998).

6. John Edward Philips, "The African Heritage of White America," in *Africanisms in American Culture*, ed. Joseph E. Holloway (Bloomington: Indiana University Press, 1990), 225–239; William D. Pierson, *Black Legacy: America's Hidden Heritage* (Amherst: University of Massachusetts Press, 1993); Shelley Fisher Fishkin, "Interrogating 'Whiteness,' Complicating 'Blackness': Remapping American Culture," *American Quarterly* 47, no. 3 (Sept. 1995): 428–466, and *Was Huck Black? Mark Twain and African American Voices* (New York: Oxford University Press, 1993); Brenda Dixon Gottschild, *Digging the Africanist Presence in American Performance: Dance and Other Contexts* (Westport, Conn.: Greenwood Press, 1996).

7. Sheila S. Walker, "Bahia: Africa in America," *Essence* (July 1977): 42–43, 64, 67; Giovanni and Michael Brewer (producers), *Bahia: Africa in America* (Boston: Broadcast Video Productions, 1987).

8. This dawning realization became the basis of my masters thesis research on the phenomenon of trance in African and African-derived religions, which was published as *Ceremonial Spirit Possession in Africa and Afro-America* (Leiden, Netherlands: E. J. Brill, 1972), and of an article linking U.S. African American religion to that of areas of more obvious African inspiration, "African Gods in the Americas: The Black Religious Continuum," special issue "Black Anthropology," eds. Johnnetta B. Cole and Sheila S. Walker, *The Black Scholar* 11, no. 8 (Nov.–Dec. 1980): 25–36.

My articles on Afro-Brazilian religion and culture are: "Candomble: A Spiritual Microcosm of Africa," *Black Art: An International Quarterly* 5, no. 4 (Fall 1983): 10–22; "Africanity Versus Blackness: The Afro-Brazilian/Afro-American Identity Conundrum," *Introspectives: Contemporary Art by Americans and Brazilians of African Descent* (Los Angeles: California Afro-American Museum, Feb. 1989): 17–21; "Everyday and Esoteric Reality in the Afro-Brazilian Candomble," *History of Religions: An International Journal for Comparative Historical Studies* 30, no. 2 (Nov. 1990): 103–128; "A Choreography of the Universe: The Afro-Brazilian Candomble as a Microcosm of Yoruba Spiritual Geography," *Anthropology and Humanism Quarterly* 16, no. 1 (June 1991): 42–50; "The Saints versus the Orishas in a Brazilian Catholic Church as an Expression of Afro-Brazilian Cultural Synthesis in the Feast of Good Death," in *African Creative Expressions of the Divine*, eds. Kortwright Davis and Elias Farajaje-Jones (Washington, D.C.: Howard University School of Divinity, 1991), 84–98; "The Feast of Good Death: An Afro-Catholic Emancipation Celebration in Brazil," *Sage: A Scholarly Journal on Black Women* 3, no. 2 (Fall 1986), published with revisions in *Women in Africa and the African Diaspora: A Reader*, 2nd edition, eds. Rosalyn Terborg Penn and Andrea Benton Rushing (Washington, D.C.: Howard University Press, 1996), 203–214.

9. Yvonne Daniel, "Dancing Divinity: Activated Philosophy in the Afro-Americas," paper presented at the conference "Africa in the Americas," David Rockefeller Center for Latin American Studies, Harvard University, October 2–3, 1998.

10. Mechal Sobel, *The World They Made Together: Black and White Values in Eighteenth-Century Virginia* (Princeton, N.J.: Princeton University Press, 1987).

11. Mechal Sobel, personal communication, Williamsburg, Va., 1990.

12. Sobel, *The World They Made Together*.

13. Loretta Johnson, personal communication, Berkeley, Calif., 1992. Most U.S. African Americans are Protestant (Baptist, Methodist, or Pentecostal), and the main service is at 11:00 on Sunday mornings.

14. Cf. George Reid Andrews, *The Afro-Argentines of Buenos Aires, 1800–1900* (Madison: University of Wisconsin Press, 1980).

15. Vatomene Kukanda, linguist and director general, and Simão Souindoula, historian and director of the Department of Cultural Programs, Centre International des Civilisations Bantu, Libreville, Gabon, personal communication, March 2000.

16. Alfredo Wagner de Almeida, Universidade Federal do Maranhão, São Luis do Maranhão, Brazil, personal communication, Austin, Tex., April 1999. In Brazil the term *quilombo* designates an autonomous maroon community created by Africans and Afro-Brazilians who escaped from slavery, hence has a positive, even heroic meaning. In addition to that specialized usage, it also has the more negative connotation of "disorder" because it referred to communities of Afro-Brazilians in a society that denigrated everything associated with Afro-Brazilians.

17. The Bantu language family covers most of Central and Southern Africa, including the Congo-Angola area from which many Africans came to the Americas. It includes such languages as Kikongo and Kimbundu.

18. Kukanda and Souindoula, personal communication, March 2000.

19. Cf. Tomás Olivera Chirimini, chapter 15 of this volume.

20. See Yvonne Daniel, *Rumba: Dance and Social Change in Contemporary Cuba* (Bloomington: University of Indiana Press, 1995); Barbara Browning, *Samba: Resistance in Motion* (Bloomington: University of Indiana Press, 1995); Marta Savigliano, *Tango: The Political Economy of Passion* (Boulder, Colo.: Westview Press, 1995).

21. Philip Curtin, *The African Slave Trade: A Census* (Madison: University of Wisconsin Press, 1969), 185.

22. Charles R. Boxer, *The Golden Age of Brazil, 1695–1750* (Berkeley: University of California Press, 1969), 174.

23. Raymond E. Dummett, *El Dorado in West Africa: The Gold-Mining Frontier, African Labor, and Colonial Capitalism in the Gold Coast, 1875–1900* (Athens, Ohio: Ohio University Press, 1999).

24. James Lockhart, *Spanish Peru, 1532–1560: A Colonial Society* (Madison: University of Wisconsin Press, 1968), 182.

25. Cf., Peter Wood, *Black Majority: Negroes in Colonial South Carolina from 1670 to the Stono Rebellion* (New York: Alfred A. Knopf, 1974) and Daniel C. Littlefield, *Rice and Slaves: Ethnicity and the Slave Trade in Colonial South Carolina* (Baton Rouge: Louisiana State University Press, 1981).

26. See W. E. B. Du Bois, *The Gift of Black Folks: Negroes in the Making of America* (New York: Johnson Reprint, 1968 [1924]).

27. Wood, *Black Majority*, 35, 26.

28. Gwendolyn Midlo Hall, *Africans in Colonial Louisiana: The Development of Afro-Creole Culture in the Eighteenth Century* (Baton Rouge: Louisiana State University Press, 1992), 121–122.

29. Wood, *Black Majority*, 56.

30. Wood, *Black Majority*, 105.

31. Littlefield, *Rice and Slaves*, xi.

32. Leland Ferguson, *Uncommon Ground: Archaeology and Early African America, 1650–1800* (Washington, D.C.: Smithsonian Institution Press, 1992), 93–94.

33. Tarikhu Farrar contrasts the nonempirical assertions that Africa was technologically underdeveloped, thus unable to contribute to the development of the Americas, with data concerning African contributions to the Americas in various areas of technology in "Reconsidering the African Impact on Colonial American Technology," paper presented at the "African Impact on the Material Culture of the Americas" conference, Old Salem, N.C., May 30–June 2, 1996.

34. Cf. Curtin, *The African Slave Trade* for the pioneering assessment of which Africans were taken from where and in which numbers, and where in the Americas and in which numbers they

wound up. Curtin's numbers have been questioned and revised, and arguments about the issues have been elaborated by, among others, Joseph Inikori, in *The Atlantic Slave Trade: Effects on Economies, Societies, and Peoples in Africa, the Americas, and Europe* (Durham, N.C.: Duke University Press, 1992), *The Chaining of a Continent: Export Demand for Captives and the History of Africa South of the Sahara, 1450–1870* (Mona, Jamaica: Institute of Social and Economic Research, University of the West Indies, 1992), and *Slavery and the Rise of Capitalism* (Mona, Jamaica: Department of History, University of the West Indies, 1993).

35. Leslie Rout, *The African Experience in Spanish America: 1502 to the Present Day* (Cambridge: Cambridge University Press, 1976), 32.

36. Robert C. West, *Colonial Placer Mining in Colombia* (Baton Rouge: Louisiana State University Press, Social Science Series, no. 2, 1952), 78, 85.

37. Akan is a language family of southern Côte d'Ivoire and Ghana, an area from which many Africans came to the Americas.

38. Lorna McDaniel, *The Big Drum Ritual of Carriacou: Praise Songs in Rememory of Flight* (Gainesville: University of Florida Press, 1998).

39. Henning Cohen, "Slave Names in Colonial South Carolina," *Speech* 38, no. 2 (May 1952): 105.

40. Lorenzo Dow Turner, *Africanisms in the Gullah Dialect* (Chicago: University of Chicago Press, 1949).

41. Wood, *Black Majority,* 181–183.

42. H. L. Mencken, "Designations for Colored Folks," *American Speech* 19 (1944): 173.

43. Sterling Stuckey, *Going Through the Storm: The Influence of African American Art in History* (New York: Oxford University Press, 1994), 58.

44. Zora Neale Hurston, *Dust Tracks on the Road* (Philadelphia: J. B. Lippincott Company, 1971 [1942]), 221, 233.

45. See Richard Price, *Maroon Societies: Rebel Slave Communities in the Americas* (Baltimore: Johns Hopkins University Press, 1979); *Maroon Heritage: Archeological, Ethnograhic, and Historical Perspectives*, ed. Kofi Agorsah (Kingston, Jamaica: Canoe Press, University of the West Indies, 1994).

46. Ibrahim Seck, "Le cycle du lièvre en Louisiane," paper presented at the West African Research Association symposium on L'Afrique de l'Ouest face au Défi Mondial, Dakar, Senegal, June 1997. For Tio Conejo, see François Bogliolo, "Contes négro-africaines et contes négro-américaines," *Ethiopiques: Revue socialiste de culture négro-africaine*, no. 8 (October 1976): 39–58.

47. Seck, "Le cycle du lièvre en Louisiane," 7.

48. Carlos Rosero, coordinator, Proceso de Comunidades Negras, Buenaventura, Colombia, personal communication, Montevideo, Uruguay, March 2000.

49. Bogliolo, "Contes négro-africaines et contes négro-américaines," 39–58; Thelma Knight, personal communication, St. Georges, Grenada, August 2000.

50. *Drums and Shadows: Survival Studies among the Georgia Coastal Negroes*, Georgia Writers Project (Athens: University of Georgia Press, 1986 [1940]), 169.

51. *Seven Tales of Uncle Remus by Joel Chandler Harris*, ed. Thomas H. English (Atlanta: Library at Emory University, 1948), 26–28.

52. Richard W. Lariviere, Dean, College of Liberal Arts, the University of Texas at Austin, personal communications, August 1999 and August 2000.

53. Olabiyi Yai, linguist and ambassador to UNESCO from the Republic of Benin, personal communication, Paris, February 2000.

54. Fernando Ortiz, *Glosario de afronegrismos* (La Habana: Imprenta "El Siglo XX," 1924); Lorenzo Dow Turner, *Africanisms in the Gullah Dialect*; Fernando Romero, *Quimba, Fa,*

Malambo, Ñeque: Afronegrismos en el Perú (Lima: Instituto de Estudios Peruanos, 1988); Winifred K. Vass, *The Bantu-Speaking Heritage of the United States* (Los Angeles: University of California Press, 1979); Joseph E. Holloway and Winifred K. Vass, *The African Heritage of American English* (Bloomington: University of Indiana Press, 1993); William W. Megenney, *Aspectos del lenguaje afronegroide en Venezuela* (Frankfurt: Vervuert, 1999), and *África en Santo Domingo: Su herencia lingüística* (Santo Domingo: Editorial Tiempo, 1990); Renato Mendonça, *A influencia africana no português do Brasil* (Porto: Livraria Figueirinhas, 1948 [1933]), *Africanisms in Afro-American Language Varieties*, ed. Salikoko Mufwene (Athens: University of Georgia Press, 1993); Nei Lopes, *Dicionário banto do Brasil* (Rio de Janeiro, Brazil: Prefeitura da Cidade do Rio de Janeiro, Centro Cultural José Bonifácio, 1995); Maureen Warner-Lewis, *Trinidad Yoruba: From Mother Tongue to Memory* (Tuscaloosa: University of Alabama Press, 1996); and Alberto Britos Serrat, *Glosario de afronegrismos uruguayos* (Montevideo: Ediciones Mundo Afro and El Galeón, 1999).

55. Clarence Major, *The Dictionary of Afro-American Slang* (New York: International Publishers, 1970). Major reminds us that hippy, meaning "a person who tries without success to be hip," "a would-be hipcat," is a derivative of hip, and notes that "in the 1960s the word fell largely into white use" (66). Hip also led to hip-hop. The dictionary was up-dated as Clarence Major, *Juba to Jive: A Dictionary of African-American Slang* (New York: Penguin Books, 1994), and included most of the Wolof origins.

56. Youssou N'Dour and le Super Étoile de Dakar, *Xippi!* Alassane Diakhate Recording Company, 1991. Cassette recording.

57. Mbaye Cham, Department of African Studies, Howard University, personal communication, Washington, D.C., January 1999. According to Dr. Cham, who is from the Gambia, *jef* or *def*, depending on the region, may also refer to someone who "does many things," which enslaved Africans and their descendants certainly did to survive, and even to thrive and create against tremendous odds.

58. *Merriam-Webster's Collegiate Dictionary*, 10th Edition (Springfield, Mass.: Merriam-Webster, 1994), 980.

59. Turner, *Africanisms in the Gullah Dialect*, 191.

60. Colin Palmer, Department of History, the Graduate Center, City University of New York, personal communication, Washington, D.C., September 1999.

61. *Webster's Collegiate Dictionary*, 23a, 26a.

62. "Dictionaries and Languages," the University of Texas at Austin General Libraries, <www.lib.utexas.edu/Libs/PCL/Dictionaries.html> (accessed 20 Aug. 1999).

63. *Webster's Collegiate Dictionary*, 23a.

64. *Webster's Collegiate Dictionary*, 26a.

65. *Webster's Collegiate Dictionary*, 26a.

66. *Webster's Collegiate Dictionary*, 808.

67. *Webster's Collegiate Dictionary*, 518.

68. *Webster's Collegiate Dictionary*, 273.

69. *Webster's Collegiate Dictionary*, 549.

70. *Webster's Collegiate Dictionary*, 541.

71. *Webster's Collegiate Dictionary*, 630.

72. *Webster's Collegiate Dictionary*, 475.

73. *Webster's Collegiate Dictionary*, 323.

74. *Webster's Collegiate Dictionary*, 178.

75. *Webster's Collegiate Dictionary*, 557.

76. *Webster's Collegiate Dictionary*, 565.

77. *Webster's Collegiate Dictionary*, 1,366.

78. *Webster's Collegiate Dictionary*, 27a.

79. David Dalby, "Americanisms that May Once Have Been Africanisms," *Times of London* (July 19, 1969): 9, also in *Mother Wit from the Laughing Barrel: Readings in the Interpretation of Afro-American Folklore*, ed. Alan Dundes (Englewood Cliffs, N.J.: Prentice-Hall, 1973), 136–140.

80. *Webster's Collegiate Dictionary*, 808.

81. Dalby, "Americanisms that May Once Have Been Africanisms," 137.

82. Dalby, "Americanisms that May Once Have Been Africanisms," 137, 139–140.

83. Dalby, "Americanisms that May Once Have Been Africanisms," 139–140.

84. Curtin, *The African Slave Trade*, 290.

85. James L. Rader, Etymology Editor, Merriam-Webster, Inc., letter to author, April 7, 2000, 2.

86. Rader, letter to author, 3.

87. David Dalby, "The African Element in American English," in *Rappin' and Stylin' Out: Communication in Urban Black America*, ed. Thomas Kochman (Urbana: University of Illinois Press, 1972), 172.

88. Jessica Harris, chapter 9 of this volume.

89. Salikoko Mufwene, personal communication, March 1999.

90. "New Orleans Menu Glossary," *Food & Wine* (Oct. 1989): 122. Reprinted with permission from *Food & Wine* magazine, October ©1989. American Express Publishing Corporation. All rights reserved.

91. Kukanda and Souindoula, personal communication, March 2000.

92. Maria Nazaré Dias de Ceita, personal communication, Lisbon, Portugal, December 1998.

93. *Webster's Collegiate Dictionary*, 224.

94. Maureen Scott, personal communication, Washington, D.C., June 2000.

95. Thanks to Ivy Noel from Trinidad for the recipe and the delicious callaloo tasting, East Orange, N.J., August 1999.

96. Leroy Romain, personal communication, Brooklyn, N.Y., September 2000.

97. Willer Océan, Haitian dentist and gourmet cook, personal communication, Cuajinicuilapa, Guerrero, Mexico, March 1999.

98. de Santana Rodrigué, Maria das Graças, personal communication, Salvador da Bahia, Brazil, December 1999.

99. *Webster's Collegiate Dictionary*, 162.

100. Yvonne Daniel, see chapter 23 of this volume.

101. Harris, chapter 9 of this volume.

102. Eddie Harris, "Mean Greens," track one on *Mean Greens*. Atlantic Records SD-1453, 1966.

103. Edna Turner, personal communication, East Orange, N.J., October 20, 2000.

104. Marcelo Montas Penha, personal communication, Washington, D.C., August 2000. In the countryside of the state of Rio de Janeiro the well-known carioca black bean feijoada may be made instead with guandu.

105. Bona Masanu, "Les survivances Bantu demeurent vivaces dans la péninsule," *L'Union* (Libreville, Gabon), (March 2, 2000), 6.

106. Joseph E. Holloway, "The Origins of African American Culture," in *Africanisms in American Culture*, ed. Joseph E. Holloway (Bloomington: University of Indiana Press, 1990), 4; also tables, 7–8.

107. Hall, *Africans in Colonial Louisiana*, 29–31, 40–41.

108. Reprinted with the permission of Simon and Schuster from *Black-Eyed Peas for the Soul: Tales to Strengthen the African American Spirit and Encourage the Heart* by Donna Marie Williams (New York: Simon and Schuster Fireside Books, 1997), 161–63.

109. Theodora Moorehead, personal communication, St. John, U.S. Virgin Islands, November 1999.

110. Mary Ellen Lane, personal communication, Washington, D.C., October 13, 2000.

111. Soukeyna Boye, personal communication, New York, February 1999.

112. Stanley Elkins, *Slavery: A Problem in American Institutional Life* (New York: Grosset and Dunlap, 1963).

113. Herbert Aptheker, *American Negro Slave Revolts* (New York: International Publishers, 1963 [1943]).

114. Melville Herskovits, *The Myth of the Negro Past* (Boston: Beacon Press, 1941).

115. E. Franklin Frazier, *The Negro Family in the United States* (Chicago: University of Chicago Press, 1966 [1948]); *The Negro Church in America* (New York: Schocken Books, 1963).

116. Mary L. Gavin, Opening Remarks from the "African Impact on the Material Culture of the Americas" conference, Old Salem, N.C., May 30–June 2, 1996.

117. W. E. B. Du Bois, *The Souls of Black Folk: Essays and Sketches* (New York: Bantam Books, 1989 [1903]); *The Gift of Black Folks: Negroes in the Making of America* (New York: Johnson Reprint, 1968 [1924]); *Black Folk Then and Now: An Essay in the History and Sociology of the Negro Race* (Millwood, N.Y.: Kraus-Thompson, 1975 [1939]), and *The World and Africa: An Inquiry Into the Part Which Africa Has Played in World History* (New York: International Publishers, 1965 [1946]); Zora Neale Hurston, *Mules and Men: Negro Folktales and Voodoo Practices in the South* (New York: J. B. Lippincott Company, 1935), and *Tell My Horse* (New York: J. B. Lippincott Company, 1938); Arturo Alfonso Schomburg, "The Economic Contribution by the Negro to America" in *Papers of the American Negro Academy* (Washington, D.C.: American Negro Academy, 1916), 49–62, and "The Negro Digs Up His Past," in *The New Negro: Voices of the Harlem Renaissance*, ed. Alain Locke (New York: Atheneum, 1992 [1925]), 231–236; and Carter G. Woodson, *The African Background Outlined* (Washington, D.C.: The Association for the Study of Negro Life and History, Inc., 1936), and *The Negro in Our History* (Washington, D.C.: Associated Publishers, 1962 [1947]).

118. Captain William Smith, *A New Voyage to Guinea* (London: Cass, 1967 [1744]), 28.

119. Wood, *Black Majority*, 180.

120. Michael Mullin, *Africa in America: Slave Acculturation and Resistance in the American South and British Caribbean, 1736–1831* (Urbana: University of Illinois Press, 1992); Gwendolyn Midlo Hall, *Africans in Colonial Louisiana: The Development of Afro-Creole Culture in the Eighteenth Century* (Baton Rouge: Louisiana State University Press, 1992); John Thornton, *Africa and Africans in the Making of the Atlantic World, 1400–1680,* (New York: Cambridge University Press, 1992); Michael A. Gomez, *Exchanging Our Country Marks: The Transformation of African Identities in the Colonial and Antebellum South* (Chapel Hill: University of North Carolina Press, 1998); Tim Carrier (director), *Family Across the Sea* (South Carolina Educational Television, 1991); Alvaro Toepke and Angel Serrano (producers/directors), *The Language You Cry In: The Story of a Mende Song* (San Francisco: California Newsreel, 1998).

121. Richard Brookhiser, *The Way of the WASP: How It Made America, and How It Can Save It, So to Speak* (New York: Free Press, 1991), and Lawrence Auster, *The Path of National Suicide: An Essay on Immigration and Multiculturalism* (Monterey, Va.: American Immigration Control Foundation, 1990).

2

Reclaiming the Black Presence in "Mainstream Culture"

Shelley Fisher Fishkin

As art historian Robert Farris Thompson has observed, "To be white in America is to be very black. If you don't know how black you are, you don't know how American you are."[1] But for hundreds of years this fact was ignored or denied. The "whiteness" of U.S. culture was so obvious to the official arbiters of that culture that it could go unnamed and simply assumed; "whiteness" as a site of privilege and power was also ignored or denied in the master narratives the United States told about itself. Today, however, this is changing. During the past decade, over a hundred books and articles published by scholars in literary criticism, history, cultural studies, anthropology, popular culture, communication studies, music history, art history, humor studies, linguistics, and folklore lend support to that assertion.

In this chapter, I will present a very brief overview of this recent scholarship. Those of you familiar with U.S. television will understand what I mean when I apologize for giving you the "Headline News" version of so much contemporary scholarship. For a more extended version, I would direct you to two articles of mine.[2] I also apologize that many of the writers and scholars that I quote will be using the word "American" when what they are referring to is the "United States."

The 1996 University of Texas at Austin conference on the African Diaspora and the Modern World bore eloquent witness to the fact that scholars in the United States are not the only ones pursuing this kind of research. As I heard colleagues from Venezuela, Colombia, Uruguay, Mexico, Peru, and elsewhere describe their efforts to reverse centuries of erasure of the Black presence in their culture's histories, I sensed that many of us were engaged in a similar challenge: revising the stories our countries tell about who and what they are. It is the challenge of trying to ensure that in the twenty-first century the master narratives will not continue to be synonymous with the master's narratives.

Today a range of aspects of U.S. culture that were previously assumed to be "white" cultural forms are beginning to be recognized as less "white" than had been supposed.

Take Mark Twain, for example. If "all modern American literature comes from one book by Mark Twain called *Huckleberry Finn*,"[3] as Ernest Hemingway declared, then all modern American literature comes, as well, from the African American speakers, rhetoric, and oral traditions that helped make that book what it is, a point I addressed in my 1993 book, *Was Huck Black? Mark Twain and African-American Voices*.[4] For example, I demonstrated that the speech of an engaging African American child Twain met in 1871 was central to the genesis of the voice with which he would endow his character Huck, and that the virtuoso "signifying" of an enslaved acquaintance from his childhood provided young Sam Clemens with his first introduction to the potential of satire as a tool of social criticism.

In recent articles literary critics Werner Sollors and Lawrence Howe examine the influence of slave narratives on themes Twain explored in *A Connecticut Yankee* and *Life on the Mississippi*.[5] And in a 1995 book, Randall Knoper explores the ways in which Twain drew on African American tactics of resistance as he negotiated his own ambivalence toward much of mainstream, middle-class culture.[6] It will be hard in the future to teach Twain without reference to the African American traditions that had such a deep influence on his work.

Current scholarship suggests that African traditions may also be essential to understanding the work of the nineteenth-century writer Herman Melville. Historian Sterling Stuckey in his 1994 book *Going Through the Storm: The Influence of African American Art in History*, Eric Sundquist in his 1993 book *To Wake the Nations*, and Viola Sachs in her 1992 book *L'Imaginaire Melville* demonstrated Melville's deep interest in African customs, myths, languages, and traditions, and pointed out the African influences on works such as *Moby-Dick* and the short story "Benito Cereno."[7] Sachs, for example, has uncovered numerous references to the Yoruba god Legba in *Moby-Dick*. Stuckey and Sundquist have examined the use of Ashanti drumming and treatment of the dead in "Benito Cereno," suggesting that the treatment of the corpse of the rich enslaver Aranda in "Benito Cereno" was not a racist allusion to African savagery, as critics have argued, but rather evidence of Melville's insight into Ashanti rituals and the shrewd political use his characters made of those traditions.

In recent studies of canonical white twentieth-century figures as well, unexpected links to African and African American culture are currently being explored. For example, while Robert Fleissner examined the influence of African myths on T. S. Eliot, David Chinitz demonstrated intriguing connections between Eliot's poetry and jazz, and Michael North addressed the dynamics of Eliot's complicated attraction to African American speech.[8]

In popular culture as well, familiar icons generally understood as "white" are being shown to have roots more complicated than previously recognized. Historians Joe Adamson and Dave Roediger, for example—Adamson in a book that came out in 1990 and Roediger in an essay published in 1994—demonstrated the African roots of that staple of American popular culture, Bugs Bunny.[9] As Roediger observed, the verb "bug," as in to annoy or vex someone, has its roots partly in Wolof, the language spoken by the largest group of Africans to arrive in the United States in the seventeenth century.[10] Moreover, Roediger writes, building on the work of historian Franklin Rosemont, "the fantastic idea that a vulnerable and weak rabbit could be tough and tricky enough to menace those who menace him enters American culture . . . largely via Br'er Rabbit tales. These stories were told among various ethnic groups in West Africa, and were further developed by enslaved African Americans before being popularized and bastardized by white collectors like Joel Chandler Harris. They were available both as literature and folklore to the white Southerner Tex Avery whose genius so helped to give us Bugs."[11]

Sociologist Howard L. Sacks and independent researcher Judith Rose Sacks argued cogently in their 1993 book, *Way Up North in Dixie: A Black Family's Claim to the Confederate Anthem,* that "Dixie," the song that became the anthem of the Confederacy, was written by the Snowdens, an African American family in nineteenth-century Ohio, and not, as previously thought, by white minstrel performer Dan Emmett who appropriated the song and presented it as his own.[12] The blend of appreciation and appropriation that the minstrel show embodied was the subject of Eric Lott's award-winning 1993 book, *Love and Theft: Blackface Minstrelsy and the American Working Class,* in which this complex nexus of cultural exchange at last received the careful attention it has long deserved.[13]

Historians investigating the African American roots of mainstream (and supposedly "white") U.S. culture in the 1990s build, of course, on the earlier extremely valuable work of Melville Herskovits and Peter Wood.[14] Herskovits, some sixty years ago, had argued in *The Myth of the Negro Past* that the brutality of the Atlantic slave trade and the oppressions of American bondage did not destroy the African cultural heritage; aspects of African culture (such as language use), Herskovits felt, both survived in the African American community in the twentieth century and influenced aspects of mainstream culture as well. And Wood, more than twenty-five years ago in *Black Majority,* demonstrated the large number of African contributions to colonial American agriculture, animal husbandry, and other fields—including rice cultivation, cattle breeding and open grazing, basketry, medicinal practices, boat building, fishing, hunting, and trapping. In the 1990s this line of argument was directly picked up by John Edward Philips in his 1990 essay, "The African Heritage of White America," in *Africanisms in American Culture,* edited by Joseph E. Holloway, and by William D. Piersen in his 1993 book, *Black Legacy: America's Hidden Heritage.*[15]

"For too long in this country," Philips writes, "whites have denied learning from blacks." In addition, he notes, some African Americans themselves have often been reluctant to acknowledge any links to Africa. Philips gives a sample of the kinds of interesting links that scholars might pursue in the future, exploring, for example, potential connections between African singing and instrumental styles and bluegrass music, probing what he calls "white Africanisms" in the fields of religious belief (particularly in Pentecostal churches), traditions of Southern hospitality and courtesy, Southern foodways and cooking techniques, and cowboys' cattle-herding techniques. Arguing that "pride in their African heritage is something that white children should be taught along with blacks," Philips presses for "a more complex paradigm to explain African cultural retentions than has hitherto been advanced," one that recognizes the constant process of cultural exchange that has continued throughout the history of the United States.[16]

Historian William D. Piersen's *Black Legacy* takes up this challenge, assembling an impressive compendium of ways in which African culture shaped white U.S. culture, particularly in the South. Piersen explores cultural phenomena including storytelling, language use, music, manners, etiquette, folk medicine, folk beliefs, cooking styles, and communal celebrations, and succeeds in persuading the reader that "the legacy of African culture is important to the understanding of America."[17] Piersen documents an impressive range of medical innovations for which enslaved medical practitioners were responsible, including being the first to use inoculation as a method of reducing the seriousness of smallpox epidemics and increasing the American pharmacopoeia stock with the addition of at least seventeen African herbal drugs. Drawing on work by Gwendolyn Midlo Hall in her award-winning 1992 book, *Africans in Colonial Louisiana*,[18] he notes that enslaved practitioners regularly cured scurvy with lemon juice thirteen years before European physicians advocated a similar cure.

In the book's strongest chapter, Piersen tracks the use of satiric traditions from Africa to the New World, pulling together a dazzling set of specific examples. He provides an overview of the use of satirical songs (sometimes called "songs of derision" by other scholars) as a mechanism of social control in eighteenth- and nineteenth-century African societies, noting the ways in which they allowed the weak to voice with impunity their grievances against the strong. After exploring the ways in which satirical songs functioned in pre-colonial African cultures, Piersen moves to their manifestations in the antebellum American South. (His explorations of this subject in an earlier article provided important background to my work on the African American roots of Mark Twain's satirical treatment of racism.)[19]

In his 1992 book, *Singing the Master: The Emergence of African-American Culture in the Plantation South*, folklorist Roger Abrahams similarly maintains that a great deal of the culture of the South took shape not in the slave quarters or the big house, but "in the yard between" the two, "in contested areas betwixt and between the two worlds."[20] Building on work by John Szwed and others, he suggests, for example, that while the American square dance grew out of European dances such as the reel and the quadrille, the distinctly American practice of calling square dance figures in rhyme has its roots in corn-shucking customs in the South, where in the plantation yard teams of enslaved African Americans entertained themselves and their masters with improvised rhymes as they husked corn.

Abrahams's careful reexamination of the intercultural dynamics of slave holidays in the antebellum South, combined with Lott's reconsideration of the role of minstrelsy in the antebellum North, lays the groundwork for new understandings of aspects of mainstream American culture today. Abrahams believes that cultural legacies of slave holiday celebrations, for example, ultimately had an impact on the Beatles, who, of course, had an era-making effect on twentieth-century popular music. The Beatles, Abrahams notes, began their career as a skiffle band, indebted to white American imitations of whites-in-blackface imitations of African American plantation musical traditions.

While the categories "humorists" and "Southern writers" tended to refer to an all-white cast of characters in the past, recent books like Roy Blount's 1994 *Roy Blount's Book of Southern Humor* changed all that. "One thing we need to get straight about Southern humor—Southern culture generally," Blount ventures, "is that it is Africo-Celtic, or Celtico-African."[21] Gene Lees made a similar observation in his 1994 book,

Cats of Any Color: Jazz in Black and White. Lees believes that what he calls "the inherent poeticism of the South" is "the consequence of the marvelous and mad love of language of the Irish and a decorative, allusive indirection of expression that is a heritage of Africa."[22]

The impact of African American humor upon mainstream "white" sensibilities was also explored in 1994 by Mel Watkins in his book, *On the Real Side: Laughing, Lying an' Signifying—The Underground Tradition of African-American Humor that Transformed American Culture from Slavery to Richard Pryor.*[23] Watkins, for example, offers a lucid and insightful analysis of the role "the street wit of the black musicians and night people with whom he associated" played in shaping the 1950s satire of comedian Lenny Bruce. Bruce's hip, irreverent, and black-inflected "comic assault on the intrinsic absurdity of race relations, religious practices, police tyranny, and hypocrisy concerning sex and drugs," left its mark on many later forms of satire including, as Watkins notes, the comedy of *Saturday Night Live.*

African American elements in mainstream "white" speech and language use were increasingly probed in the 1990s by linguists. In their 1993 book, *The African Heritage of American English*, Joseph E. Holloway and Winifred K. Vass provided a long list of "Africanisms in Contemporary American English" and their derivations. The list includes bad-mouth, banana, banjo, "be with it," bogus, booboo, bronco, coffee, cola, cool, "do one's thing," guff, gumbo, guy, honkie, hulla-balloo, jam (as in music), jazz, jiffy, jive, kooky, okay, okra, phony, rap, ruckus, tote, uh-huh, mhm, uuh-uh, and you-all. Noting the role of African cowboys in shaping American cattle culture and cowboy lore, they observed that the cowboy word "dogies" for cattle "originated from Kimbundu, *kidogo,* a little something, and *dodo,* small. After the Civil War, when great cattle roundups began, black cowboys introduced such Africanisms to cowboy language and songs."[24]

The "incontestably mulatto" nature of U.S. culture—to borrow Albert Murray's phrase—continues to be resisted in some quarters.[25] "The WASP character is the American character," trumpeted Richard Brookhiser in his 1991 book, *The Way of the WASP.*[26] "The U.S. has always been an Anglo-Saxon civilization," declared Laurence Auster in his apocalyptic 1990 book, *The Path of National Suicide: An Essay on Immigration and Multiculturalism.*[27] Auster and Brookhiser fail to understand that what they refer to as the white Anglo-Saxon Protestant civilization of the United States was itself shaped from the start by people and traditions that were not white, or Anglo-Saxon, or Protestant.

In fact, if we apply to our culture the "one drop" rule that in the United States long classified anyone with one drop of "black blood" as Black, then all of U.S. culture is Black. But well into the twentieth century, as James Horton notes, "white Americans continued to deny, yet exhibit, the complexity of their cultural heritage."[28]

We must learn to reclaim our complex roots while not ignoring the history of racism that allowed us for over two hundred years to ignore and deny who and what we really were. We must learn to appreciate the distinctive blend of cultural traditions that shaped us, while simultaneously working to dismantle the paradigms that prevented, and continue to prevent, so many African Americans from receiving credit and respect for all they did, and do, to create that common culture known as "American" throughout the world.

We need to come to terms with how the racism that denied African Americans respect, rights, and agency for hundreds of years also deformed scholars' understanding of the dynamics of twentieth-century life and thought, not only in the United States but throughout the world. How, for example, did Europeans as well as Americans disengage themselves from the nineteenth-century values of the Victorian era? Susan Curtis's 1994 cultural biography of Scott Joplin leaves the reader with the sense that any explanation that leaves out the effects of ragtime is of necessity partial and incomplete.[29]

The last decade of the twentieth century may have brought the withering away of simplistic essentialist notions of racial identity, as well as bringing increasingly sophisticated understandings of how power relations built on antiquated, discredited assumptions of racial difference sustain and perpetuate themselves. At the beginning of the twenty-first century, however, scholars may find their work increasingly at odds with the vision of the United States's past and present promoted by popular demagogues nostalgic for a time when the "whiteness" of U.S. culture was assumed, and when white privilege went unnamed, unexamined, unchallenged. In such an atmosphere, in which overt and coded racist policies are routinely sanctioned, and in which truth and justice are dismissed for political ends, scholars' efforts to revise the stories we tell about who we are to reflect what we have learned about where we have been are all the more important.

We are now and have always been a culture in which a vast range of voices and traditions have constantly shaped each other in profound ways. Our teaching and our scholarship must take into account our increasingly complex understanding of what our common culture is and how it evolved. Doing so will force us to examine how an unequal distribution not of talent but of power allowed a patently false monocultural myth to mask and distort a multicultural reality. The new vision of our culture will be truer than any that we have had before—and more interesting. It will also be a healthier base on which to build our society's future. Forging such a vision may not be easy, but it is a challenge we should be eager to embrace.

NOTES

1. Robert Farris Thompson, lecture on "The Kongo Atlantic Tradition," University of Texas, Austin, February 28, 1992.

2. The articles are: "Interrogating 'Whiteness,' Complicating 'Blackness': Remapping American Culture" in *American Quarterly* 47, no. 3 (Sept. 1995): 428–466, and a longer version (under the same title) in *Criticism and the Color Line: Desegregating American Literary Studies*, ed. Henry B. Wonham (New Brunswick, N.J.: Rutgers University Press, 1996), 251–290.

3. Ernest Hemingway, *Green Hills of Africa* (New York: Charles Scribner Sons, 1935), 22.

4. Shelley Fisher Fishkin, *Was Huck Black? Mark Twain and African-American Voices* (New York: Oxford University Press, 1993).

5. Werner Sollors, "Ethnicity," in *Critical Terms for Literary Study*, ed. Frank Lentriccia and Thomas McLaughlin (Chicago: University of Chicago Press, 1990), 288–305; Lawrence Howe,

"Transcending the Limits of Experience: Mark Twain's Life on the Mississippi," *American Literature* 63 (Sept. 1991): 420–439.

6. Randall Knoper, *Acting Naturally: Mark Twain in the Culture of Performance* (Berkeley: University of California Press, 1995).

7. Sterling Stuckey, "'Follow Your Leader': The Theme of Cannibalism in Melville's 'Benito Cereno,'" in *Going through the Storm: The Influence of African American Art in History* (New York: Oxford University Press, 1994); Eric Sundquist, *To Wake the Nations: Race in the Making of American Literature* (Cambridge, Mass.: Harvard University Press, 1993); Viola Sachs, *L'Imaginaire Melville: A French Point of View* (Saint-Denis, France: University Press of Vincennes, 1992).

8. Robert Fleissner, *T. S. Eliot and the Heritage of Africa* (New York: Peter Lang, 1992); David Chinitz, "T. S. Eliot and the Cultural Divide," *Publications of the Modern Language Association of America* 1110 (Mar. 1995): 236–247, particularly 244–246; Michael North, *The Dialect of Modernism: Race, Language and Twentieth-Century Literature* (New York: Oxford University Press, 1994).

9. Joe Adamson, *Bugs Bunny: Fifty Years and Only One Grey Hare* (New York: Holt, 1990); Dave Roediger, "A Long Journey to the Hip Hop Nation," *St. Louis Post-Dispatch* (Mar. 18, 1994): 7-B.

10. "Mandingo *baga*, to offend, annoy, harm (someone); Wolof *bugal*, to annoy, worry. Note also West African and Caribbean English *ambog*, to annoy; this form pronounced in eighteenth century with stress on second syllable may reflect the nominal prefix *m-*, in Wolof *mbugal*, hindrance, annoyance." *The African Heritage of American English*, eds. Joseph E. Holloway and Winifred K. Vass (Bloomington: Indiana University Press, 1993), 139.

11. Roediger, "A Long Journey to the Hip Hop Nation."

12. Howard I. Sacks and Judith Rose Sacks, *Way Up North in Dixie: A Black Family's Claim to the Confederate Anthem* (Washington, D.C.: Smithsonian Institution Press, 1993).

13. Eric Lott, *Love and Theft: Blackface Minstrelsy and the American Working Class* (New York: Oxford University Press, 1993).

14. Melville Herskovits, *The Myth of the Negro Past* (Boston: Beacon Press, 1958 [1941]); Peter Wood, *Black Majority: Negroes in Colonial South Carolina from 1670 through the Stono Rebellion* (New York: Alfred A. Knopf, 1974).

15. John Edward Philips, "The African Heritage of White America," in *Africanisms in American Culture*, ed. Joseph E. Holloway (Bloomington: Indiana University Press, 1990), 225–239; William D. Piersen, *Black Legacy: America's Hidden Heritage* (Amherst: University of Massachusetts Press, 1993).

16. Philips, "African Heritage of White America," 227–228, 236.

17. Piersen, *Black Legacy*, xv.

18. Gwendolyn Midlo Hall, *Africans in Colonial Louisiana* (Baton Rouge: Louisiana State University Press, 1992).

19. See William D. Piersen, "'Puttin' On Ole Massa," in *African Folklore in the New World*, ed. Daniel J. Crowley (Austin: University of Texas Press, 1977); and Fisher Fishkin, *Was Huck Black?*

20. Roger Abrahams, *Singing the Master: The Emergence of African-American Culture in the Plantation South* (New York: Pantheon, 1992), xvii.

21. Roy Blount, Jr., *Roy Blount's Book of Southern Humor* (New York: W. W. Norton, 1994), 27.

22. Gene Lees, *Cats of Any Color: Jazz in Black and White* (New York: Oxford University Press, 1994), 13.

23. Mel Watkins, *On the Real Side: Laughing, Lying an' Signifying—the Underground Tradition of African-American Humor that Transformed American Culture from Slavery to Richard Pryor* (New York: Simon and Schuster, 1994).

24. Holloway and Vass, *The African Heritage of American English*, 137–160.

25. Albert Murray, *The Omni-Americans* (New York: Vintage, 1983), 22.

26. Richard Brookhiser, *The Way of the WASP*, quoted from Stanley Fish, *There's No Such Thing as Free Speech . . . and It's a Good Thing Too* (New York: Oxford University Press, 1994), 84.

27. Laurence Auster, *The Path of National Suicide: An Essay on Immigration and Multiculturalism*, quoted from Fish, *There's No Such Thing as Free Speech*, 83–84.

28. James O. Horton, "Race, Nationality and Cultural Identity: Free Blacks in the Age of Jackson," paper presented at the Organization of American Historians Convention, Atlanta, April 1994, 33–34.

29. Susan Curtis, *Dancing to a Black Man's Tune: A Life of Scott Joplin* (Columbia: University of Missouri Press, 1994), especially chap. 6, "The Legacy of Scott Joplin," 161–189.

3

✳

Stripping the Emperor: The Africanist Presence in American Concert Dance

Brenda Dixon Gottschild

Several years ago, a student in my course at Temple University titled Black Performance from Africa to the Americas came up to me at the end of the first session and asked, "Should I take this class . . . I mean, as a white person?" The question animated her face with confusion and fear. My response was, "Honey, you're taking it right now; you've been taking it all your life!" As Americans, we are all "enrolled" in this course. [1] Some of us do not know it; some do, but deny it. For Americans, the Africanist legacy is not a choice but an imperative that comes to us through the culture.[2]

Unlike the voluntary taking on of Asian constructs in modern and postmodern practice, the Africanist legacy comes to Americans as electricity comes through the wires; we draw from it all the time, but few of us are aware of its sources. The term "Africanist" is used here to include diasporan concepts, practices, attitudes, or forms that have roots or origins in Africa. ("Diaspora" refers to the dispersion of African peoples from their homeland.) To quote Toni Morrison, it is "the ghost in the machine" or "the unspeakable things unspoken."[3] It infuses our daily existence in musical forms such as blues, jazz, spirituals, gospel, soul, rap, funk, rock, and yes, even European orchestral music. It is a considerable force in modern American arts and letters, as has been discussed by Morrison and other literary critics. It permeates American dance forms, from ballroom and nightclub floors to popular and concert stages. Finally, it pervades our everyday lifestyles, in ways of walking, talking, creating hairdos, preparing food, and acting "hip" or "cool."

But there is a problem: the Africanist aesthetic, though readily apparent in American culture, is rarely acknowledged. Morrison's "unspeakable things unspoken" describes the territory assigned to Africanisms in American culture because what is spoken or silenced depends on who is speaking. Who is doing the documenting? From whose perspective? By whose criteria? And what is being recorded? If language is the exercise of power, and the act of naming is an assertion of that power, then that which is unnamed or misnamed remains mute, inconsequential, and insignificant.

There are at least two principal American cultures: African and European, fused but also separate. Due to discrimination and segregation, cultural misunderstanding has become our normal mode of cultural exchange. As Americans, one way we could learn to embrace our conflicts is to reverse positions and see American culture as Africanist and look at the European elements in a different light. Such a revisionist perspective is the basis of my exposition of American concert dance; of dance ethnologist Joann Kealiinohomoku's signature essay, "An Anthropologist Looks at Ballet as a Form of Ethnic Dance," and of Toni Morrison's *Playing in the Dark: Whiteness and the Literary Imagination.*[4] Duke University historian Peter Wood suggested to the planners of Colonial Williamsburg that, in reconstructing that site, all roles be reversed, with African Americans depicting plantation owners and European Americans playing the enslaved.[5] That could have been a good learning experience for all involved, especially the spectators. But as anyone might have guessed, the idea did not catch on.

The Africanist presence has existed in European-American culture since plantation-era contacts between Africans and Europeans, contacts that forged and shaped a unique, creolized, Afro-Euro-American culture that all Americans embrace, consciously and subliminally, whether they admit it or not. Its impact on us, as dance people and as Americans, can be felt through many means besides dance.

Here are some cultural flashpoints. There are many cases of African-inspired beauty standards providing exotic fodder for mainstream consumption. Some examples include the European-American frizzy perm of the 1970s—in response to the Afro of the 1960s—and media figures like Bo Derek adopting braided or dreadlocked coiffures. Hardly a game of competitive sports is complete without the exchange on the field of Africanist-inspired handslaps or hip/buttock/pelvic exclamation points. European-American pop musicians have adopted the look, the sound, and the phrasing of the Africanist aesthetic. Elvis Presley is only the most famous example of a phenomenon so widespread that it is taken for granted, and its roots, unfortunately, are unacknowledged.

European Americans down South grew up living their lives with African Americans, and the Africanist legacy was almost literally in the air they breathed. Others "arrived" through music. One British writer characterized jazz as though it were marrow in the bones of European culture: "We are so accustomed to hearing jazz and American-influenced popular music—the sound of the 20th century—that our ears cannot imagine a world of sound without the freedom of syncopated jazz."[6] How telling a statement, and how true. Many of us are aware that popular American music is dominated by Africanist invention, but how many realize that concert music from Stravinsky and Milhaud to Glass and Reich is also infused with Africanisms? European composers deliberately sought to experience jazz and to add Africanist colors to their musical palette.

Theater played a large part in the appropriation of the Africanist aesthetic. To break the stranglehold of mainstream theater, many experimental groups of the 1960s and thereafter looked not only to Asian sources, which are well documented as avant-garde inspiration, but frequently to Africanisms as well. I was a member of the Open Theater, one of those pioneering groups. We used sources ranging from the cakewalk to the Candomblé, an Afro-Brazilian religion, in our theatrical explorations. The most recent work of theater innovator Jerzy Grotowski, whose small team of collaborators is based in Pontedera, Italy, provides a useful 1990s example:

> There are few discernible words, but these rhythmic, highly structured vocal works—some derived from African and Caribbean initiation rites—have an uncanny resonance and vibration. . . . Their carefully controlled movements, based on ancient forms of concentration, include a special way of holding the spine and protruding the backside, much like the warrior's position in primordial tribes. The stance, silent and attentive, is supposed to energize and enliven the body and waken a certain innate physical power and mindfulness.[7]

The vestiges of that stance, still discernible in the posture of contemporary peoples of African lineage, have been maligned in the ballet world and used as evidence to prove the inappropriateness of the African body for ballet.

Here is an especially powerful flashpoint. The African American civil rights movement of the 1950s and 1960s was the locus of origin for a nationwide revolutionary spirit and a desire for reorganization of political and social structures. It became the prototype for the subsequent women's, antiwar, and environmental protest movements, offering an immediate model for liberation. It demonstrated that an alternative form of society could exist and even thrive within an alien superculture. Contact improvisation[8] seems to have drawn unconsciously from the civil rights movement the inspiration and model for its own freedom movement in dance—not in content, of course, but in attitude. In another example of inadvertent borrowing, even the contact improviser's "jam" takes its name from the jazz musician's "jam session." These jams see contactors from far and wide converge to hold a marathon, paralleling the traditional form of African American revival meetings. In fact, our society is permeated by Africanist attitudes and forms, from the agrarian practices of Africa that were basic to the success of plantation agriculture, to such Africanist specifics as potato chips, peanut butter, and the Charleston.

So much of what we see as avant-garde in the postmodern movement is actually informed by recycled Africanist principles. The coolness, relaxation, looseness, and laid-back energy; the radical juxtaposition of ostensibly contrary elements; the irony and double entendre of verbal and physical gesture; the dialogic relationship of performer and audience—all are integral elements in Africanist arts and lifestyle, which are dreadlocked into the weave of our society, and inherited by Americans, Black and white. When Douglas Dunn creates ballet without straight legs or heroic energy, or Yvonne Rainer creates a solo, titles it a trio (*Trio A*), and bases it on movement clusters and an indirect approach to the audience, they redefine their idiom.

They may not be aware that the Africanist aesthetic is nonlinear and values dance steps that are dense, self-referential, and choreographed in clumps or clusters. This approach to dance making, from a Eurocentric perspective, has been regarded as "cluttered" or "bad." They probably do know that in hip talk "that's bad" means "that's good," and "that's down" means "that's up." Irony, paradox, and double entendre, rather than the classical European linear logic of cause, effect, and resolution, are basic to the Africanist aesthetic and offer a model for postmodernism, subconsciously as well as cognitively.

Others were touched by the Africanist presence as they reached out for the dangerous, the illicit, the hip, the *primitive*. The "seduction of the primitive" is a trope that has played havoc with the European psyche since the Age of Enlightenment. It is a love-hate relationship of binary opposites, with the black (dancing) body as the screen upon which Europeans projected their fears and phobias along with their fantasies and desires. It is the primitive trope that defines the European concept of the Other, be it the *Hottentot Venus* in nineteenth-century London, Josephine Baker in twentieth-century Paris, "Ashanti Fever" in turn-of-the-century Vienna, or the consciously non-European influences in the revolutionary work of artists such as Picasso, Braque, and Matisse.[9]

It is a well-documented fact that Picasso's art took a different course after his exposure to African sculpture. In his trailblazing work, *Les Desmoiselles d'Avignon*, two figures were influenced by African masks. The pictorial plane was broken into angular wedges. The style was termed Cubism. What if it had been called Africanism? Such a choice might have helped to advance understanding of the Africanist legacy in modernism and the place of African peoples living in the diaspora. There are innumerable examples of Africanisms in modern art, in the work of artists such as Picasso, Braque, Léger, Matisse, Modigliani, Lipschitz, right on up through American innovators from Jackson Pollock to present-day practitioners. As in contact improvisation, Pollock's work is Africanist not in content but in attitude. A serious jazz enthusiast, Pollock was known to paint while listening to jazz music and, like the traditional African artist designing patterns on fabric, worked with his canvas on the floor, transforming the act of painting into a movement process involving the whole body. Like the jazz musician, he worked directly with improvisation.[10]

Likewise, there are many examples of the primitive as a major trope in modern dance. According to dance pundit Louis Horst, "Primitive art is evident as a strong quality in every contemporary style."[11] In his book *Modern Dance Forms*, he compares modern dance poses by artists such as Martha Graham with African statuary and modern art paintings. He contends that most modern dance is "primitive to a degree," and that some have totally borrowed the primitive mold. In 1930, in an article titled "Seeking an American Art of the Dance," Martha Graham said, "We have two primitive sources, dangerous and hard to handle in the arts, but of intense psychic significance—the Indian and the Negro. That these influence us is certain."[12] This significant acknowledgment by the grande dame of modern dance has gone unnoticed. It simply fell through an interstice in history, as has the acknowledgment of those influences.

In Horst's chapter on jazz dance, he attributes its beginnings to enslaved Africans and then states that "It [jazz] does not imitate the typical ethnic African, but it retains many of the attributes brought from Africa." Among these he lists "jerky, percussive movements and accents," "syncopation," and "melancholy and lassitude."[13] He then goes on to mention the pervasive, subliminal influence of jazz in America.

> Although jazz is by now cosmopolitan and international, and has proved its affinity to the whole modern world by its popularity with all races and cultures, still it is most typically American. It is natural to all Americans, as deeply and subconsciously understood as any other folk dance is understood by the people from whom it grew. It is specifically the ex-

pression of present-day urban America. It is an intimate part of our daily life and shows in the urban walk, the posture, the rhythm of speech, the gesture, the costumes of the city. It belongs to a certain way we have of standing—a slouch, one hip thrown out—of sitting in an informal sprawl, of speaking in slangy abruptness. Jazz is the trademark of the city.[14]

The jazz characteristics described by Horst are Africanisms that infuse every aspect of American endeavor and can be summed up by the phrase, "aesthetic of the cool."

What Africanisms am I talking about? They emerge from aesthetic principles, or canons, that have been codified and discussed at length by other authors, particularly Robert Farris Thompson, Susan Vogel, Kariamu Welsh Asante, and to a lesser extent, Geneva Gay and Willie L. Baber, and Alfred Pasteur and Ivory Toldson.[15] From these sources I have designated five Africanist characteristics that occur in many forms of American concert dance, including ballet. It is important to note that these traits work together and are separated only for the sake of discussion. They are not intended to categorize phenomena. To show their interactive nature, I use the dance routine of Earl "Snake Hips" Tucker to illustrate each canon. An African American novelty dancer who attained enormous popularity in the cabarets of the 1920s, Tucker makes these Africanist principles clearly visible in his work. Ballet, the academic dance of Europe, offers the most dramatic contrast to the Africanist aesthetic. It has been regarded as the repository of European values and is characterized as a reflection of "what is thought most significant in the culture of the West."[16] For these reasons, I use ballet, rather than European vernacular dance, as the European reference point in the five principles that follow.

EMBRACING THE CONFLICT

In a broad sense, the Africanist aesthetic can be termed an aesthetic of contrariety, while the European perspective seeks to remove conflict through efficient problem solving. The Africanist aesthetic embraces difference and dissonance, rather than erasing or resolving it. Contrariety is expressed in African dilemma stories that pose a question rather than offer a solution; in music or vocal work that sounds cacophonous or grating to the untrained ear; and in dance that seems unsophisticated to eyes trained in a different aesthetic. This principle is reflected in the other four canons and they, in turn, are reflected in it. "Embracing the conflict" is embedded in the final principle, "the aesthetic of the cool," in which "coolness" results from the juxtaposition of detachment and intensity. Those opposites would be difficult to fuse in European academic aesthetics. But there is room for their pairing in Africanist aesthetics.

A routine performed by Tucker in such New York clubs as Connie's Inn and Harlem's Cotton Club—as described in Marshall and Jean Stearn's *Jazz Dance*—demonstrates this concept.

> Tucker had at the same time a disengaged and a menacing air, like a sleeping volcano, which seemed to give audiences the feeling that he was a cobra and they were mice. . . . When Snake Hips slithered on stage, the audience quieted down immediately. Nobody snickered at him, in spite of the mounting tension, no matter how nervous or embarrassed one might

be. The glaring eyes burning in the pockmarked face looked directly at and through the audience, with dreamy and impartial hostility. Snake Hips seemed to be coiled, ready to strike. Tucker's act usually consisted of five parts. He came slipping on with a sliding, forward step and just a hint of hip movement. The combination was part of a routine known in Harlem as Spanking the Baby, and in a strange but logical fashion, established the theme of his dance. Using shock tactics, he then went directly into the basic Snake Hips movements, which he paced superbly, starting out innocently enough, with one knee crossing over behind the other, while the toe of one foot touched the arch of the other. At first, it looked simultaneously pigeon-toed and knock-kneed.[17]

The conflicts are paired contraries: awkward and smooth; detached and threatening; innocent and seductive. But the most significant conflict resides in the routine's deep subtext, in the ironic playing out of power postures by the otherwise disempowered Black, male (dancing) body.

POLYCENTRISM/POLYRHYTHM

From the Africanist standpoint, movement may emanate from any part of the body, and two or more centers may operate simultaneously. Polycentrism diverges from the European academic aesthetic, where the ideal is to initiate movement from one locus: the noble, upper center of the aligned torso, well above the pelvis. Africanist movement is also polyrhythmic. For example, the feet may keep one rhythm while the arms, head, or torso dance to different drums. In this regard, Africanist dance aesthetics represents a democracy of body parts, rather than a monarchy dictated by the straight, centered spine. Again, we turn to "Snake Hips":

> The fact that the pelvis and the whole torso were becoming increasingly involved in the movement was unavoidably clear. As he progressed, Tucker's footwork became flatter, rooted more firmly to the floor, while his hips described wider and wider circles, until he seemed to be throwing his hips alternately out of joint to the melodic accents of the music.[18]

From a "get-down" posture that centered the movement in the legs and feet, Tucker adds the pelvis as another center, illustrating polycentrism. On top of the crossover step, described above, he interpolates a pelvic rhythm, exemplifying the simplest level of polyrhythm. Again, these are interactive principles; embracing opposing rhythms, coupled with a shifting center, demonstrates high-affect juxtaposition.

HIGH-AFFECT JUXTAPOSITION

Mood, attitude, or movement breaks that omit the transitions and connective links valued in the European academic aesthetic are the keynote of this principle. For example, a forceful, driving mood may overlap and coexist with a light and humorous tone, or imitative and abstract movements may be juxtaposed. The result may be surprise, irony, comedy, innuendo, double entendre, and finally, exhilaration. All traditions use contrast in the arts. But Africanist high-affect juxtaposition is heightened beyond the contrast that is within the range of accepted standards in the European academic canon. On that scale, it would be considered bad taste, flashy, or loud. "Snake Hips" demonstrates this principle, in part, through his choice of costume—a sequined girdle supporting a seductive tassel.

> Then followed a pantomime to a Charleston rhythm: Tucker clapped four times and waved twice with each hand in turn, holding the elbow of the waving hand and rocking slightly with the beat. The over-all effect was suddenly childish, effeminate, and perhaps tongue-in-cheek. The next movement was known among dancers as the Belly Roll, and consisted of a series of waves rolling from pelvis to chest—a standard part of a Shake dancer's routine, which Tucker varied by coming to a stop, transfixing the audience with a baleful, hypnotic stare, and twirling his long tassel in time with the music.[19]

Tucker shifts unpredictably from childish and effeminate to challenging and "macho" movements, disregarding European standards for consistency in characterization. In addition, with no preparation or transition, he changes from light, almost cheerleader-like hand and arm gestures, to weighted, sensual undulations centered in the lower torso. A third high-affect juxtaposition occurred with the "break," described above. Tucker cut off the movement in the middle of a Belly Roll, came to a break, or full stop, and shifted the mood and rhythm of his intricately structured routine.

EPHEBISM

Named after the ancient Greek word for youth, ephebism encompasses attributes such as power, vitality, flexibility, drive, and attack. Attack implies speed, sharpness, and force. Intensity is also a characteristic of ephebism, but it is a kinesthetic intensity that recognizes feeling as sensation, rather than emotion. It is "the phrasing of every note and step with consummate vitality," with response to rhythm and a sense of swing as aesthetic values.[20] The torso is flexible and articulate. "The concept of vital aliveness leads to the interpretation of the parts of the body as independent instruments of percussive force."[21] Old people dancing with youthful vitality are valued examples of ephebism in Africanist cultures. Moving with suppleness and flexibility is more important than maintaining torso alignment. Meanwhile, speed, sharpness, force, and attack are comparatively muted concepts in the European ballet tradition. (See descriptions later in this chapter by Balanchine dancers, who contrast his sense of speed and timing with that found in traditional ballet.) The percussive force of independent body parts, with rhythm as a principal value, is not a part of the European ballet aesthetic.

> Tucker raised his right arm to his eyes, at first as if embarrassed (a feeling that many in the audience shared), and then, as if racked with sobs, he went into the Tremble, which shook him savagely and rapidly from head to foot. As he turned his back to the audience to display the overall trembling more effectively, Tucker looked like a murderously naughty boy.[22]

Tucker's "tremble" is an excellent example of ephebism. This movement articulates the separated segments of the torso, one against the other, in a broken yet continuous movement sequence. It can be accomplished only with a totally flexible torso, which will allow the tremor-like reverberations to ripple nonstop through the body. The movement is also percussive, forceful, and intense in its attack. It racks his body. An additional fillip of ephebism is demonstrated in Tucker's "naughty boy" self-presentation.

THE AESTHETIC OF THE COOL

As Thompson so eloquently explains, the "aesthetic of the cool" is all-embracing. It is an attitude (in the sense that African Americans use the word "attitude") that combines composure with vitality. Its prime components are visibility—dancing the movements clearly, presenting the self clearly and with aesthetic clarity, luminosity or brilliance, and facial composure, or the "mask of the cool." The "cool" embraces all the other principles. Taken together, the sum total of all the principles has been characterized as "soul force."[23] It is seen in the asymmetrical walk of African American males, which shows an attitude of carelessness cultivated with calculated aesthetic clarity. It is in the unemotional, detached, mask-like face of the drummer or dancer whose body and energy may be working fast, hard, and hot, but whose face remains cool.

The aloofness, sangfroid, and detachment of some styles of European academic dance are completely different from this aesthetic of the cool. The European attitude suggests centeredness, control, linearity, directness; the Africanist mode suggests asymmetricality (that plays with falling off center), looseness (implying flexibility and vitality), and indirectness of approach. "Hot," its opposite, is a necessary component of the Africanist "cool." It is in the embracing of these opposites, and in their high-affect juxtaposition, that the aesthetic of the cool exists.

Throughout Tucker's routine, for example, he strikes a balance between the sexual heat implied in his pelvic movements and the cool attitude of his face. Luminosity and brilliance come through in his direct relationship to the audience and the choreography, and visibility is demonstrated in the fact that he dances not as a character but as himself. These traits are valued in the Africanist aesthetic.

Some people imagine that ballet is about as far away from anything Africanist as black supposedly is from white, but things are not as defined or clear-cut as that: not even black and white. In spite of our denials, opposites become bound together more often than we admit. Cultures borrow from each other and fusions abound.

The Africanist presence is a defining ingredient that separates American ballet from its European counterpart. Ironically, it was George Balanchine, a Russian immigrant of Georgian ethnicity, who was the principal Americanizer of ballet. Why and how is a story worth telling, even in brief. Balanchine cut his teeth as a choreographer in Europe during the Jazz Age of the 1920s. His early *Apollo* for the Diaghilev Ballets Russes exuded jazz references. After Diaghilev's death, Balanchine worked in major European cities as a ballet master, and choreographed revues for the popular stage to earn a living. He also created musical routines for the first feature-length English talking film, *Dark Red Roses*, made in 1929.[24]

The jazz aesthetic was familiar to him before he came to the United States. Once here, he served a long apprenticeship on Broadway, which helped him to assimilate popular, social, and vernacular dance influences in the service of creating a newly defined ballet medium. Beginning in 1936, he choreographed or co-choreographed a number of musicals, including *The Zeigfeld Follies, On Your Toes, Babes in Arms, I Married an Angel, The Boys from Syracuse,* and with Katherine Dunham, *Cabin in the Sky.* He worked with the Nicholas Brothers, two extraordinary tap-dancing kids, in *Follies* and *Babes,* and with Josephine Baker in *Follies.* Thus, he had direct contact with African American dancers and choreographers and with genres that were highly influenced by Africanisms.

It is already clear that Balanchine was a ballet choreographer who worked in the ballet medium and subscribed to a ballet aesthetic. What I hope to make equally clear is that throughout his career, he introduced to the ballet canon Africanist aesthetic principles as well as Africanist-based steps from the so-called jazz dance repertory. He introduced these innovations into the ballet context while maintaining his grounding in the ballet aesthetic. The result was still ballet, but with a new accent. My guiding premises follow:

- Ballet, like all dance, is subject to the influences and presences that are valued in its cultural context. Therefore, it can rightfully be called a form of ethnic dance.
- Influences from past and present cultures are woven into, intermeshed with, and redistributed in any given cultural mode at any given moment in time. (To paraphrase this idea in structuralist terms, every text is an intertext.)
- The Americanization of ballet by a Russian immigrant, George Balanchine, will show both African American and European-American influences.
- Looking from an Africanist perspective reveals the Africanist presence in American ballet.

There are many places in Balanchine's ballets where the Africanist legacy comes bursting through, most notably in the new movement vocabulary he introduced to the ballet stage. The displacement of hips or other parts of the torso, instead of vertical alignment; leg kicks attacking the beat, instead of well-placed extensions; angular arms and flexed wrists, rather than the traditional, rounded port de bras—all of these touches usher the viewer into the discovery of the Africanist presence in Balanchine. These elements appear in works throughout his career and are highlighted in ballets such as *Apollo* (1928), *The Four Temperaments* (1946), *Agon* (1957), *Stars and Stripes* (1958), and *Symphony in Three Movements* (1972), among others. If and when they appeared in European ballet, these elements were reserved for lesser, "ignoble" characters, and represented that which was comic or rustic, vernacular or exotic. Balanchine wielded these movements in a decidedly nontraditional fashion and assigned them central significance as movements for principals and soloists.

In the first movement of *Symphony,* the corps dancers lunge from side to side, with the straight leg turned in and one arm angularly jutting downward in a style unknown in traditional ballet. Later, a male sextet makes a prancing entrance that can only be described as an updated version of the cakewalk, with the upper torso leaning deeply backward. The second movement opens with torso isolations as a central element in the first duet, the same isolations used more baroquely in *Bagaku* (1963), which, even though it is based on a Japanese wedding ritual, reveals marked Africanist tendencies. This movement vocabulary allows Balanchine to expand the ballet idiom by introducing the articulated torso to its vertical standard.

The second and third duets of *The Four Temperaments*—the allegro tempo second duet and the adagio third—share some of the same Africanist-inflected movements. In both, ballroom dance references are as evident as the traditional pas de deux conventions into which they have been inserted. In both duets the male twirl-turns the female on one spot, as social dancers do, except that she is "sitting" in the air in plié while on point. The male then pumps his partner's hips forward and back as he grips her waist. He could pull her off the floor with this movement, and they would resemble Lindy-hoppers.

In the second duet this movement is capped off with jazzy little side lunges, straight, outstretched arms, and flexed wrists, as the two dancers face each other. They exit with "Egyptian" arms (raised to shoulder height and bent perpendicularly from the elbow). In the third duet the male leads his partner into deep, parallel-legged squats (it would be misleading to call them pliés), which she performs while still on point. Then, standing, he offers his back to her. Facing his back, she wraps her arms around his neck, drapes the full length of her body against his, and leans on him. He moves forward for several steps, dragging her along. This looks like a cleaned up, slowed down variation on a typical Lindy exit. (Only in the Lindy have I seen as much female crotch as in these two duets.)

In the first variation of the "Melancholic" section a female quartet enters. Their arms are in second position, not in a traditional port de bras, but straight, with flexed wrists. They perform high kicks that are resolved by pushing the pelvis forward on a 1-2, kick-thrust beat, and their legs are parallel as they bourrée around the male. The choreography for the male is heavy, low, intense, and marked by deep lunges and acrobatic backbends. He metaphorically follows the music and "gets down"—as if this were a melancholy blues. His ephebism is balanced by the quartet's cool. He exits in a deep, acrobatic, nonacademic backbend, his outstretched arms leading him offstage, his center in his head and arms, not only in his spine.

There are many instances in the "Sanguinic" variation, especially in the choreography for the female soloist, where the movement is danced from the hips, which are thrust forward. This and the exit in "Melancholic" are examples of the simplest version of polycentrism. Several centers may occur simultaneously, and the center has shifted from the vertically aligned spine to other parts of the body. The "Phlegmatic" solo opens and closes as a study in torso isolations and asymmetry. Paul Hindemith's score intimates the chords and intervals associated with blues and jazz.

Why did Balanchine incorporate these Africanist principles in his ballets? African American dance pioneer Katherine Dunham gives us a clue. "Balanchine liked the rhythm and percussion of our dances," she said. "Georgians have a good sense of rhythm from what I've seen."[25] Balanchine was the perfect catalyst for defining and shaping American ballet. The Georgian rhythmic sense that he had inherited culturally was the open door that allowed him to embrace the Africanist rhythmic landscape of his new homeland. With his talent and initiative he was able to merge those two principles, just as he fused ballet's cool aloofness with the Africanist aesthetic of the cool.

The 1928 ballet *Apollo* confirmed that Balanchine was an experimentalist and innovator in the same rank as those in literature, music, and painting who similarly reached out to African, Asian, or Oceanic vocabularies to expand their options. This ballet marked the first of Balanchine's collaborations with Igor Stravinsky who was influenced, in part, by Africanist principles in his radically rhythmic, chromatic scores. Balanchine described this work as a turning point in his career. As the three muses enter together, they perform the same high kicks with pelvis thrusting forward that reappear in *The Four Temperaments* nearly twenty years later. There is a delightful moment when they move by waddling on their heels, their legs straight. On another stage, and in another mood, that would be a tap-dance transition step. And the asymmetrical poses the dancers assume diverge from traditional ballet but are akin to Africanist dance, particularly the moving poses struck in African American stage and social dance styles of the 1920s.

Apollo's third solo is a twisting, lunging affair. He simultaneously jumps, bends his knees so that his heels touch his hips, and twists his hips so that they angle against his torso. His landings dig into the floor as one leg releases and kicks downward on the beat. Indeed, this solo explores the downbeat—the earth, not the air—and the soloist, like a jazz musician, hits the beat on the "one" count, not taking the preparatory "and" count that is traditional in ballet. This passage suggests a fusion between Africanisms and vernacular dance influences from Balanchine's Russian past. Another example of Balanchine's nonballetic use of phrasing and timing is recounted by Maria Tallchief, to whom he was married in the late 1940s.

> In a demonstration with Walter Terry and Balanchine, I did an eight-count *développé* straight up and out with the *port de bras* in the manner in which we most often see it done. Then George turned to me and demanded, "Now out in *one* count and hold the rest." That is an example of the simplicity of his style.[26]

The nontraditional timing Balanchine introduced into the ballet canon, like his introduction of the articulated torso, stretched the parameters of ballet and revitalized and Americanized the technique.

In his second solo, Apollo does several moves in which he pulls his weight off center as he lunges and stops short in an asymmetrical plié on the forced arch. His turns and lunges are grounded and abrupt. He stops them suddenly, as if on a dime. Unlike traditional ballet practice, the turns are not resolved; they simply stop. Both solos manifest ephebism in their speed, attack, and force. Apollo's solos and the "Melancholic" solo from *The Four Temperaments* are dances about weight and groundedness, not defying gravity but meeting it and embracing it. The jumps are performed not to highlight the going up, but to punctuate and emphasize the coming down.

Ballet's traditional airborne quality is not present here. Instead, we find the connection to the earth characteristic of Africanist dance and American modern dance. In fact, the Africanisms evident here probably came to Balanchine through modern dance as well as social and show dance. This solo is followed by an amusing vaudeville chorus that seems to come out of nowhere. The muses join him and, with no preparation and on an abrupt change in the mood of the score, they all plié in an asymmetrical position, settle back into one hip with buttocks jutting out, and bounce in unison to the rhythm. They are setting time for a change in rhythm, and this is their "break." It is a radical juxtaposition, set against the previous mood and movement. It is also a quote from popular dance styles. The work ends as the three muses lean their bodies against Apollo's back, their legs in graduated arabesques, while he poses in a lunge, legs parallel, arms raised, hands flexed.

The Africanist presence in Balanchine's works is a story of particular and specific motifs, of which there are many more examples than the ones given here, from ballets that span the course of his career. In other words, these were not dispensable, decorative touches that marked one or two ballets; rather, they were essential ingredients in his canon. However, the story only begins here. More significant are the underlying speed, vitality, energy, coolness, and athletic intensity that are fundamental to his Americanization of ballet. The tale continues with radical dynamics, off-center weight shifts, and unexpected mood and attitude changes in Balanchine's work that create a high-affect juxtaposition of elements uncommon in traditional ballet but basic to Africanist dance.

Less innovative artists might have held on to the old, but Balanchine could not settle for that. He was enticed by what he saw as American qualities of speed and coolness. Of course, those qualities are predicated as much on the African presence in the Americas as the European. It simply will not suffice to say that jazz dance influenced his work. That term, jazz, has become another way to misname and silence the Africanist legacy; systematic exclusion of African Americans from American ballet has done the same. Buried under layers of deceit, that legacy in ballet has been overlooked. Some of the hidden story is intimated in Balanchine's original intentions for his new American ballet school, as recounted by Lincoln Kirstein:

> For the first [class] he would take 4 white girls and 4 white boys, about sixteen years old and 8 of the same, *negros* (*sic*). . . . He thinks the negro part of it would be amazingly supple, the combination of suppleness and sense of time superb. Imagine them, masked, for example. They have so much abandon—and disciplined they would be *nonpareil.*[27]

Thus, even before his arrival in the United States, Balanchine was calculating how he could draw upon the energy and phrasing of African Americans. Of course, the primitive trope is at work here, with the concomitant allure of the exotic. Even so, if his dream had been realized, what a different history would have been wrought for American ballet and its relationship to peoples of African lineage. One can only imagine that, innocent and ignorant of American racism, Balanchine understood, once here, that his dream school was unfeasible.

The texts that discuss Balanchine's Broadway musical career praise the ways in which he "improved" on show dancing; none of them acknowledge what he gained from that experience and took with him back to the ballet stage. But Balanchine himself may well have been aware of the two-way exchange. He said in a 1934 interview with Arnold Haskell, soon after his arrival in the United States: "There are other ways of holding the interest (of the audience), by vivid contrast, for instance. Imagine the effect that would be produced by six Negresses dancing on their pointes and six white girls doing a frenzied jazz!"[28]

What he suggests, of course, is an example of high-affect juxtaposition. In working on *Concerto Barocco*, described by former New York City Ballet dancer Suki Schorer as a ballet with "a very jazzy feeling," he aimed for clarity in syncopation, timing, and attack, and he characterized a particular step as "like the Charleston."[29] His original intention for this work is expressed by former company member Barbara Walczak in her comparison of two versions of the ballet. Inadvertently, she points out Balanchine's use of the Africanist aesthetic:

> The difference between the original and today's *Barocco* is a timing difference, an *energy* difference. It was never meant to be lyrical. One difference was that many of the steps were *very off-center*. . . . The energy behind the steps was different. . . . They were *attacked* more than they are now.[30]

Patricia McBride, who danced for Balanchine from 1959 until his death in 1983, says, "Dancing Balanchine is harder—the patterns, the way they change in Balanchine ballets. The ballets are so fast, and they travel much more than a lot of the more classical companies."[31] Speed, timing, and attitude changes are key elements in Balanchine and are key to the Africanist aesthetic. They are not signature components of the ballet from which he emerged. It seems ironic that when Schorer compares the Russian ballet companies with Balanchinian ballet, she states that the Russians do not understand "phrasing, counting, the timing within a step. *They've never seen anything*. They only know what they know."[32]

What they don't know, and what Balanchine was exposed to, is the phrasing, counting, and timing that comes from the Africanist influence in American culture, so native to us that we take it for granted. By embracing these elements that he encountered in the United States, Balanchine expanded the definition of ballet. There is no doubt that his redefinition included both Africanist and European elements, fused into a spicy, pungent brew.

Balanchine's legacy, like the Africanist legacy, is a living one, much of which cannot be codified or contained by "the steps." Arthur Mitchell, creator of the Dance Theater of Harlem, worked well with Balanchine, and Mitchell's cultural background and training helped. His description of *Metastaseis & Pithoprakta* shows Africanisms in Balanchine's way of working through rhythm rather than steps and requiring the dancing body to be laid back, cool, and free to receive his messages:

> Suzanne Farrell and I danced a *pas de deux* that was one of those eerie things that didn't use steps per se. He'd say, "I want something like this," and he would start moving. You would just have to be free enough to let your body go and do it. I think one of the things that helped me so much with him was that, *being a tap dancer, I was used to rhythm and speed* [emphasis added]. Many times when he was choreographing he would work rhythmically and then put the step in. If you were looking for a step, it wouldn't be there. But if you got *dah, da-dah-dah-dah*, it would come out [emphasis Mitchell's]. The rhythm was always the most important. The choreography was set in time and then in space.[33]

According to Mitchell, Balanchine sometimes referred to Dunham in his work with students and sent dancers to study with her. He also regularly called on Mitchell to "come in and show these kids, because they don't know old-fashioned jazz."[34] A final statement from Mitchell is most telling about Balanchine and the Africanist legacy

Mitchell said that Balanchine described his ballerina ideal as possessing a short torso, long arms, and long legs—a designation that fits to a T the censured profile of the black dancing body.[35] By stating this preference and following through on it with his aesthetic choices, Balanchine shifted the balance of the ideal body type toward the black side and expanded the paradigm to embrace these stereotypically "black" body characteristics.

Mitchell's summation acclaims the black dancing body, and the body is the origin and outcome of my thesis. I call this chapter "Stripping the Emperor," but what needs stripping is our way of perceiving. Once we dare see the naked truth, like the child in Anderson's tale, we shall see a body, the American dancing body. It is neither black nor white, but an integrative portrait in which these two seeming opposites are embraced as two essential, complementary sides of the same coin.

NOTES

1. For a full treatment of the Africanist presence in American culture and American performance, see Brenda Dixon Gottschild, *Digging the Africanist Presence in American Performance: Dance and Other Contexts* (Westport, Conn.: Greenwood, 1996).

2. My precedent for using this term is set in recent scholarship. For example, see Joseph E. Holloway, *Africanisms in American Culture* (Bloomington: Indiana University Press, 1990), and Toni Morrison, *Playing in the Dark: Whiteness and the Literary Imagination* (Cambridge, Mass.: Harvard University Press, 1992).

3. Toni Morrison, "Unspeakable Things Unspoken: The Afro-American Presence in American Literature," *Michigan Quarterly Review* (Winter 1989): 11.

4. Joann Kealiinohomoku, "An Anthropologist Looks at Ballet as a Form of Ethnic Dance," *Impulse* (1969–70): 24–33, reprinted in *What Is Dance?*, eds. Roger Copeland and Marshall Cohen (New York: Oxford University Press, 1983), 533–549; Morrison, *Playing in the Dark*.

5. Peter Wood, personal communication, 1988.

6. Patrick O'Connor, "Josephine," *London Observer Sunday Magazine* (Jan. 19, 1986): 20.

7. Margaret Croyden, "Jerzy Grotowski—The Experiment Continues," *American Theatre* (Sept. 1992): 42.

8. Contact improvisation is a form of dance based on the premise of improvisation. Frequently performed as a duet, a contactor moves in conjunction with her partner's weight. The couple rolls, lurches, suspends, rises, and falls together, sharing responsibility for each other's weight. The important element is the process of instantaneous improvisation. Line and form, in a ballet sense, carry no significance.

9. For a full discussion of the primitive trope in various settings and perspectives, see the following sources: Marianna Torgovnick, *Gone Primitive: Savage Intellects, Modern Lives* (Chicago: University of Chicago Press, 1990); Henry Louis Gates, ed., *"Race," Writing, and Difference* (Chicago: University of Chicago Press, 1985); Sally Price, *Primitive Art in Civilized Places* (Chicago: University of Chicago Press, 1989); and Reinhold Grimm and Jost Hermand, eds., *Blacks and German Culture* (Madison: University of Wisconsin Press, 1986).

10. See Andrew Kagan, "Improvisations: Notes on Jackson Pollock and the Black Contribution to American High Culture," *Arts 53* (March 1979): 96–99.

11. Louis Horst, *Modern Dance Forms* (Pennington, N.J.: Princeton Book Company, 1987 [1961]), 53.

12. Quoted in Juana de Laban, "What Tomorrow?" *Dance Observer* (May 1945): 55.

13. Horst, *Modern Dance Forms,* 111.

14. Horst, *Modern Dance Forms,* 111–112.

15. For a thorough discussion that is applicable to both visual and performing arts, see Robert Farris Thompson, *African Art in Motion* (Los Angeles: University of California Press, 1974). Thompson compiles an Africanist aesthetic paradigm that he terms the "Ten Canons of Fine Form." See also Susan Vogel, *Aesthetics of African Art* (New York: Center for African Art, 1986), and Kariamu Welsh Asante, "Commonalities in African Dance," in *African Culture—The Rhythms of Unity,* eds. Molefi Kete Asante and Kariamu Welsh Asante (Westport, Conn.: Greenwood, 1986), 71–82, for a dance-specific discussion of African aesthetics. For a more generalized discussion of Africanisms in America, see also Geneva Gay and Willie L. Baber, eds., *Expressively Black: The Cultivated Basis of Ethnic Identity* (New York: Praeger, 1987), and Alfred Pasteur and Ivory Toldson, *Roots of Soul: The Psychology of Black Expressiveness* (New York: Anchor, 1982).

16. Rayner Heppenstall, quoted in Selma Jeanne Cohen, *Next Week, Swan Lake* (Middletown, Conn.: Wesleyan University Press, 1982), 131.

17. Marshall Stearn and Jean Stearn, *Jazz Dance* (New York: Schirmer Books, 1979 [1964]), 236.

18. Stearn and Stearn, *Jazz Dance,* 236.

19. Stearn and Stearn, *Jazz Dance,* 236–237.

20. Thompson, *African Art in Motion,* 7.

21. Thompson, *African Art in Motion,* 9.

22. Stearn and Stearn, *Jazz Dance,* 237.

23. Gay and Baber, *Expressively Black,* 11.

24. George Balanchine, *Choreography by George Balanchine: A Catalogue of Works* (New York: Viking, 1984), 25.

25. Interview with Dunham in Francis Mason, *I Remember Balanchine* (New York: Doubleday, 1991), 193.

26. Quoted in Mason, *I Remember Balanchine,* 239 (emphasis Tallchief's).

27. Letter from Lincoln Kirstein to A. Everett Austin, Jr., dated July 16, 1933, Mason, *I Remember Balanchine,* 116–117 (emphasis Kirstein's).

28. Arnold Haskell, *Balletomania Then and Now* (New York: Alfred A. Knopf, 1977), 98.

29. Quoted in Mason, *I Remember Balanchine,* 459.

30. Quoted in Mason, *I Remember Balanchine,* 259.

31. Quoted in Mason, *I Remember Balanchine,* 444.

32. Quoted in Mason, *I Remember Balanchine,* 462.

33. Quoted in Mason, *I Remember Balanchine,* 395.

34. Quoted in Mason, *I Remember Balanchine,* 396.

35. "Talk of the Town," *New Yorker* (Dec. 28, 1987): 36.

4

The African Diaspora in World History and Politics

Joseph E. Harris

In recent years the term *diaspora* has become common in studies of African, Chinese, Indian, and a host of other communities outside their original homelands. These communities reside in and have loyalty to their adopted country, but also identify with and maintain connections in their country or region of origin. They therefore have a double identity or "double consciousness," as W. E. B. Du Bois explained nearly a century ago. That helps to explain the depth of complexity and the "dialectical" contradictions in the relations between peoples in diaspora and their homelands. An assessment of these complexities and contradictions is mandatory if we are to understand the historical development and impact of the linkages between Africa and its Diaspora.

The study of diasporas is especially timely today because of the current fragmentation and population displacement in a number of countries in Eastern Europe (e.g., Czechoslovakia, the former Yugoslavia, and the former Soviet Union); Africa (e.g., Ethiopia, Eritrea, Somalia, and Rwanda); and South and Southeast Asia (especially India, Vietnam, and Cambodia). More recent and urgent for Americans is the mass immigration of Haitians, Cubans, Mexicans, Vietnamese, and Chinese into the United States. These groups have similar characteristics of ethnic identity, marginality, and homeland linkage; and one cannot understand them without an examination of their original homelands and the root causes and specific contexts within which they have been dispersed.

The case of Africans and their descendants abroad is especially complex, with a long history of international stereotypes and myths that continue to obstruct policies and practices that are intended to guarantee freedom and justice. The facts in this instance are fairly well known. Africans have since ancient times been characterized both by positive images and by negative images, such as being inferior, savage, destined to be enslaved, incapable of developing complex societies, without a meaningful history, uncivilized and thus having made no contribution to world civilization; and this list can be expanded.[1] The main point is that these myths, and variations of them, persist in spite of evidence to the contrary.

One would think that the informed reader knows about African achievements as revealed in continuing archaeological discoveries in several parts of Africa; the reconstruction of the history of ancient and complex societies in Africa and their impact on other parts of the world; the commercial relations of Africans, Arabs, and Asians in the Indian Ocean since ancient times; the creative art of Benin, the Dogon, and other African societies; the literary accomplishments of Africans in pre- and early Islamic Arabia; the roles Africans played in the rise and expansion of Islam and Christianity; the early relations between the Mali empire, the Kongo kingdom, and other African states and Portugal prior to the slave trade; and the accomplishments of Africans and their descendants in Europe and the Americas. Recent research in all of these and other areas of study demonstrates the dynamic and rich African heritage.[2]

This chapter focuses primarily on the African Diaspora in the Americas and has the following objectives: to demonstrate the global dispersion and presence of African peoples since ancient times, making a distinction between the historical and modern Diasporas; to provide evidence of the continuity of their consciousness of and identity with Africa; and to assess the gradual transformation from African to African American and the implications of that phenomenon.

THE HISTORICAL DIASPORA

Long before the transatlantic slave trade, Africans traveled voluntarily throughout much of the world. They traveled as ancient merchants and sailors, many of whom settled in Europe, the Middle East, and Asia; some fought as soldiers in those areas and remained permanently. Others served as missionaries for Islam and Christianity and settled in the Middle East, Asia, and Europe. Several Ethiopian monks accompanied European Crusaders to Rome, Florence, and Venice as well as to Portugal and Spain.

A number of Ethiopian royal emissaries traveled to and remained in Europe, Rome especially, in the Middle Ages. Itinerant entertainers performed in a number of Arab and European states, and some of them settled there. The important point here is that throughout history Africans, like other people, have traveled abroad as free persons, settled down, and made important contributions to many European and Asian countries.

It was, however, the slave trade that made the African presence essentially global (see figure 4.1). For at least fifteen hundred years prior to the European-conducted slave trade, Arabs conducted a slave trade across the Mediterranean Sea, the Red Sea, and the Indian Ocean, and took Africans to Arabia, India, and the Far East. Enslaved Africans worked in Persian Gulf salt mines, coconut groves, and date plantations; in Bahrain as pearl divers; in India as palace guards and soldiers; in Arabia and India as domestics and field hands; and as concubines and eunuchs throughout much of the Muslim world. Today several discrete communities of African descent can be found in cities, towns, and regions of Iran: Bandar 'Abbas, Jiruft, Shiraz, and Tehran; Iraq: Baghdad and Basra; Pakistan: Karachi, Lahore, and Baluchistan; and India: Hyderabad, Ahmadabad, Durat,

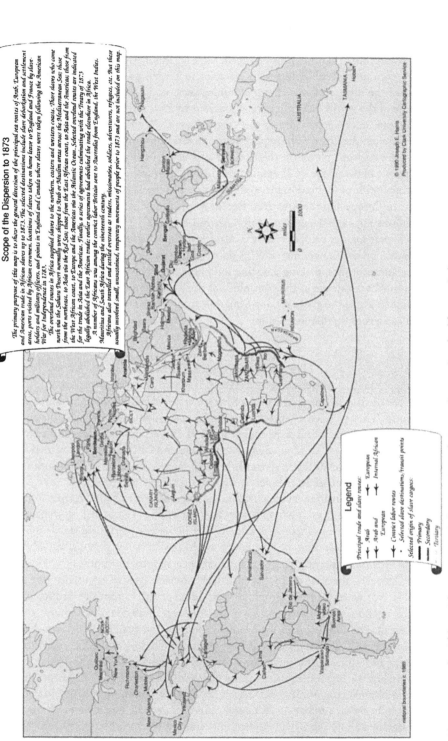

Scope of the Dispersion to 1873

The primary purpose of this map is to show the general direction of the principal sea routes of Arab, European and American trade in African slaves up to 1873. The selected destinations include slave debarkation and settlement areas, ports visited by African crewmen, locations of slaves taken on home leave to England and France by slaveholders and military officers, and points in England and Canada where slaves were taken following the American War for Independence in 1783.

The overland routes in Africa supplied slaves to the northern, eastern and western coasts. Those slaves who came north via the Sahara Desert normally were shipped to Arab or Muslim areas across the Mediterranean Sea; those from the northeast, to Asia via the Red Sea; those from the East African coast, to Asia and the Americas; those from the West African coast, to Europe and the Americas via the Atlantic Ocean. Selected overland routes are indicated for the trade in Asia and the Americas. Finally, a series of agreements culminating with the Treaty of 1873 legally abolished the East African trade; earlier agreements had abolished the trade elsewhere in Africa.

A number of Africans also travelled and settled overseas as traders, missionaries, soldiers, adventurers, refugees, etc. But these usually involved small, unsustained, temporary movements of people prior to 1873 and are not included on this map.

Mauritius and South Africa during the nineteenth century.

Africans also travelled and settled overseas as traders, missionaries, soldiers, adventurers, refugees, etc. But these usually involved small, unsustained, temporary movements of people prior to 1873 and are not included on this map.

© 1990 Joseph E. Harris
Produced by Clark University Cartographic Service

Legend

Principal trade and slave routes:

Arab
Arab and European
Coerced labor routes

European
Internal African

• Selected slave destinations/transit points

Selected origin of slave cargoes:

Primary
Secondary
Tertiary

Figure 4.1. The African Diaspora, map I. © 1990, Joseph E. Harris. Reprinted with permission.

Cutch, and Gujarat; and many individuals of African origin reside in communities of mixed descent. So far little evidence has appeared to identify contemporary descendants in China, although the historical record shows that they were taken there as well. The Portuguese even took Africans to Nagasaki, Japan, in the sixteenth century.[3]

However, it was the European Age of Exploration in the fifteenth century that led to the greatest dispersion of Africans in history. Although occurring in a much shorter time frame than that of the Arabs, the European-conducted slave trade enveloped the continent. Europeans defeated the Arabs and took control of the Indian Ocean trade routes, where they developed their own slave trade from Zanzibar and other regions of East Africa to many parts of Asia. In addition, they also captured, sold, and took Africans from what today are Kenya, Tanzania, Mozambique, and Madagascar along the southern route around the Cape of Good Hope to Buenos Aires in Argentina, Montevideo in Uruguay, and Rio de Janeiro in Brazil. Africans were marched overland from Buenos Aires and Montevideo through the passes of the Andean Mountains to enslavement in Santiago and Valparaiso in Chile, and from Rio de Janeiro to and through Paraguay and Bolivia to Lima and Callao in Peru.

The route from East Africa around the Cape of Good Hope also took Africans into the Caribbean, where some were sold and others trans-shipped to the North American cities of Mobile, Charleston, and Richmond. Cartagena in Colombia became a major port from which enslaved Africans were taken to Panama and overland to the Pacific coast area of Chocó, which today is overwhelmingly Afro-Colombian, as well as to the Pacific coasts of Ecuador, Peru, and Chile.

The well-known "slave coast" of West Africa was the area from which European dealers captured, bought, and sold most of the Africans enslaved in Europe and the Americas. As early as the 1440s Africans were taken from Arguin, in what is now Mauritania, to be sold in Portugal. Enslaved Africans became increasingly common in Spain, France, and England during the sixteenth century. Gradually the Portuguese developed tropical plantations on the offshore African islands of Cape Verde, and São Tomé and Príncipe, thereby establishing a relationship between the plantation economy and enslaved African labor, both of which they transferred to the Americas.

The other major area of intensive slave trading was around the mouth of the Congo River and upper Angola, which supplied large numbers of captive Africans to Brazil, the Caribbean islands, and North America. Most of the Africans who reached North America were transshipped from the Caribbean, where they were first "seasoned."

Although not part of the slave trade, the convict labor system that the British used to populate a number of their colonial possessions constituted another means of African dispersion abroad. Convict labor drew from the prison population, which included debtors, thieves, and other criminals. Most frequently for Africans, this meant vagrants who could not find employment in a racially biased society. While most of these convict settlers were English, recent research has revealed that hundreds of those who settled Australia were Africans. Continued research will very likely reveal a higher number of Africans who settled in that country.

There is no way to know the exact number of Africans who were transported and enslaved abroad, but the best "guesstimates" are those for the Americas, which have been the most intensively studied.[4] Based on these figures, between twelve and twenty-five million Africans reached the American hemisphere; many perished during the transatlantic voyage. Of the arrivals, by far the most went to Brazil, followed by the British Caribbean, the French Caribbean, Spanish American areas, and North America. Whereas the details of the slave system are too well known to be detailed here, what is most important to emphasize is that cultural continuities have persisted in multiple ways throughout the Diaspora:

1. Africans arrived abroad with their languages and cultures, which they continued to speak and practice, especially during the early years, in the privacy of their homes, quarters, and social groups. They continued to sing and dance as their cultures had taught them, give their children African names, and so forth.

2. Neither the Middle Passage nor the slavery system broke their awareness of their history. This is revealed in their religious practices (such as Candomblé in Brazil and Santería in Cuba) and oral traditions generally. In fact, some of the new arrivals sought their kin and friends after they had been sold into slavery. This confirms both the continuity and the consciousness of heritage, community, and common social condition.

3. Their culture and aspirations for freedom were expressed in a number of ways, often incorporated in different forms—songs, poetry, religion—and were employed to solidify mass followings in a number of resistance movements including the ninth-century revolt in Iraq, where an autonomous community replicated African traditions under the leadership of Rihan Ibn Salib; the seventeenth-century revolt led by Zumbi in Brazil, where Palmares remained autonomous for most of that century; the eighteenth-century revolt in Haiti led by African-born Boukman and Diaspora-born Christian, Toussaint L'Overture; and the unsuccessful nineteenth-century revolt led by Gullah Jack, the African, and Diaspora-born Denmark Vesey in the United States. These were all freedom movements that incorporated traditional symbols and ceremonies around which Africans and African Diasporans rallied.

As important as the struggle for freedom was, it is important to emphasize that Africans did much more than think about their enslavement. They were primarily preoccupied with daily life, and that necessitated creativity and a degree of accommodation to local conditions. Africans, for example, learned European languages and culture; in time some converted to Christianity; in Asia they converted to Islam. In both cases many of them distinguished themselves as artists, writers, poets, teachers, and inventors in Asia, Europe, and the Americas. This limited assimilation caused the double consciousness referred to above.

This necessarily brief discussion of the historical Diaspora confirms a global dispersion and settlement of Africans. They settled abroad voluntarily and involuntarily and maintained a consciousness of Africa and their identity while adapting and making positive contributions to their adopted homelands. This phase of the Diaspora was largely a heritage of the slave trade and enslavement. But it was also a period of the convergence of that slave trade and the simultaneous establishment of colonial rule in Africa during the nineteenth century. The convergence of these two phenomena resulted in the internationalization of Black economic and political dependence on Europeans, with the consequent global entrenchment of the age-old negative images, myths, and stereotypes about Africans and their descendants generally. This occurred during the modern phase of the Diaspora.

THE MODERN DIASPORA

The abolition of the slave trade led to the colonial period in African history and resulted in qualitative and quantitative differences in the dispersion of Africans abroad. Abolitionists often intercepted slave ships and freed the African captives, who were settled initially at selected points outside of Africa: Florida briefly at the outset for the Atlantic trade; India, Aden, and the Seychelles for the Indian Ocean trade. These were temporary stations.

Missionary and business groups in England and the United States soon realized that resettlement in Africa might serve as a means to rid their countries of Africans and at the same time establish communities that could expand the Christian faith and commerce and also be regarded as humanitarian gestures. Thus it was that Sierra Leone in 1787 and Liberia in 1821 became permanent resettlement communities in West Africa for freed captives from slave ships and for formerly enslaved people from the Atlantic Ocean countries. And Freretown in Kenya in 1873 became the resettlement point for formerly enslaved Africans from the Indian Ocean areas. A number of Africans on both sides of the globe saw these projects as a means to achieve freedom, launch the redemption of the African continent, and establish themselves as viable members of the world community (figure 4.2).[5]

When Sierra Leone and Kenya became British colonies, the Diaspora sentiment was muted, although not destroyed. Liberia, however, declared its independence in 1847 and became the second of only two independent African countries, after Ethiopia, until well into the twentieth century. By 1867 some twenty thousand African Americans had settled in Liberia. Many of them had been free in the United States and returned voluntarily with material resources. Liberia thus became a symbol of hope for the regeneration of Africans on the continent and in the Diaspora. Its Declaration of Independence took note of the plight of African peoples abroad, and committed the country to providing "a home for the dispersed children of Africa." Although these returnees carried with them ideas of superiority taught in the United States, they did identify with Africa, which they hoped to redeem and lead into the modern world.

This return movement from the United States coincided with a growing consciousness of and identification with Africa by African Americans. A number of church and social groups had already adopted "African" as a label (e.g., African Methodist Episcopal, or AME, Church), and engaged in activities in the Caribbean and Africa. Although they were influenced by white denominations, African American churches provided the principal opportunities for the development of sustained and meaningful links with Africa and the Diaspora, as well as the outside world generally. Thus, consciousness of

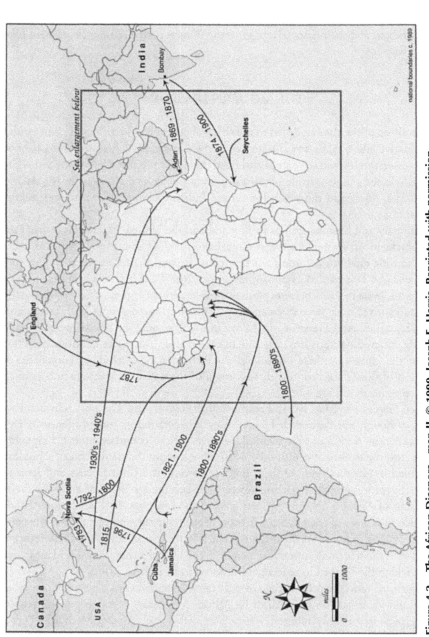

Figure 4.2 The African Diaspora, map II. © 1990, Joseph E. Harris. Reprinted with permission.

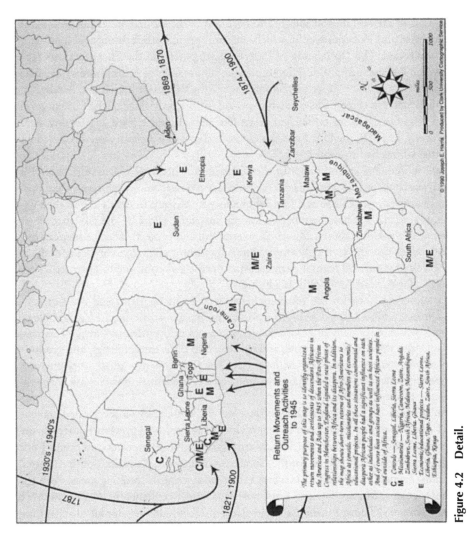

Return Movements and Outreach Activities to 1945

The primary purpose of this map is to identify organized return movements and settlements of descendant Africans to the America and Asia up to 1945 when the Pan-African Congress in Manchester, England signaled a new phase of relationships between Africa and its diaspora. In addition, the map shows short-term returns of Afro-Americans to Africa as consuls, missionaries and members of economic, educational projects. In all these situations continental and diaspora African people had a significant influence on each other as individuals and groups as well as on host societies. And of course host societies have influenced African people in and outside of Africa.

C   Consuls — Senegal, Liberia, Sierra Leone
M   Missionaries — Nigeria, Cameroon, Zaire, Angola, Zimbabwe, South Africa, Malawi, Mozambique, Sierra Leone, Liberia, Ghana
E   Economic/educational projects — Sierra Leone, Liberia, Ghana, Togo, Sudan, Zaire, South Africa, Ethiopia, Kenya

© 1990 Joseph E. Harris. Produced by Clark University Cartographic Service

Figure 4.2   Detail.

a common social condition as well as origin became more deeply embedded in the Black consciousness of the Diaspora.

That a common social condition existed and formed the basis for an international struggle stemmed largely from the centuries-old slave trade and slavery. Europeans and Americans regarded enslaved Africans as chattel and free African Americans as inferior beings. One of the best illustrations of this occurred in the United States Declaration of Independence and Constitution, in which the concepts of both freedom and inhumanity are embedded. The Declaration of Independence portrayed the European settlers as victims who had escaped political and economic inhumanity in Europe and established a refuge for liberty in the American colonies; while the Constitution defined Africans in the United States as three-fifths of a white person. Other provisions of the Constitution allowed "fugitive slaves" to be tracked down like animals and treated as property. And subsequently, in 1858, the U.S. Supreme Court declared that African Americans had no rights that whites had to respect.

While subsequent amendments to the Constitution declared citizenship rights for formerly enslaved people, there has never been a constitutional recognition of the horrendous European and Euro-American inhumanity to Africans in Africa and to their descendants abroad. Nor has there been a strong, sustained effort by the government or the people of the United States as a whole to establish and protect African American humanity, abolitionist and civil rights movements notwithstanding. Stereotypes and myths about Black physical and mental characteristics persist and continue to obstruct equity and justice for African Americans as a group.

A determining factor in the relations between Africans in Africa and their descendants abroad stemmed from decisions made by Europeans at the Berlin Conference of 1884–85, which essentially established the boundaries of the African states.[6] This partition of Africa divided some peoples and cultures into different countries, and grouped others into one country, making them "citizens" by fiat. This new phase of population displacement created internal diasporas and led to irredentist movements that still plague the continent today.

That colonial-era partition and dispersion was also marked by an accelerated gravitation of Africans to and settlement in major cities of the colonial powers: France for the Senegalese, Malians, Ivorians, Haitians, Martiniquans, Guadeloupeans, and others from French-speaking areas; England for the Ghanaians, Nigerians, Kenyans, South Africans, Jamaicans, Trinidadians, Barbadians, and others from English-speaking areas; Portugal for the Angolans, Mozambiquans, Cape Verdeans, and Brazilians; the Netherlands for the Surinamese; Belgium for the Congolese; and the United States for all of these during the late colonial period and especially after World War II. The major cities of the Western powers thus became loci for the gathering of diverse ethnic and political groups of African origin, thereby facilitating the development of an international network linking Africa to its Diaspora.

The critical point to be made about the historical and modern African Diasporas is that the former occurred prior to the partition of Africa and therefore had no basis in a consciousness of the continent as reflected by the new boundaries established during the era of colonial rule. Although the modern dispersion since the colonial era did begin to internalize a consciousness of the colonial territory, most Africans did not directly or fully confront the colonial presence. When the colonial era ended, after less than a century in most cases, the colonial identity had not fully matured. Consequently, until the 1960s, most Africans in Africa retained a primary ethnic allegiance; while their descendants abroad constituted a "stateless" diaspora without a common country of origin, language, religion, or culture. The strength of the connection between Africa and the Diaspora as a people remained essentially their common origin in Africa as a whole, and a common social condition—marginalized socially, economically, and politically—throughout the world.

THE MOBILIZED DIASPORA AND THE NEW AFRICA

A mobilized diaspora consists of people with a consciousness of the identity of their roots and of their occupational and communicational skills, social and economic status, and access to the decision-making bodies of the state. The more the political system in which people live responds to pressure at different levels, the greater their influence will be on domestic and foreign affairs. For Africans in the Diaspora this has meant the mobilization of their communities around race/ethnicity for the exertion of political pressure on elected officials. In time they have elected members of their own group to offices at virtually all levels of local, state, and national government not only in the Black-majority countries of the Caribbean, but also in the United States and recently in Brazil and Colombia.

From the early years of the twentieth century, African American migration from Southern states resulted in the gradual emergence of large segregated communities in Northern American cities—for example, Washington, D.C., Philadelphia, New York City, Detroit, and Chicago. This pattern of migration increased significantly after World War I. In these cities African Americans found better educational and employment opportunities that also attracted Black immigrants from Caribbean countries, notably Jamaica, Barbados, Trinidad, and Panama. New York City became the principal recipient of this emerging international community of African Diasporans.

A somewhat similar development was occurring in England, where London's Black community was expanding with immigrants, primarily from Jamaica, Barbados, and Trinidad. London had long been a place where Blacks from the West Indies, the United States, and Africa had become acquainted as abolitionists, businessmen, journalists, scholars, and travelers. Already in 1900, Henry Sylvester Williams of Trinidad and W. E. B. Du Bois of the United States had convened the first Pan-African Congress to mobilize African people in a coordinated international effort against racism in the African colonies and in the Diaspora.

That 1900 Congress was a wake-up call that demonstrated that Africans and their descendants abroad shared common interests and were prepared to seek a common means to satisfy their concerns. But it was not until after World War I that the Pan-African movement had a sustained impact. DuBois revived the movement and convened four more congresses, in 1919, 1921, 1923, and 1927, that had similar objectives of human rights for African peoples.

Marcus Garvey, a Jamaican, arrived in the United States in 1916 after having traveled widely in the Caribbean and South America, where he protested against white exploitation of Blacks. In the United States he organized the Universal Negro Improvement Association (UNIA), with branches throughout much of the African world. His newspaper, *The Negro World*, appeared in English, French, and Spanish, and made a strong appeal for Black unity, pride, and organization. His Black Star Line was organized not only to transport Blacks who wanted to go to Africa, but also to initiate commercial relations between Africa and its Diaspora. Although his projects failed and he was deported from the United States, Garvey contributed immeasurably to the development of a consciousness of the African Diaspora and to race pride and organization. Garveyites have continued his tradition as they have maintained branches of the UNIA and participated in numerous organizations dedicated to Black progress.

Du Bois and Garvey were giants of their time, but there were many others who contributed significantly to the cause of Africa and its Diaspora between World Wars I and II: Casely Hayford and Kwame Nkrumah of Ghana; Ladipo Solanke and Nnamdi Azikiwe of Nigeria; Duse Mohammed of Sudan; Jomo Kenyatta of Kenya; Candace Gratien of Guadeloupe; Léopold Sédar Senghor of Senegal; Léon Gontran Damas of Guyana; Aimé Césaire of Martinique; Jean Price-Mars and Dantes Bellegarde of Haiti.

A number of less well-known but important leaders and organizations either joined the better-known groups or organized their own groups to mobilize African peoples worldwide: William Leo Hansberry and William R. Steen organized the Ethiopian Research Council in the United States; Max Yergen, W. E. B. Du Bois, and Paul Robeson organized the International Committee on Africa that became the Council for African Affairs; C. L. R. James, a Trinidadian, organized the International Friends of Ethiopia in London, with branches in the United States and the Caribbean; George Padmore, also a Trinidadian, and Ras Makonnen, a Guyanese, organized the International African Service Bureau in London; Alioune Diop, a Senegalese, organized the Society for African Culture in Paris, while John A. Davis and others organized an affiliate in the United States, the American Society for African Culture.

Two Africans who physically and spiritually linked Africa and its Diaspora across the Atlantic, but who have not been accorded the recognition they deserve, were James Aggrey of Ghana and Malaku Bayen of Ethiopia.[7] Aggrey's work as an educator led to the founding of Achimota College in Ghana and influenced the founders of Fort Hare College in South Africa. Both of those institutions pursued a Pan-African perspective on Africa and the Diaspora. In the United States, Aggrey's career as professor and administrator at Livingstone College in North Carolina, and his work with the Phelps-Stokes Fund in New York, influenced many African Americans and others to devote themselves to African causes.

Malaku Bayen formed the Ethiopian World Federation in 1937 in several states of the United States and in the Caribbean as a means of organizing a movement against Italy's aggression in Ethiopia in 1935–41. The official publication of the Federation, *The Voice of Ethiopia*, not only mobilized support for the Ethiopian cause, but also promoted African/Black consciousness in the United States and the Caribbean. Slogans in *The Voice of Ethiopia* about discarding the term "Negro" and adopting "Black,"

"African," and "Ethiopian" were precursors of the 1960s movement that indeed did adopt Black and African as terms of identity.

In short, members of the mobilized Diaspora pioneered the establishment of international organizations for the promotion of African consciousness and solidarity in what essentially became a foreign relations movement. Prevented from being actors in state foreign affairs, these leaders established their own nonstate mechanisms for the conduct of foreign affairs in the interest of Africans and their descendants abroad.

The formation of the Congressional Black Caucus in 1960 represented a major step toward the official participation of Blacks in the foreign affairs of the United States. Mobilized Black voters elected three congressmen in 1960; they became the founding members of the Caucus. That membership increased to forty in 1992 and gave the organization significant political influence. Caucus leaders soon realized that their ticket to having an impact on foreign policy was in African world issues. Without conceding their right to input on foreign affairs generally, they embraced Africa and the Caribbean as their special domain. Members of their staffs followed by forming the African Forum on Foreign Affairs, which soon evolved into TransAfrica, the established lobby for African and Caribbean issues in the United States. Its influence on U.S. policy regarding South Africa and Haiti in particular has legitimized it as a force in world politics for Africa and its Diaspora.[8]

The dynamics of Black nationalism in the African world during the last generation have transformed the meaning of identity in Africa and the Diaspora. Whereas the historical Diaspora was essentially a "stateless" one that relied primarily on an Africa remembered, the post-independence Diaspora promotes a consciousness of new nations, sometimes with new names and ideologies, that challenges the older Diaspora to make choices between conflicting interests not only within the Diaspora community, but also between it and particular African countries. In addition, the existence of more than fifty African countries, with varying social and political conditions and different international interests, complicates further the relationship between Africa and its Diaspora. Moreover, the legacy of colonial internal division and the dispersion of ethnic groups forms an intra-continental Diaspora that African states must also confront.

In the United States, diverse interests and ideologies within the African American community are evident and are complicated by the continuous influx of continental Africans and Americans of African descent from the Caribbean and increasingly from South American countries. Consequently, the geographical area of focus for African Americans has been expanded to include French-, Spanish-, and Portuguese-speaking areas of the Americas.

Noteworthy in this modern phase of the Diaspora is that prior to independence, continental Africans and African Americans used nongovernmental networks (churches, social groups, schools, etc.) as the principal conduits for the promotion of their ideas and policies. With independence, however, African leaders must now negotiate their interests through governments and their representatives, thereby excluding effective nongovernmental agencies of the Diaspora. While this approach maximizes economic dimensions for African states, it minimizes the cultural and social dimensions that continue to sustain the mutual identity between them and their Diaspora, a significant political force in time of need.

Consequently, if direct and effective relations are to be expanded and sustained, Africa and its Diaspora must devise other structures to achieve their goals. This could take the form of an umbrella, nonpolitical organization/foundation that reaches across national boundaries and represents African governments, private organizations, and Diaspora groups for broad consultative purposes and humanitarian assistance. The African world would benefit greatly from having this kind of international structure with the financial capability to initiate and fund programs without reliance on outside financial or political support. This kind of autonomy would enable Africans and their descendants abroad to sustain their political presence and work with greater confidence in alliance with other groups interested in their social, political, and economic well-being.

This form of Pan-Africanism is better described as TransAfricanism, which was best demonstrated in the 1930s when Ethiopia resisted Italian aggression. Organized groups of Americans of African descent in the United States mobilized efforts that resulted in the contribution of money, supplies, and advisors to assist the Ethiopians during and after that war. Some African Americans ventured into private diplomacy, developing a code for communicating directly through their network with Emperor Haile Selassie, and ultimately persuading him to appoint a representative to the United States. These efforts demonstrated the possibilities offered when the strength of African issues compelled action by the Diaspora. Additionally, the involvement of Ethiopians in U.S. groups heightened the political consciousness of African Americans and contributed to their greater participation in the democratic process of their own country.

A problem that has prevented the fuller development of this trend has been the diversity of the groups involved and the scope of issues African Americans have attempted to address internally, while pursuing other issues under the rubric of Pan-Africanism/TransAfricanism. The obvious variety of interests in over fifty African countries and a dozen Caribbean nations continues to divert attention and diffuse limited material resources.

The last decade of the twentieth century was marked by countries and cultures being pulled closer together by technology, such as satellites, computers, and the Internet; by world health issues; by international trade; and by many other developments that continue to reduce time and distance. Moreover, the United States has emerged as the superpower that must respond to issues of world significance. As the preeminent country of mobilized diasporas, the United States can enhance its role by enlisting its diasporas as bridges to troubled lands, as agents of reconciliation, peace, and development.

Over the centuries African Americans have, by their sustained struggle and modest gains for justice, contributed mightily to the positive international image of this country's potential for real democracy. From the abolitionist travels and egalitarian appeals of Frederick Douglass and others in the nineteenth century, to Martin Luther King, Jr., and Malcolm X in the twentieth, and with the adoption by Africans, Asians, and Europeans engaged in freedom struggles of the anthem "We Shall Overcome," African Americans have aligned this country's name with struggles against racism and colonialism. It is no accident that two of the five Black Nobel Peace Prize laureates, Ralph Bunche in 1950 and Martin Luther King, Jr., in 1964, were African Americans; the other three, Chief Albert Lutuli in 1960, Bishop Desmond Tutu in 1984, and President Nelson Mandela in 1993, were South

Africans whose heritage not only parallels that of African Americans, but also has an historic link to the Pan-African movement.

Blacks in the United States are conscious of their relationship to the global African/Black presence; they also have a long and steadfast tradition of association not only with African people, but also with other minorities, the poor and disadvantaged, and with women's rights issues. They also have remained in the vanguard of the struggle for human rights and increasingly are asserting themselves in international affairs. The twenty-first century, therefore, is likely to be marked by a convergence of the rising demands of Blacks and other less-privileged groups in the developing world, and the leadership and skills of persons of African descent in the United States.

James Aggrey was right when he said many years ago that "There is a New Africa coming today and it is a challenge to civilization." I would simply add that that New Africa today is the world of African people, of Africa and its Diaspora.

NOTES

1. See St. Clair Drake, *Black Folk Here and There*, 2 vols. (Los Angeles: Center for Afro-American Studies, University of California, 1986, 1990).

2. See Hans Werner DeBrunner, *Presence and Prestige: Africans in Europe* (Basel: Basler Afrika Bibliographien, 1979); Drake, *Black Folk Here and There*; Joseph Harris, ed., *Global Dimensions of the African Diaspora* (Washington, D.C.: Howard University Press, 1993); and Bernard Lewis, *Race and Slavery in the Middle East* (New York: Oxford University Press, 1990).

3. See Joseph Harris, *The African Presence in Asia: Consequences of the East African Slave Trade* (Evanston, Ill.: Northwestern University Press, 1971).

4. See Joseph E. Inikori, *The Chaining of a Continent: Export Demand for Captives and the History of Africa South of the Sahara, 1450–1870* (Kingston, Jamaica: Institute of Social and Economic Research, 1992).

5. See Tom W. Schick, *Behold the Promised Land* (Baltimore: Johns Hopkins University Press, 1980); Akintola Wyse, *The Krio of Sierra Leone: An Interpretive History* (Washington, D.C.: Howard University Press, 1991); Joseph E. Harris, *Repatriates and Refugees in a Colonial Society: The Case of Kenya* (Washington, D.C.: Howard University Press, 1987).

6. See A. I. Asiwaju, *Partitioned Africans: Ethnic Relations Across Africa's International Boundaries, 1884–1984* (London: C. Hurst, 1985 [1984]).

7. See the papers of James Aggrey (Moorland-Spingarn Research Center, Howard University); Joseph E. Harris, *African-American Reactions to War in Ethiopia, 1936–1941* (Baton Rouge: Louisiana State University Press, 1994).

8. See Ronald W. Walters, *Pan-Africanism in the African Diaspora: An Analysis of the Modern Afrocentric Political Movements* (Detroit: Wayne State University Press, 1993).

5

The Transatlantic Slave Trade and the Making of the Modern World

Howard Dodson

Until recently, the transatlantic slave trade, like the institution of slavery itself, had not figured prominently in public discourse. The past five decades have witnessed a significant qualitative and quantitative increase in studies of the slave trade and slavery in academic circles. But the subject did not begin to become an issue of widespread public discussion and debate until the appearance of Alex Haley's "*Roots*" television series in the mid-1970s. In the midst of the U.S. bicentennial celebration, "*Roots*" provoked more discussions of slavery and the slave trade than any single event or activity since the Civil War.

Elsewhere in the transatlantic world, the government of Brazil sponsored a yearlong national celebration of the centennial of the abolition of slavery in 1988. Museums in Nantes, France, and Liverpool, England, organized and presented major exhibitions and public programs on the role of their nations in the transatlantic slave trade. Commemorations of the Columbus quincentenary throughout the Atlantic world in 1992 focused renewed public interest on these subjects on both sides of the Atlantic. And the United Nations Educational, Scientific and Cultural Organization (UNESCO), with its "Slave Route Project," is collaborating with several African, European, and American governments to heighten the awareness of the multifaceted ways in which the transatlantic slave trade transformed the economic, political, and cultural character of the peoples, nations, and continents involved in the largest, albeit involuntary, migration in the history of humankind.

Yet, despite these recent initiatives, public knowledge of the central defining role of the transatlantic slave trade in the making of the modern world remains extremely limited. Over the past five decades, scholars in Europe, Africa, and the Americas have made the slave trade the object of new historical, economic, political, and cultural studies. Gradually, they have begun to discover and assess the far-reaching impact that the slave trade and slavery had on the societies, nations, and continents of the Atlantic world and, indeed, the modern world.[1] I propose to suggest briefly some of the ways in which the intended and unintended consequences of the slave trade shaped the world we know today.

There is no general agreement about what constitutes the modern world and when it began. I have chosen to date the origins of the modern world from the first of the Columbian transatlantic voyages, for it was that voyage that ushered in the era of European colonial expansion that resulted in, among other things, the organization of the transatlantic slave trade. The slave trade, in turn, fostered the development of entirely new levels of communication, trade, cultural exchange, and economic and political interdependence between the peoples of Europe, Africa, and the Americas. The emergence and development of these interdependent continental relationships distinguishes the modern era from its predecessors.

Over the four-hundred-year history of the slave trade, upwards of twelve million Africans survived the Middle Passage and were distributed throughout the Americas. Estimates of the total number of African lives lost or impaired by the process of warfare, capture, and enslavement number up to one hundred million people. The slave trade in all its facets—capture in Africa, transshipment across the Atlantic, and sale in the Americas—took place in a market-driven, uneven fashion. It was uneven in terms of the time when the migrations occurred, the places from which the African captives were taken, and the islands, continents, and colonies in which they were enslaved. More than 40 percent of the Africans sold in the Western Hemisphere went to Brazil, while only 4.5 to 5 percent ended up in the continental United States. The tiny island of Barbados matched U.S. percentages, while Jamaica almost doubled them. Upwards of 50 percent of the survivors of the Middle Passage were transported to the Americas during the eighteenth century. More than 90 percent of the Africans involved in the trade were from the West African coast.[2]

The demographics of the slave trade take on remarkable significance when studied within the overall context of the peopling of the Americas. Contrary to popular opinion, Africans constituted the majority of the people who migrated from the Old World to the New World during the formative stages of European colonial expansion in the Americas. This basic fact suggests a much larger economic, political, and cultural role for African peoples in American colonial development than we have begun to imagine.[3]

According to historian Ralph Davis in *The Rise of the Atlantic Economy*, "Some six and a half million people migrated to the New World in the three centuries between its discovery by Columbus and the American Revolution of 1776; a million of them white, the remainder Africans, who came unwillingly to slavery."[4] Thus, more than five out of every six people who came to the Americas in the first three centuries after their "discovery" were African. And according to *The Trans-Atlantic Slave Trade: A Database on CD-ROM*, as late as 1820, three times as many Africans as Europeans had come to the Americas.[5] As a result, one of the major consequences of the slave trade was the peopling of the continents and islands of the Western Hemisphere with predominantly African peoples who constituted the demographic foundation on which the societies and cultures of the Americas were built.

We have not studied these facts in history books, and this knowledge has not been a part of our understanding of the development of the Americas. To the contrary, the histories of the Americas have been written from colonial perspectives that have neglected to take into account the economic, political, and sociocultural consequences of the undeniable fact that the overwhelming majority of the people involved in the development of the Americas were African.

Those of us who are involved in the study of the African Diaspora and the American experience are faced with two intellectual challenges: to set the record straight about the nature of African experiences in the Western Hemisphere, and to rewrite in a fundamental way the history of the Americas to include the impact of the African presence, and African economic, political, and sociocultural activity, on the shaping of the Americas and the modern world. If more than five-sixths of the peoples who developed the new societies of the Western Hemisphere have not been included in the telling of its history, then we do not know very much about this history.

Africa's multiplicity of ethnic groups, with their cultural, religious, and linguistic diversity, was represented in the populations involved in the slave trade. Frequently as much strangers to each other as they were to their European captors, Africans, upon arriving on American shores, began to refashion themselves into new peoples. They brought with them their Yoruba, Akan, Bakongo, and other cultures, which they interconnected and intertwined with the cultures and experiences of other Africans, as well as of the indigenous peoples and the peoples of the various European colonial powers. Africans, as a result, were transformed into new people who were both biologically and culturally the products of their New World experience.[6]

In the process of re-creating themselves, these New World Africans invented new forms of communication. Because the languages that had served them well in Africa did not serve them in the new environment, they created throughout the Western Hemisphere new language systems at variance with the English, Dutch, Spanish, French, and Portuguese of their colonizers.

Africans and their descendants also invented new religious expressions. Africans brought with them the religions they had practiced in Africa, and they and their descendants transformed them into new syncretic systems drawing from several African cultural streams. They took up Euro-American religions, put their cultural stamp on them, and transformed them into something new and different. The Christianity that African Americans practice and the ways in which we practice Christianity in the United States are qualitatively different from what the master class practiced or intended.[7]

New World African peoples also created new foods, new literatures, new musical forms, new dances, and new social, political, and cultural organizations. African cultural forms gave birth to the blues and jazz in the United States, the tango in Argentina, the guaguancó in Cuba, the samba in Brazil, and the cumbia in Colombia. Carnivals from New Orleans to Buenos Aires are characterized by African rhythmic and masking traditions. Gumbo in Louisiana and feijoada in Brazil are just two popular examples of dishes from the many New World African cuisines. Indeed, few if any American popular cultural forms have not been influenced in some way by the African presence. So, if there is any truth to the notion that the Americas are a New World, it was the African peoples who were central to the creation of these new forms of human existence, as expressed in new economic, social, and cultural systems and relationships, who made it new.[8]

The transatlantic slave trade also had a significant impact on the development of modern Europe, because Europeans had to reorganize their social, economic, political, and cultural institutions in order to carry out this vast trade. Eric Williams has demonstrated the central role of the slave trade and slavery in the development of British capitalism in his book *Capitalism and Slavery.*[9] The same is true for the other European nations that built their modern economies on the slave trade. New industries were created to build and supply slave ships, and new cities were created to organize the shipping activity and to exploit the products being produced in the colonies. The economic and political activities of the major European powers were, in fact, shaped and reshaped by the wars they waged with one another to gain and maintain control over the slave trade and the American colonies.[10]

It was, of course, impossible to disrupt the lives of tens of millions of Africans without having a devastating impact on their continent. If the slave trade provided the foundation for the development of Europe during the modern era, it was also the root cause of the underdevelopment of Africa. There are several immediately obvious aspects of that underdevelopment to which we might point. First was the loss of human capital—up to one hundred million disrupted or terminated lives, and more than twelve million people were actually transferred to labor in the Americas.

Another consequence was the distortion of the traditional organization of African life. As the transatlantic slave trade grew more virulent in its quest for human souls, African political and economic infrastructures were reorganized to accommodate this new kind of economic activity. Entire societies were transformed from their traditional ways of functioning into slave-catching societies, and people's lives became organized around how to make war and gather other people for the transatlantic slave trade.[11]

In conclusion, let me reiterate several points that indicate ways in which the slave trade as an economic, political, and sociocultural phenomenon was seminal in the making of the modern world. First, the slave trade was central to the development of Europe and the Americas. Second, it was central to the underdevelopment of Africa. Finally, it was through the slave trade and its related economic activities that Europe; Africa; North, Central, and South America; and the Caribbean were knit into a system of mutual interdependency, with Europe and the United States as the dominant, controlling influences that they are today.

NOTES

1. Cf. Joseph E. Inikori and Stanley L. Engerman, eds., *The Atlantic Slave Trade: Effects on Economies, Societies and People in Africa, the Americas, and Europe* (Durham, N.C.: Duke University Press, 1992); Herbert S. Klein, *The Middle Passage: Comparative Studies in the Atlantic Slave Trade* (Princeton, N.J.: Princeton University Press, 1978); and John Thornton, *Africa and Africans in the Making of the Atlantic World, 1400–1680* (New York: Cambridge University Press, 1992).

2. Cf. Philip Curtin, *The Atlantic Slave Trade: A Census* (Madison: University of Wisconsin Press, 1969).

3. Cf. Curtin, *The Atlantic Slave Trade*; Ralph Davis, *The Rise of the Atlantic Economies* (Ithaca, N.Y.: Cornell University Press, 1973).

4. Davis, *The Rise of the Atlantic Economies*, 125.

5. David Eltis, David Richardson, Stephen D. Behrendt, and Herbert S. Klein, eds., *The Trans-Atlantic Slave Trade: A Database on CD-ROM* (Cambridge: Cambridge University Press, 2000), 3.

6. Cf. Roger Bastide, *African Civilizations in the New World* (New York: Harper Torchbooks, 1972); Melville J. Herskovits, *The New World Negro: Selected Papers in Afro-American Studies*, ed. Frances S. Herskovits (Bloomington: Indiana University Press, 1966); and Sidney W. Mintz and Richard Price, *The Birth of African-American Culture* (Boston: Beacon Press, 1992).

7. Cf. Bastide, *African Civilizations*; Herskovits, *The New World Negro*; and Mintz and Price, *The Birth of African-American Culture*.

8. Cf. Bastide, *African Civilizations*; Herskovits, *The New World Negro*; and Mintz and Price, *The Birth of African-American Culture*.

9. Eric Williams, *Capitalism and Slavery* (Chapel Hill: University of North Carolina Press, 1964, [1944]).

10. Inikori and Engerman, *The Atlantic Slave Trade*.

11. Cf. Inikori and Engerman, *The Atlantic Slave Trade*; Paul E. Lovejoy, "The Impact of the Slave Trade on Africa in the Eighteenth and Nineteenth Centuries," *Journal of African History* 30 (1989); and Patrick Manning, *Slavery and African Life: Occidental, Oriental and African Slave Trades* (New York: Cambridge University Press, 1990).

6

✳

Africans and Economic Development in the Atlantic World, 1500–1870

Joseph E. Inikori

In spite of the heated debate that has surrounded the issue of African slavery in the Americas for several decades, the literature examining the role of African slavery in the economic history of the Atlantic world is relatively recent. For many years the favored subject of the debate was the politics of abolition.[1] Next in volume to the literature on abolition is that on the private profitability of slavery and the slave trade. An important characteristic of the literature on private profitability is its narrow geographical focus on the economic relationship between the individual Western European economies (England, France, the Netherlands, Portugal, and Spain) and their American colonies.[2]

The earliest work that came closest to focusing on a systematic study of the economic history of the Atlantic basin as a unit of analysis within which to locate the role of African slavery in the Americas was *The Rise of the Atlantic Economies*. Whereas the title gave the misleading impression that the Atlantic basin was being studied as an economic unit in a process of development over time, Ralph Davis actually argued that "the main influences on European economic development arose within the countries of Europe themselves," which freed him from the need to study interconnections between the economies in the Atlantic basin.[3] Consequently, *The Rise of the Atlantic Economies* is basically a story of the independent rise of the national or regional economies in the Atlantic basin, in which the economies of Western Africa are not even included.

Another dominant part of recent literature concerns the contributions of African peoples to cultural developments in the Atlantic world. A particularly disturbing trend in this part of the literature is the glorification of the cultural achievements of oppressed and exploited Africans in the Americas, with emphasis on the freedom they had that allowed them to make these cultural achievements, but no reference made to their oppression and exploitation.[4] The other currently popular part of the subject concerns various aspects of the volume of the trade that brought Africans to the Americas as enslaved people: the numbers exported and imported; the levels and causes of mortality among the enslaved and the crew in the Atlantic crossing; the shipping methods employed; the age and sex ratios of Africans exported and their determinants; and the ethnic and African regions of origin.

While all of the above issues deserve attention in their own right, their dominance in the literature on African slavery in the Americas has helped to obscure what ought to be the central focus of study—the role of the Atlantic slave trade and African slavery in the Americas in the interconnected process of economic change in the Atlantic world between 1500 and 1870. This gap in the literature is gradually being remedied. In the past decade and a half or so, a handful of scholars have begun to examine the economies of the Atlantic area as parts of one complex economic unit that went through an interconnected process of change between 1500 and 1870, centered on African slavery in the Americas.[5] This chapter attempts to highlight some of the main elements of this slowly growing new literature.

For purposes of conceptual clarity, the first part of this chapter briefly discusses the main analytic ideas that inform the arguments in the new literature. A descriptive discussion of the state of the major economies of the Atlantic basin by about 1450, and the factors constraining their development at the time, is presented in the second part. Part three examines the growth of Atlantic commerce between 1500 and 1870 and discusses the results of an attempt to quantify the contribution of African slavery to this growth of commerce. Finally, the comparative impact of this growth of Atlantic commerce on the development process in the major national and regional economies of the Atlantic basin is examined in part four.

CONCEPTUAL CLARIFICATION

Economic historians usually employ, explicitly or implicitly, some form of economic logic informed by one type of economic theory or another. Hence, searching for an appropriate set of economic theories that help pose the right set of questions concerning the problem at hand, identifying the relevant sets of evidence to look for, and ordering and interpreting the facts correctly are as important as empirical research in the field and the archives.

Clearly, a fundamental barrier in scientific discussions concerning the economics of the Atlantic slave trade and African slavery in the Americas has been conceptual. But because scholars do not usually state explicitly the theoretical assumptions that inform the questions they pose and the selection and interpretation of evidence they make, the controversies that arise often center on the conclusions reached rather than on the theoretical assumptions that informed the questions articulated, and the selection and interpretation of evidence made. The truth is that the questions raised, the information selected, and the interpretation offered all depend ultimately on the logical assumptions, stated or unstated, with which economic historians conduct their research and do their writing. Fundamental changes in these assumptions lead to major changes in the questions posed, the evidence collected, the interpretations made, and the conclusions reached.

A careful reading of the literature on the economics of the Atlantic slave trade and African slavery in the Americas offers many examples of obsolete or inappropriate theories. Because scholars have not usually stated explicitly the theories that inform their analysis, they are not debated in order to flush out inappropriate logical assumptions together with the questions and conclusions to which they lead. This section attempts to identify theoretical frameworks appropriate for the problem at hand.

The main analytical task for the economic historian concerned with the problem of economic change in the *longue durée* (very long time periods, covering hundreds of years)—the kind of problem to which the issues raised in this chapter belong—is to identify long-run patterns in the process of economic development, from a starting point of predominantly subsistence agriculture and small-scale manufacturing to a terminal point of predominantly large-scale, mechanized manufacturing and commercialized, industrialized agriculture. For many decades, going back to the eighteenth century, but more elaborately from the 1880s (when explaining the historical origins of the English Industrial Revolution became a major academic issue), the logical assumptions that informed the writings on our subject came largely from the classical economists.

Given the socioeconomic and political environment within which their theories were formulated, the classical economists devoted most of their theories to issues of long-term economic development and the factors that were critical in the process. Trade, especially overseas trade, was given much prominence.[6] Changes in the organization and technology of production in agriculture and manufacturing were viewed theoretically as a function of expanding markets. It was because of the dominant role that the classical economists assigned to trade that Adam Smith viewed government interference, which restricted the growth of foreign trade, as detrimental to long-term economic development.[7]

Neoclassical economics, the theoretical ideas of which were dominant from the late nineteenth century to World War II, was not particularly concerned with issues of long-term economic development. Hence, economic historians concerned with such issues during this period depended on the economic logic of classical economics for their understanding and interpretation of the evidence. Generally, they gave the pride of place to the growth of overseas trade—what they called the "Commercial Revolution"—in their explanation of Western European development between the seventeenth and nineteenth centuries.[8] Their works say very little or nothing at all about the role of slavery and the Atlantic slave trade. But by dealing with the issue of development and stressing the role of overseas trade, their analysis can be logically expanded to accommodate the notion of the Atlantic world as a complex economic unit that went through a process of change centered on African slavery in the Americas.

The period from the close of World War II to the early 1980s witnessed the formulation and establishment of a new set of economic theories with the apparent capacity to deal with issues of long-term development. Formulated at a time when international trade had been severely disrupted by two world wars and the Great Depression, and confidence in international trade as an engine of growth and development was badly shaken, post-war economic growth theories were inward-looking, with closed economy assumptions as their premise.[9] The influence of these post-war growth theories in the years between the late 1940s and early 1980s, among other things, undermined historical explanations of development centered on overseas trade. The role of slavery and the Atlantic slave trade as factors in the historical explanation of comparative levels of economic development in the Atlantic basin was, in consequence, drastically discounted during the period, as would be expected. These were the years when independent internal forces located in agricultural progress, population growth, sociopolitical structure, and autonomous (exogenous) change in science and technology were at the center stage of historical explanations of economic development and economic backwardness.

But not everyone accepted the change as good economics or good history. In particular, there were economists and historians who insisted that technical change and technological innovation in the preindustrial epochs were not autonomous (exogenous) variables in the development process. On the contrary, they believed, technological change in preindustrial economies was a function of market expansion and institutional transformation, all associated with the growth of population and overseas trade.[10]

Contemporary development processes in the Third World, especially Asia and Latin America, provided powerful support for these traditional positions. Apparently in response to the empirical evidence from these more recent development processes economists began fashioning new growth theories in the 1980s, with emphasis on the role of foreign trade, and technology ceased to be viewed as autonomous (exogenous) and came to be seen as a function of market growth and size.[11] The analytical tools of the new growth theory provide considerable logical strength to historical explanations of development centered on the growth and development of markets associated with overseas trade expansion and population growth.

THE ATLANTIC BASIN ECONOMIES IN THE FIFTEENTH CENTURY

In the context of the issues addressed in this chapter, the Atlantic basin economies include the economies of Western Europe, Western Africa, and the Americas. In current terms, Western Europe includes Italy, Spain, Portugal, France, Switzerland, Austria, Germany, the Netherlands, Belgium, Luxemburg, Britain, and Ireland; Western Africa includes the countries of West Africa, from Mauritania in the northwest to Chad and Cameroon in the east, and those of West-Central Africa, from Gabon in the north to Namibia in the south; and the Americas include all the countries of South and Central America, the Caribbean, and North America.[12]

Before the middle decades of the fifteenth century, the three broad regions of the Atlantic—Western Europe, Western Africa, and the Americas—operated in isolation from one another, although there were indirect trade relations between Western Europe and Western Africa through the merchants of the Middle East and North Africa. The Atlantic Ocean was then a relatively quiet sea, the Mediterranean being at the time the main center of seaborne international trade in the world. It was during the period 1500–1870 that the Atlantic was transformed into by far the greatest center of world trade, with far-reaching consequences for the economies of the Atlantic basin and those of the rest of the world.

Before the process of transformation began in the mid-fifteenth century, the Atlantic basin economies were all preindustrial and precapitalist. The bulk of the populations around the Atlantic was engaged in subsistence agricultural production (that is, the greater part of the output never reached the market, but was consumed directly by the producers themselves). Elaborate craft production also existed in all the economies. It is fair to say that these economies were able to meet the basic needs of the people within them; there was general self-sufficiency. The main elements that set them apart at this time were in the areas of market and sociopolitical development, and the driving factors that determined the relative levels of market development were population growth and export production.

Population estimates in the three regions of the Atlantic, with varying degrees of uncertainty, indicate that Western Europe reached relatively high average densities very much earlier than the other regions. The available figures show that as early as 1200, Western Europe already had about sixty-one million people, increasing to seventy-three million by 1300. As a result of the general crisis of the fourteenth century, which peaked in mid-century with the Black Death, the numbers went down to forty-five million in 1400, before resuming another round of growth and reaching sixty million in 1450 and seventy-eight million in 1550.[13] E. A. Wrigley suggests that the area of England, 50,333 square miles, represents 5.6 percent of the total area of Western Europe as defined above; the latter area, therefore, comes to approximately 898,804 square miles.[14] Thus, average population densities for Western Europe were approximately sixty-eight persons per square mile in 1200, eighty-one in 1300, sixty-seven in 1450, and eighty-seven in 1550. Since the population was not evenly distributed, certain areas had much greater densities than the average. The most densely populated areas were in northern Italy, where Florence had about two hundred persons per square mile in the mid-1550s, and several great Italian cities had total populations ranging from 100,000 to 200,000.[15]

Considerable controversy surrounds estimates of the populations of Western Africa and the Americas in the fifteenth century. Extrapolating backward from colonial censuses, and employing questionable assumptions on the impact of the Atlantic slave trade, John Caldwell estimated that the total population of Africa in 1500 would have been forty-seven million.[16] This is an extremely small population for a huge continent. If the figure is assigned to West Africa alone, with an area of 2.4 million square miles, the density in 1500 would have been approximately twenty persons per square mile; if it is assigned to Central Africa alone, with three million square miles, the density would have been only sixteen persons per square mile; assigning it to both regions, the density would have been nine persons per square mile.[17] From what is known of Africa's sociopolitical organization, agriculture, and land-use pattern, the continent's population must have been considerably greater than forty-seven million in 1500.

Based on various documents, including accounts by Arab travelers, Djibril Tamsir Niane estimated that the total population of Africa in the sixteenth century was about 200 million; the population of the Mali empire in the middle of the fifteenth century is put at forty to fifty million.[18] If Niane's figure for all of Africa is assigned to West Africa and Central Africa only, the average density would be thirty-seven persons per square mile. Thus, assigning it to Africa as a whole and excluding the areas of desert, that figure does not seem unreasonably large.

However, using a modified form of Caldwell's procedure, Patrick Manning estimated the total population of the coastal areas of Western Africa to be 22.7 million in 1850.[19] He stated in a later work that the population of the western coast of Africa in 1700 was about twenty-five million, and that of the savanna region of sub-Saharan Africa and the Horn about twenty million.[20] Under Manning's view of the impact of the Atlantic slave trade, the population of the western coast of Africa in the fifteenth century would be about the same as that of 1700, that is, twenty-five million. Assuming from the reading of Manning that the area of the western coast is one-half that of West Africa and Central Africa combined, we get an average population density of approximately nine persons per square mile for Western Africa in the fifteenth century. This seems rather low. We may settle for a figure somewhere between Manning's and Niane's, but closer to Niane's, say, an average of twenty persons per square mile, reaching forty or more in the more densely populated areas, particularly in West Africa.

Similar disagreements surround the estimates for the Americas. A summary of the literature in the form of a synthesis puts the total population of all the Americas in the late fifteenth century at 57.3 million, distributed in percentages as follows: North America 7.7; Mexico 37.3; Central America 9.9; the Caribbean 10.2; the Andes 20.1; Lowland South America 14.8.[21] Whatever one makes of the conflicting figures, the indication is that extremely low population densities characterized the territories of the Americas in the late fifteenth century. It has been said that densities below ten persons per square kilometer applied to over 90 percent of modern Latin America in 1492.[22]

The operation of these differing population densities, in conjunction with differences in other factors such as geography and access to overseas trade, meant that market institutions and sociopolitical organizations reached differing levels of development in the three broad regions of the Atlantic by the fifteenth century. In Western Europe, continuous growth of population before the Black Death led to the movement of populations from centers of early settlement to unsettled or lightly settled regions in a process of internal colonization. This population expansion and internal colonization stimulated the growth of local and interregional trade, the mechanism of which was the differing resource endowments of the old and new regions of settlement.[23] The Low Countries (the Netherlands, Belgium, and Luxemburg) and Italy became major centers of manufacturing; so too were several German city-states. Initially England specialized in the production of raw materials, especially raw wool, for export to the continent in exchange for manufactures. By the fifteenth century, however, England had become a major producer of woolen textiles, the bulk of which was exported to continental consumers.

In addition to the growing internal trade, Western Europe was also drawn into the international trade of the Mediterranean led by the merchants of the Italian city-states. Through the international trade of the Mediterranean, Western Europe had access to gold imports from Western Africa, which contributed considerably to the amount of money in circulation. The combined force of international and interregional trade, along with population expansion, led to the commercialization of socioeconomic life in much of Western Europe by the fifteenth century, particularly in Italy, the Netherlands, and England.

In Western Africa, a considerable amount of trade also developed during the same period, especially in West Africa. Geographically based resources were traded between the savanna and forest communities, and the gold trade across the Sahara stimulated a considerable amount of internal trade within West Africa. The extent of market transactions in the economies of West Africa in the early years of their contact with European traders is indirectly indicated by the structure of their imports. This is a subject that I have just begun to study systematically. What I have collected from the British archives so far suggests that the imports in the initial years were overwhelmingly in the form of money, such as cowries. This is an indication of growing market transactions that needed an expanding medium of exchange.

However, the much lower population densities in Western Africa, in addition to problems of physical geography and a disadvantageous location in relation to the major center of trade at the time—the Mediterranean—meant that West African market developments were at a much lower level in the fifteenth century than in Western Europe. In fact, in several areas of West-Central Africa, where population densities were generally about four persons per square mile by 1400, it has been said that hunting and gathering were still providing about 60 percent of the people's food in the fifteenth century, even though agriculture was already well developed.[24]

Market developments were at much lower levels still in the Americas. Added to the problem of extremely low population densities were serious difficulties of physical geography. The major centers of population concentration in Mexico, Central America, and the Andean valleys were separated from one another by high mountains and dense forests. Hence, there was very little contact between these population centers. What is more, isolation from the rest of the world meant that the Americas had no access to the trading opportunities in the Old World that would have given commercial value to the vast natural resources of the region. Given this situation, the economies of the Americas were overwhelmingly dominated by subsistence production in the late fifteenth century. Even in the major centers of population where elaborate state systems developed— the Inca, Aztec, and Maya state systems—redistributive exchange through the state was far more important than market exchange.[25]

Thus a major factor limiting economic development in the Atlantic basin in the fifteenth century was limited trade opportunity. Even in Western Europe, where trade had grown most considerably, trading opportunities had become increasingly limited by the sixteenth century. Inadequate local resources did not permit overall population size to go beyond a certain level, as the crisis of the fourteenth century shows. Also, the growth of nation-states in the fifteenth and sixteenth centuries, none of which was powerful enough to impose its will on the others, led to an atomistic competition for resources among the states of Western Europe.[26] This situation further limited trading opportunities within Western Europe as competition among the nation-states tended to encourage the growth of self-sufficiency, each state employing protective measures to stimulate domestic industrial production, with the French leading the way in the seventeenth century.

These restrictive practices, together with the other factors limiting trading opportunities in Western Europe, would produce a general crisis in the seventeenth century.[27] The colonization of the Americas and the expansion of commodity production there for Atlantic commerce from the sixteenth century, particularly between 1650 and 1850, ultimately eliminated the constraints to the growth of trading opportunities. This permitted economic development to proceed in the Atlantic basin and to produce industrial revolutions in some of the economies in the nineteenth century. The latter issues, among others, are addressed in the two remaining sections.

SLAVERY AND ATLANTIC COMMERCE

The pursuit of trading opportunities by the merchant class of Western Europe, and the need for more and more resources by the competing governments of the Western European nation-states, led to the establishment of regular seaborne contacts, first with Western Africa, then with Asia and the Americas, in the course of the fifteenth and sixteenth centuries. Seaborne contact with Western Africa from the 1440s brought Western Europeans into direct contact with West African gold and other products of the region, such as pepper, ivory, wood, and copper. Portuguese colonization of the islands off the Atlantic coast of Western Africa—Madeira, the Cape Verde Islands, and São Tomé—was accompanied by the establishment of sugarcane and cotton plantations worked by enslaved Africans brought from the mainland. In the fifteenth and sixteenth centuries, however, European trade with Western Africa was dominated by gold exports.[28]

Ultimately, it was the colonization of the Americas and the exploitation of their vast natural resources from the sixteenth century that turned the Atlantic into the greatest trading center in the world by the eighteenth and nineteenth centuries. The main products that fueled the expansion of trade all around the Atlantic during the period were silver and gold, sugar, coffee, cotton, tobacco, and rice.

In the sixteenth century, silver and gold from Spanish America were the main products, although Portuguese America (Brazil) began producing sugar on a large scale from the late sixteenth century. Spanish official records show that between 1503 and 1650 a total of about 580 million ounces of silver and 6.4 million ounces of gold were imported into Spain from the Americas. Smuggling was so widespread that the official figures do not represent total imports. Much gold was also produced in Brazil and exported to Portugal in the eighteenth century. But by far the most important product in the growth of Atlantic commerce, particularly from 1650, was sugar. By the nineteenth century cotton and coffee became relatively more important.

A recent estimate suggests that the average annual value of Atlantic commerce organized around these products in the middle decades of the seventeenth century was roughly £20 million (sterling); it rose to £40 million by the middle of the eighteenth century; and in the last decades of the eighteenth century it was running at £110 million.[29] These amounts do not include the phenomenal growth of trade within Western Europe based on the reexporting of the American products. Between 1650 and 1850 large-scale commodity production in the Americas did not only transform the Atlantic into the busiest trading mart in the world, but the American products also provided the basis for a considerable expansion of trade within Europe and between Europe and Asia. Trade between England and its European partners, France and its European partners, the Netherlands and its European partners, Spain and its European partners, Portugal and its European partners—all depended heavily on the American products during the period.

English reexports grew from £900,000 in 1663–69, when they were 22 percent of all English exports, to £5.8 million in 1772–74, by which time they made up 37 percent of all exports.[30] In addition, English domestic exports to Spain and Portugal were paid for with the silver and gold from Spanish and Portuguese American colonies, and some of these exports actually ended up in those colonies. Spanish and Portuguese imports from other Western European countries during this period were similarly paid for.[31] In turn, the silver and gold received from Spain and Portugal by these countries provided the means of exchange for their domestic trade and supported their Asian trade that could not be conducted without American bullion.

France also enjoyed a major boom in its reexporting of American colonial products to other Western European countries. Between 1730 and 1776 French reexporting of American colonial products increased by a factor of eight, while French domestic exports only tripled.[32] The redistribution of the French American products was carried out by Dutch traders, so that the trade of the Netherlands in Europe also depended heavily on the American products.

Thus, what historians refer to as the Commercial Revolution of the seventeenth and eighteenth centuries in Western Europe was a product of large-scale commodity production for Atlantic commerce in the Americas. It stimulated considerable expansion of production and income in Western Europe, whose economies were largely Americanized. For England in particular, the reexporting of the American products helped pay for the importation of vital raw materials, such as high quality iron and naval materials from the Baltic.

So what exactly was the contribution of Africans to the Commercial Revolution of the seventeenth and eighteenth centuries in the Atlantic basin? As was noted earlier, the Americas were very thinly populated in the late fifteenth century. European conquest and colonization in the early sixteenth century further worsened the situation as the preexisting population was virtually wiped out everywhere within a few decades by European exploitation and European diseases.[33] In consequence, large-scale production for export in the Americas could not be conducted on the basis of the local labor supply. Yet demographic, economic, and political conditions in Europe had not as yet resulted in large-scale migration of labor, voluntary or forced, to the Americas. The few Europeans who did migrate engaged in largely subsistence production because of the abundant supply of land.

In this situation, it was the forced migration of Africans through the Atlantic slave trade that made possible large-scale production of commodities for Atlantic commerce in the Americas. Enslaved Africans in the Americas became the forced specialized producers of the American products that fueled the growth of Atlantic commerce in the seventeenth and eighteenth centuries. According to a recent estimate, at least 75 percent of the total value of the American products traded during the period was produced by Africans and their descendants in the Americas.[34]

ATLANTIC COMMERCE AND ECONOMIC DEVELOPMENT IN THE ATLANTIC BASIN

The phenomenal expansion of Atlantic commerce in the seventeenth and eighteenth centuries removed a major constraint to the growth of trading opportunities for Western European economies. As expanding markets gave vent for domestic resources, real incomes grew, the division of labor proceeded, and industrial production developed, especially in countries like England and France, which had large colonial markets in the Americas to which they sent their manufactures. Growing industrial production created new jobs, which encouraged peasant families to abandon the long-standing tradition of tailoring their demographic behavior to access to land. This gave rise to sustained population growth for the first time in Western Europe, based on declining age at marriage and greater incidence of marriage.[35] For example, the population of England increased from 5.1 million in 1701 to 16.7 million in 1851.[36]

Population growth, greater division of labor, and increased real incomes all combined to widen the domestic market in Western European countries at the same time that non-European markets in the Atlantic basin continued to expand. It was in this environment that the first Industrial Revolution in the world took place in Western Europe, and it was the country with the largest share of Atlantic commerce in the closing years of the eighteenth century, England, that made the greatest progress in the first half of the nineteenth century. England's closet rivals in Atlantic commerce, France and the Netherlands, followed later. The example of these Atlantic seaboard economies was to be imitated forcefully in the latter half of the nineteenth century.

The defining characteristics of the English Industrial Revolution were major sustained changes in the organization and technology of industrial production. This has led some economic historians to discount the role of Atlantic commerce, believing that technological change in England was a matter of chance.[37] Both the course and regional location of technological change in England in the eighteenth and nineteenth centuries show unambiguously that the development derived its motive force from market growth and size. The same market reasons that explain England's leadership in technological change at this time also explain the preeminence of Lancashire, Yorkshire, and the West Midlands in the English Industrial Revolution. From 1086 to 1650, these three regions were among the most backward regions in England in terms of social structure and agricultural and industrial production, especially Lancashire. The success of these three regions in securing overseas markets in the period 1750–1850, relative to the previously more prosperous agricultural and manufacturing counties of the south of England, explains the miracle in the growth of their industrial production and in the pace of their technological innovation.[38]

Similarly, economic development in the United States during the period was derived from the expansion of Atlantic commerce. The process was propelled by early regional specialization in which the southern colonies employed enslaved Africans in plantation agriculture to produce commodities for Atlantic commerce, the middle colonies produced foodstuffs for the plantations of the Caribbean, and the northeastern colonies sold shipping and commercial services to New World territories producing commodities for Atlantic commerce. This regional specialization, aided by government policy and natural resource endowment, gave rise to the growth of manufacturing in the northeastern United States.

The phenomenal growth of slave-based cotton production for Atlantic commerce between 1790 and 1860 extended the regional specialization to the West, where food production grew in response to growing demand in the cotton-growing South and the trading and manufacturing Northeast. Cotton production in the southern states increased from 2 million pounds (weight) in 1790 to 1.9 billion pounds in 1860, while the enslaved population in these states grew from 642,000 in 1790 to 3,117,000 in 1850. In the 1850s, 76.5 percent of the cotton output was exported. This expansion of cotton production in the South drove regional specialization and migration into the West, all of which triggered the expansion of the domestic market. The resulting expanded domestic market, in turn, stimulated sustained technological innovation in commerce and industry in the United States.[39]

Latin America and the Caribbean also made considerable advances in the development of commodity production and trade following the growth of Atlantic commerce between 1650 and 1850. The thinly populated regions where subsistence production was overwhelmingly dominant in the fifteenth century were now dominated by production for export and for internal exchange in relatively large domestic markets. Considering the state of affairs in the late fifteenth century, this is certainly not a mean achievement. However, the socioeconomic structure that was created in the process, and the social basis of political power associated with it, did not permit an industrial revolution in these territories in the nineteenth century. Rather, their socioeconomic structure predisposed them to play more of a supporting role for the Industrial Revolution in Western Europe and North America.

Now what about Western Africa? The evidence shows clearly that the rapid growth of Atlantic commerce during the period was achieved at the expense of economic development in Western Africa. In the first instance, we have to view the development of Atlantic commerce during the period under consideration as a process in which Western Africa and the Americas ultimately competed in the production of tropical and semitropical products for Atlantic-wide commerce organized by the merchants of Western Europe. In this competition, Western Africa and the Americas had their areas of relative advantage and disadvantage. It may be conceded that the then known natural resources of the Americas, in terms of agricultural land and mineral resources, appeared to Western European entrepreneurs to be relatively more plentiful than those of Western Africa. In all probability, however, the greatest advantage of the Americas, from the viewpoint of Western European entrepreneurs of the time and their governments, was the fact that the Americas were transformed into European colonies while, apart from a few islands and limited areas of Angola, Western Africa remained practically independent. Other things being equal, the latter fact made European entrepreneurs more favorably disposed toward the Americas rather than Western Africa in the development of commodity production for Atlantic commerce.

But other things were not equal. As earlier shown, while population densities in Western Africa were low in the fifteenth century relative to those in Western Europe, densities in the Americas were even lower. To make matters worse, within a few decades of European colonization in the sixteenth century, the preexisting populations were virtually wiped out everywhere. Thus, as the process of developing commodity production for Atlantic commerce began in the sixteenth century, the Americas were seriously handicapped by an acute labor shortage. Since the labor problem could not be solved through massive migration from Western Europe, forced or voluntary, as stated above, it can be argued that Western Africa had an overall edge in the development of commodity production for Atlantic commerce during the period for as long as it retained its relative advantage in labor supply.

But it failed to retain that advantage. Because of widespread political fragmentation in the fifteenth century, and the relatively low level of market development, it was easy for European traders to present minimal material incentives that significantly altered relative prices in favor of captive production for export as enslaved laborers to the Americas at considerably low prices. In this way, the Atlantic slave trade transferred Western Africa's main advantage, labor, to the Americas. And once the process of taking captives for export was established, it generated sociopolitical and economic conditions that helped make Western Africa's economies less and less competitive in the production of commodities for Atlantic commerce. Meanwhile, the Americas continued to use Africans and their descendants to develop production for Atlantic commerce.[40]

To illustrate, the official value of West Africa's export of commodities to Britain in the 1750s was only £36,518 per annum, at which time the value of captives exported as enslaved laborers was over 90 percent of the total value of West Africa's Atlantic commerce, even though the captives were sold very cheaply.[41] After the abolition of the British slave trade in 1807, several parts of West Africa, especially Senegambia, began the difficult process of developing commodity production for Atlantic commerce under conditions inherited from the slave trade era, while European and American traders continued the slave trade. Under these mixed conditions, the value of West Africa's commodity production for Atlantic commerce rose to £821,337 per annum in the 1830s, during which time the value of captives exported was still as high as 54.3 percent of the total value of West Africa's Atlantic commerce.[42] In comparison, in Brazil, where market production scarcely existed in the fifteenth century, and where commodity production for Atlantic commerce in the period 1650–1850 was predominantly by Africans and their descendants, exports were valued at about £4.4 million (sterling) in 1750 and £5.4 million in the 1840s.[43]

In this way, the economies of Western Africa lost the stimulus for economic development that other economies in the Atlantic basin received from expanded commodity production for Atlantic commerce. What was worse, the production of captives for export, which became the specialized function of Western Africa in the Atlantic economic system, was very damaging to the process of economic development in Western Africa, given a starting point of extremely low ratios of population to cultivable land, and agricultural economies based predominantly on subsistence production, as shown earlier.

Even skeptics agree that the Atlantic slave trade kept Western Africa's population at a stationary level between 1650 and 1850. Other scholars argue that Western Africa's population declined absolutely between 1700 and 1850, and that had it not been for the Atlantic slave trade the region's population in 1850 would have been twice what it actually was.[44] I have argued elsewhere that Western Africa's population declined absolutely from 1650 to 1850, and that the region's population in 1850 would have been considerably larger had the demographic calamities of the Atlantic slave trade not occurred.[45] Whatever disagreement there is among scholars who have researched the subject, there is clear consensus that the Atlantic slave trade held back Western Africa's population growth between 1650 and 1850.

Viewed against the low densities of the fifteenth century and against the role of population growth in the development of the economies in the Atlantic basin during the period as shown earlier, we can understand that the demographic impact of the slave trade seriously retarded the development of Western Africa's economies during the period. This was in addition to the sociopolitically disruptive effects of the trade.

CONCLUSION

The employment of African peoples in the Americas to produce commodities on a large scale for Atlantic commerce was at the very center of economic development in the Atlantic World between 1500 and 1850. The forced migration of African labor to the Americas during the period represented a transfer of Western Africa's main relative advantage in the development of commodity production for Atlantic commerce. Had that transfer not taken place, Atlantic commerce would have grown much more slowly during these several centuries. But Western Africa would have gradually developed a more elaborate and intensive production of commodities for Atlantic commerce over those centuries, as it had begun to do in the fifteenth and early sixteenth centuries. Thus by using Western Africa's population to solve the labor problems of the Atlantic World in these centuries, economic development in the Atlantic basin was achieved at the expense of Western Africa's economies.

Knowledgeable people in Western Europe at the time understood the situation very well. For example, when some British traders tried to encourage commodity production for Atlantic commerce in Western Africa in the 1750s, the British Board of Trade commented:

> That the introducing of culture and Industry amongst the Negroes was contrary to the known established policy of this trade. That there was no saying where this might stop and that it might extend to tobacco, sugar & every other commodity which we now take from our colonies, and thereby the Africans who now support themselves by war would become planters and their slaves be employed in the culture of these articles in Africa which they are now employed in America. That our possessions in America were firmly secured to us, whereas those in Africa were more open to the invasions of an enemy, and besides that in Africa we were only tenants in the soil which we held at the good will of the natives.[46]

Also, in 1812, five years after Britain abolished the slave trade, officials of the English African Company wrote:

> It is a lamentable but certain fact, that Africa has hitherto been sacrificed to our West India colonies. Her commerce has been confined to a trade which seemed to preclude all advancement in civilization. Her cultivators have been sold to labour on lands not their own, while all endeavours to promote cultivation and improvement in agriculture have been discouraged by the Government of this country, lest her products should interfere with those of our more favoured colonies.[47]

Certainly the conscious policies of the European governments played a role. But it was the economics of the Atlantic slave trade and the associated sociopolitical consequences that lowered the competitiveness of Western Africa's economies in the development of commodity production for Atlantic commerce. As a Yoruba proverb says, "A person whose head is used in breaking a coconut does not participate in the eating." So the heads of Western African peoples were employed in solving the labor problems of the Atlantic world between 1500 and 1850, and Western Africa ended up not sharing in the economic development in the Atlantic basin during the period.

NOTES

1. This debate was initially led by Reginald Coupland, *The British Anti-Slavery Movement* (London: T. Butterworth, 1933) until challenged by Eric Williams, *Capitalism and Slavery* (Chapel Hill: University of North Carolina Press, 1944), who then became the focus of a voluminous literature: Roger T. Anstey, *The Atlantic Slave Trade and British Abolition* (London: Macmillan, 1975), and "The Historical Debate on the Abolition of the British Slave Trade," in *Liverpool, the African Slave Trade, and Abolition: Essays to Illustrate Current Knowledge and Research*, vol. 2, ed. Roger Anstey and P. E. H. Hair (Bristol: Historic Society of Lancashire and Cheshire Occasional Series, 1976), 157–166; and Seymour Drescher, *Econocide: British Slavery in the Era of Abolition* (Pittsburgh: University of Pittsburgh Press, 1977).

2. Joseph E. Inikori, "Market Structure and the Profits of the British African Trade in the Late Eighteenth Century," *Journal of Economic History* 41, no. 4 (Dec. 1981): 745–776; 746n3, for literature on profits.

3. Ralph Davis, *The Rise of the Atlantic Economies* (London: Weidenfeld and Nicolson, 1973), xi.

4. John K. Thornton, *Africa and Africans in the Making of the Atlantic World, 1400–1680* (Cambridge: Cambridge University Press, 1992); Larry E. Hudson, Jr., ed., *Working Toward Freedom: Slave Society and Domestic Economy in the American South* (Rochester, N.Y.: University of Rochester Press, 1994); for a critique, Colin Palmer, "Reclaiming the Past: Another View of American Slavery," paper presented at the State of Diaspora Studies Conference, University of North Carolina at Chapel Hill, Chapel Hill, February 18–19, 1994.

5. Joseph E. Inikori, "The Slave Trade and the Atlantic Economies, 1451–1870," in *The African Slave Trade from the Fifteenth to the Nineteenth Century* (Paris: UNESCO, 1979), 56–87; "Slavery and the Development of Industrial Capitalism in England," *Journal of Interdisciplinary History* 17, no. 4 (1987): 771–793; "Africa in World History: The Export Slave Trade from Africa and the Emergence of the Atlantic Economic Order," in *UNESCO General History of Africa*, vol. V: *Africa from the Sixteenth to the Eighteenth Century*, B. A. Ogot, ed., (Berkeley: University of California Press, 1992), 74–112; "Slavery and Atlantic Commerce, 1650–1800," *American Economic Review* 82, no. 2 (May 1992): 151–157; and "Slavery and the Unequal Development of Capitalism in the Atlantic Basin," 1995 C. L. R. James Lecture, St. Lawrence University, Canton, New York; William A. Darity, Jr., "A General Equilibrium Model of the Eighteenth-Century Atlantic Slave Trade: A Least-Likely Test for the Caribbean School," *Research in Economic History* 7 (1982): 287–326; Barbara L. Solow, ed., *Slavery and the Rise of the Atlantic System* (Cambridge: Cambridge University Press, 1991); Joseph E. Inikori and Stanley L. Engerman, eds., *The Atlantic Slave Trade: Effects on Economies, Societies, and Peoples in Africa, the Americas, and Europe* (Durham, N.C.: Duke University Press, 1992).

6. Darity, "British Industry and the West Indies Plantations," in Inikori and Engerman, eds. *The Atlantic Slave Trade*, 247–279.

7. Darity, "British Industry and the West Indies Plantations," in Inikori and Engerman, eds. *The Atlantic Slave Trade*, 247-279.

8. William Cunningham, *The Growth of English Industry and Commerce in Modern Times*, 3 vols. (Cambridge: Cambridge University Press, 1882); Paul Mantoux, *The Industrial Revolution in the Eighteenth Century: An Outline of the Beginnings of the Modern Factory System in England*

(New York: Harper Torchbooks, 1928 [1906]); Arthur Redford, *The Economic History of England (1760–1860)* (London: Longmans, Green and Co., 1931); Harry Elmer Barnes, *An Economic History of the Western World* (New York: Harcourt, Brace and Company, 1937).

9. K. E. Berrill, "International Trade and the Rate of Economic Growth," *Economic History Review* 12 (1960): 351–359; W. W. Rostow, *Theorists of Economic Growth from David Hume to the Present, With a Perspective on the Next Century* (New York: Oxford University Press, 1990).

10. Douglass C. North, *Structure and Change in Economic History* (New York: W. W. Norton, 1981), and *Institutions, Institutional Change and Economic Performance* (Cambridge: Cambridge University Press, 1990); Ester Boserup, *The Conditions of Agricultural Growth: The Economics of Agrarian Change under Population Pressure* (London: George Allen and Unwin, 1965).

11. Gene M. Grossman and Elhanan Helpman, "The 'New' Growth Theory: Trade, Innovation, and Growth," *American Economic Review* 80, no. 2 (May 1990): 86–91, and *Innovation and Growth in the Global Economy* (Cambridge, Mass.: MIT Press, 1991); Paul M. Romer, "The Origins of Endogenous Growth," *Journal of Economic Perspectives* 8, no. 1 (Winter 1994): 3–22.

12. E. A. Wrigley, "The Growth of Population in Eighteenth-Century England: A Conundrum Resolved," *Past and Present*, no. 98 (1983): 121–150.

13. Douglass C. North and Robert Paul Thomas, *The Rise of the Western World: A New Economic History* (Cambridge: Cambridge University Press, 1973), 71.

14. Wrigley, "The Growth of Population," 121.

15. North and Thomas, *The Rise of the Western World*, 47.

16. John C. Caldwell, "The Social Repercussions of Colonial Rule: Demographic Aspects," in *UNESCO General History of Africa*, vol. VII: *Africa Under Colonial Domination 1880–1935*, ed. A. Adu Boahen (Berkeley: University of California Press, 1985), 458–507.

17. Akin Mabogunje, "The Land and Peoples of West Africa," in *History of West Africa*, vol. 1, eds. J. F. Ade Ajayi and Michael Crowder (London: Longman, 1971), 1–32; David Birmingham and Phyllis M. Martin, eds., *History of Central Africa*, vol. 1 (London: Longman, 1983), viii.

18. Djibril Tamsir Niane, "Conclusion," in *UNESCO General History of Africa*, vol. IV: *Africa from the Twelfth to the Sixteenth Century*, ed. Djibril Tamsir Niane (Berkeley: University of California Press, 1984), 673–686, esp. 684; Djibril Tamsir Niane, "Mali and the Second Mandingo Expansion," in *UNESCO General History of Africa*, Vol. IV, ed. Djibril Tamsir Niane (Berkeley: University of California Press, 1984), 117–171, esp. 156.

19. Patrick Manning, "The Impact of Slave Trade Exports on the Population of the Western Coast of Africa, 1700–1850," in *De la traite à l'esclavage: Actes du colloque international sur la traite des noirs, Nantes 1985*, Vol. II, ed. Serge Daget (Paris: Société Française d'Histoire d'Outre-Mer, 1988), 111–134, esp. 123.

20. Patrick Manning, *Slavery and African Life: Occidental, Oriental, and African Slave Trades* (Cambridge: Cambridge University Press, 1990), 82.

21. James Lockhart and Stuart Schwartz, *Early Latin America: A History of Colonial Spanish America and Brazil* (Cambridge: Cambridge University Press, 1983), 36.

22. Arthur Morris, *Latin America: Economic Development and Regional Differentiation* (London: Hutchinson, 1981), 52.

23. North and Thomas, *The Rise of the Western World*; North, *Structure and Change in Economic History*.

24. Jan Vansina, *Paths in the Rainforests: Toward a History of Political Tradition in Equatorial Africa* (London: James Currey, 1990), 83–98, 215.

25. Morris, *Latin America*, 55.

26. Nathan Rosenberg and L. E. Birdzell, Jr., *How the West Grew Rich: The Economic Transformation of the Industrial World* (New York: Basic Books, 1986).

27. Trevor Aston, ed., *Crisis in Europe, 1560–1660: Essays from Past and Present* (London: Routledge and Kegan Paul, 1965).

28. John W. Blake, *West Africa, Quest for God and Gold, 1454–1578: A Survey of the First Century of White Enterprise in West Africa, with Particular Reference to the Achievement of the Portuguese and Their Rivalries with Other European Powers* (London: Curzon Press, 1977 [1937]).

29. Inikori, "Slavery and Atlantic Commerce," 152.

30. Ralph Davis, "English Foreign Trade, 1660–1700," *Economic History Review* 6, 2nd series (1954), and "English Foreign Trade, 1700–1774," *Economic History Review* 15, 2nd series (1962).

31. Inikori, "Slavery and Development."

32. Paul Butel, "France, the Antilles, and Europe in the Seventeenth and Eighteenth Centuries: Renewals of Foreign Trade," in *The Rise of Merchant Empires: Long-Distance Trade in the Early Modern World, 1350–1750*, ed. James D. Tracy (New York: Cambridge University Press, 1990), 153–173, esp. 163.

33. W. Borah and S. F Cook, "The Aboriginal Population of Central Mexico on the Eve of Spanish Conquest," in *History of Latin American Civilization: Sources and Interpretation*, Vol. 1, ed. Lewis Hanke (London: Methuen, 1967), 201–205.

34. Inikori, "Slavery and Atlantic Commerce," 152–155.

35. Inikori, "Slavery and Development."

36. E. A. Wrigley and R. S. Schofield, *The Population History of England, 1541–1871: A Reconstruction* (Cambridge, Mass.: Harvard University Press, 1981), 208–209.

37. Joel Mokyr, "Demand vs. Supply in the Industrial Revolution," in *The Economics of the Industrial Revolution*, ed. Joel Mokyr (Savage, Md.: Rowman & Littlefield, 1985), 97–118; "Evolutionary Biology, Technological Change and Economic History," *Bulletin of Economic Research* 43, no. 2 (1991); and "Introduction: The New Economic History and the Industrial Revolution," in *The British Industrial Revolution: An Economic Perspective*, ed. Joel Mokyr (Boulder, Colo.: Westview Press, 1993); Wrigley, "The Growth of Population," 121–150.

38. Inikori, "Slavery and Atlantic Commerce."

39. Douglass C. North, *The Economic Growth of the United States, 1790–1860* (Englewood Cliffs, N.J.: Prentice-Hall, 1961); Inikori, "Africa in World History."

40. Joseph Inikori, "West Africa's Seaborne Trade, 1750–1850: Volume, Structure and Implications," in *Figuring African Trade*, eds. G. Liesegang, H. Pasch, and A. Jones (Berlin: Dietrich Reimer Verlag, 1986); "Africa in World History"; "Slavery and Atlantic Commerce"; *The Chaining of a Continent: Export Demand for Captives and the History of Africa South of the Sahara, 1450–1870* (Kingston, Jamaica: Institute for Social and Economic Research, University of the West Indies, 1992).

41. Inikori, "West Africa's Seaborne Trade," 51–54.

42. Inikori, "West Africa's Seaborne Trade," 54–57.

43. Inikori, "Slavery and Atlantic Commerce," 153–155; Merrick and Graham, *Population and Economic Development in Brazil, 1800 to the Present* (Baltimore: Johns Hopkins University Press, 1979), 12.

44. Manning, *Slavery and African Life.*

45. Joseph Inikori, "Introduction," in *Forced Migration: The Impact of the Export Slave Trade on African Societies*, ed. Joseph E. Inikori (London: Hutchinson, 1982), and *The Chaining of a Continent.*

46. Inikori, "The Slave Trade and the Atlantic Economies," 79.

47. Inikori, "The Slave Trade and the Atlantic Economies," 79.

7

Arturo Alfonso Schomburg: A Transamerican Intellectual

Lisa Sánchez González

In her bio-bibliographical essay on Arturo Alfonso Schomburg (1874–1938), Flor Piñeiro de Rivera waxes poetic in her closing comments. Reminiscent of Schomburg's own nearly liturgical style and Espanglish rhythms, she writes:

> May God grant that all Puerto Ricans and Caribbean people take breath and catch the vision advanced by Schomburg.
>
> May the spirit of pure historical dimension, passed to Schomburg by José Julián Acosta and Salvador Brau, be honored as Puerto Ricans and other Caribbean people seek to make true Brau's dedicatory lines in *La colonización de Puerto Rico: "To my grandchildren: So that they know where they come from and be not caught off guard as to where they are going.*"[1]

Whether or not we feel there is some sort of "pure historical dimension" to be found, it is difficult not to be inspired by Schomburg's monumental effort to document the African Diaspora's rightful place as a foundational presence in transamerican civilization. In the Americas, where the majority population is nonwhite,[2] but in which, tragically, children are still contaminated by the soul sickness of racism, Schomburg has offered us a precious legacy.

This chapter introduces Arturo Schomburg to an audience interested in a politicized vision like Schomburg's, one that tests the routinely guarded boundaries of academic notions of racial belonging and disaffiliation intrinsic to both Puerto Rican and African American studies. Tracing the contours of these boundaries, then moving to a critical assessment of his work transgressing them, I elaborate on the unique role Schomburg occupies as a twentieth-century transamerican cultural intellectual. Framed by the broadest history of African descendants in the Americas, Schomburg's ideas bridge the narratives of African American and Puerto Rican racial politics in a provocative crucible of facts, fictions, and desires for an African Diasporic reinvention of *América's* history.

The story goes that sometime during the 1880s in San Juan, the young Arturo Schomburg asked his schoolteacher about the contributions of Africans and their descendants to the Americas' history. When the teacher rudely answered that they had contributed nothing, Schomburg decided that his life's work would be to prove the teacher, and his textbooks, wrong.

What began as Schomburg's indignation became for him a passion. The more he looked for documents and artifacts that chronicled Black history in the Americas and Europe, the more he found. Not only did he recuperate the lost and hidden histories and texts of such figures as Phyllis Wheatley, the first published African American poet, and Plácido, an Afro-Cuban poet assassinated by the Spanish militia (for the crime, it seems, of conspiring to discuss poetry), Schomburg also shared his knowledge by lecturing, publishing articles, and eventually making his private collection available as the African Diaspora's first public archive. Purchased by the Carnegie Foundation and donated to the New York City Public Library system in 1926, the Schomburg papers have evolved into the Schomburg Center for Research in Black Culture, housing the African Diaspora's largest combined collections of cultural and intellectual artifacts in the world today. During the 1920s, Schomburg's work was a profound inspiration for writers and artists associated with the Harlem Renaissance, and his legacy as an archivist, librarian, and curator has remained a cornerstone of twentieth-century African American studies.

What few people acknowledge about Schomburg, however, is the fact that he was Puerto Rican. Although he himself insisted that being Black and Puerto Rican were for him overlapping elements of the same proud identity, his biographers and critics tend to highlight either his "Blackness" or his "Puerto Ricanness" to the near exclusion, or even denigration, of the other.[3] Schomburg's apparent doubling in academic context is, of course, quite complicated but also quite simple; like many (if not the majority) of the Americas' racialized, subaltern communities, Schomburg's intransigent transnational identifications followed the organic course of his lived experience.

As a diasporic intellectual—both literally and figuratively deterritorialized, yet ethically and aesthetically motivated to invent a teleological narrative of his presence in the world—Schomburg's imagined communities matched his historical displacement (vis-à-vis San Juan, the Antilles, Brooklyn, Africa, Latin America, Spain, and even Germany), and making sense of this displacement required not only documentation (his primary research), but also interruptions of the very concept of nationalist subjectivity so common to even more progressive academic discourses, then and now. Somewhere between the Nation (state) and the nation (people), between statist ideologies and the Others, jettisoned quite literally by the violence of American conquest, slavery, and colonialism, Schomburg desired to situate himself (i.e., his Self, and, plurally, his Selves in the form of a historically grounded community) decisively in the world and world history, and this meant contriving a mode of understanding racism, colonialism, and their histories simultaneously.

Thus, given the currently available discourses of identity, the scholarly slicing and parsing the surfaces of figures like Schomburg to fit the depoliticized renditions of hybrid theories or to fill the gaps of (quasi-)nationalist histories, Schomburg's legacy posits a challenge to reconfigure transamerican subjectivity in a dynamic and highly politicized assessment of cultural history. Furthermore, as my research on Schomburg and other writers of the Puerto Rican Diaspora reveals, this challenge to the normalizing tendencies of identity discourses in the United States is characteristic of the narrative interventions of Puerto Rican writers in the Diaspora over the course of the entire twentieth century.

For the few Puerto Rican scholars who broach his legacy, Schomburg has become a curious footnote to the New York expatriate movement of the 1890s. In these narratives Schomburg is unquestionably Puerto Rican. But beyond his association with Cuban revolutionary José Martí and *el Club Dos Antillas*,[4] we rarely hear another word on the implications of this legacy. To date, no one has written any comprehensive, scholarly assessment of his work as a Puerto Rican cultural intellectual. Schomburg's contemporary, Bernardo Vega, makes a fleeting though positive reference to Schomburg's work in the African American community.[5] Occasionally, feature articles in Puerto Rican newspapers have introduced Schomburg's life and work in particular contexts.[6] Since my initial research on Schomburg, two major biographical sketches have appeared: Flor Piñeiro de Rivera's introduction to her anthology of his work and Victoria Ortiz' biographical essay.[7] But Schomburg has not yet been moved from margin to center in Puerto Rican studies, either on the island or in the mainland context.

On the other hand, the scholars who discuss his legacy in terms of African American/Black West Indian archival and community politics are very quick to dismiss Schomburg's native Puerto Rico's relevance to his life and life's work, and they seem to misunderstand the intricacies of Puerto Rican social and intellectual history when they do attempt to describe his family's background and the formative years he spent in San Juan and Cangrejos,[8] as well as the importance of his early educational experiences with José Julián Acosta.[9] His only biographer, Elinor des Verney Sinnette, has gone so far as to mention his Puerto Rican baptismal certificate only to deny its relevance as a meaningful historical document. In her assessment:

> The certificate of record in Santurce's Church of San Francisco de Asís indicates that Schomburg was baptized on January 28, 1874, as the "hijo natural" (out-of-wedlock) son of María Josepha Schumburg. *Strangely*, the same certificate lists his "abuela materna" (maternal grandmother) as Susana Schumburg.
>
> Another source, however, gives a rather different version of Arturo Schomburg's family history, a version provided by Schomburg himself. He offers much more information about his mother's side of the family than his father's, leading us to conclude that he really did not know or care to record that much about his father's people. According to Schomburg, his mother was born free in St. Croix, Virgin Islands in 1837.[10]

Unless, of course, she means to imply that the Church records are falsifications (which is doubtful or, at the very least, as yet unproven), Sinnette suggests that the "strange" aspect of Schomburg's baptismal certificate is that it indicates, first, that Schomburg's single mother retained her mother's surname and, second, that Schomburg was possibly born into the Catholic faith. However, neither of these historical details, in and of themselves, and in Puerto Rican context, is "strange" at all. As Sinnette herself emphasizes, Schomburg had his own version of his family history, which he shaped and reshaped over the course of his lifetime. In a rather romantic fashion that, arguably, follows certain discursive tendencies in Caribbean fiction, Schomburg concocted a heroic lineage for himself, with a noble, maternalistic slant, and rooted in the slave societies of the Lesser Antilles. We could guess (as Sinnette and others have) at Schomburg's motivations for fictionalizing his family history,[11] but until researchers can confirm such educated guesses with new evidence, Schomburg's St. Croix descent is, at best, uncertain.

As far as his imbrication with Catholicism is concerned, it is probable that Schomburg went to a Jesuit-run academy in his youth, since it is the sect most likely to have had a school open to less affluent children. Thus, whether or not he embraced Catholicism, and whether or not his baptism was merely a formal event, his humanist intellectual tendencies must have been influenced to some degree by Jesuit educators (the most radical intellectual sect, historically, in Latin America's Catholic church). For better, or for worse, as his earliest experiences of racism in the classroom would imply, it is highly unlikely that Schomburg would have emerged untouched by the intellectual traditions specific to Puerto Rico's Catholic educational establishment.

This is not to categorically exclude St. Croix from Schomburg's biography and cultural or intellectual formation. Certainly Schomburg may have had family ties in St. Croix, given the proximity between Cangrejos's port community and the Virgin Islands, the common transantillean routes of trade and migration in the nineteenth century, as well as his own recollections. Yet, opting to cite Schomburg's occasional references to himself as a West Indian as the only valid line of inquiry, Sinnette loses track of perhaps the most fascinating aspects of Schomburg's life and work, which are in fact the conscious, kaleidoscopic complexity of his identity as a bilingual and (at least) quadri-cultural member of the African Diaspora; characteristics, moreover, at the core of the lower-income, stateside Puerto Rican community, and acknowledged as often as not by members of this community. Furthermore, creatively reinventing Schomburg's biography, particularly in the context of a rhetorical maneuver that serves to obliterate the fact of his Puerto Rican background, is as much a moment of relaxed scholarly rigor in Sinnette's otherwise meticulously researched biography as it is a moment that forges a conceptual wedge between social histories that, I would argue (for equally politicized purposes), should be read in tandem rather than conflict (as Schomburg himself read them).

Indeed, while Schomburg was an extraordinary cultural worker by any standards, his predicament as a nonwhite, Spanish-speaking yet de facto U.S. citizen who was born in the Caribbean (with intergenerational ties to various islands) and who, through force of historical circumstances, settled in New York City, marks him as the rule of the Puerto Rican colonial Diaspora rather than as the exception. We might even argue that his automythological storytelling is also characteristic of the Puerto Rican colonial Diaspora, in which written as well as oral traditions foment innovations often conducive to teleological, nation-based personal or allegorical narratives.[12] What is perhaps most important for a contemporary dialogue about the African Diaspora is that Schomburg's complicated family ties through routes of Euro- and Afro-Caribbean transmigration are illustrative of the complexities of Caribbean subjectivity since the advent of Spanish, Portuguese, British, French, Danish, and Dutch colonization in the Americas, and most definitely characteristic of Puerto Rican social history.[13]

Similar in spirit to Sinnette's biography on Schomburg, Winston James has recently averred that Schomburg's race consciousness only makes sense if we understand him as, in the final analysis, not *really* Puerto Rican. While James gives us a much more closely argued account of Schomburg's political trajectories than Sinnette, the conclusion boils down to the same dismissal: Puerto Ricans in general have false race consciousness (i.e., we do not know or do not choose to recognize our *real* racial identity), so any Puerto Rican who broaches the subject and identifies with some form of African diasporic identity is an aberration. James, picking up the narrative thread of the St. Croix connection, argues that Schomburg's aberrant consciousness is the result of his mother's family ties to the Virgin Islands.[14] Again, the figure of Schomburg's mother stands in for a critical analysis of race relations in Puerto Rico, much of which is deeply encoded in the island's intellectual debates and literary allegories since the nineteenth century, and little of which has been translated into English, not to mention the bulk of historical evidence that might help us examine this history *as* history, which still waits to be discovered in the archives.[15]

The question of racism within both island and mainland Puerto Rican communities is not complicated; Puerto Rican versions of color prejudice are not any less profound or real than in other social contexts of the Americas. The majority of the Puerto Rican population—70 percent by current estimates—is of various degrees of African descent.[16] What is complicated is the *narration* of this racism in Puerto Rican social history, which has been to a large extent neglected by scholars in a critical milieu that has privileged macroeconomic analysis over race and gender analysis. In this sense, Puerto Rican scholarship may very well suffer from what Florestan Fernandes identifies in Brazilian culture as the prejudice among Brazilians of thinking they have no prejudice,[17] which is a clever way of describing the strong and willful belief in many Latin American contexts in a multiracially homogenous (and democratic) national identity.[18] Similarly, in leftist social scientific narratives, class identification becomes the prime metaphor for social struggle within the bulk of twentieth-century Puerto Rican studies.

While it is obviously problematic, there are strong determinants at work in the development of this historical perspective in Puerto Rican scholarship, not least of which is the primacy of state nationalism as a crux of resistance to U.S. imperialism and colonization. A brief sketch of this development is important here for pointing out the socialist and anticolonial imperatives implied or contested over the century in this scholarship. On a popular level, Puerto Rico's entry into modernity at the turn of the twentieth century was the anarcho-syndicalist tendency,[19] galvanized into a social movement under the leadership of Spanish immigrant Santiago Iglesias and the *Federación Libre de Trabajadores* (Free Federation of Workers). With the onslaught of U.S. colonialism after 1898, this tendency shifted in tandem with various generations of intellectual debates, helping to spawn and shape today's most prevalent trend—Marxist political economy, which is characteristically fueled by desires for national autonomy.

This is evident in the major research consortia prevailing in Puerto Rican studies: the *Centro de Estudios Puertorriqueños* at Hunter College, which was led by political economist Frank Bonilla for most of its history, the *Centro de Estudios de la Realidad Puertorriqueña* (CEREP) in San Juan, and the *Centro de Investigaciones Sociales* (CIS) based at the island's flagship public university in Río Piedras.[20] This trend seems to parallel developments in post-colonial countries struggling to shape a viable nationalist agenda in the face of a new global political economy that privileges "free market" imperial policies over organically contrived regional or national planning principles; a conflict that, of course, implies ideological struggle as well, particularly concerning the nature of the state itself.[21] Given this theoretical milieu, Puerto Rican scholarly attention to race is usually restricted to economically inflected studies of slavery, and cultural analyses of African descendants are more often than not folkloric.[22]

Though rarely mentioned in the same breath, I would like to suggest here that the problem of racial invisibility in Puerto Rican social sciences and literary criticism may be akin to similar maneuvers in Brazilian cultural intellectual history. In a concise article on the myth of harmonious racial relations in Brazilian scholarship, historian Thomas Skidmore claims that discourses of racial democracy have been a constant in Brazilian scholarship, serving in the final analysis as a rhetorical device for obfuscating the racial determinants so clearly at work in Brazilian class formation.[23] I would likewise argue that this is the hostile discursive context in which the Caribbean Négritude and Afro-Criollo movements and their precursors should be understood.

This century's Caribbean intellectuals have struggled to make sense of racism and colonialism in an anti-imperialist tradition that has had to be contested and, in some cases, revised, in order to make race a determining historical factor. Within francophone and anglophone Caribbean studies, this complex revision has been duly evaluated as a core episteme for twentieth-century cultural intellectual history. But we have yet to see similar comparative and more comprehensive scholarship concerning the hispanophone Caribbean; until we do, it would be premature to cast judgment on race consciousness among Puerto Rican, Dominican, and Cuban populations collectively. Within the next generation of scholars, racial subjectivity in the reevaluation of social history may very well be the most compelling concern.

Again, just because, collectively, scholars have yet to prioritize the study of racial subjectivity does not mean that there is no such cultural intellectual legacy to be found. As the late María Milagros López suggested, those of us from the United States have helped challenge the normative notions of sexuality and cultural citizenship in island-based criticism.[24] Certainly Schomburg, who spent most of his life in the United States facing specifically Puerto Rican Diasporic realities, is part of this obscured legacy.

Here, José Luis González's[25] polemical treatise *The Four-Storeyed Country* (*El pais de cuatro pisos*) is instructive.[26] The González controversy is too involved to exhaust in the space of this chapter, but for any student of Puerto Rican studies, his work is imperative to understanding the shape and direction of cultural intellectual politics concerning race in Puerto Rico.[27] González is firmly entrenched in the Marxist tradition but offers the first explicit analysis of racism (as opposed to race) as a defining trope in Puerto Rican political economy. His argument is that the Puerto Rican autonomist movements (largely socialist) throughout the twentieth century have not been able to garner popular support among the nonwhite majority of Puerto Ricans because the roots of our oppression are dyed in the very threads of the island's social fabric.

For González, the pattern of nostalgic "Creolism" that characterizes Puerto Rico's autonomist movements after 1898 romanticizes the era of Spanish colonial rule as a sort of antediluvian paradise (the Deluge being the U.S. invasion). In one of the most controversial passages of his work, González writes of this nostalgia, which he configures as a white racial fantasy:

> [T]hose who reason thus either don't know or have forgotten an elementary historical truth: the experience of racism of Puerto Rican Blacks came not from American, but from Puerto Rican society. In other words, those who have discriminated against Blacks *in Puerto Rico* haven't been Americans, but white Puerto Ricans, many of whom moreover have always taken conspicuous pride in their foreign ancestry (Spanish, Catalán, Mallorcan, etc.). What a Puerto Rican Black, or for that matter what any poor Puerto Rican, even a white (and everyone knows that there has always been a much higher proportion of poor people among the Blacks than whites) understands by "returning to the Spanish era" is this: returning to a society in which the white and property-owning part of has always oppressed and despised the nonwhite and non-property-owning part.[28]

This argument attests to a particular *narrative* predicament in a characteristically polemical body of scholarship, in which race and class consciousness have been generally juxtaposed as mutually exclusive concerns in post-1898 intellectual politics.[29] At the risk of oversimplifying the issue, we might say that the critique of racism among the leftist activist intelligentsia in Puerto Rico is often viewed as a suspicious cover for pro-U.S. (therefore pro-imperialist, pro-colonial, or even pro-statehood) desires. Conversely, Marxist theoretical affinities are often viewed among critics of racism as an apologetic cover for domestic regimes of white supremacy. Rarely do the two perspectives meet, let alone compromise. Among other things, this may help us to understand Schomburg's virulent anticommunist sentiments, nationalist leader Pedro Albizu Campos's[30] apparent silence on race matters, and José Luis González's decision to spend the rest of his life writing and teaching in Mexico City.

Given that Schomburg's intellectual activities occurred during the formative moment of the twentieth-century Puerto Rican nationalist program, perhaps Schomburg (a solid patriot of a colonized nation) disengaged from the Antillean independence struggle due to dynamics akin to the ones sketched by González. Schomburg himself never directly explained his break with Puerto Rican and Cuban nationalist politics (although, immediately after 1898, there really was not much of an organizational structure with which to be involved in New York). But he has left testimony to his own notion of Creole identity—that is, anyone of even the most remote African ancestry—which (if in fact it was a popular concept among his contemporaries in Puerto Rico) seems to have been utterly reconfigured in post-1898 nationalist renditions.

Like José Luis González much later in the twentieth century, Schomburg understood the historical and popular presence of Africanity as a definitive characteristic of the latent Puerto Rican nation, a conceptualization that echoes in later discourses of "Négritude"[31] and "Créolité"[32] in twentieth-century French Antillean anti-colonial writing. Perhaps too, Schomburg's new ties in the New York community, particularly his initiation into and strong participation with the Prince Hall Masons, prompted him to reassess his commitments in a new context, one in which he and his colleagues were less concerned with national struggle per se, than with mutual aid in a specific social, economic, and political context.

This racially segregated lodge, which was founded in Massachusetts in 1784 by Black Caribbean immigrant Prince Hall (for whom it is named) was, according to Schomburg, "built upon" the "character, fidelity and trust" of its African American and other African Diasporic members, who sought companionship and mutual support among their peers.[33] Therefore, however we might speculate as to his personal motivations, Schomburg never again concentrated his energies in explicitly political mobilization, neither among African Americans nor Caribbean expatriates. Instead, enjoying more personal support and encouragement from fellow Masons, Schomburg dedicated the rest of his life to researching and constructing an archive of the African Diaspora.

Schomburg's subsequent allusions to racial politics are almost exclusively articulated within discussions of aesthetics, usually in the histories of African Diasporic art, theater, and literature in the Americas and Spain. A prolific essayist, Schomburg's published and unpublished manuscripts include reviews of plays (particular favorites were the performances of Ira Aldridge) and exhibitions; commentaries on Cuba, Panama, Mexico, Haiti, and Africa (the Italo-Ethiopian crisis figures here, and a consistent interest in Abyssinian culture); polemical editorial pieces on the Prince Hall Masons; and reflections on his recuperation of Black writers and artists, as well as the African heritage of writers and artists not yet recognized as Black in various national traditions—Aleksandr Pushkin (Russian), Juan Latino and Sebastian Gómez (Spanish), José Campeche (Puerto Rican), and Alexandre Dumas (French) are some examples. A fascinating unfinished manuscript titled "Negroes in the Discovery and Development of America" poses his only attempt to consolidate his research into a synthetic study of the African Diaspora in the Americas.[34]

In an almost astounding dimension of its own, Schomburg's legacy—which is as vast as his virtuosity (and curiosity) as a writer and archivist were—includes more material than might seem humanly possible for one person to collect in a single lifetime (especially considering the fact that he did his research almost completely at his own expense). In all his work, Schomburg's inspiration is clearly humanist; his passion was righting the historical record by testifying to the contributions of African descendants to a progressive version of the Americas' history. Thus, despite his decided aversion to party radicalism in his later years, we can find traces in his writing and curating of an implicit critique of prevailing discourses of nationalism, racial subjectivity, and historical narrative politics, all of which formed an important precursive contribution to what would later emerge as Black cultural intellectual movements in twentieth-century Caribbean and North American history. In this sense, Schomburg's work has valences that purely biographical accounts cannot fathom, and also attests to the often underestimated significance of (autodidactic) librarianship to twentieth-century cultural intellectual history in the United States.

Within this corpus, an important aspect of Schomburg's legacy is a reading of racial power dynamics in Caribbean national contexts. His Puerto Rican childhood is of central importance here to the broader exploration of transamerican racial identifications, the limits of national discourses of harmonious heterogeneity, and the implicit critique of the (white-ish) Caribbean intellectual status quo of the early twentieth century. Throughout this work, Schomburg recalls his experiences growing up in Puerto Rico as anecdotal illustrations of the erasure of African ancestry in the chronicles of cultural history. In his article on José Campeche, he explains how the most important figures in Puerto Rican arts and letters have been reinscribed into the Euro-Caribbean tradition by those in power in Puerto Rico:

> Imagine a boy living in the city of his birth and not knowing who was the most noted native painter! . . . The white Spaniards who knew, spoke not of the man's antecedents. A conspiracy of silence had been handed down through many decades and like a veil covered the canvases of this talented Puerto Rican. Today we understand the silence and know the meaning of it all. In Puerto Rico there lived an artist whose color prevented him from receiving full recognition and enjoying the fame his genius merited.[35]

José Campeche (1752–1809) is in fact the only Puerto Rican figure whom Schomburg discusses in his various essays, which perhaps suggests his desire to move away from the delimitations of exclusively Puerto Rican identity politics. As Piñeiro de Rivera comments, "this essay is a sad lament deploring the disregard of Puerto Ricans for their island's history and racial prejudice."[36] Yet at the same time, this essay functions as an allusion to Schomburg's description of his life and work as well, in which he was eager to position himself as part of the Black cultural intellectual tradition he knew existed in Puerto Rican history.

Like Campeche, Schomburg's occasional references to his father centered on the detail that he was born and raised in Puerto Rico and, like the immigrant background of Campeche's mother (an emigrant from the Canary Islands), Schomburg represented his mother as a member of a prominent family in St. Croix. In terms of character, Schomburg underscores Campeche's high ethical standards as a man who "lived as an example of virtue" and whose memory "lives in our minds as the embodiment of a moral man," which is akin to the way Schomburg also took conspicuous pride in the ethical dimensions of thought and action intrinsic to his critical interventions as an essayist.[37] Finally, Schomburg calls attention to the notoriety that, "by dint of hard work," Campeche enjoyed outside Puerto Rico; for Schomburg, Campeche's relevance as a member of the African Diaspora forms one of the most important legacies of his career, one nearly identical to Schomburg's own aspirations as an Afro-Caribbean scholar.[38]

The "conspiracy of silence" that Schomburg examines in the Campeche essay suggests Schomburg's conceptualization of himself as an African Diasporic cultural intellectual as well; in this regard, he positioned himself and his work centrally in what scholars now recognize as the foundational moment of Pan-African historical discourse. Schomburg defined himself as a transnational intellectual, evidenced in the way he underscored the need to build coalitions across the standard national lines, along with his focus on outlining the contours of a hemispheric African Diasporic consciousness. These two concerns dovetail in the impetus behind his most cited essay, "The Negro Digs Up His Past," published during the Harlem Renaissance in *Survey Graphic*, in which he composed this call to action:

> The American Negro must remake his past in order to make his future. Though it is orthodox to think of America as the one country where it is unnecessary to have a past, what is a luxury for the nation as a whole becomes a prime social necessity for the Negro. For him, a group tradition must supply compensation for persecution, and pride of race the

antidote for prejudice. History must restore what slavery took away, for it is the social damage of slavery that the present generations must repair and offset. So among the rising democratic millions we find the Negro thinking more collectively, more retrospectively than the rest, and opting out of the very pressure of the present to become the most enthusiastic antiquarian of them all.[39]

Thus, while fin-de-siècle Puerto Rican activists and writers were hailing the collectivization of the working classes under the banner of trade-unionism (as Bernardo Vega's memoirs attest) and, later in the 1920s and 1930s, of nationalism, Schomburg was thinking about African Diasporic "group tradition" and race pride as the bases of both archival research and an insurgent, collective subjectivity. Importantly, Schomburg posited the shared history of slavery as the crux of the transamerican African Diaspora's mobilization in the United States.

This and other essays implicitly reject the idea of more traditional nationalisms as an "antidote" to the hostile context of Afro-Caribbean and African American political discourse. Schomburg alludes to this critique in his essay on the Cuban poet Gabriel de la Concepción Valdés, popularly known as "Plácido," whom he celebrates as a "*mulato*" with "an aesthetic soul great and heroic with more wings than space and *with more genius and heroism than fatherland.*"[40] Confined within the limits of racism and class prejudice—both in the "fatherland" and in the continental United States—Schomburg argues that the African Diaspora cannot be conceptualized within the rather strict constructs of class constituency and state nationalism that characterized the work of his contemporary Puerto Rican and Cuban colleagues.

Overall, Schomburg challenges his contemporaries to redesign cultural and political analysis. His essays always negotiate the historical "we," the metacritical third person, and his own personal involvement with the issues, figures, and histories he discusses. Since Schomburg traveled throughout Europe and the Americas in his search for what he termed "Negroana," his essays are often tales of his meandering journeys through streets and towns, as in the essay "In Quest of Juan de Pareja":

> Late one afternoon I came to Grenada [Spain], where Sebastian Gómez, the "Mulato de Murillo" and Juan de Pareja, the slave of Velázquez, were born.
>
> I strolled through the spacious avenue of El Gran Capitán; tarried in the beautiful, filigree sculptured cathedral and saw the sarcophagus of Ferdinand and Isabella, the patrons of Columbus. I walked through the cloisters of the University where one may still see the minutes attesting the fact that a black man, Juan Latino, received here, on May 4, 1546, his B.A. degree before the archbishop of Grenada, the learned men of Spain and the élite of the city. I saw the house where he wrote his famous epigrammatic poems. . . . I saw the home of Leo Africanus, "A Moor born in Grenada and brought up in Barbarie," and the home of the Negro priest who was seen now and then with Latino and the King of Spain, walking through the streets of Grenada.
>
> I walked up the hill to the Alhambra and saw in the sunshine the legacies of that civilization, which grew luxuriantly like an exotic plant native, yet foreign, to Spain.[41]

Schomburg transforms archival research into a narrative journey, one that unravels the apparent paradox of the African Diaspora's "native" yet "foreign" locations in Spain and the Americas. Here, as in many of his pieces, he elaborates how people of African ancestry have contributed to American and European art and culture through the palimpsests he finds inscribed, like filigree, around and within the places he visits in his various "quests" for an erased history. This notion of historical understanding as travel, as a nomadic trek that enables the archivist to witness and then to map the subsumed histories of the African Diaspora, is for Schomburg an alternative mode of making meaning out of a lost legacy, while literally and metaphorically "strolling" and "walking" through the "cloisters" of Grenada, history, and the imagined possibilities of globalized African identities.

The legacy of Arturo Schomburg provokes the question: Can African Americans and Puerto Ricans embrace a shared African Diasporic cultural legacy, revolving around the intricacies of Caribbean–New York transmigration starting at the turn of the twentieth century, and punctuated by the cultural workers whose ideas and activities offered creative alternatives to standard, often nationalist, racial identities? Can Puerto Rican critics accept a figure like Schomburg as a central, definitive thinker for the Puerto Rican Diaspora? And can African American scholars accept him as a definitively Puerto Rican member of the African American intellectual tradition?

There is still so much research to be done on nuancing the African Diaspora's cultural history in ways that illuminate—without losing sight of specificities—the rich mosaic of intellectual trajectories we have only recently begun to piece together in the Americas' history. I for one have hope that we can answer these provocative challenges with an affirmative effort that can begin the necessary dialogue and rapprochement in the interstices of Puerto Rican, African American, Caribbean, and Latin American studies. Indeed, there are undeniable historical and intellectual ties between the African American and Puerto Rican communities in the United States that deserve serious reflection. And Arturo Schomburg's legacy offers a unique opportunity for beginning to narrate these connections within the broader scope of transamerican cultural intellectual history.

NOTES

1. Flor Piñero de Rivera, ed., *Arturo Alfonso Schomburg: A Puerto Rican Quest for His Black Heritage* (San Juan, Puerto Rico: Centro de Estudios Avanzados de Puerto Rico y el Caribe, 1989), 50.

2. Of course, the official statistics make it impossible to "objectively" tabulate nonwhiteness in the Americas at large, and there are no such demographic surveys available for many countries. However, my preliminary analysis of the demographic tables available through the U.S. Census Bureau's online International Data Base suggests that the nonwhite population is indeed larger than the white population in the Caribbean, Mexico, Central America, and most of South America. This holds true for the near future in many areas of the United States as well, and according to the statistical summaries on Canada, "white" is not even a significant enough category to list (ethnicity in Canada seems to be determined by linguistic, ex-national, and tribal affiliations). For an overview of the problems inherent to racial codification and an educated estimate of the Black population in Latin America, see Rodolfo Monge Oviedo, "Are We or Aren't We?" *Report on the Americas* 25, no. 4 (February 1992): 19.

3. A glaring exception is Piñeiro de Rivera's arduously researched and celebratory anthology of Schomburg's writing, *Arturo Alfonso Schomburg: A Puerto Rican Quest for His Black Heritage*, which was issued in both English and Spanish.

4. A Cuban and Puerto Rican organization, based in New York City, that was dedicated to armed resistance against Spanish colonial rule on both islands.

5. Bernardo Vega, *Memorias de Bernardo Vega*, ed. César Andreu Iglesias (Río Piedras, Puerto Rico: Ediciones Huracán, 1988), 106.

6. Some examples of this interest, beginning in the late 1970s in Puerto Rico, are Marta Aponte's review of Schomburg's political trajectories for *Claridad* (then the socialist-independence party newspaper), "Del Club Dos Antillas al renacimiento de Harlem," *Claridad*, section "*En Rojo*" (Jun. 16–22, 1978): 10–11; C. Orama Padilla's story, "Por fin, Schomburg," *El Mundo* (Mar. 6, 1979): 9A; and Peggy Ann Bliss's cover story, "More than a Library," *San Juan Star* magazine (Mar. 30, 1980): 2–3, 15.

7. Piñeiro de Rivera, *Schomburg: A Puerto Rican Quest*, 17–50; Victoria Ortiz, "Arturo A. Schomburg: A Biographical Essay," in *The Legacy of Arthur A. Schomburg: A Celebration of the Past, A Vision for the Future*, Exhibition Catalogue, ed. Glenderlyn Johnson (New York: New York City Public Library, 1986).

8. Historically, Cangrejos (near the port area of San Juan) was a long-standing free Black community in Puerto Rico; today the area is called Santurce.

9. José Julián Acosta (1825–1891), one of the founders of the *Atenéo Puertorriqueño*, published a number of historical essays during his lifetime and was also a deputy to the Spanish Cortes (the seat of Spanish legislation for the Americas), in which he was an active abolitionist.

10. Elinor des Verney Sinnette, *Arthur Alfonso Schomburg, Black Bibliophile and Collector: A Biography* (Detroit: Wayne State University Press, 1989), 7–8.

11. An anecdote from Bernardo Vega's memoirs illustrates the paternalistic anxiety over "legitimacy" and moralistic codes of sexual conduct among the Puerto Rican expatriate community around the time Schomburg became a leader in this community in New York. According to Vega, José Martí himself was nearly expelled from the Club Dos Antillas because of rumors of his extramarital affair with a woman named Carmen Mantilla (*Memorias de Bernardo Vega*, 81–83). Apparently, Martí was vindicated on the grounds that his private life was irrelevant to his politics.

12. I cannot think of a single exception to this tendency in fiction. And in conversation, when asked about our identity, the short answer in the Puerto Rican colonial Diaspora is usually Puerto Rican, Boricua, or Nuyorican. When pressed for the long answer, it will include quite a few nation-states, "races," and regional and/or neighborhood affiliations. Given our eternal colonial condition and the Diaspora's collective experiences in urban North America, complex identifications (as opposed to a simple national identity) and sensibilities about belonging to multiple historical constituencies, might well be expected.

13. Continental, and even intercontinental, transmigration may very well be a defining characteristic of Caribbean social history, although it seems to aggravate the national(ist) paradigms of subjectivity that have formed the basis of most cultural intellectual paradigms. Some partial examples more or less in and around North America: C. L. R. James (Trinidadian) in London, Coyoacán, New York; Anaïs Nin (Cuban) in Paris, New York, Los Angeles; Piri Thomas (Nuyorican) in San Juan, San Francisco; Luisa Capetillo (Puerto Rican) in Ibor City, New York, Havana; Ana Mendieta (Cuban) in Iowa, Mexico, New York; Derek Walcott (St. Lucian) in Trinidad, New England. The list is virtually endless, and I think it attests to a complicated facet of Caribbean history that is as common for Caribbean intellectuals as it is confusing for those who prefer simpler evocations of national identity.

14. Winston James, *Holding Aloft the Banner of Ethiopia* (London: Verso, 1998).

15. Jalil Sued Badillo and Angel López Campos have begun this examination in their work, *Puerto Rico Negro* (Río Piedras, Puerto Rico: Editorial Cultural, 1986). The starting point of this exploration—the early period of colonization—indicates that there is a complicated web of gender, race, and economic struggles definitive of Puerto Rican social formation. This struggle is evidenced by the various patterns in Spanish colonial rules governing the colonists' (free, indentured, or enslaved) bodies, labor, and personal relationships along a spectrum in which men and women were racialized and assigned limits to a number of material, spiritual, and other expressions, including (for women) self-stylization in the form of clothes and jewelry and (for men, generally) economic policies that favored white (Catholic European) entrepreneurs over others, as well as (for everyone) a vigilant policing of any social interactions colonial administrators deemed immoral (unChristian) or otherwise problematic. These thematic struggles, generally, have yet to emerge and develop as central concerns in terms of nineteenth- and twentieth-century Puerto Rican cultural, intellectual, literary, and political theory.

16. Jorge Duany, "Ethnicity in the Spanish Caribbean: Notes on the Consolidation of Creole Identity in Cuba and Puerto Rico, 1762–1868," in *Caribbean Ethnicity Revisited*, vol. 6, ed. Stephen Glazier (New York: Gordon and Breach Science Publishers, 1985): 99–123.

17. Florestan Fernandes, *The Negro in Brazilian Society*, trans. Jacqueline D. Skiles, A. Brunel, and Arthur Rothwell, ed. Phyllis B. Eveleth (New York: Columbia University Press, 1971 [1969]).

18. This question of the rhetorical politics of "*mestizaje*" is a crucial concern for many Latin American theorists. As Xavier Albó has argued in "Our Identity Starting from Pluralism in the Base," in *The Postmodernism Debate in Latin America* (eds. John Beverley, José Oveido, and Michael Aronna [Durham, N.C.: Duke University Press, 1995], 18–33), new configurations of identity imply "pluralism at the base" in grassroots contexts, in which specific forms of cultural expression must be analyzed as the primary articulation of these new/old identities. Consequently, he claims that "*mestizaje*" can be a cover for erasing insurgent, more contemporary complexes of identities and identifications in national and transnational contexts, and that this erasure tends to reassert the privileged castes or constituencies of the modern Latin American state. Yet there are, as he contends, other potential readings of the nation and territory more relevant to grassroots mobilization in Bolivia, Albó's case in point.

19. This socialist trajectory was especially popular in Spain at the end of the nineteenth century, and many political exiles continued this movement in Cuba and Puerto Rico. The anarchism of the period in these contexts favored regional autonomy (as opposed to a centralized bureaucracy and/or a national government structure) and localized socialist economic reorganization. For further background on anarchism in Puerto Rico, see Igualdad Iglesias de Pagán, *El obrerismo en Puerto Rico: epoca de Santiago Iglesias, 1896–1905* (Palencia de Castilla, Spain: Ediciones Juan Ponce de León, 1973), and Gervasio L. García and A. G. Quintero Rivera, *Desafío y solidaridad: breve historia del movimiento obrero puertorriqueño* (Río Piedras, Puerto Rico: Ediciones Huracán/CEREP, 1982).

20. Judging mainly by conference presentations and personal contacts, there is, however, some semblance of a post-Marxist schism among younger Puerto Rican scholars, most of whom are teaching or pursuing graduate study in U.S. colleges and universities.

21. See Aijaz Ahmad, *In Theory: Classes, Nations, Literatures* (London: Verso, 1992); Samir Amin, *Eurocentrism* (New York: Monthly Review Press, 1989); Khachig Tölölyan, "Rethinking Diasporas: Stateless Power in the Transnational Movement," in *Diaspora* 5, no. 1 (1996): 3–36; and Arturo Escobar, *Encountering Development: The Making and Unmaking of the Third World* (Princeton, N.J.: Princeton University Press, 1995).

22. The Centro de Estudios Puertorriqueño's journal, *Centro*, attempted a break with this critical tendency in its 1996 special issue on race in the Puerto Rican community.

23. Thomas Skidmore, "Fact and Myth: Discovering a Racial Problem in Brazil," working paper, Universidade de São Paulo: Instituto de Estudios Avançados, 1992.

24. María Milagros López, "Post-Work Selves and Entitlement 'Attitudes' in Peripheral Postindustrial Puerto Rico," in *Social Text*, no. 38 (Spring 1994): 111–134.

25. José Luis González (1926–86) is a central figure in twentieth-century Puerto Rican cultural intellectual history, as the controversial legacy of his scholarship has made evident. On his life and life's work, see his memoir, *La luna no era de queso: Memorias de infancia* (Río Piedras, Puerto Rico: Editorial Cultural, 1989 [1988]). On González' literary legacy in Puerto Rico seeCésar Salgado, "El entierro de González: Con(tra) figuraciones del 98 en la narrativa ochentista puertorriqueña," *Revista Iberoamericana* (special issue: "1898–1998: Balance de un siglo") (July–Dec. 1998): vol. 54, 184–185, 413–439.

26. José Luis González, *Puerto Rico: The Four-Storeyed Country*, trans. Gerald Guiness (Princeton, N.J.: Markus Wiener Publishing, 1980).

27. For a detailed exploration of González's significance for contemporary ethnography and historiography in insular Puerto Rican studies, see Arlene Torres, "La gran familia Puertorriqueña 'ej prieta de beldá" (The Great Puerto Rican Family Is Really Really Black)," in *Blackness in Latin America and the Caribbean: Social Dynamics and Cultural Transformations*, eds. Arlene Torres and Norman E. Whitten, Jr. (Bloomington: Indiana University Press), 285–306.

28. González, *The Four-Storeyed Country*, 24.

29. Near the end of his life, living in exile in Mexico City, González wrote that he was convinced that indeed the African Diasporic community in Puerto Rico (who, in his analysis, are the definitive community of Puerto Rican cultural history) had voiced its own understanding of "*patria*" ("fatherland," or national belonging) *extra-discursively* in popular music and dance: González, *The Four-Storeyed Country*, 102.

30. Pedro Albizu Campos (1891–1965) was a central figure in the Puerto Rican nationalist movement after 1930. For an assessment of his role in this movement, see Luis Angel Ferrao, *Pedro Albizu Campos y el nacionalismo puertorriqueño* (Río Piedras, Puerto Rico: Editorial Cultural, 1990).

31. Aimé Césaire, *Cahier d'un retour au pays natal* (Paris: Présence Africaine, 1956).

32. Edouard Glissant, *Le discours antillais* (Paris: Les Editions du Seuil, 1981).

33. Arturo Schomburg, "Prince Hall Masons of the State of New York," in *Fraternal Review* 2, no. 12 (December 1923): 1–2.

34. There are various pieces of this manuscript, "Negroes in the Discovery and Development of America," in his collected papers (Schomburg Papers, Schomburg Center for Research in Black Culture, New York Public Library). One of the most complete texts includes an enthusiastic handwritten preface contributed by a lifelong friend, James Boddy, who comments at the end of his correspondence: "Such a colored man has never yet been born; to do what you have done."

35. "José Campeche 1752–1809: A Puerto Rican Negro Painter," in Piñeiro de Rivera, *Schomburg: A Puerto Rican Quest*, 201 (essay originally published in April 1934).

36. Piñeiro de Rivera, *Schomburg: A Puerto Rican Quest*, 32.

37. Piñeiro de Rivera, *Schomburg: A Puerto Rican Quest*, 207.

38. Piñeiro de Rivera, *Schomburg: A Puerto Rican Quest*, 204.

39. Arturo A. Schomburg, "The Negro Digs Up His Past," in *Survey Graphic* 6, no. 6 (March 1925): 670–672.

40. In "Plácido: An Epoch in Cuba's Struggle for Liberty," in Piñeiro de Rivera, *Schomburg: A Puerto Rican Quest*, 60 (essay originally published in *1909* [emphasis added]).

41. Piñeiro de Rivera, *Schomburg: A Puerto Rican Quest*, 139 (essay originally published in July 1927).

8

✳

"It Don't Mean a Thing If It Ain't Got That Swing": The Relationship Between African and African American Music

Olly Wilson

African American music developed as a unique musical tradition reflecting the experiences of people of African descent within the Western Hemisphere; this musical tradition has been influenced, however, by African cultural patterns in profound as well as subtle ways. This is because in its seminal stages it was a music of Africans in America, as well as of African Americans. Any study of the history of African American music must take this basic fact into serious consideration.

For several years I have been interested in exploring the nature of the relationship between West African music and African American music of the United States. My quest was stimulated by what appeared to my ears to be an obvious similarity between certain aspects of West African and African American musical genres, although both musical traditions are clearly distinct. Moreover, the significant role of sub-Saharan cosmology, coupled with the obvious historical-cultural relationship of peoples of African descent throughout the Diaspora, suggested that West Africans and African Americans may share some common modes of musical practice—that there may be a set of common basic elements that help define each tradition and establish their relationship.

The effort to define the peculiar qualities of African American music is made difficult by the fact that music of African Americans, like that of all ethnic groups within the United States, exists within a larger multicultural social context. Thus, African American music has both influenced, and been influenced by, several non-African musical traditions, thereby making it difficult to pinpoint precisely the essential aspects of the music that make it a part of a larger African music tradition. In spite of this fact,

[T]he empirical evidence overwhelmingly supports the notion that there is indeed a distinct set of musical qualities that are an expression of the collective cultural values of peoples of African descent. This musical tradition has many branches that reflect variations in basic cultural patterns over time, as well as diversity within a specific time frame. However, all of

153

these branches share, to a greater or lesser extent, a group of qualities that, taken together, comprise the essence of the Black musical traditions, share a "critical mass" of these common qualities. It is this common sharing of qualities that comprises and defines the musical tradition.[1]

In an article published in *Black Perspectives in Music*, I proposed a theoretical approach to the problem of definition of that broader musical tradition. The substance of that approach is that the essence of the relationship between African and African American musical traditions consists of

> the common sharing of a core of conceptual approaches to the process of music-making, and hence is not basically quantitative but qualitative. The particular forms of Black music that evolved in America are specific realizations of this shared conceptual framework, which reflect the peculiarities of the Black American experience. As such, the essence of their Africanness is not a static body of something that can be depleted, but rather a conceptual approach, the manifestations of which are infinite. The common core of this Africanness consists of a way of doing something, not simply something that is done.[2]

My approach to this question is based in large part on the model Melville Herskovits put forward in his monumental study, *The Myth of the Negro Past*.[3] His notions of "cultural reinterpretation," "syncretism," and African "cultural areas" are central to my formulation of "shared conceptual approaches to the process of music-making." The weakest part of Herskovits's model was his attempt to quantify specific cultural patterns. A closer reading of Herskovits by subsequent scholars has, however, focused on his formulation of the notion of "cultural heritage" as opposed to a quantification of cultural practices.

As Sidney Mintz and Richard Price indicate in their 1976 book, *The Birth of African American Culture*:

> An African cultural heritage, widely shared by the people imported into a new colony, will have to be defined in less concrete terms by focusing more on values, and less on socio-cultural forms, and even by attempting to identify unconscious "grammatical" principles, which may underlie and shape behavioral response. To begin with, we would call for an examination of "cognitive orientations" on the one hand, basic assumptions about social relations (what values motivate individuals, how one deals with others in social situations, and matters of interpersonal style), and on the other, basic assumptions and expectations about the way the world functions phenomenologically (for instance, beliefs about causality, and how particular causes are revealed). We would argue that certain common orientations to reality may tend to focus the attention of individuals from West and Central African cultures upon similar kinds of events that may seem quite diverse in formal terms.[4]

And later, Mintz and Price state quite explicitly:

> In considering African American cultural continuities, it may well be that the more formal elements stressed by Herskovits exerted less influence on the nascent institutions of newly enslaved and transported Africans than did their basic assumptions about social relations or the workings of the universe.[5]

Other scholars of African American culture have also come to similar conclusions:

> It is obvious that Black Americans were prevented from maintaining in North America the large numbers of African cultural institutions and traditional customs which have survived in the Caribbean and South America. It has been less obvious to outside observers, however, that Black Americans have succeeded in preserving a high degree of their African "character" on the much deeper and more fundamental level of interpersonal relationships and expressive behavior.[6]

The thrust of this scholarship is to underscore the significance of basic "underlying principles" that define social behavior—to focus in on the fundamental "concepts" of collective cultural orientation. Such an approach to the study of culture is obviously influenced by conceptions of cultural "deep structures" though not necessarily adhering to a strict structuralist view of reality. My hypothesis of fundamental conceptual approaches to the process of music-making is consistent with the basic notion of "deep structural" cognitive assumptions in cultures.

It is important to note that the scholars of the past twenty years who have studied the relationship between West African and African American religion, art, vernacular traditions, and literature—Albert Raboteau, Robert Farris Thompson, Houston Baker, and Henry Louis Gates, Jr.—have all focused independently on the pivotal role of West African "cognitive assumptions" in exploring the various aspects of culture that comprise the respective areas of inquiry.[7]

Henry Louis Gates, Jr., for example, begins the second paragraph of his seminal study of African American literature, *The Signifying Monkey*, with the following observation:

> Common sense, in retrospect, argues that these retained elements of cultures should have survived, that their complete annihilation would have been far more remarkable than their preservation. The African, after all, was a traveler, albeit an abrupt, ironic traveler, through space and time; and like every traveler, the African "read" a new environment within a received framework of meaning and belief. The notion that the Middle Passage was so traumatic that it functioned to create in the African a tabula rasa of consciousness is as odd as it is a fiction, a fiction that has served several economic orders and their attendant ideologies. The full erasure of traces of cultures as splendid, as ancient, and as shared by the slave traveler as the classic cultures of traditional West Africa would have been extraordinarily difficult. Slavery in the New World, a veritable seething cauldron of cross-cultural contact, however, did serve to create a dynamic of exchange and revision among numerous previously isolated Black African cultures on a scale unprecedented in African history. Inadvertently, African slavery in the New World satisfied the preconditions for the emergence of a new African culture, a truly Pan-African culture fashioned as a colorful weave of linguistic, institutional, metaphysical, and formal threads. What survived this fascinating process was the most useful and the most compelling of the fragments at hand. Afro-American culture is an African culture with a difference as signified by the catalysts of English, Dutch, French, Portuguese, or Spanish languages and cultures, which formed the precise structures that each discrete New World Pan-African culture assumed.[8]

African American music, then, from this perspective, exists as a code of patterned sound and behavior by which human beings exchange experiences in a specific cultural context. This particular "code," although formed by the basic "cognitive assumptions" or conceptual approaches to music-making that are African in origin, is fundamentally shaped by experiences in the American reality. The music thus reflects, in a profound way, the duality of which W. E. B. Du Bois speaks so eloquently in *The Souls of Black Folk*, which is a fundamental theme of African American experience.[9] It is precisely this "duality" or "double consciousness" that gives the music its distinctive position, its ability to be part of the broader fabric of shared American culture, and simultaneously to be rooted in aspects of culture that are fundamentally African. It is also this feature that creates important differences of perspective toward that experience.

Earlier, I mentioned conceptual predispositions in African American music. These predispositions also reflect basic values in the culture. It is the reaffirmation of these values that forms the basis of "aesthetics" in African American music. I define "aesthetics" broadly, by which I mean the full range of attitudes, values, and assumptions about the fundamental nature of the musical experience; the criteria by which a culture assesses quality and assigns meaning to music, and the relationship of the musical experience to the overall system of reality.

The exploration of aesthetics in African American music is necessarily multidimensional. In the first instance, consideration must be given to the determination of what constitutes the musical experience. Ethnomusicology, influenced by developments in anthropology, semiotics, and philosophy, has developed an approach that views meaning in music in a broad cultural context. As John Blacking indicates in describing the goal of ethnomusicology:

> The central problem is to describe all the factors which generate the pattern of sound produced by a single composer or society; to explain music as signs and symbols of human experience in culture and to relate form to its social and cultural content.[10]

If one accepts this definition, the musical experience would include structural aspects of the musical event as well as a wide range of encoded meanings of social and cultural significance. Music as an aspect of culture proceeds from what postmodern scholars such as Roland Barthes and others have called an ideological basis.[11] A meaningful study of music must take both these factors into consideration. It may be convenient to view the musical experience as one of a system of interactive concentric circles in which each sphere represents a layer of meaning radiating in and out of one another.

The African influence on African American music has been reflected historically in shared and similar conceptions regarding (1) the fundamental nature of musical experience; (2) specific approaches to musical form, patterns of continuity, and syntax; and (3) performance practices, the processes involved in actively making music.

The term "African music" is much too broad to have meaningful significance, given the size of the African continent and its extraordinary cultural diversity. Most scholars divide the continent into at least two large major parts: North Africa, that part north of the Sahara where most inhabitants speak Semitic and Afro-Asiatic languages and have cultures that manifest the impact of Arab culture and Islamic religion; and sub-Saharan

Africa, the area south of the Sahara that encompasses the large Niger-Congo language family (West Sudan, Bantu, and Kordofanian). Studies of the slave trade have demonstrated that the majority of Africans were taken from sub-Saharan Africa, primarily from the Guinea Coast or West Sudan and Congo Basin regions. The music of Africa that has the greatest influence on African American music has been from these regions.

HISTORICAL BACKGROUND

In addition to the African origin of African Americans, there are several historical factors that contributed to the influence of African music on African American music. First, during the slave trade, African music and dance were often encouraged on slave ships. This practice existed because slave traders believed their human cargoes were better able to survive the horrible, inhumane conditions of the Middle Passage if they were permitted to dance aboard the ships. The concomitant effects of this practice were to provide opportunities for Africans of diverse ethnic groups to learn one another's music, and also to literally bring African musical practices to the New World every time a new cargo of Africans arrived. Because the African slave trade existed for almost four hundred years and involved an estimated twelve to fifteen million people, depending on how one counts, the developing eighteenth- and early nineteenth-century African American community was continually exposed to new Africans who brought fresh knowledge of traditional African music.

A second historical factor that contributed to the influence of African music on African American music in the United States was the performance of African music in colonial America. From the seventeenth century through part of the nineteenth, various "African Festivals," or mass public gatherings of enslaved and free African Americans, where traditional African music was performed, were held in the colonies. Musical scholar Eileen Southern has pointed out that among these were the Pinkster Day festival in Albany, Manhattan, and other parts of New York; Lection Day in Hartford; Jubilees at Potter's Field in Philadelphia; and the John Connu Christmas festival in North Carolina and Virginia. The most famous of these gatherings, cited by several contemporary chroniclers, was in New Orleans at Place Congo. Here, every week from as early as 1786 until well into the nineteenth century, large numbers of African and African Americans assembled, organized themselves into "nations," and performed music that had all of the characteristics of African music.[12]

The significance of both historical factors cited above is that during the formative period of African American culture, Africans who thought of themselves as exiles and African Americans at various degrees of acculturation to the new nation were brought into contact with traditional African music and thereby increased its possible influence on the new music of African Americans.

INFLUENCE OF AFRICAN CONCEPTS OF THE NATURE OF MUSIC

African conceptions of the fundamental nature of music are among the most important influences on African American music. Although there are important differences between musical practices of various sub-Saharan African people, a basic conception that music is an essential, obligatory aspect of life is commonly held. Music is used with almost every human activity and has had a persistent central role in African culture. Moreover, it is generally believed that music has an affective power and functions as a force or causal agent. This is reflected most vividly in the role music plays in African views of the cosmos.

"The Gods will not descend without song" is a common aphorism in West African cultures. It is extremely significant because this phrase embodies a fundamental conception concerning the role of music in sub-Saharan African cultures. It is critical that we understand this in order to grasp fully the nature of the musical experience in Africa, and by extension, the African American musical experience.

Although there are differences in the cosmological concepts of the various sub-Saharan peoples, numerous scholars have noted that the universe is conceived of as containing a dynamic flux of forces that are constantly interacting with one another. Everything has a certain degree of force, and hegemony is determined by the relative strength of a force in relationship to other forces. Also, most sub-Saharan cultures conceive the universe as consisting of at least three tiers reflecting relative power and authority. At the top is the supreme being or supreme force, the omnipotent, omniscient, begetter of all things and ultimate source of all force. This supreme deity is called various names by various cultures—Onyame, the shining one, or Odomankoma, the boundless one, by the Akan people of Ghana, or Olodumare by the Yoruba of Nigeria, or the dualistic male-female deity Mawu-Lisa, by the Fon people of Benin. This supreme force is generally uninterested in the day-to-day affairs of humans and, having created the world, maintains a distance from it.

A second tier or middle level of deities, by contrast, represents various forces of nature and presides over various activities, constantly interacting with humankind, which is the third level of the cosmos. These deities, such as the Yoruba Eshu-Elegbara, the god of the crossroads, the source of divination, the interpreter of the other gods; Ogun, the Yoruba god of iron and war; or the Otu gods of war of the Ga people of Ghana, all have specific domains over which they exercise power and authority. Humankind must implore and appease them in order to achieve its goals. Hence, the humans who are particularly knowledgeable about a specific deity (perhaps priests or devotees of that deity) are approached for guidance about how to seek the support of that deity. The central most important act that occurs during this process is the communion between a devotee of a deity and that deity—a process that is generally known in scholarly literature, if not by most practitioners, as "possession."[13] This occurs at the height of the musical performance when the drumming, dancing, and singing are most intense and the participants become completely absorbed with the music.

During this act it is believed that the deity actually possesses the body of the devotee, who then takes on the character of that deity. This process strengthens the devotee and empowers her or him with greater force. Of critical importance is the fact that the deities will not descend to possess the devotees unless implored. The means of calling forth the deities is the playing of specific music associated with each deity.

"The Gods will not descend without song." The Gods will not descend without the proper song. Music, then, plays a powerful role in African cosmology. It is absolutely essential, or indispensable, in order for the cosmos to function properly. Musicians, because they are the reservoirs of knowledge of the specific music associated with a specific deity, are therefore extremely important to the culture. That is perhaps why many cultures state that "a musician in the art of making music must not be disturbed." Musicians facilitate the vital communion between human and god.

What I have described is common in sub-Saharan African cultures and in the African Diaspora in those places where the conditions of slavery enabled much of the original African culture to be retained or syncretized in large degrees. Hence, Vodun in Haiti, Candomblé in Brazil, and Santería in Cuba all reflect the overall cultural patterns just described. The situation in the United States was/is different. The patterns of slavery and the conscious attempts to obliterate vestiges of African culture—including outlawing the usage of the drums—made it impossible to retain the specificity of musical practices that occurred in the Caribbean and South American regions. What persisted, however, were the general concepts and values of the old culture, devoid of the specificity of its predecessors.

In attempting to understand the various levels of meaning that occur in the experience of African American music, it is important to take cognizance of the critical role of music in African cultures, including in "possession," or, in general terms, in transcending normal states of consciousness. It is important because this process, which is so critical in African cosmological terms, also shapes the African American musical experience. Although devoid of the specificity associated with African culture, the underlying concept of music as "ritual" is extremely important in many African American musical genres. The notion that music is a vehicle for the inducement of an altered state of consciousness is very important to its understanding. It is, if you will, an important "extra-musical text" to be read when experiencing performances of certain African American music genres.

It is perhaps this factor that contributed to the adoption of the form of Christianity that most African Americans accepted in eighteenth-century colonial America. The Methodist and Baptist denominations were the most successful in converting African exiles and African Americans to Christianity. I believe this was true, in large measure, because the religious practices of the then evangelical movements of John and Charles Wesley openly embraced ecstatic expressions of religious fervor. Consequently, "speaking in tongues," fainting, moving with the "shakes," uncontrollably going into trance-like states were all practices in which white Methodist and Baptist religious celebrants engaged. In other words, religious behavior of eighteenth-century evangelical Methodists and Baptists was very consistent with religious behavior of eighteenth-century West Africans, although the religious ideology was not. This congruence of religious behavior was what anthropologist Melville Herskovits suggests was fertile ground for cultural syncretism to occur.

Although the adoption of Christianity by African Americans indelibly altered their traditional view of the cosmos, the reinterpretation of African concepts of religion to conform with the realities of the American experience resulted in a new or syncretic religious practice in which fundamental African concepts were retained, but manifested in ways that were consistent with preexisting similar Euro-American religious practices.

Hence, although specific music used to call specific deities was rarely practiced in the continental United States (there are exceptions, such as New Orleans), the concept of music functioning as a vital part of the religious service in which members become possessed by the Christian Holy Ghost became well established. The idea of possession and the role of the music in inducing possession was retained, though the specific nature of the possession was new. The African American notion of music as a causal agent that fosters religious ecstasy is a clear example of a reinterpreted African cultural concept.

It is easy to observe the "ritual" function of the music in the realm of African American religious practice. From the eighteenth-century adoption of Christianity and Richard Allen's subsequent establishment of the African Methodist Episcopal Church as an independent institution in 1794 up to the present, music has remained a powerful and pivotal force in religious practice. The genre of the "spiritual" of the eighteenth and nineteenth centuries, and its twentieth-century successor, gospel music, represent a continuing legacy of sacred liturgical music. But in addition to their role as carriers of the ritual, they function as affective forces to induce altered states of consciousness.

Observers of eighteenth- and nineteenth-century African American religious practices, from the camp meetings and prayer house revivals to the religious dance known as the "ring shout," consistently refer to a climactic point or points in the service in which an emotional pinnacle of religious ecstasy is reached among the celebrants.[14] This high point is usually occasioned by the music in conjunction with the minister's sermon. And it is well known that contemporary gospel music has certainly functioned as a catalyst for similar expressions of religious fervor.

The role of music in inducing states of emotional fervor exists outside of the religious practice as well. Charles Keil in his book *Urban Blues* describes the ritual-like practice obtained in a B. B. King blues concert, and cites the similarity between the oratory of the Rev. Martin Luther King, Jr., and the blues playing of B. B. King:

> I was struck by the stylistic common denominator that binds the sacred and the secular realms of the two Kings into one cultural unit. The preacher used two phrases over and over again as he improvised the conclusion of his address, "Let freedom ring from . . ." followed each time by a different range of American mountains, and then, "I have a dream . . . that someday . . ." used to introduce each item on the list of promises to the Negro that have yet to be kept. This relentless repetition of phrases, the listing of the American landmarks, and the long enumeration of Negro goals, gradually moved the audience to an emotional peak, a fitting climax to a stirring demonstration. Employing a standard twelve-bar blues form, repeated over and over again in song after song, turning out well-known phrases in every chorus yet always introducing novel combinations and subtle new twists in each performance—in short, using the same patterns—B. B. King rarely fails to give his listeners much the same kind of emotional lift.[15]

And Albert Murray in his insightful book *Stomping the Blues* describes the role of the blues performance, in contra-distinction to those feelings of sadness and melancholy that he characterized as the "Blues as such":

> [T]he fundamental function of the blues musicians (also known as the jazz musicians), the most programmatic mission of whose performance is not only to drive the blues away and

hold them at bay at least for the time being, but also to evoke an ambiance of Dionysian revelry in the process.

Which is to say, even as such blues (or jazz) performers as the appropriately legendary Buddy Bolden, the improbable but undeniable Jelly Roll Morton, the primordially regal Bessie Smith, played their usual engagements as dance-hall, night-club, and vaudeville entertainers, they were at the same time fulfilling a central role in a ceremony that was at once a purification rite and a celebration the festive earthiness of which was tantamount to a fertility ritual.[16]

As the above quotes illustrate, Murray and Keil recognize an extramusical level of meaning that exists in performances of blues and jazz. The performance is viewed as a group ritual designed to drive away a sense of melancholy and to celebrate life in the present moment, or, as Murray puts it, "the downright exhilaration, the rapturous delight of sheer physical existence."[17] The point I wish to make here is that this dimension of musical performance that is shared in both sacred and secular music-making is derived from concepts that are vestiges of African cosmological beliefs. It is a subtext that is expected to exist in a performance, but how it is manifested is up to the ingenuity of the particular performers. We know that repetitive cyclical structures will be used to achieve the moment of catharsis. But the skill, imagination, and ingenuity displayed in their usage will determine the quality of the performance.

A second African musical conception that influenced African American music is the view that music is a communal activity. Music is an interactive human activity in which everyone is expected to participate: there are no detached listeners, but rather a communion of participants. The social structure of music-making thus involves a hierarchy of participants whose responsibilities are variable over a continuum from the highly complex to the very simple. Nevertheless, the basic conception of music entails the notion of inclusion, of participatory, integrative engagement of the entire community. This ideal is also a fundamental principle of traditional African American folk music, and is reflected in all genres of traditional African American religious and secular music of the eighteenth and early nineteenth centuries.

The notion of "inclusion" in the music-making process becomes another "extramusical" dimension of the performance process in both African and African American music. That is, given the cultural bias toward privileging participation, the society tends to place a higher value on those performers who are able to engage the entire community in actively participating in the performance. The performance itself is structured in ways designed to provoke a dynamic interaction between the principal performers and everyone else; and the listeners sing, clap, dance, and most importantly, respond to the "call" of the principal performers.

The performers who by their striking musical imagination elicit the most response from the audience are generally the most highly regarded. Louis Armstrong, Bessie Smith, Duke Ellington, Mahalia Jackson, Ray Charles, Aretha Franklin, and Charlie Parker all possess(ed) this quality in abundance. They are valued because they were/are able to bring about the highest degree of communal participation in which everyone is working toward the same focused musical goal. In a broad sense, a successful performance is a musical realization of the traditional communal social values that place great value on the entire group functioning as an interdependent single entity.

One thing to "read" in traditional African or African American music is the degree to which the music actively engages the audience. When teenagers listen to their favorite rap performer, a measure of the success of that performer is the degree to which the listeners move in synchrony with the rapper. The establishment of a communal bond is a significant goal of the musical experience.

A third basic conception underlying the practice of African music is the assumption that music is integrally related to language. Within most sub-Saharan African cultures, a special relationship exists between language and music, and this relationship has had an important impact on determining the nature of African American music. At the root of the relationship is the fact that language and music are both modes of communication that use sound and exist in time, and hence may share some general principles, although there are important differences between them. Moreover, many African languages are tonal, using tonal or pitch level as a means of defining a specific word. Two words with the same syllables and rhythm may have entirely different meanings if they have different tones. The simulation of the rhythm and tonal levels of speech enables uniquely constructed drums to imitate some speech and develop a repertoire of musical speech. These drums are generally referred to as talking drums. One well-known example is the Yoruba *dun dun* drum.

In his classic study *Drumming in Akan Communities of Ghana*, musicologist Kwabena Nketia has demonstrated that much of Akan drumming has a verbal basis.[18] He shows that Akan drum and metallic bell patterns are, literally, musical simulations of verbal proverbs, poems, common exhortations, and other statements. Hence, music is inextricably related to language, or put most directly, instrumental performers often involve literal musical statements of poetic phrases. Therefore, music often exists as a multi-leveled form of communication. It is literally as well as figuratively "saying something."

In addition, African musicians characteristically use nonsemantic or onomatopoetic syllables to reproduce an aural pattern analogous to the pitch contour and rhythm of a drum pattern that they wish to convey to another person. This verbalization of drum patterns is commonly used in recalling musical patterns or teaching music to novices. This verbal-musical interaction is doubtlessly enhanced by the fact that many African languages are tonal languages and use tonal levels as a means of defining specific words.

The basic conception of music as a multidimensional verbal-music experience profoundly influences African American music, as is reflected in the frequently used continuum from speech to song. The most vivid expressions of this continuum are the "sing-performance sermons" of African American preaching; the "talking, shouting" blues tradition; the speech and dialogue simulations common in jazz instrumental improvisations (especially by muted brass instruments); the phenomenon of jazz poetry performances of the 1920s, 1940s, and 1960s; and the hip hop and rap of contemporary African American popular music since the 1980s.

In *The Signifying Monkey*, Henry Louis Gates, Jr., traces the relationship of the Yoruba deity Eshu-Elegbara to the African American figure the "Signifying Monkey," and shows how "signifying"—the vernacular verbal practice of engaging "in rhetorical games through the free play of associated rhetorical and semantic relations," and "troping"—reinterpreting, revisiting, or "repeating previous existing texts with a difference" and, hence, reinventing and transforming them, describes processes that are fundamental to African American literature.[19] Other scholars have pointed out how these same processes are fundamental to traditional African and African American music.[20]

I concur with this observation and note that the common sharing of similar rhetorical strategies in verbal and musical exposition underscores or recalls the special relationship between language and music in traditional African societies. The usage of cyclical structures, significant repetition, improvised variations within an established framework, and call-and-response structures on many architectonic levels, abounds in and defines the character of both language and musical play. It also explains why musicians so often regale in obliterating the boundaries between speech and music as in the practices of "scat singing," or simulating speech by playing with mutes. African American music history is full of such examples in blues, jazz, and gospel music as well as in the various genres of popular music. This interesting notion of music as language and language as music represents another level of meaning that can be read in performances of African American music.

INFLUENCE OF AFRICAN CONCEPTS OF MUSICAL ORGANIZATION AND SYNTAX

Much of the scholarship devoted to a consideration of the relationship of African music to African American music has focused on comparative analyses of the formal aspects of the two musical traditions. The predilection in African music for cyclical musical structures that also employ antiphonal or call-and-response forms on multiple structural levels has been well documented as a common organizational principle by many observers. This basic principle has profoundly influenced African American music. The earliest documented genres of distinctly African American music, the spirituals, work songs, and fiddle and banjo secular music, all demonstrate the pervasiveness of this principle. Each genre, however, utilizes this formal principle in a manner unique to its musical and social function.

The adaptation of similar formal techniques for different musical types is one of the factors that makes various genres of the music sound similar. In addition, each musical type evolves its own genre-specific techniques of exploiting common formal devices. For example, the twelve-measure, three-poetic-line blues structure, with its intrinsic responsorial structure determined by the statement relationship of the first two lines to the answering third line of the form, also developed the convention of a call-and-response relationship between the singer and his or her instrument within the four-measure stanzas.

The blues developed as a post–Civil War musical genre that evolved in part from the wordless "hollers, cries, and moans" that preceded it, and contained the musical outpourings of an individual expressing his or her reactions to the world. Although it continued to develop as a distinct genre that found its most characteristic and exquisite forms in the twentieth century, its formal principles were reinterpretations of concepts associated with earlier African American music and influenced by African music.

African conceptions of rhythm have had an important impact on African American rhythmic ideas. The fundamental principle governing African rhythm cited by Nketia,

Alan Merriam, and other researchers is what A. M. Jones has referred to as "the clash of rhythm," or what might be referred to as the principle of rhythmic contrast.[21] The basic notion is that such music will evince a disagreement of rhythmic accents, cross-rhythm, and/or implied metrical contrast as an ideal. Syncopation, off-beat accents, and anticipation and retardation of foreground accents that clash with the prevailing metrical framework are the expected norm. The terms polyrhythm and multimeter have been used by some ethnomusicologists to describe specific subsets of this rhythmic quality. Others have chosen to use the broader, more inclusive concept of rhythmic contrast.

African American music reflects its usage of the basic principle of rhythmic contrast in many ways. Although complex examples of extended multilayered texture are not as common in African American music, rhythmic contrast in some form is found as an intrinsic quality within all genres of African American music. It is the imposition of techniques of rhythmic contrast on previously existing music of European American origin that is one of the major factors that transforms that music into styles that are distinctly African American.

One common means of creating contrast in African and African American music is to establish musical textures in which there is a built-in dichotomy between a repetitive rhythmic pattern that exists on one level, and simultaneously occurring variable rhythmic patterns that exist on other levels. This interaction between fixed and variable rhythmic strata that exists within an interlocked rhythmic-metrical framework is a means of establishing rhythmic contrast. In African music one finds expression of this practice in ensembles in which a group often consisting of a metal bell, a gourd rattle, hand claps, and sometimes high-pitched drums or instruments performs a fixed rhythmic pattern that has a metronomic function. This "time line" is used in contrast to other drums, instruments, and voices that perform variable rhythms.

In African American music the same basic rhythmic structure is apparent in instrumental genres from the fiddle and banjo music associated with the eighteenth and nineteenth centuries, to the complex instrumental ensembles of jazz and popular music that evolved in the twentieth century. In all of these genres, the organization of instruments into the "rhythm section" that plays recurring fixed rhythmic patterns, and the "front line" or lead instruments that play changing rhythmic patterns, is characteristic.

Within African and African American music, the dynamic relationship between the fixed and variable rhythmic strata is a process that determines one aspect of the syntax of both musical traditions. The organizational structure of both African and African American music is shaped on a large scale as well as on a foreground level in important ways by the interaction of fixed and variable rhythmic strata in conjunction with the usage of antiphony. This operates in different ways and is affected by other musical parameters to varying degrees in the two musical traditions. But the fundamental concept is present in both.

INFLUENCE OF AFRICAN CONCEPTS OF PERFORMANCE PRACTICE

Of great importance to the development of African American music is the retention in some instances, and adaptation in others, of performance practices associated with

African music. Among these practices is the approach to singing or playing any instrument in a percussive manner, a manner in which the greatest volume level occurs at the beginning of a sound, the attack phase, and the subsequent duration of the sound has a rapid decay of volume. The result is music that is characterized by qualitative stress accents. Performances of African and African American music tend to use instruments that are percussive in nature, and performance on all instruments is usually approached in a percussive manner.

Another common performance practice idiomatic of African American music clearly derived from African music is the incorporation of body motion as an integral part of the music-making process. In sub-Saharan cultures, body motion and music are viewed as interrelated components of the same process. Hence, singing or playing musical instruments is characteristically associated with elaborate body movements. These movements are not extraneous gestures, but are actions necessary to produce a desired effect in the musical performance; they are an intrinsic part of the music process. The most obvious example of this is the African usage of various arm, waist, and ankle rattles that adorn the bodies of dancers and produce a characteristic buzzy timbre when they move. The sounds produced by this movement are important components of the music. The dance becomes the music, and the music is the dance. A similar situation occurs in the work songs in both cultures when the physical action of work produces a sound that becomes an integral part of the music.

The common usage of body percussion (hand claps and slapping of hands against the body) and the history of African American dances that produce sounds created by the feet, from the shuffling sounds of the nineteenth-century religious dance called "ring shout" to twentieth-century tap dancing, are examples of the association of body motion with music. The approach to African and African American music assumes that body motion will be an integral part of the musical experience.

Another African practice that shaped African American musical performance practice is the predilection to create various ensembles comprised of contrasting timbres (sound colors). African instrumental ensembles characteristically consist of combinations of instruments whose individual colors are distinct—bells, drums, horns—and vocal ensembles in which the vocal qualities of individual performers may be discerned. I call this performance practice predilection the "heterogenous sound ideal."[22] African American music utilizes the same practices. The fact that individual singers are identified by distinct vocal timbres that contrast with others, such as Louis Armstrong, Billie Holiday, and Aretha Franklin, and that most performers use a wide range of vocal timbral nuances is a reflection of this ideal. This common practice is most notable in the performance of blues and gospel music. Thus, in ways that are both obvious and subtle, African American music owes a considerable debt to African performance styles.

Kofi Agawu, in his recent book, *African Rhythm: A Northern Ewe Perspective,* demonstrates through a careful study of northern Ewe music that the concept of rhythm is multidimensional. That is, "rhythm refers to a binding together of different dimensional processes, a joining rather than a separating, an across-the-dimensions instead of within-the-dimension phenomenon."[23] He also presents a conceptual model of the "domain of rhythmic expression" that is inclusive of "gesture-spoken word-vocal music-instrumental music and dance."[24] The point here is that the notion of rhythm, like the notion of music in many African cultures, consists not simply of an abstraction of a single dimension of music, as is the case in Western thought, but rather is inclusive of several dimensions of inextricably related human activities. For example: "the Ewe word 'vu' refers simultaneously to dance, music, and drumming." The context determines which of those dimensions is being signified in a particular instance.[25]

In an important sense, though Agawu wisely limits himself to a discussion of the specifics of northern Ewe musical culture, I, in an admittedly more speculative mode, would assert that the "conceptual approaches to the music-making process" cited above are all interrelated and generally shared by many West African cultures; further, that these concepts also collectively form the basis of a "critical core" of qualities associated with African American music; and finally, that they are important factors in the development of African American music.

Analysis of African American music must take cognizance of the above underlying conceptual approaches. To fail to do so shifts the focus away from those qualities that are the most significant in the musical experience to those that are of lesser significance. For example, in much African American music the parameters of music that are most important in shaping moments of rhythmic contrast are the heterogeneous sound ideal and the structural principles of antiphony, among other factors, the interaction among these qualities establishing the processes of greatest importance.

Specifically, among these processes is the propensity to create musical situations in which dynamic tension is developed between a fixed and usually cyclical metrical background framework and a variable musical foreground that inevitably contrasts or clashes with that framework in terms of rhythm, phrase structure, timbre, texture, melodic contour, and/or harmony. This exists on a number of different architectonic levels, sometimes in the form of simple syncopation or off-beat accents, but also at larger levels in the form of shifts of an entire motive, phrase, or section of a piece. This basic process, which perhaps also explains the presence of the unique quality of "swing" that is so pervasive in African and African American music, is fundamental to this tradition. From the point of view of aesthetics, what is important about this observation is that value appears to be accorded to certain kinds of musical processes—specifically musical processes that reaffirm, usually in ingenious ways, fundamental conceptual assumptions about the music process. High value is placed on those musical events that bring fundamental underlying conceptions into sharp relief by means of a fresh or novel musical approach.

It has been well documented that the traditional African and African American musical experience is an inclusive one in which the ideal is one of involvement of everyone who experiences the event as well as the principal performers. Part of this participation involves spontaneous reaction in the form of applause, verbal interjections, physical movement, or other outward responses to specific events in the music. It thus becomes possible to monitor moments of particular musical significance in a performance as judged by the collective response of a particular communion of participants by noting when they occur. It would then be possible to determine if there are musical qualities that these moments share.

Although a systematic exploration of "significant musical moments" remains to be undertaken, I have made some general observations of this phenomenon that I think are relevant to the present discussion. First, as is the case with most musical traditions, instances in a performance that reveal extraordinary technical virtuosity often elicit an immediate response from the audience-participants. This is perhaps akin to the reactions of a circus crowd when a trapeze artist performs a triple somersault, or the reactions of a nineteenth-century Italian opera audience when the soprano sang a series of reiterated florid passages around high "C."

But there are other moments in traditional African American performances that commonly elicit audience reaction. These are those moments when the artist performs a particularly unique phrase in which rhythmic, timbral, melodic, or harmonic displacement is ingenious. It is these moments that reveal the quality of the artist's musical imagination. An analysis of the musical performance must take these moments into consideration because often they reflect the high point of a particular improvised performance. These moments, which I call "soul focal points," often involve the combination of an ingenious rhythmic and timbral modification.

In summary, I have attempted to show that African American music is related to African music by a common sharing of a basic core of conceptual approaches to the process of music-making. As stated earlier, African American music reflects the duality of the African American experience. The aesthetics of this situation, though grounded in concepts that are essentially African, are also clearly influenced by non-African cultural traditions. The English language, functional tonality, European instruments, European socioeconomic structures, and Western concepts of time and space have all influenced the African American music tradition and impacted its aesthetics and historical development in varying degrees, in different genres, and in different historical periods. The central defining qualities of this musical tradition, however, are rooted in African concepts of music mediated by the American experience of its creators. Careful consideration of this basic fact enables one to gain greater insight into the nature of the music and a clearer understanding of the dynamics of its historical development.

NOTES

Title drawn from Edward Kennedy "Duke" Ellington and Irving Mills, "It Don't Mean a Thing If It Ain't Got That Swing" (Brunswick Records #6265, 1932).

1. Olly W. Wilson, "Black Music as an Art Form," *Black Music Research Journal* 3, no. 2 (1983), 1–22.

2. Olly W. Wilson, "The Significance of the Relationship Between Afro-American and West African Music," *Black Perspectives in Music* 2, no. 1 (1974): 2, 3–22. See also Alan P. Merriam, *The Anthropology of Music* (Evanston, Ill.: Northwestern University Press, 1964).

3. Melville J. Herskovits, *The Myth of the Negro Past* (Boston: Beacon Press, 1990 [1941]).

4. Sidney W. Mintz and Richard Price, *The Birth of African American Culture* (Boston: Beacon Press, 1976), 9–10.

5. Mintz and Price, *The Birth of African American Culture*, 11.

6. David Dalby, "The African Element in American English," in *Rappin' and Stylin' Out*, ed. Thomas Kochman (Urbana: University of Illinois Press, 1972), 173.

7. See Albert J. Raboteau, *Slave Religion: The "Invisible Institution" in the Antebellum South* (New York: Oxford University Press, 1978); Robert Farris Thompson, *African Art in Motion* (Berkeley: University of California Press, 1974); Houston Baker, *Blues Ideology and Afro-American Literature: A Vernacular Theory* (Chicago: University of Chicago Press, 1984); and *"Race," Writing and Difference*, ed. Henry Louis Gates, Jr. (Chicago: University of Chicago Press, 1984).

8. Henry Louis Gates, Jr., *The Signifying Monkey: A Theory of Afro-American Literary Criticism* (New York: Oxford University Press, 1988), 4.

9. W. E. B. Du Bois, "The Souls of Black Folk," in *Three Negro Classics* (New York: Avon Books, 1965 [1903]).

10. John Blacking, *How Musical Is Man?* (Seattle: University of Washington Press, 1973), 69.

11. Roland Barthes, *The Pleasure of the Text*, trans. Richard Miller (New York: Hill and Wang, 1976 [1973]).

12. Eileen Southern, *The Music of Black Americans: A History* (New York: W. W. Norton, 1983 [1971]).

13. Sheila S. Walker, *Ceremonial Spirit Possession in Africa and Afro-America* (Leiden, Netherlands: E. J. Brill, 1972).

14. Sterling Stuckey, *Slave Culture* (New York: Oxford University Press, 1987).

15. Charles Keil, *Urban Blues* (Chicago: University of Chicago Press, 1966), 97.

16. Albert Murray, *Stomping the Blues* (New York: McGraw-Hill, 1976), 17.

17. Murray, *Stomping the Blues*, 20.

18. J. H. Kwabena Nketia, *Drumming in Akan Communities in Ghana* (London: Thomas Nelson and Sons, 1963), 32–50.

19. Gates, *The Signifying Monkey*, 4.

20. Samuel A. Floyd, "Ring Shout! Literary Studies, Historical Studies, and Black Music Inquiry," *Black Music Research Journal* (1991).

21. A. M. Jones, *Studies in African Music* (London: Oxford University Press, 1959).

22. Olly W. Wilson, "The Heterogeneous Sound Ideal in African American Music," in *New Perspectives on Music: Essays in Honor of Eileen Southern*, ed. Josephine Wright (Warren, Mich.: Harmonie Park Press, 1992).

23. Kofi Agawu, *African Rhythm: A Northern Ewe Perspective* (Cambridge: Cambridge University Press, 1995), 7.

24. Agawu, *African Rhythm*, 28.

25. Agawu, *African Rhythm*, 7.

9

✳

Same Boat, Different Stops: An African Atlantic Culinary Journey

Jessica B. Harris

Malian scholar Amadou Hampâté Bâ once said, "*Chaque viellard qui meurt en Afrique, est comme une bibliothèque qui brule*" (Each old person who dies in Africa is like a library that is burned).[1] Nita Villapol, at a UNESCO conference on Africa in Latin America, put it in more culinary terms: "*en todo pais de América Latina donde hay influencia negra, cada vez que muere una cocinera vieja, se pierde todo un mundo de tradición oral y popular*" (in all Latin American countries where there is a Black influence, each time an old cook dies, a whole world of oral and popular tradition is lost).[2]

It has become popular to say that you are what you eat. In the case of Africans in the Diaspora, this saying takes on new meaning. For despite unspeakable treatment and privations, we have kept many of our foodways in this so-called New World. Cuban poet Nicolás Guillén in the poem "Mi Apellido" ("My Last Name") reminds us that "*sin conocernos nos reconoceremos en . . . los fragmentos de cadenas adheridos todavia a la piel*" ("without knowing each other we will know each other by the fragments of chains still stuck to our skin").[3] I would like to add "and by the okra on our plates." Indeed this African native—okra—and other foods and cooking techniques from the mother continent remain uniquely African American in hemispheric generality. Our food defines us, and because of our position in the kitchen, at the bottom of the culinary pecking order, our food has subtly defined the taste of the Americas.

Archaeologists now feel certain that eastern and southern Africa provide the world's earliest and most continuous record of human evolution. This history includes what is arguably some of humankind's earliest food production. In *Africans: The History of a Continent,* John Iliffe reminds us that "there is evidence as early as 20,000 to 19,000 years ago of intensive exploitation of tubers and fish at waterside settlements in southern Egypt near the First Cataract, soon followed by the collecting of wild grain."[4] One of these early grains was millet, which is still widely used throughout the African continent. Highland Ethiopia was another area of early plant domestication. In the grassy northern highlands and their eastern margins, teff (*Eragrostis tef*), finger millet (*Eleusine coracana*), noog (*Guizotia abyssinica*), sesame (*Sesamum indica*), and mustard (*Brassica juneca*) were all brought under cultivation. Ensete (*Ensete ventricosa*) and coffee (*Coffea arabica*) seem to have developed in the heavily forested uplands of southwest Ethiopia.[5] While the Sahel and the Sudan developed plants later, they were responsible for two agricultural systems: one based on sorghums and millets, and the other on African rice.

It must be noted that while much emphasis has been placed on cereal cultivation, there is increasing evidence that tubers played an important role in African diets as well, beginning seventeen thousand to eighteen thousand years ago.[6] Yams became so important in Africa that they took on mythical proportions, with festivities marking their planting and harvesting in countries like Ghana even today.

It is difficult to reconstruct the foodstuffs that were cultivated and eaten in Western Africa prior to European contact. But from archaeological evidence and early Arab chronicles, it is possible to make some deductions. From them we learn that while the African larder was significantly smaller prior to the Columbian exchange, there were nonetheless sufficient foodstuffs to provide a varied diet. There were grains that were prepared as fritters, porridges, mashes, and couscous-like dishes, much as they are throughout the continent today. One of the grains of preference was indigenous pearl millet (*Pennisetum typhoideun*). The botanical origins of this grain become clear when given its names in French and German, where it is known respectively as *millet* or *mil africain* and *negerkorn*.[7] Other grains included sorghum (*Sorghum vulgare*) and an African variant of rice (*Oryza glaberrima*), a wet rice that was cultivated in what is today the Casamance region of lower Senegal and in the area that would later become known as the Grain Coast.[8] The Grain Coast, though, was not named for this grain, but rather for the "grains of paradise" (*Amomum* or *Aframomum melegueta*) that were exported to Europe.

Other foodstuffs eaten in the western segment of Africa prior to European arrivals were pumpkins (*Telfairia pedata*). They are reported by chroniclers as being eaten in Timbuktu and Gao on the Niger River and in other areas within the Niger Basin. By the fourteenth century there were turnips (*Brassica rapa*), which were probably imported from Morocco to the north; cabbage (*Brassica oleraca*), which most likely arrived earlier from Morocco and Muslim Spain; eggplant (*Solanum melongena*); and cucumbers (*Cucumis sativus*), which some scholars feel may have originally come from Central Africa.[9] In addition, there were onions and garlic.

There was also okra, which is indigenous to the continent. It was used both fresh and dried, appeared in soups and stews, and was used to thicken sauces. A number of legumes were available including the black-eyed peas (*Vigna sinensis*), which have found their way into many dishes emblematic of the African American experience, and congo, or gunga peas (*Cajanus cajan*), which have been found in Egyptian tombs. Native to the continent, their names in English and French, congo peas and *pois d'Angole*, hint at a Central African connection. There were also broad, or fava beans (*Vicia faba*), and more than likely chick peas, kidney beans, and lentils. All were eaten in ancient Egypt and had made their way to the western part of the continent through trade.[10] The beans were used in soups and stews, and Ibn Battuta, during his 1352 C.E. journey through

Iwalatan and Mali observed, "They dig from the ground a crop like beans and they fry and eat it. Its taste is something like fried peas."[11] He also commented on women selling a type of bean flour from which porridges were prepared.[12]

There were also fruits such as tamarind, which was, and still is, consumed as a cooling beverage called *dakhar* in today's Senegal, and which is also used medicinally for its prodigious laxative qualities. Wild lemons and oranges were available in parts of the Sahel; the Portuguese traveler Diego Gomes found lemon trees growing in Senegambia in 1456.[13] There were also melons, including watermelon (*Citrulus vulgaris*), which has been cultivated in Africa for millennia and seems to be indigenous to tropical Africa, as well as dates (*Phoenix dactylifera*) and figs (*Ficus carica*).

Other more unusual foodstuffs included akee (*Bligha sapida*), the bland-tasting tripartite red tropical fruit that turns up in one of Jamaica's most popular dishes. While akee originated in West Africa, it can be found from Senegambia to Gabon and is eaten by the Yoruba of southwestern Nigeria, seemingly used more for medicinal than culinary purposes.[14] It is considered a sacred plant in parts of Côte d'Ivoire, where it is used medically, and it is employed by the Krobos of Ghana to wash clothing and to fix dyes.[15] Brought to the Caribbean by Captain Bligh in 1793, it became a major component of a favored Jamaican Sunday meal, akee and saltfish.

The baobab tree (*Adansonia digitata*) that grows from Senegambia to Zimbabwe offers virtually all of its parts for culinary purposes. The leaves are dried and pulverized for soup, the pulp of the white gourdlike fruit is eaten, and the seeds are roasted and taste like almonds. The latter are occasionally ground into a powder and used to thicken soups and stews.[16] Leo Africanus recorded that there were truffles, some of which were so large that a rabbit could make its burrow in them. They were peeled and roasted on coals or cooked in a fat broth, but were probably some other form of vegetable fungus than the black and white truffles we know today.[17]

Sesame oil was used for cooking, as were vegetable butters like shea butter, or *karité* as it is known in French. It is mentioned by Ibn Battuta and called *gharti*, a variant on the Soninke *kharite*.[18] Farther south there was also the red oil of the oil palm tree (*Elais guineensis*) that crossed the Atlantic to become Brazil's *dendê*. The same tree also provided palm wine that could be cooling and refreshing or, if allowed to sit and ferment, could pack the kick of a country mule—an early variety of white lightning, no doubt!

Aside from palm wine, there were other beverages for cooling off, including meads, all manner of beers, and drinks prepared from tree barks. There was also the drink prepared from the deep red flowers of a bush of the hibiscus family (*Hibiscus sabdariffa*). It is consumed today as *carcade* in Egypt, as *bissap* in Senegal, and on the other side of the Atlantic, as *sorrel*, the Caribbean region's most popular Christmas beverage.

Meat was used sparingly and was mainly for seasoning. At times of feasting, though, meat was important. And there was fish and the bounty of the sea, lagoons, and rivers. Dishes tended to be soupy stews served over or alongside a starch. To spice things up there were members of the pepper family, some native, others acquired through trade, most notably grains of paradise (*Amomum or Aframonum melegueta*) as well as other variants like long pepper (*Piper longum*); West African, Guinea, or Ashanti pepper (*Piper guineense*); Monk's pepper (*Agnus castus*); and cubebs (*Piper cubeba*). In the Middle Ages, these were much prized in Europe and traded in limited competition with pepper from the East (*Piper nigrum*). They were, and still are, used in conjunction with ginger to season dishes calling for a more spicy outlook. They are also found in the more elegant variations of *Ras al Hanout*, Morocco's legendary spice mixture. Salt was highly prized and used mainly as a preservative.[19]

In addition, there was kola (*Cola acuminata*). The nuts of this plant are chewed as a stimulant, containing kolatine and small quantities of theobromine, which allow people to function for extended periods of time without rest or nourishment.[20] The plant's importance is also religious, as it is used in divination by the Yoruba and several other groups. In many parts of Western Africa, kola has social and ceremonial importance, notably in the payment of dowries and in other exchanges of gifts and demonstrations of wealth. The sharing of kola is still considered a sign of friendship in many West and Central African countries. Known as *obí*, kola is also used for spiritual purposes by some Afro-Brazilians who have perpetuated African religious systems.

Prior to the Columbian exchange, the West African crucible that was the matrix of much of the food of the Western Hemisphere was a world where food was abundant and readily available, if not as diverse as it would become. Ingredients were prepared according to time-tested recipes in time-honored manners. Cooking and eating utensils were made from earthenware, wood, or metal, and many of the dishes and food storage vessels were prepared from calabashes and other gourds, a habit that would be duplicated in the new American life.

Anthropologist William Bascom researched the cooking of the Yoruba people of southwestern Nigeria and found six basic preparation techniques that can arguably be extended to much of West Africa and are assumed to have been known to West Africans before Columbus. They are:

- Boiling in water,
- Steaming in leaves,
- Frying in deep oil,
- Toasting beside the fire (this can also be described as grilling),
- Roasting in the fire, and
- Baking in ashes.[21]

To Bascom's culinary techniques, it is possible to add seven culinary tendencies that traveled from West Africa to the Americas and are emblematic of African-inspired cooking in the hemisphere. They are:

- The preparation of composed rice dishes,
- The creation of various types of fritters,
- The use of smoked ingredients for flavoring,
- The use of okra as a thickener,
- The abundant use of leafy green vegetables and the consumption of the "pot likker,"
- The abundant use of peppery and spicy hot sauces and condiments, and

- The use of nuts, beans (such as peanuts, which are beans, not nuts), and seeds as thickeners.[22]

With the arrival of Europeans and the extension of the culinary cornucopia, the West African larder (and indeed the world larder in general) expanded to include such American foodstuffs as chiles, tomatoes, and manioc or cassava. Indeed, it is impossible to think of the food of Africa without the addition of members of the capsicum family, or of Senegal's *chebujen* without tomatoes, or the food of southwestern Nigeria and the coastal République du Bénin without the cassava meal called *gari*.

The cuisine of Western Africa, both with and without the American additions to the diet, drew praise from missionaries and explorers in their travel logs. René Caillié, who traveled overland from Morocco through Mali into Guinea, repeatedly speaks of the foods he ate. He mentions a "copious luncheon of rice with chicken and milk" that he ate with delight and that filled the travelers for their journey.[23] He also speaks in his 1830 travel account of a meal offered to him by the poor of a village he was visiting, which consisted of a type of couscous served with a sauce of greens. He was astonished by the lavish hospitality, as the hosts ate only boiled yams with a sauce prepared without salt.[24]

The prodigious hospitality to which visitors were treated was worthy of commentary by virtually all writers, and Caillié and others were as astonished by the sophisticated tastes of the food as they were by the hospitality they were offered. Theophilus Conneau, another Frenchman, records that on December 8, 1827, he partook of an excellent supper

of a rich stew which a French cook would call a sauce blanche. I desired a taste which engendered a wish for more. The delicious mess was made of mutton minced with roasted ground nuts (or peanuts) and rolled up into a shape of forced meat balls, which when stewed up with milk, butter, and a little malaguetta [*sic*] pepper, is a rich dish if eaten with rice en pilau. Monsieur Fortoni of Paris might not be ashamed to present a dish of it to his aristocratic gastronomes of the Boulevard des Italiens.[25]

While Caillié was a traveler and chronicler, Conneau was on the continent in connection with an infamous trade: the Atlantic slave trade that would force millions of Africans from the continent of their birth and indirectly result in the transfer of African foodways to the Western Hemisphere. Conneau and thousands of others like him transformed Africa and changed the complexion and palate of the Western Hemisphere forever.

The almost four-century-long period of the transatlantic slave trade was marked by a second trade in foodstuffs necessary for the enslaved Africans to survive their arduous and unspeakable journey. Their survival was of prime importance to the traders, who were more sagacious about West African cultures and habits than many thought. James A. Rawley, in *The Transatlantic Slave Trade*, presents his observations, noting that captives from the Bight of Benin were accustomed to yams, while those from the Windward and Gold Coasts were accustomed to rice. The newly enslaved Africans were also said to have a "good stomach for beans."[26]

The nationality of each slave trader was associated with specific rules and regulations. As early as 1684, Portugal enacted rules limiting the number of captives to be transported and regulating the amount of provisions and the size of ships. North American slavers commonly fed their captives rice and corn, both of which were readily available on the African coast and in America. They also gave them black-eyed peas. The rice was boiled in iron cauldrons, and the corn was fried into cakes. The beverage was water, occasionally flavored with molasses. Some slavers noted an African taste for the "bite-y" and offered rice wine flavored with hot pepper. Usually though, wine and spirits were only used medicinally. British ships fed the Africans horse beans that were brought from England and stored in vats. They were later mixed with lard and turned into a pulpy mash.[27]

William Richardson, in *A Mariner of London*, speaks of his experiences aboard a slaveship: "Our slaves had two meals a day, one in the morning consisting of boiled yams and the other in the afternoon of boiled horse beans and slabber sauce poured over each. This sauce was made of chunks of old Irish beef and rotten salt fish stewed to rags and well seasoned with cayenne pepper."[28]

Others suggest that the infamous and repellently named slabber sauce was a mixture of palm oil, flour, water, and chile.[29] On some ships the allowance of water was a half pint per meal unless the ship was put on short rations.[30] This for the enslaved Africans who would become African Americans was a period of trial; a period in which they underwent a sea change on the waters of the Atlantic to become new and different people; a period in which the human will to survive triumphed over the impossible.

Many have told tales of the newly enslaved Africans bringing with them in their hair or their clothing okra and sesame seeds, thereby transplanting them to the New World. The truth is that with the exception of necklaces and amulets, beads from which have been found in archaeological digs on this side of the Atlantic, most Africans arrived with no belongings and little idea of their ultimate fate. Some, in fact, thought that they would be eaten by white cannibals!

The arrival of African foodstuffs in this hemisphere during the period of the transatlantic slave trade is the result of a more brutal reality. The economics of slavery were such that it made sense for slavers and plantation owners to feed the Africans a diet on which they would survive to work. Much ink flowed on how to feed the enslaved Africans inexpensively and in a manner that would allow for their survival. Foods like breadfruit from the South Pacific found their way to the Caribbean to provide inexpensive fodder for them. Many African foodstuffs, such as akee, also arrived in the Americas in this manner.

The peanut, which originated in Brazil or Peru, was transported to Africa by the Portuguese. It came to the northern part of the Americas aboard slave ships along with its African name from the Kimbundu word *nguba*—goober.[31] As came the peanut, so came okra, black-eyed peas, watermelons, and other foodstuffs popular in Africa. True (white) yams did not come to the northern part of the hemisphere. They were replaced in the diet by sweet potatoes, which in many parts of the American South are still called by the name of the tuber they replaced. The confusion between the sweet potato (*Ipomea batata*) and the (yellow or orange) yam (*Discorea sp.*) still exists, particularly in the southern United States.

Botanically, sweet potatoes and yams are two different species. The former is of New World origin, and the latter comes from various areas of tropical Africa and Asia. They neither look nor taste alike. The confusion comes as they may be prepared in similar ways. Once rooted in this hemisphere, African plants such as okra, black-eyed peas, and watermelon went on to become emblematic of the food of Africans in the North American Diaspora.

The American Diaspora began as a trickle with the African crew members who were aboard the vessels of explorers from Columbus to (Pedro Alvez) Cabral (who "discovered" Brazil). It grew to a flood in the early years of the seventeenth century and became a tidal wave that transformed the hemisphere with the sugar economy of northeastern Brazil and the Caribbean and the cotton culture of the southern United States. The tidal wave began in Brazil, where the first enslaved Africans arrived in large numbers in the sixteenth century. One of the places they first saw in this hemisphere was the circular customs house in the bay by the city of São Salvador da Bahia de Todos os Santos. Africans were becoming African Americans.

The climate of coastal northeastern Brazil was similar to the one that they had left, and many African foodstuffs were transplanted. Okra was grown and called *quiabo*. The tenth edition of the *Pequeno dicionário brasileiro da lingua portuguesa* offers variants and synonyms for *quiabo*, "*gombo, guingombo, quingombo, quingobo, quimbombo, quinbombo, and quibombo*," all derived from the Bantu languages of Central Africa. It would seem that the word quiabo in current usage is a corruption of one of the Bantu forms.[32]

In fact, okra retains traces of its African origins in all of the names by which it is called in the Romance languages. In French the word *gombo* owes its origin to the Bantu languages, most notably to the Chiluba of Zaire or Kimbundu of Angola: *quingombo* or *chingombo* or *ochingombo*. Spain's and Cuba's *quimbombó* is an almost direct transliteration. Caribbean English's *okro* and U.S. English's okra originate from one of the Akan languages of Ghana. The Dominican Republic's variant, *malondrón*, is of uncertain origin.

Palm oil, called *dendê*, is another of the transplanted foods, and the northeastern section of Brazil is one of the few places in the Americas, if not the only place, where the oil of the Central African native has become a hallmark of African-inspired cooking. The likely origin is the Angolan Kimbundu term *ndende* (*elaeis guineensis*), designating the oil palm tree that gives the palm nuts that furnish the unctuous red dendê oil.[33]

While many of the enslaved Africans were put to work in the cane fields of Bahia and Pernambuco, there was also the growth of urban slavery that, at times, allowed them to pursue a trade with the profits going to the master or mistress. In many cases the vending of foodstuffs, fresh produce, confections, and savories was a popular trade. Perhaps more than any of the other European powers in the hemisphere, the diet of the Portuguese colonists changed radically from that of the mother country. The Afro-Bahian culinary holy trinity of hot chiles, dendê, and coconut milk was established and came to mark their tastes.

The African specialties of steaming in leaves, grilling, frying in deep oil, and the preparation of composed rice dishes were all maintained. *Angú* is an African-type porridge or mash prepared from corn or manioc flour and water. It is thought that the name angú comes from the elision of the Yoruba terms *a ni e gun*, meaning a crushed or smashed thing.[34] The gelatinous paste of rice or corn flour and water wrapped in banana leaves and steamed is called *acaçá*, a word close enough to have its Ewe origins as *akatsa* recognized.[35] The Yoruba bean fritter known as *akará* is prepared in Bahia with black-eyed peas and called *acarajé*, a corruption of *akará ije* (an akará meal) or *akará je* (akará to eat).[36]

One of the most important influences on Brazilian cuisine, and most particularily Afro-Bahian cuisine, was the ritual cooking of the Yoruba, Fon, and Ewe religions from Nigeria, Benin, and Togo, which became known as Candomblé in Brazil's northeastern state of Bahia where people from these African ethnic groups were concentrated. In their bodies and their heads the enslaved Africans brought to this hemisphere their Orishas, the demanding gourmet gods who insisted on having their ritual meals prepared according to centuries-old exacting recipes that allowed for little variation, as they prescribed not only ingredients, but even methodology. Foods in Bahia's most traditional Candomblé houses of worship are still prepared on wood-burning fires using ingredients cut and diced, stirred and seasoned according to recipes that crossed the Atlantic as part of the oral baggage of enslaved Africans.

Ogun, the blacksmith god and patron of all those who work with metal, ate and still eats roasted yam and black-eyed peas, and *feijoada*, a Brazilian mixture of black beans and smoked meats. Oyá, or Yansã, the Orisha of the whirlwind and owner of the precincts of the cemeteries, still craves her bean fritters, the *akará* of Nigeria, which she calls *acarajé* on the American side of the Atlantic. Over the years these dishes went from the religious houses of worship, or *terreiros*, to the *casas grandes,* or "big houses," where Afro-Brazilian cooks were in charge of the kitchens. From there they became a part of the culinary consciousness of the country. Yansã's *acarajé* is a favorite snack food in much of the country, and Ogun's *feijoada* became Brazil's national dish.

Like their counterparts in Brazil, many of the Africans who arrived in the Caribbean region were immediately initiated into the brutal task of cultivating sugarcane, the sugar-bearing reed that had become King Sugar. The cane arrived from the Canary Islands with Columbus on his second voyage in 1493, and more than a century later became part of the revolution that dramatically transformed the agriculture, complexion, history, and culture of the Caribbean region.

In the Caribbean, though, tastes would not only be influenced by a combination of African culinary techniques, the bounty of the sea, local produce, brief contact with Native Americans, and one colonial power as in Brazil. Those first four factors interacted in the Caribbean with the prevailing cuisine of four colonial powers—English, Spanish, French, and Dutch—to produce a regional cuisine that has an ethos all its own, a multicultural cuisine that speaks of the region as much as does its music and art.

Itinerant merchants hawked their wares and presided over tables at markets in cities like Kingston, Jamaica, Port-au-Prince, Haiti, Pointe-à-Pitre, Guadeloupe, and Bridgetown, Barbados. Vendors, although in most cases enslaved, were major forces in the marketplace. Advertisements in the Barbados newspapers of the mid-eighteenth century testify to the participation of enslaved market women in the country's domestic economy. They, in fact, so dominated the market that huckstering became punishable by law, only becoming legal in Barbados in 1794.[37] Despite their outlawing, five basic types of hucksters worked on the streets, including "specialists, often domestics who sold on the streets on their owners' account," and "petty hucksters who sold sweets and drink."[38]

The manners of selling of these Caribbean women, seated on a stool on the ground or carrying a flat tray on the head, and indeed many of the tastes that were to be found on the trays, were similar to those sold by their Brazilian sisters:

[A]rticles of various kinds. . . . These they carry on their heads in wooden trays, and call at different doors as they pass. From these peoples, eatables . . . may be purchased, but the things for which they find the most ready sale are pickles and preserves with fruit, sweetmeats, oil, noyau, annisette, and more.[39]

Sugar cakes, peanut or other nut patties, and fritters were particularly popular. The influence of the enslaved Africans on the economy of markets was so strong that many of the islands have to the present retained their traditional market days. In Jamaica, for example, the tradition of a Sunday market has been maintained in some outlying parishes.

The African influence was felt not only in the manner of selling foodstuffs, but also in the manner of seasoning them, as the general African taste for the "bite-y" and the hot that had been noted by the explorers and then the slavers and the plantation owners still prevailed. It is shown in myriad hot sauces, pepper sauces, *moyos*, and *sauce piments* that make ample use of the fiery local chiles that are called by names that sing with the humor and poetry of the region—Scotch Bonnet for the tam o'shanter-shaped chile that appears frequently in the food of Jamaica, *wiri wiri* for the small incendiary cannonballs of heat that "fire up" the food of Guyana, and *Bonda Man' Jacques* for the super-hot fat red chile that comes to the table in Martinique and Guadeloupe (this chile's name is Kréol for Madame Jacques's backside!).

The mixing of foodways in the Caribbean also parallels that of Brazil in the use of such native American staples as cassava bread, which appears on virtually all of the islands in one form or another. In Jamaica it is *bammie*, in the Dominican Republic it is *pan de casaba*, and in the French Antilles it has given its name to the famous zouk music group—Kassav.

Pork, which was brought to this hemisphere by the Spaniards, became one of the quintessential meats. Its popularity is due in large measure to the fact that pigs could be raised easily, the meat was adaptable to most cooking methods, and there was very little waste. The choice parts could be eaten by the enslavers and the rest consumed by the enslaved. In the Caribbean it turns up as everything from sausages to barbecue. Deep-fried pork skins become *chicharrones* in Puerto Rico and Cuba, and the meat is one of the several that go into the *locrio* or multimeat stew of the Dominican Republic.

Rubbed with garlic, pork is transformed into Puerto Rico's and Cuba's Christmas and festive homage to Spain, *lechón asado*. It is equally transformed into the garlic pork of Guyana and the *grios de cochon* of Haiti. It is the traditional meat for the jerk of Jamaica, the war food of the Maroons that has become one of that island's most popular culinary exports. It even shows up in unusual mixes like Guadeloupe's and Martinique's pork curry or *colombo de porc*, which speak of the mixing of African foodways with those of southern Indians who arrived as indentured servants in the mid-nineteenth century.

For most people, the Caribbean's best-loved contribution to the art of eating well is rum. A sugarcane by-product, it is a commodity complexly involved with the presence of Africans in the hemisphere in that, ironically, this fruit of the labor of enslaved Africans served to pay for yet more Africans. This uniquely Caribbean beverage has played a major role in the history of the hemisphere, lubricating the wheels of the "triangular trade" between Europe, Africa, and the Americas. It was one of the trade goods that was used to barter for Africans in the slave trade, and it fueled the sailors of the ships. The beverage was also used to lure voters to the polls in the United States in the early years of the Republic.

In the present it is possible to recognize and distinguish the identity of a Caribbean neighborhood in any part of the world by the brands of rum for sale. For the Haitians, there is Barbancourt; the Puerto Ricans drink Don Q, Palo Viejo, Barrilito, and Bacardi, the latter having moved from Cuba. In the United States Virgin Islands, it is Cruzan rum, while in the British Virgin Islands it is Pussers, the rum of the Royal Navy. Rhum St. James and Rhum Mauny are two of the rums that mark Martinique, while Mount Gay and Cockspur speak of Barbados. Trinidadians settle down to Old Oak at their local rum shops, while Guyanese sip "a tip" of XM, and Dominicans savor the three B's—Barceló, Brugal, and Bermudez. It is consumed neat, in piña coladas, in a seemingly endless array of house drinks, in *'ti ponchs* and in rum punches. Most sippers, though, would be unable to identify the beverage's infamous history as a contribution of African labor to the foodways of the Western Hemisphere.

Like Brazil, the Caribbean region retains many culinary Africanisms. Small packets of cornmeal with savory or sweet fillings are steamed in banana leaves. In Barbados, they are called *conkies*, which is thought by some to be a corruption of *kenkey*, as the dish (without the filling) is known in Ghana. In Jamaica they are known as blue drawers for the color that the banana leaves turn, and are also called *dokono*, an African survival, as Leonard Barrett found out:

> In 1969, on my first trip to Africa, our party stopped at the Koromantyn market at the foot of the famous Koromantyn Castle from which most Jamaican slaves embarked on their Atlantic journey to Jamaica. Walking in the market, I came upon a woman with a stall of the same banana leaf preparation. I pointed to it and said "*dokono!*" The woman, who spoke no English, was startled. She ran and called a man who spoke English and Twi. On their way back to me, the woman was frantically explaining something to him. He finally caught up with me and asked how I knew the items were *dokono*. I told him that my mother used to make them and referred to them by that name in Jamaica. In a few minutes I was in the midst of a noisy admiring crowd of old men and women all talking to one another. Some came close, hugging my hands in a most caressing manner. The gentleman explained to me

that the elders were giving me an African welcome because I was the son of an ancestor who was sold in slavery.[40]

As Barrett's poignant memoir reminds us, in the case of many of the foodways of the southern part of the African Atlantic world, thanks to climates that allowed for the cultivation of African foodstuffs or similar species, the circle is indeed unbroken.

It was more complex for the enslaved Africans who arrived in the northern segment of the hemisphere. Like their "cousins" who arrived in South America and the Caribbean, they were initiated into the cultivation end of the food chain and placed in charge of big house kitchens, where they instituted what historian Eugene D. Genovese has called, "the culinary despotism of the slave cabin over the big house."[41] Unlike others who shared their enslavement in other parts of the hemisphere, they found unfamiliar, and in many cases unhealthy, climates and had to adapt to different foods. The taste for the "bite-y" persevered, and chiles, when available, were still used, notably bird chiles (*Capsicum frutescens* or *Capsicum annuum*). Preserved in vinegar, they formed a table condiment that was much prized. This in more recent years has become the long thin bottles of hot sauce that are hallmarks of good African American cooking.

African techniques still played an important role in the antebellum South. Both testimonials gathered in the 1930s from people who had been enslaved and archaeological evidence reveal that foods were prepared using open-hearth cooking techniques that depended on flames, charcoal, and ash.[42] Indeed, many of these methods were similar to those the enslaved Africans had left behind. On small plantations many enslaved people prepared food either in their cabins or outside when the weather was too hot to allow for indoor cooking. Large plantations often had communal kitchens with a few cooks preparing the food for the others. The habit of eating stews and thick soups was retained, along with the Africanism of using a starchy mass—cornbread, hoecakes, ashcakes, and the like—to sop the gravy.

The African ingredients that could be transplanted—okra, black-eyed peas, sesame, rice, watermelon—became emblematic of the food of African Americans. To these were added New World ingredients like corn and the sweet potatoes that were promptly baptized "yams" by some, thereby leading to the institutionalization of a misnomer.

Game, when it could be hunted, was a delicacy with preference being given to small game such as rabbits and squirrels. Opossum, although requiring careful preparation, was also prized and often found its way into cook pots. The animal's nocturnal habits made it most likely to be abroad after dark, when enslaved people had more liberty for hunting.[43] Chicken, which could be raised with minimal outlay, was usually reserved for special occasions or Sundays, hence its name the "Gospel Bird," and pork was king for all Americans.

Tradition has it that African Americans ate, and in many cases still eat, everything on the pig "but the oink." The desire to "eat higher on the hog" is testified to by much "Massa and John" humor from the antebellum South. Many enslaved people felt that a Northern victory in the Civil War would allow them to live higher on the hog. Yet ironically, the Civil War had the reverse effect of introducing many white Southerners to the dishes that had been previously relegated to African Americans. Many dishes that had been African American food became known as Southern food, the African origins of the cuisine that still typifies the region being unavowed in the former bastion of racial segregation.

The early years of the twentieth century marked the beginnings of the northern migrations of many African Americans. They went in search of jobs, equality, and a place away from Jim Crow. Just as sure as the Delta Blues gave birth to the Chicago Blues and, as many African Americans would say, "just as sure as grits is groceries," rapidly urbanizing African Americans took their foods with them. African American neighborhoods can to this day be distinguished by their produce and meat shops. In them are sold a full range of leafy green vegetables that serve as the basis of African-inspired dishes and a seemingly endless array of pork products, including snouts, feet, ears, tails, and innards—hog maws and chitterlings, or more properly, "chit'lins"—that hark back to tastes acquired during the period of enslavement.

Throughout the history of the United States, African American cooks, like their counterparts throughout the hemisphere, have worked unheralded and underpaid in many of the nation's finest public and private dining establishments, including the White House. Their tastes have influenced the taste of the nation. Yet unlike their "cousins" in other parts of the hemisphere, their contributions to the culinary ethos of the United States have been largely ignored until the present.

Finally, as the twenty-first century dawns, the culinary contributions of Americans of African descent are being recognized and documented not only in the United States, but throughout the hemisphere. They are being linked together to form a culinary continuum that bears gustatory witness to the African Diaspora—an umbilicus that joins all people who shared the yoke of enslavement in an unending chain that begins in Africa, spreads throughout the Western Hemisphere, and gives true meaning to the expression "same boat, different stops!"

NOTES

1. Amadou Hampâté Bâ, "La parole africaine dans des instances internationales" speech at the UNESCO General Conference, Paris, 1960.

2. Nita Villapol, "Hábitos alimentários africanos en América Latina," in *África en América Latina*, ed. Manuel Moreno Fraginals (Paris: UNESCO, 1977), 328.

3. Nicolás Guillén, "Mi Apellido" in *Patria o muerte: The Great Zoo and Other Poems* (La Habana: Editorial de Arte y Literatura, 1973), 160–161.

4. John Iliffe, *Africans: The History of a Continent* (Cambridge, U.K.: Cambridge University Press, 1995), 6.

5. James L. Newman, *The Peopling of Africa: A Geographic Interpretation* (New Haven, Conn.: Yale University Press, 1995), 51–52.

6. David A. Phillipson, *African Archeology*, 2nd ed. (Cambridge, U.K.: Cambridge University Press, 1995), 102.

7. Newman, *The Peopling of Africa*, 54.

8. Jessica B. Harris, *The Welcome Table* (New York: Simon and Schuster, 1995), 20.

9. Thadeuz Lewicki, *West African Food in the Middle Ages: According to Arabic Sources* (Cambridge, U.K.: Cambridge University Press, 1974), 64. These are the botanical designations as reported by Lewicki. Some scholars, however, have problems with some of the particular species being too modern or otherwise inaccurate. As I am not a botanist, I offer Lewicki's suggestions as a point of departure for future study.

10. Hilary Wilson, *Egyptian Food and Drink* (Princes Risborough, U.K.: Shire Egyptology, 1988), 25–26.

11. Said Hamdun and Noel King, eds., *Ibn Battuta in Black Africa* (Princeton, N.J.:) Markus Wiener Publishers, 1994), 40.

12. Hamdun and King, *Ibn Battuta*, 41.

13. Lewicki, *West African Food*, 72.

14. William Bascom, "Yoruba Food," *Africa* 21, no. 1 (Jan. 1951): 41–53.

15. Anthony K. Andoh, *The Science and Romance of Selected Herbs Used in Medicine and Religious Ceremony* (San Francisco: North Scale Institute, 1986), 180.

16. Andoh, *Science and Romance*, 150–151.

17. Lewicki, *West African Food*, 77.

18. Hamdun and King, *Ibn Battuta*, 40 and note.

19. Paula Wolfert, *Couscous and Other Good Food from Morocco* (New York: Harper and Row, 1973), 26.

20. Bascom, "Yoruba Food," 48.

21. William Bascom, "Yoruba Cooking," *Africa* 21, no. 1 (April 1951), 125–37.

22. Harris, *The Welcome Table*, 2.

23. René Caillié, *Voyage à Tombouctou*, vol. 1 (Paris: Editions F. Maspéro/La Découverte, 1982 [1830]), 353.

24. Caillié, *Voyage à Tombouctou*, 353.

25. Captain Theophilus Conneau, *A Slaver's Log Book of 20 Years' Residence in Africa* (Sheffield, Mass.: Howard S. Mott. Inc., 1976), 117.

26. James A. Rawley. *The Transatlantic Slave Trade: A History* (New York: W.W. Norton, 1981), 298.

27. Rawley, *Transatlantic Slave Trade*, 298.

28. Richardson quoted in George Francis Dow, *Slave Ships and Slaving* (New York: Dover, 1970), 13.

29. Dow, *Slave Ships and Slaving*, 144.

30. Dow, *Slave Ships and Slaving*, 13.

31. Lorenzo Dow Turner, *Africanisms in the Gullah Dialect* (Ann Arbor: University of Michigan Press, 1974 [1949]), 194.

32. Aurelio Buarque de Holanda Ferreira and Hildebrando de Lima, *Pequeno dicionário brasileiro da língua portuguesa* (Rio de Janeiro, Civilização Brasileira, 1968)—"*quiabo.*"

33. Olga Guidolle Cacciatore, *Dicionário de cultos afro-brasileiros* (Rio de Janeiro: Forense Universitária/SEEC, 1977), 104; Ana de Sousa Santos, *A alimentação do muxiluanda* (Luanda, Angola: Cooperação Portuguesa, Embaixada de Portugal, 1996).

34. Guidolle Cacciatore, *Dicionário de cultos afro-brasileiros*, 48.

35. Guidolle Cacciatore, *Dicionário de cultos afro-brasileiros*, 34.

36. Guidolle Cacciatore, *Dicionário de cultos afro-brasileiros*, 34.

37. Guidolle Cacciatore, *Dicionário de cultos afro-brasileiros*, 86.

38. Hilary McD. Beckles, *Natural Rebels: A Social History of Enslaved Black Women in Barbados* (New Brunswick, N.J.: Rutgers University Press, 1989), 79.

39. Beckles, *Natural Rebels*, 80.

40. Leonard Barrett, *The Drum and the Sun: African Roots in Jamaican Folk Tradition* (Kingston, Jamaica: Heinemann, 1976), 21–22.

41. Eugene D. Genovese, *Roll Jordan Roll: The World the Slaves Made* (New York: Vintage, 1976), 543.

42. Harris, *The Welcome Table*, 26.

43. Harris, *The Welcome Table*, 147.

10

✳

Roots and Branches: Historical Patterns in African Diasporan Artifacts

John Michael Vlach

The image of the tree that serves so well as an operative metaphor in the study of genealogy and the recovery of family history provides effective guidance for the study of African American material culture. Just as in the search for family origins where the quest for "roots" is so essential, so too does the study of historic artifacts demand pursuit of the earliest-known examples in order to understand how technology-based traditions first took hold and began to develop. But just as a tree may over time assume a character or shape not anticipated when it was first planted, so too may a cultural expression evolve unexpected features.

The contingencies of experience and environment or the unique peculiarities of personality or place will often combine to induce novel and unforeseen outcomes. Put another way, the branches of a tree do not always follow the intent of its roots. Applying this insight to the study of traditional artifacts, we must ready ourselves to encounter divergent personal innovations as well as the soothing reassurance of stable, deeply rooted customs. Where a customary technology begins may not always explain how it ends up.

The arts and crafts created by African Americans are perhaps the least acknowledged of their cultural traditions. Worldwide recognition of African American achievements in music and dance has overshadowed significant accomplishments in the area of material culture. So that while African Americans are seen as gifted performers, they are rarely described as even adequate producers of objects. But in times past African American artisans were numerous, and they are to be credited with making a wide array of artifacts, particularly in the southern states. It is important to recall that during the preindustrial era most rural people made things: tools, utensils, containers, clothes, houses, musical instruments, toys. African Americans were not exempt from this pattern; indeed their lives were characterized by repeated acts of material self-reliance. Whether held in slavery or working as free people, African Americans created a multitude of necessary, useful, and often beautiful, objects[1] (figures 10.1 and 10.2).

Figure 10.1.   Pearl Davis, rendering of *Hickory Rocking Chair* from Sam Houston home, Huntsville, Texas. Index of American Design. © 2001, Board of Trustees, National Gallery of Art, Washington, D.C.

The reasons for which African Americans would be skilled at making domestic arts and crafts are not hard to fathom. In the plantation context they often had little choice when they were ordered to learn particular trades by their owners. But more often, because they were provided with so few domestic items, they either had to make most of their furnishings and utensils or do without. After emancipation, the arts and crafts that African Americans had developed while in bondage continued to prove useful. Reduced

Figure 10.2. Joe Brennan and Jesús Peña, rendering of *Writing Desk* from Red River Valley, Texas. Index of American Design. © 2001, Board of Trustees, National Gallery of Art, Washington, D.C.

to a condition of near servitude by continued racial exploitation and poverty, African American artisans used their traditional skills to get themselves and their families through tough times, and some still do today.

Arts and crafts have always played dual roles in the African American community, serving both as a means of making a living and as a means for creative self-expression. While many craft items produced by African Americans are indistinguishable in form, technique, and style from works produced by white Americans, there is a stream of African inspiration that runs through traditional African American material culture, especially in the South. The most distinctive works in cultural terms are those that manifest a linkage to African origins.[2] The remainder of this chapter provides a survey of a few examples of artifactual expressions linked in some manner to an African genealogy.

BASKETRY

Coiled-grass baskets have been produced in the United States by African American artisans for more than three centuries. Once integral items on plantations along the former "rice coast" extending from North Carolina to Florida's northern border, the craft is today most publicly on display in and around Charleston, South Carolina. Here hundreds of "sewers" are daily at work fashioning baskets. Using "sweetgrass," rush, pine needles, and strips of leaves from the palmetto tree as their primary materials, they produce a seemingly limitless variety of forms that they sell on street corners, in the central open-air market, and at more than a hundred stands along the main highway entering the city.

What one sees here are mainly "show baskets" (figure 10.3), a subgenre within this tradition that was initiated probably in the mid-nineteenth century. Included under this category are all sorts of decorative containers: flower baskets, serving trays, purses, sewing baskets, casserole holders, umbrella stands, and cake baskets. As is evident from this partial inventory, the show basket is intended to be used in the home where it will

Figure 10.3. "Show baskets." Photo by Martin L. Linsey.

be prominently displayed. The basket-makers explore at every opportunity new creative possibilities in form and decoration to make these baskets fancy. A show basket is, then, a highly personalized artwork shaped extensively by individual imagination.

Yet, matriarch basket-maker Mary Jane Manigault explains, "All baskets begin as a hot plate,"[3] meaning that all works, no matter how imaginative and seemingly without precedent, trace back to a common ancestry rooted in basic forms and techniques: all coiled baskets start out as a disk form. The oldest African American coiled baskets were "work baskets" (figure 10.4). They were made with bundles of stiff rushes and often sewn with strips of oak. With coils generally an inch in diameter, these were tough, durable baskets intended to be used outside either in the fields or in the farm yard.

They are easily distinguishable from the lighter, more delicately formed show baskets. Most work baskets were large, heavy, round containers made to carry produce; they all had flat bottoms and straight walls that flared out slightly from the base. One specialized work basket, the fanner, was a large tray about two feet in diameter with a

Figure 10.4. Work basket. Photo by Martin L. Linsey.

low outer rim. Primarily an implement for processing the rice harvest, it was a basic kitchen tool. Rice could not be properly cooked unless it had first been fanned to separate the kernels from the husks.

These baskets were but one element in a set of African practices upon which the production of rice was based. Planters specifically sought out Africans from the rice-growing regions of West and Central Africa, and with these people came a knowledge of rice cultivation and of the technology for its harvest and preparation. While planters were generally wary about allowing overt African expressions among their enslaved workers, they tolerated those features such as basketry production that enhanced the productivity of their estates. In so doing, these planters unwittingly facilitated the maintenance of a decidedly African tradition.

While the end of the plantation era understandably brought an end to the large-scale work basket tradition, it did not cause coiled basketry to disappear. These baskets remained a feature of home craft on small African American farms in the area, and there was from 1910 to 1950 an attempt at the Penn School on St. Helena Island to revive the practice. While this particular effort ended with disappointing results, the tradition was able to flourish in the Charleston area, where show baskets became popular among tourists who sought them as souvenirs of their visit.

The basket-making tradition was necessarily transformed as artisans shifted from a rural to an urban venue, and as artisans made baskets more often for sale than for domestic use. Yet venerable traditions were still honored. The sewing baskets and serving trays were still old-timey baskets, even if their origins did not trace all the way back to Africa like the work baskets. But the entrepreneurial energies released in this boot-straps commercial effort led mainly to free-wheeling displays of personal imagination. Soon basket-makers were as proud of new unprecedented forms that they called "own style baskets" as they were of more conventional flower baskets or clothes hampers.

But even within this spirited and open-ended creativity, there are still signs of historical memory. Fanner baskets, for example, can occasionally be found for sale in the Charleston market, albeit as lightweight show basket facsimiles. But more importantly, the techniques for coiling and stitching remain unchanged regardless of the type of basket. This continuity of process allows contemporary basket-makers to place themselves in the flow of a tradition that traces back through time and space to African roots. The personal satisfaction these artisans derive from making coiled baskets is amplified by a keen awareness of that history, which increases their motivation to preserve this custom.[4]

BOATBUILDING

That African American competence in agriculture was matched by maritime abilities should not be surprising. Many Africans brought to the New World were captured from coastal or riverine environments and thus had had experience with a variety of small watercraft. When set to work on plantations, often located near the coast or along prominent rivers, these Africans had ample opportunity to display their navigational skills. Eighteenth-century commentators were quick to acknowledge how adept enslaved boatmen were in paddling log canoes difficult to maneuver in swift current. In the Charleston area African American watermen working out of hewn dugouts called pettiaugers (an Anglicized version of the French *pirogue*) had by 1750 achieved almost complete domination of the local fishing trade. White people depended on African American boating skills from Georgia to Maryland, as enslaved watermen literally provided the backbone for the local transportation system during a period when there were few roads.[5]

In this context enslaved Africans also built boats. While the surviving descriptions tend to be somewhat vague with respect to details, it seems that West Indian watercraft, and thus in some measure African-derived maritime traditions, provided the basic models. The pettiauger was a well-known Caribbean vessel with a hull consisting of a log dugout extended upward by the addition of extra planks. Fitted with sails for open water voyaging, it could also be propelled by teams of oarsmen. Boats of this sort are described repeatedly as the usual type of plantation "barge" used to ferry people, supplies, and produce.

A second type of plantation vessel was a canoe hewn from a single log. Derived from either African or Native American precedents, it was less than twenty feet in length and relatively light due to the thinness of the hull. This was an excellent vessel for navigating the shallow marshes and streams surrounding the barrier islands of the South Carolina and Georgia coasts. Plantation mistress Fannie Kemble recorded in 1838 that two carpenters on her Butler Island estate had made such a canoe, which they sold for the sum of $60.[6] A type of multilog dugout canoe common to the waters of the Chesapeake Bay is credited to a man from York County, Virginia, remembered only as Aaron.[7] In form this craft, with a hull shaped from as many as nine logs, seems related to the West Indian pettiaugers. When fitted out with a mast and sail, these vessels were well adapted for dredging for oysters, and it is estimated that in 1900 there were as many as seven thousand such craft plying the Chesapeake (figure 10.5).

In Virginia and Maryland, African Americans were extensively involved in a full range of shipbuilding trades as ship's carpenters, caulkers, sail-makers, and blacksmiths. A remarkable account from the *Raleigh Star* in 1811 describes how a brig launched in Alexandria, Virginia, was "drafted by a coloured man belonging to Col. Tayloe and under his superintendence built from her keel to her topmast."[8] Here the design sources were unquestionably Anglo-American. But the fact that an enslaved African American was given such broad authority suggests that he was working in a context in which most of the men under his command must have been African Americans as well. This event suggests that African Americans could have done quite well as shipbuilders had they been afforded the chance. But there were few opportunities, as African American watermen were diverted mainly to fishing and oyster dredging, where they would be employed for their brawn rather than for their designing and woodworking skills.

MUSICAL INSTRUMENT-MAKING

In the testimonies of formerly enslaved African Americans about their domestic experiences, there is frequent mention of homemade musical instruments. Litt Young, who was held on a plantation near Vicksburg, Mississippi, recalled exciting events around

Figure 10.5.   Multilog dugout canoe common to the waters of the Chesapeake Bay. Drawing by C. B. Hudson, 1890. Reprinted with the permission of the U.S. Fish and Wildlife Service.

1860 when, "Us have small dances Saturday nights and ring plays and fiddle playin' and knockin' bones. There was fiddles made from gourds and banjos from sheep hides."[9] The inventory here of stringed and percussive instruments identifies two of the main classes of musical instruments frequently made by African American artisans. To Young's short list one can add rattles, gongs, scrapers, fifes, whistles, pan pipes, and drums. All of these had verifiable African antecedents, as did many of the songs they were used to playing and the dances they were intended to accompany.

The drums that were so essential not only to African musical performance, but also to religious and healing rituals, were frightening to enslavers, who realized that these instruments could be used to send private messages that they were unable to decipher. Laws were passed in South Carolina shortly after the Stono Rebellion of 1739, and later in other states, banning the playing of drums expressly to eliminate this means of communication. But such prohibitions were less than effective as deterrents. Well into the nineteenth century enslaved people, particularly those who had more recently arrived from Africa, were still making drums. They commonly affixed some type of animal skin with thongs or pegs across the open end of a hollowed log or large gourd. Apparently such drums were made often enough that even as late as the 1930s elderly African Americans living in the coastal regions of Georgia could still describe the practice in detail. Even though the custom was fast fading into obscurity by that time, a few of these informants claimed to have made drums themselves.

The banjo is a very old African American instrument that ironically continues to enjoy considerable popularity among white aficionados of so-called country music. This is an instrument which, according to no less an authority than Thomas Jefferson, was "brought hither from Africa." In the earliest examples, the body of the instrument was shaped from a gourd sliced in half lengthwise that was then covered with a stretched animal skin. A fretless neck was inserted at one end and four gut strings ran from its top to the base of the gourd (figure 10.6).

Today's banjos made in factories are different in every respect, except that they continue to have a membrane-covered drum underneath the strings. Thus, when the instrument is strummed, one can still hear the distinctive combination of melodic tone and percussive thump that was present in the original plantation instruments. Once a mainstay of African American music, the banjo is rarely played today by African American musicians, and the only reported contemporary makers of banjos with gourd bodies are white.

The experience among fife-makers is more positive. In the delta area of northwestern Mississippi, a small number of families continues to play fifes, or as they might say, "blow canes," as the entertainment at picnics and barbecues. The process seems deceptively simple: a foot-long section of bamboo cane is hollowed out and a mouth hole and four finger holes are pierced into it with a red hot poker. Calculating the correct placement for the holes so that notes of the correct pitch can be played is, however, quite complex. Considerable experimentation is required, since each piece of cane has a

Figure 10.6. *The Old Plantation.* **Artist unknown. Water color, circa 1810. Reprinted with the permission of the Abby Aldrich Rockefeller Folk Art Center, Williamsburg, Virginia. The banjo and drum are seen to the right.**

slightly different tonal range. In Mississippi, the fife is played as the lead instrument together with an ensemble of drums; a performance that resonates with similar performances among the Akan peoples of Ghana.[10]

POTTERY

Enslaved African and African American potters made two very different types of wares. The earliest, produced during the seventeenth and eighteenth centuries, were earthenware vessels shaped by hand and fired to very low temperatures in open bonfires. These pots, recovered from many early plantation sites in South Carolina and Virginia, consisted mainly of small, round-bottomed bowls suitable for eating and drinking, and larger round-bottomed cooking vessels. Only discovered by archaeologists in the 1950s, for decades these vessels were believed to be Native American in origin and were labeled as Colono-Indian ware. Subsequent investigation has shown that given the sheer quantity of Colono shards at the sites occupied by enslaved African Americans, and their relative absence in Native American villages during the same period, there can be no other conclusion than that this type of pottery was being made by enslaved African American artisans. Comparison with African wares lends further support to the claim of manufacture by enslaved artisans, so that some of this eighteenth-century earthenware is now referred to as Afro-Colono pottery.

Many plantation-made bowls have a cross or an "X" scratched into their bases. While the function of these intriguing marks remains open to speculation, these are signs that have mystical associations in Central Africa, where they are used in acts of prayer, particularly in summoning the protective power of ancestral spirits. As scholars have puzzled through the significance of these marks, they have surmised that the first Africans must have looked to their own inventory of cultural forms and simply used a familiar craft tradition.[11]

A second episode of African American ceramic history unfolded during the nineteenth century in west-central South Carolina after the production of plantation earthenware had come to an end. By then there were relatively few knowledgeable African potters left in the enslaved population to carry on the practice. More importantly, enslavers were now providing more everyday food preparation items such as storage crocks. The first quarter of the nineteenth century witnessed as well an upsurge in the production of stoneware pottery, a durable type of ware shaped on a potter's wheel and fired to very high temperatures in a kiln. This type of pottery was produced mainly at small family-run shops owned by whites. Occasionally African Americans were employed in these shops chiefly as laborers who cut the firewood or dug and mixed the clay; the more prestigious role of potter or turner was reserved for a white artisan. There was, however, one site where African Americans were allowed more extensive participation, and it is there that one can identify a nineteenth-century tradition for African American pottery.

In about 1810, Abner Landrum, a prosperous planter–physician–newspaper editor–businessman living in the Edgefield district of South Carolina, opened a pottery works and was soon producing high-quality wares recognized as superior to any in the region. His shop would quickly grow into a booming industrial village, and soon Landrum was selling stock in his operation. His financial success, however, did not go unchallenged. Other entrepreneurs also set up potteries in the area, luring away many of Landrum's skilled white artisans. When he solved this crisis by training his enslaved African Americans to make pottery, other pottery shop owners soon followed his example.

Most of these African American artisans remain unnamed, but various records suggest that about fifty were employed at various shops throughout the Edgefield district. The best known of this group was a man named Dave, who had been enslaved to Abner Landrum. Trained first as a typesetter at Landrum's newspaper, Dave continued to display the fact that he was literate by signing and dating his pots and occasionally inscribing them with rhymed couplets. The terse captions on the sides of these vessels indicating the time of manufacture and their maker's identity are exceptional documents of the local pottery industry. More importantly, they publicly present the written words of an African American at a time when it was illegal for enslaved people to be literate. Consequently, these pots were also statements of overt resistance. Other enslaved African Americans, upon seeing Dave's works, were likely to know that one of their own was mocking the white man's law; and they may have derived some measure of inspiration from his audacious example.

Certainly many would have noticed Dave's pots, for he made some of the biggest vessels ever produced in Edgefield. The largest one, inscribed "Great and Noble Jar" (figure 10.7), has a capacity of almost forty-five gallons and stands thirty inches in height. Many of his other pots are in this same size range and are distinctively shaped with walls that flare boldly from a relatively narrow base to a wide shoulder close to the top of the vessel. While white potters also made large storage jars, none of their works seem as daring. With their widest sections nearer their middles, they appear to squat safely on the floor, while Dave's pots seemingly leap up and threaten to teeter back and forth. The form of Dave's pots further emphasizes the rebelliousness signaled by his inscriptions.

Even though Dave's works grew out of commonplace African American experiences in the South, his pieces, as objects, are expressions of European ceramic traditions. The pot forms for which he is so famous take their lines from the bread pots of northeastern England, and his use of pottery wheels, kilns, and glazes are manifestations of standardized Anglo-American ceramic technology. Yet within the community of African American potters in Edgefield, there were opportunities for artisans to revisit ancestral aesthetic forms.

In a series of small vessels averaging about five inches in height, African American potters were apparently able to rekindle memories of African sculpture. Pots decorated with faces are known in every ceramic tradition on the globe. But those attributed to African Americans in Edgefield have several attributes not seen elsewhere. Their most distinctive feature is the use of a different clay body to mark the eyes and teeth: white porcelain clay contrasts sharply with the dark glaze covering the rest of the stoneware vessel. The riveting gaze and seeming snarl that result from this mode of decoration recall the mixed-media approach to sculpture found in West and Central Africa, where all sorts of contrasting materials are applied to wooden forms for dramatic effect, particularly in the rendering of eyes and teeth on statues and masks (figure 10.8).

Figure 10.7. "Great and Noble Jar." Made by Dave the Potter. Stoneware with ash glaze, signed and dated May 3, 1859. Edgefield district, South Carolina. Reprinted with the permission of the Charleston Museum, Charleston, South Carolina.

That a white substance is used in Edgefield is very significant, for the same visual effect might have been achieved by simply coloring the eyes and teeth with a light-colored slip. That the look of an Edgefield face jug was created by the rather difficult technique of embedding an entirely different clay body into the walls of the pot suggests that both the material and the behavior were charged with important symbolic meanings. In Central Africa, homeland to 75 percent of all Africans imported into South Carolina, white clay has sacred associations with ancestral authority.

Among the Kongo people, white is the color of the dead, so that white objects are offered to them and effigies of the dead are marked with white eyes. The strong stylistic affinities between Kongo sculpture and Edgefield vessels suggest that enslaved artisans took full advantage of their access to ceramic technology. Why they did so is not completely certain, but they may have been motivated by a desire to practice African-inspired funerary rituals. The custom of placing ceramic ornaments on graves observed widely in

Figure 10.8. Decorated pot from Bath, South Carolina, similar to West and Central African Sculpture. Artist unknown. Stoneware, kaolin, ash glaze, circa 1860. Reprinted with the permission of the National Museum of American History, Smithsonian Institution, Washington, D.C.

Central Africa was still being followed in South Carolina in the late antebellum period. Certainly the sculpted face vessels fashioned by Edgefield artisans would have served well as funerary pots. Rituals utilizing African-looking sculpture clearly would have posed a threat to enslavers' sense of social order and would have been stopped if discovered. But the demographic pattern of the region favored the survival of secret funerary customs, since during the late antebellum period African Americans outnumbered whites in the Edgefield district by more than four to one.

The evident Africanity revealed in Edgefield ceramic art was reinforced by smuggling operations that brought new African captives into the area. In fact, one of the last known cargoes of Africans was a group of Kongo people who landed first on the Georgia coast, were then carried up the Savannah River to Augusta, and were sold in Edgefield County in 1858. The face vessels of Edgefield are then evidence of how African American artisans could, when circumstances allowed, counter the assimilationist trajectory of their experiences and use whatever means were available to reestablish ties to their African roots.[12]

WOODCARVING

The prodigious woodcarving skills of African artisans are widely recognized, and their masks and statues are granted honored places in first-rank museums along with noteworthy masterpieces of Western art. Since these works, so abundant in Africa, seem to be noticeably absent in the United States, assessments of African American culture often begin by lamenting the loss of these skills. This carving tradition, while diminished in scale, is not, however, altogether absent.

Enslaved African Americans seem to have remembered their traditions for woodcarving. According to an old man from Georgia who was interviewed in the late 1930s: "I remember the African men used to all the time make little clay images. Sometimes they like men, sometimes they like animals. Once they put a spear in his hand and walk around him and he was the chief. . . . Sometimes they try to make the image out of wood."[13] In 1819 a banjo seen in Congo Square in New Orleans by architect Benjamin Latrobe had an unmistakable African figure carved at the top of the instrument's neck just above the tuning pegs (figure 10.9). A remarkable table was built sometime in the 1850s on a plantation in north-central North Carolina with each of its legs carved into figures highly reminiscent of African figures (figure 10.10). From this smattering of examples, one can conclude that African proclivities for working creatively in wood did not end upon arrival in the Americas. These skills were carried on when and wherever possible.[14]

Most often, African woodcarving skills were turned away from sculpture and generally to the production of useful household objects like bowls, trays, mortars and pestles, and handles for various metal tools. The severely functional nature of these items did not provide much opportunity for creative expression, even if the artisan did his work with diligence and commitment. African American carving became, then, mainly American carving. Yet in the carving of wooden canes, some degree of African inspiration was seemingly able to reemerge. Numerous walking sticks carved by African Americans, from the nineteenth century to the present, bear distinctive marks that may relate to African traditions kept alive mainly among country people.

These canes are often decorated with a wide range of media including brass tacks, colored beads and marbles, aluminum foil, and other shiny materials. In one case from Mississippi, the carver attached a silver thermometer to the handle of a cane that was already elaborately carved with figures of humans and serpents. Yet it was not judged as complete without the bit of flash that a seemingly incongruous temperature gauge could provide. While this decorative gesture could be nothing more than a whimsical act of personal innovation, the fact that such acts are commonplace among African American cane-makers in the South implies the presence of a shared style. Certainly one senses in these decorated canes a parallel to the African use of mixed-media assembly in sculpture.

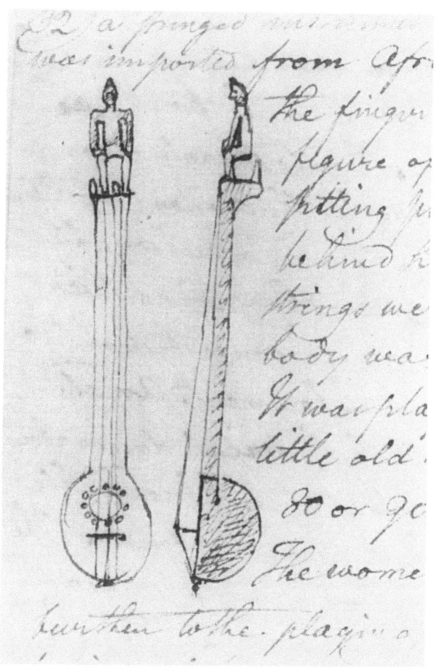

Figure 10.9. Drawing of banjo with African statue carved on neck discovered in New Orleans in 1819, from the papers of Benjamin Henry Latrobe. Reprinted with the permission of the Maryland Historical Society, Baltimore, Maryland.

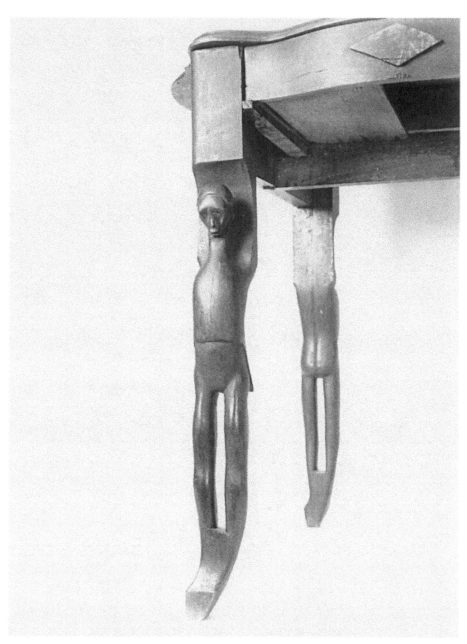

Figure 10.10. Detail of African figures carved into the legs of a table. Artist Unknown. Wood, circa 1850s. Reprinted with the permission of the North Carolina State Museum of History, Raleigh, North Carolina.

Closer African affinities are seen in the selection of certain motifs. Reptiles dominate the shafts of most of the walking sticks that have clear attributions to African American carvers; in addition to snakes (which are common to woodcarvers of canes everywhere), African American artisans also render alligators, turtles, and lizards (figures 10.11 and 10.12). Often combined with figures of human beings, the contrast may be read as symbolic of supernatural communication. According to widely held African beliefs, reptiles are appropriate symbols of messages between the spirit and human domains because they are creatures able to travel in two realms—in the water and on the land, or underground and above ground. They, like spiritual messengers, move between the human environment and another unseen place.

The chief linkage between this symbolism and African American traditions in woodcarving may lie in the fact that throughout the nineteenth century traditional healers or "root doctors" are said to have carried carved walking sticks decorated with reptiles as a sign of their authority. Since their cures are likely to have been based on African practices, it follows that the rest of their paraphernalia (which was often as instrumental in effecting a cure as the medicines that they administered) was also African-derived. Consequently, when an African American carved a snake or an alligator on a walking stick, it may have carried a different meaning and function than a similar animal carved by a white artisan.[15]

QUILTING

Quilted bedcovers are unknown in tropical Africa. However, some West African ceremonial textiles are decorated with colorful appliqué figures, and large pieces of cloth for use as clothing as well as covers are assembled by sewing narrow woven strips together. Thus, while the actual quilting process was new and different—that is, the binding of two large pieces of cloth together with a layer of batting in between by means of thousands of geometrically patterned stitches—extant quilts said to have been made by enslaved women demonstrate that these women were certainly capable of mastering the task.

Very little about the oldest surviving African American quilts seems to demonstrate any affinity for African textile traditions. What one sees is mainly the strict guidance of the plantation mistress. However, during the last decades of the nineteenth century Harriet Powers of Athens, Georgia, produced two quilts filled with images that seem to come straight out of Dahomey, a prominent kingdom on the West African coast in what is now the Republic of Benin (figure 10.13). While her links to a specific part of Africa are less than certain, and would have been, at best, indirect, the figures on her two "bible" quilts compare closely with appliqué figures found on sewn narrative textiles of the Fon people.[16]

More commonplace and perhaps more profoundly and directly associated with African textiles are the strip quilts that appear with great regularity wherever African Americans make quilts. In this type of bedcover, long, thin strip units are sewn edge to edge to form the large square or rectangular quilt top. The "strips" may be single pieces

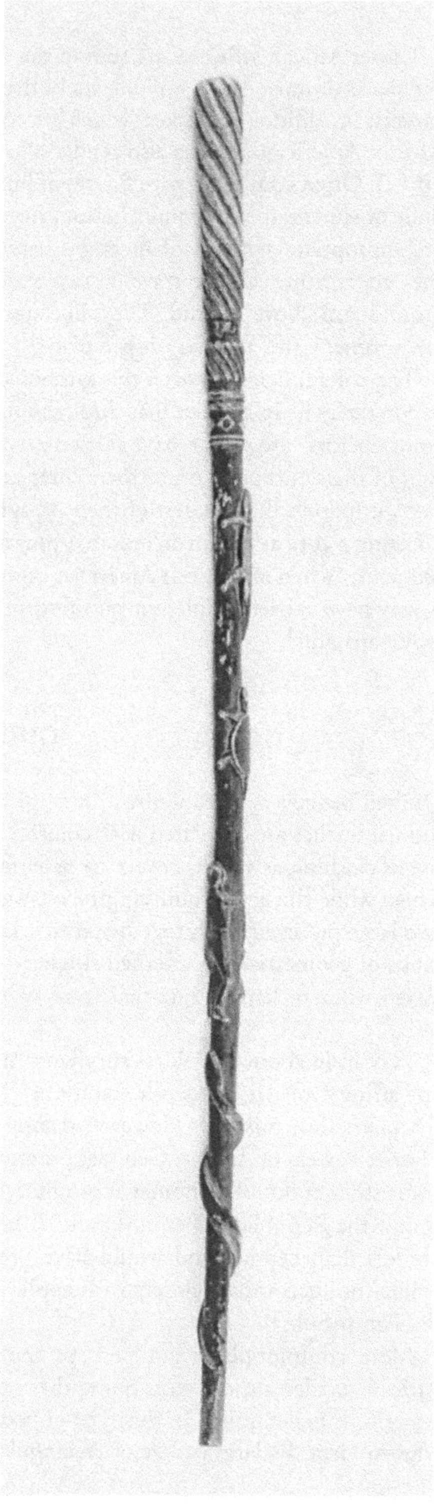

Figure 10.11. Carved walking stick. Henry Gudgell. Wood, circa 1863. Reprinted with the permission of the Yale University Art Gallery, Director's Purchase Fund, Yale University, New Haven, Connecticut.

Figure 10.12. Detail of carved alligator on walking stick. Howard Miller. Mahogany, circa 1920. Photo by Martin L. Linsey. Reprinted with the permission of the Cleveland Museum of Art, Cleveland, Ohio.

Figure 10.13.   Quilt produced in the late nineteenth century by Harriet Powers of Athens, Georgia. The figures on this quilt compare closely with appliqué figures found on sewn narrative textiles of the Fon people of the Republic of Benin. Courtesy, Museum of Fine Arts, Boston, Massachusetts. Reproduced with permission. © 2001. Museum of Fine Arts, Boston. All rights reserved.

or may be assembled from blocks, from thin remnants called "strings," or from assorted remnants. Regardless of the technique employed, the overall linear composition of the top cannot be missed (figure 10.14).

Since most contemporary African American quilters claim that quilts of this type are the oldest pattern they know, there is a good possibility that such quilts were made during slavery. They resemble in form and technique the strip cloths of West and Central Africa. These textiles are assembled from narrow pieces about five inches wide and eight feet long that are sewn edge to edge to create a large rectangular panel. This format may be observed, albeit in a modified form, in the African American strip quilt.

Even if this mode of quilt-top assembly proves not to be African in origin, it is certainly a marker of African American style. While strip quilts are made by white quilters too, they will usually protest that they were a simple type made when they were "just learning," or that they were quilts merely "thrown together" and thus were not something about which they are particularly proud. African American quilters, on the other hand, celebrate strip patterns as among the most significant in their repertories and produce them from childhood to old age. They work at refining the form as they explore the nuances of the genre. These quilters are aware of the geometric patterns common in Euro-American quilting, patterns usually generated from block units, but they prefer to use strips.

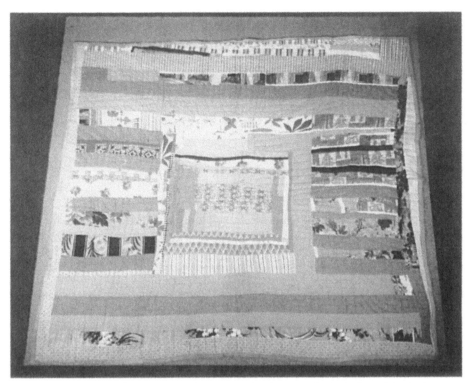

Figure 10.14.   Example of a strip quilt by Mrs. Floyd McIntosh of Pinola, Mississippi, 1934. Reprinted with the permission of the Collection of the Old Capitol Museum, Mississippi Department of Archives and History.

The strip format is innovative, open-ended, and considerably less bound by the formal conventions so common in Euro-American quilt patterns. There is a sense of design permission about strip quilts; even a sense of liberation. This is an attribute that African American artisans would appreciate for a host of reasons both personal and social. For African American quilters and the multitudes who sleep under their handiwork, the strip quilt has become simply the "right" quilt and thus a representative expression of African American art.[17]

CONCLUSION: LOOKING BACKWARD AND FORWARD

Because only a relative handful of scholars has been interested in the topic of African American material culture, research on African American arts and crafts remains in its infancy. More investigation will undoubtedly bring to the surface more discoveries of important African connections. While we need to know where these traditions came from, we also must consider what African American artisans have done with them and anticipate what may come next. Historian Lawrence W. Levine has observed that the study of African American material culture "requires a scholarship with the requisite patience and tolerance for complexity: a scholarship not prone to jump to simple or familiar conclusions, not content to remain on the surface or to make unreflective connections; a scholarship not unmindful of syncretic developments with other cultures; a scholarship not rooted too deeply in only one disciplinary mode."[18] To return to the arboreal metaphor that launched this chapter, what is needed is a mode of study and investigation that grants serious consideration both to "branches" and to "roots."

NOTES

1. For a general overview of the tactics useful in the study of African American material culture in the United States, consult Leonard Price Stavisky, "Negro Craftsmanship in Early America," *American History Review* 54 (1949): 315–325; Robert Farris Thompson, "African Influence on the Art of the United States," in *Black Studies in the University*, eds. Armstead I. Robinson, Craig C. Foster, and Donald H. Ogilvie (New Haven, Conn.: Yale University Press, 1969), 128–177; James E. Newton and Ronald L. Lewis, eds. *The Other Slaves: Mechanics, Artisans, and Craftsmen* (Boston: G. K. Hall, 1978); Phil Peek, "Afro-American Material Culture and the Afro-American Craftsman," *Southern Folklore Quarterly* 42 (1978): 109–134; John Michael Vlach, *The Afro-American Tradition in Decorative Arts* (Athens: University of Georgia Press, 1990 [1978]); Clarence Mohr, "Black Artisans and Craftsmen, Colonial Era Through 1900: A Select Historical Bibliography," in *Afro-American Folk Art and Crafts*, ed. William Ferris (Boston: G. K. Hall, 1983), 405–418; and John Michael Vlach, *By the Work of Their Hands: Studies in Afro-American Folklife* (Charlottesville: University Press of Virginia, 1991).

2. The foundational work for tracing the African roots of African American cultural expression was done by Melville J. Herskovits, *The Myth of the Negro Past* (New York: Harper and Brothers, 1941). A more recent work following the same scholarly path is Joseph E. Holloway, ed., *Africanisms in American Culture* (Bloomington: Indiana University Press, 1990).

3. Mary Jane Manigault, personal communication, 1995.

4. The coiled-grass basket tradition is thoroughly presented by Dale Rosengarten in her book *Row Upon Row: Sea Grass Baskets of the South Carolina Lowcountry* (Columbia: McKissick Museum, University of South Carolina, 1986). Consult as well Vlach, *Afro-American Tradition*, chap. 1; Gerald L. Davis, "Afro-American Coil Basketry in Charleston County, South Carolina" and Mary Twining, "Harvesting and Heritage" in Ferris, *Afro-American Folk Art and Crafts*, 235–271.

5. See Peter Wood, *Black Majority: Negroes in Colonial South Carolina from 1670 through the Stono Rebellion* (New York: Norton, 1974), 122–124, and Philip Morgan, "Black Life in Eighteenth-Century Charleston," *Perspectives in American History* (1984): 1–55, for discussion of the role played by African American watermen in the colonial South.

6. Frances Anne Kemble, *Journal of a Residence on a Georgian Plantation in 1838–1839* (Athens: University of Georgia Press, 1984 [1863]), 62.

7. M. V. Brewington, *Chesapeake Log Canoes and Bugeyes* (Cambridge, Md.: Cornell Maritime Press, 1963), 31.

8. Quoted in Vlach, *Afro-American Tradition*, 102.

9. Cited in Norman R. Yetman, *Life Under the "Peculiar Institution": Selections from the Slave Narrative Collection* (New York: Holt, Rinehart and Winston, 1970), 337.

10. See Vlach, *Afro-American Tradition*, chap. 2. Consult as well: Harold Courlander, *Negro*

Folk Music, U.S.A. (New York: Columbia University Press, 1963); William Ferris, *Gravel Springs Fife and Drum* (16mm film) Memphis, Tenn.: Center for Southern Folklore, 1971; Dena J. Epstein, "The Folk Banjo: A Documentary History," *Ethnomusicology* 20 (1976): 347–371; Eliot Wigginton, ed., *Foxfire 6* (Garden City, N.Y.: Anchor/Doubleday, 1980); Robert Lloyd Webb, *Ring the Banjar!: The Banjo from Factory to Folklore* (Boston: MIT Museum, 1984); Cecelia Conway, *African Banjo Echoes in Appalachia: A Study of Folk Traditions* (Knoxville: University of Tennessee Press, 1995).

11. The key source on early period African American pottery is Leland Ferguson, *Uncommon Ground: Archaeology and Early African America, 1650–1800* (Washington, D.C.: Smithsonian Institution Press, 1992), especially chap. 1.

12. The history of African American potters in Edgefield is covered in Vlach, *Afro-American Tradition*, chap. 5. Other useful works on this topic include: Robert Farris Thompson, "The Structure of Recollection: The Kongo New World Tradition," in *Four Moments of the Sun: Kongo Art in Two Worlds* (Washington, D.C.: National Gallery of Art, 1981), 157–165; John A. Burrison, *Brothers in Clay: The Story of Georgia Folk Pottery* (Athens: University of Georgia Press, 1983), chap. 8; John Michael Vlach, "International Encounters at the Crossroads of Clay: European, Asian, and African Influences on Edgefield Pottery," in *Crossroads of Clay: The Southern Alkaline-Glazed Stoneware Tradition*, ed. Catherine Wilson Horne (Columbia: McKissick Museum, University of South Carolina, 1990), 17–39; Cinda K. Baldwin, *"Great and Noble Jar": Traditional Stoneware from South Carolina* (Athens: University of Georgia Press, 1993).

13. Georgia Writers Project, *Drums and Shadows: Survival Studies Among Georgia Coastal Negroes* (Athens: University of Georgia Press, 1941), 106

14. Benjamin Henry Latrobe, *Impressions Respecting New Orleans*, ed. Samuel Wilson, Jr. (New York: Columbia University Press, 1951), 50–51; an image of the North Carolina table can be seen in *The Clarion* (Spring 1980): 59.

15. Useful works regarding African American woodcarving include, in addition to Vlach, *Afro-American Tradition*, chap. 3, the following works: Robert Farris Thompson, "African Influence on Art;" Elizabeth Mosby Adler, "George 'Baby' Scott (1865–1945): A Carver and His Repertoire" in Ferris, *Afro-American Folk Art and Crafts*, 149–159; and George H. Meyer, *American Folk Art Canes: Personal Sculpture* (Bloomfield Hills, Mich.: Sandringham Press, 1992).

16. For a biography of Harriet Powers, consult Gladys-Marie Fry, "Harriet Powers: Portrait of a Black Quilter," in *Missing Pieces: Georgia Folk Art, 1770–1976*, ed. Anna Wadsworth (Atlanta: Georgia Council for the Arts and Humanities, 1976), 17–23.

17. For further discussion of the African American quilting tradition, consult Vlach, *Afro-American Tradition*, chap. 4; Robert Farris Thompson, *Flash of the Spirit: African and Afro-American Art and Philosophy* (New York: Random House, 1983), chap. 4; Laurel Horton, *Social Fabric: South Carolina's Traditional Quilts* (Columbia: McKissick Museum, University of South Carolina, 1985); Eli Leon, *Who'd a Thought It: Improvisation in African-American Quiltmaking* (San Francisco: Craft and Folk Art Museum, 1988); Gladys-Marie Fry, *Stitched from the Soul: Slave Quilts from the Antebellum South* (New York: Dover Studio Books, 1990); Cuesta Benberry, *Always There: The African-American Presence in American Quilts* (Louisville: Kentucky Quilt Project, 1992); Maude Southwell Wahlman, *Signs and Symbols: African Images in African-American Quilts* (New York: Studio Books, 1993).

18. Quoted in "Preface" to Vlach, *By the Work of Their Hands*, x.

11

Cultural Passages in the African Diaspora: The West Indian Carnival

John O. Stewart

For some time now it has been the case that elements of Black culture emanating from the western Atlantic have been adopted in a widening geographical area around the globe. Perhaps the best illustration of this movement is to be found in the world of music. From jazz to calypso, hip-hop, rumba, and reggae, music from Black American and Caribbean cultures has found its niche in metropolitan sites of the northern Atlantic region and beyond, to places such as Japan, the Gulf States of western Asia, and back to Africa. Two distinct but related processes attend this widening spread of Western Black culture: globalization in entertainment marketing, and the incidence of migrations from the Caribbean and Brazil.

The marketing of Black music from the Americas by way of live performances has been a lucrative practice ever since the second half of the nineteenth century, when plantation songs and American minstrelsy became popular stage items. Since then, and with both the advancements in recording technology and the marketing of mega-stars, the energizing rhythms and mass poetry of Black American music have mushroomed into a worldwide phenomenon, particularly among the urban youth in industrialized and modernizing societies. Jamaica, Brazil, the United States, Trinidad, Cuba, Martinique, and Guadeloupe are all significant sites for the production of Black music heard and adopted around the world. One result of this is that music has come to be taken as a core expression of Black American culture and the basis for constructed identities throughout the African Diaspora.[1]

Not as widely marketed or promoted as Black music, but nevertheless making an increasingly popular appearance internationally, is the street festival known as carnival—a moveable feast that celebrates the ideal of a grand humanity that precedes and remains superior to entrenched social categories such as race, class, and nationality. The three centers where carnival has been most seriously developed in the Americas are New Orleans, Brazil, and Trinidad. They are all sites where the dynamic mixing of cultures—

commonly known in American societies as creolization—has been achieved to a high degree, particularly in religious and aesthetic values and activities. Of the three, the Trinidad carnival has had the greatest influence beyond its island center, largely because there has been heavier migration from Trinidad than from the other two sites.

Migration from New Orleans, when it occurs, is mostly to other urban centers of the South, or west to California. New York, Washington, D.C., and San Francisco have been attractive sites for Brazilians who have emigrated for political as well as economic reasons. Small enclaves of Brazilians are also to be found in London and Toronto. Trinidadians, on the other hand, are among the West Indians who emigrate in numbers to all of the principal English-speaking North Atlantic metropolitan centers. There has also been a small but steady migratory stream from Trinidad to Venezuela and Panama.

Although by regional standards Trinidad is a prosperous society, emigration has long been, among the working class, a principal path to more lucrative employment and a better life. Many Trinidadians were among the West Indian workers who flocked to Panama for work on the canal. From Panama, many found their way to the United States after the canal was completed. Again, Trinidadians were a significant percentage among West Indians who flocked to the United Kingdom and Western Europe to work on the rebuilding of London and other cities that had suffered severe damage during World War II. Apart from these surges, which resulted in the overnight establishment of overseas communities in London and elsewhere, there has been a steady migratory stream from the West Indies for most of this century to sites such as Harlem, Queens, London, Boston, Toronto, Los Angeles, Houston, Washington, D.C., and other metropolitan sites where work can be found.

Under Spanish rule from 1498 to 1797, then a British colony until 1962, Trinidad has itself been historically an attractive destination for colonists and migrant workers within the Caribbean. In its early years as a Spanish colony, the island had been used mainly as a staging area for expeditions to the South American mainland and had remained largely undeveloped until the 1780s, when the Spanish opened it up to Catholic settlers, both white and mulatto, from the neighboring territories. Catholic colonists fleeing from revolutionary upheavals in Haiti, and in Martinique and Guadeloupe in the French West Indies, took the greatest advantage of this opportunity to relocate themselves and their many African workers. It was in their hands that Trinidad began its sustained development as a sugar colony and as one of the most racially and culturally mixed sites in the West Indies. By the end of the eighteenth century the island population included Spanish and French colonists, a diversified group of African workers—mainly Mandingos, Congos, Yorubas, and others from the African west coast—and surviving populations of Caribs and Arawaks.

The Spanish ceded Trinidad to the British near the close of the eighteenth century, the transatlantic slave trade came to an end in 1807, and the emancipation of enslaved African workers followed in 1834. These three conditions led to a revised population policy for the colony. To maintain the flow of workers necessary for continued agricultural development, the British opened the island to Protestant immigrants from European Catholic countries, Black soldiers mainly from the United States who had served in the British military, and indentured laborers from Africa, China, and India.

No provision was made for any of these groups to maintain a native culture. In fact, the British observed an aggressive policy of suppressing all but the colonial culture, which was then the policy of the British empire. While the colony was not to be a direct extension of the colonizing center as was the case with French-controlled territories, it was yet expected to be a respectable dependency. Cultural policy therefore favored "Protestant Britishness" in all formal circles, a civil hostility toward Roman Catholic paganism, and vigilance against the non-European rest. This policy could not be fully enforced, however, largely because the British were vastly outnumbered. Catholicism was the religion of the French and Spanish colonists and their mulatto offspring, and a majority of Blacks had already found Catholicism to be a satisfactory correlate of African Orisha worship of Yoruba origin and a medium for the direct retention of essential Orisha practices.[2]

The Trinidad carnival originated as a pre-Lenten fête among the island's eighteenth-century Catholic elite. This festival, which has occupied a place in the Catholic calendar since medieval times, has a deep and rich ancestry going back through the Calends and Lupercalian rites of ancient Rome, the Bacchanalia of ancient Greece, to even earlier ritual traditions from the civilizations of Egypt and the Near East where the mystic dimensions of the festival were dominant.

In its early years in Trinidad, the carnival was designed, officially, as a fête exclusively for the elites. "Wealthy citizens . . . gave elaborate masked balls, and in the evening during Carnival the leading members of society would don masks and drive through the streets of Port of Spain, visiting houses thrown open for the occasion."[3] But carnival is not an easily controlled event. Even then the debarred African masses managed not only to participate in the festival, but even to be its most creative dancers. According to a diarist writing in 1831, "The dances are usually African dances, and the enthusiasm of the negroes and negresses amuses us very much, for these dances are stupendous. We play smart and look on at the ball for a short time from the street, and then return home and go to bed."[4]

The pretense of an exclusively elite carnival came to an end after emancipation in 1834. The Africans who had been brought to Trinidad to work the plantations had festive traditions of their own, some elements of which were revitalized in the post-emancipation carnival. By the 1870s, Blacks had taken over the street parade, costuming, and the ritual ascension of carnival kings and queens. By the 1880s the whites had mostly withdrawn from the festival, and the carnival became essentially a Black parade that privileged warriorhood and rebellion against authority. Intense violence between rival bands representing different communities drew the attention of the authorities. And in the mid-1880s, after two major clashes between carnival bands and the local constabulary led to a reduced incidence of fighting between bands, whites returned to participating in the festival.

In time Asian Trinidadians of Chinese and Indian descent, as well as a small but influential enclave of Lebanese, also joined in the festival, enriching it with contributions from their own celebratory traditions. Arawaks and Caribs were no longer present in numbers, but the brave indigenous warrior family soon became established as a preferred masquerade. The steady stream of migrants from the neighboring islands of Grenada, Barbados, St. Vincent, St. Lucia, and Antigua, who came to Trinidad in search of work once a petroleum industry got under way in the 1920s, also added their accents to the song and dance forms of the carnival and to the local creole culture in general.

By the middle of the twentieth century Trinidad could credit itself with being, socially and aesthetically, the cosmopolitan society of the West Indies. It accommodated a range of cultural images and values, all subject to the judgment of a creole sentiment that was itself being shaped by the multiplicity of cultural encounters in the everyday world. Contributions from all the various ethnic sources were grafted, however, to what is essentially an Afro aesthetic and social sensibility at the core of the local culture. For the carnival, this is evident in the combination of African-originated music, dance, and spiritual temper with an Afro insistence on the primacy of liberated sociation and unfettered creativity. In this context, the carnival acquired a sanctioning and censorial dimension and came to serve as a mass expression of those cultural images and values the society held in esteem as well as those it found deserving of ridicule.

The broad range of ethnic styles and cultural nuances became a source of enrichment in Trinidadian culture generally, as well as a resource for the imaginative scope and design of the carnival in respect to costuming, song themes and lyrics, and the mimicry that are essential elements of the festival. Modern art as it has developed in the United States also became an instrumental source of concepts and techniques in the carnival, as more and more Trinidadian artists undertook training at various art institutes in New York, Chicago, and elsewhere.

Following the transition from colony to independent state in the 1960s, the carnival was officially adopted as a ritual expression of Trinidadian national culture. It is now regarded as emblematic of the successful integration of diverse cultural segments into a cosmopolitan society that values productive tolerance and promotion of the general good over sectional interests. This image and ideal is announced in the national saying, "All ah we is one."

The Trinidad carnival has been an inspiration and resource for similar festivals throughout the West Indies, where carnival has emerged as a pan-regional festival that takes place serially from island to island at various times throughout the year. Music and costuming styles originally from Trinidad—and often transferred directly by specialists brought in from Trinidad—are featured elements in island festivals from Grenada to Jamaica. Tourists and musicians from the other islands as well make themselves present at the Trinidad carnival for both professional performances and to participate in the general revelry. But key factors in the success of the Trinidad carnival, both at home and abroad, are the intense cosmopolitan background out of which it emerges and the eventual triumph of a Black aesthetic in the forging of a Trinidadian cultural sensibility—not an easy or simple achievement.

The tension between form and creativity, a condition present in every culture, is a fundamental condition in creole society where the formal is usually affronted by contradictions and lacks true consensus. A great deal of the compulsive energy, the kinesis that is a source of the carnival's great appeal, derives from this tension. In common with other colonial territories in the Americas, Trinidad did not, early on, officially embrace its culture of African origin. In fact, under British rule a concerted effort was made to stamp out African expressions in religion and popular culture through the adoption of restrictive ordinances and intense police surveillance.[5] The effort was never fully successful. But it did much to broadcast and confirm a negative attitude toward African cultural forms and to stimulate a paranoid ambivalence toward them, especially among Trinidadians with middle-class values and aspirations. This was so even though some of the most creative contributions to the creole culture—especially in the carnival—were clearly African-derived.

The drum genius that drives the pulse of the carnival has its roots in Central and West African percussive traditions, and its most vibrant and extended elaboration is in the steelband—a Trinidadian invention that came into existence among lower-class Trinidadians in the 1930s and survived against formidable official resistance all through the 1940s. Despite the eventual widespread recognition of the steelband as one of the singular musical inventions of the twentieth century, relations between the steelband community and the governing carnival authorities continue to be contentious, particularly with respect to the terms under which steelbands may officially participate in the carnival.

Calypso, the song style of the carnival, emerged as a local song variant in the nineteenth century. It integrates melodic and lyrical elements from the *bel air* (French), the *kalinda* (Congo), the *pasillo* (Spanish), and the *oriki* (Yoruba) and could be in its lyrics a praise song or a song of derision and disrespect.[6] As the gazetteers of the people, calypsonians often had and still have critical or satirical observations to make about the elites or governing authorities, and in colonial times were considered outcasts from respectable society. The rhythm of the calypso is definitely African in origin, and this rhythmic quality dominates even in the case of soca, a recent outgrowth from calypso that features Latin American and East Indian nuances. While calypso is now regarded as the national song form, the carnival audience still frequently divides on the freedom to criticize or satirize when particular songs offend officials or various segments of the society.

In dance, pelvic rotation, or "wyning," stepping, and jumping, all well-known African-derived patterns, are core movements in the Trinidad carnival, with individual virtuosity being privileged over group choreography even in bands that number into the thousands. This freedom of individual movement and inattention to group choreography is one of the significant differences between the Trinidadian/West Indian and the Brazilian carnivals. There is no equivalent to the Brazilian samba school in Trinidad, and no authority that determines when a band dances well enough to occupy a place in the parade.

The mixing of races and cultures is seldom a benign affair, and in West Indian creole societies the concern with managing the potential for social conflict has long been fundamental. One of the ways in which the potential is confronted is the repeated assertion that out of the many, a social unity is being achieved. This civic mantra is announced in many forums that West Indians conduct among themselves, but in none so powerfully as in the carnival, and among none so aggressively as among Trinidadians. With its tight and complex demography, Trinidadian society has been forced to confront the tension across racial and social lines more copiously and consistently than most of the other West Indian territories. The characteristic Trinidadian response to this has been an unreserved idealization of the life force and the creative powers at the core of its endowment. This attitude is at the center of the local belief that "Trinidadians know how to live," a belief that for a long time has had its most ardent adherents among Afro-Trinidadians. The fête is very much a part of Trinidadian living, and carnival is the grandest fête of all.

In recognition of this, the government of Trinidad has invested a great deal in making carnival a ritual expression of transcendent nationhood. A government committee (first the Carnival Development Committee, later the National Carnival Commission) has been in place for several years now. It oversees government-sponsored national performances and competitions during the carnival season and provides small subsidies to selected bands and individuals. It must be emphasized, however, that government interest is preceded by the enormous fervor with which Trinidadians on their own embrace the carnival. Schools, social clubs, banks, and other private businesses also sponsor local competitions in calypso and costuming; and the constabulary, defense forces, workers' unions, and other public establishments sponsor fêtes and seasonal entertainments. Carnival activities and music are so pervasive during the carnival season that even those who hold themselves aloof from participating in the festival would nevertheless have some knowledge about it and be exposed to the music and news about it by way of daily newspapers, radio, and television.

Superficially, the festival might enact to some measure the social ideals of racial tolerance and solidarity between the classes. But far more profoundly, the carnival releases Trinidadians—performers, those who parade in costumes, and nonmasqueraders alike—into a state of sensual spirituality that is at once narcissistic and communal. Little wonder, then, that Trinidadians, wherever they congregate, tend to reinvent the carnival, or that they emerge as leaders where carnival is concerned in overseas West Indian communities.

Carnival is an open and eclectic ritual that involves the actual participation of those present. For each carnival season, a series of smaller fêtes and entertainments lead up to the grand days when the festival moves outdoors and culminates in a street parade, public dancing, theatrics, and days-long cavorting. Individual masqueraders and bands of costumed players dance through the streets along routes jammed with spontaneous participants, spectators, vendors, strollers, and the police, who vary numerically in their presence depending on whether they expect trouble or not. The parade can move along some streets, and not along others. It may begin at a certain hour, it must end at another.

Costumes range from simple personal masquerades to huge pageants hauled along on wheels or skillfully designed to be worn on the shoulders of individual "kings" and "queens." The pageant presents humorous, diabolic, or warrior figures; it satirizes or honors contemporary outstanding citizens; it shows off local flora and fauna; and it depicts technological achievements on a grand scale. It brings alive images from antiquity and classical drama, all dancing to the beat of the drum, electric keyboards, voices, and horns raised in calypso. Some of the costuming is traditional, some ultra-contemporary. Some costumes emphasize nudity; others in their size and complexity completely obscure the masquerader. All are very colorful. Dancing costumed bands may number fewer than ten, or up to four or five thousand. The ambiance is visually opulent.

The assemblage of arts and crafts that are the graphic media serves mainly as a decorative framework for the kinetic milieu that blooms out of the overpowering sound of celebratory music and the repetitive motions of congregational dancing. The vibrating drums are everywhere; the spirit they invoke is infectious. Dancing, eating, drinking, and spontaneous socializing—all are driven by the pulsing rhythms and chanting melodies of the season's music, delivered by thundering steelbands or sound trucks loaded with massive banks of amplifiers between which calypsonians, disc jockeys, and brass bands perform.

In waves of imaginatively layered colors and syncopated motion, everyday social order and decorum give way, and the music, the kinetic force generated by thousands of bodies in the dance, enraptures. Masqueraders and spectators who want to wyne, wyne. Those who are moved by the exuberance of the occasion to jump, jump. Many are happily satisfied with just chipping to the music.

The usual formalities in dress, body language, and even social attitude are set aside. And perhaps the grandest sense of community of which the people are capable surfaces around them. This is the people's festival. In this masquerade no desire need be secret. The incongruous and the beautiful are equally allowed. People from all walks of life celebrate themselves and the gifts of humane sociability. This, ideally, is the carnival in Port of Spain, Trinidad. With some variation it is, ideally, the carnival in New York, London, Toronto, Miami, Montreal, Washington, D.C., and several other sites now home to sizable enclaves of West Indian migrants who have reinvented or been instrumental in the reinvention of the carnival.

In each case the carnival is a multilayered social art event that is anchored in the intention to achieve a seamless continuity between social and spiritual domains that is really the domain of the aesthetic, art, and in this case the festival as social art. Hypnotic in its sound and motion, tantalizing in its display of imaginative figures and liberated socializing, open in its format, the metropolitan carnival increasingly engages the imagination and participation of others beyond the nucleus immigrant enclave. It is open to all people, irrespective of origins or affiliation, who wish to experience the festive dismissal of exclusive identities, who will escape all urges to alienation.

In the metropolitan centers of the United States, Canada, and the United Kingdom, the street parade becomes even more inclusive ethnically and culturally than it is in the West Indies. If Trinidad is a singular site in that region for the meeting of peoples and cultures from around the world, it is not yet as richly clustered with ethnic cultures as are Toronto, London, or New York. These and other major cities of the North American continent and Western Europe are indeed the international crossroads of the modern era, and the carnival invites all to the dance that evokes the bonds people have in common with one another.

Organized by the West Indian American Day Carnival Association, Inc., the West Indian carnival on Brooklyn's Eastern Parkway takes place on Labor Day—the first Monday in September. Trinidadians, Jamaicans, Barbadians, Antiguans, Guyanese, and other West Indians are out in numbers for this annual celebration. Also among the throngs are a fair number of Puerto Ricans and Brazilians. They have festivals of their own on different days and do not emphasize their unique ethnicity in this parade, but they are present. A Jewish rapper made his appearance on a sound truck one year, but Jews who live in the neighborhood mainly stay indoors and peek at the parade from behind closed windows. Relations between Jews and West Indians are not the best, and this carnival in its principal features is a "Black thing."[7]

Haitians are also in the parade. They do not sport extravagant costumes, and they dance in a tight crowd to their own music. Small bands of Ghanaians and other Africans are in the parade, and increasingly, although they produce no bands as yet, African Americans join in the street dancing behind steelbands and the booming sound trucks.

Overall, participation is focused less on costuming and more on the dance. People gather for the dance and the exuberant conviviality. Even though salsa, reggae, and rara join soca and calypso in the air, there is sufficient commonality in their meters and syncopations to give a musical harmony to the occasion.

The West Indian carnival in New York had its genesis in Harlem, the "capital of the Black world," during the 1930s. There had been a trickle of West Indian migrants to New York and other eastern seaports since the late nineteenth century. But West Indian migrants first came to Harlem in significant numbers following the close of building operations at the Panama Canal. They were numerous enough to be recognized as a noticeable enclave during the Harlem Renaissance, and according to several observers the carnival began as a pre-Lenten indoor fête organized by a Trinidadian woman, Jessie Waddle, who was unable to go home for carnival. But carnival is not to be contained as a mere indoor event curtailed by wintry weather. In the early 1940s, she obtained the first permit to celebrate carnival outdoors on Lenox Avenue on Labor Day.[8] As the demographics changed with the migration of Caribbean Americans and African Americans from Harlem to Brooklyn, Trinidadian Rufus Goring took the carnival south across the river.[9]

In 1998 the carnival had the sponsorship of the New York mayor's office, the City Department of Cultural Affairs, the New York State Council on the Arts, the Brooklyn borough president, the Brooklyn Museum, and the Brooklyn Botanical Gardens. There were also a number of corporate sponsors including AT&T, American Airlines, ABC-TV, Chase Bank, Citibank, the New York Daily News, and Time-Warner. Official support came from the New York Police Department, the Fire Services, the Emergency Medical Services, and the Parks, Sanitation, and Transportation Departments. The festival now takes place over five days instead of just one.

Activities leading up to the street parade mirror the pattern established in Trinidad, with some variation. There are competitions in music and costuming, a children's street parade, a variety show on stage on the eve of the main parade (*Dimanche Gras* in Trinidad), and a reggae festival. An activity in which the Brooklyn carnival varies dramatically from the Trinidad "mother" festival is in the collection of funds to support programs for children around the world. This practice, begun in 1993 by the Caribbean American Community Comprehensive Center, Inc., has volunteers soliciting single dollars among the carnival crowds, which are sent as donations to different parts of the world. So far donations have been made to children's funds in Rwanda (through UNICEF), Haiti, Antigua and Barbuda, Jamaica, and Grenada. Future collections are earmarked for Trinidad and Tobago, St. Lucia, and Dominica. The success of the Brooklyn carnival has led to spin-off celebrations in Washington, D.C., Jersey City, Boston, and Baltimore. It has also stimulated a contest over the leadership and control of the festival.

"Carnival has out-grown its humble beginnings and has moved into the realm of big business. [It] is poised to be the number one tourist attraction and money maker of both New York City and New York State."[10] The Brooklyn festival generates millions of dollars. It also serves to define a cultural constituency of over two million people in the borough, and both of these are attractive potentials for local politicians and entrepreneurs. The West Indian American Day Carnival Association, which has led the organization and production of the festival for thirty years, consequently finds itself under challenge by several other organizational cliques. This, in turn, has led to a growing caution against divisive eruptions in the West Indian American community, and promotion of an ideology that would put the community in a position to benefit maximally not only from the ecstatic rewards of the festival, but also from its political and economic potential as well.

Caribana in Toronto is organized by the Caribbean Cultural Committee. Thousands from the West Indies and the United States journey to Toronto for the event. Calypso, calypsonians, soca, steelbands, the massive sound trucks, and dancing masqueraders—they are all there. As in New York, ethnic communities represented in the parade are numerous. Toronto has the reputation of being the world's most culturally diverse city. But here, much more than is the case with their counterparts in New York, white Canadians participate in numbers. They march in organized bands, are numerous among the onlookers and supporters, and they are among the officiants. On occasion, provincial political figures lead the parade. Native Americans too take part in the parade, not as masqueraders per se, but as themselves, driven along serenely in their ceremonial dress that is the inspiration for costumes in Trinidad, New Orleans, Brooklyn, and London; but in Canada they wear their own dress as the emblem of their own sacred majesty.

Leading up to the parade are the customary competitions in music and costuming, excursion boat rides, concerts of Caribbean music, and a junior carnival parade. The postparade event in Toronto is unique. On the two days following the parade—usually Sunday and a Monday bank holiday—a Caribbean Arts and Cultural Festival is held on Olympic Island in the Toronto harbor. This is an occasion when families usually picnic amid a festival of crafts, theatrical presentations, and music. Altogether, Caribana is not only a celebration of West Indian/Caribbean cultural identity, it is also a Canadian event, a time when the country celebrates itself.

Caribana was begun in 1967 as part of Canada's Centennial Celebration, and has over the years grown into a great commercial success. It is estimated that Caribana generates $200 million in tourism revenue, and an additional $40 million in tax revenues each year.[11] Little from these revenues, however, makes its way to the West Indian Canadian community or even to the Caribbean Cultural Committee. While the committee receives some funding from the provincial government for the festival, it is yet some $400,000 in debt, the result of accumulated shortfalls over the years.

The committee has been faced with a great deal of criticism, charges of incompetence in representing the needs of the festival to the provincial authorities, and charges of mismanagement in its organization of the festival. In disaffection with the state of affairs, several of the regular bandleaders opted to boycott the carnival in 1997, a year that marked the thirtieth anniversary of the festival, and organize a Carnival Jam and Picnic of their own. The result was a fragmented, and for many a diminished, carnival. There was an eruption of smaller fêtes taking place at the same time as the grand event. In addition, there was a dearth of costumes along the parade route, while hip-hop and rap music by Black American performers displaced calypso and soca in the parade. The committee has made some changes in its personnel, and there is hope in some quarters that the carnival will return to its ebullient, all-conquering state in the future.

The Notting Hill (London) carnival had its origins in a pan–West Indian fête organized by another woman from Trinidad at the St. Pancras Town Hall in 1958. This was the same year as one of the worst race riots in Britain, when West Indian Blacks were violently targeted by marauding bands of white youths inspired by the virulent antiforeigner rhetoric of certain politicians. The riot precipitated a sense of unity among West Indians, who had brought their inter-island rivalries to the United Kingdom with them. The St. Pancras fête became an annual event at which islanders set aside their differences and celebrated their common cultural roots.

The street parade that spun out of this event was, however, first organized by a London-born social worker in Notting Hill in 1966. Here, West Indian, Irish, and Eastern European immigrants clustered with the local English in a working-class neighborhood where tensions subsequent to the race rioting remained high. The social worker promoted the outdoor parade as a revival of the Notting Hill Annual Fair, which had traditionally been held in the area until the turn of the century. "There was no suggestion that it would imitate a West Indian or any other foreign form of carnival." The political intention was to foster amity among neighborhood dwellers and cohesion in the struggle they all faced against overcrowded housing and lagging social services.[12]

In 1970, as a result of continuous clashes between the police and West Indian residents, the social worker called for a cancellation of the carnival. West Indians resisted the call and took over leadership of the event. They organized the 1970 festival, then sent a representative to Trinidad to study the conventions of the "mother" carnival. Under his guidance, the Notting Hill celebration took on the principal elements of the Trinidadian festival in a more or less direct fashion.[13] The preliminaries of a calypso monarch competition, a steelband competition, a competition for kings and queens of the bands, as well as various concerts and dance fêtes, all took place leading up to the days of the parade. On carnival day the bands came out to play and dance in the streets. They passed before judges stationed along the route of the parade, and prizes were awarded for the best costumes and best musical performances. The carnival came to be accepted as a community art event and in this way continued to qualify for government funding.

Never enough to produce the festival in its entirety, government funding nevertheless kept the authorities in touch and gave them some decision-making role in how the carnival would deploy itself from year to year. As many carnivalists have claimed, government funding put the authorities in a position not only to influence the carnival, but also to undermine and dissipate its integrity. Two ways in which the influence of external authorities is most strongly evident are the stimulated competition among community groups for the privilege of disbursing allocated funds, with the result being a splintered rather than a stable representative leadership for the festival, and excessive authority in the hands of the police, who have been placed in a position to dictate the structure of the festival and given freedom to be as forceful as they wish in containing it.

Since 1970, Notting Hill has been the site of a number of violent clashes between carnivalists and the police, who treat the festival as a dangerously anarchic event in a dangerously anarchic community, both of which ought to be eliminated. This position has the support of various politicians, the cadre of English yuppies who have recently moved into the neighborhood, and other citizens who oppose the carnival and view it as an intrusive, economically wasteful, and socially disruptive affair. In spite of this opposition, the carnival has persisted as a result of the continued commitment of the bandleaders, musicians, craftspeople, and others who actually live for and make the festival.[14]

Massive sound trucks have joined steelbands in providing music for the parade. Samba schools have sprung up, producing bands in the Brazilian style. Reggae, dancehall, and hip-hop have joined calypso, soca, and samba as nightclub music, and audiences have been increasingly integrated into the parade. Thousands of spectators and participants from across the United Kingdom and neighboring European countries now flow into Notting Hill during the last weekend in August for the celebration. On the Internet, Notting Hill is advertised as a "diverse community" with a population of 150,000 that plays host to a weekend crowd numbering over a million during the carnival.

In 1996 a major soft drink company was one of the principal sponsors of the event, and a fresh observer could report, "Apart from what it must have looked like at the Tower of Babel, I know I've never seen so many shades, cultures and nationalities concentrated in one place at the same time. . . . A world as racially harmonious as the one I experienced at Notting Hill has got to be a bigot's worst nightmare."[15] "This festival should be called 'the United Nations of Fun'," this observer continues, for Anglo-Saxons, Caribbeans, second and third generation Black-Britons, Black Muslims, white Muslims, Arabs, Indians, and others from nations as varied as Kenya, Bulgaria, South Africa, New Zealand, Japan, and Colombia were present not only as spectators but as die-hard participants as well. The artistic and organizational leadership of the carnival is still heavily controlled by West Indians, but "nowadays over half of the groups participating in London carnival are people of non-Caribbean origin."[16] The aspect is a great mixing of peoples and cultures, in the face of mixed official resistance and support, demonstrating to themselves and the world that they do indeed share an identity that transcends racial, cultural, and political categories.

In San Francisco the carnival, which takes place on Memorial Day, the last Monday in May and official start of the summer season in the United States, also had its early start with a woman from Trinidad who migrated to New York in the 1920s and later relocated to San Francisco in 1956. She, with the help of a costume-maker also from Trinidad, organized the area's first carnival in 1960. As a result of failing health, she is no longer involved in the organization of the festival. In its current version the carnival is organized by the Mission Economic Cultural Association, a mixed but largely Latino organization, in company with the Mission Neighborhood Centers and the support of several San Francisco city departments, and takes place in the Mission District, a largely Latino neighborhood.

The parade is dominated by a Brazilian-Latino ambiance. Samba bands and blocos dominate. Costumes and music from the Andean countries, Argentina, and Central America are also frequent in the parade. So too are bands of Polynesian, Filipino, and other Pacific origins. A West Indian presence is still here. There are costumes and one or two bands direct from Port-of-Spain. There are calypso and soca and a steelband or two. But West Indians have not relocated to this city in numbers. Those who come to California tend to settle mostly in Los Angeles, or if in the northern part of the state, in the warmer East Bay or the suburbs of the Peninsula.

West Indian carnivalists and revelers in the area are at the same time not too enthusiastic about the barricaded route of the San Francisco festival or the intensively organized and choreographed pattern of the parade. Some complain that the festival here is baldly dominated by an economic, rather than an artistic and culturally liberating, interest. Many save their energies for Carijama in Oakland and other newly founded "Afribbean" festivals in the city of Mountain View, some thirty-five miles south of San Francisco, and in Los Angeles. Carijama is largely a staged music festival at a lakeside park, with some of the gaiety and dance of the carnival. The others are minor street festivals, again with certain features of the carnival—music, dance, food, some costuming—but they are not yet developed events of scale.

West Indian carnival is at once an expression of the challenges faced in multiracial, multicultural societies and an invitation into the aesthetic arena where citizens may indulge an urge toward freedom from the routine of social identities. Racial and cultural tension in West Indian life, with its roots in the region's colonial history, underlie to a great extent the intensity with which West Indians embrace the carnival and take it along as they relocate outside the region. Art and politics commingle to such a degree in the carnival that it may be as easily accessed by a politics of rebellion as by a politics of repression. Which it does depends heavily on who controls it.

In Trinidad, control of the carnival shifted from the landed gentry to the masses immediately following the nineteenth-century emancipation, then into the hands of a creole business class during the early years of the twentieth century. Since independence in the 1960s, it has been under the control of a bourgeois government struggling with the divisive race, class, and cultural relations inherited from the colonial period, as well as with the plethora of trade, finance, and geopolitical problems that small Caribbean economies must face on the international front. The ambition toward an integrated and equitable society based on common respect has not survived well against the cross-hatch of power struggles, grand and small, that tends to dominate everyday life. This is reflected in the organized carnival, which has in recent years been drifting into an eclectic amalgam of domains, each with its own individual leadership that negotiates its participation directly with the National Carnival Commission. On their part, the Trinidad Unified Calypsonians Association, National Carnival Bands Association, and Pan Trinbago representing the steelbands are fairly well organized under relatively stable and respected leaderships. At its metropolitan sites the carnival has not yet reached this stage of development.

In New York and London there has been a growing concern among carnivalists that established politicians and venturesome corporations may be scheming to take control of the festival out of the hands of current West Indian leadership, and this may be a catalyst for accelerating organizational development among the carnivalists themselves. If the San Francisco case is an indication of what might follow should such a takeover occur, however, it may be expected that the West Indian carnival will migrate away from the sites of great central control to neighboring domains where authority is less focused on the event and less dominating. The difference between the Trinidadian and the metropolitan cases in this instance would turn on the issue of scale. On the small, ethnically complex island of Trinidad, because of the limitations on both geographical and calendrical space, carnivalists who withdraw from the festival have great difficulty crafting alternative instances for a celebration. In metropolitan situations the sort of space required is usually available.

In each instance of its development, the West Indian carnival is a site where a constellation of artistic, social, political, and economic interests converge. Most of the postevent reports dwell on its social achievements. This is understandable, because the carnival is a one-of-a-kind social event of great dimensions. The massive congregation of numerous racial, ethnic, and cultural groups demonstrating without rancor against one another, in an aesthetically ebullient atmosphere taut with energy and a potential for misbehavior, is an extraordinary achievement. So, too, is the cavalcade of violence and destruction when clashes occur either between carnival bands or between carnival bands and the police. Both can have far-reaching social effects.

The carnival as a social and aesthetic event is inevitably framed by political dimensions at its core and in its relations with the surrounding conventions by which it is contextualized. On the inside, there is contention over standards of masquerade, the terms of participation, musical choices for the parade, leadership and the role of the organizing committee, and so forth. Surrounding the event are issues of its reception and control. Local officials and nationalists may choose to emphasize individual solidarity with racial and ethnic constituencies by joining in the parade. In Toronto, one provincial leader actually made it a point to be seen leading the parade. On the other hand, right-wing politicians in London made the carnival a staple in their anti-immigration campaign, during which they cultivated an ideology of racial and cultural purity among underprivileged English youth who then targeted Blacks and foreigners as parasitic polluters of the English state.

The carnival also provides an opportunity for West Indians to address the issue of their own insular divisions and deal with the need to "come together" and constitute themselves as a political presence in the metropole. In this there is an artistic-political pulse that recalls the "Négritude" movement of the 1930s, when immigrant intellectuals from the West Indies and Africa discovered that as far as Paris was concerned, they were all "*des nègres*," then went on to find something positively productive in their common condition.

Economically, carnival is a boon to the cities where it occurs. Merchants derive substantial income from the marketing of costuming materials. The fête is a great tourist attraction and generates lots of income for local hotels, food and beverage markets, and by extension the official tax collectors. One of the enduring complaints of West Indian organizing committees in New York, London, and Toronto is that the local government's support of the carnival is poor in contrast to the income that flows into the cities as a result of the festival.

Yet carnival is much more than the annual parade and its satellite entertainments. It is the context within which many artists, musicians, and dancers find their professional calling. In addition to producing for the parade, several have been hired to teach dance, music, and theater arts at metropolitan schools with multicultural enrollments, as well as at other institutions where art and music therapy are part of the curriculum. Some steelband players and pan makers have been hired by music production companies.

Others have found niches as instructors at universities and colleges in New York, Illinois, California, Georgia, Minnesota, and elsewhere.

Good costume designers are always in demand, and some are engaged year-round designing for the carnivals in different locations. The costume designer Peter Minshall was hired by the International Olympic Committee to design costumes for the opening and closing ceremonies of the Summer Olympics in Barcelona and Atlanta. The entertainment industry sees more stage performances by calypsonians, and steelbands are regularly heard in an increasing number of musical commercials. Some private entrepreneurs have begun their own steelband schools for youngsters in California and Arizona.

The carnival has been especially useful for West Indians as a medium through which to engage and perhaps bring partial resolution to the enduring tensions surrounding the African presence in the post-colonial world. The reliance on property—material and social—as a way of ascertaining human worth has a lot to do with the construction and survival of such tensions. Africans were integrated into the European colonial enterprise in the Caribbean as enslaved workers for over three hundred years. It is interesting that in Trinidad they chose to mark and confirm the event of their emancipation, not with the expected outburst of revengeful violence, or even with sullen subversion of any kind, but with the carnival, an occasion for the acting out of unrestrained liberty. This suggests an understanding that the deeper barriers to liberty rested not in the absence of property—material or social—but in its presence. They probably learned a great deal about property from having been dealt with as if that was what they were. This would have led to an understanding of the alienating effects of property and led to the attractive occasion to transcend it in mockery, satire, and exuberant excess.

Openness, creativity, and a strong association between aesthetics and personal politics are among the principal conditions through which the carnival is carried forward. The main intention of the fête is to fête, or achieve itself as aesthetic experience. While the construction of carnival as the ritual enactment of a unity that transcends racial, ethnic, and national identities is worthy, the festival has been around for much longer than neoteric plural society, and its genius must rest in an older and more profound set of associations. In the carnival, revelers resurrect a metaphysical force, much in the way that devotees do in houses of African-style worship. They are possessed. In possession, they are liberated from history.

Carnival is often described as ritual reversal. The sensibility at the core of the West Indian carnival is, however, not an alternative or subterranean sensibility. It is pervasive and anchored in its stand against the construction of "otherness"—a construct so necessary to the grand achievements in Western history, so much a source of African agony. It is a sensibility that, with good reason, occupies privileged space in New World African culture. For West Indians, carnival is neither the masking nor the unmasking of an alternative face of the civic deity. But it is the deifying force itself, confirming the original gift of creativity and liberty.

The deity of this carnival remains unnamed, but it is aesthetically quite African in orientation and the festival itself decidedly New World African in its inspiration and ethos. Freedom, liberty, and creativity are major celebratory interests. Much more than the practice of frivolous misbehavior or the playing out of any contest between good and evil, the West Indian carnival is at once an expression of the challenges people face in their relations with transhuman forces, and an empowering event.

In his work on the Black Atlantic tradition, Robert Farris Thompson draws attention to the "streams of creativity and imagination, running parallel to the massive musical and choreographic modalities that connect Black persons of the western hemisphere, as well as the millions of European and Asian people attracted to and performing their styles, to Mother Africa."[17] In the Western world, Africa has been maligned with such power and consistency over the past four centuries that here, any performance of Africa requires, or is itself, an act of transcendence. In Thompson's remark there is the suggestion of a sort of West-to-East cultural flow carried principally by Black people of the West unabashedly reclaiming their African identities, and in so doing sweeping others along with the force and authentic power in this reclamation.

The reclamation of an African identity, accompanied as it must be by the discarding of an earlier identity, has to be seen as indicative of complexities prior to the reclamation itself. What these complexities are for West Indian creoles, and the pathway for their reclamation, is fairly transparent. What the prior complexities and pathway for Europeans and Asians might be are more obscure. In any case, the carnival, like Black music, is clearly a medium cultivated for its liberating thrust into transcendence without the required allegiance to any specific identity. In ideal form it is a festival with unlimited access, and this has made it an event of great appeal.

NOTES

1. Paul Gilroy, "Fractured Blackness and the African Diaspora," talk given at the University of California at Davis, 1995.

2. Andrew Carr, "A Rada Community in Trinidad," *Caribbean Quarterly* 3 (1953): 36–54; Melville Herskovits and Frances Herskovits, *Trinidad Village* (New York: Farrar, Straus, and Giroux, 1976 [1947]).

3. Donald Hill, *Calypso Calaloo* (Gainesville: University Press of Florida, 1993), 20.

4. Hill, *Calypso Calaloo*, 20.

5. David Trotman, *Crime in Trinidad: Conflict and Control in a Plantation Society, 1838–1900* (Knoxville: University of Tennessee Press, 1986).

6. Jacob D. Elder, "Evolution of the Traditional Calypso of Trinidad and Tobago," Ph.D. dissertation, University of Pennsylvania, 1966.

7. See Remco van Cappelleveen, "The Caribbeanization of New York City" in *Feasts and Celebrations in North American Ethnic Communities*, ed. Ramón A. Gutiérrez and Geneviève Fabre (Albuquerque: University of New Mexico Press, 1995), 159–171.

8. Jean P. Alexander, "Carnival: Past, Present and Future" <http://www.carnaval.com/main.htm> (accessed April 3, 2000).

9. Lamuel Stanislaus, "WIADCA is 30" <http://www.carnaval.com/cityguides/newyork/wiadc.htm> (accessed April 3, 2000).

10. Alexander, "Carnival: Past, Present, and Future," 2.

11. Raynier Maharaj, "Of Caribana and the CRTC," *Caribbean Camera* (August 7–13, 1997, Toronto), 4.

12. Abner Cohen, *Masquerade Politics* (Berkeley: University of California Press, 1993), 11–13.

13. Cohen, *Masquerade Politics*, 21–32.

14. See Michael La Rose, *Mas in Notting Hill* (London: New Beacon Books, 1989), and *Police Carnival* (London: Association for a People's Carnival, 1989).

15. Loretta Henry, "The United Nations of Fun," *So Yu Going to Carnival*, No. 1 (1997).

16. Henry, "The United Nations of Fun," 63–68.

17. Robert Farris Thompson, *Flash of the Spirit: African and Afro-American Art and Philosophy* (New York: Random House, 1983), xiii–xiv.

12

The Study of New York's African Burial Ground: Biocultural and Engaged

Michael L. Blakey

THE DISCOVERY AND SIGNIFICANCE OF THE AFRICAN BURIAL GROUND

In October of 1991, a press conference was held at a construction site in New York City announcing the discovery of a colonial cemetery to which an historic map referred as the "Negroes Burying Ground." It was later renamed the "African" Burial Ground to conform to the earliest recorded term that New Yorkers of African descent had applied to themselves and the term preferred by living descendants in New York City. The U.S. General Services Administration's Public Buildings Service was excavating for the foundation of one of its most ambitious office buildings. Thirty-four stories high, the office tower at 290 Broadway would eventually come with a price tag of $300 million for its construction.

The implications of the discovery of the earliest and largest African cemetery found in North America have been immeasurable in their scientific, social, political, emotional, and spiritual dimensions. Some have called the events surrounding the site's discovery a watershed for African American anthropology and history. Whether or not that is so, these events certainly represent a powerful exposé of the problems racism continues to present for African American people. The African Burial Ground phenomenon is an important event in the African American struggle for self-definition against the customary forces of white supremacy, which quickly took on monumental significance for the African American community.

THE POLITICS OF OMISSION AND THE DISTORTION OF HISTORY

Not surprisingly, many of the most obvious issues emerged immediately in the wake of the announcement of the cemetery's existence. Here were the physical, skeletal remains of Africans who had lived and died in colonial New York sometime between the late 1600s and 1794. Although the archaeologists responsible for the excavation had initially estimated finding no more than fifty skeletons, by the summer of 1992 more than four hundred burials had been excavated, and an upper estimate of twenty thousand original burials in the total 5.5-acre burial ground was being discussed.

What more substantial evidence could there be of the presence and participation of Africans, in very significant numbers, during the founding of the great city of New York? But that was not supposed to be. Whether educated in New York City or elsewhere, the public had been led to believe that the city was built by Europeans, with precious little, if any, mention of Africans. Blacks and whites alike were shocked by the revelation of the cemetery. But for African Americans, here was dramatic evidence of the lies of omission and distortion about their contributions as a people; lies that Euroamerica seemed casually, or deliberately, to conspire to tell; lies of omission that denied African Americans their place in the founding of the nation.

Equally profound was the truth that emerged as the Burial Ground focused attention on historical information that was available to scholars of New York history[1] but that had previously made no headway against popularized notions about "the North." These dead Africans had not, for the most part, been free wage laborers. They had been enslaved, just as in the American South. As public discourse over the African Burial Ground ensued, layer by layer the distortions of American education rapidly peeled away, exposing a simple set of facts:

1. Africans had been brought to the original Dutch colonial city of New Amsterdam in 1626, the second year of that colony, thus being among its founders. In fact, Jan Rodriguez, a free Black trader, had set up the first long-term trading post in Manhattan prior to the establishment of the Dutch colony, making a person of African descent Manhattan's first foreign (i.e., nonindigenous) businessman.

2. Africans had constituted 40 percent of the population of the Dutch colony and about 15 percent of the subsequent larger, English colony of New York.

3. Most New York Africans lived under the harsh conditions of slavery from 1626 until emancipation took effect in 1827. In fact, large numbers of African Americans continued to be enslaved until the mid-1840s as a result of a special condition of that emancipation law, which allowed visitors from slave states to maintain their enslaved workers in that condition for as long as their stay might last, even indefinitely. Fewer than two decades prior to the Civil War, the North's economy and society was a slave economy and society. Northerners had little special claim to being "the good guys" on the issue of slavery. White supremacy had reigned in the North in dimensions that were subsequently denied and were omitted from the historical accounts with which the vast majority of modern Americans were familiar.

4. At least as important as these historical issues, a sacred cemetery had been covered with fill by the early 1800s and forgotten, and was the target of desecration by anthropologists and developers under the direction of the U.S. government. In the

1990s there was no respect for the African American past, its sacred space, or the sensibilities of living descendants on the part of the government in general, or of many involved Euroamericans in particular.

The distortions of history are not simply academic. All of what a people knows itself to be is historic. The future is an ideal, and the present is a fleeting moment that becomes the past in an instant. We know ourselves to be what we are according to what we have been. The distortion of African American history is a distortion of the identity of each and every person who is a member of that ethnic group.

African Americans have long viewed the construction of history as politically disempowering and demeaning. Frederick Douglass's "Claims of the Negro Ethnologically Considered,"[2] written during slavery, provides the evidence of that community's early awareness and incisive critical debate with anthropologists and archaeologists about such distortions. During the early twentieth century, Marcus Garvey, perhaps the most effective Black nationalist leader in U.S. history, would argue that "a people without knowledge of its history is like a tree without roots." Like Douglass, Garvey referenced Africans in biblical history to correct their disempowering exclusion from the history created by the hands of white interpreters. During the twentieth century, works by W. E. B. Du Bois and Carter G. Woodson were the most exemplary.[3] It was Woodson who founded the Association for the Study of Negro Life and History and who began Negro History Week, now evolved to African American History Month, to rectify the demeaning effects of white distortions of African American history and identity.

Throughout the civil rights and Black nationalist movements of the 1950s, 1960s, and early 1970s, "Black Studies" was fought for and established at many universities in order to rectify the distortions or "miseducation" of Eurocentric curricula.[4] Although African American studies curricula were established, at least marginally, in many public primary and secondary schools, many of these modest inroads were dismantled by the late 1970s as the pressure of "the movement" had waned.[5]

During the 1980s and 1990s, an Afrocentric educational movement emerged in the Black community, along with more broadly based efforts to establish "multicultural" curricula, because African American children were continuing to be taught a Eurocentric distortion of global and American history. That history included a romantic view of European and Euroamerican identity, and an omitted African and African American presence in important societal developments of which they were an integral part. Throughout the nation, independent African American schools have sprung up in the interest of Black children's education and need to know themselves as a means of avoiding the psychological wounds often inflicted by white supremacist public schools.

The issues that sparked the African Burial Ground situation were sometimes represented by whites as solely matters of spiritual and religious concern. But the politics of history and anthropology were also on the minds of African Americans as they considered the Burial Ground. Although an important element of concern, the exclusive emphasis on the spiritual and emotive aspects of African American sensibility constitutes a stereotypic distortion consistent with white supremacist assumptions.

The dignity of these dead Africans and African Americans was nearly disregarded in 1991 as the U.S. General Services Administration (GSA)[6] sought to expedite the building project that unearthed them. While many people looked on from around the nation, the living African American descendants of the people buried there struggled to gain control of the Burial Ground. African American political leaders Congressman Gus Savage, New York Mayor David Dinkins, and New York State Senator David Paterson challenged violations by the federal government in its expeditious approach to the removal of the African Burial Ground. A federal steering committee representing the descendant African American community was established by those elected officials and was chaired by historian Howard Dodson, chief of the Schomburg Center for Research in Black Culture. A broad cross-section of religious leaders, grassroots community leaders prominently including cultural nationalists and Pan-Africanists, and concerned citizens in New York City held mass demonstrations and confronted the GSA. Together, they succeeded in stopping part of the excavation, putting together a plan for a fitting memorial, and placing the scientific tasks of constructing these ancestors' history in the hands of the leading African American research university, Howard University in Washington, D.C.

The transfer of the scientific project to Howard was made difficult by competing anthropologists at Lehman College of the City University of New York who, having had a contract to do the original excavating, had possession of the remains and whose local political allies had mobilized in an attempt to obtain the lucrative contract to do scientific research on them. The City University underwent intense conflict over the issue of who should have the project. African American and progressive faculty tended to support the Howard University option, while many whites and opportunistic Blacks tried to keep the remains in the hands of an all-white team of anthropologists at Lehman who were inexperienced with African American research.

The very act of asserting our control of the Burial Ground signals who we are as a people, now and in the past. The protests in New York City showed that we believed in our dignity; the fact that the federal government's intent to disregard us was thwarted demonstrates our capacity for power; the fact that we could peel the City University's fingers away from the remains and take them to Howard University on the basis of superior scientific facilities and a commitment to self-determination signals both our expectation of control and our respect for our own intelligence. Had such control not been taken, African Americans would have signaled to ourselves and others whatever is meant when a formerly enslaved people must rely upon the descendants of our former enslavers for an elucidation of who we were and are as a people.

In November 1993 the last of these 408 excavated remains was brought to Washington, with ceremonies upon their departure and arrival. Religious observances, cultural events, and scientific meetings—each with distinctive African Diasporic cultural and intellectual elements—celebrated the significance of our achievement of control in New York City and at Howard University.

BIOCULTURAL AND ENGAGED APPROACHES

By 1996 more than three hundred ancestral remains had been cleaned, reconstructed, measured, photographed, and analyzed by a team of Howard University anthropologists who are African American, Jamaican, Trinidadian, Nigerian, Ghanaian, Ethiopian, Euroamerican, and South Asian. One purpose of the project has been to enhance educational and research opportunities for African American students. The persons trained in our W. Montague Cobb Biological Anthropology Laboratory, which has been responsible for the scientific analysis, constitute more Black osteological technicians than have ever before existed.

The project's theoretical approach is biocultural and biohistorical, consistent with both modern trends in anthropological theory and the Cobbian tradition (W. Montague Cobb was the first African American Ph.D. in physical anthropology) at Howard. We seek to enculture and engender the physical remains through interdisciplinary contextualization. We have rejected the now passé "race" concept preferred by the Euroamerican forensics researchers who had bid for control of this project, in favor of determining ethnic and national identifications through a mix of genetic, chemical, cultural, and historical data. In essence, the difference in our scientific approach is analogous to the difference made by the descendant community when it changed—or resurrected—the name of the site from "Negroes Burying Ground" to the "African Burial Ground."

Anthropological studies of Blacks tended to approach them as subjects for the study of presumed natural categories of race.[7] But "Negroids," as constructed, have no history or cultural interest. Races are social categories constructed with biological traits in an attempt to make social status differences appear to be natural. Racial identity conveys a static, ahistorical, and accultural definition of a human population. We are seeking to identify these skeletons as deriving from the Ashanti, Yoruba, Bakongo, or the Lenni Lenape, Dutch, and English, as they might be found to be. As biological categories (breeding populations), these groupings are more realistic genetic populations than are racial types, which lump together diverse genomes. They are also culturally defined societies whose histories can be known. In this sense, the African Burial Ground Project is "creating" more sophisticated identities of the people buried there by choosing nonracial units of population analysis.

As "engaged anthropologists" we view the descendant community as the project's ethical client. The cemetery belongs to them on humane grounds consistent with the Principles of Professional Responsibility and Ethics of the American Anthropological Association and the First Code of Ethics of the World Archaeological Congress. Newly proposed principles of "public engagement" have been drafted for the discipline that are consistent with those being applied by the African Burial Ground Project.[8] Yet our case mainly follows in the long African American tradition of "activist scholarship."[9]

Our research design was disseminated and discussed among members of the community in order to derive the kinds of scientific questions in which they were most interested and ultimately to obtain their approval. That engagement improved our research not only by fine-tuning our questions and language, but also by making this project their project. The engagement process helped bring about a public commitment to the broad scope of our research. Without such public support or pressure, the government was not likely to have provided funding for so extensive a research program. Our engaged and activist scholarship also submits our scientific evidence to a critical public dialogue.

Because archaeological skeletal remains and artifacts are material, they are graphic, powerful teaching devices that bring history near at hand. The W. Montague Cobb Biological Anthropology Laboratory has provided tours to thousands of people of all walks of life from four continents and the Caribbean. The project's main clearinghouse for information, the Office of Public Education and Information (OPEI) of the African Burial Ground, also gives tours of the artifacts in New York, holds teacher workshops, gives lectures at New York public schools, and publishes a quarterly newsletter going out to eleven thousand interested persons throughout the United States. Thus far, the OPEI has served more than 100,000 visitors under the directorship of cultural anthropologist Dr. Sherrill Wilson. Through these means, the project exchanges information with the broader public.

The project has been dedicated to the idea that the African Burial Ground population constituted a "bridge" between Africa and the Diaspora. The remains were of African- and American-born people, being studied by mostly African- and American-born researchers. For these reasons our project is well suited to a substantive transatlantic discussion, one that must take place in order to help confront our common history realistically. The project should help clear the air in ways that contribute to the extension of Pan-African relationships.

In 1993, for example, a discussion of the African Burial Ground was initiated by Nigerian scholars interested in reparations and African American political pressure for U.S. aid to Africa. In 1995, a royal delegation of the National House of Chiefs of Ghana visited Howard's laboratory and the cemetery in New York. They were reaching out to African Americans in an act of "atonement" for their responsibility in the slave trade and seeking to further strengthen economic and political ties. If the slave dungeons lining Ghana's coast were to attract African American tourists, Ghana would need to confront and acknowledge its contradictory involvement as both enslaved and enslavers when expressing its fraternity with the American Diaspora. Such a dialogue around the bones of the ancestors would not have had the same meaning of familial reconciliation had the remains been in Euroamerican hands. The project was uniquely positioned for this confluence of events.

Similarly, Euroamerica's psychologically deep denial of the implications of its practice of slavery and institutional racism should be confronted by our scientific findings. At the beginning of the twenty-first century, however, there has been no Euroamerican expression of atonement nor reconciliation toward African Americans for the costs of slavery. The scientific method would not create that discussion on its own. The public hearings on the research design did, however, help to make researchers conscious of a broad range of public concerns regarding the biases of traditional African Diasporic history and their alternatives.

The project seeks to answer four main questions about the African Burial Ground: Where did the people come from who were buried there? What was the physical quality of life during their enslavement? What biocultural transformations had and had not taken place during their lifetimes? In what ways did they resist slavery? Our initial biological data have begun to answer these questions, especially that of the physical quality of life.

PRELIMINARY RESULTS OF THE AFRICAN BURIAL GROUND PROJECT

Thus far, the skeletal biology facet of this project has moved ahead of the other disciplinary components due to prolonged contract negotiations with the GSA. Some archaeological and historical information has, nonetheless, emerged. Our preliminary findings presented here are based on a sample of the three hundred burials that had been processed (cleaned, reconstructed, inventoried, measured, photographed, and assessed) as of 1996.

Dental enamel hypoplasia (a developmental defect of dental enamel that results from childhood malnutrition and disease) is common (over 60 percent) in children under twelve years of age. This frequency is high for children and comparable to the enslaved African American plantation populations studied by our laboratory and others. Approximately 49 percent of adult dentitions have defects that occurred during childhood. This frequency is about half that of nineteenth-century African American plantation populations.[10] These data suggest a more benign or healthy, possibly African, context of childhood for many of those who died as adults than for those dying as children in New York City.

We are also finding childhood cases of rickets and porotic hyperostosis indicative, respectively, of vitamin D deficiency and anemia. The observed cases of craniosynostosis (premature closure of cranial sutures) in children is well above modern rates. Children's skeletons often show combinations of two or more of these effects. Indeed, 50 percent of the population died by age twelve, approximately 35 percent of them dying in infancy. These data on children clearly represent a highly stressed population.[11]

What strikes us as particularly profound in frequency and severity is the evidence of work- and load-bearing stress in adults. Most men and women show hypertrophic (enlarged) muscle attachments in bones of the shoulders, arms, and legs. Cases of enthesopathy (large pits and grooves in bones resulting from the tearing of muscles and ligaments where they attach to the skeleton) are evident in most individuals, male and female, in the upper and lower limbs. Heavy lifting and other work would have caused these changes. These individuals performed work that pressed the musculoskeletal system to its limits and arguably beyond those limits.[12]

Osteophytosis (degenerative arthritis) of the cervical (neck) vertebrae has often been observed. We are exploring our best hypothesis for this excessive degeneration of the bones of the neck as caused by carrying heavy loads on the head.[13] This highly efficient axial loading technique is used throughout African societies. Cases of fractures of the base of the skull and upper neck (first and second cervical vertebrae) have frequently been found. Perimortum circular fractures of the skull base that we have found were also probably caused by loading on top of the head in such a rough way and with sufficient weight and force to kill. Other accidental or deliberate trauma to the head and spine might also account for these fractures. If the former explanation prevails in these cases, then load-bearing stress exceeded human capacity.

Finally, there are a few other cases of trauma, most of which involve women. Burial no. 25 is the most graphic case in point. A woman approximately twenty-two years (plus or minus eighteen months) of age and 51 inches tall was found to have a musket ball in her thoracic (chest) area. The projectile appears to have entered through the upper back or side (left scapula). Blunt force fractures of the lower face and a torsion fracture due to the twisting of her right arm are also present. All trauma occurred within a short time prior to her death. These data are beginning to tell of the hardships of slavery in a northern colony.

Archaeological data have just begun to focus our attention on Akan-speaking West African origins with the discovery of what we believe is an Ashanti Adinkra symbol, Sankofa, on the coffin lid for burial no. 101. This symbol can be interpreted as meaning, "look to the past to inform decisions for the future; one can correct one's mistakes."[14] Those who initially excavated the site, having little or no background in African history and culture, had assumed that this important symbol had the meanings normally associated with the European geometricized heart shape. The geometricized Sankofa is a particularly elaborated "heart-shaped" symbol.

The fourteen cases of modified anterior dentition (front teeth) observed thus far, comprising at least seven different styles of filing, direct our attention to West and Central African societies where dental modification had been widespread and to which these variations might be usefully compared.

Historical data have also begun to provide a context within which to consider likely explanations for the skeletal indicators of African origins and the physical quality of life of the people who worked at the docks and on the farms; cleared the land; constructed roads, walls, and buildings; maintained the European domestic sphere; rebelled, worshiped, and negotiated the establishment of their own families and communities. These were the people who built and maintained colonial New York. Yet they are also people who often had had a life in Africa, the Caribbean, or the American South prior to arriving in New York. Our African Diasporic historians and archaeologists, conscious of this fuller life, are in the process of re-creating the larger identity of these ancestors in such a way that one might understand them as "enslaved African people" rather than simply as "slaves" or as Negroids.

The New York African Burial Ground is phenomenal because of the rich combination of institutions, symbols, information, and politics that weave through it. Here we have an original community of African North Americans, a revelation of Northern slavery and African contributions to the creation of New York and, indeed, the Western world. The issues surrounding the Burial Ground include who should speak for the past, a Diasporic dialogue, group rights, educational opportunities, business interests, racism, the need for a more balanced education, the value of interdisciplinary research, and relationships between science, politics, culture, and spiritual belief.

This is a story, also, of the importance of having African American representation "in every room." Bringing this situation under control depended mightily upon African

Americans with key access to information, influence, and power. They ranged from construction workers to holders of high public office who closed ranks in myriad ways that secured significant descendant oversight of the cemetery. Differences in the range of African American participation in all American institutions influence how we can and will construct history and culture. Similarly, ongoing geopolitical changes throughout Africa and the Diaspora have empowered whole nations and ethnic groups to rewrite their pasts as they forge new futures.

NOTES

1. T. J. Davis, *Rumor of the Revolt: The "Great Negro Plot" in Colonial New York* (New York: Free Press, 1985). See historical review in Howard University and John Milner Associates, *Research Design for Archaeological, Historical, and Bioanthropological Investigations of the African Burial Ground, New York: Broadway Block* (Washington, D.C.: Howard University), 131.

2. Frederick Douglass, "The Claims of the Negro Ethnographically Considered," in *The Life and Writings of Frederick Douglass*, ed. Philip S. Foner (New York: International Publishers, 1950 [1854]), 289–309.

3. See, for example, W. E. B. Du Bois, *The Gift of Black Folks: Negroes in the Making of America* (New York: Johnson Reprint, 1968 [1924]), and Carter G. Woodson, *The Mis-Education of the Negro* (Washington, D.C.: Associated Publishers, 1969 [1933]).

4. See "An Assessment of Black Studies Programs in Higher Education," a special issue of the *Journal of Negro Education*, no. 53 (1984).

5. For example, in Washington, D.C., where I was raised, we nearly had to shut down the public school system in order to be taught about our own people. By 1970–71 my high school classmates and I had courses in an African language, African American literature, and African music to augment our studies in European languages, literature, and art. Three years after my class graduated, all of these courses were removed from the curriculum.

6. The GSA, the nation's landlords, had responsibility over the Burial Ground, including the excavation, as mandated by the Historical Preservation Act of 1966. For more information, see Leland Ferguson, *Uncommon Ground: Archaeology and Early African America, 1650–1800* (Washington, D.C.: Smithsonian Institution Press, 1992), xxxiii–xl.

7. Michael L. Blakey, "Skull Doctors: Intrinsic Social and Political Bias in the History of American Physical Anthropology, with Special Reference to the Work of Ales Hrdlicka," *Critique of Anthropology* 7 (1987): 7–35.

8. Shepard Forman, ed., *Diagnosing America: Anthropology and Public Engagement* (Ann Arbor: University of Michigan Press, 1994), 295–312.

9. Leslie Rankin-Hill and Michael L. Blakey, "W. Montague Cobb (1904–1990): Physical Anthropologist, Anatomist, and Activist," *American Anthropologist* 96 (1994): 74–96.

10. Mark E. Mack, Michael L. Blakey, and M. Cassandra Hill, "Preliminary Observations of the Dental Pathologies of the African Burial Ground Skeletal Population," paper delivered at the 64th Annual Meeting of the American Association of Physical Anthropologists, Oakland, California, 1995.

11. Mark E. Mack, M. Cassandra Hill, and Michael L. Blakey, "Preliminary Analysis of Skeletal Remains from the New York African Burial Ground," paper delivered at the 94th Annual Meeting of the American Anthropological Association, Washington, D.C., 1995.

12. M. Cassandra Hill, Michael L. Blakey, and Mark E. Mack, "Women, Endurance, Enslavement: Exceeding the Physiological Limits," paper delivered at the 64th Annual Meeting of the American Association of Physical Anthropologists, Oakland, California, 1995.

13. Hill et al., "Women, Endurance, Enslavement."

14. Kwaku Ofori-Ansa, "Identification and Validation of the Sankofa Symbol," *The Update, Office of Public Education and Interpretation of the New York African Burial Ground and Five Points Archaeological Projects* (New York, 1995), 3.

13

New African Diasporic Communities in the United States: Community-Centered Approaches to Research and Presentation

Diana Baird N'Diaye

The African Immigrant Folklife Study (AIFS) Project is a collaborative project of the Smithsonian Institution Center for Folklife Programs and Cultural Studies and community-based African-born scholars, cultural organizers, and culture bearers from the Washington, D.C., area. The goals of the AIFS Project have been to research, interpret, and present programs on the uses of traditional skills and knowledge in new contexts within communities of recent African immigrants in the United States. In this chapter I will report on the project and discuss some of the issues relevant to African Diaspora research that we encountered in the course of the study.

Whether designated as African immigrants, American Africans, African transnationals, hyphenated African-Americans, or Africans of the new Diaspora, new communities of Africans have emerged in the post-slavery and more recent post-colonial era, joining older African American populations in the United States. These recently formed communities of African immigrants extend the considerable diversity that has existed for centuries within the population of African descent in the United States; a broad diversity of language and regional and ethnic culture enhanced by immigration from the Caribbean and Central and South America. African American cultural diversity has until recently been largely unacknowledged.

The growth of post-slavery communities of African-born immigrants dates back to more than one hundred years ago, when families from the Cape Verde Islands off the West African coast were driven by harsh conditions of drought and economic hardship to settle in New England, where they played a large role in seafaring and the cranberry industry.

Since the 1960s, several complex circumstances have contributed to attracting increased immigration and transnational activity of Africans to the United States. Some of these factors, both political and economic, include the decline of European colonization and economic influence in Africa, the concurrent growth of United States participation in African political affairs, changes in U.S. immigration laws, and the existence of an established African American population.

Whatever the circumstances that compelled Africans to make the transatlantic journey and settle in the United States, communities of Africans residing in the United States have begun to take their places within the multicultural landscape of the nation. The constituents of this new African Diaspora in the United States came from all regions of the African continent. According to figures available from the U.S. Census bureau, the overall African-born population of the United States in 1990 was 363,819. Informal estimates indicate that numbers may now be more in the low millions.

While recent African transnational communities share some social characteristics with those of the African Diaspora created by the slave trade and with immigrant groups in general, the circumstances that brought them to this country vary significantly. Some came to attend American universities, others fled oppressive political situations, many came with entrepreneurial aspirations. The communities constructed by these new African arrivals vary in size from under one hundred to several thousand people. They also vary in the duration of their settlement in the United States, in the extent to which they remain in contact with their countries and regions of origin, and in the ideas upon which they base their sentiments of shared identity.[1]

A few examples will serve to illustrate the diversity of contexts for cultural expression created by these new immigrants. Senegalese residents of New York City organize traditional wrestling matches called *lambes* at local parks, and they transform apartment buildings in Harlem into "vertical villages" where apartment restaurants serve midday fish, rice, and news from home as good as any available back in Dakar. Like a village in Senegal, these living arrangements provide security, communication-networks, information, easy social and economic reciprocity, health care, and contexts for cultural performances.

Immigrants whose members originate in the Horn of Africa and who may identify themselves as Ethiopians, Amhara, Tigray, or Oromo celebrate or choose not to celebrate the evening of the Coptic new year in separate restaurants and clubs in the Adams Morgan neighborhood of Washington; Yoruba-speaking Nigerians establish houses of worship in the city, such as the International House of Prayer for All People and the Celestial Church of Christ. These churches, part of an indigenous Nigerian prophet-centered independent religious movement called Aladura, combine aspects of traditional Yoruba cultural practice and Christian belief. And Ghanaians of the Ashanti ethnic group appoint local leaders from Atlanta, Georgia, to Oakland, California—with the ceremony and regalia of the Akan tradition in Ghana.

African-born immigrants come together as self-identified sociocultural communities for social and symbolic events that help their members create and maintain a sense of shared identity. They do this through creatively selecting, transforming, recontextualizing, and privately and publicly enacting aspects of expressive culture as traditions from their countries of origin. As they do so, they take an active role in inventing and reinventing their communities.

While these communities have grown in size and visibility in the urban landscape, the diversity and richness of their cultures remains largely invisible to Americans at large. Practices, occasions, and agreed-upon artistic standards for cooking, presenting, and consuming food; dressing; dancing; worshiping; decorating homes; and producing festivals and other celebrations are all bases for shared identity. In these and other ways, African-born immigrants in the United States debate, perform, present, transform, transmit, and create expressive culture to define and redefine who they are to one another and to the world.

RESEARCH BACKGROUND

The research objectives of the AIFS Project and the questions that accompany them are grounded in a set of working assumptions about the culture-building processes of immigrant groups. The theoretical bases for these concepts have been explored in the burgeoning literature on ethnicity and tradition,[2] on the "new" post-1965 immigrants,[3] and in studies of African culture and its Diaspora as exemplified in Joseph Harris's edited volume *Global Dimensions of the African Diaspora*.[4]

Initial analytic constructions of the relationship between ethnicity and tradition conceived of ethnic groups and their traditions as set entities. Members of immigrant groups were seen as possessing uniformly shared items of culture brought over from the home country, which they reenacted with less and less accuracy or "authenticity" as the immigrants became more acculturated to the new society to which they had come.[5]

More recent views, beginning with the work of Fredrik Barth,[6] understand ethnicity as created by the negotiation of boundaries between insiders and outsiders; it is fluid and situationally performed,[7] and constantly being reconstructed by the creative use of expressive culture as symbolic of group identity.[8] Contemporary views understand that tradition is used continuously and dynamically to legitimate, to indicate, or to reify cultural identity in ever-changing social contexts.[9] Studies of the development of ethnic identity within urbanized and creolized communities in Africa and the Caribbean have recognized the changing construction of cultural identity. Barbara Koptyoff notes, for example, that:

> A striking finding of recent research on ethnic groups in Africa has been the flexibility of ethnic identity and ethnic group boundaries. While ethnic identity does not normally change very much in an individual's lifetime if he stays in the same place, surrounded by the same people, migration may result in redefinitions of ethnic group boundaries and of the basis of ethnic identity itself. One finds such ethnic redefinition in multi-ethnic African cities and towns today.[10]

The theoretical understanding of cultural identity as continually and actively negotiated fits well with a methodological approach to folklife as contextualized performance.[11] Hence, the project proceeds from the standpoint that recent African immigrants have some agreed-upon (and some disputed) concepts of the culture they bring with them from Africa. The forms of this culture embody shared values, skills, knowledge, and culturally determined perceptual lenses through which members experience the world. These symbolic forms are enacted as part of traditional performance genres practiced in everyday life and on special occasions.

These cultural forms—chosen among others from a wide universe of possibilities—become part of a discourse used to construct cultural identity. Group members continually and consciously reconstruct this discourse using symbols claimed by individuals and groups as metaphors for identity. The selection of traditions to acknowledge through practice is informed by, and has consequences for, a culturally defined ethical system. The dynamics of this culture-building seem to be affected by, among other factors, the immigrants' changing images of the place they have come to and the place they have left. The images change over time and from member to member, and bear significance for the selection of symbols in the performance of identity.

ISSUES OF CULTURAL DEFINITION

African newcomers to the United States include those who consider their residence as temporary and plan to return to live in their countries of origin at a later date. Many actively move between residences on the African and North American continents. Some have chosen to reside permanently in the United States but still find it important to teach their children everything they need to know to maintain ties with relatives in Africa, if only during brief visits "home."

Alexander Okechukwu, director of a youth program organized by the Ibo-speaking Nigerian community, notes that, "Having lived here for some time and away from home, we begin to have children; we see that this area, the Washington metropolitan area, is full of cultural mix. And we find out . . . what is missing . . . it appears our culture is missing, and we would like our children to know some of the facets of our culture. We decide we would like to create . . . an awareness of our culture and the way of life of our people . . . the Anioma people—so that we will create a kind of community."[12]

In discussions with African-born residents of the United States, some of the same issues and concerns kept coming up. These concerns included:

1. The social, emotional, and economic need to maintain connections with people and things from home in order to survive in America;
2. The need to pass on to children of African-born parents growing up in the United States a sense of cultural grounding in the key values, beliefs, and knowledge that will also enable them to have smooth social relations in the home of their parents as the children learn to function in American society;
3. The wish for Americans to have more balanced and informed representations of Africa and Africans; and
4. The desire for more dialogue and closer relationships with other Americans, especially those of African descent with whom they invariably felt strong historical and cultural links.

The urgency of these concerns is, of course, familiar to both continental and diasporic Africans across a wide range of geographical and ethnic origins. As Remi Aluko, founder of a summer camp that teaches children about African culture, says of her own children, "I started teaching them and talking to them right from when they were babies, and I saw it worked." When she took her children to visit Nigeria in 1990, "It was tremendous. When they would go to the people they would understand the language. They could eat the food. Everybody felt as if these kids had been part of them."[13]

THE AFRICAN IMMIGRANT FOLKLIFE STUDY GROUP: A PARTNERSHIP WITH COMMUNITY SCHOLARS

In the past, much of the formal study and documentation of culture and of traditional folklife has been considered the professional domain of anthropologists, folklorists, and other formally trained specialists, usually from outside the communities that have been studied. Recent work in reflexive anthropology and folklore has stressed the importance of the perspectives of culture bearers and of acknowledging the orientations researchers carry with them into the field. The development of this ethical knowledge coincides with cultural communities' increasingly asserted right to be agents of their own representation and explication, rather than merely objects of study.

The AIFS Project is grounded in community-centered research that places the tools and methods of research and access to forums for public presentation in the hands of those whose communities are represented. Although community-based research has a long history of practice within social change movements, this project in the context of the Smithsonian Institution faced several challenges in regard to support and funding. The project was sustained in part because individuals in key positions at the Smithsonian Institution and especially in its Center for Folklife Programs and Cultural Studies believed in its mission. However, it proved very difficult to fund through conventional research sources. Many potential funders both within and outside the Smithsonian questioned whether such research would be "good enough." They focused on the absence of sanctioned, published, institutionally based "experts" as primary researchers, and questioned the ability of community members to seriously research their own cultures.

Some potential funders mistakenly assumed that African immigrants were too close, culturally, to African Americans for the project to be taken seriously as a cross-cultural project. Others assumed that the involvement of community members in the project would be only superficial, that the Smithsonian had little to learn from a partnership with people outside of academia producing research for the benefit of their own communities, and that as in other "community outreach" efforts by large cultural institutions, the community relations benefit could be achieved with much less effort through conventional programs. Although the project had the benefit of the participation of several African scholars who were, in fact, credentialed in fields related to folklore and anthropology, the fact that they were not known by reviewers, and were not necessarily academically based, seems also to have made a difference.

The project also had a long hard road to walk to win the trust of members of the African immigrant communities that eventually became involved. Cultural gatekeepers stood on both the institutional and the community sides of the gate. The Smithsonian had made little effort in the past to reach out respectfully to the African communities, even though it held at least two substantial collections of African art and historical artifacts. Africans complained that they had been represented in the former African Hall of the National Museum of Natural History as if caught in a European colonial fantasy. In the National Museum of African Art, the cultural production of African people was, they noted, also limited to the usual favorite eras and categories of Western representation and tended to be portrayed out of context and without much regard to the creators as living, breathing, ongoing communities in the contemporary world.

Because their participation in Smithsonian programming had not been previously solicited to any great extent, many potential participants were suspicious of the aims of an invitation coming from the institution, initially scoffed at the idea that any project based there held the possibility of an authentic partnership, and questioned how the research would be used. Others felt that the project stipends that the Smithsonian offered were not comparable to what more traditional researchers would receive for similar research.

By no means have all of these issues been resolved. However, the AIFS Project managed to gain community trust through the production of programs and publications that reflected African immigrant voices. Community-based scholars, educators, and organizers also participated in advisory capacities in the planning for the new African Cultures Hall at the National Museum of Natural History, as well as in symposia and presentations at the National Museum of African Art. The challenges remain, however, in creating a sustainable community-centered base for ongoing cultural work that focuses on community-building and bridging.

PROJECT DESCRIPTION

This documentation, interpretation, and presentation project was an ideal opportunity to work with researchers within the communities who displayed a strong commitment to and passion for the collection and preservation of culture. Stating their personal goals for the project, community scholars emphasized the social action aspects of their work. In response to the recruitment application, many stated a desire to provide opportunities for dialogue among residents of Washington on issues of identity between members of various communities of African descent as well as with the public at large.

Some community scholars mentioned that the documentation and presentation of African immigrant community culture would enhance the public image of Africans. This would lead to enhanced communication and better relations between African-born immigrants and their neighbors. Others mentioned that both the collective research and the resulting presentations provided support for community-building efforts and community and individual self-discovery, and contributed toward shaping an inclusive cultural identity.

Anna Ceesay, a fabric-resist artist and merchant who learned her traditional craft skills from her grandmother in the Gambia, wrote that her reasons for participating in the project were that, "As Africans we are faced with prejudice and unfair treatment in our everyday immigrant life. This is due to ignorance and lack of understanding. This project will . . . give us opportunities to reveal and teach something of our traditional ways of life, our culture, and therefore make more people know and understand us better."[14]

A twelve-session training program began in the spring of 1994 with sixteen community scholars identified through recommendations from established scholars at the Smithsonian National Museum of African Art, the Anacostia Museum, and other sources. As director of the AIFS Project, I designed and facilitated the training program with the assistance of other Smithsonian staff folklorists, especially educational specialist Dr. Betty Belanus. Applicants for the program revealed their many activities in and commitment to cultural preservation.

A Smithsonian staff review panel looked for individuals rooted and respected in their own communities. We tried to configure the group to include representatives from each community, varying in ethnic affiliation, gender, age, length of residence in the United States, prior research experience, and skills and aptitudes as tradition-bearers. Initially the composition of the group, the members of which we referred to as "community scholars," reflected most of the largest African immigrant populations in the area: Egyptian, Nigerian, Ghanaian, Senegambian, the Horn of Africa (Ethiopian/Oromo/Somali), and Southern African (Lesotho). Community scholars from other countries and regions of African origin joined the project as it developed. The program ultimately included the participation of people from over thirty African countries of origin.

In early sessions our study group discussed and unpacked eclectic concepts of community, tradition, and folklife. Individuals wrote cultural autobiographies locating themselves within their cultural community or communities. Later sessions included visits by Smithsonian-based researchers, guest lecturers from area universities, and presentations by community-based scholars from the group on methods of documentation through interviews, participant observation, surveys, and the use of recording technologies (video and audio taping, photography, note-taking, and archiving).

In order to shape the fieldwork plan collectively, the AIFS group needed to decide which aspects of the African population and which forms of expressive culture to document. To this work community scholars brought knowledge of the dominant discourses occurring in their communities relevant to identity and culture. They were familiar with the types of institutions and businesses that African-born residents were forming and what needs they were meant to address. They came to the research knowing subtleties of practice and meaning rarely available to outside scholars.

The group visited the Smithsonian's Field to Factory exhibition at the National Museum of American History, and learned that many African Americans whose ancestors were forced to emigrate from Africa centuries ago had experienced additional migration from the fields of the lower South to the factories of the urban North during the 1930s and 1940s.[15] Other African descendants had come to the United States post–World War I from the Caribbean and South America. It was noted in the discussions that followed that both groups and their descendants living in the Washington area are often the neighbors, clients, patrons, and religious co-congregants of African newcomers to the area.

The twelve weekly meetings also served as occasion to examine collectively the meaning of a number of terms. The examination of these terms was critical to designing research plans, to the fieldwork process, and to curating Festival of American Folklife presentations. Defining the terms "African," "immigrant," "community," and "folklife" in the context of the Washington area were key to our dialogue, to the substance of the fieldwork, and to the process of designing public presentations. Terms such as African American, African immigrant, and voluntary immigration were all problematized. "African" could refer to people born on the continent and residing abroad, what Ali Mazrui has characterized as "the diaspora of colonialism," but it could also refer to historical communities of Africans born in what he terms "the diaspora of enslavement."[16]

The group searched for a better term than "immigrant" to describe how they saw their status as nonnative-born residents of the United States. Some argued that the use of the word immigrant implies voluntary separation from one country and exclusive adoption of another; it does not account for Africans in this country as refugees. It implies a permanency of residence that precludes the eventual return that many people hope for; it does not describe the conditions of dual residence and transnationality that more precisely define the contemporary experience of many Africans here.[17]

The AIFS group concluded that an "African immigrant community" did not yet exist as a clearly defined and coherent entity. We found that we could not always define a community by geographical nation-state of origin without grouping together people who saw themselves as part of fundamentally different groups. For example, Oromo community scholars refused to be defined as Ethiopian nationals. They preferred instead to define themselves as citizens of a colonized Oromo state. Other community scholars defining themselves as Ethiopian insisted that their community included all of those within the United Nations–sanctioned, internationally accepted boundaries of Ethiopia.

We tried looking at ethnic groups within countries as the primary unit of community, and found that in the United States, religious affiliation united people across ethnic, geographical, and political boundaries while dividing others with similar language and geographical origin. We met with groups organized on the basis of the town or region they had come from, such as the River States Forum, named after a region in Nigeria, or the Volta Club from the similarly named region in Ghana. The confluence of immigrant alliances and professional activities is reflected in the names of community associations such as the Ghanaian Registered Nurses Association. Although the community scholars recognized that they could not document or interview immigrants from every country in Africa, they felt that it was important that no region of the continent be completely left out.

Consequently, members decided to focus on exploring their own self-identified communities in depth, but also to assign responsibility for contacting cultural organizations from other countries and regions. "Community" was finally defined for working purposes as a group whose members define themselves as such and that constructs and reinforces feelings of shared identity through reference to common heritage, traditions, religious or political beliefs, language, geography, values, and experience. This formulation of the concept, close to contemporary scholarly notions of community, as noted earlier, paved the way for the research plans that the group designed.

Initially, when people in the group spoke about African "traditions," it was often about those ways of doing things just the way that they were done back home; customs brought over like so much baggage from home and set up in the new place. As the fieldwork results began to come in and we moved toward planning the presentations, it became clear that Africans were not merely reproducing customs that they remembered from home, but were also actively and explicitly using the *language* of tradition—ways of cooking food, of dressing, of dancing—to name themselves and to make statements about their identity as Africans to one another and to the world.

At the same time, because of more reliable telephone communications, frequent and less expensive flights, and accessible home audio and video recording, it has become easier in recent years to maintain a closer connection with family and friends at home. Goods, ideas, and expressive culture flow back and forth much more easily. Just as the expressive culture of African-born residents of Washington receives constant new infusions through visitors from home and from their own trips to the continent, popular and grassroots culture in Africa are influenced by new music, language, and goods from America.

RESULTS AND CONCLUSIONS

The AIFS Project can boast of success in several areas. We began in March 1994 with a group of community activists from different African countries and ethnicities with distinct religions and mother tongues. The group included professional folklorists and other academics, traditional artists, cultural organizers, and cultural entrepreneurs. Their research focused on some of the largest African immigrant populations in the metropolitan area and on some of the most visible by virtue of the range of their organized cultural activities.

With Smithsonian staff they produced a body of fieldwork and a workable conceptual framework and site plan for the 1995 Festival of American Folklife (FAF) program. The training, discussion, fieldwork, planning, and preview presentations of African immigrant community culture at the festival yielded much evidence of the research value embedded in the process of community-centered folklife studies. Activities at the FAF included a two-part concert series on African immigrant music, dance, and verbal arts; an exhibition of films by and about African immigrants cosponsored by the National Museum of African Art; a photo exhibition: "New Ties: Portraits of African Immigrant Community Folklife in Metropolitan Washington, D.C."; and an online exhibition on the World Wide Web about a Yoruba Naming Ceremony in Washington, D.C.[18] In addition, community scholars and Smithsonian staff produced a body of audio, video, and still photography, and identified and showcased the work of several African-born traditional craftspeople residing in the Washington area.

More than four hundred African-born residents of the Washington area participated in the program, presenting and interpreting their community culture to the public in the form of published articles, panel discussions, music and dance performances, demonstrations of crafts, and social events. Among the many special events of significance to local and national communities held during the festival, perhaps the most spectacular was the inauguration of a Ghanaian community leader, the Asantehene-Kuo of metropolitan Washington, which was attended by representatives of Akan communities throughout the United States and Canada.

The 1997 Smithsonian FAF program, "African Immigrant Folklife: Community Building and Bridging," was also conceived and accomplished as a collaborative effort through partnerships between African immigrant community members, other interested institutions, and the Center for Folklife Programs and Cultural Studies—with African immigrants playing central roles. The major presenters were African immigrant traditional artists, cultural educators, cooks, musicians, radio and television show hosts and organizers, craftspeople, shop owners, and cultural activists from social clubs and self-help and cultural organizations from several ethnic and cultural communities around the Washington area. Identified on the basis of interviews and participant observation, they shared their expertise, skills, and perspectives on the role of tradition in community building with visitors to the festival and with each other.

Several years have passed since the participants in the AIFS Project met for the first time to exchange stories about their personal odysseys to the United States, to share knowledge about their own community traditions with the rest of the group, and to learn the basic tools of folklife research and programming. During this time an evolution has occurred—from unacquainted but like-minded individuals with a strong interest in the presentation and preservation of their respective African cultures, to a network of people with ongoing relationships and alliances that reach beyond the Smithsonian and beyond their separate organizational affiliations.

Although the AIFS Project stopped short of engaging in the process of incorporating as an independent and ongoing group, individual community scholars and the organizations they work with in the Washington area have used the research/presentation/dialogue process in their own presentations in order to make their cultures more accessible and more valued as an important part of the area's cultural heritage. As community scholar and Howard University professor of art Dr. Kwaku Ofori-Ansa puts it:

> We used to have a saying in Ghana that any town without a Nigerian in it is a bad town. It means that people who come from outside a culture and live within that other culture always bring with them something that helps that new home to improve, to develop. . . . One cannot appreciate what people have brought in if people do not have an idea of what they do or what they are.[19]

When asked to describe his cultural community, filmmaker Olaniyi Areke summed up the way many participants felt as a result of the project:

> Being an African was not a big thing when I was in Nigeria. I never knew the importance of my culture until I came here. I used to think the cultures of other ethnic groups in Nigeria and other African countries were different. I know now that there are more similarities than differences. My community is not limited to Yoruba, Nigeria and Africa; the whole world is now my community since African people are all over the world.[20]

NOTES

Portions of this text have appeared in Diana Baird N'Diaye and Betty Belanus, "The African Immigrant Folklife Study Project," *Smithsonian Festival of American Folklife* (program book), ed. Peter Seitel (Washington, D.C.: Smithsonian Institution, 1995), 90–96.

1. Several articles in the *New York Times* and the *Washington Post* have highlighted the unique attributes and characteristics of new immigrant communities throughout the United States: Deborah Sontag and Celia W. Dugger, "New Immigrant Tide: Shuttle Between Worlds," *New York Times* (July 19, 1998): 1(1); Pamela Constable and D'Vera Cohn, "Lives Transplanted, a Region Transformed; Immigration Changes Face of the Region; Schools Up Immigrant Costs," *Washington Post* (Aug. 30, 1998): 1A; "Immigrants: More Boon Than Burden; Woven Economic Fabric Is Strength of Foreign Threads," *Washington Post* (Aug. 31, 1998): 1A; and "Culture Clashes Put Immigrant Women on the Front Lines," *Washington Post* (Sept. 1, 1998): 1A. The articles seem to concur that new immigrants tend to be from Asia, Latin America, and Africa rather than Europe, that they are intent on maintaining many aspects of their cultural traditions and perspectives, and that they are keeping in touch more effectively and more easily with their countries of origin than did earlier generations of immigrants. When it is an option, many carry dual citizenship in the United States and in the country of their births. In fact, the new immigrants, in the context of a global economy and an increasingly global cultural environment, may be more accurately characterized as transnational.

2. Surveyed by Stephen Stern and John Allan Cicala, eds., "Introduction," in *Creative Ethnicity: Symbols and Strategies of Contemporary Ethnic Life* (Logan: University of Utah Press, 1991). See also George De Vos and Lola Romanucci-Ross, "Ethnicity: Vessel of Meaning and Emblem of Contrast," in *Ethnic Identity: Cultural Continuities and Change*, eds. George De Vos and Lola Romanucci-Ross (Palo Alto, Calif.: Mayfield Publishing Company, 1975), 363–390; Stephen Stern, "Ethnic Folklore and the Folklore of Ethnicity," in *Studies in Folklore and Ethnicity*, ed. Larry Danielson (Los Angeles: California Folklore Society, 1978), 7–32; Benedict Anderson, *Imagined Communities* (London: Verso Editions, 1983); Elliot Oring, *Folk Groups and Folk Genres: An Introduction* (Logan: University of Utah Press, 1986); Ellen Badone, "Ethnicity, Folklore and Local Identity in Brittany," *Journal of American Folklore* 100 (1987): 161–190; Olivia Cadaval, "Making a Place Home: The Latino Festival," in *Creative Ethnicity*, 204–222; John Sorenson, "Essence and Contingency in the Construction of Nationhood: Transformations of Identity in Ethiopia and its Diasporas," *Diaspora* 2, no. 2 (1992): 200–228.

3. Won Moo Hurh, Hei Chu Kim, and Kwang Chung Kim, "Cultural and Social Adjustment Patterns of Korean Immigrants in the Chicago Area," in *Sourcebook on the New Immigration: Implications for the United States and the International Community*, ed. Roy Simón Bryce-Laporte (New Brunswick, N.J.: Transaction Books, Rutgers University Press, 1981), 295–302.

4. See Elliot P. Skinner, "The Dialectic Between Diasporas and Homelands," in *Global Dimensions of the African Diaspora*, ed. Joseph E. Harris, 2nd edition (Washington, D.C.: Howard University Press, 1993 [1982]), 11–40; Okan Edet Uya, "Conceptualizing Afro-American/African Relations: Implications for African Diaspora Studies," in *Global Dimensions*, 69–84; Adell Patton, Jr., "Howard University and Meharry Medical Schools in the Training of African Physicians, 1868–1978," in *Global Dimensions*, 109–123; Ibrahima B. Kaké, "The Impact of Afro-Americans on French-Speaking Black Africans, 1919–1945," in *Global Dimensions*, 249–261; St. Clair Drake, "Diaspora Studies and Pan-Africanism," in *Global Dimensions*, 351–514.

5. Melford E. Spiro, "The Acculturation of American Ethnic Groups," in *American Anthropologist* 57 (1955): 1240–1252; Milton M. Gordon, *Assimilation in American Life: The Role of Race, Religion, and National Origin* (New York: Oxford University Press, 1964).

6. Fredrik Barth, ed., *Ethnic Groups and Boundaries: The Social Organization of Culture Difference* (Boston: Little, Brown and Company, 1969), 9–38.

7. J. A. Nagata, "Adaptation and Integration of Greek Working Class Immigrants in Toronto: A Situational Approach," in *International Migration Review* 1 (1969): 44–70.

8. Shalom Staub, *Yemenis in New York City: The Folklore of Ethnicity* (Philadelphia: Balch Press, 1989); Charles F. Keyes, "Towards a New Formulation of the Concept of Ethnic Group," *Ethnicity* 3 (1976): 202–213; Keyes, "Introduction" in Charles F. Keyes, ed., *Ethnic Adaptation and Identity: The Karen on the Thai Frontier* (Philadelphia: ISHI Press, 1979), 1–23; Keyes, "The Dialectics of Ethnic Change," in *Ethnic Change*, ed. Charles F. Keyes (Seattle: University of Washington Press, 1981), 4–30; and Stern and Cicala, *Creative Ethnicity*.

9. Barbara Kirshenblatt-Gimblett, "Studying Immigrant and Ethnic Lore," in *Handbook of American Folklore*, ed. Richard M. Dorson (Bloomington: Indiana University Press, 1983), 39–47; Staub, *Yemenis in New York City*.

10. Barbara Kopytoff, "The Development of Jamaican Maroon Ethnicity," in *Caribbean Quarterly* 22 (Jun.–Sept. 1976): 34.

11. Dell Hymes, "The Ethnography of Speaking," in *Anthropology of Human Behavior* (Washington, D.C.: Anthropological Society of Washington, 1962), and "Breakthrough into Performance," in *Folklore: Performance and Communication*, eds. Dan Ben-Amos and Kenneth Goldstein (The Hague, Netherlands: Mouton, 1975), 11–74; Richard Bauman, *Verbal Art as Performance* (Prospect Heights, Ill.: Waveland Press, 1977); M. M. Bakhtin, "The Problem of Speech Genres," in *Speech Genres and Other Late Essays*, ed. Caryl Emerson and Michael Holmquist (Austin: University of Texas Press, 1986 [1979, written 1952–53]), 60–102; Joel Sherzer, "A Discourse-Centered Approach to Language and Culture," *American Anthropologist* 89, no. 2 (1987): 295–309; Charles Line Briggs, *Competence in Performance: The Creativity of Tradition in Mexicano Verbal Art* (Philadelphia: University of Pennsylvania Press, 1988); Leigh Swigart, "Wolof: Language or Ethnic Group? The Development of a National Identity" (unpublished paper, 1991).

12. From the transcript of an interview with Alexander Okechukwu by Diana Sherblom, African Immigrant Folklife Study Project (AIFS), Washington, D.C., 1997.

13. Transcript from African Immigrant training sessions, AIFS, Washington, D.C., 1994.

14. Anna Ceesay, Washington, D.C., personal communication, March 1994.

15. See Ira De Augustine Reid, *The Negro Immigrant: His Background, Characteristics and Social Adjustment, 1899–1937* (New York: Arno Press, 1969 [1943]).

16. Ali Mazrui, "Global Changes and the Future of Higher Education in Africa," in *James Smoot Coleman Memorial Series* no. 4 (Los Angeles: James S. Coleman African Studies Center, University of California at Los Angeles, 1993).

17. See note 1.

18. See "A Nigerian Yoruba Naming Ceremony in the Washington, D.C. Area," Smithsonian Institution, <http://www.si.edu/folklife/vfest/africa/start.htm> (accessed Mar. 9, 2000).

19. Kwaku Ofori-Ansa, Washington, D.C., meeting notes, African Immigrant Folklife Project scholars meeting, August 1995.

20. Olaniyi Areke, Washington, D.C., personal communication, 1995.

14

African Diasporan Concepts and Practice of the Nation and Their Implications in the Modern World

Olabiyi B. Yai

a la hija de Changó y Ochún (to the daughter of Changó and Ochún)

Perhaps one of the most urgent tasks of ours and the next generation of Africanists—by which I restrictively mean those who are committed to the understanding of the past, present, and future of Africa for the defense and promotion of the interests of Africa's children on the continent and in the Diaspora, as opposed to those who prey on Africa for a living—is to effect a thorough terminological, epistemological, and hermeneutical overhauling of the field. It is sad, and scientifically unsound, to uncritically "inherit" and endorse the conceptual tools forged by one's oppressors' organic intellectuals to discourse on oneself and one's realities.

This task is a long-term agenda that will restore African terms and African languages as media of scientific discourse. It will equally involve African Diasporan creoles and the European languages creatively and idiosyncratically used by Diasporan Africans for over four hundred years. In this context, the term *nation* deserves a special place as an entry in a prospective dictionary of African Diasporan concepts for reasons that will soon be made clear.

It is now a truism to say that the right to name confers on the namer a special hegemonic power over the named, be it an object or a person. Africans, for whom a name is sacred, know this all too well. But we must daily ponder the vast operation of denaming—therefore of desecration of humans, things, and concepts—that slavery was. That systematic enterprise of "thingification" of the African by the European enslaver produced such words as *pieza* and *bois d'ébène*[1] to refer to Africans as individuals, and *horde*, *tribe*, and *peuplade* to refer to them as sociopolitical entities.

But have we paid sufficient attention to the profound message encoded in the words Black folks choose to refer to themselves? Instead of such derogatory words as pieza and bois, with which they certainly were familiar from the African coast, they chose from the white man's language lexicons *neg* (Haitian Creole), *nego* (Brazilian Portuguese), and *man* (Caribbean and U.S. English) to unambiguously assert their humanness and identity. These words occur in contexts where the standard European languages would use *people, one, on* (French), *uno* and *la gente* (Spanish).

Likewise, Diasporan Africans' terminologies and discourse markedly depart from their masters' when they refer to themselves as communities or to social institutions they have created. I surmise that it is no accident that they have discarded all negative and derogatory terms that were, and still are, available in the conceptual panoply of European languages to refer to themselves. Instead, they have invariably selected the term nation. I believe they did this not so much because the white folks used it to refer to themselves, but perhaps more significantly, because nation was perceived by them as the closest approximation, in translation, to concepts used in their respective African languages to refer to themselves in the Old World, Africa.

Africans in the Americas were thus applying what St. Clair Drake was later to call a "vindicationist perspective" to their lived history in their new, imposed habitat. This terminological continuity is a reflection of Africans' conceptual and experiential retention and invention. It was made possible because Africans were able to take the initiative (in the sense of Aimé Césaire's "*le droit à l'initiative,*" the right to initiative) to invent unmistakably African institutions. It is no surprise, therefore, that nation is one of the rare terms anthropology—the colonial and hegemonic discipline par excellence—begrudgingly borrowed from the African Diasporan vocabulary.

I say begrudgingly because most writers still use "nation" with quotation marks, as if to say "so-called nation." Most specialists do not take seriously the African nations of the Americas. Imperial mentalities and prejudice prevent them from accepting and conceptualizing the legitimacy and credibility of this nationhood. They are in good company, for alienated African élites of the homeland do not trust their nations either, as is often reflected in the official use of the term nation throughout the continent. For example, the "national" anthem of Nigeria, adopted at independence in 1960 and discarded only recently, contained this line: "Though tribes and tongues may differ, In brotherhood we stand," which betrays the poverty of the alienated African élite's political imaginary. For them, a nation is a conglomerate of "tribes," a notion they uncritically borrowed and endorsed from ethnologists, missionaries, anthropologists, and other organic intellectuals of colonialism. This tragic irony—a nation of tribes—was sung by millions of school boys and girls for over two decades. Fortunately, alternative internally generated ideas of the nation do exist in Africa and the African Diaspora.

The widespread use of the word nation in its African acceptation testifies to its significance among Diasporan Africans. That it is found in the four most important European languages imposed on Africans in the Americas, and in the creoles the Africans invented, is due neither to chance nor to conspiracy:

nação in Brazilian Portuguese
nación in Spanish-speaking America
natchon in French Creole
nation in English (e.g., the Nation of Islam)

In the United States, for example, nation and its derivative national have become emblematic of African American identity, in fact serving as code words for "African American," as exemplified in the long-standing National Medical Association and National Bar Association, and more recently the National Brotherhood of Skiers, National Association of Black Scuba Divers, and Hiphop Nation.[2]

If chance and a conspiracy theory are ruled out to account for this consistency in the use of the concept over such a vast area, it then becomes legitimate to hypothesize an explanation based on antecedents from the homeland. When an Afro-Brazilian says: "*Eu sou de nação jeje*," (I am of the Jeje nation), when a Cuban refers to herself as "*de nación ijecha*," or when a Haitian claims *rada* nationality, they all consciously or subliminally refer to time-honored African worldviews and practices on the continent. I will briefly delineate a West African paradigm of the concept of nation, and suggest how it deeply informs African Diasporan models of nação/nación/natchon/nation.

Pre-colonial states of the Bight of Benin, from the Edo state in the east to the Ajá states in the west, shared strong cultural traits, developing among themselves an intricate system of hierarchy, allegiance, seniority, and mutual obligations. This arrangement was based on the family model, and therefore was rightly termed "*ebi* social theory" (meaning family in Yorubá, with, of course, the African extended connotation of the term) by historian Adeagbo Akinjogbin.[3]

Religions based on Orishas and/or Voduns were freely exchanged from one state to the other throughout the area, and the introduction of the transatlantic slave trade intensified this tradition of exchange of ideas, worldviews, and institutions.[4] One important religious feature or practice that has not received the critical attention it deserves, and that is relevant to the understanding of the concept of nation in Africa and its instantiations in the New World Diaspora, is the existence, permanence, and indeed cultivation of the phenomenon of double or multiple religious and cultural loyalties— across geopolitical entities.

As is well known, an Orisha or a Vodun, the spiritual beings of the Yorubá and Fon people, has a mythical or an historical home. For example, Ire is Ogun's home, Oya hails from Ira, and Kétu is Eshu's home. It was, and still is, mandatory for the devotees of an Orisha or Vodun to learn the language, the history, the cuisine, and other mores of the birthplace of their respective spiritual beings and, indeed, to regard themselves as citizens of that city-nation. This sacred rule applies to devotees irrespective of their place of birth or residence. For example, a Shango devotee from Kétu will learn and speak the Eyò language of Òyó because Shango hails from Òyó, and the devotee regards him- or herself as an Òyó citizen.

Moreover, if in the course of his or her history an Orisha or Vodun becomes more prominent in an area outside his or her birthplace, the devotees will add to the corpus of their traditions the language and mores and sometimes the taboos of this new adoptive or second birthplace. Generally speaking, an Orisha or Vodun attains prominence in a second place if that place reinforces his or her *àse* (life-power or spiritual energy) through new rituals and other accomplishments in the spiritual and nonspiritual realms.

Among all Orishas, Obaluayé (also known in various parts of the area as Babaluayé, Omolu, Sànpànná, Onile, and Sapatá) best epitomizes this ethos. This is hardly surprising, since he is the earth deity and the oldest deity. In many parts of Yorubáland this deity is widely believed to hail from the Fon-Ajá area, as clearly indicated in parts of his praise names. Paradoxically, in the Fon-Ajá area the same deity is believed to be of Yorubá origin. This is evidenced not only in his praise names in the local languages, but also and more significantly in the name given his devotees: *Anagónu*, a Yorubá person or citizen.

Historical and linguistic evidence based on fieldwork recently conducted on the Fon plateau and in adjacent territories offers a plausible solution to this puzzle. The early inhabitants of the Fon plateau were the Anagó, the primordial ancestors of modern Yorubá. Sànpànná or Babaluayé, as his names suggest, was their major deity. In Yorubá, Babaluayé means Father/Lord/Owner-of-the-World or primordial father of the world. When the Fon later settled in the region, they borrowed this deity, now called Sapatá, a phonetic cognate of Sànpànná. In the hands of the Fon-Ajá group, Sapatá gained more àse (*axé* in Portuguese, *ashe* in English, *aché* in Spanish), presumably because his devotees invented an antidote to smallpox. Consequently, Obaluayé devotees in Yorubáland came to Fonland to strengthen their knowledge of and spirituality in Sapatá. The impression was thus created in Yorubáland that the home of this Sànpànná/Sapatá renaissance, in reality his second home, was his birthplace.

The story of Sànpànná/Sapatá is interesting for many reasons. First, it is regarded by the knowledgeable people of the area as their real history. For them it is as important, perhaps more important, than the conventional history of kings, dynasties, wars, and treaties. So attentive are we scholars to these conventional factors of history that we tend to overlook other peculiar cultural features that are more significant for the history of the area. A case in point is the immunity as a rule enjoyed by Orisha/Vodun devotees and *babaláwo* (diviners). They could move freely from one state to another without fear, even in wartime. This war protocol was, of course, violated by unscrupulous rulers encouraged by European powers at the height of the Atlantic slave trade. The methodological issue here is that historians have not given due attention to the implications of this war protocol, and its violation, in their attempts to explain the diffusion of certain cultural features and patterns in the area, as well as in the New World Diaspora.

Second, the corpus of praise poetry (*oriki* in Yorubá, *ako* in Fon) about Sànpànná/Sapatá suggests that religion is a vital ingredient in the conceptualization of the notion of nation. The double/multiple allegiance ethos promoted by the Orisha/Vodun religion in the area has been for centuries a defining trait of the concept of nation. For example, a Gun, a native of Hogbonu (Porto-Novo) in today's Republic of Benin, who worships Oduduwa, will regard him- or herself as a citizen of the Yorubá town of Ife in Nigeria. A Fon devotee of Nàná Bùùkúù will speak the Nchà dialect of Yorubá from the central part of Benin and claim Nchà nationality.

This belief in double nationality is made evident in the Fon ritual sentence "*E yi Ife*" (He has gone back to Ife) pronounced at the death of a diviner. In other words, in the Fon imaginary a diviner never dies; he returns to Ife, the birthplace of Orunmila, the Yorubá deity of divination. A Fon diviner thus conceives of himself as a citizen of Ife, irrespective of his birthplace. Consequently, he will learn Yorubá, usually attaining conversational proficiency. As a diviner, he must memorize the *Ifa* divination texts in

Yorubá and recite the appropriate verses verbatim to his clients. He will then translate and interpret them into the Fon language if the client happens to be a nonbilingual Fon-Yorubá speaker. This is still largely the practice today among serious Fon, Ajá, Waci, and Gun diviners and is a marker of their claim to legitimacy.

From this discussion, it can be seen that double nationality, a tardy discovery in Europe and still a taboo in many "modern" African states, was common practice in the Bight of Benin area. To be sure, many kings and other officials have tried to control and manipulate religions in the area. In ancient Dahomey, for example, kings had their ancestors divinized under the name of Nesuxue and appointed the *mivede,* or head priest, of this new Vodun. He determined the calendar of annual Vodun celebrations and ensured that the Nesuxue opened the season. But the Orisha and Vodun communities have, as a rule, consistently functioned as, in today's parlance, *forces of transnational civil society,* countering the hegemonic state policies that tended to promote unconditional allegiance to one state. This explains why, strictly speaking, there were no European-style nation-states in the area.

We have difficulty understanding this transnational community phenomenon today because the religious and political situations have drastically changed under the combined deleterious effects of Jihadist-type Islam, missionary Christianity, colonialism, and the European nation-state template and ideology, with their well-known intolerance. The impact of Orisha/Vodun communities in forging a (trans)national consciousness in the sense described above was, however, paramount. An Orisha or Vodun community was defined as the total number of men, women, and children who regarded themselves as worshipers of a specific Orisha or Vodun. For example, a Shango community would consist of devotees at various levels of initiation and responsibility in the worship of this Orisha, nondevotees whose families traditionally owed allegiance or a debt of gratitude to Shango for a variety of reasons, and other individuals who were friends or allies of these two categories.

When these structures were intact, each town or village would have no fewer than ten Orishas or Vodun, half of which may not have originally belonged to the area where the town or village was located. In such a context, and given the double/multiple nationality ethos delineated above, it is little surprise that many citizens were "plurinational," which softened their unconditional allegiance to particular states. Alterity was inscribed, so to speak, in the very idea of the nation, as well as in personal identity. Both personhood and personality were also important defining elements of the nation concept, since a person's *ori* ("inner head," idiosyncratic characteristics) could be an essential factor in the determination of his or her Orisha or Vodun. These defining traits of the concept and practice of nation in West Africa were retained, sometimes reinforced, in the Americas.

In the Americas, Africans had to invent new institutions within which they could cultivate their customs and perpetuate the memory of Africa, and thus live a meaningful life. *Cabildos de nación* in Cuba, which were associations of Africans based on cultural affinities, Afro-Catholic lay brotherhoods and sisterhoods in Brazil, and more importantly religious institutions such as Candomblé in Brazil, Santería in Cuba, Kumina in Jamaica, and the African American church in the United States are prominent instances of such invented institutions.

Some official historians claim that enslavers, for fear of slave revolts, implemented the age-old divide-and-rule principle and organized Africans along nation lines. This preemptive, anticonspiracy-conspiracy theory is a half truth. It may be plausible, but it is simplistic in that it assumes the absence of African agency in these scenarios. The reality is that Africans had a role to play in the genesis of cabildos and other similar oases of relative freedom in slavocratic societies. They displayed a wealth of diplomacy or/and discrete pressure/threats to conquer what they perceived as social and cultural free time.

The "civilizing mission" of the Catholic church, which sought to use African nations as steppingstones for conversion, must have been perceived by most Diasporan Africans, certainly by their intellectuals, as a *felix culpa*, a blessing in disguise. Such institutions as cabildos de nación were based on a quid pro quo, a *mal entendu bien entendu*. This must have been the case when in seventeenth-century Cuba the head of the Catholic church, Monsignor Morell de Santa Cruz, persuaded the reluctant white enslavers to grant their enslaved Africans some free time on weekends for entertainment and Christian instruction. The Africans used this free time gained through negotiation to reinvent time-honored African institutions and practices cloaked in Christian garb.

Let us for a moment imagine a plausible scenario of cabildo formation. The aim of the enslaver was ideally to bring together Africans of the same nation, meaning in European terms "nation-state." This would have proven impracticable in most cases. Most Africans would have based their *choice* of a cabildo on real or perceived cultural or national—à la African, that is—affinities. It is not unreasonable to surmise that those Africans who had no alternative other than isolation and ostracism would have based their choice simply on their Négritude—the sum total of Black values, according to Aimé Césaire. The point being made here is that local constraints as well as African traditions could not have generated conditions that would have been conducive to the arrangement of cabildos strictly along the lines of exclusive African nations conceived as nation-states.

Concretely, it would have been permissible for an Anagó/Ijesha who found himself as a minority on a plantation to join a Congo cabildo, as it was conceivable and indeed likely to find Africans from Angola in a cabildo whose members were Fon and Mahi in their majority. This trend of *deliberate African nationalization* was further encouraged by the well-documented gender imbalance on plantations. Because of the scarcity of women, further aggravated by the white master's lust and *droit de cuissage*, it would have been natural to expect enslaved males to have a preference for African nations with a significant female presence.

Let us illustrate this scenario of an African idea of the nation with an historical case from Cuba. In 1810 the Afro-Cuban José Aponte organized and led one of the most extensive liberation movements in colonial times. The rebellion threatened the colonial system and was such a blow to the plantation system that it left an indelible scar on the Cuban Spanish language by way of a proverb with racist overtones. *Mas malo que Aponte* (worse than Aponte) is used to describe a situation of extreme severity. Aponte's was therefore a proverbial revolt, even in the literal sense of the word.

What both official history and the proverb fail to tell us is that José Aponte was a prominent member of a cabildo called *Chango-tedo*, in Yorubá "founded by Shango," the

Yorubá Orisha of thunder and justice. This was a cabildo with mostly Yorubá membership. But José Aponte's rebellion could not have been a national and popular movement if his cabildo had been exclusively Yorubá and perceived as such by other African nations in Cuba. Similarly, in Brazil, the sisterhood of *Nossa Senhora da Boa Morte* (Our Lady of Good Death) and the brotherhood of *Nossa Senhora do Rosário* (Our Lady of the Rosary), which have both played significant roles in African cultural maintenance, were initially Yorubá and Angola respectively. Both subsequently admitted Afro-Brazilians of other nations through a process of African nationalization and internationalization that is still in process in the Diaspora today.

In today's Bahia, any Candomblé, when invited to declare its identity, will invariably refer to one of three African nations, *nagô, jeje,* or *angola.* These three nations correspond broadly to the Yorubá, Fon, and Kongo-Angola cultural areas on the African continent. Each of these three nations refers to a generic entity that could be further qualified, for example, Nagô-Kétu, Nagô-Ijexá, Jeje-Mahí, Angola-Monjola. These subspecifications demonstrate that Diasporan Africans have maintained an acute sense of difference within sameness, and of complementarity between the local and the global, an ageless tradition in African cultures. As Antonio, an enslaved Yorubá, put it in Bahia during court proceedings following the famous 1835 Malê rebellion, *"Ainda que todos são Nago, cada um tem a sua terra"* (Even though they are all Nagô, each one has his own homeland).[5]

On the Bahian Candomblé much has been written since the pioneering work of Raimundo Nina Rodrigues by scholars such as Roger Bastide, Pierre Verger, Vivaldo da Costa Lima, Julio Santana Braga, and Juana Elbein dos Santos. I will therefore stress some of the features of the concept of nation that have escaped the critical attention of analysts. The Bahian concept of *nação* cannot be dissociated from that of *família de santo* (African-type socioreligious community).[6] This *família* or family is a reformulation, under Brazilian conditions, of the *ebi,* of the continental African extended family or village community. The Yorubá and the Fon supplied the theology, the rituals, and the structure of initiation of all Candomblés, irrespective of the nation. This led Nina Rodrigues to suggest a *"Jeje-Nagô"* model, in Bahia the term Jeje designating the Fon and Nagô the Yorubá, as will be elaborated further on. This, however, is unfortunate reductionism not endorsed by Afro-Bahians themselves. They are conscious of commonalities between nations as well as of idiosyncrasies. Each nation is distinct, and even within the same nation each family has its idiosyncratic rites.

A nation is composed of all *terreiros* or families that claim descent from the same primordial African nation. In an attempt to distinguish the African and Afro-Bahian concepts of the nation, Vivaldo da Costa Lima says the following:

> A nação, portanto, dos antigos africanos na Bahia foi aos poucos perdendo sua conotação política para se transformar num conceito quase exclusivamente teológico. Nação passou a ser, desse modo, o padrão ideológico e ritual dos terreiros de Candomblé da Bahia, estes sim fundados por africanos angolas, congos, jejes, nagôs—sacerdotes iniciados de seus antigos cultos, que souberam dar aos grupos que formaram a norma dos ritos e o corpo doutrinário que se vem transmitindo através os tempos e a mudança nos tempos.

Esse processo, entretanto, não eliminou de todo a consciência histórica de muitos descendentes de africanos, que conhecem bem suas origens étnicas a ponto de serem capazes de discorrer—os velhos informantes iletrados—sobre a situação política e geográfica da terra de seus antepassados no tempo da escravidão.[7]

(The nation of the old Africans in Bahia, however, little by little lost its political connotation and became an almost exclusively theological concept. The nation, thus, became the ideological and ritual model for Candomblé houses in Bahia, which were founded by Angola, Congo, Jeje, Nagô Africans who were priests initiated in their ancient religions and who succeeded in giving to the groups they constituted the ritual norms and the body of doctrines that have been transmitted through time and changing times.

This process, however, did not completely eliminate the historical consciousness of many descendants of Africans, who knew their ethnic origins so well that these old illiterate informants could comment on the political and geographical situation of the land of their ancestors during the time of slavery.) [Author's translation]

Da Costa Lima is right on the issue of the continuity of African consciousness among Afro-Bahians. But when he claims that "the nation of the old Africans in Bahia little by little lost its political connotation and became an almost exclusively theological concept," he is a victim of Eurocentrism, as he is wrongly attributing to Africans the European idea of the nation, which he apparently unconsciously endorses (i.e., the nation-state in which the political dimension is inflated to the point of becoming hegemonic or exclusive). For him, Afro-Bahians have operated, as it were, a "transfer" of the concept of the nation from the political realm to the "exclusively theological" (i.e., religious) domain.

But as I have demonstrated in the first part of this chapter, the African concept of nation cannot be reduced to politics alone. The notion of the African as a *homo politicus* is a recent myth being made reality by the imposition of colonialist and neocolonialist policies within notoriously artificial nation-states. At any rate, with reference to "*antigos africanos na Bahia*" (old Africans in Bahia) the polarization of the "political" and the "theological" must have been as meaningless as it was in the pre-colonial African areas from which they originated.

We should perhaps pay more attention to the deep meaning of the ethnonyms by which Diasporan Africans have chosen to identify themselves. In Brazil, all nations of the Fon-Ajá-Gun-Gen-Waci-Mahí continuum have selected Jeje for self-identification. Jeje is a numerically and politically insignificant member of this continuum located in the southern Ouémé province of today's Benin Republic. Had the political (state) dimension been the main ingredient in the nation as conceived by enslaved Africans of this continuum, Danxomé (or Dahomey), being the most powerful state in the area, would have been the natural name chosen by them for self-identification. There were thousands of enslaved Fon in Brazil including, although exceptionally, members of the Danxomé royal families.[8] But why choose the name of an insignificant group? Asking the question assumes, perhaps Eurocentrically, that size and political power are the only or the main criteria of a group's significance and identity. The experience of Diasporan Africans invalidates the universality of such an assumption.

One can only venture a hypothesis to account for the choice of the ethnonym Jeje to represent all ethnic groups of the Fon-Ajá-Gun-Gen-Waci-Mahí cultural continuum. It may be that the first men and women who founded a Vodun cult in the area were Jeje. Subsequently, waves of enslaved Fon, Gun, Aja, or Mahí would have had no problem endorsing the ethnonym, since their respective languages and the Jeje language are mutually intelligible and they worship the same deities. The conditions for double nationality were met.

In the same manner, in Bahia all Yorubá groups (Kétu, Ijeshá, Sabe, Ègbá, Ègbádò, Òyó, Ijebu) have endorsed the ethnonym Nagô, the primordial name given to their ancestors, as they did in Cuba. Here again, Òyó would have been the ideal ethnonym if the political/hegemonic dimension were a significant defining criterion of the concept of nation. The choice of Rada (Alada) in Haiti, and Anagó-Lucumí in Cuba seem to obey similar principles of reference to the same ancestral cultures. Alada is the primordial kingdom from which ancient Dahomey is derived. Similarly, the Yorubá refer to an ancient stage of their culture called Anàgó.

All these facts seem to suggest the following. What matters in the definition of nation in Africa and in the African Diaspora is not so much the place where one was born (Latin: *natus*, the root of nation). It is rather the set of values this place stands for, or the set of values invested in it by conscious agents. This is why Africans may claim or desire several nations without any sense of contradiction. It is indeed possible that one's ori (inner head) suggests or selects one's nation, by divination for example.

Mãe Aninha, the most prestigious *iyalorixa* (priestess) in the history of the Brazilian Candomblé, significantly exemplified this deliberate choice of a nation, this *nationalization*, to which I refer elsewhere as a gesture of *"deliberate alienation."*[9] She was born of enslaved Gurunsi parents, and she knew it. Her parents, therefore, hailed from what is now Burkina Faso. She was entrusted to a Yorubá priestess who initiated her, and she became *Nagô Kétu* (i.e., a Yorubá national from the Kétu subgroup). Under her leadership, the Nagô community in Bahia tremendously reinforced its axé, its spiritual energy. As a result, the primordial female deities of her Gurunsi ancestors, Cajapriku and Iya by names, have been adopted in the Bahian Yorubá pantheon. This is a not uncommon, if little researched, aspect of inter-African syncretism.[10]

In the course of time, various nations have established bridges among themselves. Both devotees and uninitiated members of the family interact across nations through various structures and channels: ceremonies, initiations, visits. The result is that each nation always has some features of all other nations. Esmeraldo Emetério de Santana was voicing a truism not easily acknowledged by analysts who prefer to emphasize differences when he made the following statement at a celebrated meeting of the three Afro-Bahian nations: *"Eu acho que cada qual deve cuidar da sua nação. Claro que debe aprender também um pouco da outra, porque hoje foram todas na milonga, como ja disse, mistura."*[11] (I think that everyone should take care of his/her nation. Of course, one must also learn a bit about the others, because today we are all in a milonga, as I said, a mixture.) [Author's translation].

The African international structure of interaction par excellence is the *axexé*, the funeral rite for a departed Candomblé devotee. The axexé is a grand exercise in tridimensional solidarity, especially when the departed devotee is a priest(ess) or an *ebomim*, an initiate.[12] It is above all a massive exercise in Pan-African solidarity. During seven nights, special rites are performed with the participation of those who, initiated or uninitiated, knew the deceased. Among the initiated the tridimensional solidarity involves:

1. Those who share with the deceased the same Orisha/Vodun or the same function in the family irrespective of their nations. This satisfies the personal or individual dimension.
2. Various families of the same nation. This satisfies the vertical dimension.
3. Delegations from various nations, which horizontally reinforces the Pan-African *milonga* (mixture, in Kikongo and some other Bantu languages).

The three constituencies are lavishly recognized in the chants and songs: laments and celebration songs in praise of the Orisha of the deceased devotee, songs and chants belonging exclusively to the repertoire of the family and the nation, as well as songs of all three Bahian-African nations, often including their subdivisions. As the last rite of passage, the axexé, thus, emphasizes the historically constituted Africanness of the devotee, above and beyond the birthplace of his or her ancestors in Africa, which may still be known, and beyond his or her nation by heritage or selection in Brazil.

CONCLUSION

The conceptualizations and instantiations of the nation sketched above have far-reaching implications for us as Africans in the modern world. We should value, endorse, revive, cultivate, and update the multiple allegiance tradition inherited from our ancestors. One major implication of this endorsement is that modern states on the continent should be regarded as strictly provisional arrangements, particularly as we were no party to the birth of the colonies from which they evolved. Were Africans present at the conference table in Berlin in 1884–85?

For over three decades now, African élites in the homeland have embarked on a *white elephant* project called "nation building." In the name of this white mythology, derived from the not-so-successful historical experience of Europe, African élites have indulged in unspeakable human rights abuses and have produced everywhere on the continent bloody "kleptocracies."[13] The Berlin Conference was an accident in African history, yet African élites have sought to turn the nation-states that were "inherited" (how can we inherit that which did not belong to our ancestors?!) from its aftermath into a permanent feature of African political culture. That which was a potentially crippling accident in our history they aspire to turn into a permanent feature of our political life. But today, the nation-state based on the European definition and model of the nation has lamentably failed and is being rejected in the European matrix and its peripheries, as exemplified positively in the creation of the European Union. The implication of this failure is that we must turn to our own models, our own intellectual heritage, to redefine and refine the nation in the context of our current predicament.

Certainly in 1963, when African heads of state met in Addis Ababa to effect the parturition of the Organization of African Unity (OAU), most of them naively thought they were creating the first Pan-African political entity. They did not know that various OAUs in the African Diaspora had predated theirs. Today some of us know better, and we should put ourselves in a position to know even better. The Quilombo of Palmares, an independent maroon community created in Brazil by Africans who escaped from the institution of slavery, like other *quilombos* and *palenques* before and after it in the Americas, are perhaps better models or instances of an "Organization of African Unity"; although, sadly enough, we seldom envisage them in that perspective. We Africans have to constantly remind ourselves that the Occident is an accident in our millennial history. Only by reclaiming our African intellectual heritage can we minimize the deleterious effects of this accident. Otherwise we run the risk of being permanently handicapped by self-Europenalization.

In this age of deepening globalization, we Africans are constantly relegated to the periphery of the world. On a daily basis we witness the erosion of our fundamental rights to decency. The gains of the glorious days of the civil rights movement are contested in the United States. We now realize that "integration" is no solution, for how can we integrate a structure we deemed intrinsically vicious in the first place, as were most socioeconomic structures that legitimately evolved from colonial economic systems. In this age of globalization, it would seem that the only viable long-term agenda is to dream of, and work for, entirely new sociocultural and socioeconomic systems and relations in Africa and all parts of the world where Africans have been enslaved, with our people as our architects on the basis of equality and mutual respect.

In Cuba, the collapse of the Soviet system and the attendant recrudescence of racism and economic and cultural discrimination against Afro-Cubans clearly show that there was no wisdom in the ontologization of class and the nation-state, as some of us had been lured into believing. Race matters. On the continental motherland itself, the OAU's impotence and its inability to address problems of wars, displacement, debt, and poverty point to a major lesson: African nation-states are not sacrosanct, and we must seriously question the premises of the Berlin Conference. For African peoples, the borders arbitrarily imposed after Berlin lack legitimacy.

I suggest, therefore, that we work out a research agenda that will target concepts and institutions that harbor redemptive potentials. For example, cabildos, quilombos, and palenques should be studied with an African agenda in mind, rather than as anthropological curios. What, for example, were their language policies? How did they tackle the problem of the plurality of religions? What modalities of Pan-Africanism did these polities individually and collectively display?

The Romans used to say: "*Ex Africa semper aliquid novi*" (Out of Africa always something new). Admittedly, the Romans' knowledge of Africa was limited, and the Africa the authors of this saying had in mind was limited to parts of North Africa. But they were right and the adage is still valid today, and should be extended to the entire continent and its Diaspora. *Yes, there is always something novel to be learned from Africa.* It is possible to build a new, healthy, and democratic Africa if—and perhaps only if—we tap into those ideas, concepts, and practices enshrined in microcosmic institutions in the African Diaspora.

NOTES

1. See introduction by Sheila Walker.
2. I am grateful to Dr. Sheila Walker, who brought these African American examples to my attention.
3. Adeagbo Akinjogbin, *Dahomey and Its Neighbours* (Cambridge: Cambridge University Press, 1967).
4. Sandra T. Barnes, ed., *Africa's Ogun* (Bloomington: Indiana University Press, 1989).
5. João José Reis, *Slave Rebellion in Brazil: The Muslim Uprising of 1833 in Bahia* (Baltimore: Johns Hopkins University Press, 1993 [1986]), 139.
6. Vivaldo da Costa Lima, "A familia-de-santo nos candomblés jeje-nagô da Bahia: Um estudo de relações intergrupais (Master's thesis, Universidade Federal da Bahia. Salvador, Bahia, Brazil 1977).
7. Vivaldo da Costa Lima, "O conceito de "nação" nos *candomblés* da Bahia," *Afro-Ásia*, (Salvador, Bahia, Brazil), no. 12 (June 1976): 77.
8. So numerous were the Fon that their language became a lingua franca in the Minas Gerais area of eighteenth-century colonial Brazil. Fon was the common language or *lingua geral* among enslaved Africans of what was then called "Mina," roughly between today's Ghana and Benin Republic. See Antonio da Costa Peixoto, *A obra nova de lingua geral de mina traduzida ao nosso idioma* (Lisbon: Agência Geral das Colônias, 1945).
9. Olabiyi Babalola Yai, "The Concepts of 'Tradition' and 'Creativity' in the Transmission of Yorubá Artistry Over Time and Space," in *The Yorubá Artist: New Theoretical Perspectives on African Arts*, eds. Henry Drewal, Rowland Abiodun, and John Pemberton III (Washington, D.C.: Smithsonian Institution Press, 1994).
10. Waldir Freitas Oliveira and Vivaldo da Costa Lima, *Cartas de Édison Carneiro a Artur Ramos* (São Paulo: Corrupío, 1987), 53 sq; Deoscóredes Maximiliano dos Santos (Mestre Didi), *História de um terreiro nagô* (São Paulo: Max Limonad, 1988 [1962]), 45.
11. Esmeraldo Emetério Santana, as quoted in Vivaldo da Costa Lima, et al., *Encontro de nações-de-candomblé* (Salvador, Bahia, Brazil: Centro Editorial e Didático, Universidade Federal da Bahia1984), 39.
12. An *ebomim* is an initiate with at least seven years in the family. He or she must have gone through a graduation ceremony called "*confirmação*" (confirmation) to sanction this status.
13. Suffice it to evoke the events in Bosnia, Chechnya, Russia, Northern Ireland, Spain (Basques), among others.

15

Candombe, African Nations, and the Africanity of Uruguay

Tomás Olivera Chirimini

There is little research about Afro-Uruguayans and our history as a community, and our role in Uruguayan history has not yet been written. Our African history before our ancestors were enslaved in Uruguay, which might be a source of pride, and which in any case is part of the nation's reality, has been erased. Hence, there is little teaching about Afro-Uruguayan history and culture in the curricula of educational institutions, and the response to the challenge of correcting this omission has only recently begun.

The way out of this absence and selective amnesia is by confronting this discrimination against the Afro-Uruguayan community and by both acknowledging and researching our contributions to the national culture. Acknowledging the role that Africans and their descendants played alongside Europeans and their descendants in developing our common Uruguayan culture should help increase pride in our heritage and contributions on the part of Afro-Uruguayans, and decrease discriminatory attitudes and behaviors toward Afro-Uruguayans on the part of whites.

Africans first arrived on the banks of the Río de la Plata (Plate River) between what are now Uruguay and Argentina in 1527, with the expedition of Diego García Hernández, a navigator in the service of the Spanish Crown. He had made previous expeditions with Juan Díaz de Solís, the man who "discovered" the Río de la Plata, and the goal of this voyage was to further explore the Americas. It is believed that the Africans he brought with him were intended for sale in Spain after the American expedition was completed. In 1530, the Spanish Crown hired Sebastian Cabot, the son of John Cabot (whose "discovery" of the east coast of North America was the basis of British claims to that area), to explore and chart the coasts of the Río de la Plata as well as the Paraguay and Paraná Rivers. Cabot also brought Africans on his voyage and, like García Hernández, probably intended to sell them upon his return to Spain.[1]

As early as 1534, the Spanish Crown licensed the commerce in African captives in the Viceroyalty of Río de la Plata—which included modern Argentina, Uruguay, Paraguay, and Bolivia—with Buenos Aires as the capital. The first royal *licencia* seems to have been granted to Domingo Martínez de Irala to ship one hundred Africans to the Río de la Plata. Spain's system of authorizations for the enslavement of Africans passed through three phases: 1493–1595, the period of licencias, royal authorizations to individuals to introduce captive Africans into the colonies, with a tax to be paid to the Crown for each African; 1595–1789, the period of *asientos* or *capitulaciones*, pacts between the Crown and trading companies; and 1789–1812, when trading in captive Africans became free enterprise.[2]

Don Pedro de Mendoza, a Spanish knight, was appointed in 1536 as the first *adelantado* (governor) of the Río de la Plata, and was granted a licencia to import two hundred Africans.[3] The post of adelantado was awarded by the Crown to men of distinction whose mission was the armed conquest and colonization of the Americas. Buenos Aires was founded in the same year but was razed by indigenous forces. In 1570, Juan Ortiz de Zárate was appointed adelantado of the Río de la Plata. Arriving in 1573 with the mission of founding two cities and colonizing the conquered territory, he was commissioned to bring two hundred colonists and three hundred soldiers, along with cattle, goats, sheep, and horses, and was granted a licencia to import one hundred Africans.[4]

Contraband trading in enslaved Africans in the Río de la Plata was extremely significant during the late sixteenth and early seventeenth centuries. The "forced docking" of many ships, especially Portuguese ships coming from Brazil with both merchandise and enslaved Africans, was a frequent ruse by merchants and local officials to avoid paying taxes to the Spanish Crown. Complicit local officials "forced" ships' captains to dock and unload their cargo for various reasons. Their human cargo was then quietly and cheaply sold to their collaborators. Sometimes "bad weather" was the cover for the extensive and profitable contraband trade. Portuguese traders founded the Sacramento Colony in 1680 primarily to facilitate the contraband trade, their clandestine activities including both sides of the Río de la Plata. A small number of Africans escaped from the traders and settled as free people.[5]

The city of Montevideo was founded between 1724 and 1730, beginning when the Spanish king Felipe V ordered the governor of Buenos Aires to establish a fortified settlement on the east side of the Río de la Plata. By 1730, 450 settlers lived within the walls. In 1738, a request was made for the king's permission to bring three boatloads of enslaved Africans from Brazil to serve as a labor force for the settlers, but the request was apparently not fulfilled. In 1741, Thomas Navarro was granted the first regional licencia for introducing enslaved Africans into the port of Montevideo from "Guinea," a term generally designating the west coast of Africa. The first boatload of enslaved Africans probably arrived in Montevideo in about 1743.[6]

Between 1751 and 1810, during the first wars of independence, there was an intense period when enslaved Africans from both Africa and Brazil were introduced into the Río de la Plata province, reaching a zenith between 1791 and 1809. The largest number of documented Africans arrived in Montevideo in 1805 and 1806, 3,235 and 2,742, respectively. During this turbulent period, the Spanish Crown granted exclusive rights for selling enslaved Africans for the Río de la Plata, Chile, and Peru to colonial authorities in Montevideo by royal decree on November 24, 1791. The decree was ignored and the intense contraband trade continued.[7]

At the beginning of the nineteenth century Afro-Uruguayans formed nearly a third of the Uruguayan population. In 1801 "Black and Brown" army troops fought for independence from Spanish colonialism, and in 1803, the most important Afro-Uruguayan revolt in the nation's history occurred. A group of twenty enslaved and free men tried to establish a maroon community in a forested area on an island on the Yi River. Overcome by government troops, they represent the only documented attempted maroon settlement in Uruguayan history.[8]

The abolition of slavery was a gradual process, the first step being the first *Libertad de Vientres* (Free Womb) declaration in 1813, in which the colonial General Constituent Assembly declared the child of any enslaved woman free at birth. In 1825, the first independent Uruguayan House of Representatives proclaimed a second Free Womb Act, as well as prohibited the trade in enslaved Africans, which continued despite the declaration. In 1839, Uruguay and Argentina both signed a treaty with Great Britain to end the slave trade, which continued legally for two more years until the treaty was ratified in 1841.[9]

Slavery was abolished for Afro-Uruguayan men in two phases during the Great War, an international conflict in which Argentina on one side, and England and France on the other, supported different Uruguayan political factions. In 1842 and again in 1846, the government guaranteed freedom to enslaved men for the purpose of increasing the number of men who could be drafted into the army. Hence, for these men, abolition meant not freedom, but rather a transfer from individual colonial masters to governmental military masters.[10]

There were two main slave trading routes into Montevideo: directly from Africa, and indirectly from Rio de Janeiro, Santa Catarina, Santos, and Salvador da Bahia in Brazil, with an estimated half of the enslaved coming from Brazil and half from Africa.[11] Because of the pervasive contraband trade, as well as the fact that the place of origin of Africans was often designated as their point of embarkation in Africa rather than their ethnic name or original geographical location, we cannot know the exact number or places of origin of Africans who arrived in Uruguay. Nineteenth-century archival records and newspapers from the Río de la Plata, however, provide a sense of at least relative origins based on the names of the African *nations* or *societies* that were important institutions in both the Afro-Argentinean and Afro-Uruguayan communities.

The nations were associations created by Africans from the same or related ethnic groups or regions who, although their organizational structures and rules were formally determined by colonial authorities, attempted to keep alive their traditions and identities by functioning as mutual aid societies and organizing social activities. The nations represented from Central Africa were the Angolas, Congo de Gungas (Augungas), Benguelas, Bomas, Cabindas, Casanches, Congos, Molembos, Monyolos, and Mozambiques; from the current nations of Angola, the two Congos, and Mozambique. Those from West Africa were the Ardras (Alada) and Magíes (Mahi) from the current nations of Benin and Nigeria; Mandingas from the current Mali, Guinea, Senegal, Gambia, Burkina Faso, Sierra Leone, and Côte d'Ivoire area; and Minas, Akan-speaking people from the current Ghana and Côte d'Ivoire, who acquired the designation "Mina" in the Americas because they left Africa from the "Mina Coast" or the port of El Mina.[12] These nation names referred to ethnic groups such as the Mandinga and Mahi, places of departure from Africa such as Mina, and large geographical areas such as Angola, Congo, and Mozambique. Central African Bantu-speaking peoples were in the majority.

Of the African nations, Ildefonso Pereda Valdés says:

> From the beginning of their introduction in large quantities, in cities all over the Americas enslaved and free Blacks created organizations based on their original African communities and cultures. Known as "nations," "cofradías" [brotherhoods], or "cabildos" [after the colonial town councils], they were recognized and supported by the colonial authorities. These "nations" had their "kings" or "governors," and within them survived some traditional festivities as well as certain religious practices camouflaged by the Catholic forms that were imposed on them. In some areas they functioned as mutual aid societies, and they often adopted the form of initiatic secret societies, as in Cuba.
>
> In our country, the "nations" had their own meeting places called "*salas*" [halls] in which on holidays they held dances presided over by their kings. These more or less secret societies had a public existence. Over and above their rather precarious functions of aid to their members, such as holding wakes for the dead of specific "nations" in the corresponding "salas," their major purpose was to celebrate collective dances (*candombes*) coinciding with Christian religious festivities such as Christmas, New Years', and the Kings, an occasion on which was held, in addition, a procession culminating with a mass at the cathedral.[13]

As a way of bringing Africans into the Catholic church and trying to acculturate them to European norms, priests organized the Africans into *cofradías*, lay brotherhoods devoted to specific saints, especially the Black Saints Benedict and Balthazar, whom the Africans venerated with great respect and fervor. Born near Messina, in Sicily in southern Italy, of pious Christian African parents enslaved to a wealthy landowner, Benedict, because of his devoutness, was nicknamed when only ten years old "the Holy Moor." As an adult he joined a community of hermits and became a solitary, being selected as Superior against his will. He later became a lay brother and the cook at St. Mary of Jesus convent near Palermo. "His goodness so permeated him that his face, when he was in chapel, often shone with an unearthly light and the brethren told each other that angels had been seen assisting him in the kitchen. Moreover food seemed to multiply miraculously under his hands." He was later appointed guardian of the convent, although he could neither read nor write. "The holy Guardian's reputation for sanctity and miracles quickly spread over Sicily . . . such that clergy and people turned out to meet him, men and women struggling to kiss his hand or obtain a fragment of his habit to treasure as a relic." He was able to "expound the Holy Scriptures to the edification of priests and novices alike, and his intuitive grasp of deep theological truths often astonished learned inquirers." He asked to be returned to his former position of cook. But his holiness, reputation for miracles, and fame as a confessor brought hordes of visitors from all stations in life, including the Viceroy, requesting prayers and advice.[14] Saint Benedict the Holy Moor was canonized in 1807 and is the patron saint of Sicily's capital city of Palermo and of many Blacks in the Americas.[15]

In Montevideo, Saint Benedict had an altar in the Archicofradía del Cordón and in the parish of San Francisco de Assisi. He was also honored on church altars in the interior of the country, the presence of the Black saint, who in Uruguay was a patron saint of the Black population, suggesting that there had been a significant Afro-Uruguayan historical presence. Concerning the other Black saint popular among Afro-South American communities, Ortiz Oderigo says, "Saint Balthazar, an African king canonized as a saint, was also an object of sacred worship for both Afro-Argentineans and Afro-Uruguayans."[16]

It has been suggested that the Africans saw in the carved wooden statues of these Black saints the kinds of material representations of immaterial spiritual power they knew from Africa, and that they therefore attributed to these images meanings quite different from those intended by the Catholic establishment. Such behavior in Uruguay would have been consistent with behavior documented elsewhere in the Americas, especially in Brazil and Cuba. These institutions, thus, provided contexts in which Africans were able to express some of their own religious and festive behaviors in the context of Christian rituals, celebrating, for example, Catholic saints in public processions with music and dance of African origin.

African storytelling traditions were also preserved by Afro-Uruguayan domestic servants who used stories to entertain and educate white children as well as their own. The "Little Black Shepherd Boy" is a popular rural legend passed on by enslaved Afro-Uruguayans. An enslaved orphan about twelve years old was taking care of a wealthy farmer's livestock. One day the boy was so tired, and the heat so intense, that he fell asleep and failed to return to the corral on time. While the boy was asleep, a lamb strayed from the herd. Realizing that the boy had not returned, the owner went looking for him and found him sleeping. Furious about the missing lamb, he gave the child a severe beating, then ordered his enslaved workers to tie the boy over an ant hill so that the ants would eat him alive. Fireflies intervened and carried the child to heaven. Since then, when something is lost, rural people especially pray to the "Little Black Shepherd Boy" for its return. A prayer is said while kneeling to the "little saint of lost things," and an offering of lit candle stubs is made in gratitude for finding the lost object.

After emancipation, Afro-Uruguayans became concentrated in communities on the edges of Montevideo. Although they began to integrate into the society as free people in the latter half of the nineteenth century, their access and mobility were impeded by their historical position at the bottom of the social ladder, their lack of access to formal education, and, during the final quarter of the century, economic competition from European immigrants, mostly Spaniards and Italians. Thus, they continued doing the same kinds of work they had done during the colonial period, especially as domestic servants. Women were wet nurses, laundresses, and cooks, as well as street vendors of pastries, porridge, and flowers. Men worked as day laborers, drivers, artisans, lamplighters, bakers, and shoemakers, and sold brooms, feather dusters, and other items in the street. Men were also soldiers in the infantries of all of the century's wars: the wars of independence (1810–30), the Great War (1842–51), and the War of the Triple Alliance against Paraguay (1865–70), as well as being active between wars in the many armed conflicts between political opponents.

Some Afro-Uruguayans made a slow climb up the social ladder at the end of the nineteenth and beginning of the twentieth century. Their upward mobility occurred mainly through music and sports, particularly boxing and soccer, a very few moving up via vocational or college education. In spite of their reduced absolute and relative numbers due to wartime losses and demographically overwhelming European immigration, as well as their limited educational attainment and scarce resources, Afro-Uruguayans engaged in community-based institution-building and cultural production. Two Afro-Uruguayan newspapers were begun in the final quarter of the nineteenth century, *La Conservación* (1872) and *La Propaganda* (1893–95). *Ecos de Porvenir* (1901) and *La Verdad* (1911–14) were published daily at the beginning of the twentieth century in Montevideo, and the newspaper *Acción* was founded in the town of Melo in the state of Cerro Largo. Magazines have also been published in Montevideo, such as *La Vanguardia* (1928), *Nuestra Raza* (1933–48), *Bahía-Hudan-Jacks* (1958–96), and *Revista Mundo Afro* (1987–present).

Afro-Uruguayans are best known for contributions to the national culture in the form of *candombe*[17]—music, dance, and instrumentation that continues to evidence its Central African origins. Candombe is similar in rhythm and style to the Afro-Brazilian *congada*, *maracatú*, and *batuque*. The first written mention of the term candombe was in an 1835 poem, "*Canto patriótico de los negros celebrando a la ley de libertad de vientres y a la constitución*," attributed to Francisco Acuña de Figueroa, author of the words of Uruguay's national anthem.[18] From the Central African Kimbundu word *ndombe*, meaning black, and the qualifier "*ka*," the term candombe designates things having to do with Black people. Candombe refers to private Afro-Uruguayan music and dance events and the places in which these take place, to public music and dance festivities, to the music and dance performed, and to the candombe drums. As a result of the subordinate position of Afro-Uruguayans, and the disdain expressed toward them and their culture by the white elite, the term also connotes poor Afro-Uruguayan neighborhoods, and by extension, immorality and disorder.

The candombe developed from the *calenda*, *bámbula*, *chica* or *congo*, and *semba* or *zamba*, music/dance forms popular in the eighteenth century. Also found elsewhere in the Americas, they were characterized by polyrhythmic drumming, pelvic rotations and thrusts, and circle formations. Candombe, which became popular in the nineteenth century, developed by the twentieth century into contemporary Afro-Uruguayan carnival *comparsas*, processional street dance groups that have contributed drum sections, songs, dances, fashions, and symbols that have become the basic ingredients giving Montevideo's carnival its contemporary character and ambience.

The calenda, or *calinda* or *caringa*, was recorded as early as 1763 or 1764 in the Río de la Plata. It was performed by facing couples who danced toward each other and moved away after making the characteristic pelvic thrust gesture originating in some Central African dances and best known from the *vacunao* of the contemporary Cuban rumba. The calenda was danced in many African Diasporan communities including Cuba, Haiti, and Trinidad, and in Congo Square in New Orleans, where it was regularly performed until it was prohibited by city authorities in 1843 because of its "lascivious nature."[19]

The bámbula, based on a syncopated 2/4 beat, was similar to the calenda, the chore-ography typically picking up speed toward the end of the song. A group of women dancers circled around the musicians and around one or more male solo dancers, who sometimes executed athletic flips. The dancers' ankle bells provided additional layers of rhythmic complexity.[20]

The chica or congo was also performed in much of African America. The basic moves, characterized by early chroniclers as erotic, were made with the shoulders, hips, and arms, while the rest of the body remained immobile, evidencing the bodily isola-tion characteristic of much Central African and related African Diasporan dance styles. The dance continued to be danced out of the view of whites in the same way that so many other African cultural expressions prohibited by white ecclesiastical and political authorities continued to exist in various guises.[21] The semba or zamba was an evolution of the calenda, bámbula, and chica, with a slower rhythm and cadence. Semba, in Kim-bundu, means navel, referring to the coming together of navels in the pelvic thrust.[22]

The *Candombe de Reyes* (Candombe of the Kings) was the annual celebration of the coronation of the Kings and Queens of the Congo and Angola, beginning on Christ-mas Day and culminating on January 6, Three Kings Day,[23] which for some Afro-South American communities was the feast day of Saint Balthazar, the African among the three kings or wise men who brought gifts to celebrate the birth of Jesus Christ. This cele-bration represented an interesting juxtaposition, perhaps conflation, of the sense of Central African kings in exile in the Americas, and the African King Balthazar, the pop-ularly canonized patron saint of Afro-Uruguayan and other Afro-South American com-munities. The dance style of the coronation pageantry included elements from the *con-tredanse* brought to Uruguay from the Spanish royal court. The term candombe, thus, embraced a range of meanings, including pageantry for African kings who became Catholic saints celebrated in the Americas with European court dance forms trans-formed with African moves by enslaved Afro-Uruguayans.

The candombe coronation commemorated African royal ceremonial in a manner that integrated aesthetic and religious elements of European origin. Africans from a variety of ethnic traditions blended their own ritual styles first with each other, then with elements of the European pageantry of colonial Montevideo. According to both contemporary chroniclers and my own archival and oral history research with Afro-Uruguayan elders, the nineteenth-century Candombe de Reyes was a dramatic pan-tomime dance reenacting the coronation of the Kings and Queens of the Congo and Angola with a syncretic choreography and all the pomp and circumstance appropri-ate to such an occasion. The presiding king and queen and the members of the royal court were selected from among the most respected elders of the community (figure 15.1).[24]

The characters of the candombe were the king and queen, symbols of authority and reminiscences of African royal traditions; the *bastonero*, the standard bearer or master of ceremonies, who led the procession and directed the choreography; and the *gramillero*, the traditional herbal doctor of the African nations. These characters were followed by a cortege of members of the royal court, men and women dressed in their owners' cast-off finery, after whom came the musicians playing drums, mazacallas (two-headed rat-

Figure 15.1.   Ruben D. Galloza, *Coronación de Reyes* (1998). From *Postales de Candombe*
© 1998 Juan Antonio Varese and Ruben D. Galloza.

tles), and marimbas (xylophone in Kimbundu). The royal procession was preceded by a
carved wooden statue of Saint Balthazar.

The choreography reflected in six figures a synthesis of African and European features
involving the line formation, which included the pelvic thrust; the circle; and the *entrevero*, a period of free improvisation based on African-derived dance movements. The
court entered in a (1) royal procession, formed a (2) double line with men and women
facing each other. They danced toward each other, (3) performed the pelvic thrust as in
the calenda, and danced back to their lines. Then there was (4) European-style couple
dancing by the court. The dancers then moved into a (5) turning circle that signaled the
approaching end. The final sequence was the period of (6) improvised dance, in which
the earlier staged and staid choreography was abandoned, and everyone danced freely
and spontaneously, ending the European court-inspired performance in a climax of
African-inspired candombe.

Candombe as a music/dance form may be divided into three phases. For the
first, eighteenth-century phase, we have descriptions of individual precursor dances
to what came to be generically called candombe. This phase evolved at the end of
the eighteenth and the beginning of the nineteenth centuries into the practice of

institutionalized Sunday social gatherings organized by African nations. Members of the nations danced to the music of drums, mazacallas, and marimbas outdoors in vacant areas in the Cubo del Sur near the wall surrounding the city, and in the Plaza del Mercado (Market Square) in the center of town. As a Sunday outing, white families would watch the candombes of their enslaved domestics, buying foods sold by the Afro-Uruguayan women street vendors, who were a common feature of colonial Montevideo. Candombes in which Africans could socialize and remember and recreate traditional knowledge and behaviors began to be held indoors when the nations became able to accumulate enough money to acquire structures in which to house their salas.

The vestibule of one sala had two doors, one leading to a chapel in which there was an altar with a statue of Saint Benedict, and the other leading to the throne room, which had a dais on which chairs where placed for the royal couple.[25] Weekly festivities began with a brief ceremony over which the king presided. Candombe salas proliferated during the first part of the second half of the nineteenth century, but died out along with the nations between 1880–90 due to the death of the last generation of people born in Africa.

The salas that still existed in 1885 included that of the Congos on Paraguay Street between Canelones and Soriano, and that of the Benguelas on Ibicuy (now Gutiérrez Ruiz) Street between Durazno and Maldonado in what is now downtown Montevideo. Vestiges of the traditional candombes persisted into the early twentieth century, as the old dances were danced at the beginning of newer styles of festivities held in the *conventillos*, multifamily tenement-like dwellings with shared facilities, in which Montevideo's Afro-Uruguayan population became concentrated and segregated.

The second phase of candombe involved the integration of European styles, such as the introduction of the contredanse, into the choreography of the annual coronations. Beginning as an English peasant "country dance" in the sixteenth century, it was danced in the British royal court by 1600. The dance spread to the royal courts of Europe, including Spain, from which it arrived in Uruguay by 1752.[26] The line formation characteristic of the European contredanse culminated in the candombe coronations, uncharacteristically, in a very African pelvic thrust. This phase, thus, involved the perpetuation of private African social and public performative dance, with the accretion of Africanized European forms used in public performances for Christian holidays celebrating African royalty in European style. This era was the high point of candombe, with regular Sunday festivities in the African nations' salas, and annual public performances of candombe for Christmas, New Year's, and especially Three Kings Day.

The third phase, beginning at the end of the nineteenth century, involved the demise, along with the African-born population, of the institutionalized context and physical spaces in which candombe existed—the African nations and their salas. The years 1870 to 1890 marked the period of coexistence and transition between the beginning of Afro-Uruguayan participation in carnival and the demise of the African nations. During this time the African candombe was being transformed into the Afro-Uruguayan carnival comparsa, with music and dance still characterized by polyrhythmic percussion and pelvic rotations. Hence, the three phases of Candombe might be characterized as African, mixed African-European, and Afro-Uruguayan, as Afro-Uruguayans continue to affirm and promote a distinctive African-based cultural form as an essential element of both their own specificity and of their contribution to the more general Uruguayan national identity.

The first documented reference to Afro-Uruguayan participation in carnival was in an 1832 article in the newspaper *La Matraca,* which referred to their dancing the "*tango.*"[27] Carnival seems to have been interrupted by wars until about 1870, judging by the absence of mention of it in the press. In 1867 Afro-Uruguayans began forming "philharmonic societies" whose members, seeking social integration and upward mobility by abandoning traditions of obvious African origin and trying to assimilate to Euro-Uruguayan styles, composed songs and dances to be performed by carnival comparsas. They created a space for integrating Afro-Uruguayans from the city's de facto segregated neighborhoods into the previously elite white event.

By 1870 Afro-Uruguayans had become the major participants in the carnival. The comparsas, *la Raza Africana* (the African Race), *los Pobres Negros Orientales* (the Poor Oriental Blacks, referring to the República Oriental del Uruguay's position east of the Río de la Plata, as opposed to Argentina's to the west), and *los Negros* (the Blacks), participated with great success in carnival festivities. They initiated the definitive Afro-Uruguayan contribution to this principal expression of Uruguayan popular culture.[28] Annual Afro-Uruguayan celebrations of African monarchs in honor of Afro-Catholic saints in the context of religious commemorations evolved into participation in annual secular celebrations of national festive integration.

In about 1875, when carnivals had become quite popular, whites joined the comparsas with blackface performances mimicking Afro-Uruguayan traditions. The first group was founded by two Argentineans, Crewell and Escalera, who called themselves *los Negros Lubolos* (the Black Lubolos) from the name of an important Central African nation in Buenos Aires. Lubolo was also the name of an African nation recorded in 1812 as being located on Sierra (now Fernández Crespo) and La Paz Streets in the Cordón Norte neighborhood of Montevideo.[29] Young white businessmen and professionals painted their faces, necks, and ears black, wore clothing supposedly modeled on that of enslaved Africans from Brazilian and Cuban plantations, and mimicked the *bozal*, the disoriented, newly arrived African, whom they represented as a simpleton. They spoke the "broken Spanish" of Africans obliged to communicate in a language foreign to them, and mocked their naïveté and presumably obsequious behavior.[30]

These annual performances became very popular with all social classes; elite white families competed to host such groups, and Negros Lubolos were featured at society balls. Eventually, young Afro-Uruguayans began to imitate the songs and expressive styles of these whites who were performing burlesque representations of their own African ancestors. An ironic benefit of the phenomenon of whites imitating Afro-Uruguayans was that it demonstrated to those Afro-Uruguayans who believed that in order to be successful, they had to imitate the philharmonic societies of the whites, the error of turning their backs on their own ancestral culture.

The white Black Lubolos, thus, performed a task of cultural rescue, reviving some African-based music and dances and compiling and making more widely known some characteristic movements, albeit in a simplified choreography that merely evoked the complexity of the original African gestures. Although based on African rhythms and gestures, their recodification developed its own characteristic style. In further irony, "lubolos" became a generic term designating carnival groups based on African-derived styles, which included both Afro-Uruguayan groups and white groups imitating them in blackface. Today the carnival category *Sociedades o Agrupaciones de Negros y Lubolos* (Black and Lubolo Societies or Groups) designates candombe-based groups, few of which remain in majority Afro-Uruguayan.

When the Candombes of the Kings died out and carnival comparsas took their place, a legacy that remained was the *personajes típicos* (dramatic characters). Modified in their attributes and meanings from the candombe coronations to the carnival comparsas, they are the *mama vieja* (old mammy), the gramillero (herbal doctor), and the *escobero* or *escobillero* (sweeper). These three figures are indispensable in any candombe-based comparsa involved in carnival parading and competition. They are also the key elements of "folkloric" and tourist performances of Afro-Uruguayan culture, major subjects of representation by both well-known and unknown visual artists, and standard images on souvenirs of Uruguay, such as T-shirts. Some individuals have become famous for their portrayals of these characters (figure 15.2).

Figure 15.2.   Ruben D. Galloza, *Mama Vieja y Gramillero* (1998). From *Postales de Candombe* © 1998 Juan Antonio Varese and Ruben D. Galloza.

Each of the personajes típicos has a characteristic attitude and social persona, as well as costuming and dance steps. The mama vieja wears a cotton blouse, long full skirt, and head tie, and carries a fan with which she coyly fans herself and hides her face as she dances seductively. Some consider the mama vieja a re-creation of the colonial era's candombe queen, some say she is a vestige of the pastry vendors typical of the streets of nineteenth-century Montevideo, and others contend that she is a symbol of the "mammies" working for wealthy white families. There was probably no incompatibility between these roles for Afro-Uruguayan women of that era, queens of African nations on Sundays and on January 6 being pastry vendors and/or domestic servants in everyday life.

The gramillero, an elderly man with white cotton hair and beard representing wisdom and experience, formally dressed in tails and a top hat, leaning on a cane, and carrying a doctor's bag, dances a trembling but agile step as he avidly pursues the mama vieja. The escobero represents the contemporary transformation of the bastonero of the old Candombe of the Kings, who directed the processions with his baton.[31] Over time the character substituted a broom for the baton, which he twirls with amazing expertise. The broom in some African and African American traditions is used for symbolic purification from negative influences.[32] The transition from a baton representing royal service to African kings, to a broom representing menial service to white elites, suggests a significant decline in status symbolism perhaps associated with the ending of the link with and memory of an autonomous African past with the death of the Africans, the African nations, and the Kings and Queens of the Congo and Angola.

Since 1949 the Black and Lubolo comparsas have incorporated a new figure, *la vedette* (the star, in French), beginning when *Añoranzas Negras* added this inspiration from French cabaret acts to their carnival competition choreography. Today a comparsa's success is in direct proportion to the popularity and attractiveness of its vedette, suggesting that commercial appeal has replaced the value of tradition (figure 15.3).

The other unique characteristic of the Afro-Uruguayan musical tradition, also based on candombe, is *las llamadas de tambores* (the calls of the drums). Spontaneous groups constitute themselves beginning with a few people and pick up others who hear the rhythm and join them to parade through Montevideo's streets playing candombe. The practice dates back to the era of the African nations. Given permission to hold festivities, members of the nations "called" each other using the distinctive languages of their drums. When Montevideo was a small walled city, musicians from the nations would go through the streets drumming calls to their members with the distinctive rhythms by which each nation could be recognized. People would join the members of their nation as they passed by. At the end of the nineteenth century, members of Afro-Uruguayan carnival comparsas also called one another with their distinctive drum rhythms, and in the twentieth century groups from one traditional Afro-Uruguayan neighborhood would call their members to visit another neighborhood to play candombe with groups there, each showing off its prowess (figure 15.4).

During the summer season, from December—Christmas Eve, Christmas Day, New Year's Eve, New Year's Day, and Three Kings Day—through the end of carnival, groups of drummers dressed in everyday clothes still parade in what were the traditional Afro-Uruguayan neighborhoods, accompanied by neighbors and others who join in the

Figure 15.3.   Ruben D. Galloza, *Noche de Llamadas* (1998). Carnival comparsa featuring the personajes típicos: the escobero, gramillero, and mama vieja and the candombe drummer and vedette. From *Postales de Candombe* © 1998 Juan Antonio Varese and Ruben D. Galloza.

drumming and dancing. These spontaneous llamadas epitomize Afro-Uruguayan, and Uruguayan, popular culture, and are the nation's most important instrument of social identification and unification. Groups that parade through the streets for their weekend entertainment are now sometimes all white.

The importance of the llamadas in both the Afro-Uruguayan and national communities is such that they have become an indispensable part of all significant events—from sports to national and international politics. The expansion of Afro-Uruguayans from a few population concentrations to a presence throughout the capital, the existence of relatively important Afro-Uruguayan populations in several states in the interior, and the racial integration of candombe-based carnival comparsas favored the extension of this current manifestation of Afro-Uruguayan celebratory and performative styles throughout Montevideo and the interior of the country.

Based on an initiative from ASCU (Asociación Social y Cultural Uruguaya, Uruguayan Cultural and Social Association), now ACSUN (Asociación Social y Cultural Uruguaya Negra, Uruguayan Black Social and Cultural Association), in 1956 the Municipal Festival Commission formalized carnival llamada performances into an official event, which has become such a success and tourist attraction that it is now a centerpiece of the carnival, with a day set aside for it. On the first Friday of the carnival sea-

Figure 15.4. Tomás Olivera Chirimini, *Desfile de Llamadas en el Barrio Reus al Sur* (watercolor, 1991).

son, groups from different neighborhoods, as well as more and more groups from the interior, participate in the Parade of the Llamadas through the traditional Afro-Uruguayan Reus al Sur and Palermo neighborhoods. Montevideo's municipal government, with the support of the Ministry of Tourism, organizes and finances the parade, qualifies the participants, chooses the judges for the competition, and supplies both trophies and cash prizes for the winners. A few days before the parade, a beauty pageant is held to select the queen—although no longer of the Congo and Angola—and runners-up, who lead the parade of thematic floats. Since 1990, the government has also sponsored Parades of the Llamadas in the city of Durazno in the center of the country.

Throughout the twentieth century, candombe, through its various expressions in instrumentation, rhythm, music, song, dance, clothing, and scenic choreography, has decisively and indisputably influenced other Uruguayan cultural and artistic manifestations, including popular and classical music, ballet, and the sociopolitical movement called *canto popular*, as well as poetry and painting. Thus, Afro-Uruguayan culture is central to the nation's artistic, representational, and expressive traditions.

Candombe, the *milonga* and its slower version the *milongón*, and the tango, the most characteristic current musics and dances of the Río de la Plata, are related musical genres characterized by a rhythmic structural core reflective of their common African origins. The candombe and the milonga were important rhythmic influences on the contemporary Uruguayan tango. The milonga is a popular song-and-dance style with humorous and witty lyrics that first appeared in Uruguay around 1870. The milonga rhythm, played on a guitar, became the accompaniment for the *payada de contrapunto*, a clever verbal duel sung in verse. The milonga developed into a dance at the end of the nineteenth century on both sides of the Río de la Plata, in Montevideo's "dance academies" and in Buenos Aires' *perengüidines*, lower-class dives in which Afro-Uruguayans and Afro-Argentineans were an important human and cultural presence.

The current version of the tango developed in 1880–90 accompanied by drums and originally based on rhythms and movements from candombe and other African-derived dances. Its melody and harmony were derived from rural musical traditions of nineteenth-century Uruguay, as well as from newly introduced Spanish and Italian traditions. The tango began to distinguish itself from these predecessor dances and acquire its contemporary style between 1894 and 1900, the now-dominant European influences resulting from the massive immigration that occurred at this time.[33]

The candombe drum made its first appearance in contemporary popular music in the 1930s as an accompaniment to milongas and to candombe-based piano compositions. In the 1940s drums were introduced into orchestras that had typically played tangos, waltzes, and milongas, so that they could add candombe rhythms to their repertoires. Since then, Afro-Uruguayan rhythms have become standard for orchestras that play the dance hall circuit, now playing candombe as well as the popular international styles of various periods such as jazz, bolero, mambo, rumba, and samba. Thus, as a fundamental source and indicator of Uruguay's national identity, candombe is present today in all artistic, as well as commercial, and even educational expressions. Candombe is, in fact, now taught as an Uruguayan musical form in primary and secondary school music classes.

Uruguayan classical music fits into two basic categories, universalist and nationalist. Universalist music consists of the adoption and imitation of European genres. Nationalist music began in the early decades of the twentieth century to incorporate traditional and regional elements so as to create a specifically Uruguayan flavor representing and symbolizing the expression of a pluralistic national spirit. The nationalist style was consolidated by a group of classical composers interested in capturing popular cultural expressions in their compositions. Carlos Giucci pioneered the use of Afro-Uruguayan musical themes in nationalist classical music with his 1928 piano composition, *Candombe–cuadro de coloniaje* (Colonial Sketch), in which the rhythm was inspired by the candombe.

Another musician who followed Giucci's lead was composer, pianist and violinist, and choir director Luis Cluzeau Mortet. His early phase was European in style, initially romantic and then impressionist. His second phase was nationalist in inspiration, and in his third phase he composed *Tamboriles (Drums)*, a piano composition, in 1954. According to Fantina Signorelli, in her study, "*Vivencia de lo afro a través de algunas obras de artistas nacionales*" (The Afro Presence in Some Works of National Artists), "The distinguishing characteristic of this work is rooted in its Afro rhythm. Many features demonstrate the most characteristic element of Black music: an emphasis on rhythmic syncopation."[34]

Juarés Lamarque Pons was the nationalist composer whose music reflected the strongest Afro-Uruguayan presence in the realm of the musical and movement repertoire of contemporary Uruguayan ballet, in works such as his ballet pantomime, *"El Encargado"* (The Messenger), a one-act farce; his *"Suite Rioplatense"* (Río de la Plata Suite), a one-act sketch accompanied by two pianos and a candombe-inspired percussion section; and his *"Suite de Ballet según Figari"* (Ballet Suite According to Figari), Figari being an artist many of whose paintings were inspired by scenes from candombe.

The culmination of this phenomenon was the 1989 production of the *"Candomballet,"* a collaborative work by Cuban choreographer Gustavo Herrera and Uruguayan musicians Hugo Fattoruso, Silvia Contenti, and Fernando Condón. Candombe has also been represented in religious liturgy. Afro-Uruguayan author and composer Gilberto Silva crafted the *Misa Candombe* (Candombe Mass), which premiered in 1984 in the Tierra Santa Catholic Church, further broadening the range of stylized versions of candombe, and adding another element of Afro-Uruguayan culture to the national scene.

Canto popular (popular song) was a leftist artistic movement in music and poetry that emerged during the 1960s as an expression of the material and spiritual realities of ordinary people, as poets, singers, and composers tried to raise their audiences' consciousness. They did extensive research into many traditional musical styles and incorporated into their compositions elements of both urban Afro-Uruguayan and rural folk music. During the 1970s military dictatorship, canto popular thrived as a vital political voice of dissent. Although the artists were almost exclusively white, they used Uruguay's most popular rhythmic genres, the Afro-Uruguayan candombe and milonga, as the basis of their compositions. Some examples of this music are *Doña Soledad* by Alfredo Zitarrosa, *Yacumensa* by José Carbajal, *A mi gente* by Rubén Lena, and *Ta' llorando* by Los Olimareños.

Uruguayan poets regularly compose verses, and often musical lyrics, based on Afro-Uruguayan themes. Some of the more important Afro-Uruguayan poets are Pilar Barrios, Virginia Brindis de Sala, Juan Julio Arrascaeta, Isabelino José Gares, and Cristina Rodríguez Cabral. Among Euro-Uruguayan poets using Afro-Uruguayan themes are Ildefonso Pereda Valdés, Fernán Silva Valdés, Ruben Carámbula, Gladys Cancela, and Carlos Paéz Vilaró.

Many visual artists have also been inspired by Afro-Uruguayan motifs. One of the most celebrated Euro-Uruguayan artists, Pedro Figari (1861–1938), painted Afro-Uruguayan festivals featuring people who were at the same time both servants and occasional kings and queens. As a child Figari had been dazzled by his experiences of candombe. Later in life he read books about European explorations of Africa and especially enjoyed the works of Blaise Cendrars (1887–1961), a French writer and Négritude aficionado who traveled in Africa and whose best-known work was *Antologia negra* (*The African Saga*), a collection of African expressive culture translated into several languages, as well as *Una noche en la selva* (*A Night in the Forest*), and *Cuentos negros para los hijos de blancos* (*Black Stories for White Children*).[35] From his memories, Figari attempted to recapture candombe's visual splendor, spirituality, and powerful rhythms using a vibrant palette and a well-developed gift of observation and memory. His images have become part of the standard repertoire of the Uruguayan visual imagination.

Other outstanding Euro-Uruguayan artists who have portrayed Afro-Uruguayan themes are Eduardo Vernazza (b. 1911), Carlos Paéz Vilaró (b. 1923), and Leonel Pérez Molinari (1927–89). Molinari was one of Uruguay's most representative painters of popular scenes and carnival festivities. His corpus of work includes an extensive series of well-researched historical paintings depicting candombes in colonial Montevideo. Some of his most memorable works, reflecting details of candombe, are *Fiestas de San Baltasar, Corejo, Cuplés y Ruedas, Entrevero, Ombligada*, and *Noche de Llamadas*.[36]

Afro-Uruguayan painters from a variety of stylistic schools have also represented Afro-Uruguayan themes, beginning with Victor Ocampo Vilaza (1881–1960). Ramón Pereyra (1919–54), who died early in his promising career, was best known for his skill as a stylist and for his sensitive palette. Ruben Galloza (b. 1926) has enjoyed wide-ranging success as one of Uruguay's major and most prolific Afro-Uruguayan contemporary artists (see figures 15.1–15.3). His canvases depict everyday scenes and characters of Afro-Uruguayan life in Montevideo, including characteristic candombe subjects such as mamas viejas, gramilleros, escoberos, dancers, conventillos, carnival comparsas, llamadas, and drums. Galloza's work has been exhibited in South America (Argentina, Brazil, Bolivia, and Chile), Europe (Germany, Spain, the Netherlands, and England), in Pretoria and Cape Town in South Africa, and in Miami and New York in the United States.

Thus, although now a small proportion of the total population, Afro-Uruguayans have made significant contributions to Uruguay's history, military, arts, and popular culture. More research will no doubt add to our knowledge of the fundamental Afro-Uruguayan role in the creation of a unique Uruguayan national identity. Afro-Uruguayan organizations are working to recapture this history and to make it broadly available through formal and informal educational programs, exhibits, and artistic manifestations. Our African traditions are so clearly present in so much of Uruguayan life that they should only need to be acknowledged for all Uruguayans to appreciate their full value.

NOTES

This chapter was translated from Spanish by Lisa Sánchez González.

1. According to Diego Luis Molinari, *La Trata de negros: datos para su estudio en el Río de la Plata* (Buenos Aires: Universidade de Buenos Aires, 1944 [1916]), as cited in Eugenio Petit Muñoz, *La condición jurídica, social, económica y política de los negros durante el coloniaje en la Banda Oriental* (Montevideo: Talleres Gráficos "33," 1949 [1947]), 29.

2. See Ildefonso Pereda Valdés, "El negro en el Uruguay, pasado y presente," in *Revista del Instituto Histórico y Geográfico del Uruguay* 25 (Montevideo, 1965): 29; Daniel Vidart and Renzo Pi Hugarte, *El legado de los inmigrantes* (Montevideo: Editorial Nuestra Tierra, 1969), 30.

3. Eduardo Thomas, *Compendio de historia national* (Montevideo: Monteverde y Companía, 1943), 46.

4. Marisa Rey Bruno, "Nuestras raices: negritud y orientalidad" (unpublished manuscript), 9.

5. Bruno, "Nuestras Raices," 9.

6. Ema Isola, *La esclavitud en el Uruguay desde sus comienzos hasta la extinción, 1743–1852* (Montevideo: Publicaciones de la Comisión Nacional de Homenaje del Sequicentenario de los Hechos Históricos de 1825–1975, 1976), 55.

7. Homero Martínez Montero, "La esclavitud en el Uruguay," *Revista nacional*, no. 32 (Montevideo: Ministerio de Instrucción Pública, 1940), 257.

8. Carlos M. Rama, *Los afro-uruguayos* (Montevideo: Editorial El Siglo Ilustrado, 1967), 21.

9. Rama, *Los afro-uruguayos*, 21.

10. Rama, *Los afro-uruguayos*, 21.

11. Pereda Valdés, "El negro en el Uruguay," 16.

12. The list, without the geographical explanations, is from Vidart and Hugarte, *El legado de los inmigrantes*, 30.

13. Pereda Valdés, "El negro en el Uruguay," 17.

14. Alban Butler, *The Lives of the Saints*, vol. 4, eds. Herbert Thurston and Norah Leeson (London: Burn, Oates and Washbourne, Ltd., 1933 [1756–59]), 52–54.

15. John L. Delaney, *Dictionary of the Saints* (Garden City, N.Y.: Doubleday and Company, Inc., 1980), 98.

16. Néstor Ortiz Oderigo, *Aspectos de la cultura africana en el Río de la Plata* (Buenos Aires: Edición Plus Ultra, 1974), 33.

17. See Tomás Olivera Chirimini and Juan Antonio Varese, *Memórias del tamboril* (Montevideo: Editorial Latina, 1996), and Tomás Olivera Chirimini, *El candombe* (Montevideo: El Galeón, 1992); Tomás Olivera Chirimini and Juan Antonio Varese, *Los candombes de reyes: las llamadas* (Montevideo: El Galeón, 2000).

18. Lauro Ayestarán, *La música en el Uruguay* (Montevideo: Servicio Oficial de Difusión Radio-Eléctrica (SODRE), 1965 [1953]), 71.

19. Ortiz Oderigo, *Aspectos de la cultura africana*, 78.

20. Ortiz Oderigo, *Aspectos de la cultura africana*, 84–85.

21. Ortiz Oderigo, *Aspectos de la cultura africana*, 87–88.

22. Ortiz Oderigo, *Aspectos de la cultura africana*, 180.

23. Ayestarán, *La música*, 101.

24. Special thanks to Juan Antonio Varese and Ruben D. Galloza for their kind permission to reprint figures 15.1–15.3 from *Postales de candombe* (Montevideo: Juan Antonio Varese, 1998).

25. Ayestarán, *La música*, 452–453.

26. Ayestarán, *La música*, 452–453.

27. Antonio D. Plácido, *Carnaval: evocación de Montevideo en la historia y la tradición* (Montevideo: Ediciones Ciudadela, 1966), 56–57.

28. Plácido, *Carnaval*, 71–76.

29. Ayestarán, *La música*, 84.

30. Pereda Valdés, "El negro en el Uruguay," 172.

31. Ayestarán, *La música*, 101.

32. Alberto Soriano, *Tres rezos augúricos y otros cantares de liturgia negra* (Montevideo: Universidad de Montevideo, Facultad de Humanidades y Ciencias, Cátedra de Etnología Musical, 1968), 53.

33. Oscar Natale, *Buenos Aires, negros y tango* (Buenos Aires: Ediciones Peña-Lillo, 1984), 249-251.

34. Fantina Signorelli, "Vivencia de lo afro a través de algunas obras de artistas nacionales," unpublished thesis (Licencia de Musicología, Facultad de Humanidades y Ciencias, Universidad de Montevideo, 1971), 4.

35. Blaise Cendrars, *The African Saga*, trans. Margery Bianco (New York: Payson and Clarke Ltd., 1927), *Une nuit dans la forêt (A Night in the Forest: First Fragment of an Autobiography)*, trans. Margaret Kidder Ewing (Columbia: University of Missouri Press, 1985), and *Petits contes nègres pour les enfants des blancs* (Paris: Au Sans Pareil, 1929). See also: Francisco Melitón Merino Burghi, *El negro en la sociedad montevideana* (Montevideo: Ediciones de la Banda Oriental, 1982), 87.

36. Juan Antonio Varese, "Molinari: pintor de carnavales y candombes," in *Almanaque del Banco de Seguros del Estado* (Montevideo: F. Oliveras, 1995), 112.

16

*

"Catching Sense" and the Meaning of Belonging on a South Carolina Sea Island

Patricia Guthrie

For African American Sea Islanders living on St. Helena, South Carolina, during the first half of the twentieth century, "catching sense" denoted the socialization process that occurred between the ages of two and twelve, at which point children joined the Baptist church and became members of their home plantation communities. Developed during slavery, catching sense provided the mechanism by which African Americans on St. Helena were recruited into community life. The process exemplified a creative strategy, developed by enslaved people in the Americas, to ensure that all children, regardless of the circumstances of their birth, belonged to a community.

Plantations historically provided the framework on St. Helena within which individuals came to belong or to catch sense. To belong in the cultural and social sense, one must have resided in a plantation community during one's formative years. What makes the notion so compelling for the anthropologist is that this was a concept of belonging that was not based on filial ties. To the contrary, despite whatever filial relationships existed, one caught sense because of location rather than through ties of kinship.

In this chapter I describe what it meant to catch sense on St. Helena in 1976 when I first conducted field research on the island. My data resulted from what I witnessed and, more importantly, what I was told by islanders. The individuals with whom I spoke and whom I observed at that time were the last to remember, understand, and appreciate the significance of catching sense.[1]

PLANTATIONS AND THEIR ANTEBELLUM ROOTS

The literature about St. Helena focuses primarily on linguistics and folklore. The linguistics literature attempted to establish whether Gullah, the spoken language of most African American Sea Islanders, was a variation of standard American English or a creole based on a combination of English and various West African languages. Folklorists devoted considerable time to recording Gullah songs, practices, and customs, many of which appear to be African in origin.[2]

In *Black Yeomanry: Life on St. Helena Island*, Thomas J. Woofter, Jr., represented an exception to these two primary areas, in that he concentrated on the historical development of the St. Helena community. His study provided a starting point for my work with his focus on the definition and meaning of "plantations." Woofter's writings described how island plantations developed from the end of slavery through the 1920s and showed the importance of plantation communities as residential units.[3] During my research I found that inhabitants still described their place of residence as, for instance, "Fripp Plantation."

By the close of the Civil War era, numerous white St. Helenian planters had abandoned their land, most of which had been dedicated to the lucrative rice plantations characteristic of the region (figure 16.1), because they could not pay the taxes. Freed

Figure 16.1.   Woman "fanning" rice (separating the rice from the husks). Photo by Patricia Guthrie.

African Americans, both local and from other parts of the antebellum South, purchased portions of abandoned plantations from the federal government. The changeover in ownership resulted from the efforts of the federally sponsored Port Royal Experiment,[4] which made it possible for formerly enslaved people to purchase ten-acre tracts of land, subdividing antebellum plantations into numerous African American-owned parcels.

St. Helena is currently composed of approximately forty-five plantation communities,[5] inhabited primarily by the descendants of formerly enslaved people, with whites scattered here and there. The latter are descendants of the antebellum planter class, as well as outsiders with no family ties to the island. One plantation, previously inhabited entirely by African Americans, is now a private, upscale residential development occupied by both African Americans and whites. A special pass is needed to enter its gated grounds. As is the case in much of the Sea Islands region—Hilton Head Island, South Carolina, is the best-known example—outsiders are purchasing land as it becomes available. In some cases, African American heirs to island property no longer reside in the area and decide to sell.[6] In other instances, African Americans are forced to sell because they lack the funds needed to pay the rapidly escalating property taxes.[7]

THE PLANTATION SETTING—1976–1990

In 1976, plantations—increasingly referred to in the late 1990s as "plantation communities" or just "communities"—contained cultivated land, brush, young forest growth, waterfront, marshes, land where trees were planted for future sale and for building materials, houses with adjoining yards, and burial grounds. Before the 1950s, more farming had been done on St. Helena, but as farming became a less viable livelihood, islanders began to secure nonagricultural jobs, and farmlands were neglected.

Homes were built of brick, wood, or cinder block, and most of them stood in good repair. Some islanders had purchased mobile homes because of affordability and ease of installation. Residence sites contained anywhere from one to six individual homes, as brothers tended to live in close proximity to their parents, sharing a "yard." Since closely related kinsfolk were close neighbors, there were few fences. Islanders took pride in the overall appearance of their yards. The grounds were clean, and many residents cultivated decorative plants and flowers. It was this network of individually owned dwelling sites that constituted a plantation community.

Today, St. Helena remains much the same. Brothers still build together in the yard. Most sites are easily accessible by paved roads and, unlike the 1970s, paved and dirt roads are now all named, many bearing names of popular deceased plantation members. The biggest change on the island is the increase in both local businesses (e.g., gas stations and convenience stores) and residence sites. But the breathtakingly beautiful old live oak trees with their dripping Spanish moss remain fixed in time. The island's Baptist churches, some expanded and updated, retain their stately charm and splendor.

CATCHING SENSE AND THE EXPERIENCE OF ENSLAVED PEOPLE

The phenomenon of catching sense is central to understanding African American life and history on St. Helena Island. How do you give people a sense of identity and belonging in a situation in which kinship ties have been intentionally interrupted, as was the case during slavery? How do you construct a social reality in such a way that all persons can potentially attain full social standing in a community in which there is recognized filiation only on the side of one parent, the enslaved parent in the case of people with white genitors? Catching sense, I speculate, grew out of this experience, and was practically designed for providing security and acceptance in people's lives under the most barbaric of circumstances.

Cross-culturally, it is usually the filiation of people, along with questions concerning legitimacy of birth (however that is defined) that determines their place in society. During the antebellum period, using birth filiation as a primary criterion for determining an African American individual's place in society would have been unworkable. What would happen to kinless children, purchased and placed on a plantation without family members? What mechanisms would enable them to have a place in society? Since most enslaved people were not allowed to marry, legitimacy by birth would not work as a criterion either. Catching sense, therefore, was the "ideal" response to the conditions of slavery. It was a survival strategy. During slavery on St. Helena, even when people were sold onto another plantation, they still belonged to the people with whom they had grown up and learned about the meaning of life and proper social relationships.

Children became eligible for plantation "membership" because they held membership in a household on the plantation where they caught sense. But, although household membership was a prerequisite to catching sense, it was not by itself sufficient to connote belonging. Catching sense represented the socialization process experienced by African American children who came of age on St. Helena. On the psychosocial level, the essence of catching sense was remembering and understanding the meaning of social relationships beyond the natal household. Initially children knew only their own house, yard, and yard members, but in the process of catching sense, their knowledge and experience extended eventually to include their entire home plantation community, as they learned how to behave socially, and get along peacefully, and, among other proper behaviors, show respect to elders.

CATCHING SENSE AND RIGHTS

Catching sense conferred three rights: the right to sanctuary, the right to be buried in the plantation graveyard, and the right to succeed to office. The first two rights applied to men and women equally, while the third accrued only to men, St. Helena, like the rest of the United States, being patriarchal. St. Helenians were also patrilocal, and at marriage, women usually moved to their husband's home plantation.

The Right of Sanctuary

If a person moved to another plantation or off the island and then returned, the people of the plantation saw to it that the returnee had a place to live. If a person belonged, he or she was taken into a home or given shelter in an unoccupied dwelling. Once a person belonged to a certain plantation, there was always a place for that person upon his or her return.

The Right to Be Buried in the Plantation Graveyard

On St. Helena, each plantation has its own burial ground. Individuals who caught sense together were ultimately laid to rest together. The exceptions to this were women who caught sense elsewhere but married and resided on the plantation where their husband belonged. Such women were buried in their husband's plantation graveyard.

The Right to Succeed to Office

A man who caught sense on a plantation became eligible for leadership positions both locally and island-wide. Access to the office of praise house leader most clearly separated male members of a plantation from male nonmembers. The praise house leader had to have caught sense on the plantation where the praise house operated, and a man residing on a plantation where he had not caught sense was ineligible for the office.[8]

CATCHING SENSE, PRAISE HOUSES, AND CHURCHES

Plantation praise houses were related to the concept of catching sense. In his analysis of St. Helena, Woofter wrote, "After the slave laws discouraged the gathering of slaves away from their own plantations, masters allowed their people to worship in plantation groups, usually at the house of one of the older people, sometimes in a special praise house."[9] Praise houses of the 1970s were small private buildings (figure 16.2). When I first began research on St. Helena, I was unable to identify one since there were no signs, symbols, or markers.[10] The interiors were plain and bare, especially when compared with the well-appointed interiors of local churches. A praise house contained wooden benches or chairs and a podium. A single naked light bulb hung from the ceiling.

Membership in a given praise house was open to all plantation residents who were members of the church congregation connected to it, each praise house being affiliated with an island Baptist church, with one to four praise houses connected to each church congregation. The number of praise houses reflected the number of plantation communities with members belonging to that church. To become a praise house member, a plantation resident formally accepted the "right hand of fellowship" that the leader extended on behalf of the congregation. The approximate age at which islanders joined the church and the praise house coincided with that time when the process of catching

Figure 16.2.   Sea Island praise house. Photo by Patricia Guthrie.

sense approached completion. In other words, entrance into adult religious life paralleled the time when catching sense became fully realized.[11]

People attended praise house meetings for devotional purposes: to sing, to praise their Creator, and to pray to God the Father and His Son, Jesus Christ. Services began with a welcome given by the leader. Next came a Bible reading, testifying, praying, and singing of hymns. While the leader called on specific members to read hymns, give the Bible reading, and offer prayer, any member or visitor was free to raise songs, pray, and testify.[12] Services closely paralleled the devotional segment that began the regular Sunday Baptist church services, but lacked musical accompaniments and a pastor, the small, local-level congregations being composed entirely of plantation community residents.[13]

Praise houses reinforced a sense of belonging on the plantation level through worship and through a system of dispute settlement. When disputes or problems arose among members, settlement was reached through the "just law" of the praise house system. Church law demanded that all grievances go before the leader and three or four leadership committee members. Instances of trouble were reported to the leader by praise house members, committee members, or the parties involved in a grievance. The leader then assigned the case to the committee, who attempted to have the aggrieved parties agree to a meeting with the committee in one of their homes. The dispute was "thrashed out" as each party was given the opportunity to explain her or his side. When a peaceful settlement was reached, the quarreling parties confessed to wrongdoing and "took [shook] hands," thus restoring peace and harmony.

Should the aggrieved individuals refuse to meet in one or the other's home, the case could be adjudicated by the committee at a meeting in "the middle of the road." Committee members and disputants literally met in the middle of a plantation road and employed the same mechanisms for dispute settlement. If the committee could not solve a case, it was taken before the praise house leader, who alone decided guilt or innocence.

Taking disputes to the secular court was a last resort and was almost exclusively reserved for instances involving non-Baptist St. Helenians. A church member who went to the "unjust law," the secular court, when trouble developed with another Baptist church member was censured both informally and formally. Informally there was much gossip and general disapproval. Islanders complained that a person who would take a grievance to the secular authorities really did not want peace and harmony restored to the community.

In fact, the person who went to the court was accused of stirring up more trouble. The court imposed hardships by holding sessions during working hours, fining guilty parties, and sending them to jail. Whereas the praise house had as its primary function to restore peace and harmony to the community, the secular court had as its apparent purpose to establish guilt and seek restitution. This approach, local people believed, exacerbated rather than resolved problems.

A church member who went to the secular law when trouble arose "took a back seat" in the church, losing his or her rights as a member of the religious community and, before the 1970s, literally sitting in the back of the church. Such a person could attend services but could not sing in a choir, serve as an usher, or take part in church or praise house programs. A person who took a back seat at any one of the island's churches took a back seat in all of them. In order to regain his or her place in the community, the person had to make a public announcement in the church: "Forgive me for the wrong course I have taken." Once the public apology was made, the person resumed his or her place in the community.

A successful praise house leader stood an excellent chance of becoming a church deacon, and deacons remain highly respected and powerful leaders. This leadership chain based on catching sense connected churches and praise houses. A man who wanted to become a deacon had to catch sense on an island plantation, reside on the plantation where he caught sense, become a successful praise house leader, and then be confirmed as a deacon by the church members.

CONCLUSIONS AND SUGGESTIONS

Catching sense was developed not by choice, but because enslaved persons were "mobile"—an involuntary and forced mobility. Enslaved persons were bought and sold and moved around wherever and whenever the white planter class saw fit to do so. There are, for example, instances in which enslaved children, even infants, were given as door prizes at house parties. What would happen to the social world of that child because of such forced mobility? On St. Helena the child belonged where he or she caught sense.

The church, the praise houses, the dispute settlement systems—all were connected to catching sense. Because it represented the socialization process on St. Helena, catching sense gave people their guiding principles, their knowledge of how to interact with one another. The process ended when the person belonged, when he or she left childhood and entered adulthood. Children became true members of their community when their social world and their social relationships expanded to include the public as well as the domestic domain. The individual moved from being a private person to a public person—to a sense of self that others in the community were able to recognize, acknowledge, and affirm. For islanders who belonged, that recognition, acknowledgment, and affirmation was crystallized through praise house and Baptist church membership and participation—that is, participation in both worship and dispute settlement.

Today we too live out our lives in a mobile society, albeit voluntarily. Perhaps we can begin to understand and appreciate not only the uniquely creative aspects of catching sense, but also the appropriateness and practicality of such a system. We might even apply the concept to ourselves and to people around us, in urban as well as rural settings.

Outside the limits of St. Helenian society, we are locked into the importance of where we were born. Every application we complete, every form we fill out, from grade school through social security, asks for a place of birth. Yet in conversation, people will say, "Oh, yes, I was born in New York City, but I grew up in California." For all of us, the significance in this statement lies in the qualification "I grew up in California" or, put another way, "I caught sense in California." In reality, it does not really matter much today where a person was born unless the concern is specifically with national or regional origin. When it comes to how we interpret the world in an increasingly mobile society, what is really important is that formative period—where we were and with whom we were in communication when our sense of self was formed, when we "caught sense."

NOTES

1. The data in this paper are based on two primary field research projects conducted on St. Helena Island, S.C. Besides being a participant observer, I also collected material by means of intensive open-ended interviews. Additional research was carried out on St. Helena Island in 1992, 1996, and 1998.

2. See, for example, John G. Williams, "Is Gullah a Corruption of Angola?" *Sunday News* (Charleston, South Carolina), Feb. 10, 1895; J. Jenkins Hucks, *Plantation Negro Sayings on the Coast of South Carolina in Their Own Vernacular* (Georgetown: Charles W. Rouse, 1899); John Bennett, "The Comedie Humaine of the Gullah Darkey," *The State* (Columbia, S. C.), Dec. 17, 1922; Lorenzo Dow Turner, *Africanisms in the Gullah Dialect* (New York: Arno Press, 1949); Julian Mason, "Etymology of Buckaroo," *American Speech* 15 (February 1960): 51–55; P. E. H. Hair, "Sierra Leone Idioms in the Gullah Dialect of American English," *Sierra Leone Language Review* (1965): 79–84; Irma Aloyce Ewing Cunningham, "A Syntactic Analysis of Sea Island Creole," Ph.D. dissertation, University of Michigan, 1970; Henry Carrington Bolton, "Decorations of Graves of Negroes in South Carolina," *Journal of American Folklore*, vol. 4, (July–Sept. 1891): 214; S. E. Steward, "Seven Folk-Tales from the Sea Islands, South Carolina," *Journal of American Folklore*, no. 32 (Lancaster, Pa., 1919): 394–396; Elizabeth Ware Pearson, ed., *Letters from Port Royal* (Boston: W. B. Clarke Company, 1906); Ambrose E. Gonzales, *Two Gullah Tales: The Turkey Hunter and At the Cross Roads Store* (New York: Purdy Press, 1926); Guy B. Johnson, *Folk*

Culture on St. Helena Island, South Carolina (Columbia: University of South Carolina Press, 1930); Hermes Nye, "Animal Tales Told in the Gullah Dialect," *Saturday Review* (Oct. 13, 1956): 40; Patricia A. Jones-Jackson, *When Roots Die: Endangered Traditions on the Sea Islands* (Athens: University of Georgia Press, 1989); Margaret Washington Creel, "Gullah Attitudes Toward Life and Death" in *Africanisms in American Culture*, Joseph E. Holloway, ed. (Bloomington: Indiana University Press, 1990); and Josephine A. Beoku-Betts, "She Make Funny Flat Cake She Call Saraka" in *Working Toward Freedom: Slave Society and Domestic Economy in the American South*, ed. Larry E. Hudson, Jr. (Rochester, N.Y.: University of Rochester Press, 1994).

3. Thomas J. Woofter, Jr., *Black Yeomanry. Life on St. Helena Island* (New York: Henry Holt and Company, 1930).

4. For a detailed discussion of the Port Royal Experiment and the changeover in land ownership, see Willie Lee Rose, *Rehearsal for Reconstruction: The Port Royal Experiment* (New York: Vintage Books, 1964); also Carol K. Rothrock Blesser, *The Promised Land: The History of the South Carolina Land Commission, 1869–1890* (Columbia: University of South Carolina Press, 1969).

5. The plantation communities are: Brisbane, Capers, Cedar Grove, Paul Chaplin, Cherry Hill, Club Bridge, Coffins Point, Corner, Croft, Cuffy, Dataw, Eddings, Eddings Point, Fripp Point, Ann Fripp, John Fripp, Lawrence Fripp, Oliver Fripp, Tom Fripp, Frogmore, Fuller, Goodman, Hopes, Indian Hill, Mary Jenkins, Land's End, McTureous, Mulberry Hill, Oakland, Oaks, Orange Grove, Pineland, Pollywanna, Pope, Pritchard, Saxtonville, School Farm, Scott, Scott Hill, Sixty Acres, Tombee, Wallace, Warsaw, Dr. White, White Church.

6. Starting with the end of the Civil War a steady stream of St. Helenians has left the island. Islanders move to urban areas such as New York City, Boston, and Atlanta, and routinely leave for college and for military service. Many of those who leave do not return except for holidays, vacations, or when they retire. See Vernon Kiser, *Sea Island to City* (New York: Columbia University Press, 1969) for an analysis of early St. Helena out-migration.

7. Property costs on St. Helena and the entire Sea Islands region have risen steadily since the 1970s, as an increasing number of tourists, land developers, and retirees from the mainland are overrunning the area.

8. For a more detailed discussion of catching sense and rights, see Patricia Guthrie, *Catching Sense: African American Communities on a South Carolina Sea Island* (Westport, Conn.: Bergin and Garvey, 1996).

9. Woofter, *Black Yeomanry*, 236.

10. During the late 1980s, islanders posted a sign on one of the last remaining praise houses. The sign resulted, I believe, from the newly developed local interest and pride in the historical, cultural, and societal significance of praise houses.

11. Viewed cross-culturally, the completion of catching sense brings to mind other rites of passage, such as the bar mitzvah when a Jewish boy, age thirteen, assumes religious responsibility and becomes an adult member of the Jewish community.

12. As of June 1998, one praise house on the island still held services.

13. While it may appear that churches and praise houses are two separate institutions, they are in fact parts of the same structure. Enslaved persons were forbidden for the most part from attending church (although drivers delivering plantation owners to service could sit in the narrow gallery of St. Helena's Brick Church), and so praise houses were the loci of both their worship and dispute settlement. With emancipation, they superimposed churches onto the praise house system (Woofter, *Black Yeomanry*, 236). What continues to link praise houses and churches is the system of dispute adjudication and male leadership.

17

Demystifying Africa's Absence in Venezuelan History and Culture

Jesús "Chucho" García

In 1985, I made my first trip to the Republic of the Congo in search of information about Venezuela's historical relationship with Central Africa. My purpose was to seek information to demystify the African, particularly the dominant Central African Bantu, presence in Venezuela in order to fill in the African absence in the construction of our national identity.[1] This was an important task since the official versions of Venezuelan history, akin to the histories of the rest of so-called Latin America, reduce Africa's contributions mainly to drums and "witchcraft." Many attribute what they consider the irrational behavior of Latin America's leaders to their "magical sense of reality," a legacy presumably inherited through the breast milk of the enslaved *ayas negras*, the Black "mammies" responsible for their socialization, "such that when they took power, they reproduced this magical concept of reality."[2]

From 1937 to the present, Arturo Uslar Pietri, the celebrated Venezuelan writer with the greatest influence on the white elite, has kept this official discourse alive in his writings and his addresses to Venezuelan intellectuals concerning issues of modernity and the nation. Uslar Pietri's premise is that "Blacks did not arrive" in Venezuela "with a culture that visibly affected the construction of our national identity."[3] He asserts that "Blacks did not make a racial contribution beneficial to the nation. Our racial blend has not enabled us to transcend the original ingredients. In general terms, those members of what we might call the current Venezuelan race are as incapable of comprehending modern and dynamic concepts of work as were their ancestors. This means that if we cannot substantially modify the ethnic composition of our population, it will be virtually impossible to change the course of our history and to make our country a modern nation."[4]

When I began to understand the nature of this hegemonic position in Venezuela's historical discourse, a perspective imposed in compulsory school curricula, and became aware of how this point of view negatively affected Afro-Venezuelans, I felt obliged to deconstruct and reconstruct the discourse, or really the absence thereof, about the

Africanity of Venezuela's national formation. This meant that my version of Afro-Venezuelan history would have to serve to combat both the racism expressed in schoolbooks and the trauma of internalized racism for the Afro-Venezuelan community.

The words of my grandmothers, traditionalist elders born in the nineteenth century in San José de Barlovento, one of the Black communities in the subregion of Barlovento in the state of Miranda, offered me an alternative source of our history, one that contradicted that of my formal education. Their words inspired me—their stories, songs, and lyric poems. Our daily life outside of school also inspired me. I realized that our oral traditions had been banished from the classroom in the interest of creating a social science program that reproduced official versions of Venezuelan history that endorsed the stories of conquering Europeans. I also became aware of exactly how we, the "others," were erased from the history, geography, music, and cultural curricula taught in the nation's schools.

My first step was to investigate seventeenth-, eighteenth-, and nineteenth-century documentary evidence in the national archives. I went to the same sources used by those who created and defended the official historical narratives.[5] My next task was to decode the declarations, the discourse, of runaway Africans—*cimarrones*/maroons—who had been captured and brutally tortured in their efforts to resist enslavement, making allowances, of course, for the demeaning and insulting tone of these sources.[6]

The data led me to classify *cimarronaje*/marooning as either passive or active. Passive marooning refers to those ways in which Africans and their descendants fought against their enslavement in colonial contexts by taking advantage of available institutional resources, such as the law and the Catholic church. Beginning in the middle of the eighteenth century, for example, enslaved people could, if they amassed adequate resources, purchase their own freedom, or even that of babies in the wombs of enslaved mothers; or they could "inherit" their freedom if their owners made such provisions in their wills.

Active marooning refers to enslaved people fighting directly against the system of slavery in order to reclaim their freedom at any cost. This active resistance to the different modalities of colonial oppression by Africans and their descendants filled many archival files, which clearly indicated that active marooning signified a sustained politics as well as a concept of anticolonial liberation. As such, the African contribution to the Venezuelan nation was both moral and political.

We find evidence of this moral and political activity in the archival documentation concerning Miguel Luango, for example, who headed a rebellion of enslaved people in Caracas in 1749. Luango, whose name refers to his Central African origins (Africans often being named for their points of departure from the continent), demanded that the colonial authorities establish a nonracist government. Had this rebellion succeeded, administrative posts were to be assigned to Francisco Loango as lieutenant general, Manuel Loango as mayor, and Simón Loango as attorney general.[7]

Already beginning in 1552, with the rebellion headed by "El Negro" Miguel in the Buria Mountains, in the 1749 Kongo and Loango Rebellion in Caracas, and later in the 1795 uprising instigated by a Loango man called Cocofío and led by José Leonardo Chirinos, we see evidence for the construction of a specifically African idea of "independence" in Venezuela. This idea was distinct from what Francisco de Miranda, the "precursor of Venezuelan independence," intended as the incipient nation's moral and political imperative. Miranda preferred to capitulate to the Spanish Crown, rather than strike an alliance with the Black insurgents in the Barlovento valleys, for fear that Venezuela would become another Black maroon republic like Haiti, the nation where independence for the entire population was born in the Americas.[8]

Even Simón Bolívar, the "Liberator" of five South American nations—Venezuela, Colombia, Peru, Bolivia, and Ecuador—included abolition as part of his platform for national liberation in 1816.[9] But this was conditional freedom, and soon after the wars of independence had subsided, previously enslaved people were reenslaved. Provoked to indignation, they increased their marooning. Reneging on abolition during the independence era was consistent with the Eurocentric notions of Venezuela's white creole "paladins of liberty," who could not accept the insurgent and more complete ideal of liberty contributed by the African rebels whose quests for freedom had helped to destabilize and defeat the Spanish colonial regime.

Reconstructing this other history also meant elaborating strategies to demystify the erasure of the Africanity of Venezuela's national formation, which remains one of my main preoccupations. This is a general problem in Latin American and Caribbean historiography. When Black insurrection erupted at the end of the eighteenth century, it was explained as the product of French revolutionary thinking, hence the cliché "Black Jacobins." This idea, which is the focus of Marxist historian Federico Brito Figueroa's book *El problema tierra y esclavos en la historia de Venezuela*, is historically inaccurate.[10]

Long before the French decreed *liberté, egalité, et fraternité*, Africans imprisoned in cacao, sugarcane, and cotton fields in the Americas were already revolting against their exploitation. They rallied against oppression and exploitation based on skin color and social position and in favor of human redemption. This trend had been evident by the beginning of the seventeenth century with the Quilombo dos Palmares in Brazil and the Yanga Rebellion leading to the *palenque* (maroon community) of San Lorenzo de los Negros, now known as Yanga, in Mexico. These initial rebellions that led to the creation of multiethnic free maroon communities were led by Central African Bantu-speaking people. The names of leaders like Zumbi of Palmares in Brazil, Yanga in Mexico, and the Loangos in Venezuela, bespeak their origins.

Rethinking history to demystify Africa's political and moral contributions to the Americas, and pursuing this line of inquiry into both comparative marooning and the contributions to "the idea of independence" in the Americas by Africans and their descendants, is an important task. We must debunk the dishonest and inconsistent historical discourses that assume Eurocentric hegemonic authority and ignore and distort African contributions to the formation of the American nations. Unraveling hegemonic discourses of the "other"—discourses about descendants of Africans the world over—has been and continues to be necessary.

If, as Marcus Garvey said, history is a tree with roots, a tree that falls when we disavow it, then culture is the body of a tree lush in leaves. According to the eminent Senegalese scholar Cheikh Anta Diop, historical factors are "the cultural cement that brings together the elements of a people's existence, forming a oneness as a consequence of the sense of lived historical continuity that a collectivity shares."[11] And another extraordinary African thinker, Amilcar Cabral of Guinea-Bissau, asserted that "Culture, despite whatever may be the ideological or idealistic characteristics of its manifestations, is therefore an essential element of history, like a flower that springs forth from a plant."[12] The doubled term "history-culture" is indispensable when we sketch the process implicit in our reconceptualization of the Afro-Venezuelan and Venezuelan, in fact the American, story.

The culture of Africans and their descendants in the Americas reflects a history of survival, a survival that has been possible because of processes that have been, and continue to be, both painful and triumphant. The problematic representational politics that disregard the body as a site of cultural expression force a rapprochement to not only what I characterize as a "culture of resistance," but also to our own cultures of origin. In these origins we can find ways of reconceptualizing ourselves in a contemporary way that makes organic cultural sense, given our shared Bantu heritage.

The very language we use to describe our bodies' life forces can be a key in reconceptualizing ourselves as African descendants. According to interviews I conducted with *ngangas*, traditional healers, in various regions of the Republic of the Congo, the body is constituted of four substantial elements: the *nitu*, or physical body, the *menga*, or blood, the *moyo*, or eternal soul, and the *mfumu kutu*, or double or shadow soul in Kikongo, the language of the Kongo or Bakongo people.[13] The nitu is a kind of box in which ancestral spirits dwell. The menga, the motor principle of life whose vital center is the heart, is the seat of the soul, thus blood sacrifices play the role of liberating powerful forces during transcendent ceremonies. The moyo represents the principle of resistance to death, and the mfumu kutu is the principle of sensory perception and self-consciousness that defines the continuity of the life and identity of the person.

The verb "to live" is translated by three terms: *zinga*, the continuity of life in the sense that the dead and unborn, not only the living, are part of the totality of human life; *moyo*, the spiritual aspect of all living beings; and *kala buna*, the physical life of the body. This conceptualization of the body and spirit, present among our Bantu ancestors who were transported to the Americas, was the basis of their understanding of their new lives and of their survival in their New World. We can interpret our cultures of resistance as reflecting and being products of these principles of resistance to death, which are still a part of our resistant worldview and behavior even if we have forgotten the words that define them and have to return to the source to recall them. These principles will continue to guide us in the new millennium. In other words, intentions of denying the profound philosophical foundations of our behavior by trivializing them as "folklore," as has been done by colonially minded "scholars," has catalyzed our collective mfumu kutu into a dynamic stance of continual resistance.

This is why many Afro-Venezuelans have in recent years been implementing a process of self-reconceptualization, of stripping ourselves of concepts that Eurocentric social scientists have imposed on us and our realities, fraudulent foreign concepts that, lamentably, still continue to plague us, and that we must identify and deconstruct when we sit down to write about our own communities. When we refer to accounts of African culture in the Americas, we often have to contend with its "folklorization" by those who characterize our cultural productions as "folk music," "religious folklore," "folk arts," and so forth—stereotypical and prejudiced conceptual terminologies that serve as road signs and tricks or traps in the colonial imaginary.

We need to develop a pedagogy of self-perception. Those of us who are musicians and/or members of African-derived religions, for example, must fight against efforts made to folklorize us. To fail to do so is to continue to view ourselves through borrowed eyes. African cultures in the Americas, rather than quaint but superficial folklore, are cultures of resistance based on African philosophical principles that we must rediscover, that persist and reshape themselves as time passes and as changes occur in our communities.

What do we mean by cultures of resistance? We mean a dynamic process in which original cultural elements are set in opposition to the pressure of colonial and post-colonial religious and governmental authorities' attempts to "disappear" them. We deliberately imagine the possibility of cultural exchange in the Americas on an equal plane of mutual respect and tolerance, insisting upon the possibility of a reciprocal process of cultural transformation that guarantees the peaceful coexistence of both colonial European and African cultural traditions in contemporary social contexts.

The cornerstone of our ideas is that for the past five hundred years African history-culture has searched for ways to reproduce itself in the Americas, ways such as cimarronaje/marooning in *quilombos, cumbes,* and *palenques,* as well as in *cabildos, cofradías,* and other alternative spaces of African-inspired religious celebration. Cumbes, quilombos, and palenques were the liberated spaces that the enslaved created in rebelling against the system of slavery, such as the Ocoyta Cumbe led by Guillermo Rivas during the end of the eighteenth century in Barlovento, Venezuela, and the still extant Palenque de San Basilio in Northern Colombia. These expressions of history-culture have created scenarios in which Bantu cultural codes, based on profound philosophical concepts, have been (re)produced in music, dance, and religion, in relationship with other ethnic configurations emanating from Native American, Hispano-Arabic, and Anglo-Saxon cultures.

Bantu cultural (re)production in the Americas has maintained a distinct historico-cultural presence. Unable to maintain itself in its original state, it has gestated new creative processes. Its imaginary breathed in new air, and its original modes transformed themselves in the heat of new experiences. Out of this cultural reproduction came its own style of modernity, as manifest in music/dance such as Bantu-derived *mambos, rumbas,* and *cumbias,* and in the use of Bantu words in everyday language in the European languages of the Americas, words such as *bilongo, nganga,* and *cafunga,*[14] Kikongo terms used in hispanophone America. All of these syncretic elements mark the shifting of a modernity that emerges from a specific cultural root growing against the grain of a reductive, homogenizing, and heavy soil.

We can describe this modernity as a continuous process of cultural recycling for African, especially Bantu, cultures in the Americas that have struggled to minimize the cultural desolation imposed on them by forces that would have them become passive and uniform. In contemporary reality there are new palenques and quilombos, translated as militant practice that allows us to reappropriate our own self-perceptions. This new practice in the case of Venezuela includes festivals such as "Multicultural Day," initially created for Afroamérica 92, and now celebrated every year in the heart of Barlovento.

As Venezuela celebrated the annual Dia de la Hispanidad (Hispanicity Day), commemorated all over Hispanic America on October 12, 1992, in honor of the so-called discovery of the Americas by Columbus, we created the Afroamérica 92 festival celebrating Afro-Venezuelan culture. Within that event, we organized Multicultural Day on October 12 as a more honest meaning of the results of Columbus's encounter. Out of Afroamérica 92 grew the Fundación Afroamérica (Afroamerica Foundation), which began in 1993 with the support of UNESCO, the United Nations Educational, Scientific, and Cultural Organization. The foundation's goal is to research the sub-Saharan African presence in Venezuela and the Caribbean. We publish the journal *Afroamérica* and have developed nine compact discs of Afro-Venezuelan music as a part of the Memoria Musical de Orígen Africana en Venezuela (African Musical Memory in Venezuela) project.

The foundation has also published sixteen *Cuadernos de historia regional* (Regional History Notebooks) based on both historical research in regional and national archives and on the oral traditions of our communities. The notebooks are used in primary and middle schools in Barlovento, and we also organize educational seminars and workshops about this new conceptualization of our history for teachers and administrators. We are planning to extend this Barlovento educational model to fifteen other regions with 90 percent Afro-Venezuelan populations. We also produced a documentary, *Salto al Atlántico*, filmed in the Republic of the Congo and in Barlovento, in which Congolese and Afro-Venezuelans discovered and compared their common cultural ground.[15]

All of these new programs and activities reaffirm the experience of constructing our own modernity in our own image, a process that goes well beyond academia and comes closer to accurately representing our reality than do the "intermediaries" who pretend to speak for us.

NOTES

This chapter was translated from Spanish by Lisa Sánchez González.

1. My first six-month field research trip in 1985 was the basis for my book *La diáspora kongo en Venezuela* (Caracas: Fundación Afroamérica and CONAC [Consejo Nacional de la Cultura de Venezuela], 1995).

2. Arturo Uslar Pietri, "Identidad nacional," paper presented at a meeting of the Grupo Santa Lucía, August, 1983, p. 5.

3. Arturo Uslar Pietri, 1983, as cited in Senta Essenfeld de Bruwer, *La cara oculta del desarrollo* (Caracas: Ediciones Monte Ávila, 1987), 16.

4. Arturo Uslar Pietri, *El país necesita inmigración* (Caracas: Boletín de la Cámara de Comercio de Caracas, February 1937), 1,235.

5. *Archivo General de la Nación, Sección Diversos*, vol. 29, "Autos criminales contra varios negros que se sublevaron en el Tuy contra los blancos," 1749; *Archivo General de la Nación, Sección Real Cédula*, vol. 1, "Asientos de negros," 1675; *Archivo General de la Nación, Sección Interior y Justicia*, vol. 175, "Levantamientos de negros en Curiepe," 1822.

6. Jesús García, *Afrovenezuela: una visión desde adentro* (Caracas: Editorial Fundación Afroamérica, 1993), 2.

7. Jesús García, *África en Venezuela* (Caracas: Edición de Lujo, 1990).

8. Jesús García, *Barlovento: tiempo de cimarrones* (San José de Barlovento: Editorial Lucas y Trina, 1990), 83.

9. Simón Bolívar, *Escritos fundamentales* (Caracas: Biblioteca Bolivariana, 1966), 102.

10. Federico Brito Figueroa, *El problema tierra y esclavos en la historia de Venezuela* (Caracas: Universidad Central de Venezuela, 1982).

11. Cheikh Anta Diop, *De la identidad cultural africana* (Paris: UNESCO, 1978), 65.

12. Amilcar Cabral, *Liberation national et culture* (Praia, Cape Verde: Partido Africano da Independência da Guiné e Cabo Verde, 1978 [1970]), 202.

13. In the Bantu languages, the pluralizing prefix "ba" means people and is often left off.

14. In the Republic of the Congo, *bilonga* is a medicine bundle. In Venezuela it refers to herbal medicine and is the name of a community known for its healers, and in Cuba it means witchcraft, or a charm used on someone. *Nganga*, which in the Republic of the Congo designates a healer, is also the name of a Venezuelan community near Bilonga, also known for its healers. Hence these two Venezuelan toponyms are derived from African occupational activities. *Cafunga* in the Republic of the Congo is a style of food preparation involving wrapping in banana leaves, especially *chikuanga*, balls of cassava flour steamed in the leaves. In Venezuela *cafunga* is a dessert of ripe bananas, coconut, brown sugar, and cloves, baked in banana leaves.

15. *Salto al Atlántico*, produced by the Organización Salto al Atlántico (Maria Eugenia Esparragoza and Jesús García), Caracas, Venezuela, 1989.

18

*

Fárígá/Ìfaradà: Black Resistance and Achievement in Brazil

Gilberto R. N. Leal

Fárígá—absolute refusal; *Ìfaradà*—fortitude, endurance—in Yoruba—expressing principles of both active and passive resistance.

It is important to establish the current social reality of the Afro-Brazilian population by presenting the facts in black and white. Of Brazil's population of 150 million people, Afro-Brazilians represent 53 percent and whites 47 percent. Illiteracy among Afro-Brazilians is 28.5 percent versus 11 percent for whites as of the 2001 census results. Income distribution shows that the poorest 20 percent of the population owns only 2.6 percent of national wealth, while the wealthiest 10 percent commands 48.1 percent. If we compare ourselves with India, where the poorest 20 percent of the population has 8.8 percent of national wealth and the wealthiest 10 percent commands 27.1 percent, the extent of how skewed the distribution of wealth is in Brazil becomes apparent.[1] Without these facts it is impossible to understand the Brazilian nation and the historical and current reality of Brazilians of African descent.

The year 1995 was a landmark for the Black movement in Brazil, during which we took the opportunity to reflect upon the history of Afro-Brazilian resistance as we commemorated the three-hundredth anniversary of Zumbi of Palmares, one of the greatest Black leaders of the Americas. Zumbi, who escaped from slavery, became the leader of the Quilombo of Palmares in what is now the state of Alagoas. Palmares was the largest and most important of the *quilombos,* the seventeenth-century maroon communities composed of Africans and Afro-Brazilians who escaped from bondage, which were based on the ideal of preserving African traditions. Quilombo dwellers, or *quilombolas* (maroons), struggled simultaneously against the internal strife of a newly created community in a constant state of siege as a result of aggressive Portuguese colonial policies and against military attacks by the colonial army throughout the seventeenth century.[2]

Although historical documents beginning in 1516 record instances of resistance by the first Africans who arrived in Brazil to the violence practiced against them, conservative symbologies have defined the roles of Africans and Afro-Brazilians during the period of slavery to emphasize their contributions to the system of order and their conformity with the necessities of the country's development. These stereotyped roles included the *mãe preta*, the docile Black "mammy" figure, and the *mucama* (from *mukamba* in Kimbundu), a young enslaved female held in high regard by the master, often chosen to serve in his house as a female companion or wet-nurse and sometimes share his bed. Young Black boys were portrayed as willingly "accepting" beatings and abuse from their young masters. These images, produced and reproduced by conservative interests, remain to this day. They serve, however, as a counterpoint to true Afro-Brazilian libertarian sentiments as reflected in both active and passive resistance.

Passive resistance often took the form of *banzo* (lingering melancholia) in which newly arrived Africans opted for physical inactivity with accompanying psychophysical symptoms as an expression and resolution of their profound longing for Africa. Active resistance ranged from suicide and the assassination of one's own children or of other enslaved people, to the organization of quilombos, and to revolts aimed at seizing political power. The latter included guerrilla fighting in the forests, participation in social movements, armed resistance of the quilombolas against their oppressors, and personal and collective action against masters and/or overseers. Thus, parallel to the role of enslaved Afro-Brazilians in sustaining the growing national economy with their labor was the simultaneous growth of Afro-Brazilian participation in the negation of this economy.

The formation of the economic basis of the Brazilian nation occurred during the colonial period, essentially in the sixteenth and seventeenth centuries, based on sugarcane cultivation in the northeast coastal region. During this two-hundred-year period, the Afro-Brazilian majority were the "workers," the creators of wealth, while the white minority reaped the benefits of this unrenumerated labor, setting the basis for the current unequal distribution of wealth. Afro-Brazilians also participated in the construction of the economic base of the nation through their work in mining based on skills and knowledge they brought from Africa. Mining, introduced into Brazil at the beginning of the sixteenth century and culminating at the beginning of the eighteenth century, was responsible for the transfer of the economic axis of the colony from the northeast to the south-central region.

In the nineteenth century, a coffee- and entrepreneurial-based economy, also sustained by the enslaved Afro-Brazilian workforce, emerged in the south-central region. Afro-Brazilians were transformed into laborers in the newly industrializing sectors of the economy that eventually replaced more traditional economic forms such as sugar plantations. From 1830 on, coffee cultivation drove this new economy, generating sufficient income for the embryonic rise of capitalism. Soon afterward, along with incipient urbanization, the first banks developed, along with companies involved in enterprises such as insurance, urban transportation, coastal trading, and railroad, maritime, and river transportation. Hence, Brazil's economic foundation was constructed with the violence of colonial slavery.

Brazil's colonial ideology supported the myth that Afro-Brazilians accepted slavery passively, an absurd notion that is countered by abundant historical data. The forging of Afro-Brazilian leaders through rebellion has been a constant in Brazilian institutional life, for which systematic repressive brutality has been the preferred tonic. This version of Afro-Brazilian history contradicts the "official" portrait of gentle paternalism as promoted, for example, in widely accepted works such as Gilberto Freyre's *Casa grande e senzala* (The Masters and the Slaves).[3] To make such a claim is not to deny that there has always been interracial accommodation, underscored by the existence of Afro-Brazilians who freely submitted to the Catholic church, hunted Afro-Brazilian fugitives from enslavement, or performed services for their enslavers in exchange for pseudo-advantages.

During the first half of the sixteenth century, Afro-Brazilian resistance was marked by acts of rebellion that varied in degree from the passivity of banzo to the assassination of enslavers. Although there are few surviving historical records from that period, references to the form of organization that constitutes the major reference point for Afro-Brazilian resistance, the quilombos, began to appear during the second half of the century (1559–1600). Quilombos proliferated throughout the territory in what we might call the political project of transforming enslaved people into self-emancipated maroons, a process that continues in contemporary forms. As a landmark of historical resistance, the greatest success was represented by the Quilombo of Palmares, whose most important and final leader was Zumbi.

Three hundred years ago, in 1695, on a mountain in the state of Alagoas, one of the most glorious pages of Brazilian history ended with the assassination of the first great leader and true Brazilian hero risen from the oppressed masses, Zumbi of Palmares. Among the episodes of our history, it is for us Afro-Brazilian activists an incontestable fact that the Quilombo of Palmares held and still holds an unparalleled relevance for the entire Brazilian community as a model for the fight for national independence from Portuguese colonialism.

Palmares and other quilombos represented important moments in the development of Brazil's national consciousness, in the affirmation of liberty against institutionalized genocide, and against the brutality and murder that were an inherent part of slavery and colonialism. All those oppressed by the colonial system—enslaved and even free Africans and Afro-Brazilians, landless indigenous people, and mestizos and whites without fortunes—found refuge in this fertile land covered in dense vegetation and crowned with palm trees.[4] The motto of Palmares in its almost century of resistance (1595–1695) was "*Quem vier para amor à liberdade, fica*" (Whoever comes for the love of liberty, stays).

Historical research tells us that Palmares was a democratic and multiracial state. The prolonged repressive fury that fell upon this community of revolutionaries can only be explained by the impossibility of the coexistence in the same territory of two states organized upon viscerally antagonistic bases—the "official" Brazilian colonial state and the Quilombo. Although the rulers of Palmares assumed the title of "king," a reflection of their African roots and their colonial context, historical research shows that these monarchical regimes were democratic rather than dictatorial. Decisions in the capital,

Macaco, were made by the supreme council composed of leaders of the various constituencies of the community. Occupying an area of approximately 27,000 square kilometers, Palmares was a gigantic agglomeration of villages, or *mocambos*. The central supreme council oversaw the authority of each local village council, and both the council members and the local leaders were elected. Important decisions, especially those concerning the economy, security, and internal and external politics, were made in an assembly that included all adult inhabitants, both male and female. Palmares was a multiethnic state of people oppressed by the colonial system, with a nucleus of Africans and Afro-Brazilians at war against slavery.[5]

The Quilombo of Palmares spread throughout the captaincy of Pernambuco and was particularly concentrated in what was then the *comarca*, or district, of Alagoas. Based upon Portuguese reports, the communities of the Quilombo grew to a population of between twenty and thirty thousand inhabitants, a large number for that period.[6] Palmares resisted for almost a century the successive expeditions organized by the captaincy's troops to combat the rebel community. Indeed, historical registers record that up to forty such expeditions were defeated by the Palmarinos. But they were unable to resist the final massive assault by a heavily armed Portuguese colonial army. Although this final onslaught exploded into the massacre of a freedom-seeking population, official Brazilian history has long proclaimed the commander of the massacre, Domingos Jorge Velho, a hero.

In effect, Palmares was an embryonic "country for everyone," in that the means of production, the main factor being the land, was never private property in quilombo communities. The annual commemoration of the death of Zumbi on November 20 as the Dia Nacional da Consciência Negra (the National Day of Black Consciousness), in addition to commemorating the major Afro-Brazilian hero, also represents a contemporary protest against the *latifundio* system, the concentration of large tracts of lands in very few hands, which today as yesterday is the principal generator of social problems in the countryside. Zumbi is the great national hero whom "official" Brazilian history has long kept hidden. He represents for us Afro-Brazilians the symbol of resistance to oppression and injustice.

Besides establishing quilombos, Afro-Brazilians practiced other forms of resistance. During the eighteenth century, for instance, Afro-Brazilian rebellions broke out in the new urban centers. The *Revolta dos Alfaiates* (Revolt of the Tailors) at the end of the century stands out. Also called the *Revolta das Argolinhas* or *Revolta dos Buzios* (Revolt of the Earrings or Revolt of the Cowrie Shells), the event took place in 1798 in the city of Salvador, capital of the state of Bahia. The revolt drew its titles from some of the characteristics of its participants. Men's tailors formed an important component of the rebellion, with many rebels self-identifying by wearing earrings and/or cowrie shell bracelets. This event in which Africans and Afro-Brazilians, allying themselves with other social sectors, played a preponderant role, was the first great urban revolt in Brazil.[7]

White intellectuals, professionals, and businessmen involved in the rebellion called for social justice and an end to Portuguese domination, claiming inspiration from the ideas of the French Revolution. Afro-Brazilians called for the liberation of Brazil from the Portuguese yoke and an ensuing regime of equality for all, in which every individ-ual would be evaluated on his or her own merits without prejudice of class or race. What is most significant for our concerns is that when this revolutionary movement was sup-pressed and its leaders imprisoned and judged, the only participants who received cap-ital punishment were four Afro-Brazilian men, who were hanged in a public square: Lu-cas Dantas, twenty-four; João de Deus, twenty-four; Manuel Faustino, twenty-six; and Luis Gonzaga, thirty-six.[8]

Despite such setbacks, Afro-Brazilian resistance continued. In the period 1808 to 1835, as Brazil ended its colonial phase and entered the period of empire, various urban and rural insurrections took place throughout the country, especially in the state of Bahia, which had a large African and Afro-Brazilian population. Two especially notable examples of resistance occurred during this period. The first was the re-creation of the Yoruba Ogboni society, the Yoruba having become the culturally dominant African eth-nic group in Bahia at this time. In Nigeria, the present-day nation from which most of the Yoruba originated, the Ogboni society held great civil, religious, and political power, overseeing the spiritual aspects of harvests, reproduction, and funerals. Some historians have attributed to the Afro-Brazilian Ogboni society the secret support that sustained rebellious processes of the period.[9] The Ogboni exercised much of its power through the Candomblé, an Afro-Brazilian religious institution of Yoruba origin. Interestingly, in Brazil the Ogboni organization was always directed by a woman.[10]

The second distinctive aspect that marked the revolutionary activity of this period was the presence of Islamicized Yorubas and Hausas in roles of leadership among other rebels. The period culminated with the *Revolta dos Malês* (Revolt of the Malês) in 1835. This most significant of Brazil's urban revolts was based on a sophisticated strategy that included synchronization with revolts of quilombolas in nearby rural areas. The betrayal of the secrecy of the plan led to the massacre of the freedom fighters by government troops and the condemnation to death of the surviving leaders.

The nineteenth century was, in fact, marked by extensive Afro-Brazilian participation in insurrectionary movements and revolts, often in alliance with other sectors of society dissatisfied with imperial rule. Examples of other such movements include the War of the Farrapos in southern Brazil, and the Cabanagem Rebellion in the north in 1835. Other rebellions, such as the Sabinada Rebellion in Bahia in 1837 and the Balaiada Re-bellion in the state of Maranhão in 1838, were also notable for the presence of strong Afro-Brazilian leaders like Santa Eufrasia in the Sabinada, and Manuel Balaio and Prêto Cosme in the Balaiada. All of the rebellions were suppressed.[11]

Between 1860 and 1870 there was a marked increase in the killing of enslavers, as well as a great increase in the flight of enslaved people. These events were influenced by the growing number of quilombos and urban revolts resulting from and reflecting the enslaved population's increasing determination to rebel against their enslavers. They were encouraged in these confrontations by the examples of those who had already fled or been manumitted.

In the state of Ceará in 1881 and 1884, a movement called the *Organização Libertadora Cearense* (Ceará Liberation Organization) arose. Led by Afro-Brazilian Francisco Nasci-mento, "the Dragon of the Sea," its main objective was to impede the now-clandestine maritime slave trade by closing the port of Fortaleza, the capital of the state. The slave trade had been officially outlawed in 1850, and slavery was officially abolished in 1888 by the *Lei Aurea* (Golden Law, because it was signed with a golden pen). A major goal of this "abolition" was actually to curb the increasing tendency among Afro-Brazilians to revolt and to extinguish the flames of what could have been one of the most shattering social revolutions in the Americas. As a result, most Afro-Brazilian militants consider absurd the characterization of the official act as the "abolition of slavery."

During the period of the First Republic, proclaimed in 1889, Afro-Brazilians continued to revolt. In 1910, members of the Brazilian navy led by Afro-Brazilian João Cândido organized the *Revolta da Chibata* (the Revolt of the Lash).[12] The marked presence of Afro-Brazilians among military personnel was due to the elitist and racist character of the navy, whose leadership was from the white upper and middle classes, while Afro-Brazilian enlisted men formed the majority of the crew. The military structure mirrored that of the larger society, so when rebellious Afro-Brazilian sailors took control of naval ships anchored in Rio de Janeiro's Guanabara Bay, they threatened the power structure. Demanding the elimination of disciplinary tortures such as whipping, the sailors also called for better working conditions and salaries. The rebellion was put down and its leaders were imprisoned, then discharged after serving their sentences.

A major accomplishment expressing another aspect of Afro-Brazilian resistance took place during the period 1915–67 with the rise of the Black press. During this time, approximately thirty Afro-Brazilian newspapers began publication. The first newspaper, *O Menelik* (the name of an Ethiopian ruler), began publication in 1915, and the period of Afro-Brazilian publishing culminated in 1963 with the appearance of the *Correio d'Ébano* (The Ebony Courier). The growth of the Black press saw a parallel upsurge in the growth of Afro-Brazilian organizations that engaged in a variety of events and activities.[13]

A second critical event in the first half of the twentieth century, as an indirect result of the proliferation of Afro-Brazilian newspapers, was the organization of the *Frente Negra Brasileira* (FNB; the Black Brazilian Front), one of the strongest institutions in Afro-Brazilian organizational history. Created in São Paulo on September 16, 1931, the FNB came to include about two hundred thousand members, and in 1936, became Brazil's first all-Black political party. The party was short-lived, however, and never managed to involve its candidates in the electoral process because all Brazilian political parties were dissolved with the onset of President Getúlio Vargas's dictatorship (1930–45; 1951–54). Prohibited from engaging in politics, Afro-Brazilians refocused their organizational energies on the creation of sports, dance, and leisure clubs.[14]

Another important mid-twentieth-century development was the creation in 1944 of the *Teatro Experimental do Negro* (TEN; Black Experimental Theater), which created cultural space for Afro-Brazilians in the arts, particularly the theater. Led by Abdias do Nascimento, the TEN also played a decisive role in organizing meetings and congresses for the discussion of Black realities in Brazil. Important events organized by the TEN included the 1945 *Convenção Nacional do Negro Brasileiro* (National Convention of Black Brazilians), the 1949 *Conferencia Nacional do Negro* (National Black Conference), and the 1950 *Primer Congresso do Negro Brasileiro* (First Congress of Black Brazilians). The *Teatro do Povo* (Theater of the People), founded in 1945 by Solano Trinidade, marked another significant event in Afro-Brazilian history. This group was responsible for the development of revolutionary neo-African poetry and for the promotion of Black artists.

The preoccupations of the associations of the 1950–64 period were the denunciation of prejudice based upon skin color, access to education and professional training, and the improvement of living conditions, including demands for the elimination of slum housing, the improvement of existing housing, and the construction of affordable housing. At this phase of the process, a critical analysis of Brazil's social model had not yet been developed.

With the military takeover of the government in 1964 and the beginning of the dictatorship that lasted two decades, the Black movement slumbered and only began to revive in the early 1970s with the advent of a new musical aesthetic movement. This movement was heavily influenced by the Black pride and Black nationalist movements in the United States and the politico-aesthetic slogan, "Black Is Beautiful." Centered in Rio de Janeiro, the main manifestation of the "Black Rio" movement was in soul music dances. Black Rio was a Black youth response to the mechanisms of exclusion imposed upon them by Brazil's social system, responding particularly to the racist notion that only white skin is beautiful, as well as to such social problems as unemployment, ghettoization, and the lack of leisure activities for Afro-Brazilians. Black Rio leaders and events were victims of government repression.

In the mid-1970s politico-cultural institutions devoted to understanding Afro-Brazilian history and culture and promoting cultural events were founded, as were *Centros de Estudos Afro-Brasileiros* (Afro-Brazilian Studies Centers) at some universities. Some of the more important Afro-Brazilian institutions founded at this time in Rio de Janeiro include the *Instituto de Pesquisas das Culturas Negras* (IPCN; Institute for Research on Black Cultures) and the *Gremio Recreativo de Arte Negra e Escola de Samba Quilombo* (Recreational Association for Black Arts and Quilombo Samba School). In Bahia, the *Bloco Carnavalesco Ilê Aiyê* (Ilê Aiyê Carnival Group) and the *Núcleo Cultural Afro-Brasileiro* (Afro-Brazilian Cultural Center) were founded.

The 1970s ended with one of the most important developments for Black resistance in Brazil. Harkening back to the spirit of the quilombos, the movement waged a frontal struggle to occupy greater social and cultural space, as well as to establish connections with Africans and with other segments of the African Diaspora. Toward this end, the *Movimento Negro Unificado Contra a Discriminação Racial* (MNUCDR; the United Black Movement Against Racial Discrimination) was formed in 1978. Its first action was the organization of a public event in São Paulo to protest the murder of a Black man by police torture and the expulsion of Black athletes from a social club.

On November 4, 1978, an assembly of the MNUCDR in Salvador, Bahia, instituted the *Dia Nacional da Consciência Negra* (National Day of Black Consciousness). The decision to commemorate this day is now considered one of the most significant moments in the development of Afro-Brazilian awareness. The drive to commemorate a National Day of Black Consciousness united various institutions and individuals with the intention of creating a unified force to express and realize the aspirations of Afro-Brazilians. The MNUCDR, however, had difficulty maintaining its unifying role and soon simplified its name to Movimento Negro Unificado (MNU; United Black Movement). Despite its partial maintenance of the original name, the MNU has become just one among many institutions, no longer playing the role of organizational coordinator.

The 1980s began with the assumption of new postures by existing entities, and new groups were formed. The *Núcleo Cultural Níger Okàn* (Níger Okàn Cultural Center) was created in Bahia in 1984, as was the *União de Negros pela Igualdade* (UNEGRO; Union of Blacks for Equality). The SOWETO Group, among others, was established in São Paulo, as was *Geledes*, an Afro-Brazilian women's organization. During the 1980s Afro-Brazilian conferences were organized in the north, northeast, south, southeast, and central-west regions of the country, and approximately one thousand Afro-Brazilian cultural and political organizations were established, a figure that does not take into account the large number of Afro-Brazilian religious institutions.

The demonstrations and lobbying carried out by the Black movement during the 1980s led to the creation of *Conselhos Estaduais de Participação da Comunidade Negra* (State Councils for the Participation of the Black Community). These councils, composed of Afro-Brazilian community representatives, were designed to respond to the specific situations existing in each state, and in several states Afro-Brazilians began to occupy important political positions and were elected to public office. They came to occupy positions in left and center-left political parties such as the *Partido dos Trabalhadores* (Workers Party), the *Partido Democrático Trabalhista* (Democratic Workers Party), and the *Partido do Movimento Democrático Brasileiro* (Party of the Brazilian Democratic Movement). As a result of this party involvement, some Afro-Brazilians also acquired positions of influence in the executive branch of government, an example being the establishment of the *Secretaria de Defensa e Promoção do Negro* (SEDEPRON; Secretariat for the Defense and Advancement of Blacks) in the state of Rio de Janeiro, whose first secretary was longtime activist Abdias do Nascimento. The governmental organization failed to achieve its objectives, however, due to a lack of commitment on the part of the head of state.

An additional result of the efforts of Afro-Brazilian institutions during this decade was the creation in 1986 of the Zumbi Memorial, a national historical park established at the site of the Quilombo of Palmares. In 1988, the *Fundação Cultural Palmares* (Palmares Cultural Foundation) was created by the federal government as a further fruit of this effort. Members of the Black movement who helped promote the creation of the foundation to act as a bridge between the government and the Afro-Brazilian community are critical of it for representing government policy rather than serving community interests.

The 1990s began with the first *Encontro Nacional de Entidades Negras* (National Meeting of Black Organizations), one of the most important achievements by the Afro-Brazilian movement in the recent past. At this meeting the *Coordenação Nacional de Entidades Negras* (CONEN; National Coordinating Body of Black Organizations) was created to unite the majority of Afro-Brazilian organizations. A major success in 1991 was the government's invitation of South African President Nelson Mandela to Brazil as a result of the initiative of several Black organizations.

In 1994 two Afro-Brazilian women were elected to the senate, Benedita da Silva and Marina Silva, which was a major step in the direction of promoting Black participation in the political arena. In the same year, Afro-Brazilian organizations initiated on the national level a struggle to ensure the land rights of communities descended from quilombos. They managed to have included in the federal constitution article 68, the Act of Transitory Constitutional Dispositions, which established property titles for the inhabitants of these communities. Although some communities actually received titles, all did not, and there is still an unresolved polemic surrounding the issue.

In 1994, the *Seminário Nacional de Comunidades Rurais* (National Seminar of Rural Communities) was organized along with the *Primer Seminário de Planejamento Estratégico da Coordinação Nacional de Entidades Negras* (First Seminar for Strategic Planning of the National Coordinating Body of Black Organizations), an important moment in the process of Afro-Brazilian resistance. Finally, in 1995, a great moment in the struggle to ensure land tenure rights for the communities descending from quilombos took place, the *Primer Encontro Nacional das Comunidades Negras Rurais* (First National Meeting of Rural Black Communities).[15]

Other significant achievements for 1995 included three events associated with the memory of the Quilombo of Palmares: the commemoration of Three Hundred Years of Immortality for Zumbi of Palmares; the Zumbi of Palmares March Against Racism and for Equality and Life; and the selection of "Zumbi, 300 Years of Courage" as the theme of the Bahian carnival.[16] Two major international events also took place: the *Encontro Continental dos Povos Negros das Américas* (Continental Meeting of Black Peoples of the Americas), and the *Seminário Internacional: Stratégias e Políticas de Combate à Discriminação Racial* (International Seminar on Strategies and Policies to Fight Racial Discrimination), both in São Paulo.

Brief mention must also be made of the role of Afro-Brazilian religions in the process of resistance. As a major focus of cultural production, they have played a fundamental role in the maintenance of our spiritual values in a universe in which Catholicism has always been the "official" religion. The influence of Afro-Brazilian religions on Brazilian culture in general permeates music and dance, literature, visual arts and crafts, culinary arts, fashion, lay medicine, and popular celebrations. Afro-Brazilian religions also play an important role in the contemporary re-Africanization of the consciousness, identity, and cultural production of the Afro-Brazilian population.

In 1889, at the beginning of the republican period, Afro-Brazilian religions began to suffer persecution at the hands of the state's police apparatus, and only within the past two decades have practitioners been legally free to celebrate their religion openly. During this same period, however, they have come under assault by the growing evangelical Protestant movement. Yet Afro-Brazilian religious institutions continue to prosper. There are approximately 3,000 Afro-Brazilian temples in the state of Bahia alone, and many more in São Paulo. Today there are a variety of organizations devoted to the development and defense of Afro-Brazilian religions, the largest of which is the *Instituto da Tradição dos Cultos Afro-Brasileiros* (Institute of the Traditions of Afro-Brazilian Cults).

My motivation for highlighting half a millennium of resistance against their oppressors by Africans and their Afro-Brazilian descendants is an awareness of the official denial of many of these historical facts. It is essential for the present generation of Afro-

Brazilians to understand our ancestors' heroic trajectory for the sake of our sense of identity and our appreciation of our role in the nation. We must engage in constant and intense research into the history of the participation of Africans in the Diaspora, and especially in Brazil, which will inevitably lead to the conclusion that the foundation of Brazilian society was created by Black people.

NOTES

This chapter was translated from Portuguese by Cynthia Baker.

1. See *Os números da cor: boletím estatístico sobre a situação socio-econômica dos grupos de cor no Brasil e em suas regiões* (Rio de Janeiro: Centro de Estudos Afro-Asiáticos, Universidade Cândido Mendes [CEAA], 1990); *Relações raciais no trabalho e no sindicalismo* (São Paulo: Centro de Estudos das Relações de Trabalho e Desigualdades, Textos de Apoio 1, 1994); *Encontro de negros do norte e do nordeste: o negro e a educação* (Recife: Editora Pernambuco, 1988); Lélia Gonzales and Carlos Hasenbalg, *Lugar do negro* (Rio de Janeiro: Editora Marco Zero, 1982), and *Cor da população: síntese de indicadores 1982–1990* (Rio de Janeiro: Instituto Brasileiro de Geografia e Estatística [IBGE], 1995).

2. See E. Bradford Burns, *A History of Brazil* (New York: Columbia University Press, 1993); Julio José Chiavenato, *O negro no Brasil: da senzala à guerra do Paraguai* (São Paulo: Editora Brasiliense, 1980); and Décio Freitas, *Palmares: a guerra dos escravos* (Porto Alegre: Editora Mercado Aberto, 1984).

3. Gilberto Freyre, *Casa grande e senzala* (Rio de Janeiro: Schmidt Editor, 1938). Significantly, this is the Brazilian book most translated into English.

4. Freitas, *Palmares.*

5. Clôvis Moura, *Rebeliões de senzala: quilombos, insurreições, guerrilhas* (São Paulo: Conquista, 1981).

6. There is some controversy over these estimates. See Moura, *Rebeliões de senzala.*

7. *Anais do Arquivo Público do Estado da Bahia* (Salvador: Arquivo Público do Estado da Bahia, 1971).

8. *Anais do Arquivo Público do Estado da Bahia.*

9. Chiavenato, *O negro no Brasil*; Freitas, *Palmares.*

10. *Anais do Arquivo Público do Estado da Bahia.*

11. Chiavenato, *O negro no Brasil.*

12. Edmar Morel, *A revolta da chibata*, 3rd ed. (Rio de Janeiro: Editora Graal, 1979 [1959]).

13. Freitas, *Palmares.*

14. Florestan Fernandes, *A integração do negro na sociedade de clases* (São Paulo: Editora Ática, 1978).

15. The principal remaining quilombo communities are Calunga in the state of Goiás; Rio das Rãs, Bananal, and Barra in Bahia; Turiaçu and Frechal in Maranhão; Oriximina in Pará; Ivoporanduva in São Paulo; and Mucambo in Sergipe. A national survey of the remaining quilombo communities reveals that the state of Maranhão has the largest number of former quilombos, with a total of four hundred sites statewide out of an estimated five thousand sites that may once have existed.

16. Gilberto R. N. Leal, *Carnaval "Valeu Zumbi 300 Anos": tema de carnaval de Salvador* (Salvador, Bahia: Núcleo Cultural Níger Okàn, 1995).

19

Quilombos and Rebellions in Brazil

João José Reis

Uprisings of enslaved people and their subsequent formation and defense of maroon communities, called *quilombos* or *mocambos* in Brazil, were common facts of Brazilian slavery. Whereas quilombos and conspiracies occurred throughout the history of slavery and everywhere in the vast territory of Brazil, actual revolts of enslaved people were concentrated in specific areas and periods. For example, over one hundred quilombos have been identified in the rich mining region of Minas Gerais in the eighteenth century. But there is no record of a revolt in this period, and only three aborted conspiracies in 1711, 1719, and 1756. On the other hand, most quilombos in Minas and elsewhere involved few fugitives, often very few, for the colonial government defined a quilombo as the gathering of five or more fugitive Africans or Afro-Brazilians settled in an unpopulated area. That definition in part accounts for the large number of quilombos in the official records.[1]

Revolts of enslaved people happened with special virulence in the plantation areas of the northeast, particularly in the captaincy and later province of Bahia during the first half of the nineteenth century. Some of these were linked to or benefited from political conflict among the free classes after the independence of Brazil in 1822–23. In the coffee regions to the south, which became prosperous and came to concentrate the majority of the enslaved population in the second half of the nineteenth century, small but numerous local rebellions and conspiracies took place parallel to, or more rarely in combination with, the abolitionist movement in the last two decades of slavery, which ended in 1888.

The colonial era, however, did involve one very big maroon phenomenon, the Quilombo of Palmares, which survived for almost one hundred years. Located in the present-day state of Alagoas in the northeast, the population of Palmares has been estimated at a few thousand, although there is debate about this estimate. The often quoted higher figures—twenty to thirty thousand—are taken from reports written by colonial authorities who sought to impress the Portuguese Crown and justify their failure to destroy the quilombo. Recent historiography has revised these figures down in the light of the plantation demography of the period without, however, offering any precise alternative.[2]

Palmares survived assaults from colonial forces between about 1605 and 1695, when it was finally destroyed and its last celebrated leader, Zumbi, was killed. The question of whether Zumbi was the name of a man or a political title, an issue in Palmares historiography since the nineteenth century, has not been resolved. Décio Freitas's attempt to resolve it in Palmares: *a guerra dos escravos,* based on documents that described the last leader's life under slavery, is inadequate. That particular Zumbi could have been just the final leader to hold the title.[3]

Palmares was actually a confederacy of several mocambos (settlements), well protected by palisades, and toward the 1670s ruled by a "king" who lived in the largest village, Macaco. Its political structure has been loosely defined as "republican" by some scholars, who mistakenly understood the expression *republica* in its modern political meaning, and as monarchical by others. Although lesser leaders and mocambo chiefs were apparently elected on the basis of military expertise, very valuable knowledge in a community under constant military pressure, there are also signs of royal lineage. Zumbi himself was allegedly the nephew of the previous king Ganga Zumba, which suggests matrilineal descent, a characteristic of the Africans from the Central African matrilineal belt, who probably founded Palmares.

The population of the quilombo initially consisted of formerly enslaved Africans from several ethnic groups from the present-day Angola-Congo areas. Some of its military and political organizations have been linked to an Imbangala military society called *kilombo.* This institution was probably reinvented, although not entirely reproduced, by the Palmarinos to respond to the military circumstances that they faced in Brazil. It was only after Palmares was established that the word quilombo became synonymous with mocambo, the term most often used until then to describe maroon settlements, as if Palmares had become symbolic of future maroon communities.[4]

Although Africans predominated in Palmares, indigenous people and Europeans as well as Afro-Brazilians were also present. In addition to sparse news in contemporary sources, the pottery found in archaeological excavations under way in the mountains where Macaco was probably located, the Serra da Barriga near Maceió, capital of the state of Alagoas, indicates a significant presence of indigenous material culture. We must be cautious here, for the pottery has not been dated, and even if it belonged to the Palmares era, it could indicate the adoption by African Palmarinos of indigenous crafts without the physical presence of members of Brazil's indigenous population.[5]

The economy of Palmares was based on slash-and-burn agriculture and on periodic raids of villages, farms, and sugar plantations for supplies and the recruitment of new members, especially women, who were very scarce both on plantations and in quilombos. Surplus produce was exchanged for arms, ammunition, and food in local markets or with farmers and traveling merchants. Little is known of the internal social structure of Palmares, but there seems to have been a social hierarchy based on lineage, military distinction, age, and access to land.

There was a kind of temporary slavery for captives taken in raids, but fugitives who joined the rebels spontaneously were not enslaved. This aspect of the community has produced reactions from both historians and Afro-Brazilian militants, who would prefer to represent the quilombo as an egalitarian society. Much of Brazilian Marxist historiography, which demystified many aspects of Palmares, also created new myths to serve contemporary political projects. Décio Freitas, for example, discovered "popular assemblies" in Palmares, probably inspired by early 1970s Maoist China! The widely popularized, romantic idea of an egalitarian Palmares, depicted as an eternal carnival by Caca Diegues's 1980s feature film, *Quilombo*, is only made possible through a very partial, not to say distorted, reading of the available sources.

The production and appropriation by the state of agricultural surpluses is typical of tributary structures in complex societies, and I believe that Palmares was such a society. It is clear that there was an elite surrounding the main leaders, which exercised social and political power. Control over people more than control over land was probably the basis of social hierarchies, as it was in many African societies contemporary with the great quilombo. He who controlled the people controlled the military machine essential to a community in an almost permanent state of war.

As Palmares grew and expanded, it became clear to the Portuguese government that slavery, and even colonial rule in the northeast, could collapse due to the systematic loss of enslaved people to the quilombo and to the military threat it would represent if consolidated as a state formation. Military expeditions were sent one after the other against the Palmarinos, who tried to reduce the pressure through peace proposals. In 1678, their leader, Ganga Zumba—also a name considered by some to be a royal/religious title rather than a proper name—signed a treaty with the colonial government that would guarantee land and freedom for those born in the quilombo in exchange for loyalty to the Portuguese Crown and a promise to return fugitives from slavery. The treaty, which was not honored by the Portuguese, divided the rebels into two hostile camps. Zumbi's supporters apparently poisoned his uncle, Ganga Zumba, and Zumbi became the supreme ruler.

Although there were new offers of peace, Zumbi made no concessions to the colonial authorities. The Portuguese government continued to send expeditions against Palmares during the 1680s, and in the 1690s decided to employ the services of Paulista *bandeirantes*—groups based in the captaincy of São Paulo and dedicated mainly to the enslavement of indigenous people in the interior—to conquer Palmares. After several attempts, Palmares was finally defeated in a bloody battle in February 1694. Zumbi escaped the massacre with a few Palmarinos but was captured and finally killed on November 20, 1695, a date now designated as the National Day of Black Consciousness by Afro-Brazilian civil rights and cultural movements.[6]

Although the quilombolas (maroons) of Palmares effectively organized production and developed new kinship and power structures, not much is known about these and other aspects of the internal life of the quilombo. Historians tend to generalize to the entire history of Palmares information from sources that depict, sometimes vaguely, specific local conditions and isolated moments of a society formed by several different settlements, which were destroyed and rebuilt many times during almost one hundred years of history. The institution of polyandry, for instance, has been pointed out as typical of the quilombo on the basis of a 1677 document that—if it did not distort reality to "prove" before Christian eyes the "barbarous" behavior of quilombolas—could have referred specifically to recently formed villages where a high male/female ratio was more severe than in older, more demographically stable mocambos.[7]

Palmares was a maroon community of revolutionary stature. Nothing like it would ever be allowed to happen again in Brazil. Although some quilombos were, like Palmares, located in well-protected mountainous country and combined agriculture with raids against relatively distant plantations and villages, most maroon communities were located near farm areas, mining fields, and villages, and were short-lived and quickly dismantled by military force and by *capitães-do-mato* (slave patrollers).[8]

During the first three decades of the nineteenth century, the forests surrounding important colonial and post-colonial cities Vila Rica, Pelotas, São Paulo, Rio de Janeiro, Salvador, and Recife hid numerous maroon communities. These suburban quilombos often functioned as "rest stations" for enslaved urban Afro-Brazilians, who ran away from their enslavers' rule for a few days and later returned. Whatever punishment they received for their *petit marronage* did not prevent new flights to the urban periphery, where they socialized with free(d) Africans and Afro-Brazilians and immersed themselves in African religious practices such as *Calundú* or *Candomblé*, involving drumming and dancing for African deities, divination sessions, and ritual healing.[9]

Other quilombos brought together enslaved people of one specific plantation, as happened in the large Engenho Santana in southern Bahia at the end of the eighteenth century and again between 1824 and 1828. On the latter occasion, more than two hundred people from the Engenho Santana established themselves in a forest near the plantation, where for four years they planted a diversified crop of cassava, coffee, sugarcane, and cotton, in addition to fishing, hunting, and using looms to make cloth from the cotton they grew. In 1828 they were subdued and put back to work on the plantation by troops sent from Salvador, four hundred kilometers away.[10]

The formation of quilombos has been viewed until recently as attempts to recreate Africa in isolated areas of the interior. Brazilian scholars such as Arthur Ramos and Edison Carneiro have called this a *"processo contra-aculturativo"* (counter-acculturative process). It is true that in many early quilombos such as Palmares, Africa would be reinvented based on cultural syncretisms involving several different African ethnic groups interacting with one another as well as with local populations. Quilombos, however, were almost never completely isolated from the surrounding society but maintained both conflictive and cooperative relationships with it. Their members raided and kidnapped, but they also traded and kept a network of friends and often lovers with both free people and people still in bondage. Even whites such as farmers and merchants developed friendly relationships with quilombolas. Recent studies call attention to the intensity of these relationships, which were fundamental to the survival of the quilombos.[11]

Although most quilombos were started peacefully by small groups of maroons, some developed from insurrections. The original maroons who organized Palmares seem to have been involved in a sugar plantation rebellion in the village of Porto Calvo. Two hundred years later in 1838, the parish of Pati do Alferes in the province of Rio de

Janeiro witnessed a movement involving more than one hundred enslaved men and women, the majority from a large coffee plantation, who, after killing the overseer, ran away under the leadership of Manoel Congo, an artisan. As in Palmares, most of the fugitives were Central Africans from the Angola-Congo and Mozambique areas. But a few Brazilian-born Creoles, especially women, also joined the movement. Carrying firearms and other weapons, they tried to organize a quilombo in a nearby mountain range but were soon attacked. Seven people were killed on the spot and twenty-two were arrested. Manoel Congo was sentenced to be hanged. Although most runaways later returned to their owners, some managed to escape.[12]

If there were insurrections that led to the formation of quilombos, there were also quilombos behind some insurrections and conspiracies by enslaved people. Some of the famous nineteenth-century Bahian revolts were initiated by groups of recent runaways. In 1809, fugitives from the city of Salvador, Bahia's capital, and from sugar plantations in the neighboring Recôncavo area formed a quilombo on the banks of a river, from which they attacked and nearly took control of Nazaré, a food-producing village. They were defeated by local militias and troops sent from the capital; many were killed, and eighty-three men and twelve women were arrested. The rebels were Hausa, Ajà-Fon (locally known as Jeje), and Yorubá (locally known as Nagô) from West Africa, some of whom escaped in small groups to a life of raiding in the Recôncavo.

The clearest collaboration between quilombolas and urban rebels in Bahia happened during the rebellion of the Quilombo do Urubú in 1826, which received many new escapees from slavery on the day before Christmas, when the rebels had planned to occupy Salvador. But capitães-do-mato spotted the runaways, who reacted by killing two of them. Militia and regular troops sent by the government surrounded the quilombo and overpowered it. A valiant woman named Zeferina led the battle of mainly Nagô people, a rare case of female leadership of a revolt.[13]

The combination of quilombos and insurrections can be found elsewhere in Brazil. In the village of Viana, Maranhão, in 1867, a group of about two hundred people from the quilombo São Benedito do Céu—named for the Black Saint Benedict—attacked several farms and incited enslaved people to rebel. The movement, which lasted several days, had a clear abolitionist goal. In a letter the rebels forced a plantation *feitor* (overseer) to write and send to the authorities, they proclaimed that enslaved people were tired of waiting for their freedom, which they demanded immediately. This was a rare episode in which quilombolas clearly expressed an ideology of complete freedom for both themselves and those still enslaved. They were not influenced by the predominantly white abolitionist movement, which was then in its early days.[14]

Quilombos have been seen by some scholars as an important escape valve for the tensions of slavery. U.S. historians Donald Ramos, writing about Minas Gerais in the eighteenth century, and Mary Karasch, writing about Rio de Janeiro in the nineteenth, have both suggested that the very large enslaved populations of both regions never revolted in large part because they could instead easily form quilombos in the mountains surrounding the mining region, including its capital Vila Velha, and around the city of Rio, capital of the colony and later the empire of Brazil. This may be an explanation for these two regions, but certainly not for the city of Salvador and the plantation areas in the state of Bahia, which were also surrounded by quilombos, yet witnessed several uprisings and conspiracies.[15]

Bahia was by far the region that experienced the greatest number and the most serious revolts and conspiracies in the nineteenth century. There were more than twenty uprisings and plots in Bahia between 1807 and 1835. Some were local affairs in the sugar plantation area of the Recôncavo, carried on by enslaved people protesting against working or living conditions. Other Africans and Afro-Brazilians made bolder attempts to bring down the system.

Both smaller, short-lived rebellions, and more extensive and sophisticated conspiracies and uprisings in Bahia were frequently, but not always, organized and implemented by enslaved Muslims. The earliest Muslim Africans to come to Bahia were probably Islamicized Mandinga brought from West Africa in small numbers from the sixteenth through the eighteenth centuries. We know little about their religious practices beyond the fact that they gave their name to the famous *bolsas de mandinga* (Mandinga pouches), a kind of Islamic amulet that came to designate various types of good-luck charms, the term mandinga becoming synonymous with "witchcraft" in modern Brazil.[16]

The great wave of African Muslims, however, arrived during the first half of the nineteenth century. They were primarily Hausa and Yorubá, and less frequently Bornu, Nupe, and Fulani, brought to Brazil to work in the mines, in cotton and coffee fields, in cities, and above all on the sugar plantations of Bahia. Bahia practically monopolized the Brazilian slave trade from the Bight of Benin ports, where most Muslims embarked. Historians have estimated that at least 354,100 Africans, including a significant number of Muslims, were imported from the Bight of Benin between 1791 and 1850. Most were captured during political and religious conflicts within what is present-day Nigeria, mainly in the succession of revolts that led to the demise of the Yorubá empire of Òyó, and the Islamic Jihad, or Holy War, initiated by Usuman Dan Fodio in Hausaland that led to Islamic expansion in Yorubáland and the formation of the large Sokoto Caliphate.[17]

In Brazil, enslaved Muslims were initially known by the Hausa term *Musulmi*, and later by the Yorubá term *Imale,* or *Malê,* a reflection of the greater number of Yorubás in the Muslim community in the 1820s and 1830s. This religious culture became interwoven with the political history. There is documented evidence of Muslim participation and leadership in at least two rebellions and two important conspiracies, but Malês were probably present in other African resistance movements of the period as well.

In May 1807, an extensive conspiracy involving people from both the city and plantations, mostly Hausas from Salvador and the surrounding region, was uncovered by the governor, the Count of Ponte, who was famous for his heavy hand in the control of the enslaved. According to results of the inquiry, the plot was very ambitious. Organized under a complex hierarchy of leaders, some of whom were in charge of inciting the different neighborhoods of the city and the sugar plantations, the rebels planned to surround Salvador and seal it off from food provisioning, conquer the besieged city, establish contact with enslaved Muslims in the northern province of Pernambuco, and organize a quilombo in the interior.

In the capital, Catholic churches would be stormed, and altar images would be gathered in public squares and burned. Whites would be massacred, while creoles and mulattos would be spared to be enslaved by the rebels. Command of this operation was in the hands of a Muslim leader, who intended, on being victorious, to assume the titles of both bishop and governor of Bahia, reflecting the merging of religious and secular governments in the Muslim tradition. The Hausa rebels never had a chance to begin to implement their plan.[18]

In February 1814, enslaved fishermen from whaling warehouses on the coast revolted with the help of runaway and free Africans and Afro-Brazilians from Salvador. More than two hundred men set fire to fishing nets and warehouses, attacked a nearby village, and tried to reach the plantation area. They killed more than fifty people before being overpowered by troops sent from the capital. Rebel ranks were overwhelmingly Hausa, but included a few Nupe, Bornu, and Yorubá. Their principal leader, João, was described in documents as a *malomi,* or priest, the term malomi probably being a variation of *malam,* a Hausa word for a Muslim priest. The Muslim role in the episode is confirmed by confiscated papers written in Arabic.

Three months later, the Hausas again plotted a rebellion involving both urban *negros de ganho* (Blacks-for-hire) organized in *cantos* (work gangs) and suburban quilombos.[19] Here again a malomi was mentioned, who was the same man who had led the February rebellion and apparently escaped. Other African *nations* and even indigenous people—a group more commonly found among the forces dedicated to capturing fugitive Africans and Afro-Brazilians—are said to have been invited and to have agreed to join the rebel party. But the scheme was discovered and dismantled by the government.[20]

A more serious episode would take place ten years later on January 25, 1835. During this Malê revolt, some five hundred rebels fought for nearly four hours in the streets of Salvador, more than seventy dying before the defeat. They were mostly enslaved Yorubá and Hausa, as well as free Africans and Afro-Brazilians, who paid dearly for their actions. They received varying punishments that involved as many as one thousand lashes, fifteen years of prison with hard labor, and for four of them the extreme—the death penalty.

The movement was led by Muslim religious leaders, most of them elders, who had promised to protect their followers with Islamic amulets. Some students of this movement have suggested that it was a continuation in Bahia of the Fulani Jihads, or Islamic Holy Wars, in West Africa, an interpretation that overemphasizes the religious dimension of the rebellion to the exclusion of social and historical processes specific to the Bahian context. Jihadic ideology may have inspired some of its leaders, but that does not make the movement itself a Jihad, and much less a continuation of the Fulani Jihad.

The use of and dependence on amulets in Bahia was a form of magical behavior against which the Fulani Jihadists had fought in Africa. Also, there were very few Fulani among the enslaved Bahians, and none involved in this movement. The majority of Muslims in 1835, including the leaders, were Yorubá, who lacked a tradition of Jihads. Unlike the 1807 plot, nothing in the more than two hundred testimonies indicates a particularly violent opposition to Catholicism and its symbols. Plus, during the uprising, the Africans, among whom there were also non-Muslims, did not attack any of the many dozen churches of Salvador.

Although there is no reason to believe that the rebels sought to establish an Islamic state or saw the movement as a Jihad, the uprising did have a Muslim ritual dimension. For instance, it was planned to occur at the end of Ramadan, probably after the Lailat al-Qadr festival of 1250 A.H. (January 25, 1835), a time normally dedicated to peaceful retreat, but not in this case. It may be that the Muslims counted on the help of Allah precisely at a time when they were presumably on the best terms with the Almighty. Participants' testimonies at the trial that followed revealed a network of Muslim practices: the celebration of Muslim holidays, daily prayers, the observance of food taboos, initiation rites, meetings for Koranic reading, the teaching of the Arabic language, and especially the making of Muslim clothes and amulets. There is evidence that a strong process of conversion to Islam was under way at the time of the rebellion, particularly among the numerous enslaved and free Yorubá.[21]

The brutal repression that followed the revolt disrupted and dispersed the Muslim community. Hundreds of free people were deported to Africa, and others went voluntarily to avoid continued discrimination and police violence. Many enslaved rebels were sold to prosperous Southern coffee plantations. Elsewhere in Brazil, and especially in Bahia, Africans found with Arabic writings were considered suspect. Recent literature on slavery in several regions of Brazil indicates that the Malê rebellion had a tremendous impact on enslavers' policies all over the country. News of the episode reached as far as the United States, where the abolitionist newspaper *The Liberator* published a long article in May 1835 praising the heroic behavior of the Muslims during the fight.[22]

After 1835, in Bahia and elsewhere in Brazil, a situation of hostile mistrust of Muslims by the authorities and enslavers persisted for most of the nineteenth century. Yet after the abolition of slavery in 1888, formerly enslaved Muslims could still be found as isolated practitioners of their faith. Some became well known as makers of amulets, reflecting a very unorthodox Muslim way of life. Beyond this fact and the sporadic presence of Islam in the symbolic realm of Afro-Brazilian religions, mostly in fragmented form, Islam was unable to penetrate the national Afro-Brazilian community, which developed a pluralistic worldview combining Catholicism and African ethnic religions.

As in other New World regions, revolts of enslaved people in Brazil, especially in Bahia, have been explained by the degree of concentration of enslaved people in the total population, of Africans in the enslaved population, and of particular ethnic groups within the African population, many revolts being, in part, ethnic rebellions. In the case of Bahia, we must add to these factors the role of Islam as a rebellious religious ideology that, because adopted by two large ethnic groups—the Hausa and the Yorubá—reinforced ethnic allegiances. In 1835, in fact, the war cry of the rebels was ethnically, not religiously, defined: "Long live the *Nagôs!*"

The term Nagô in the Bahian uprising referred to a coalition of different groups of Yorubá-speaking peoples—mainly from Òyó, Egba, Ketu, Ilesbá—who were linguistically and culturally related but who had not been politically unified in Africa. A similar process happened with the so-called *Angolas*, part of a "Bantu proto-nation," according to one scholar, that consisted of several different Bantu-speaking peoples from present-day Angola and surrounding areas.[23] So when I speak of identity and ethnic concentration, I am speaking of African ethnicity as *recreated* in the New World, not African ethnicity as *transferred* to the New World.

In any case, ethnic concentration and ethnic identity alone cannot explain rebelliousness. The Angolas, for example, represented half of the enslaved people in the city of Rio de Janeiro during most of the first half of the nineteenth century. Yet they did not rise up in arms. One has to consider who, that is, which African group, was ethnically concentrated, as well as the surrounding socioeconomic and political circumstances. In Bahia, for instance, most rebellions were waged by enslaved men who had been captured on African battlefields. These rebellions happened parallel to revolts waged by free people, a political situation that facilitated the decision of the enslaved to revolt. That was not the case for enslaved Angolans, who were concentrated in the generally peaceful and well-guarded city of Rio de Janeiro, capital of the Brazilian empire.[24]

Nor was Islam the only African ideology behind the rebelliousness of enslaved people in Bahia and elsewhere in Brazil. Many Bahian revolts do not seem to have been touched at all by Allah's blessings. In the Quilombo do Urubú, for example, when the revolt took place in 1826, there was a Candomblé, or Yorubá Orisha, temple involved. And an extensive conspiracy in the coffee region of Campinas, São Paulo, in 1832, was led by African priests, who distributed protective herbs, or *feitiçarias* (literally "witchcraft," as written in the police records) with the same function as the Muslim amulets—to protect the rebels against their enslavers' and the police's bullets.[25]

At the same time, non-African ideological currents were also adopted as a language of rebellion among enslaved people. Although Afro-Catholicism, which flourished within Afro-Brazilian brotherhoods and sisterhoods throughout Brazil, became primarily a mechanism of peaceful negotiation, it also fueled a few cases of rebelliousness. In 1836 in Salvador, members of Afro-Brazilian brotherhoods joined an uprising against the prohibition of burials inside church buildings in an effort to preserve the sacredness of their burial practices. The 1849 rebels in Queimado in the province of Espírito Santo trusted their enslaved leader's confidence that a local white Catholic priest would obtain their freedom with the good offices of Saint Joseph, whose church they had helped to build. And Saint Anthony seems to have been the accomplice of a large conspiracy in 1847 among enslaved people in the coffee region of the Paraíba River valley in Rio de Janeiro and southern Minas Gerais.[26]

Secular ideologies can also be found in the roots of freedom-seeking movements, such as the influence of the Haitian revolution, referred to as *haitianismo*, the liberal discourse peculiar to a time of decolonization, and after the mid-nineteenth century, to abolitionist ideas. Enslaved Afro-Brazilians were more in tune with these ideologies than were newly arrived Africans, and in Bahia and other northern provinces they joined several revolutionary movements of free people between 1823 and 1840.

The movement known as the Balaiada, which exploded between 1838 and 1841 in the province of Maranhão, mobilized thousands of poor rural people under the leadership of liberal and federalist rebels, who, similar to Brazilian rebels elsewhere in this period, had no abolitionist plans. Enslaved Maranhenses, however, took advantage of the rebellion to carry on their own movement guided by an extraordinary leader, Cosme

Bento das Chagas, a free Afro-Brazilian from the province of Ceará, who sought the destruction of slavery and the establishment of a color-blind republic. Faced with defeat, radical liberals eventually had to accept an uncomfortable alliance with forces that included hundreds of fugitives from slavery. But the very presence of enslaved people in the Balaiada alienated white and *mestiço* supporters. Thus weakened, both enslaved and free rebels became easy prey for the numerous troops sent from Rio de Janeiro to put down the rebellion. Chagas was captured, accused of murder and of leading a rebellion of enslaved people, and hanged.[27]

Federalist movements in the northeast and in Rio Grande do Sul also recruited enslaved Afro-Brazilians to their ranks. But no independent enslaved faction such as that within the Balaiada ever developed. And in Bahia, rebellions of enslaved people and liberal revolts punctuated the two decades after independence without ever converging.[28]

The 1870s and 1880s, especially the last years before abolition in 1888, saw a significant increase in tensions between enslaved people and their enslavers, especially in the prosperous coffee regions and outlying areas of Rio de Janeiro and São Paulo. Recent studies have shown that individual flights from and violent crimes against enslavers and overseers grew in the police statistics of this period, most of them committed by enslaved people imported to the South from the declining sugar areas of the northeast, and therefore foreigners in the coffee region. This unrest became a strong argument for politicians and militants of abolitionist persuasion.

As abolition approached, small uprisings, collective flights, and the formation of quilombos around urban areas multiplied. Between 1885 and 1888, São Paulo alone witnessed more than two dozen uprisings. Most, however, were either small, localized, and hastily improvised, or only potentially serious conspiracies that never materialized. During the same period, on several occasions flames destroyed plantations in the sugar districts of Campos in Rio de Janeiro. The radicalization of the freedom-seeking movement among enslaved people radicalized the sectors of the abolitionist movement that supported them. Some of these pre-abolitionist movements of enslaved people, however, were still immersed in religious, even messianic, ideologies. A syncretic Afro-Catholic religion with spiritist elements, akin to present-day Umbanda, has been detected by recent scholarship in the early 1880's São Paulo coffee region.[29]

Thus, in explaining the rebelliousness of enslaved people in Brazil, we must reject a rigid evolutionary line that runs from religious to secular ideologies. This evolutionary model has been suggested by scholars such as Eugene Genovese who, although pointing to important changes provoked by the Age of Revolutions, in particular the Haitian Revolution, neglected the fact that African-derived or rather African-reconstituted ideologies in the Americas would still play an important role long after the passing of the Age of Revolutions.[30] What is certain is that enslaved people elaborated their rebellious discourse and actions from a number of ideological elements, be they originally African, local, or European.

The recent historiography of resistance by enslaved people in Brazil has gone far beyond a focus on just revolts and quilombos. Day-to-day resistance, crimes, flights, and legal action by enslaved people against their enslavers have been major subjects of analysis.[31] These studies suggest that the majority of enslaved people confronted slavery through methods that, without threatening the system as a whole, helped them avoid being completely objectified by it. At the same time, enslaved people who were involved in the creation of quilombos and the organization of revolts kept the enslaver class and police authorities on the defensive, thus weakening their position of authority in the eyes of enslaved people remaining on plantations. Enslavers often chose to negotiate in order to avoid further rebellion. Of course, the dialectics of power, control, and rebellion cannot be so simply represented; and the best attitude for the historian is to avoid generalizations and interpret each episode of resistance within its specific circumstances.

NOTES

1. On quilombos and rebellions in Minas Gerais, see Carlos Magno Guimarães, *Uma negação da ordem escravista* (São Paulo: Ícone, 1988); Julio Pinto Vallejos, "Slave Control and Slave Resistance in Colonial Minas Gerais, 1700–1750," *Journal of Latin American Studies* 17 (1985): 1–34; Kathleen Higgins, "Masters and Slaves in a Mining Society," *Slavery and Abolition*, no. 11 (1990): 1; and chapters by Carlos Magno Guimarães, Laura de Mello e Souza, Donald Ramos, and Silvia H. Lara in *Liberdade por um fio: história dos quilombos no Brasil*, eds. João José Reis and Flávio dos Santos Gomes (São Paulo: Companhia das Letras, 1996).

2. Stuart B. Schwartz, *Slaves, Peasants, and Rebels* (Urbana: University of Illinois Press, 1992).

3. Décio Freitas, *Palmares: a guerra dos escravos*, 5th ed. (Porto Alegre: Mercado Aberto, 1984).

4. Schwartz, *Slaves, Peasants, and Rebels*, 125–128; see also Kabengele Munanga, "Origem e história do quilombo na África," *Revista da Universidade de São Paulo* 28 (1995–96): 56–63.

5. A report on the excavations can be found in Pedro Paulo de Abreu Funari, "A arqueologia de Palmares—sua contribuição para o conhecimento da história da cultura afro-americana," in Reis and Gomes, *Liberdade por um fio*, 26–51.

6. Four or five books form the basic Palmares library: Ernesto Ennes, *As guerras nos Palmares* (São Paulo: Companhia Editora Nacional, 1938); Edison Carneiro, *O quilombo dos Palmares*, 4th ed. (São Paulo: Companhia Editora Nacional [orig. 1946 in Spanish and 1947 in Portuguese]); Freitas, *Palmares*; and Ivan Alves Filho, *Memorial dos Palmares* (Rio de Janeiro: Xenon, 1988). See Waldir Freitas Oliveira, "Apresentação" in Carneiro's *O quilombo dos Palmares* for a critical appraisal of Palmares bibliography.

7. See Richard Price, "Palmares como poderia ter sido," in Reis and Gomes, *Liberdade por um fio*, 52–59.

8. For methods of repression against quilombos, see Silvia H. Lara, "Palmares, capitães-do-mato e o governo dos escravos," in Reis and Gomes, *Liberdade por um fio*, 81–109.

9. See most chapters in the book edited by Reis and Gomes, *Liberdade por um fio*. See also Mary Karasch, *Slave Life in Rio de Janeiro, 1808–1850* (Princeton: Princeton University Press, 1987), 311–315; Magna Ricci, "Nas fronteiras da independência: um estudo sobre os significados da liberdade em Itú," master's thesis, Universidade de Campinas, 1993, pp. 62–63; and João José Reis, "Quilombos baianos no século XIX," unpublished manuscript, 1995.

10. Stuart B. Schwartz, "Resistance and Accommodation in Eighteenth-Century Brazil," *Hispanic American Historical Review* 57 (1977): 69–81; João José Reis, "Resistência escrava em Ilhéus," *Anais do APEBA (Arquivo Público do Estado da Bahia)* 44 (1979): 285–297.

11. See works referenced in note 1; Carneiro, *O quilombo*; Arthur Ramos, *A aculturação negra no Brasil* (São Paulo: Companhia Editora Nacional, 1942) Reis and Gomes, *Liberdade por um fio*.

12. See João Luiz Pinaud et al., *Insurreição negra e justiça* (Rio de Janeiro: Expressão e Cultura/OAB, 1987), and especially Flávio dos Santos Gomes, *Histórias de quilombolas* (Rio de Janeiro: Arquivo Nacional, 1995), chapter 2, which is the best and most complete study of this revolt.

13. João José Reis, *Slave Rebellion in Brazil: The Muslim Uprising of 1835 in Bahia* (Baltimore: Johns Hopkins University Press, 1993), chap. 3.

14. Mundinha de Araújo, *Insurreição de escravos em Viana, 1867* (São Luís: SIOGE, 1994), 42.

15. Donald Ramos, "O quilombo e o sistema escravista em Minas Gerais do século XVIII," in Reis and Gomes, *Liberdade por um fio*; Karasch, *Slave Life*, 324–325.

16. Laura de Mello e Souza, *O diabo e a terra de Santa Cruz: feitiçaria e religiosidade popular no Brasil colonial* (São Paulo: Companhia das Letras, 1986), 210–212.

17. Reis, *Slave Rebellion*.

18. João José Reis, "Nova luz sobre a conspiração haussá de 1809 na Bahia," unpublished paper, 1995.

19. *Negros de ganho* (Blacks-for-hire) were enslaved people, who hired out their labor as a source of revenue for their owners and of which they received a part.

20. On the May 1814 aborted conspiracy, see Stuart B. Schwartz, "Cantos e quilombos numa conspiração de escravos haussás—Bahia, 1814," in Reis and Gomes, *Liberdade por um fio*, 373–406.

21. Reis, *Slave Rebellion*, esp. part 2. I have discussed the 1835 historiography in "Um estudo sobre as revoltas escravas da Bahia," in *Escravidão e invenção da liberdade*, ed. João José Reis (São Paulo: Brasiliense, 1988), 87–140. See also João José Reis and P. F. de Moraes Farias, "Islam and Slave Resistance in Brazil," *Islam et societé au sud du Sahara* 3 (1989): 41–66. The Jihad interpretation goes back to Raimundo Nina Rodrigues, *Os africanos no Brasil* (São Paulo: Companhia Editora Nacional, 1976), chap. 2, which was written at the turn of the twentieth century. The most recent proponent of this interpretation that I know of is Paul Lovejoy, "Background to Rebellion: The Origins of Muslim Slaves in Bahia," *Slavery and Abolition* 15, no. 2 (1994): 151–180. As a contrast to Lovejoy's position, see Rosemarie Quiring-Zoche, "Glaubenskampf oder machtkampf? Der aufstand der Malé von Bahia nach einer Islamischen quelle," *Sudanic Africa: A Journal of Historical Sources* 6 (1995): 115–124, who mentions that a learned Turkish Muslim interviewed enslaved Bahians in the 1860s. Based on this document, she supports the thesis of a political rather than a religious revolt. An expanded version of this article was published as "Luta religiosa o luta política? O levante dos malês da Bahia segundo uma fonte islâmica," in *Afro-Ásia*, no. 19–20 (1997): 229–238.

22. "Interesting from Bahia," *The Liberator* 5, no. 19 (May 9, 1835): 73.

23. On the "Bantu proto-nation" see Robert Slenes, "'*Malungu Ngoma vem*': África encoberta e descoberta no Brasil," *Revista da Universidade de São Paulo* 12 (1991–92): 48–67.

24. Karasch, *Slave Life*, 152–153, 324–326, and Thomas Holloway, *Policing Rio de Janeiro* (Stanford, Calif.: Stanford University Press, 1993), 114. Karasch maintains that Rio's enslaved population was ethnically dispersed, and I have suggested elsewhere that it was not more dispersed than Bahia's: João José Reis, "Nos achamos em campo a tratar da liberdade," *Revista da Universidade de São Paulo* 28 (1995): 23–27.

25. Suely Robles Reis, *Escravidão negra em São Paulo* (Rio de Janeiro: José Olympio, 1977), 207–232.

26. João José Reis, *A morte é uma festa* (São Paulo: Companhia das Letras, 1991); Afonso Claudio, *Insurreição do Queimado* (Vitória, Espirito Santo: Fundação Ceciliano Abel de Almeida, 1979); Slenes, "'*Malungu Ngoma vem*'," 64–66.

27. Maria Januária Vilela Santos, *A Balaiada e a insurreição de escravos no Maranhão* (São Paulo: Ática, 1983).

28. See Marcus Joaquim de Carvalho, "Hegemony and Rebellion in Pernambuco (Brazil)," (Ph.D. diss, University of Illinois at Champaign-Urbana, 1989); Clovis Moura, *Rebeliões da senzala*, 4th ed. (Porto Alegre: Mercado Alberto, 1988), chap. 3; João José Reis, *Slave Rebellion*, chap. 2; Paulo César Souza, *A Sabinada* (São Paulo: Brasiliense, 1987), chap. 7; Mario Maestri, *O escravo gaúcho* (Porto Alegre: Editora da Universidade, 1993), 76–82; Helga Piccolo, "A questão da escravidão na revolução farroupilha," *Anais da V Reunião da SBPH* (São Paulo: SBPH [Sociedade Brasileira de Pesquisas Históricas], 1986), 225–230.

29. Ronaldo Marcos dos Santos, *Resistência e superação do escravismo na província de São Paulo (1885–1888)* (São Paulo: Paz e Terra, 1987); Lana Lage Gama Lima, *Rebeldia negra e abolicionismo* (Rio de Janeiro: Achamé, 1981); and Maria Helena Machado, *O plano e o pânico* (Rio de Janeiro/São Paulo: Editora da Universidade Federal do Rio de Janeiro/São Paulo, 1994).

30. Eugene Genovese, *From Rebellion to Revolution* (New York: Vintage, 1981).

31. For a small but representative sample of this historiography, see works by Sidney Chalhoub, *Visões da liberdade* (São Paulo: Companhia das Letras, 1990); Silvia H. Lara, *Campos da violência* (São Paulo: Paz e Terra, 1988); Leila Alfranti, *O feitor ausente* (Petrópolis: Vozes, 1988); Kátia Mattoso, *Etre esclave au Brésil* (Paris: Hachette, 1979); Stuart Schwartz, *Sugar Plantations in the Formation of Brazilian Society* (Cambridge: Cambridge University Press, 1985); Karasch, *Slave Life*; Marcus Carvalho, "Quem furta mais e esconde: o roubo de escravos em Pernambuco, 1832–1855," *Estudos Econômicos* 17 (1987): 89–110; Marica Odila S. Dias, *Quotidiano e poder* (São Paulo: Brasiliense, 1986); João José Reis and Eduardo Silva, *Negociação e conflito* (São Paulo: Companhia das Letras, 1989); José Roberto Goes, *O cativeiro imperfeito* (Vitória, Espirito Santo: Linearte, 1993); Keila Grinberg, *Liberata: a lei da ambigüidade* (Rio de Janeiro: Relume Dumará, 1994); Maria Helena Machado, *Crime e escravidão* (São Paulo: Brasiliense, 1987); Robert Slenes, "'*Malungu Ngoma vem*'"; and Eduardo Spiller Pena, "Liberdades em arbítrio," *Padê* 1 (1989): 45–57.

20

The Afro Populations of America's Southern Cone: Organization, Development, and Culture in Argentina, Bolivia, Paraguay, and Uruguay

Romero Jorge Rodríguez

Dominant, well-known cultures do not necessarily have more to say or show than others. They have, however, the power to share with broad publics what they know, think, and wish to project about themselves. The Afro societies of Latin America are disadvantaged as a result of having been politically, economically, and socially subjugated during slavery and colonialism. They have also suffered for centuries from both the disdain of others and from having been commodified—bodily during the slave trade and culturally thereafter—for the benefit of others. These conditions have generated a low standard of living and a resultant lack of access to technology, impeding our communication with other African Diasporan communities and preventing us from sharing our cultural production with broad publics from our own points of view.

A major challenge for South America's Afro communities is to make a qualitative leap into the future, to get up to speed with the revolutionary new world of current technology. Our leaders are setting new goals for our communities, among which is the recuperation and reaffirmation of the unique memories that have been preserved and transmitted in our oral traditions. Our cultural creativity and knowledge offer us invaluable resources for reconstructing our histories on our own terms, in ways relevant to understanding our present and as foundations for developing our futures. Many of our traditions have already contributed a great deal to our nations' multicultural heritages. And we are now beginning to use modern technology to further share our cultural riches with local and global audiences.

Culture and the teaching of culture is the topic of one of the contemporary world's most pressing philosophical debates. Today we Afro-Uruguayans can speak of our own ethnic identity and of issues of diversity and pluralism that have surfaced from centuries of struggle with hegemonic culture and the ignorance and intolerance it spawns. Fewer than twenty years ago it would have been inconceivable in the context of the societies of the Southern Cone of South America to admit that the Uruguayan population, for example, was composed of a rich mosaic of cultures, and that each of these cultures has evolved according to its own historical specificities. And it was not very long ago that we had lengthy and intense debates and were often misunderstood when we defended our Afro-Uruguayan identity at the University of the Republic of Uruguay. In these debates we tried to exchange ideas on diversity and argued that cultural difference was a defining characteristic of Uruguayan society.

Developing this multicultural paradigm of our national identities, and gaining recognition for our cultures and their contributions to the larger society, has required a sustained effort from our Afro communities. It has been difficult for others to accept the fact that we have our own ancestral models that include, for example, a resistance to the very idea of cultural homogeneity. Today it is finally understood, if only by the most enlightened segments of our societies, that our Afro cultures are an inextricable part of the character of the Americas.

African Diasporan arts, traditions, and customs influence all of South America's popular expressions. *Candombe*, a music/dance form of Central African origin, has spread beyond the Afro-Uruguayan community to be adopted as a collective expression of Uruguayan identity. In Argentina, enslaved Africans created the *tango*, the word itself deriving from the Kikongo *tanga*, meaning "party, festival, banquet."[1] Today this African-derived dance, the cultural feature that most characterizes Argentina and by which it is known globally, is studied and taught as an Argentinean invention, usually with its Central African origins unavowed. Brazil's *samba*, also adopted from the cultural expressions of the nation's Afro population, is likewise a national art form symbolizing the society's collective identity, in this case with its African origins acknowledged.

A major goal of and challenge for the Afro movements in these Southern Cone nations is to empower our communities by improving the conditions of our everyday lives, and to ensure that we can affirm, transmit, and promote the appreciation by others of our cultures without demeaning stereotypes. In this process it is imperative that, while charting the common denominator of our ancestral roots, our network of activists, intellectuals, and research partners also understand and appreciate each community's unique characteristics.

Our Afro communities are currently living in a state of permanent dialectic, in large part because of legal changes and transformations in regional economies due to the creation of the *Mercado Común del Sur* (MERCOSUR), the Southern Common Market, uniting Argentina, Brazil, Paraguay, and Uruguay, with Bolivia and Chile as associate members. Our big challenge is to figure out how to organize ourselves regionally, eliminating obstacles imposed by national borders along the lines of MERCOSUR. We are strategizing about how to create individual and collective spaces for our communities within this new political and economic framework.

Our nations, which suffer from skyrocketing inflation, high mortality rates, double-digit unemployment rates, and a rise in illiteracy and preventable diseases such as cholera, have proposed to accelerate the process to accomplish within ten years the goal of regional integration via the free market system with neoliberalism as the economic model. In contrast, the European Union, with its stable economies, single-digit inflation rates, and without the pockets of often racially based abject poverty that we have in our *chabolas, favelas, cantegriles, cayampas, villas miserias,* shanty towns, has undergone a forty-year process to arrive at the Treaty of Maastricht. It is the responsibility of the leaders of our Afro movements to strategize as to how our communities are going to confront the challenges of the new system.

Getting Afro groups to dialogue, exchange ideas, and establish common goals in the context of South American neoliberalization is our current objective. In the face of these regional challenges, we created *la Red de Organizaciones Afro-Americanas* (the Network of Afro-American Organizations) as a mechanism to facilitate communication among the Afro communities of the Americas. Since its establishment at the *Primer Seminario Internacional de Racismo, Discriminación y Xenofobia* (First International Seminar on Racism, Discrimination, and Xenophobia), organized December 8–10, 1994 in Montevideo, Uruguay, by *Organizaciones Mundo Afro,* the network has developed linkages with more than twenty Southern Cone organizations, as well as with other groups throughout the Americas. It has not only familiarized each group with the others' situations, but by identifying areas of common concern, has also led to collaborations in resolving specific problems. For the new millennium, our analysis of the cultural politics in South America must take into account the region's economic integration and must develop collective formulas and proposals for influencing contemporary sociocultural processes that affect us.

Mundo Afro's *Centro de Estudios y Investigaciones Afro* (Afro Study and Research Center), in addition to organizing training courses on the national, regional, and international levels, also helps local communities research and recover their historical legacies. Fruits of this collective enterprise are evident in oral history projects undertaken in Argentina, Bolivia, and Paraguay, as well as Uruguay. I have chosen not to speak of Brazil, where we also work closely with Afro groups, but to speak about Bolivia because of our desire to emphasize the special importance of our work in creating supportive ties with small, less-known communities. Highlighting key issues in the evolution of these four Afro populations, and providing examples of their organizational activities, will offer a context for discussing their current activities of cultural affirmation as distinctive groups that are also claiming credit for their contributions to their nations' collective identities.

ARGENTINA: A "DISAPPEARED" PEOPLE

Beginning in 1538, Buenos Aires was one of the principal ports of entrance for Africans to South America. Buenos Aires also served as a stopover for thousands of Africans en route to the mines and the Casa de la Moneda (the Mint) in Potosí, Bolivia. Many enslaved Africans remained in Argentinean villages and towns along the way. Census figures from the colonial period demonstrate a significant African presence. As early as 1778, one-third of the population of Buenos Aires was of African origin, and according to the 1810 census, in some cities Blacks comprised 60 percent of the population.[2] Thus, the Black population was demographically, hence socially and culturally, significant in Argentina's early history.

Both the total and the relative numbers of Blacks diminished drastically during the second half of the nineteenth century, and by 1887, only 8,005 out of 433,375 people were identified in the census as Black, representing less than 2 percent of the population.[3] George Reid Andrews, author of *The Afro-Argentines of Buenos Aires, 1800–1900*, the most important study of Buenos Aires' Black community, says that the disappearance of Afro-Argentineans has been explained by four arguments:

1. the ending of the slave trade in 1813 radically diminished the influx of Africans;
2. Afro-Argentinean men, who were freed from slavery to be obliged to join the military, constituted an important part of the nation's armed forces, and their disproportionate participation in numerous armed conflicts radically diminished the male population and consequently the Black birth rate;
3. the Afro-Argentinean population suffered from high mortality rates because of their marginal status and resultant poor living conditions, and they were the community most impacted by the 1871 yellow fever outbreak in Buenos Aires;
4. the wave of European immigration instigated by state policies accelerated the process of ethnic mixing, diluting the relative significance of the Afro-Argentinean population in the overall gene pool.[4]

The first three arguments are self-explanatory. But the "European immigration" hypothesis only acquires its full significance if we analyze it in the context of the myth of "white Argentina." This myth was fashioned on the eve of the twentieth century by the "Eighties Generation," whose ideological forerunners were educational reformer Domingo Faustino Sarmiento, who was president of Argentina from 1866 to 1874, and Juan Bautista Alberdi, author of *Bases y puntos de partida para la organización política de la República Argentina* (Bases and Premises for the Political Organization of the Republic of Argentina),[5] which influenced the national constitution of 1853. These profoundly Eurocentric intellectuals were part of the "scientific racism" school of thought that was based on a belief in the innate superiority of the white race.

Sarmiento was the "Father of Argentina's educational system,"[6] whose thinking provided the conceptual basis of the nation's educational enterprise. He argued that because thoughts and ideas were inherited genetically, Argentina could not progress through education alone. According to Sarmiento, what the Argentinean nation desperately needed was, in fact, an infusion of white genes as the only way to rescue itself from the barbarism that was the product of its mixed indigenous, African, and European heritage.[7]

We can confidently affirm today that in the interests of a national development policy based on the premise of a "white Argentina," the Argentinean state consciously engineered the genocide of Afro-Argentineans to hasten their disappearance. Thus, the decline of the Afro-Argentinean population between the 1830s and 1880, a period characterized by many military conflicts, resulted from a policy of extermination based on the four aforementioned points. This provoked "disappearance," resulting from the desire among Argentinean statesmen, historians, and writers of the era to see Argentinean society whitened, also prompted them to claim that indigenous people and Blacks had, in fact, disappeared from the country. They thus wrote Afro-Argentineans out of the national history and present and erased from most of the national consciousness those who continued to exist.[8]

In spite of their decreasing numbers as a result of the campaign to "disappear" them, late nineteenth-century Afro-Argentineans continued to organize to both affirm their existence and to seek to participate in the society. They developed autonomous institutions such as mutual aid societies. The most significant of these, *la Protectora* (The Protector), became an important force in the defense of Afro-Argentineans in the last quarter of the century and was the first group to introduce the concept of seeking to secure equal rights in Argentinean society for the Black population.

After a century of trying to assimilate into Euro-Argentinean society in the belief that that was their only recourse, Afro-Argentineans are now trying to organize the country's diminished and dispersed Black community, improve their economic and social situation, and inform them and others of their historical and cultural contributions to the nation. It is estimated that about fourteen thousand Afro-Argentineans live in towns such as Santa Fe, Salta, and Corrientes, as well as in certain neighborhoods of Buenos Aires.[9]

The *Casa de la Cultura Indo-Afro-Americana* (House of Indo-Afro-American Culture) in Santa Fe is currently the most dynamic and productive of the groups working to recuperate and promulgate Afro-Argentinean culture. They have organized regional and international conferences on Afro-American, especially Afro-Argentinean, realities, published the results of their research on Afro-Argentinean culture, and promoted cultural events to create public awareness of Afro-Argentinean contributions to the nation.[10]

BOLIVIA: A TRADITION REVIVED

A series of deep, wide valleys spanning a broad area east of the Altiplano marks the Nor (north) and Sur (south) Yunga provinces in the Department of La Paz, the passageway from Bolivia's highlands to the tropics, where tobacco, coffee, cacao, sugarcane, and coca leaves are cultivated in the temperate climate.[11] During the colonial period the Spaniards, finding the workforce composed of the conquered indigenous people insufficient to adequately exploit the region's mineral wealth, began to use enslaved Africans in the mines and mint of Potosí. In 1807 there were 458 Africans in Potosí.[12]

Beginning in 1535, at least 1,536 people from the Congo-Angola area and Mozambique were sent to a region over 4,000 meters above sea level, where they suffered a very high mortality rate. Because the Africans could not adapt to the altitude and cold, the Spanish colonists began to use them in agricultural work in the tropical valleys, supplying miners with coca and other agricultural products. In 1883 the enslaved Black population consisted of more than six thousand people.[13] Not enumerated in the 1996 National Census, Afro-Bolivians did their own count and concluded that currently an estimated ten thousand Afro-Bolivians are concentrated mostly in the Yungas provinces in rural towns and villages such as Coroico, Chicaloma, Coripata, Irupana, Chirca, Mururata, and Carmen Pampa.[14]

Especially dynamic Afro-Bolivian communities are found in the town of Coroico, the provincial capital; in the village of Chicaloma, which has about 1,200 residents divided roughly into two hundred families; and in the village of Tocaña. Migrants from the Yungas also live in the nation's capital, La Paz. The majority of the rural Yungan population works in coca production for legal pharmaceutical purposes, the only agricultural product for which there is a market that provides an adequate income. Other produce, such as citrus fruits, is abundant and of low market value. The communities' needs are numerous, including potable water, sanitation facilities, hospitals, roads, and schools.

Although slavery unified Africans from diverse ethnic origins into a community of common interest and laid the groundwork for an Afro-Bolivian culture, the small African population also adjusted to its human environment by adopting much of the technological and economic organization and cultural norms, such as dress, of the indigenous Aymara people. Their work ethic is communitarian, which was already familiar to the Africans, and their religion is Catholic.

The Yungan communities' most important religious holiday is el Día de la Santísima Trinidad o del Señor Jesús del Gran Poder (the Day of the Most Blessed Trinity or the Day of Lord Jesus of Great Power). Afro-Bolivians observe the Catholic event by dancing the *saya,* the music and dance of their African ancestors that is the most obvious surviving aspect of their distinctive cultural heritage. Accompaniment is played on *bombos,* drums made of treated wood with sheepskin heads, and other percussion instruments. Saya lyrics were traditionally used for the preservation and transmission of oral history and now have been adapted to convey messages having to do with current Afro-Bolivian consciousness-raising efforts and assertions of their place in the nation.

Only in 1952 could the Afro-Bolivian population begin to make organizational advances as a result of Bolivia's revolution and agrarian reform, which abolished the system of virtual enslavement to which Afro-Bolivians and other peasants had been subjected under the feudal hacienda regime. Properties of large landowners were redistributed to the people who had worked them, including the Afro-Bolivians concentrated in the Yungas. As a result, the Yungas region has become an important Afro-Bolivian cultural space.

The reclaiming of Afro-Bolivian culture has been manifest in and spurred by the creation of the Movimiento Cultural (Saya) Afro-Boliviano (Afro-Bolivian [Saya] Cultural Movement), which was developed as Afro-Bolivians joined the process of consciousness-raising undertaken by other African Diasporan communities concerning their Afro identity and role in the nation. The organization has promoted increased Afro-focused cultural activity among community groups in Tocaña, Mururata, and Coroico. Youth groups have also been created in Chicaloma and in other communities such as Laza, Chulumani, Dorado Chico, and Caranaguí. In addition to the revitalization of the saya, which had been dying as a result of assimilationist pressures, and as a further manifestation of their renewed sense of their distinctive cultural identity, Afro-Bolivians have also begun to research other music and dance expressions of African origin, such as the dance called the *zemba* or *cueca negra,* of Central African origin, and the *mauchi,* a funeral song.

A striking Afro-Bolivian phenomenon is the existence of *el rey negro,* the Black king of the town of Mururata in Nor Yunga. Respected and beloved elder Bonifacio Pinedo was recognized as king by members of his community in the 1940s. Every Easter he dressed in a cape and crown and was carried around the town in a palanquin accompanied by a cortege of people dancing the zemba. Although Pinedo was an important lay leader in the church, the Catholic hierarchy disapproved of the community's honoring him as royalty.

Reviving this tradition after a hiatus of three decades after Pinedo's death in 1962, the people of Mururata crowned Julio Pinedo, Bonifacio's great-grandson, king on Easter in 1992. While this title has no political relevance, it does contribute to the vindication of Afro-Bolivian historical memory. Some people say that Pinedo's title was inherited through an African royal lineage. One might also speculate that this tradition could be reminiscent of the coronations of the kings of the Congo and Angola practiced in other Afro–South American communities.[15]

In response to the initiative of Afro-Bolivian community leaders who met with the vice president of the nation, Bolivia's under-secretariat of ethnic relations helped them to create a community oral history project that involved constituting an oral history and visual archive, implementing a pilot project to develop a community research methodology, and developing social activities to strengthen community organizations. Workshops have been set up to teach leadership skills and train community oral history researchers. Thus, an Afro-Bolivian agenda is taking shape as Afro-Yungans take steps to both learn about their own cultural heritage and increase public awareness of it throughout Bolivian society by participating visibly and successfully in cultural festivities and contests and by recording and broadcasting their message-conveying music.

PARAGUAY: RESISTANCE AND CULTURE AMONG THE CAMBÁ CUÁ

Africans arrived in landlocked Paraguay from the ports of Buenos Aires and Montevideo and as a result of the very vigorous contraband trade from Brazil.[16] In 1782 the free and enslaved Afro-Paraguayan population numbered about 10,000 in a population of 89,178, so more than 10 percent of the total. In 1846 they were 17,212 of 232,862. This number was based on the numbers of Afro-Paraguayans in the major areas of concentration in the towns of Areguá, Tabapy, and Emboscada, and in the Barrio de San Blas de Asunción, a neighborhood in Paraguay's capital, where they worked mainly in domestic service. The importation of Africans was reduced, although the contraband trade continued, after the end of the colonial regime in 1811. Slavery, however, did not officially end until December 2, 1869, making Paraguay the last country in hispanophone South America to abolish the institution. Afro-Paraguayan numbers declined precipitously as a result of their over-representation in the front lines of the military in mid-century warfare, which by the end of the War of the Triple Alliance in 1870 had decimated half of Paraguay's population.[17]

The enslaved Afro-Paraguayan population, characterized in euphemistic irony as *amparado*, "sheltered," worked especially in agriculture and cattle-raising for Catholic religious orders, mainly in Areguá, established in 1538 by the Order of Our Lady of Mercy, and Tabapy, southwest of Asunción, established in 1653 by the Dominicans. Some of these "sheltered" Afro-Paraguayans were relocated as free people to settlements created by the government to serve as military barriers to prevent indigenous people from attacking the "Spanish towns" of the colonial invaders. San Augustín de la Emboscada (Saint Augustine of the Ambush), north of Asunción near the Paraguay River, was established in 1740, and the inhabitants were forbidden to travel away from the settlement. Tevegó was established on the Paraguay River with Afro-Paraguayans sent from Tabapy in 1813 to serve as a barrier to attacks by the Mbayá people. Destroyed by the Mbayá in 1823 and reestablished by the government with more Afro-Paraguayans in 1848, Tevegó disappeared in 1870 as a result of the War of the Triple Alliance.[18]

Largely as a result of their depopulation due to warfare, most of the original Afro-Paraguayans faded, so to speak, into the larger community of the European and numerically dominant indigenous Guaraní populations. Some of their descendants remain visible in Tabapy, now known as Roque González, and especially in Emboscada, particularly in the area of Minas, where African somatic characteristics are still quite noticeable.[19] The current Afro-Paraguayan population is, in fact, composed primarily of descendants of Afro-Uruguayans who arrived at the beginning of the nineteenth century and settled as a distinct population. Called Cambá Cuá, Guaraní for "well or place of the Blacks," they adopted much Guaraní culture, such as the language, Paraguay being a bilingual Guaraní/Spanish–speaking republic, while also maintaining some of their African-derived traditions.

In 1820 General José Gervasio Artigas, Uruguay's major national hero for his leadership in the fight for independence from Spain, arrived in Paraguay as a political exile after suffering defeat in Uruguay. Artigas was accompanied by 175 to 200 Afro-Uruguayan soldiers and his personal guards, the Lancer Squadron. Some of the troops were accompanied by their families. With Artigas was Joaquín Lenzina, known as Ansina, his Afro-Uruguayan confidant and strategist, who has become a hero for the Afro-Uruguayan population. There is a statue of Ansina in Montevideo, and several Afro-Uruguayan organizations bear his name.

Paraguayan dictator José Gaspar Rodríguez de Francia granted Artigas and his troops land that has become the communities of Lomas Campamento, on which I focus here, and nearby Laurelty. The Afro-Uruguayan troops took with them to Paraguay a statue of Saint Balthazar, the African king among the Magi (the Three Wise Men who presented gifts at the birth of Jesus), who, as elsewhere in South America, was the patron of the Black community. They honored Saint Balthazar on January 6, *el Dia de los Reyes* (the Day of the Kings), with a candombe procession of polyrhythmic drumbeats and Central African-style dancing.

Saint Balthazar is still venerated annually with candombe by the descendants of the original Cambá Cuá in the chapel of Lomas Campamento, as the community's major public event and the principal expression of their identity. On that occasion the Grupo Tradicional de Danza Cambá Cuá (Traditional Cambá Cuá Dance Group) plays and dances candombe in honor of the African king in his role as Afro-South American saint. The Cambá Cuá's preservation of their Afro-Uruguayan culture as expressed in the drum rhythms and dances of candombe is the most obvious evidence of their cultural resistance and ethnic self-representation.

Presently a community of three hundred families, the Cambá Cuá of Lomas Campamento, now in the municipality of Fernando de la Mora in Paraguay's capital, Asunción, are in a precarious socioeconomic situation due largely to the loss of most of the hundred hectares of land given to their ancestors. For the past decades their principal goal has been to recuperate some of this land. A number of African Diasporan communities are similarly confronting the threat of losing their ancestral lands. Examples include efforts to gain legal titles to land inhabited by quilombo-descended communities in Brazil and in the majority Afro-Colombian state of Chocó in Colombia, as well as the struggle to keep control of the prime coastal land settled by their ancestors and now coveted by the multinational tourist industry by the Garifuna people of Honduras in Central America.

Whereas the lands settled by the Cambá Cuá were rural and used for agriculture and cattle-raising in 1820, Lomas Campamento has now become a part of suburban Asunción as a result of urban growth. The land is on the Avenida Mariscal López, the highway linking Asunción with the important town of San Lorenzo, and its value has risen steeply because of its prime location. The Cambá Cuá community is now surrounded by apartment buildings, and a recently built shopping center has further encroached upon what had been their ancestral land.

The government's intention to expropriate Cambá Cuá lands began years ago. In the 1940s the government laid plans to use part of the Cambá Cuá lands for a university, which culminated in the 1950s with the construction of the Agro-Meteorological University. In the 1960s, government soldiers on horseback invaded the community. Their violent attack was met with active resistance, and several community leaders had to go into hiding to avoid military persecution. There was also a government scheme, which the Cambá Cuá successfully resisted, to relocate the community three hundred kilometers away in Gaguazón.

The Cambá Cuá contend that the land belongs to them because Paraguay's head of state gave it to Artigas to distribute among his soldiers almost two centuries ago. Their elders' oral histories offered useful starting points for research into official documents listing names of the ancestors of current residents of Lomas Campamento, which provided a way of establishing the legitimacy of their land claims. During the community's struggle to retain and reclaim the land, the Network of Afro-American Organizations organized a support campaign and joined the Cambá Cuá in public demonstrations. The municipal council of Fernando de la Mora eventually recognized the validity of Cambá Cuá claims and gave them title to 10 hectares of land. Now the community has plans to develop improved housing and other social and cultural facilities to help improve their standard of living and maintain their distinctive identity.

Cambá Cuá leaders have been a major presence in the Southern Cone branch of the Network of Afro-American Organizations, playing an important role in efforts to create ties between Afro communities. For the Cambá Cuá, the Network has also been essential in their success in creating contacts outside of Paraguay, which have helped their efforts at land reclamation, economic development, and cultural affirmation at home.

URUGUAY: AFRICAN TRADITIONS TRANSFORMED

We cannot know the real numbers of Africans brought into Uruguay because, in addition to those who arrived legally via the port of Montevideo, which in 1791 the Spanish Crown declared the only port of entry for enslaved Africans into Spanish America, as many or more arrived as contraband.[20] Although most were domestic servants in Montevideo or worked in the meat-processing industry, they were also craftspeople, fishermen, water carriers, and pastry sellers. The very significant colonial-era Afro-Uruguayan population was estimated at 36 percent of the total population in 1810, and decreased to about 25 percent in 1819 and 15 percent in 1829.[21] Their numbers diminished significantly during the nineteenth century because Afro-Uruguayan men were freed from slavery to be obliged to serve in the military during the many wars among the Southern Cone countries, as well as because of massive late nineteenth-century European migration.

The national census does not currently include a breakdown by ethnicity, but in 1995, Afro-Uruguayan community leaders initiated negotiations with the Instituto Nacional de Estadísticas y Censos (National Institute of Statistics and the Census) to urge the inclusion of ethnic categories so that there would be a better understanding of the ethnic and cultural identity of the Uruguayan people. According to statistics compiled by the Dirección General de la Extensión Universitaria (University Extension Office), Afro-Uruguayans constitute between 4 and 6 percent of the population, thus about 180,000 people. Seventy percent of this community lives in the capital, Montevideo, with the other 30 percent distributed throughout the rest of the country but concentrated especially in the north and northeast near the Brazilian border in the Departments of Artigas, Rivera, Cerro Largo, Treinta y Tres, and Rocha. There is also a significant concentration in the Department of Durazno and the central zone.[22]

Our perspective as a community is based on our social, economic, and educational experience as the nation's most underserved constituency. Seventy-five percent of our women work as maids or have other low-paying jobs in factories or fish processing plants. Men have low-paying jobs as doormen, janitors, street cleaners, and the like, or as low-level military personnel. Their resultant precarious economic conditions lead to family situations in which children have a high dropout rate from school, with the attendant negative implications. Fewer than two hundred Afro-Uruguayans have a college education, and there is no history of business ownership or labor leadership and no parliamentary representation.[23]

In nineteenth-century Montevideo, Africans of similar ethnic and regional origins organized themselves into *nations*, which gathered regularly to recreate ancestral sociocultural behaviors in festivities called candombes.[24] Providing mutual aid and protection, the nations also managed to maintain some African ritual behavior and music and dance forms.[25] Although they had few resources, each nation managed to acquire a *sitio*, a meeting place in which to locate the *sala* (hall) where they held their meetings and festivities. The first dances held in these salas were referred to by the Africans as *tambor y tango*.[26]

In 1839, in response to complaints from whites concerning the noise and disturbances caused by these Afro-Uruguayan festivities, candombes were prohibited by police decree from taking place within the walls of the city and had to be relocated outside. Although slavery was officially abolished in 1842, Africans and Afro-Uruguayans continued to suffer the repression of their candombes and other forms of cultural policing, as well as being generally denigrated as a community under the ideological pressure of the white elite.

Although the African nations suffered from social control imposed by the government, which determined their organizational structures and rules, it was also through these institutions that Afro-Uruguayans maintained and recreated elements of African culture. The African nations began dying out in the middle of the nineteenth century with the death of the last generation born in Africa. Out of these cultural expressions, generations born in Uruguay developed new organizational and aesthetic forms in keeping with the social transformations of the times.[27] Candombe rhythms and dance styles were perpetuated in the *comparsas*, the processional street dance groups of the modern carnival.

The only attempt to construct an Afro-Uruguayan ethnic politics was the Partido Autóctono Negro (PAN; Autochthonous Black Party), founded in Montevideo on May 9, 1936, and recognized by the electoral college on January 5, 1937. PAN cells were also created in Rivera on the Brazilian border in the north, and in Melo, capital of the Department of Cerro Largo, in the center of the country. PAN's agenda centered on three issues: unifying the interests of Uruguay's most disenfranchised communities, fighting employment discrimination against Blacks, and promoting electoral action in the pursuit of Afro-Uruguayan parliamentary representation.[28]

Although stressing racial identification, the party's goals were integrationist. In spite of its efforts to project its message to a broad community, its appeal was limited. The party had no middle-class vanguard, since there was no Black middle class. It was created by four intellectuals who, in spite of their efforts to share their ideas with a broad public, remained a closed circle: Elemo Cabral (1887–1969), brothers Ventura Barrios (1896–1952) and Pilar Barrios (1899–1974), and lawyer Salvador Betervide (1903–1936). The vanguard's polemics were articulated in the *Revista Nuestra Raza* (Our Race Magazine), published from 1917–48. Two other Afro-Uruguayan publications also stand out—the newspapers *La Conservación* (The Preservation), 1871–1915, and now *Revista Mundo Afro* (Mundo Afro Review), 1987–present.

Over the years various organizations have formed the nucleus of Afro-Uruguayan community life, such as the Centro Cultural de Ansina de Melo-Cerro Largo, the Club Ansina de Castillo-Rocha, the Asociación Cultural y Social Uruguaya Negra (ACSUN), the Fundación Ansina Afro Uruguaya (FUNDAFRO), the Asociación de Arte y Cultura Afro Uruguaya (ADACAU), the Centro de Estudios por la Paz y la Integración, the Centro Cultural Afrouruguayo, and Organizaciones Mundo Afro. The oldest groups are the Centro Uruguayo del Departamento de Melo and the Asociación Cultural y Social Uruguaya Negra in Montevideo, both of which focus on culture and the arts and have had a significant impact in these areas.

As with the mid-nineteenth-century outlawing of the candombes of the African nations because of white objections, in recent decades Afro-Uruguayans once again fell victim to government policies whose goal was the destruction of the Black community. This most recent dramatic blow to the Afro-Uruguayan community was the military dictatorship's decimation of Montevideo's Black neighborhoods. In 1976 the government ordered the removal of all Afro-Uruguayans from the center of the city. Afro-Uruguayans were forced out of their homes and relocated in makeshift living quarters in abandoned warehouses and factories on the outskirts of town. The pretext was that the buildings in which they lived were in poor condition and had to be condemned. The real motive was to destroy the concentration of Afro-Uruguayan families and the perpetuation and spread of Afro-Uruguayan culture.

The three most important traditional Afro-Uruguayan neighborhoods before the expulsion were Gaboto, Ansina, and Cuareim, named after major streets in each area and all within walking distance of one another. Gaboto was located in the Cordón Norte zone, and Ansina and Cuareim were in the Sur and Palermo zones near downtown Montevideo. Ansina, a street a block long named after the Afro-Uruguayan military hero, ran in front of a housing complex known as Barrio Reus al Sur. On Cuareim Street (Zelmar Michelini Street today) there was one large building known as Mediomundo. Gaboto had the same sort of buildings, known as *conventillos*, large tenement-like dwellings in which whole families lived in one or two rooms and shared sanitary facilities with their neighbors. The painful and violent process of this mass eviction suffered by the great majority of the Afro-Uruguayan population meant not only physical dispersion to worse housing and the destruction of a sense of organic community, but also cultural destruction, since the nuclei of creation were shattered.

The inhabitants of the Gaboto conventillo had been evicted in 1965, and the building was demolished and a police station was built on the vacated property. Although part of the destruction of the Afro-Uruguayan community, this phase had taken the form of a peaceful eviction in the name of "urban renewal" under a democratic regime. The 1978 evictions from Reus al Sur and Mediomundo were done under a dictatorship with government-sanctioned violence that the community tried, unsuccessfully, to resist. The residents were brutally evacuated by military force for sociopolitical and commercial objectives. The lower-class, mainly Afro-Uruguayan residents were considered an obstruction to the upscale development project under way for Montevideo's nearby riverfront. Yet today, the land where both conventillos stood remains unused. Reus al Sur, in which skeletons of the old buildings remain, has been turned into a vacant lot into which people throw garbage, and Mediomundo is an abandoned shell. Both remain as vivid reminders and symbols to the Afro-Uruguayan community of their former lifestyle and culture that were deliberately destroyed by the state.

The evicted residents were not resettled together, which made it impossible for them to reconstitute their communities and their culture. Most people from Mediomundo were taken to the Cerro Norte area, where levels of delinquency were already very high. The rest were taken elsewhere on the city's outskirts. The residents of Reus al Sur were taken to the abandoned, unrenovated La Aurora blanket factory in the Aguada neighborhood, in which they lived in deplorably overcrowded conditions. Some of these families were then relocated to housing facing the Corralón Municipal (the municipal garbage dump). Those left behind in the blanket factory until very recently were finally relocated to the Borro neighborhood, also plagued by problems of delinquency. Over the years, a very few families have been able to move back to the historically Afro-Uruguayan district of Palermo in the center of town.

As a result of these traumas, the mortality rate of elderly community members, unable to adjust to these brutal changes, was tremendous. The loss of these elders was in itself a blow to the culture. Another very obvious index of destruction has been in the loss of community values. One indication of this cultural loss has been in the realm of candombe, which is not surprising since it is a core cultural complex. Previously each neighborhood had its own recognizable styles. With the destruction of the neighborhoods and the dispersal of the people, candombe has lost its distinctive styles and become increasingly homogenized.

The creation of Organizaciones Mundo Afro was a response to this situation. The largest Afro-Uruguayan institution, Mundo Afro is a national federation of institutions involving about four thousand people. Its priorities are promoting the active participation of Afro-Uruguayans in all issues affecting our communities' living conditions; combating all forms of discrimination and racism; improving our quality of life by raising our level of self-esteem, an integral element for advancing our capacity as human beings; raising our economic indices by making more effective our social integration via concrete, viable, and effective development projects; linking our efforts in solidarity with the world's Black communities, especially those in greatest need; promoting cooperation and exchange with other Afro communities; and recuperating and promoting knowledge of our historical memory. Organizaciones Mundo Afro engages in research, publishes a newspaper and books, organizes exhibits and conferences, and teaches classes in Afro-Uruguayan culture, among other activities. Our most recent event was the March 2000 Instituto Superior de Formación Afro (Advanced Afro Training Institute), a one-week event, inaugurated by the president of the republic, involving more than 140 leaders of North, Central, and South American Caribbean Afro organizations.

Mundo Afro has also been concerned with the reconstitution of the Afro-Uruguayan community dispersed by the government. We are currently involved, with the assistance of the municipal government, in the building of thirty-six apartments for Afro-Uruguyan female single heads of household in downtown Montevideo, symbolically only one block from Mediomundo, and facing the riverfront from which members of these women's own families had been violently evicted. There was opposition to this project, again from the white middle class as in the nineteenth century, to the presence of these Afro-Uruguayans in their neighborhoods. But we overcame the opposition and the project is progressing.

ORGANIZING AFRO COMMUNITIES: LA RED DE ORGANIZACIONES AFRO-AMERICANAS (THE NETWORK OF AFRO-AMERICAN ORGANIZATIONS)

The experience of racial discrimination and the awareness of the social and cultural conditions of our communities in Uruguay inspired Organizaciones Mundo Afro to create a mechanism, the Network of Afro-American Organizations, within which to collaborate with other similar communities in reflecting on and creating proposals for the development of Afro-American populations. In preparation for the 1994 conference at which the Network was created, Mundo Afro held a conference titled "The Afro-American Development Program," which served as a starting point for implementing communications and training networks and building alliances based on our communities' shared interests. This meeting generated strategies for regional and continental exchange and development among grassroots organizations. A fundamental activity of the international Black movement in the past twenty years has been getting to know one another and developing a dialogue. Since creating the network, Mundo Afro has held innumerable follow-up meetings involving a variety of associated organizations. The resulting relationships have allowed us to strategize and collaborate on regional, continental, and intercontinental programs.

Given the difficulties our communities share, we knew that creating an instrument to articulate our activities regionally and internationally would not be easy. Yet since the formation of the network, we have been maintaining contact and sharing knowledge among our communities on a regular basis. Within the first two years of the Network's existence, we were able to develop a general understanding of the realities and predicaments of our diverse communities and to meet and act in solidarity with members of communities of which we had previously only heard.

In learning about the other societies in the Southern Cone on which I have focused here, we realized that a very important common denominator in our histories, which contributed to the objective conditions in which our communities live today, and which severely impacted our roles in our nations, is that we have all been systematically victimized by our national governments, even beyond the general violence done to all people of African descent in the Americas by the institutions of slavery and post-slavery racial discrimination. Prior to the 1950s revolution and agrarian reform, Afro-Bolivians, along with other Bolivian peasants, were held in a situation of virtual servitude as agricultural peons on feudal haciendas controlled by the national oligarchy. Afro-Bolivians had no property, no rights, and no recourse.

Whereas the exploitation of the Afro-Bolivian population was also common to the general Bolivian peasant population, although aggravated by racism, in the other three countries the Afro populations were specifically victimized. Afro-Argentineans, from a very significant proportion of the population in the early nineteenth century, were "disappeared," reduced to virtual physical and cognitive invisibility as a result of the government's deliberate genocidal "whitening" project. The very existence of Afro-Argentineans is now usually denied, although their cultural contributions continue, mostly without acknowledgement, to characterize the nation.

Afro-Uruguayans during slavery suffered systematic physical violence as a result of the conscription of men, like other Black men in the Southern Cone, as military cannon fodder. They also suffered cultural violence in the nineteenth century, as the efforts of Africans to preserve their traditions in their candombes were outlawed as part of a larger effort to destroy manifestations of African culture in the Americas. The violence to which Afro-Uruguayans were subjected in recent years, like that suffered by the Cambá Cuá of Paraguay since the 1950s, represented a new wave of government aggression targeting Afro communities. The Cambá Cuá were deprived of most of their ancestral lands and were threatened with being relocated a great distance from their homes as their lands became valuable to government and elite interests.

We Afro-Uruguayans were forcibly evicted from our homes, and our communities were destroyed, also because of government interest in our potentially valuable, but still undeveloped, land. The desire of the Paraguayan and Uruguayan governments to move their Afro populations away from central urban zones to more peripheral areas might also be interpreted as a kind of "disappearing" of them from sight and hence from the national consciousness, as well as an attempted destruction of the cultural integrity that is the basis of their identities and, ironically, of our contributions to our respective national cultures. Hence, both communities have been victims of land loss, relocation, and cultural destruction as the result of state and elite interests.

Thus, meeting and learning about one another and about our historical and more recent circumstances has made us all aware of the kinds of harsh common realities to which our communities have been subjected, of which we are products, and which are part of the consciousnesses of our leaders and community members. We are seeking, through our efforts at communication and solidarity, to use the strengths acquired while surviving these experiences of oppression and exploitation to mobilize our collective resolve to forge a more positive future. Given our knowledge of this history, we are especially able to appreciate the triumphs of members of the Network in overcoming tremendous obstacles.

The Afro-Bolivian movement's interventions vis-à-vis state organizations have helped spread awareness of the cultural riches of that community, including creating research initiatives and study programs, organizing artistic groups, and creating a space for recognizing Afro-Bolivian contributions to the nation. In Paraguay, the mere presence of the Cambá Cuá, a group that has maintained distinctive African-derived traditions, counters official versions of the nation's history. Erupting on the national scene by promoting their cultural expressions in music and dance, the Cambá Cuá, in reclaiming their entitlements—their rights to their land, to expressions of their unique customs, and to self-determination—are important actors in Paraguay's current reality.

In Argentina, the Second Workshop on Afro-American Culture, an international conference organized in 1993 by the Casa de la Cultura Indo-Afro-Americana in Santa Fe and attended by members of many Afro organizations from the Americas, impacted the nation as Black organizations began to insist upon occupying a self-conscious and self-determined role in the cultural sphere and to demand that the educational system incorporate knowledge about Afro-Argentineans. Among the results are the fact that today the University of Argentina in Buenos Aires allows the study of Afro-Argentinean art, and the San Telmo neighborhood in Buenos Aires, which has a concentration of Afro-Argentineans, is witnessing a renaissance of Black cultural expressions such as carnival comparsas.

In Uruguay, Black community organizations that are a part of Organizaciones Mundo Afro are, among other activities, coadministrating public areas. In addition to implementing small business projects, Mundo Afro, in conjunction with Montevideo's Municipal Council, both operates a multicultural space in the city's historic district and plays an advisory role in the nation's parliament on issues such as racism in the educational system.

Workshops, courses, and training sessions; commercial exchanges of crafts; protest and solidarity marches and demonstrations; petitions to and meetings with heads of state; discussions with international institutions such as the Inter-American Development Bank, the World Bank, and the Ford Foundation concerning the creation of development programs; the promotion of reforms in public education to incorporate our proposed Black studies programs into school curricula; the furnishing of legal services for intervening in racist court proceedings; the formation of regional commissions to foster our communities' involvement in MERCOSUR and other programs of regional integration—all of this and more has occurred through the Network's efforts, giving our organizations the opportunity to interact with, support, and vindicate our communities as never before. The Network has subheadquarters in the MERCOSUR region, the Andean Pact region, and the Central American region, as well as collaborative relationships with many diverse Afro organizations in the United States.

The Network suffered birthing pains in facing obstacles that we have had to overcome in organizing across the Americas, obstacles having to do with differences in institutional forms and processes. But despite difficulties created by our differences, a great deal of creative potential is also embedded within them, as well as within our commonalities. We have only begun to tap this potential through the Network, whose fundamental virtue is the unity, strength, and possibility for exchange that it offers us.

Leaders of our Afro communities are calling for the international Black movement to make a clear articulation of its goals, to unite in mutual defense of our communities' interests, and to commit to a campaign of immediate solidarity. To speak of culture and community is to insist upon playing an active role in the global dimension of humankind's most pressing challenges. It is increasingly evident that no community, no nation, no continent can develop without considering the cultural dimensions as well as the material conditions that forge people's lives.

The challenge continues to be the need to organize the cohabitation of many humans on a single planet in a way that enables us all to live in peace and freedom, without wars and threats, free from oppression and fear, free from hunger, poverty, and solitude. Above all, this challenge requires us to respect and tolerate one another, and to keep in focus the ways that culture influences humankind's constantly changing shape. It is through the efforts of their Afro communities that the nations of the Americas are beginning to tackle the potentially problematic and mutually enriching issues of the diversity and differences of which they are composed.

NOTES

This chapter was translated from Spanish by Lisa Sánchez González.

1. Vatomene Kukanda and Simão Souindoula, Centre International des Civilisations Bantu (CICIBA), personal communication, March 2000.

2. Marta Goldberg, "La población negra y mulata de la cuidad de Buenos Aires, 1810–1840," *Desarollo Económico* 16 (Apr.–June 1976): 79.

3. *Censo general de la cuidad de Buenos Aires, 1887*, vol. 2 (Buenos Aires, 1889), 55–56.

4. George Reid Andrews, *The Afro-Argentines of Buenos Aires, 1800–1900* (Madison: University of Wisconsin Press, 1980), 4–5. [Editor's note: Andrews's book was translated into Spanish as *Los afroargentinos de Buenos Aires, 1800–1900,* trans. Antonio Bonanno (Buenos Aires: Ediciones de la Flor, 1989).]

5. Juan Bautista Alberdi, *Bases y puntos de partida para la organización de la República Argentina* (Buenos Aires: Ediciones de Palma, 1964 [1852]).

6. Andrews, *The Afro-Argentines,* 103.

7. See Domingo Faustino Sarmiento, *Civilización y barbarie: la vida de Juan Facundo Quiroga* (Buenos Aires: Editorial Lajouane, 1889) and *Conflicto y armonía de las razas en América* (Buenos Aires: Imprenta M. Moreno, 1900 [1883]).

8. See Andrews, *The Afro-Argentines,* chap. 6.

9. *Dossier de la organización* (Santa Fe, Argentina: Casa de la Cultura Indo-Afro-Americana, 1994), and Lucía Dominga Molina and Mario Luis López, *El aporte africano a la cultura popular Argentina* (Santa Fe, Argentina: Casa de la Cultura Indo-Afro-Americana, 1996).

10. *Dossier de la organización;* and Molina and López, *El aporte africano.*

11. Major references on the Afro-Bolivian population are Alberto R. Crespo, *Esclavos negros en Bolivia* (La Paz: Ediciones Juventud, 1995); David Mendoza Salazar, *El negro no es un color, es una saya* (La Paz: Gobierno Municipal de La Paz, 1993); Mónica Rey Gutiérrez, *Aspecto socioeconómico de la población negra boliviana* (Mar de Plata, Argentina: Movimiento Saya Afroboliviano, 1994); and Juan Angola Maconde, *Raíces de un pueblo: cultura afroboliviana* (La Paz: Producciones Cima, 2000).

12. Crespo, *Esclavos negros,* 26.

13. Crespo, *Esclavos negros,* 26.

14. Juan Iriondo Alaca, Juventud Saya Afro-Boliviana, personal communication, Montevideo, Uruguay, March 2000.

15. For a discussion of the Candombe de Reyes in Uruguay, see Tomás Olivera Chirimini, chapter 15 of this volume.

16. Research in collaboration with the Cambá Cuá community has also been done by the Centro de Estudios y Investigaciones Afro (CEIAF) of Organizaciones Mundo Afro: Juan Pedro Machado, *Informe preliminar sobre la comunidad Cambá Cuá* (Montevideo: CEIAF, Organizaciones Mundo Afro, 1996), *Cambá Cuá, una forma de resistencia étnico-cultural* (Montevideo: CEIAF, Organizaciones Mundo Afro, 1996), and *Síntesis informativa de la comunidad Cambá Cuá* (Montevideo: CEIAF, Organizaciones Mundo Afro, 1996); and Juan Pedro Machado, Araceli Suárez, and Lázaro Medina, *Informe general primário de la situación de las comunidades negras de América del Sur* (Montevideo: CEIAF, Organizaciones Mundo Afro, 1996).

17. Germán de Granda, "Origen, función y estructura de un pueblo de negros y mulatos libres en el Paraguay del siglo XVIII (San Augustín de la Emboscada)," *Revista de Índias* 43, no. 1171 (Jan.–June 1983): 229–230.

18. De Granda, "Origen," 230.

19. De Granda, "Origen," 229–234.

20. Major references on the Afro-Uruguayan population are: *Programa de desarrollo—objectivos* (Montevideo: CEIAF, Organizaciones Mundo Afro, 1994); *Propuesta de acción institucional, municipal, y nacional* (Montevideo: Organizaciones Mundo Afro, 1994); *Estudio preliminar para la realización de un programa de instalación y funcionamiento de la Casa de la Cultura Afrouruguaya* (Montevideo: Organizaciones Mundo Afro, 1991); *Instalación de una universidad afro de carácter regional en la ciudad de Montevideo, Uruguay* (Montevideo: Organizaciones Mundo Afro, 1993); *Encuentro de entidades negras del Cono Sur (Uruguay-Brasil-Argentina)* (Montevideo: Organizaciones Mundo Afro, 1990); *Primer Seminario Internacional sobre Racismo, Discriminación y Xeno-*

fobia (Montevideo: Organizaciones Mundo Afro, 1994), and *Instituto de Formación de las Organizaciones Mundo Afro* (Montevideo: Organizaciones Mundo Afro, 1995).

21. Ernesto M. Campagna, *La población esclava en ciudades puertos del Río de la Plata, 1750–1830* (São Paulo: CEDHAL/Universidade de São Paulo, 1989), 15.

22. *Anuario estadístico de Uruguay 1988* (Montevideo: Dirección General de Estadística y Censos, 1989).

23. *Anuario estadístico de Uruguay 1988.*

24. Lauro Ayestarán, *La música en el Uruguay* (Montevideo: Servicio Oficial de Difusión Radio-Eléctrica, 1953), 103–110.

25. Lino Suárez Peña, *Apuntes y datos referente a la raza negra en los comienzos de su vida en esta parte del Plata* (Montevideo: Colección de manuscritos del Archivo y Biblioteca Pablo Blanco Azevedo, Museo Histórico Nacional, 1924), 51–56.

26. Ayestarán, *La música,* 68.

27. Vicente Rossi, *Cosas de negros* (Buenos Aires: Hachette, 1958 [1926]), 93–99.

28. Álvaro Gascué, "Partido Autóctono Negro: un intento de organización política de la raza negra en el Uruguay," unpublished manuscript, Montevideo, November 1980.

21

Afro-Argentineans: "Forgotten" and "Disappeared"—Yet Still Present

Lucía Dominga Molina and Mario Luis López

¿A qué cielo de tambores
y siestas largas se han ido?
Se los ha llevado el tiempo,
El tiempo, que es el olvido.

—Jorge Luis Borges[1]

THE AFRICAN PRESENCE IN ARGENTINA

Look carefully at most Argentinean history books and you will find nothing on the presence and participation of Africans and their descendants in the formation of the nation. Should we be represented at all, we appear dancing happily in *candombes*,[2] or happily selling *mazamorra*[3] and milk in the streets during the colonial period, or washing clothes and cleaning houses, also happily, and then—nothing. Nothing except "forgetting," as Argentinean writer Jorge Luis Borges would say.

We believe that this absence is a consequence of prejudice regarding the racial composition of our national identity, in which European characteristics have been prioritized, valorized, and glorified, in denial of the indigenous and, above all, African roots of Argentinean culture. We also believe that denying the contemporary existence of Blacks in Argentina, in addition to "forgetting" and "disappearing" the indisputable historical roles of Africans in the development of the nation, is a denial of our true national identity. Hence the imperative to vindicate the African presence in Argentina, beginning with slavery.

Buenos Aires was, along with Montevideo, one of the two principal South Atlantic ports for the slave trade. At the end of the sixteenth century the destiny of the port of Buenos Aires became linked to that of the town of Potosí, in modern Bolivia. A mining center, Potosí was Latin America's most important and wealthiest center of commerce and as such required a massive influx of laborers. Enslaved Africans became a substitute labor pool for the indigenous peoples who, initially enslaved for Potosí's intensely dangerous, and equally profitable, mining industry, were rapidly dying off.

Between 1623 and 1680, 22,892 Africans were brought to Buenos Aires legally, based on *licencias*, the authorizations to traffic in African lives that were awarded to merchants as rewards for their loyalty by the Spanish Crown. An example is the case of Viceroy Liniers of the Viceroyalty of Río de la Plata that became the modern nations of Argentina, Bolivia, Paraguay, and Uruguay. As an expression of royal gratitude for his help in defending Buenos Aires from English invasions of the city in 1806–7, the Viceroy was given permission to import two thousand Africans, which he raised to four thousand, thus becoming the most important trader in African captives in the Southern Cone of South America. The first of his human cargos arrived on two frigates, the *Venus* and the *Caña Dulce* (Sugar Cane), and were sold in the public squares of Buenos Aires, Montevideo, Santiago de Chile, and Lima.[4]

Parallel to the legal market, the demand for enslaved labor and the desire to increase profits by avoiding government taxation gave birth to an intense contraband trade in enslaved Africans with the complicity of the Spanish colonial authorities. According to Diego Abad de Santillán, there is evidence that 8,932 Africans arrived in the port of Buenos Aires between 1606 and 1625, 5,553 of whom arrived between 1618 and 1623 under the ruse of "emergency docking."[5] This practice consisted of feigning problems on board ship to get permission to dock, then covertly unloading a small amount of contraband in the form of "confiscation" by local authorities, who would earn illicit profits by selling the "confiscated (human) cargo" in "public" auctions closed to all but the traffickers and their local accomplices. Africans were sold at very low prices during these auctions (80–100 pesos), enabling traffickers in human lives to resell them for 250–300 pesos and make a large profit.[6]

Between 1710 and 1739 nearly ten thousand Africans were imported via Buenos Aires. Some stayed there, and others were left in smaller towns en route to the primary destinations of Potosí, Chile, or the Banda Oriental (the eastern shore of the Río de la Plata that became present-day Uruguay). According to the *Padrones de Esclavos* (Slave Schedules) 12,706 Africans arrived between 1792 and 1806, of whom 1,000 were sent to Alto Peru, Chile, and various destinations in the Río de la Plata. Fifty-five and thirty-seven were sent to the towns of Salta and Córdoba, respectively, and an undetermined number was sent to Paraguay, the Banda Oriental, and southern Brazil, with more than half remaining in and around Buenos Aires.[7]

According to the 1778 census more than a third of the inhabitants of the "civilized areas" of the Spanish settlements in Tucumán, Cuyo, and Río de la Plata were Afro-Argentinean (African, mulattos and *zambos* [Afro-indigenous people]). In the interior, the percentages of Afro-Argentineans were 54 percent in Santiago del Estero, 64 percent in the rural part of Tucumán, 50 percent in Catamarca, 46 percent in Salta, 44 percent in Córdoba, and 15–20 percent in Mendoza, La Rioja, and San Juan.[8] There are no data for Santa Fe, Corrientes, and Entre Rios in the first census, but the second census in 1782 shows almost 20 percent Afro-Argentineans in these populations.[9] Between 1780 and 1810, 30 percent of Buenos Aires' population was Afro-Argentinean.[10]

Perhaps Argentina's historical amnesia concerning slavery is a result of the fact that the power elite of the era, many of whose names are widely respected today, owed their wealth to the slave trade. Historian María Cristina de Liboreiro reads in this fact an important explanation for the "forgetting" of everything related to Africans in the nation's history. She asks, "Could it be that it is difficult to remember the 'illustrious families' of that era, the ancestors of contemporary ones, as creators of the wealth of the colonial and republican periods based on the legal and illegal buying and selling of human beings?"[11] Perhaps we also wish to forget that not only affluent families, but also religious orders such as the Dominicans, Franciscans, Jesuits, and others owned large numbers of enslaved Africans.

A term repeated ad nauseum whenever slavery is mentioned in the history of Argentina is "benign." The argument is that the treatment of enslaved Africans in Argentina was benign in comparison with other parts of the Americas. Clearly there must have been differences between the treatment of the domestics and artisans who constituted the majority of enslaved people in Argentina, as compared with miners and plantation workers elsewhere. But to term any form of slavery "benign" is absurd. The forced submissiveness, the discrimination and humiliation, the pain, torment, and torture to which our enslaved ancestors were subjected everywhere in the Americas was anything but "benign."

One common act of brutality was to brand enslaved people on the forehead or cheeks, like cattle. Although branding was prohibited by royal decree in 1784, many enslaved men born after 1784, who were drafted into military service in the nineteenth century, had been branded, making it clear that this heinous practice continued long after it had been outlawed.[12]

Official colonial codes of punishment for enslaved people also demonstrated how brutal, rather than "benign," conditions were. An enslaved person who missed up to four days of work could be given fifty lashes of the whip, then tied up and left in the sun until nighttime. Missing up to eight days of work or straying a mile from the city was punishable by one hundred lashes, followed by being shackled for two months with a twelve-pound ball and chain attached to each ankle. An absence of a few months could result in two hundred lashes, with one hundred more if the returnee had associated with bands of *cimarrones* (maroons) who had escaped from slavery. Staying with maroons for more than six months could be punished by the gallows. Taking up arms against a Spaniard, even in self-defense, and even if the Spaniard was not injured, was punishable with one hundred lashes and a spike nailed through the hand for a first-time offender; for a repeat offense, the person's hand could be cut off.[13] In Buenos Aires these punishments were inflicted in public at the walls of the city hall. Today one of the city's most treasured colonial landmarks, this site is for Afro-Argentineans a painful symbol of the suffering of our ancestors.

Although the most common occupation for enslaved people was domestic service, they were also important as craftspeople and, in rare cases, as master artisans. They were most prevalent as shoemakers and tailors, but also worked in more lucrative crafts such as masonry and metalworking. Many enslaved artisans were contracted out, their wages becoming the primary source of income for their owners' families.

During time off, enslaved people could work as street vendors and in other service capacities and keep those earnings. Women sold pastries, especially empanadas, pickled olives, and dairy products, and did laundry at the river. Men sold brooms, feather dusters, and candles, specialized in exterminating insects or selling water, or worked as porters.

One well-documented fact is the massive Afro-Argentinean participation in the military during the nineteenth century. Yet these contributions are not generally elaborated in official histories, and the heroic accomplishments of Afro-Argentineans who distinguished themselves as military leaders, rising to ranks as high as colonel, have been "forgotten." Some of the most illustrious Afro-Argentineans in our military history were:

Soldiers: Joaquín Chaves (b. 1813), battalion chief (active into his nineties); Josefa Tenorio (who managed to hide the fact that she was a woman); and Gregorio Badía (b. 1907); *Sergeants*: José Cipriano Campana (born at the end of the eighteenth century, died a hundred years later, having fought with General San Martín as well as in the Paraguayan War); Carmen Ledesma, sergeant first class (a.k.a. "Black Mother Carmen," who bore sixteen children while she was in the army); and Felipe Mansilla (1814–79), sergeant major; *Captains*: Antonio Videla; Andrés Ibañez (who fought with General San Martín); Casildo Thompson (1826–73) and his son Casildo G. Thompson (1856–1928); *Lieutenant Colonels*: Manuel Macedonio Barbarín (1781–1836); Inocencio Pesoa (b. 1775); and Agustín Sosa (1775–1820);[14] *Colonels*: Lorenzo Barcala (1795–1835); José María Morales (1818–94); Nicolás Cabrera (1780–1876); and José Narbona (d. 1850).[15]

Many enslaved men were promised their freedom in exchange for five years of military service, or were forcibly drafted. According to Liboreiro, "Undoubtedly, the lure of future freedom would entice people to volunteer to participate in the bloody battles. But we should also note that not all Afro-Argentinean soldiers joined the military voluntarily to win their freedom. Many were, in fact, sent as replacements by their owners. In times of national emergency, the government would solicit aid in the form of armed and equipped soldiers, which would be satisfied with the donation of horses, clothes, arms and . . . an enslaved black man."[16]

Afro-Argentineans enjoyed a brief period of favor during the administrations of President Juan Manuel de Rosas (1829–31 and 1835–52), who used them as support for his political project. But when the Rosas administration lost power to the opposition, this favorable treatment quickly ended.[17] Although the Spanish Crown had abolished slavery during Argentina's first wars of independence at the beginning of the nineteenth century, the decree was not enforced. Slavery was only made officially illegal with the 1853 constitution of the independent republic, which declared all Argentinean citizens equal under the law. Abolition did not take effect in Buenos Aires, however, until 1861, when the city finally joined the nation.

Despite abolition, the effects of the discriminatory system elaborated under the colonial regime remain a heavy legacy, the effects of which continue. The most obvious manifestations are in the educational system and in public institutions. There was de facto segregation in the form of separate schools for Black children, and Afro-Argentineans were often barred from theaters and other public venues at the turn of the century. "Is it that we are willfully forgetting all of this?" Liboreiro asks.[18]

Even after independence and abolition, such educational segregation made it virtually impossible for Afro-Argentineans to compete for employment. The most common routes of economic mobility were the military, the police, and low-wage jobs. But even in these job sectors Afro-Argentineans were quickly supplanted by late-nineteenth-century waves of European immigrants. This socioeconomic competition is well documented in Black newspapers from the turn of the century. Thus, during the second half of the nineteenth century Afro-Argentineans were likely to work as domestic servants, musicians and performers, and low-level government employees.

NEWER AFRO-ARGENTINEAN POPULATIONS

In contrast with the rest of the country, especially Buenos Aires, in which the Afro-Argentinean population declined precipitously in the nineteenth century, the Black population in and around the town of Corrientes rose. The presence of Black soldiers in transit may explain this demographic increase. During the War of the Triple Alliance (1865–70), in which Argentina, Brazil, and Uruguay fought against Paraguay, all of the allied armies included large numbers of Black troops, some of whom camped close to Corrientes in a spot still known as Cambá Punta, or Blacks' Point. At the close of the war many soldiers, especially Afro-Brazilians, soldiers chose to settle in Corrientes, since slavery continued in Brazil until 1888.[19]

Other Black soldiers from the three armies had also deserted during the war and had settled near Corrientes in an area covered with thick undergrowth and natural caves on the banks of the Paraná River. These caves had served as places of refuge during the colonial period for indigenous people fleeing the European invasion, and later for African and Afro-Argentinean fugitives from slavery. The resultant settlement came to be known as Cambá Cuá, the Well of the Blacks in the indigenous Guaraní language of the area from which the term *cuá* comes.[20] Since *cambá* is not a Guaraní term for the color black, it is likely that it is an African ethnic name that was incorporated into Guaraní and generalized to designate Black people.[21] The source could be the Kikongo-speaking Kamba or Bakamba people of the Republic of the Congo.[22]

The Black community in the town of Vera in the province of Santa Fe seems also to be of mostly exogenous origin. The construction of a railroad connecting Vera with the town of Reconquista began in 1887. In 1889 the tracks were laid as far as the Vera Station in what was then called Jobson Town and later renamed Governor Vera after the station. The French company that was contracted to build the railroad brought in laborers from the French colonies of Guadeloupe and Martinique in the Caribbean and Senegal in West Africa. It is easy to surmise that the workers who lived in the area for years while constructing the railroad had children with local women.[23] In both Corrientes and Vera we find the typically Afro-Argentinean January 6 Festival of Saint Balthazar, which celebrates the African king among the Magi. The festival is also held in other areas in the interior such as Empedrado, Concepción, Saladas, and Solari, suggesting an historical Afro-Argentinean presence.

The newest Afro-Argentinean community is composed of immigrants from the Cape Verde Islands off the west coast of Africa. As a result of their Portuguese nationality due to their colonial status until Cape Verde's 1975 independence, and because article 25 of the Argentinean constitution, which is still enforced, requires the state to promote European immigration, many Cape Verdeans were allowed to immigrate. Their migrations, the result of economic hardship in the often drought-stricken islands, came in three waves: 1910–20, 1927–33, and post-1946. Estimated at eight or nine thousand people concentrated in Dock Sud, the southern port zone of Buenos Aires, and in Ensenada, a port near the city of La Plata, capital of the province of Buenos Aires, they have traditionally been employed in shipping and port-related industries. Whereas George Reid Andrews noted two decades ago that "Cape Verdeans have not integrated into the larger Afro-Argentinean society, keeping to themselves instead,"[24] Cape Verdean Argentineans are now involving themselves in Afro-Argentinean institutions.

AFRO-ARGENTINEAN ORGANIZATIONAL LIFE

Enslaved Africans and their descendants developed distinctive organizational forms. First, there were the *cofradías*, lay brotherhoods organized to bring Africans into the Catholic church, allowing their members a Christian funeral and masses in their memory. The first of these, the *Cofradía de San Baltasar* at the *Iglesia de Piedad* in Buenos Aires, dates to 1772. In 1780 three more were formed: the *Cofradía de San Benito de Palermo* in the *Convento de San Francisco*, the *Cofradía de la Virgen del Rosario* in the *Convento de Santo Domingo*, and the *Cofradía de Santa María del Corvellón* in the *Iglesia de la Merced*. Brotherhoods of Saint Balthazar, the Black king among the Magi, of Saint Benedict the Moor, and of the Virgin of the Rosary were developed among Afro-Argentineans in interior cities as well. In Córdoba the *Cofradía de la Virgen del Rosario* is also known as *Nuestra Señora de los Negros y Mulatos* (Our Lady of Blacks and Mulattos), shortened to *La Virgen Mulata* (the Mulatto Virgin).[25] The brotherhoods reflected well-defined policies of both racial segregation and social control that also sought to reconcile Afro-Argentineans with their social condition.

African *nations* or African *societies*, organizations based on African ethnic and regional origins, began to become institutionalized around 1770. In 1821 a government mandate formalized the process for establishing an African nation or society, with a standardized constitution defining their objectives, electoral procedures, membership criteria, and financial accounting. The government entity charged with overseeing these institutions was the police.[26] The nations organized community activities in an effort to recreate their African cultures in the form of festive social gatherings involving music and dance, as well as to offer support of various types to their members and amass resources to buy members' freedom from enslavement.

George Reid Andrews lists the following nations in Buenos Aires by area of African origin:

West Africa: Abayá, Auza (Hausa), Borno, Carabarí (Kalabari), Goyo, Main, Maquaqua, Mina (Mina Mají, Mina Nagó), Moros, Sabalú, Santé (Ashanti), Tacuá, Yida.
Congo: Augunga, Basundi, Cambundá (Cabinda), Congo, Loango, Lubolo, Lumboma, Mayombé, Momboma, Mondongo, Umbonia, Zeda, Zongo.
Angola: Angoloa, Benguela, Casanche (Kasanje), Ganguelá, Huombé, Lucango, Majumbi, Muñandá, Quipará (Kibala), Quisamá (Kisama), Umbala.
East Africa: Malavé (Malawi), Mancinga, Mauinga, Mozambique, Muchague, Mucherengue, Muñambani.
Afro-Argentinean: Argentina Federal.
Afrobrasilian: Brazilian Bahianos, Brazilian Nation.
Unknown Origin: Bagungane, Hambuero, Monyolo, Villamoani.[27]

When the African nations declined beginning in the mid-nineteenth century with the deaths of the last generation of people born in Africa, Afro-Argentineans began to form mutual aid societies. These were the first autonomous Afro-Argentinean organizations since, unlike the brotherhoods and nations whose constitutions had to be ratified by the Church and the provincial government respectively, the mutual aid societies drafted their own constitutions. *La Sociedad de la Unión y de Socorros Mútuos* (the Society of the Union and of Mutual Aid) was formed in 1855, followed by *La Sociedad Protectora Brasileira* (the Brazilian Protective Society) and *La Fraternal* (the Brotherhood) later in the 1850s, and in 1877 *La Protectora* (the Protector). In 1932, immigrants from Cape Verde founded *La Sociedad de Socorros Mútuos Unión Caboverdeana* (the Mutual Aid Society Cape Verdean Union).[28]

The twentieth century saw the development of Afro-Argentinean recreational and social centers and associations. These groups included, in the interior, *Los Negros Santafesinos* (Blacks of Santa Fe), which was formed on December 25, 1900, and was active until 1950;[29] and in Buenos Aires El Shimmy Club, which organized annual dances attended by the entire community from 1922 to the 1970s; *El Centro Centenário* (the Centennial Center) founded in 1910, a century after the May 25, 1810 beginning of the revolution that brought independence from Spain, by Afro-Argentinean Walter Forna, and that met at the prestigious Marconi Theatre in downtown Buenos Aires; *La Asociación General San Martín* (the General San Martín Association), named for the leader of the army of liberation from Spain of much of southern South America; *El Centro Patriótico* 25 de Mayo (the May 25 [independence day] Patriotic Center); and *La Fraternidad* (the Brotherhood).[30] The names associated so obviously with the creation of the Argentinean nation suggest a desire to reject the past of the African nations in favor of integrating and assimilating into the whitening Argentinean nation.

More recently formed Afro-Argentinean organizations in Buenos Aires include *El Movimiento Afro Argentino* (Argentinean Afro Movement), which issued two editions of its newspaper *El Mandinga* in 1991; *El Movimiento Argentino Contra el Apartheid* (the Argentinean Anti-Apartheid Movement); *El Centro Cultural Afro* (the Afro Cultural

Center); and in 1995, *La Organización de Afroamerianos en Argentina* (the Organization of Afro-Americans in Argentina). In the interior, Santa Fe's *Casa de la Cultura Indo-Afro-Americana* (the Indo-Afro-American Culture House) has functioned since 1988, organizing the *Primeras Jornadas de la Cultura Negra* (the First Workshops on Black Culture) in 1991 on a national level, and the *Segundas Jornadas de la Cultura Negra* (the Second Workshops on Black Culture) on an international level in 1993. The Casa also has an Afro Documentation and Bibliographic Center, publishes articles and newsletters, and organizes events such as lectures, exhibits, and public events to create greater awareness of the Afro-Argentinean presence.

THEORIES OF AFRO-ARGENTINEAN "DISAPPEARANCE"

Since Afro-Argentineans were clearly present during the formation of the nation, we must search for the motives behind the "disappearance" of our ancestors from official Argentinean history. The primary motive is that the new nation's discourses of identity were integrally bound with a discourse of "whitening" the Argentinean "race," which created racist institutional imperatives that persist to this day. During the late nineteenth century, while European immigration was being intellectually elaborated and politically, economically, and socially promoted, the decline in Afro-Argentinean demographics was artificially accelerated by the misleading use of government statistics and corresponding analyses by Argentinean historians and other writers.

According to official documents, by 1887 the Afro-Argentinean population had dropped from its early nineteenth-century high of 30 percent to a mere 1.8 percent.[31] Empirical evidence contradicting the tale of Afro-Argentinean "disappearance," however, includes a surge in the numbers of Afro-Argentinean institutions and publications in the late nineteenth century, as well as the frequent visual presence of Afro-Argentineans in photographs of public scenes.

Froilán P. Bello (1822–93) founded and edited the magazine *El Eco Artístico,* and journalist Manuel Posadas (1841–97) founded several newspapers and edited *El Eco Artístico* after Bello. Afro-Argentinean periodicals included: *La Ortiga*; *La Raza Africana* (eight issues) founded in 1858; *La Igualdad* (eight issues) founded and discontinued in 1864 (unknown number of issues) and published again on a weekly basis in 1873; and *El Artesano/El Tambor* and *El Candombero* (no extant copies), which appeared in 1873. *La Perla, El Unionista, El Aspirante, La Aurora del Plata,* and *La Idea* appeared between 1870 and 1873; *La Juventud* (published every ten days) and *La Broma* appeared between 1876 and 1878; *La Protectora* and *El Látigo* were published between 1876 and 1880; and *La Razón* and *El Obrero* began publication in 1880.[32]

Thus, to understand the process of the alleged "disappearance" of Afro-Argentineans—while they remained visibly and actively present—we must analyze the myth of "White European Argentina" in the formation of Argentina's racial philosophy. This myth was produced in the second half of the nineteenth century, and although it has been challenged, it persists into the present. Historians have advanced four classic causes to explain this "disappearance."

The most pervasive argument, and justification, is that Afro-Argentineans disappeared because of their massive participation in all of Argentina's many nineteenth-century wars.[33] Indeed, Afro-Argentineans did serve as cannon fodder in repelling the British invasions and were heavily involved in the revolutionary armies that fought for Argentina's independence, as well as in the numerous civil and other wars. According to this explanation, the War of the Triple Alliance dealt the final blow to—or served as the "final solution" for—Argentina's Black population. So many Black men died on battlefields that Afro-Argentineans could not recover from their demographic losses and reconstitute themselves as a community.

While affirming the above thesis, many authors add the subtext of racial miscegenation to the script.[34] The idea here is that Afro-Argentineans disappeared through the process of miscegenation, based on tales of Black women seeking white mates because of the scarcity of Black men. Another ingredient here is Black women's presumed desire to have lighter-skinned babies to favor their social mobility. This argument runs in tandem with the fact of the massive influx of European immigrants.

The third argument is that Afro-Argentineans disappeared because of their poor socioeconomic conditions as reflected in inadequate housing, food, clothing, and medical care, which ostensibly produced a low birth rate and a high mortality rate. This explanation culminates in the yellow fever epidemic of 1871, which supposedly gave the coup de grace to the Afro-Argentinean community.[35] The fourth argument is that Afro-Argentineans disappeared because of the outlawing of the slave trade in 1813. But as detailed above, the official decree did not end the importation of Africans because of the extensive contraband trade.

Historian George Reid Andrews states, however, that "These explanations, which have been repeated by Argentine historians and foreigners writing on Argentina for the last one hundred years, are logical, coherent, and eminently reasonable. Indeed, there is only one criterion that they fail to meet: little or no effort has been made to prove them."[36]

We contend that despite the partial truth of these arguments, "these four logical and reasonable causes do not explain the worst aspect of our supposed disappearance, which is that we have been erased from history. We do not exist."[37] These rationalizations have obscured and minimized Afro-Argentinean roles in the history and formation of the nation. It is in the society's Eurocentric project of "whitening" the population that we must seek the response to the question of why most Argentineans prefer to ignore the African part of our historical heritage in the interest of conceptualizing themselves as more European than mestizo.

THE FORMATION OF ARGENTINA'S RACIAL CONSCIOUSNESS

Argentineans seem prone to wishful thinking, willful mythologies often flagrantly contradicting the historical record. One of the most repeated myths in the cache of the national imaginary is that Argentina is white and European. Argentina is proud of its socalled whiteness, which marks its supposed difference from the rest of Latin America.

But if we consider that our nation is located in an area that has been inhabited by aboriginal ethnic groups for thousands of years, and then by tens of thousands of Africans brought during the European invasion and conquest of the native peoples, and later by Europeans jettisoned by misery from their countries of origin, we have to ask ourselves from whence this racial pride, this self-miscognition as "white" emanates. Argentina's "whiteness" being such a centerpiece of national identity, especially in Buenos Aires, we must ask how and where this "white pride" idea developed. This is important not only because this "white" identity has become popularized as common sense and as consensus, but also because it tends to blind most research and scholarship to the evidence that so flagrantly contradicts the myth.

Nineteenth-century discourses of Spanish colonialism and Argentinean national unification established the foundation of the myth. The end of the Rosas regime helped produce the conditions for the elaboration of a politics and philosophy of liberalism that rode on the tails of European ideals considered progressive at the time. Ricardo Rojas argues that influential figures of the era borrowed their ideals of national independence from European models: Domingo Faustino Sarmiento from the United States, and Juan Bautista Alberdi from England. They wanted to detach themselves from the Spanish colonial past and transform their colonial heritage by embracing the modernity of these exemplary nations.[38]

Early-twentieth-century Argentinean writer Carlos O. Bunge presented a theory of Spanish American psychology in his monograph *Nuestra América (Our America)* that helps account for the racist underpinnings endemic to philosophies of national unification. Bunge claimed that a certain sense of "decorum" characterized Spanish colonists in the Americas, imbuing them with a kind of seriousness, affectation, uniformity of customs, arrogance, indolence and, above all, an aversion to manual labor, which was considered undignified in the settler culture. Bunge characterized indigenous people as resigned, passive, and vengeful, and Blacks as servile, treacherous, and malleable in ways that made them tricksters. From this mixture, he maintained, there resulted "Spanish Americans whose common traits were laziness, sadness, and arrogance." Given this situation, Bunge's ultimate solution for modernizing Argentina involved "Europeanizing" the national character via the work ethic.[39]

Bunge's ideas are indicative of the kind of "scientific racism" that is entrenched in South America's brand of liberal positivism and embedded in the cultural intellectual history of the Americas. With this ideological basis of national formation came the belief that the creation of a modern nation based on European models required a European population. As a doctrine, scientific racism affirmed the innate superiority of the "white race" and the innate inferiority of indigenous, African, and any other groups included in the rubric of "nonwhite races."[40]

The imperative for European immigration began as early as 1820 and intensified in the 1850s. These Eurosupremacist discourses and practices emerged in official form with the Generation of the '80s, an intellectual group that was the product of the combined interests of the mercantile bourgeoisie in Buenos Aires and the cattle ranching bourgeoisie in the provinces. Imbued with the European liberal positivist tradition, the core idea of this movement was "progress."

The ideological template for the Generation of the '80s was elaborated in the work of Argentinean President Domingo Faustino Sarmiento (1866–74), who was also the "Father of Argentinean education." From the provincial town of San Juan, Sarmiento's thinking was shaped by a Catholic conservatism typical of the Argentinean provinces and later influenced by North American liberalism. In Sarmiento's work *Civilización y barbarie: la vida de Juan Facundo Quiroga* (Civilization and Barbarism: The Life of Juan Facundo Quiroga), we find a concept of Argentinean history that pits against each other two conflicting aspects of the nation's social evolution: the "civilized" Europeanized cities, and the "barbarous" countryside that maintained its "colonial" character (i.e., its mestizo culture). In Sarmiento's words, this city/countryside friction "is an ingenuous, frank, and primitive struggle between the modern progress of the human spirit and the rudimentary principles of savagery, that is, between the populous cities and the dark forests." [41]

This "struggle" has a precise, well-populated ethnic significance: the cities Sarmiento idealized were predominantly white, while the countryside was predominantly mestizo. Sarmiento later refined this theme in explicitly racial terms when he argued that racial conflict was manifested in the Americas by the very different levels of civilization that the two coexisting social groups had achieved. [42] Sarmiento admired the United States, attributing its "progress" to the fact that its white colonists had not permitted the "servile races" or "secondary races" to mix with them and thus become a part of their society. He also admired the fact that North Americans had segregated indigenous people and marginalized Black people, and that they had not permitted these groups to participate genetically, socially, or politically in the nation's formation. He believed that this was what had made the United States a great nation. [43]

Rosalia Cornejo Parriego, in her analysis of Argentinean racial philosophy, notes that Sarmiento claimed in his essay "Conflicto y armonía de las razas en América" (Racial Conflict and Harmony in the Americas) that Afro-Argentineans "had made no important contribution to the nation's culture." [44] Thus, Sarmiento obviously realized that Argentina's population was not "white," but rather mestizo and mulatto, a situation that he felt needed correcting. He believed that he had discovered the origin of Argentina's incapacity for civil democracy precisely in this "inferior" racial condition. Argentina's only hope was European immigration.

George Reid Andrews's commentary on Sarmiento's profoundly racist thought is that "despite the fact that he was the father of Argentina's educational system, he paradoxically believed that ideas and enlightenment were not so much learned as inherited. Thus, instruction alone would not be enough to pull Argentina from its barbarism; an actual infusion of white genes was required." [45]

Political philosopher Juan Bautista Alberdi, author of *Bases y puntos de partida para la organización política de la República Argentina* (Bases and Premises for the Political Organization of the Argentinean Republic), was as important as Sarmiento for the formation of Argentina's racial philosophy. Alberdi's book, in which he expressed sentiments almost identical to Sarmiento's, provided the basis of the national constitution of 1853. Alberdi's inspiration came from Great Britain, and his thinking was likewise informed by an intensely Eurocentric perspective. "Although we call ourselves 'Americans,' we are just Europeans born in the Americas. Our brains, blood, color—this all comes from abroad." [46]

According to influential sociologist José Ingenieros, seven sociological premises formed the backbone of Alberdi's treatise and the Argentinean constitution:

1. That "Argentina is absolute, loyal, and firm like no other nation." This marks the beginning of what we might call a national sociology.
2. That Argentineans are Europeans (not indigenous peoples) adapted to life in the Americas. And everything that may be called civilization in the Americas is European.
3. That it is necessary to form a white national population.
4. That to govern is to settle the nation. "Settling means to instruct, educate, morally train, and improve the racial composition of the citizenry; civilize, enrich, and spontaneously and quickly expand the nation as was done in the United States; and reinforce and affirm the nation's liberty, endowing it with the intelligence for and habit of self-governance, and the means with which to accomplish this end. Furthermore, civilizing the citizenry means the need for civilized peoples who can educate our part of America about liberty and industriousness, which in turn means that we must settle the country with Europeans who are more advanced in terms of liberty and industriousness."
5. That education be adapted to the environment as an essential condition for the development of this new citizenry that we desire.
6. That the conception of a political economy be inspired by liberal economies.
7. That a work ethic be developed that would be opposed to the "Spanish ethic that disdained work."[47]

At the beginning of the twentieth century Ingenieros went further than his nineteenth-century intellectual predecessors in formulating the nation's racial philosophy in *Al margen de la ciencia* (On the Margin of Science), *Sociología argentina* (Argentinean Sociology), *La locura en la Argentina* (Madness in Argentina), and his essay, "La formación de una raza argentina" (The Development of an Argentinean Race), which appeared in Sarmiento's *Conflicto y armonía de las razas en América*.[48] Ingenieros's ideas were heavily influenced by "social Darwinism," the concept of history as a process of "racial struggle" more than class or institutional struggle. In *Sociología argentina* he wrote, "The superiority of the white race is accepted even among those who deny the existence of racial struggle. Natural selection, an inviolable truth among humans as well as all other species, tends to extinguish the colored races wherever these races come into contact with the white races."[49]

Ingenieros analyzed Argentina's role in the South American context and concluded that the future would depend on Argentina, Chile, or Brazil based on the combination of four elements: territorial size, climate, natural resources, and race. He then explained that Chile lacked size and fertile soil, Brazil lacked the proper climate and race, but Argentina united all four factors with a vast territory, a temperate climate, fertile soil, and a racially white population.[50]

In "La formación de una raza argentina" Ingenieros wrote:

The indigenous races, eternally alien to our political and social national identity, are now reduced to near extinction; they are now confined to the territories whose physical characteristics were not hospitable for the European races. Blacks have also become extinct; the mulattos of the temperate zone are becoming whiter and whiter. In Buenos Aires a Black Argentinean is an object of curiosity.[51]

Ingenieros's opposition to racial mixing went well beyond Sarmiento's; he went so far as to propose the separate development of the white and nonwhite races in a particularly Argentinean species of apartheid.

These racist goals of eliminating Afro-Argentineans from the population were concretely implemented through military action by using our ancestors as cannon fodder in all of the wars, and were intellectually implemented by "disappearing" them from the pages of Argentinean history. A paragraph from the 1895 census is instructive: "It will not be long before the population will be completely united, forming a new and beautiful white race produced by the contact between all of the European nations and nurtured in American soil."[52]

CONCLUSION: ARGENTINA'S ORIGINAL SIN

We contend that the kind of racism expressed by these influential authors is the "original sin" in the definition of our Argentinean national identity. This original sin especially affects Afro-Argentineans who, in addition to our drastic demographic decline, have also suffered from the stigmatizing and devaluing of our Blackness. We have not had a Black pride movement because we have not developed a collective Black consciousness, an idea of who we are, of our worth, of our history, and of our integral role in the creation and evolution of the Argentinean nation. Except for the Cape Verdean community, we do not have a reference group with which we can identify. Afro-Argentineans are dispersed and lost in the society around us, a society that attacks our self-esteem by marking us as "different." Being "Black" implies the pejorative connotations that Argentinean society attaches to the term. This racism often creates a contradiction between phenotype and consciousness of Black people without a corresponding Black consciousness.

This deficiency of consciousness began with the "whitening" that was a fundamental process in Argentinean social history and that affected Black as well as "white" Argentineans. This is evident in our generation's sense that our elders, who were victims of this process, have withheld from us much of our cultural legacy. They were forced to accept "white" values, going in some cases to the extreme of being ashamed of their own cultural traditions of African origin, such as candombe. The historical and present existence of Afro-Argentineans, to say nothing of our ancestors' historical contributions to the nation, are practically unknown even to us because of the "whitening" imperative that has resulted in the deliberate "disappearing" of African and Afro-Argentinean cultural production.

Without recognizing the negritude of Argentinean history, however, all Argentineans are ignoring a significant part of the demographic and cultural factors that contributed to the construction of our national identity. To help us all transcend nearly a century of confusion and error, we need an intense process of unlearning and of consciousness-raising. We must develop a new critical attitude and new strategies for confronting a national history that has falsified elements of the historical record that are fundamental to our full understanding of Argentina.

NOTES

This chapter was translated from Spanish by Lisa Sánchez González.

1. "To what heaven of drums / and long siestas have they gone? / Time has taken them away, / the time that is forgetting." From Jorge Luis Borges, "Milonga de los morenos," in *Obras completas II* (Buenos Aires: Emecé Editors, 1996 [1965]).©María Kodama, 1996. Reprinted with permission. [Ed. note: Translation by Lisa Sánchez González.]

2. *Candombe* is a music/dance form of Central African origin.

3. *Mazamorra* is a corn-based sweet.

4. Eduardo Luis Duhalde, "Los negros, nuestros primeros desaparecidos," in *Humor*, no. 168 (Buenos Aires) (Feb. 1986): 82.

5. Diego Abad de Santillán, *Gran enciclopedia argentina* (Buenos Aires: Ediar, 1964), 105.

6. Luis Romero, "La lucha por el Puerto," in *Buenos Aires: historia de quatro siglos*, vol. I (Buenos Aires: Editorial Abril, 1983), 51.

7. Daniel Santamaría, "La población, estancamiento y expansión, 1580–1855," in *Buenos Aires: historia de quatro siglos*, vol. I (Buenos Aires: Editorial Abril, 1983), 212–214.

8. María Cristina de Liboreiro, "Un olvido histórico: los negros en Argentina. Ensayo sobre un ejemplo de racismo historiográfico," *Cuaderno*, no. 1 (Santa Fe: Casa de la Cultura Indo-Afro-Americana, 1996): 4.

9. Narciso Binayán Carmona, "Pasado y permanencia de la negritud," in *Todo es historia*, special issue "Nuestros negros," no. 162 (Nov. 1980): 68.

10. José Luis Moreno, "La estructura social y demográfica de la cuidad de Buenos Aires en el año 1778," in *Anuario del instituto de investigaciones históricas*, vol. 8 (Buenos Aires: Rosario, 1965), 166.

11. Liboreiro, "Un olvido histórico," 8.

12. Duhalde, "Los negros," 83.

13. Duhalde, "Los negros," 82.

14. Marcos de Estrada, *Argentinos de origen africano* (Buenos Aires: Editorial Universitaria de Buenos Aires [EUDEBA]), 1979: 179.

15. George Reid Andrews, *The Afro-Argentines of Buenos Aires, 1800–1900* (Madison: University of Wisconsin Press, 1980), 229–231. [Editor's note: Andrews's book was translated into Spanish as *Los afroargentinos de Buenos Aires, 1800–1900*, trans. Antonio Bonanno (Buenos Aires: Ediciones de la Flor, 1989).]

16. Liboreiro, "Un olvido histórico," 11.

17. Andrews, *The Afro-Argentines*, 96–101.

18. Liboreiro, "Un olvido histórico," 11.

19. Andrés Alberto Salas, *Los cambá, el cambá cuá y cambaltasar* (Corrientes: Editorial Aguaradas, 1990), 11.

20. Salas, *Los cambá,* 11.

21. José Miguel Irigoyén, "Etimología de cambá cuá," in *Revista historia de los Corrientos y sus pueblos*, no. 6 (1985): 187.

22. Jesús García, *La diáspora de los kongos en las Américas y el Caribe* (Caracas: Fundación Afroamérica, 1995), 187.

23. Juan Antonio Giordano, assistant director, Colegio Nacional Superior de Vera, Santa Fe Province, Argentina, personal communication, September 19, 1991.

24. Andrews, *The Afro-Argentines*, 209.

25. Andrews, *The Afro-Argentines*, 138–142.

26. Alberto González Arzac, "Abolición de la esclavitud en el Río de la Plata," in *La esclavitud en la Argentina* (Buenos Aires: Editorial Polémica, 1974), 51.

27. Andrews, *The Afro-Argentines*, 233–234.

28. Andrews, *The Afro-Argentines*, 151–154.

29. Mario Luis López, "Comparsa los negros santafesinos: presencia negra en la cuidad de Santa Fe (República Argentina) en la primera mitad del siglo," in *Cuaderno*, no. 2 (Santa Fe: Casa de la Cultura Indo-Afro-Americana, 1996).

30. Nestor Ortiz Oderigo, "Las naciones africanas," in *Revista todo es historia*, special issue "Nuestros negros," no. 162 (Nov. 1980): 34.

31. *Censo general de la cuidad de Buenos Aires, 1887*, vol. 2 (Buenos Aires, 1889), 56–57.

32. Andrews, *The Afro-Argentines*, 179–200.

33. For several versions of this theory see *Segundo censo de la República Argentina: 10 mayo, 1895*, vol. 2 (Buenos Aires: Taller Tipográfico de la Penitenciaria Nacional, 1989), xlvii; José Ingenieros, *La locura en la Argentina* (Buenos Aires: Cooperativa Editorial Limitada, 1937 [1920]), 30; Domingo Faustino Sarmiento, *Conflicto y armonía de las razas en América*, vol. 1 (Buenos Aires: Imprenta Mariano Moreno, 1900 [1883]), 72–73; Alvaro Yunque, *Calfulcura: la conquista de las pampas* (Buenos Aires: Ediciones A. Zamora: 1956), 187–188; and Andrés Avellaneda, "Prohibe la junta el ingreso de esclavos," in *La Opinión* (May 28, 1976): 8.

34. See Juan José Soiza Reilly, "Gente de color," in *Caras y Caretas* (Nov. 25, 1905); Máximo Simpson, "Porteños de color," in *Panorama* (June 1967): 85; Marta B. Goldberg, "La población negra y mulata de la cuidad de Buenos Aires 1810–1840," in *Desarrollo económico* (Apr.-June 1976): 85; and Emiliano Endrek, *El mestizaje en Córdoba, siglo XVIII y principios del XIX* (Córdoba: Dirección General de Publicaciones, 1966), 18–19.

35. See Ricardo Rodríguez Molas, "El negro en el Río de la Plata," in *Polémica* 2 (May 1970): 55–56; Sir Woodbine Parish, *Buenos Aires y las provincias del Río de la Plata* (Buenos Aires: Hachette, 1958), 179; and Nicolás Besio Moreno, *Buenos Aires: puerto del Río de la Plata, capital de la Argentina: estudio crítico de su población, 1536–1936* (Buenos Aires: Talleres Gráficos Tuduri, 1939), 24, 290, 380.

36. Andrews, *The Afro-Argentines*, 5.

37. Lucía Dominga Molina, "Negros en Argentina: racismo, autoestima, reseña histórica y el lugar del negro en una sociedad pretendidamente blanca," paper presented at La primera Jornada de Mujeres Negras y Derechos Civiles (the First "Black Women's Civil Rights" workshop), Lima, Peru, May 1994, published in *Boletín ALAI* (Agencia Latinoamericana de Información), No. 195 (Quito, Ecuador, July 1994): 4–5; also see Lucía Dominga Molina and Mario Luis López, *Negros en Argentina: presencia y ocultamieto*. (Oiartzun, Guipúzcoa, Spain: Sendoa Editorial y Universidad de Alcalá de Henares, 2001).

38. Ricardo Rojas, *Eurindia* (Buenos Aires: Centro Editorial de América Latina, 1980 [1924]), 18.

39. Carlos O. Bunge, *Nuestra América: ensayo de psicología social* (Buenos Aires: Casa Vaccaro, 1918), 142.

40. Proponents of scientific racism included French diplomat and essayist Josef Arthur de Gobineau, whose *Essai sur l'inégalité des races* (Essay on the Inequality of the Races*)*, written in 1855 (Paris: Firmin-Didot, 1884), was later used by the Nazis to support their own racist ideologies, and Houston Stewart Chamberlain, whose anti-Semitic *Die grundlagen des neunzehnten*

jahrhunderts (Foundations of the Nineteenth Century) (Munich: F. Brickmann, 1900), was also embraced by the Nazis.

41. Domingo Faustino Sarmiento, *Civilización y barbarie: la vida de Juan Facundo Quiroga* (Buenos Aires: Editorial Lajouane, 1889), 6–7.

42. Sarmiento, *Ambas Américas* (Buenos Aires: Imprenta Mariano Morena, 1899), 301–302, and *Conflicto y armonía de las razas en América*, vol. 1 (Buenos Aires: Imprenta Mariano Moreno, 1900 [1883]), 70–71.

43. Andrews, *The Afro-Argentines*, 103.

44. Rosalia Cornejo Parriego, "El discurso racial in Amalia de José Marmol," in *Afro-Hispanic Review* 13, no. 2; (Fall 1994): 22.

45. Andrews, *The Afro-Argentines*, 103.

46. Juan Bautista Alberdi, *Bases y puntos de partida para la organización política de la República Argentina* (Buenos Aires: Editorial Tor, 1948), 33.

47. José Ingenieros, *Sociología argentina* (Buenos Aires: Editorial Losada, 1946), 340–352.

48. Ingenieros, *Al margen de la ciencia* (Buenos Aires: Lajouane, 1908); *Sociología argentina*; *la locura en la Argentina*; and "La formación de una raza argentina," in *Conflicto y armonía*.

49. Ingenieros, *Sociología argentina*, 35.

50. Ingenieros, *Sociología argentina*, 76.

51. Ingenieros, "La formación de una raza argentina," in *Conflicto y armonía*, 460.

52. *Segundo censo de la República Argentina: May 10, 1895*, vol. 1: xlviii.

22

Stories and Images of Our People: Propositions for a Future

Gloria Rolando

To the memory of Felipe Alfonso, son of Obatalá

In September of 1991 I had my first experience directing a documentary, *Oggún: An Eternal Present*, and a few months later I attended the funeral of one of the singers who had given life and personality to the film. There was crying and much sadness. But this sadness was also expressed in singing and dancing to the sound of a rumba, to the sound of drums that paid homage to Felipe.

Even the coffin helped reinforce the contagious rhythm. With the coffin carried on men's shoulders, we sang and danced all the way into the cemetery. Good-byes were said to a friend, to the Son of Obatalá, who dedicated his last breath to singing to all of the African deities who have found another home on the island of Cuba. Music had accompanied Felipe Alfonso's birth many years ago when he was initiated into the Regla de Ocha, the worship of the Yoruba Orichas. The music, the dance, and the drum are inseparable from the culture of our people.

I did not have a camera on hand to record those images, nor were there others interested in capturing those scenes that for me are now very difficult to narrate. I ask myself, why do things like this happen? Why don't we give these events all of the importance that they deserve?

With the experience of these years—after finishing *Oggún*—I have realized that the stories and images of our people are still blowing around in our countries like loose pages from an anonymous book. Anyone who wishes uses a paragraph of this collective book as he or she pleases when preparing to speak, opportunistically, about Blacks, or when a "folkloric" touch is necessary.

In the world of images there is very little concern with discovering the true stories, with discovering a way of being, with respecting the elders who are the source of popular wisdom. After a century in which a homogenizing cultural model of generalized violence and consumerism was imposed, authentic values and ancestral knowledge struggle to prevail but at an enormous disadvantage.

The result of this disinformation and distortion is that Black children and adolescents do not identify with the history of Africa and all of its diverse contributions to science and the arts. As an African proverb says, "The tree always follows its roots." But these roots need to be tended, need to be protected, need to be enriched within the dynamics of their contributions to the modern world, which include the multiple experiences of Black men and women in their paths throughout the Americas and the Caribbean.

We have a worldview in which our dialogue with nature is extraordinary because everything has life and is a carrier of energy. In spite of our languages or colonizers, our people carry in their blood an eternal sequence of rhythms that translates into the language of the drums and transcends contemporary cultural expressions. Nevertheless, we also bear, in some places more than others, the heritage that our cultures have not been accepted by the establishment.

I am referring to cultures that were disarticulated, were dismembered in such a brutal manner that it is still difficult to imagine what the social conditions of an enslaved man or woman could have been like. Through their rebelliousness, however, our ancestors offered admirable resistance and made their legacy to us possible because they did not allow themselves to die spiritually. How can we be indifferent to this heritage? It is logically impossible, although throughout our education we have never been taught enough, or accurately enough, about it.

The world of images—cinema and video—is extremely attractive when the resources exist to create good productions. It speaks a powerful and direct language that develops our imagination. And it can reveal to us the anonymous actors rarely highlighted in official history—the musicians and singers and the ordinary small-town people with their tragedies and their laughter. Most of all, it can bring the audience into contact with our ways of being beyond the usual prefabricated cultural stereotypes that make cultivating an effective narrative style both difficult and of the utmost importance.

When I had the opportunity to produce *Oggún*, I was certain that a good portion of the documentary would consist of songs of Yoruba origin sung by Lázaro Ros, with his distinctive voice and style. My objective was to leave proof of that ancestral language. That man or woman who sings and dances, those hands that play the *batá* drums, have stories to tell. And it is important that they tell them. For this reason, throughout the documentary I included an interview with Lázaro Ros that, far from following a linear biographical structure, seeks to communicate his life as a religious person. He knows many legends and myths that reveal the deep humanism of these African sources. People like Lázaro Ros are the last links of a long cultural chain that still connects enslaved Africans and their descendants in the New World.

In preparing the script for the documentary, I interviewed Lázaro on many occasions. I wanted to discover something beyond his extraordinary voice. One day as I listened to him, I realized that he was like a Caribbean *griot* who, throughout the years, has assumed the task of collecting stories—*patakines* of the old Yoruba gods. That is how he told me the beautiful story of how Oshún, goddess of love, conquered Oggún, god of war and lord of metals, with her *oñí* (honey). With her action, Oshún helped to reestablish the equilibrium of the universe. Lázaro's story led me to introduce fictional elements into the documentary, and I believe that one of the accomplishments of the film is this blending of different styles.

Oggún is not a documentary describing a religion or showing rituals. I am interested in the religion, but I am much more interested in human beings. The ultimate objective was to leave the viewer intoxicated with the worldview of this Caribbean man and to inspire reflection. Lázaro's final words are, "For me, Oggún has been and is my life force. He is a humble God, kind and loving, and I love him very much."

Oggún was a very special experience. My subsequent film, *My Footsteps in Baraguá*, deals with a different theme. It tells the story of immigrants from the English-speaking Caribbean in the eastern part of Cuba. It represents one of the many chapters in the economic history of the Caribbean, caused by the constant migratory movements, the other diasporas, the dispersions and separations our people have suffered. Haitians, Jamaicans, Barbadians, men and women from other islands of the Caribbean came in an economic migration that added new nuances to the ethno-cultural composition of eastern Cuba. In the early years of this century Cuba was the "promised land" due to its booming sugar industry. The protagonists of this story were first part of the great migration induced by the construction of the Panama Canal, who later traveled to Cuba with hopes of a new life and a better future.

When I began my research in Guantánamo and Baraguá (in the Province of Ciego de Ávila), the immigrants and their descendants were amazed and happy that someone was interested in their story, the story of their parents, and their customs. Their faces lit up as they remembered the past when they were referred to as "the English," since they were subjects of the British Crown. I slowly won their confidence, and they started sharing memories and taking out the old photographs that I used in the documentary. These old photographs were of great value because they helped create an imaginary closeness to the past.

There are no prescribed formulas for the production of a documentary of this nature. The aesthetic organization of the script comes to life based on knowing what we want to relate and on loving the characters. We have to return to the past in order to see what remains in the present. I remember walking through the *batey*, the sugarcane fields during harvest, with the aroma of sugarcane permeating the atmosphere they loved, an atmosphere they created with their humble houses, the churches they founded, and the breadfruit and akee trees they planted. Even when they told very personal stories, they were narrating important passages in a process common to many people in the Caribbean.

Resources? Financing? None existed during the preparation and filming of the documentary. Only a group of friends, assistance from the Baraguá Sugar Mill, and my family's support helped me initiate this first project of the video group, "Caribbean Images." I could not wait any longer because I ran the risk of losing the testimony of Miss Jones, the last immigrant from Barbados to Baraguá. No one could tell how long the pleasing smile of the Jamaican Ruby Hunt would be with us on this earth. Moreover, when we begin to think about all that has been lost, we must impose on ourselves and others the task of recording such testimonies. This can only be achieved with faith, tenacity, and passion.

The stories and images of our people are sometimes fortunate enough to be promoted by prestigious producers and directors who have the economic means. Most of us, however, cannot compete with the big market of commercial cinema. Nevertheless, with video we can accomplish projects with the help of universities, nongovernmental organizations, other institutional sources, and private monies.

More than as a theoretical presentation, I would like for my modest thoughts to be taken as a proposition. We have an audience, a public that needs and wants our cultural products, our artistic creations. We can help this audience get closer to our realities, a task that should be a major concern for cinematographers and videographers. If we want to contribute to building a historical consciousness, we must begin with ourselves. For this new century let us create video series telling and showing the "Stories and Images of Our People."

NOTE

This chapter was translated from Spanish by Sheila S. Walker.

23

Embodied Knowledge in African American Dance Performance

Yvonne Daniel

I have been researching dance behavior as an artist and as an anthropologist for some time now. What has become most important to me are those Caribbean performances and practices that are found also within niches of transnationality in the United States and elsewhere around the globe. It is within the domain of aesthetic expressions that the modern world has had to contend continuously and rigorously with African-derived structures. It is in the dance domain especially that many African principles and moral values continue to vibrate, and often where other domains of interest—botany, mathematics, philosophy, economics, history, religion, ethics—are revealed and reinforced.

This chapter presents a sample of my ongoing research on "embodied knowledge," which is, within the dance, a branch of knowledge, a method of knowing, that receives little academic attention in a technologically oriented world. Such attention is sorely needed. I am suggesting that we take a sharper look, in our modern contexts around the globe, at the significance of body knowledge and at the well-being of its recognized and treasured elders, savants, and scholars.

My examples are taken from recognized ritual dance practices in what is called Yoruba, Lucumí, or Santería, an Afro-Caribbean religion that has crossed the Americas from Cuba. Devotees within this and similar African American religious practices in Haiti, Brazil, and the United States understand the function of dance performance as a primary vehicle for spiritual communication, physical healing, and social balance. Through their bodies, they access and store music and dance scores. These scores, however, relate to belief, politics, and economics, and not simply to social relaxation.

Devotees interpret the stories of dancing divinities called Orichas as statements on human behavior. Proper social relationships and culturally appropriate behaviors are outlined and retold in chants, proverbs, religious liturgy, and both oral and written histories.[1] Also, these relationships and behaviors are vividly repeated through codified gestures, expressive movement sequences, and a range of kinesthetic responses.[2]

In the dance practices of Yoruba/Lucumí/Santería,[3] the physical body becomes the social body, both the repository of knowledge from the collective memory of a variety of African ethnic groups, and the sensitized reactor of modern transnational culture.[4] The body is dressed in memory and spiritual clothing while in performance; it drinks of archaic chants and ancient rhythms as well as from synthesized and electronic sound concoctions. This body is fed by organic movements of old as well as by particularized contemporary gestures, until it generates a power within that is capable of the transformation of the self and of others.

OYÁ'S DANCE

With one example of a public dance performance we can see its powerful objective, balance, drawn on the ground through the dancer's foot pattern. Oyá, the Oricha or spirit and energy of air, visually forms a sequence that alternates from left to right, tracing the cardinal directions by traveling forward, backward, and then, with three steps, to both sides. The arms are held majestically and authoritatively above the head and, at this beginning point, they mark the soft curving of a breeze in space, blowing gently in one direction and then in the opposite direction.

In John Mason's *Orin Orisa*,[5] we find literal translations of the Yoruba chants that invoke the presence of the cosmic spirits within Yoruba cosmology. His translations of Oyá's chant refer to Oyá as a mighty power that has the potential to clean, destroy, or change. He says:

Oyá de, iba ri iba; (a)'se ke (a)'se.
  Ago ile; ago lona. Oyá de ire O, Oyá de.
  (The Tearer arrives. Homage finds homage; authority hails authority. Make way in the house; make way on the road. The Tearer comes with goodness, the Tearer comes.)[6]

The chant, the rhythm, the gestures, and the hundreds of family stories, or *patakines,* concerning Oyá describe her as the cosmic essence that is most associated with air: the wind, the breeze, the hurricane, but especially the tornado. This cosmic power is also referenced in animal form as a buffalo, quiet and massive, but also overwhelmingly fierce. Judith Gleason has given a meteorological analysis of wind patterns that govern western Africa and the fierce atmospheric conditions that became associated with the force of Oyá in and around the Niger River, Oyá's original shrine or worship site.[7] She is associated with the Niger River and with two rivers that flow in opposite directions, thus aligning her and her devotees with places and times of dynamic change, whether in revolution, the market place, the carnival and masking, or simply with the last breath of all life. She is a female warrior.[8]

These references anticipate the second series of songs that are performed to a different set of rhythms called generically *llongo.* With this faster pace, we hear words that summon images of Oyá with increased tension. The songs for the second stage of an Oyá dance/ music offering say, "One who turns in another direction is perplexing. . . . Please come,

I will be happy . . . [when you] gush into the house. Oyá is strong and capable . . . the Tearer continually speaks, continually speaks."[9] In the dance patterns, Oyá begins to gallop and lope like the massive buffalo with which she is aligned:

Oyá, the one who tears the leaves,
The one who turns things and changes them,
The woman who you make way for when she turns,
Massive structure that sits on the ground;
The woman who wears short pants (is ready to fight).
Who can capture the head of Oyá?
Oyá, the quick-eyed, we salute you.[10]

Her danced body rhythms play a three against two pattern and encourage dynamic mathematics, both in the drumming and in dance practices, a demonstration of skill, craft, intelligence, and inventiveness.[11] Singer, chorus, and drummers transition from the slow *jueso* rhythm of the first section that marks the cardinal points, to the second llongo rhythm section, which quickens the pace and intensifies the danced pattern. With the third section, the *chacha* rhythmic pattern of the *batá* drums, and with chants of the *tratao,* or the order of chants for one Oricha, the dancer can alternate at an even swifter pace between the cardinal points step and the horse or galloping step.

The prayer, or *meta,* is sung over the fourth section, or *tuitui* rhythm, which is distinct from previous rhythms and is not usually alternated with any other dance steps. The tuitui pattern consists of three huge, percussive torso undulations that alternate side to side and finish with the arms, which are carrying an *iruke,* or horse's tail, slashing downward from high in the air to hip height. Ultimately, Oyá's dance is wild, aggressive, and provocative; she engages the full physical force of women, and simultaneously, the affinity for mental challenge and problem-solving that is more commonly associated with men in European and Euro-American cultures.

In Cuba, Oyá is guardian of the cemetery and is feared and avoided at times because she is thought to associate with the living dead spirits. Her proximity to death and the living dead is explained beyond the chants and dance within the patakines, the praise stories; devotees are told of her devotion to her nine still-born children, and how she tries to stay near and to guard them in the cemetery.

At other times she whirls, spins, and churns the air like tornadoes, hurricanes, and cyclones. Her spinning force connotes that she has little fear of others, of death, or even of fear itself; she is female all powerful. Her basic foot pattern is close to that of the male Oricha Ogún, Oricha of iron and war, creating a physical parallel with maleness. She carries the iruke and gallops with Changó, Oricha of lightning and thunder and another male warrior, across space and through time.

DANCE ANALYSIS

Through the examination of multiple channels of sensory perception that dance behavior comprises, and through keen observation and analysis of emotive body states that are demonstrated in devotional performance, spectators and analysts become acquainted with some of the knowledge that practitioners access. In the case of Oyá's dance, transformations take place.[12] First, humans are transformed into the divine being called Oyá, the goddess if you will, through imposed recognition of complementary relationships. Humans recognize and acknowledge relationships between animals, plants, and themselves. They construct, experience, and come to recognize relationships between vocal sentiment, instrumental sound, and human movement. They become increasingly aware of all the senses—taste, smell, touch, seeing, hearing—and in acutely recognizing these, gain familiarity with their personal relationship to the senses as channels of awareness and learning, and submit themselves fully to sensory stimuli.

Humans acknowledge the relationship between the principles of cooperation and reciprocity and the dancing Oricha in the present. For example, in order to prepare for Oyá's appearance and consequent advice, humans are bathed in or dusted with particular leaves and herbs, perhaps sugar water or rain water with *bari'a* (*cordia gerascanthus*) or *caimitillo* (*chrysophylum oliviforme*).[13] Plants are cooked with an emphasis on Oyá's preference for eggplant, sweet potatoes, and black-eyed peas. Animals, for example goats, hens, pigeons, and guinea hens, are dedicated to her and her community of godchildren and are later eaten as social medicine for the well-being of the community as well as for the human part of a reciprocal relationship with the Orichas.

In order for a transformation to occur from invisible to visible energy, the entire family of ancestors is praised and acknowledged. The ancestors are accorded recognition within a plant-animal-human connection with offerings of foods, flowers, and liquids, particularly water. These are symbolic affirmations of social cohesion among family members in the present by restating the locus of interpersonal relations and invoking the requisite behavior that is proper for reciprocity to succeed. In other words, the present community is reminded of its common heritage and of its elders; it is encouraged to perform respectful, and thereby specific behaviors in order that reciprocity and balance between the spirit and human worlds continue. Humans reaffirm their interconnections with all life when animals and plants are transformed into nourishment, into food for the dancing spiritual entities, food for the ritual community, and food for the participant-observing public.

Humans, plants, and animals, transformed as music and dance, are utilized jointly to effect transformations. Transformed plants, as wooden drums and beaded shakers, create a solitary, demanding, resultant call. Wood, bamboo, and gourds join with metal bells and combine again with solo and group voices to collectively implore social and spiritual communication. Transformed animals, as drum heads that give impulse to instrumental sound and as blood that expresses the utmost sincerity and seriousness of the endeavor, are employed in concert with the lead singer and the chorus to initiate and access spiritual transformations. Thus, abstract rhythm, melody, and gesture are transformed into visual but also mathematical configurations—los Orichas, the dancing divinities.

Once all ceremonial elements combine, the notion of time itself is transformed. Specific time becomes nonspecific or relative time. In these situations, there are only four times that are relevant. Time is calculated as before and after sunrise or before and after sunset.[14]

After the dancing divinities appear, another transformation presents itself. The divinities themselves are transformed into advisers, godmothers and godfathers, therapists who bathe people with body sweat and herbal waters, who greet them, dance with them, eat with them, and then sit down and talk to them with symbolic counsel for present problems and everyday situations.

Behavior speaks as Oyá joins the human community. She demands cognitive action, for example, by forcefully hugging an uninitiated "stranger" for a noticeable period of time and then specifically dancing with him or her. In so doing, she gives her demand for incorporation silently but physically in danced movement. Or she might take the hands of quarreling neighbors and forcibly shake them together. No one speaks, but the advice is heard in physical movement and recognized behavior. The principles of incorporation, respect, generosity, and sharing are made evident in danced movement. Oyá imposes chores, at first glance seemingly trivial and unrelated obligations, but which in time are understood to provide individual tranquility and peaceful respect within the group. Ultimately, the Orichas teach balance in the universe.

DANCE IN THE TRANSNATIONAL SETTING

In the contemporary setting, we read in news and popular media such as the *New York Times*[15] and *Hispanic Magazine*[16] that Yoruba/Lucumí/Santería beliefs and customs are spreading. Also, we can perceive the existence of Oyá and her still powerful, but often disregarded, dance and music in mainstream transnational popular culture. Nina (Simone) had a powerful Oyá at the piano and in her voice; Aretha's (Franklin) Oyá used to speak loudly and publicly as archetype when Black communities especially, but also mainstream North, South, Central America, and Europe, Japan, and Australia buzzed with "R-E-S-P-E-C-T" a few decades ago. More recently, the lyrics and preaching of Queen Latifah also resonate with the spirit of Oyá in Yoruba understanding. She and the current literary goddesses, Toni Morrison, Alice Walker, and Terry MacMillan, express traditional Oyá in contemporary form with poignant words and burning assertions of female strength and wisdom. Nia Love and Jawole Willa Jo Zollar's Urban Bush Women, to cite a few examples in dance, provide contemporary Oyá charters for strength and are modern models of vivacious power in the midst of struggle through contemporary, cultural fusion, mixed-media work.

The music industry has generally understood and dealt with what I call the "contagious remedies" of African American music/dance performance. It has never failed to target the spirit, and often wisdom, of African American artistry that is grounded in Yoruba and other African models. This industry has consistently garnered every talent in sight—Black, Latina, or white—that assures its reliable market and continuous profits due to the contagious, satisfying responses that African and African-derived music and dance conjure. Irrespective of who the popular artist or current commodity is around the globe, she or he owes tremendous acknowledgment to the principles that Oricha dance and music reflect, as is fully documented from an historical perspective and for the concert stage by Brenda Dixon Gottschild in her book *Digging the African-*

ist Presence in American Performance,[17] and referenced in the performances of break dancers dancing onstage with the San Francisco Ballet, and with the music of Prince as the basis of choreographic work for the American Ballet Theater on television.

However, as Maya Angelou describes so painfully in her latest poems, and as Judith Jamison originally danced in Alvin Ailey's "Cry," who aids and supports both women and men in the most desperate hours, the most agonizing cruelty, the most hurtful instants of contemporary life? Devotees of the Orichas and other African American religious communities would answer kinesthetically with the jerking or undulating, unabashedly asymmetrical, and rhythmically sophisticated movements and splendor of the humanized divinities.

If and when performed, Oricha dance movements provide for historical catharsis and contemporary release, but also for meaningful social action; these are dances of human resilience. In the moment of performance, the nonverbal messages—both displayed visually and experienced physically—of persistence, deliberation, dedication, reliability, resourceful resilience, and ultimately calm and strength, are all taught, learned over time, and transferred beyond the dance/music event to other arenas of social life.

Transformed as Oyá, for example, the dancer soars through space and time and reestablishes maintenance patterns that confront and resist the magnetized dehumanizing elements within contemporary situations. The dances express the collective memory and understanding of the cosmos, but they also relate to wholeness in the present. The dance performances teach balance, discipline, and humanity in a silent lecture within a loud, multicolored, and multisensory experience. The social body experiences the remembered patterns that constitute the balance of each interfacing realm of knowledge and integrates those experiences into daily routine.

CONCLUDING COMMENTARY

Dancing keeps us healthy, sane, balanced, strong, vital, vivacious, continually growing! It does so by enlivening and continually revitalizing the transformational process of living. The concrete act of dancing affords the immediacy of both the learned and intuitive realms of knowledge, and empowers humans as well as transforms and identifies them with and as spiritual entities.[18]

In this chapter, in effect, I am challenging the issue of what kinds of knowledge are considered reliable and/or important. I am addressing the categorization of all sorts of knowledge and their ranking.[19] My position is that the embodied knowledge or physical/cognitive/emotional/spiritual knowledge that is found in dance behavior has too often been devalued. Additionally, I offer dance performance and its analysis as a method for perceiving, understanding, and knowing particularly an African American cultural system, but others as well.[20] If we use body knowledge or knowing through dancing, we are better able to understand and relate what is embedded in the bonds of social relations and cultural interaction.

Without the deep knowledge that comes from body/mind/emotion/spirit immersion in combination with the study of institutions, social interaction, and the like, I suggest, with other critics, that the researchers do not "know" social or ritual communities in the manner of the participants, even if they put "native" voices within the texts. They remain distant from the studied group due to training as rigorous skeptics. This distance reinforces the devaluation of "body knowledge." The knowledge that is received is fragmented and lacks the relevance of interdependent spheres of knowledge that dance behavior can regularly access.

In conclusion, I must recall my professional foremothers Katherine Dunham,[21] Pearl Primus,[22] and now another sister dancer, Emmika Hearadi of Suriname (who has recently passed on in frustration around this subject). Ms. Dunham first wrote of what I speak; she and the others dared to dedicate a portion of their lives to knowing through dancing. Both Ms. Dunham and Dr. Primus received the highest medals of honor that the United States gives for artistic contribution to our nation and the world. Yet both were/are in desperate financial and social situations. Dr. Primus told me that she asked President George Bush, "Will this medal buy me a bus ticket home?" when he pinned it on her breast! She, at seventy-five years old, was hustling, trying to make academic institutions value the embodied knowledge that she had first researched in Africa four decades previously. She died almost penniless in 1995. Ms. Dunham too, still living at ninety years old, has been slighted in anthropology, although also honored, but mainly curtailed in her attempts to validate what can be learned when analyzing the human body in dance performance and performance contexts.

In the future, I urge more deliberation upon this deep concern: dance analysis should be included in future social analyses because it does not polarize, prioritize, nor fragment knowledge.[23] Instead, it integrates and explicates diverse realms of knowledge as it provides still another route to understanding human behavior and social/political/economic action. For the present, however, I look to the physical sciences of physics, chemistry, and neuropsychology that will ultimately prove what social scientists and dance researchers are so far inferring about embodied knowledge.[24] Embodied knowledge and other knowledge systems are reconcilable and, like sound waves in relation to light waves, are truths and knowledge of different orders, but nonetheless, equally valuable.

NOTES

1. George Brandon, *Santeria from Africa to the New World: The Dead Sell Memories* (Bloomington: Indiana University Press, 1993); Margaret Thompson Drewal, *Yoruba Ritual and Thought: Play, Performance, Agency* (Bloomington: Indiana University Press, 1992); Karen McCarthy Brown, *Mama Lola: A Voodoo Priestess in Brooklyn* (Berkeley: University of California Press, 1991); Natalia Bolívar, *Los orichas en Cuba* (La Habana: Ediciones Unión, 1990); Sandra T. Barnes, ed., *Africa's Ogún: Old World and New* (Bloomington: Indiana University Press, 1989); Joseph Murphy, *Santeria: An African Religion in America* (Boston: Beacon Press, 1988) and *Working the Spirit* (Boston: Beacon Press, 1994); Judith Gleason, *Oyá, In Praise of the Goddess* (Boston: Shambhala Publications, Inc., 1987); Diane Brown, *Umbanda: Religion and Politics in Urban Brazil* (Ann Arbor, Mich.: UMI Research Press, 1986); Roger Bastide, *The African Religions of Brazil* (Baltimore: Johns Hopkins University Press, 1978); Mercedes Cros Sándoval, *La religión*

de los orichas (Hato Rey, Puerto Rico: Colección Estudios Afrocaribeños, 1975); Migene González-Wippler, *Santeria: African Magic in Latin America* (Garden City, N.Y.: Anchor Press/Doubleday, 1975); George Simpson, *Black Religions in the New World* (New York: Columbia University Press, 1978); Alfred Métraux, *Voodoo in Haiti* (New York: Knopf, 1964 [1951]); Miguel Barnet, "La religión de los yorubas y sus dioses," in *Actos de Folklore* (La Habana: Instituto de Etnología y Folklore, 1961); Pierre Verger, *Notes sur le culte des Orisa et Vodun á Bahia* (Dakar: Institut Fondamental d'Afrique Noire, 1957); Maya Deren, *Divine Horsemen: The Living Gods of Haiti* (New York: Thames and Hudson, 1985 [1953]); William Bascom, "The Focus of Cuban Santería," in *Southwestern Journal of Anthropology* 6, no. 1 (Spring 1950): 64–68, "Two Forms of Afro-Cuban Divination," in *Acculturation in the Americas*, ed. Sol Tax (Chicago: University of Chicago Press, 1952), proceedings of the 29th International Congress of Americanists, vol. 2, 169–179, *Shango in the New World*, Occasional Publication of the African and Afro-American Research Institute, no. 4 (Austin: University of Texas, 1972), and *Sixteen Cowries: Yoruba Divination from Africa to the New World* (Bloomington: Indiana University Press, 1980); Ruth Landes, *The City of Women* (Albuquerque: University of New Mexico Press, 1994 [1947]); Romulus Lachatanere, *Manuel de santería* (La Habana: Editorial Caribe, 1942); Edison Carneiro, "The Structure of African Cults in Bahia," in *Journal of American Folklore*, no. 53 (1940): 271–278, and *Candomblés da Bahia* (Rio de Janeiro: Civilização Brasileira, 1978); Lydia Cabrera, *Cuentos negros de Cuba* (La Habana: La Verónica, 1940), *El monte* (Miami: Colección del Chicherekú, 1983 [1954]), *Anagó: vocabulario lucumí* (La Habana: Ediciones C.R., 1957), *La sociedad secreta abakuá* (Miami: Ediciones C.R., 1970 [1958]), *Yemayá y Ochún* (New York: Colección del Chicherekú, 1974), and *Reglas de congo, palo monte mayombe* (Miami: Ediciones Universal, 1986 [1979]); Fernando Ortiz, *Los bailes y el teatro de los negros en el folklore de Cuba* (La Habana: Editorial Letras Cubanas, 1985 [1951]); Carlos Carnet, *Lucumí: religión de los yorubas en Cuba* (Miami: AIP Publications Center, 1973); Arthur Ramos, *O folk-lore negro do Brasil: demopsychologia e psychoanalyse* (Rio de Janeiro: Civilização Brasileira, 1935); and Harold Courlander, *The Drum and the Hoe* (Berkeley: University of California Press, 1974).

2. Graciela Chao Carbonero, *Bailes yorubas de Cuba* (La Habana: Editorial Pueblo y Educación, 1980); Graciela Chao Carbonero and Sara Lamerán, *Folklore cubano*, vols. 1, 2, 3, 4 (La Habana: Editorial Pueblo y Educación, 1982); Yvonne Daniel, "The Ethnography of Rumba: Dance and Social Change in Contemporary Cuba," unpublished dissertation, Department of Anthropology, University of California at Berkeley, 1989; Kariamu Welsh-Asante, "Afro-Cuban Religion in the Diaspora," in *International Journal of African Dance* 1, no. 1 (1993): x–xx; Stephen Feld, *Sound and Sentiment* (Philadelphia: University of Pennsylvania Press, 1982); also cf. J. H. Kwabena Nketia, "The Interrelations of African Music and Dance," in *Studia Musicologia* 7 (1965): 91–101; Rex Nettleford, *Dance Jamaica: Cultural Definition and Artistic Discovery* (Kingston: National Dance Theater Company of Jamaica, 1985); Olly Wilson, "Association of Movement and Music as a Manifestation of a Black Conceptual Approach to Music Making," in *Essays on Afro-American Music and Musicians*, ed. Irene V. Jackson (Westport, Conn.: Greenwood Press, 1981), 1–23; and Lavinia Williams Yarbrough, *Haiti: Dance* (Frankfurt am Main: Bronners Druckeri, 1958).

3. Currently there are disputes as to the naming of this belief system. See Brandon, *Santeria from Africa to the New World*, 55–59.

4. Sidney Mintz and Richard Price, *An Anthropological Approach to the Afro-American Past: A Caribbean Perspective* (Philadelphia: Institute for the Study of Human Issues, 1976); Paul Connerton, *How Societies Remember* (New York: Cambridge University Press, 1989); Maurice Halbwachs, *The Collective Memory* (New York: Harper and Row, 1980); and Robert Friedman, "Making an Abstract World Concrete: Knowledge, Competence and Structural Dimensions of

Performance among Bata Drummers in Santeria," Ph.D. diss., University of Indiana–Bloomington, 1982.

5. John Mason, *Orin Orisa* (New York: Yoruba Theological Archministry, 1992).

6. Mason, *Orin Orisa*, 327.

7. Gleason, *Oyá, In Praise of the Goddess*.

8. Mason, *Orin Orisa*, 336.

9. Mason, *Orin Orisa*, 321–326.

10. Mason, *Orin Orisa*, 70.

11. Friedman, *Making an Abstract World Concrete*; Roberto Burrell, personal communications, Oakland, California, June-August, 1995.

12. For more information on trance, possession, and altered states of consciousness, see Sheila S. Walker, *Ceremonial Spirit Possession in Africa and Afro-America* (Leiden, Netherlands: E. J. Brill, 1972), and "A Choreography of the Universe: The Afro-Brazilian Candomblé as a Microcosm of Yoruba Spiritual Geography," in *Anthropology and Humanism Quarterly* 16, no. 2 (1985), 42–50; Deren, *Divine Horsemen*; Gleason, *Oyá, In Praise of the Goddess*; Margaret Thompson Drewal, "Symbols of Possession in an Anago-Yoruba Performance," in *Dance Research Journal* 8, no. 2 (1978): 15–24; Robert Farris Thompson, *Black Gods and Kings* (Los Angeles: Museum of Ethnic Arts, 1971), *Flash of the Spirit: African and Afro-American Art and Philosophy* (New York: Random House, 1983), and *Face of the Gods: Art and Altars of Africa and the African Americas* (New York: Museum for African Arts, 1993); and Erica Bourguignon, *Possession* (San Francisco: Chandler and Sharp, Inc., 1976).

13. Cabrera, *El monte*, 335, 349.

14. Ana Pérez, personal communications, Matanzas, Cuba, January–July 1987; Maria das Graças de Santana Rodrigué, personal communications, Salvador, Bahia, Brazil, August 1991 and June 1995.

15. Lizette Alvarez, "A Once-Hidden Faith Leaps Out into the Open," *New York Times*, Metro Section (Jan. 27, 1997): B1, 3–4.

16. Mali Michelle Fleming, "Santeria: Magic or Religion?" in *Hispanic Magazine* (1993): 32–34.

17. Brenda Dixon Gottschild, *Digging the Africanist Presence in American Performance: Dance and Other Contexts* (Westport, Conn.: Greenwood Press, 1996).

18. Cf. Arturo Lindsay, ed., "Santeria Aesthetics," in *Contemporary Latin American Art* (Washington, D.C.: Smithsonian Institution Press, 1996).

19. Cf. Israel Scheffler, *Conditions of Knowledge: An Introduction to Epistemology and Education* (Glenview, Ill.: Scott, Foresman and Co., 1965), 5; Fela Sowande, "Black Folklore," in *Black Lines* 2, no. 1, special issue on folklore (Fall 1971): 5–21; Howard Gardener and Thomas Hatch, "Multiple Intelligences Go to School: Educational Implications of the Theory of Multiple Intelligences," in *Educational Researcher* 18, no. 8 (1989): 4–10; see also Kim Greenberg, "Transformations: The Teaching of Afro-Cuban Sacred Dance," master's thesis, Teachers College, Columbia University, 1996, pp. 38–57.

20. For example, Cynthia Novack, *Sharing the Dance: Contact Improvisation and American Culture* (Madison: University of Wisconsin Press, 1990); Deirdre Sklar, "Invigorating Dance Ethnology," *UCLA Journal of Dance Ethnology* 15 (1991): 4–15; Sally Ness, *Body, Movement, and Culture* (Philadelphia: University of Pennsylvania Press, 1992); Marta Savigliano, *Tango and the Political Economy of Passion* (Boulder, Colo.: Westview Press, 1995).

21. See Katherine Dunham, *Island Possessed* (Garden City, N.Y.: Doubleday, 1969).

22. See Pearl Primus, "Life Crises: Dance from Birth to Death," American Therapy Association, proceedings from the Fourth Annual Conference, Philadelphia 1969, pp. 1–13.

23. See Frederique Apffel-Marglin and Stephen A. Marglin, *Decolonizing Knowledge: From Development to Dialogue* (Oxford: Clarendon Press, 1996), and Delmos Jones, "Toward a Native Anthropology," in *Human Organization* 29, no. 4 (1970): 251–259.

24. For example, Joe Martinez, "Physiological Psychology," a presentation at the Ford Foundation Fellows' Conference, Washington, D.C., November 1991; Deirdre Sklar, "Can Bodylore Be Brought to Its Senses?" *Journal of American Folklore* 107 (1994): 9–22; Joyce Avrech Berkman, "To Feel It Viscerally: Empathetic Knowing," unpublished paper presented at Vermont Council on the Humanities, November 1994; also Marlo Morgan, *Mutant Message from Down Under* (New York: Harper Collins, 1994).

Index

About the Contributors

Michael L. Blakey is professor of anthropology and anatomy and curator of the W. Montague Cobb Skeletal Collection at Howard University, where he is also director of the African Burial Ground Project.

Yvonne Daniel is a dance anthropologist and associate professor of dance and of Afro-American Studies at Smith College.

Brenda Dixon Gottschild, professor emerita of dance studies at Temple University, writes for *Dance Magazine* and is a freelance performer and lecturer.

Howard Dodson, chief of the Schomburg Center for Research in Black Culture of the New York Public Library since 1984, is a specialist in African American history and a noted lecturer, educator, and consultant.

Shelley Fisher Fishkin is professor of American studies and English at the University of Texas at Austin.

Jesús "Chucho" García is president of the Fundación Afroamérica, in Venezuela and an author, filmmaker, and educator concerning Afro-Venezuelan traditions.

Patricia Guthrie is an anthropologist and professor of human development and director of women's studies at California State University at Hayward.

Jessica B. Harris is a culinary historian and a professor of English at Queens College, New York.

Joseph E. Harris is Distinguished Professor of History at Howard University.

Joseph E. Inikori is professor of history at the University of Rochester.

Gilberto R. N. Leal is coordinator of Níger-Okàn, a leading political and cultural organization in Bahia, Brazil.

Lucía Dominga Molina and **Mario Luis López** founded the Casa de la Cultura Indo-Afro-Americana in Santa Fe, Argentina, in 1988.

Diana Baird N'Diaye is a cultural specialist/folklife curator on the staff of the Center for Folklife Programs and Cultural Studies at the Smithsonian Institution in Washington, D.C.

Tomás Olivera Chirimini, is director of Culture of the Asociacion Cultural y Social Uruguaya Negra (ACSUN) and founder and artistic director of Conjunto Bantú.

João José Reis is a professor of history at the Federal University of Bahia in Salvador, Bahia, Brazil.

Romero Jorge Rodríguez is director general of Organizaciones Mundo Afro, a federation of Afro-Uruguayan organizations, and general coordinator of the Red de Organizaciones Afro-Americanas (Network of Afro-American Organizations), an international organization linking groups in the African Diaspora in the Americas.

Gloria Rolando is a filmmaker, and directs Imagenes del Caribe, in Havana, Cuba.

Lisa Sánchez González is a literary critic and assistant professor of English at the University of Texas at Austin.

John O. Stewart is an anthropologist and professor and former director of African American and African Studies, University of California at Davis.

John Michael Vlach is professor of American civilization and anthropology at George Washington University in Washington, D.C.

Sheila S. Walker, organizer of the international conference on the African Diaspora and the Modern World that is the basis of this volume, was the director of the Center for African and African American Studies, and is a professor of anthropology and the Annabel Irion Worsham Centennial Professor in the College of Liberal Arts at the University of Texas at Austin.

Olly Wilson is a composer and professor of music and former chairman of the department of music at the University of California at Berkeley.

Olabiyi B. Yai is a linguist and the ambassador to UNESCO from the Republic of Benin.

CPSIA information can be obtained
at www.ICGtesting.com
Printed in the USA
LVHW051509101218
599931LV00023B/1217/P

9 780742 501652